# 1 MONTH OF
# FREE
# READING

## at

## www.ForgottenBooks.com

By purchasing this book you are eligible for one month membership to ForgottenBooks.com, giving you unlimited access to our entire collection of over 1,000,000 titles via our web site and mobile apps.

To claim your free month visit:

www.forgottenbooks.com/free975067

ISBN 978-0-260-83852-0
PIBN 10975067

/395 United States /389

# Circuit Court of Appeals

## For the Ninth Circuit.

---

DEA HONG, DEA CHUCK, DEA TON and DEA FONG,

Appellants,

vs.

OHN D. NAGLE, as Commissioner of Immigration, Port of San Francisco,

Appellee.

---

# Transcript of Record.

---

Upon Appeal from the Southern Division of the United States District Court for the Northern District of California, Second Division.

---

# FILED

APR 1 1 1924

F. D. MONCKTON,

CLERK.

---

Filmer Bros. Co. Print, 330 Jackson St., S. F., Cal.

# United States
# Circuit Court of Appeals

## For the Ninth Circuit.

---

DEA HONG, DEA CHUCK, DEA TON and DEA FONG,

Appellants,

vs.

JOHN D. NAGLE, as Commissioner of Immigration, Port of San Francisco,

Appellee.

---

# Transcript of Record.

---

Upon Appeal from the Southern Division of the United States District Court for the Northern District of California, Second Division.

---

# INDEX TO THE PRINTED TRANSCRIPT OF RECORD.

[Clerk's Note: When deemed likely to be of an important nature, errors or doubtful matters appearing in the original certified record are printed literally in italic; and, likewise, cancelled matter appearing in the original certified record is printed and cancelled herein accordingly. When possible, an omission from the text is indicated by printing in italic the two words between which the omission seems to occur.]

Index.                                    Page

# NAMES OF ATTORNEYS OF RECORD.

For Petitioners and Appellants:
  STEPHEN M. WHITE, Esq., San Francisco.
For Respondent and Appellee:
  UNITED STATES ATTORNEY, San Francisco.

---

In the Southern Division of the United States District Court for the Northern District of California.

CLERK'S OFFICE.—No. 18,009.

DEA HONG et al.

vs.

JOHN D. NAGLE, etc.

## PRAECIPE (FOR TRANSCRIPT ON APPEAL).

To the Clerk of Said Court:

Sir: Please issue copies of the following papers to be used in preparing transcript on appeal:

1. Petition for writ of habeas corpus.
2. Order to show cause.
3. Demurrer to petition.
4. Minute order regarding immigration record.
5. Judgment and order dismissing order to show cause and denying petition for writ.
6. Notice of appeal.
7. Petition for appeal.
8. Assignment of errors.

9. Order allowing appeal.
10. Stipulation and order regarding immigration record.
11. Clerk's certificate.
12. Citation on appeal—original and copy.

STEPHEN M. WHITE,
Attorney for Appellant.

[Endorsed]: Filed Mar. 12, 1924. Walter B. Maling, Clerk. By C. M. Taylor, Deputy Clerk. [1*]

---

In the Southern Division of the District Court of the United States in and for the Northern District of California, Second Division.

### No. 18,009.

In the Matter of DEA HONG, DEA CHUCK, DEA TON and DEA FONG, Ex. SS. "TAIYO MARU," May 26, 1923. Nos. 22186/5–6, 5–14, 5–7 and 5–5, on Habeas Corpus.

## PETITION FOR WRIT OF HABEAS CORPUS.

To the Honorable United States District Judge, now Presiding in the Above-entitled Court:

It is respectfully shown by the petition of the undersigned, Dea Chung Wing, that his sons, Dea Hong, Dea Chuck, Dea Ton and Dea Fong, hereinafter referred to as "the detained," are unlawfully imprisoned, detained, confined and restrained of

---

*Page-number appearing at foot of page of original certified Transcript of Record.

their liberty by John D. Nagle, Commissioner of Immigration for the Port of San Francisco, California, at the United States Immigration Station at Angel Island, California, county of Marin, State and Northern District of California, Southern Division thereof, that the said imprisonment, detention, confinement and restraint are illegal and that the illegality thereof consists in this, to wit:

That it is claimed by the said commissioner that said detained are Chinese persons and aliens not subject to nor entitled to admission into the United States under the terms and provisions of the Acts of Congress of May 6, 1882, July 5, 1884, September 13, 1888, May 5, 1892, November 3, 1893, and April 29, 1902, as amended and re-enacted by Section 5 of the Act of April 7, 1904, which said Acts are commonly [2] known and referred to as the Chinese Exclusion or Restriction Acts; and that he, the said commissioner intends to deport the said detained away from and out of the United States to the Republic of China.

That the said commissioner claims that the said detained arrived at the port of San Francisco on or about the 26th day of May, 1923, and thereupon made application to enter the United States as sons of a native-born citizen thereof, and that the application of the said detained to enter the United States as citizens thereof was denied by a Board of Special Inquiry; that an appeal was thereupon taken from the exclusion decision of the said Board of Special Inquiry to the Secretary of the Department of Labor, and that the Secretary of the Department of Labor thereafter dismissed the said appeal; that it is claimed by the said Commissioner of Immigration that in all of the proceedings had herein the said detained were accorded a full and fair hearing, and that the action of the said Board of Special Inquiry and the said Secretary of Labor was taken by them in the proper exercise of the discretion committed to them by the statute in such cases made and provided, and in accordance with the regulations promulgated under the authority contained in said statute.

But, on the contrary, your petitioner alleges, on his information and belief, that the hearing and proceedings had herein, and the action of the said Board of Special Inquiry, and the action of the said Secretary of Labor was and is in excess of the authority committed to them by the said rules and regulations and by the said statute, and that the denial of the said application of the said detained to enter the United States as sons of a native-born citizen thereof was and is an abuse of the authority committed to them by the said rules and regulations and by the said statute in each of the following particulars: [3]

1. That your petitioner alleges upon his information and belief that the excluding decision of the said Board of Special Inquiry and the said Secretary of Labor is based upon so-called "prior testimony" of Dea Chung Wing, the alleged father, given on the 28th day of February, 1900, at a hearing before a referee appointed by the District Court of the United States, in and for the Northern Dis-

trict of California, in a proceeding on habeas corpus, No. 12029, the record of which is now on file with the clerk of the aforesaid court; that it is claimed by the said Board of Special Inquiry and the said Secretary of Labor that the so-called "prior testimony" of the alleged father shows conclusively that Dea Chung Wing, the alleged father of the said detained, was not married in the year of 1900, or prior thereto, and that therefore his paternity to the said detained is precluded.

But, on the contrary, your petitioner alleges, that the aforesaid mentioned claim of the said Board of Special Inquiry and the said Secretary of Labor, is not based upon evidence or facts, in that, at the said hearing before the said referee, the alleged father did not give so-called "prior testimony" or any testimony, to the effect that he was not married; for the purpose of showing that the aforesaid mentioned claim of the said Board of Special Inquiry and the Secretary of Labor is not a fact, and is without foundation, your petitioner has annexed hereto, and marked Exhibit "A," a true and correct copy of the full and complete hearing before the said referee.

That your petitioner alleges that the said Board of Special Inquiry and the same Secretary of Labor have acted in excess of the authority and in abuse of the discretion committed to them in attributing to the said father so-called "prior testimony," which did not, or does not, exist; that in basing their excluding decision on so-called "prior testimony" [4] which in fact does not exist, the said Board of

Special Inquiry and the same Secretary of Labor
have denied the said detained the full and fair
hearing to which they and each of them are entitled.

2. Your petitioner alleges, upon his information
and belief that the said Board of Special Inquiry
and the said Secretary of Labor, admit that Dea
Chung Wing, the alleged father of the said detained,
is a native-born citizen of the United States; that
upon the hearing of the said applications of the
said detained before the said Board of Special Inquiry, the said detained were denied admission into
the United States without being accorded or granted
an opportunity to prove their relationship to the
aforesaid Dea Chung Wing; that the said Board of
Special Inquiry and the said Secretary of Labor in
denying the said detained admission into the United
States, without affording the said detained an opportunity to prove their relationship to the alleged
father upon the hearing of their applications before
the said Board of Special Inquiry, acted arbitrarily
and in abuse of the discretion and in excess of the
authority committed to them; that the said detained
were thereby denied the full and fair hearing to
which they and each of them are entitled.

Your petitioner has not in his possession the record of the proceedings had before the said Board
of Special Inquiry and the said Secretary of Labor,
and it is therefore impossible for your petitioner
to annex hereto the said Immigration record, but
your petitioner is willing and hereby consents that
the original immigration record, when presented

by the immigration authorities, may be introduced in evidence and considered as part and parcel of this hearing. [5]

That the said Commissioner of Immigration has given notice of his intention to deport the said detained away from and out of the United States on the SS. "Shinyo Maru" which sails from the port of San Francisco on October 10th, 1923, and unless this Court intervenes the said detained will be deprived of residence within the land of their citizenship.

That the said detained are in detention as aforesaid; for this reason they are unable to verify this petition upon their own behalf, but your petitioner is the father of the said detained and does upon his own behalf and upon the behalf of the said detained verify the said petition.

Wherefore, your petitioner prays that a writ of habeas corpus issue herein as prayed for, directed to the said Commissioner of Immigration, commanding and directing him to hold the body of the said detained before this Court at a time and place to be specified in this order, together with the time and cause of their detention so that the same may be inquired into to the end that the said detained may be restored to their liberty and go hence without day.

STEPHEN M. WHITE,
Attorney for Petitioner. [6]

State of California,
City and County of San Francisco,—ss.

Dea Chung Wing, being duly sworn, deposes and says:

That he is the petitioner named in the foregoing petition; that the said has been read and explained to him and he knows the contents thereof; that the same is true of his own knowledge, except as to those matters which are therein stated on his information and belief, and as to those matters, he believes it to be true.

DEA CHUNG WING,

Also Known as Taytong Wing.

Subscribed and sworn to before me this 9th day of October, 1923.

[Seal]        IRENE CAMPBELL,

Notary Public in and for the City and County of San Francisco, State of California.   [7]

EXHIBIT "A."

In the District Court of the United States, in and for the Northern District of California.

Hon. E. H. HEACOCK, Special Referee.

No. 12029.

In the Matter of DEA CHUNG WING, on Habeas Corpus.

Wednesday, Feb. 28, 1900.

Appearances:

JAMES H. HANLEY, Esq., for the Petitioner.

No appearance for the United States.

DEA CHUNG WING, the petitioner, sworn.

Mr. HANLEY.—Q. What is your name?

A. Dea Chung Wing.

Q. How old are you?     A. 25.

Q. Where were you born?

A. #618 Jackson Street, San Francisco.

Q. What year, month and day were you born?

A. February 3, 1876.

Q. What is your father's name?

A. Dea Leong Jit.

Q. What is your mother's name?

A. Yee Shee. [8]

Q. Did you ever leave this city to go to China?

A. I went to China in 1880.

Q. With whom?

A. With my father and mother.

Q. Where have you resided since you went to China?

A. Wong Son How Village, Sun Ning District.

Q. And had you resided there until your departure a short time ago for this country?

A. Yes, sir.

Q. Has anyone been to see you in China from this city since your departure?     A. Yes, sir.

Q. Who?     A. Yee Nee Jung.

Q. Is he related to you?

A. He is a friend of my father's; who is interested in business with him.

Q. Has anyone else visited you in China who has resided in this country?     A. No, sir.

Q. Has your uncle ever been to China?

A. My uncle has been in China.

Q. When has he been there?     A. In 1895.

Q. What is his name?     A. Dea Leong Foon.

Q. Where is your uncle now?

A. He is in this city.

Q. Where is that friend that visited you in China and where is he now?

A. He is in this city. [9]

The REFEREE.—Q. Is your uncle married, Dea Leong Foon? A. Yes, sir.

Q. When was he married?

A. He was married before I was born.

Q. Is his wife living, do you know?

A. Yes, sir.

Q. Where is she now?

A. She is living in China.

Q. Where? A. Wong Son How Village.

Q. How large is your village; how many houses?

A. There are 10 alleys.

Q. How many buildings are there in the village, as near as you can tell? A. Between 60 and 70.

Q. In what row is your house?

A. It is the 2d house, in the 5th alley, in the 5th row.

Q. In what row is your uncle's house in which his wife lives? A. In the 5th row.

Mr. HANLEY.—Q. In the same row as yours?

A. Yes, sir.

The REFEREE.—Q. What number is your house? A. The 2d house.

Q. What number is your uncle's house?

A. The 3d house.

Q. Then it is the next house to yours, is it?

A. Taking this for my house, my uncle lives in the adjoining house, and then he lives also in the 6th house, the 6th house from me. When it rains he moves from the 3d house into the 6th house; the 3d house leaks. [10]

Q. Which house did he live in while he was in China, and when you saw him there?

A. He lived in the furthest house.

Q. All the time he was in China?

A. He first lived in the house nearest my house, and then it leaked and then he moved into the other one.

Q. What part of the time did he live in the 3d house?

A. He moved into the other house last year, before that time he lived in the 3d house.

Q. When did your uncle return to this country?

A. I don't remember when he returned.

Q. When did he leave China?

A. I do not remember.

Q. Tell me as near as you can?

A. He left to come back here in 1895, in the 8th month (September).

Q. And when did he arrive in China?

A. In April.

Q. Then he was there only four months?

A. Yes, sir.

Q. Did he live at home all the while he was there?

A. Yes, sir.

Q. How long did he continue to live in the 3d house before he moved into the 6th house while he was home on that trip?

A. He lived in the 3d house all the while he was in China.

Q. Who lived with him there while he was in China?    A. My aunt.

Q. Anybody else?    A. That is all.    [11]

Q. How often did you see him?

A. I saw him frequently.

Q. What do you mean by frequently—daily?

A. Yes, sir, daily.

Q. Did you ever stay overnight at his house while he was there?    A. No, sir.

Q. Did he ever stay overnight at your house?

A. No, sir.

Q. Did he visit your house daily?    A. No, sir.

Q. How often would he come to your house?

A. Every four or five days.

Q. Any oftener?    A. No, sir.

Q. Who was living with you in your house besides your mother when your uncle was in China?

A. No one else.

Q. Did he ever eat a regular meal in your house, your uncle, while you were there?    A. Yes, sir.

Q. How often?    A. A great many times.

Q. Tell as near as you can tell me—I do not expect *me* to tell the exact number, but as near as you can tell me?    A. 6 or 7 times.

Q. What meal—morning, noon or night?

A. The morning meal, I think.

Q. Did he ever eat a noon meal there?

A. Did he ever eat an evening meal was it?    [12]

Q. A noon meal.    A. No, sir.

Q. Did he ever eat any regular evening meal at your house?    A. No, sir.

Q. Always in the morning?

A. He only took the morning meal.

Q. Did his wife come with him any time he took the morning meal?

A. Yes; she would come occasionally.

Q. With him? A. Yes, sir.

Q. And would she eat at the same table with you and your uncle and your mother?

A. My aunt ate with my mother.

Q. Would they eat at the same time that you and your uncle were eating? A. Yes, sir.

Q. Where did you and your uncle eat—in the reception-room, or in one of the kitchens?

A. In the reception-room.

Q. And where did your mother and aunt eat?

A. In the kitchen.

Q. When you say the 6th house, do you mean in the same row as your house?

A. Yes, sir.

Q. When has your uncle's wife, your aunt, lived in the 6th house?

A. She moved there last year in the 10th month.

Q. Has she lived there ever since?

A. Yes; she is living there now. [13]

Q. Did she ever live there before? A. No, sir.

Q. Did you often talk with your uncle?

A. Yes; I talked with him frequently.

Q. Were you examined on the mail dock on January 8th, 1900, by the officers of the Chinese Bureau?

A. Yes, sir.

Q. Have you any other uncle besides Dea Leong Foon? A. I have two maternal uncles.

Q. Any paternal uncle? A. No, sir.

Q. Were you asked this question among others, referring to your uncle's wife, your paternal uncle's wife, "Did she live in your village?" and did you answer, "Yes"?    A. Yes, sir.

Q. And were you next asked, "Does she live in your house, and did you answer, "No"?

A. Yes, sir.

Q. And were you asked, "Are your houses close together?" and did you answer, "Yes, sir"?

A. Yes, sir.

Q. And were you next asked, "Any house between them?" and did you answer, "Yes, sir"?

A. I did not say there was.

Q. And were you asked, "How many houses between the house you lived in and the house your uncle's wife lived in?" and did you answer, "Six houses between"?

A. I said from my house to my uncle's house there were six houses.

Q. Did you ever have any other paternal uncle than Dea Leong Foon at any time?

A. He is the only one.  [14]

Q. Now, were you further asked in that examination, "Has your father any brothers?" and did you answer "Yes, two elder brothers"?

A. No, sir.

Q. And were you next asked, "Where are they now?" and did you answer, "They are farmers in China"?

A. Those two are my maternal uncles who are farmers.

Q. And were you next asked, "Have they ever

been in this country?" and did you answer, "My maternal uncles have not been here"?

A. Yes, sir.

Q. Were you next asked, "Has anyone else visited you in China?" and did you answer, "No, sir"?

A. No, sir.

Q. Were you next asked, "Has Dea Leong Foon been to China to see you?" and did you answer, "Yes, in 1895"?    A. Yes, sir.

Q. And were you asked, "Did he visit you very often while he was in China?" and did you answer, "Yes"?    A. Yes, sir.

Q. And were you next asked, "Were you talking to him frequently?" and did you answer, "No"?

A. No, sir.

Q. And were you next asked, "Did he call at your house to see you?" and did you answer, "Yes, sir"?    A. Yes, sir.

Q. And next, "He comes there very often, did he not?" and did you answer, "Once"?  [15]

A. I said he went to my house frequently.

Q. And were you next asked, "How long did he remain at your house on that visit?" and did you answer, "About half an hour"?    A. Yes, sir.

Q. And were you next asked, "Were you in the same room during that half hour?" and did you answer, "Yes, sir"?    A. Yes, sir.

Q. And were you next asked, "Did you not say a word to him?" and did you answer, "No, sir"?

A. I said that I spoke to him.

Q. And were you next asked, "He did not say

a word to you?" and did you say, "I spoke to him and he answered"?     A. Yes, sir.

Mr. HANLEY.—How many children has your uncle?     A. One son.

Q. Where is he?

A. He is going to school in China.

Q. Has he any other child?

A. He only has one son.

Q. Did he ever have any other children?

A. He had two sons.

Q. Where is the other son, if you know?

A. He has gone to Jew Foo.

Q. Was that boy who is now in Jew Foo in China when your uncle was there in 1895?

A. Yes, sir.

Q. Where was he living?

A. He was living in that house.     [16]

Q. With his father and mother?     A. Yes, sir.

The REFEREE.—Q. Did he come to that house with his father and mother, and eat at the same time?     A. Yes, sir.

Q. Where was this other son at the time your uncle was in China, the one who is now in Jew Foo?     A. He was living there too.

Q. Did he come to your house with your uncle and aunt also, and eat at your house?     A. Yes, sir.

Q. Where did the two sons eat—at the table with your uncle and you, or with your mother and their mother?

A. They are with my uncle and me.

Q. Whenever they (your uncle and his wife)

came on those visits and ate at your house, did the sons come with them? A. Yes, sir.

Q. Every time? A. Yes, sir.

DEA LEONG FOON, called for the petitioner, sworn.

Mr. HANLEY.—Q. What is your name?

A. Dea Leong Foon.

Q. What is your business?

A. General merchandise.

Q. How long have you been in this country?

A. 28 years. [17]

Q. Have you been a merchant all of that time?

A. Yes, sir.

Q. What business are you engaged in now, what is the name of your firm?

A. Formerly in the drug business. Now in the general merchandise business.

Q. Where? A. 742 Sacramento Street.

Q. What is the name of your firm?

A. Wah On Hai.

Q. Do you know the petitioner (pointing to the petitioner)? A. Yes, sir.

Q. Is he related to you? A. My nephew.

Q. Do you know where he was born?

A. In San Francisco on Jackson Street.

Q. What number? A. 618.

Q. Do you know when. A. In 1876.

Q. What was his mother's name?

A. Yee Shee.

Q. And his father's name?

A. Dea Leong Jit.

Q. Do you know *what* this boy ever went to China? A. In 1880.

Q. Do you know who he went with?

A. His parents.

Q. Have you ever been to China since the boy left here? A. Yes, sir.

Q. When did you go? A. In 1895. [18]

Q. Did you ever see the boy on your visit there? Yes, sir.

Q. What village, district and house did you reside in? A. Wong Son How Village.

Q. When did you return to this country?

A. In 1895, in the 12th month I got back here.

Q. When did you start to return to this country from your village? A. In the 11th month.

Q. And when did you arrive in your village?

A. In the 4th month.

Q. Have you any children?

A. Yes, sir; I have two sons.

Q. What are their names.

A. Dea Seong Fong and Dea Sheong Gee.

Q. Where are they now?

A. Dea Seong Fong is in Australia.

Q. And where is the other one?

A. The other one is home.

Q. Do you know where the father of this boy is?

A. He is dead in China.

Q. Where is his mother? A. Living in China.

Q. Have you a wife? A. Yes, sir.

Q. Where does she live? A. In China.

Q. Where did you reside while in China?

A. Wong Son How Village?

Q. What row of houses?

A. The 5th row. [19]

Q. The same street, or row, as the boy?

A. Yes, sir.

Q. What house, with reference to the boy's house?

A. I am in the 3d, and the boy is in the 2d.

Q. Did you ever reside in any other house in that row?

A. I got a letter from there stating that the old house needed repairing and they may have moved from it.

Q. Was your house in good condition when you left there? A. It was leaking.

Q. Did the leak ever cause you to move at any time?

A. I always lived in that one house, the old house, and it was all right; but afterwards I got a letter saying it was in bad condition, and they might have moved now.

Q. Do you know in what house your wife lives in now?

A. Since I have returned here, I don't know. Maybe on account of the house being broken up, she might have moved, but when I was home we lived in the 3d house.

The REFEREE.—Q. Did she say anything about moving in her letter to you?

A. She wrote a letter to me for me to come back and fix the house as it was out of repair, and if I did not come she would have to move.

Q. Did you own any other house in that village?

A. I only own that one house: if she moves, she will have to rent another one.

Q. Have you the letter now that she wrote you?

A. It is a long time ago, last year.

Q. Have you more than one brother?

The INTERPRETER.—I asked him if he had another brother, and he says "We are two brothers." [20]

The REFEREE.—Q. Did you ever have more than one brother?

A. Dea Leong Jit is dead, and I have no other.

Q. How many houses are there in that village, as near as you can tell me?

A. 20 or 30 houses.

The REFEREE.—I wish to ask the petitioner a few questions before going any further with this witness. (The witness here leaves the courtroom.)

DEA CHEONG WING, the petitioner, recalled.

The REFEREE.—Q. You told me there were 60 to 70 houses in your village, did you not?

A. Yes, sir.

Q. How many houses were there in the village when your uncle was there?

A. When he came to this country there were 20 to 30 houses.

Q. How many houses were there when he was there in 1895?    A. Twenty or so.

Q. They have built pretty lively there in the last 5 years?    A. Yes, sir.

Q. Is there any ancestral hall in that village?

A. No; not at that time.

Q. Is there any there now?

A. Yes, there is a schoolhouse.

Q. How many houses were there when your uncle was there in 1895, and lived there in the 3d house?     A. 7.

Q. Then your town has not increased any?

A. There has always been 7 houses in that 5th row, and it is the same now.

Q. How many rows of houses were there in 1895, when your uncle was there?   [21]

A. There were 6 rows at that time.

Q. And now there are ten, I understand you?
A. 10.

### DEA LEONG FOON.

The REFEREE.—Q. How many houses were there in the 5th row in which you lived when you were in China in 1895?     A. 7 houses.

Q. Was there any ancestral hall, if so, where was it?

A. No, there was a schoolhouse there.

Q. Was there any ancestral hall beside the schoolhouse?     A. No, sir.

Q. Did you ever live in any house but that third house in that row?     A. No, sir.

Q. Where were your two sons when you were in China in 1895?     A. Both of them were home.

Q. Did you or did you not, go frequently to your brother's house?     A. Many times.

Q. Did you ever eat any regular meal at his house?     A. Yes, sir, he also in mine.

Q. What meal did you eat in his house—morning, noon or evening meal?

A. Sometimes the evening meal, and sometimes the morning meal.

Q. (The INTERPRETER.) I asked him any noon meal, and he said he did not eat any noon meal. [22]

The REFEREE.—Q. Where would the boy be when you were eating *there* meals?

A. Both at the morning and evening meal the boy would be present.

Q. You say this would happen frequently, and that you would eat the meal?    A. Yes, sir.

Q. On the occasions when you would be there, who would be present?

A. Women would eat with women and men would eat with men.

Q. Who ate with you when you would be there, at the same table?

A. Sometime we would eat a holiday meal, and sometime we would eat an ordinary meal.

Q. I am speaking of the ordinary meal, not holiday meal.

A. The four of us; my two boys, this boy and myself.

Q. Would your wife be there?

A. She would be with the women.

Q. With the boy's mother?    A. Yes, sir.

Q. When did they eat?

A. After we would go out, the women would eat, they would not eat with us.

Q. Did they eat at all while you were there?

A. No, sir.

Q. Where would they be when you would be eating?

A. In the bedroom; the meal would be prepared before I was invited to eat.

Q. While you were eating, they would be in the bedroom, do I understand you? Do not state so unless you remember it. [23]

A. They might come in and out, and so on, but they did not eat with us or stay with us.

Q. And did they eat while you were in the house?

A. No, sir. They did not eat in the bedroom. They would eat after the men would go out.

Q. Did they eat in the kitchen while you were there? A. How would I know?

Q. Well, you say they would go in and out.

A. They did not eat until after we left the house.

Q. You say you never ate a noon meal?

A. Sometimes there would be a noon meal.

Q. Did you eat at any time at a noon meal there with the boy when you were there in 1895?

A. Yes, sir.

Q. How often?

A. Forenoon we would eat, and noon we would eat.

Q. How many times did you eat a forenoon meal there when the boy was present?

A. Many times; I don't remember how many times.

Q. And how many times did you eat that evening meal there in 1895 when the boy was present eating with you?

A. 6 or 7 in the morning, and 12 to 1 in the noontime, and in the evening at 7 o'clock sometimes; but the regular meals are the morning and noon, and occasionally a meal at 2 o'clock.

Q. How many times did you eat the evening meal there with the boy?

A. I don't remember how many times.

Q. Well, about how many?

A. Many times. How could I remember? When there was anything they would invite me. [24]

Q. Well, I do not expect you to remember the exact number of times, but I want you to tell me as near as you can.    A. I do not know exactly.

The INTERPRETER.—I asked him, "Tell me how many," and he says, "Approximately in the morning 6 or 7 times, and the noon 5 or 6 times, and the evening 3 or 4 times; this is approximately only."

Mr. HANLEY.—Q. As a rule, you ate your meals home, did you not?    A. Yes, sir.

Q. With your own family?    A. Yes, sir.

Q. And occasionally you had meals with the boy?

A. Yes, sir.

Q. Now, would you state as to the number of meals you had with the boy and his mother as you best recollect?

A. I am just giving you up and down, allowing space to go up, and a space to go down.

Q. Then you may have had 10 meals in the morning, and one or two at noon?

A. Well, maybe; I do not know; I cannot say exactly.

Q. Most of your testimony on this point is guess-work, is it not?

A. Well, I am just saying about. When they invited me, I went; and when they did not, I did not go.

The REFEREE.—Q. Are you certain that you did eat morning and noon and evening meals at the boy's house when the boy was there? To say now for sure without saying the number of times that you are with the boy in the morning. [25]

A. Yes, sir.

Q. You say the same regarding the noon meal?

A. Yes, sir.

Q. And also the same about the evening meal?

A. Yes, sir.

[Endorsed]: Filed Oct. 9, 1923. Walter B. Maling, Clerk. By C. W. Calbreath, Deputy Clerk. [26]

---

In the Southern Division of the District Court for the United States, in and for the Northern District of California, Second Division.

### No. 18009.

In the Matter of DEA HONG, DEA CHUCK, DEA TON and DEA FONG, Ex. SS. "Taiyo Maru," May 26, 1923. Nos. 22186/5–6, 5–14, 5–7 and 5–5 on Habeas Corpus.

### ORDER TO SHOW CAUSE.

Good cause appearing therefor, and upon reading the verified petition on file herein,—

IT IS HEREBY ORDERED, that John D. Nagle, Commissioner of Immigration for the port of San Francisco, appear before this Court on the 22d day of October, 1923, at the hour of 10 o'clock A. M. of said day, to show cause, if any he have, why a writ of habeas corpus should not be issued as prayed for, and that a copy of this order be served on said Commissioner;

AND IT IS FURTHER ORDERED, that the said John D. Nagle, Commissioner of Immigration as aforesaid, or whoever acting under the orders of said Commissioner of the Secretary of Labor shall have the custody of the said Dea Hong, Dea Chuck, Dea Ton and Dea Fong, are hereby ordered and directed to retain the said Dea Hong, Dea Chuck, Dea Ton, and Dea Fong within the custody of the Commissioner of Immigration [27] and within the jurisdiction of this Court, until further orders herein.

Dated at San Francisco, California, October 9, 1923.

JOHN S. PARTRIDGE,
Judge of the U. S. District Court.

[Endorsed]: Filed Oct. 9, 1923. Walter B. Maling, Clerk. By C. W. Calbreath, Deputy Clerk. [28]

In the Southern Division of the United States District Court, for the Northern District of California, Second Division.

No. 18009.

In the Matter of DEA HONG, DEA CHUCK, DEA TON, and DEA FONG on Habeas Corpus.

## DEMURRER TO PETITION FOR WRIT OF HABEAS CORPUS.

Comes now the respondent, John D. Nagle, Commissioner of Immigration, at the port of San Francisco, in the Southern Division of the Northern District of California, and demurs to the petition for a writ of habeas corpus in the above-entitled cause and for grounds of demurrer alleges:

### I.

That the said petition does not state facts sufficient to entitle petitioner to the issuance of a writ of habeas corpus, or for any relief thereon.

### II.

That said petition is insufficient in that the statements therein relative to the record of the evidence taken of the said applicant are conclusions of law and not statements of the ultimate facts.

WHEREFORE, respondent prays that the writ of habeas corpus be denied.

JOHN T. WILLIAMS,
United States Attorney,
THOMAS T. CALIFRO,
Asst. United States Attorney,
Attorneys for Respondent.

[Endorsed]: Filed Dec. 17, 1923. Walter B.
Maling, Clerk. [29]

---

At a stated term of the Southern Division of the
United States District Court, for the Northern
District of California, held at the courtroom
thereof, in the city and county of San Francisco, State of California, on Monday, the seven-
teenth day of December, in the year of our
Lord, one thousand nine hundred and twenty-
three. Present: The Honorable   JOHN  S.'
PARTRIDGE, Judge.

No. 18009.

In the Matter of DEA HONG et al., on Habeas
Corpus.

## MINUTES OF COURT—DECEMBER 17, 1923— ORDER SUSTAINING DEMURRER AND DISMISSING PETITION.

This matter came on regularly this day for hearing on order to show cause as to the issuance of a
writ of habeas corpus herein.  Attorneys were present for and on behalf of respective parties.  Attorney for respondent filed demurrer to petition,
and all parties consenting thereto, it is ordered that
the immigration records be filed as respondent's Exhibits "A," "B," "C," "D" and "E" and that
the same be considered as part of original petition.
After argument by the respective attorneys, the
Court ordered that said matter be and the same
is hereby submitted.  After due consideration had

thereon, ordered that said demurrer to petition be and the same is hereby sustained and that said petition be dismissed. [30]

---

In the Southern Division of the United States District Court, for the Northern District of California, Second Division.

No. 18009.

DEA HONG, DEA CHUCK, DEA TON, DEA FONG,

Appellants,

vs.

JOHN D. NAGLE, as Commissioner of Immigration for the Port of San Francisco,

Appellee.

NOTICE OF APPEAL.

To the Clerk of the Above-entitled Court, to John D. Nagle, Commissioner of Immigration, and to John T. Williams, Esq., United States Attorney, His Attorney:

You and each of you will please take notice that the above-named appellants, hereby appeal to the United States Circuit Court of Appeals for the Ninth Circuit, from an order and judgment made and entered herein on the 17th day of December, 1923, sustaining the demurrer to and denying the petition for a writ of habeas corpus in the above-entitled causes.

Dated this 24th day of December, 1923.

STEPHEN M. WHITE,

Attorney for Appellants.   [31]

---

In the Southern Division of the United States District Court, for the Northern District of California, Second Division.

No. 18009.

DEA HONG, DEA CHUCK, DEA TON, DEA FONG,

Appellants,

vs.

JOHN D. NAGLE, as Commissioner of Immigration for the Port of San Francisco,

PETITION FOR APPEAL.

Come now, the above-named appellants, through their attorney, Stephen M. White, and say:

That on the 17th day of December, 1923, the above-entitled court made and entered its order denying the petition for a writ of habeas corpus, as prayed for, on file herein, in which said order in the above-entitled cause certain errors were made to the prejudice of the appellants herein, all of which will more fully appear from the assignment of errors filed herewith.

Wherefore the appellants pray that an appeal may be granted in their behalf to the Circuit Court of Appeals of the United States for the Ninth Circuit thereof for the correction of the errors as complained of, and further, that a transcript of the record, proceedings and papers in the above-entitled cause, as shown by the praecipe, duly authenticated, may be sent and transmitted to the said United States Circuit Court of Appeals for the Ninth Circuit thereof, and further, that the said appellants be held within the jurisdiction of this Court during the pendency of the appeal herein, so that they may be produced in [32] execution of whatever judgment may be finally entered herein, or that they be released upon bond in the sum of $1,000.00, each, during the further pendency of this action.

Dated at San Francisco, California, December 24th, 1923.

STEPHEN M. WHITE.

Attorney for Appellants. [33]

---

In the Southern Division of the United States District Court for the Northern District of California, Second Division.

No. 18009.

DEA HONG, DEA CHUCK, DEA TON, DEA FONG,

Appellants,

vs.

JOHN D. NAGLE, as Commissioner of Immigration for the Port of San Francisco,

Appellee.

## ASSIGNMENT OF ERRORS.

Comes now the above-named appellants, by Stephen M. White, their attorney, and file the following assignment of errors upon which they will rely in the prosecution of their appeal in the above-entitled causes to the United States Circuit Court of Appeals for the Ninth Circuit, from the order and judgment made by this Honorable Court on the 17th day of December, 1923.

### I.

That the Court erred in sustaining the demurrer to the petitions for a writ of habeas corpus in the above-entitled causes.

### II.

That the Court erred in denying the petition for writ of habeas corpus in the above-entitled causes.

### III.

That the Court erred in refusing to grant the writ of habeas corpus as prayed for in the above-entitled causes.   [34]

### IV.

That the Court erred in holding that the allegations contained in the petition herein for a writ of habeas corpus and the facts presented upon the issues made and joined herein were insufficient in law to discharge the above-named appellants from custody as prayed for in said hearing.

### V.

That the judgment made and entered herein is contrary to law.

## VI.

That the judgment made and entered herein is not supported by the evidence.

## VII.

That the judgment made and entered herein is contrary to the evidence.

## VIII.

That the Court erred in holding that the above-named appellants were, or either or any of them, subject to exclusion from the United States.

Dated this 24th day of December, 1923.

STEPHEN M. WHITE,

Attorney for Appellants.

[Endorsed]: Filed Jan. 11, 1924. Walter B. Maling, Clerk. By C. W. Calbreath, Deputy Clerk. [35]

---

In the Southern Division of the United States District Court for the Northern District of California, Second Division.

No. 18009.

DEA HONG, DEA CHUCK, DEA TON, DEA FONG,

Appellants,

vs.

JOHN D. NAGLE, as Commissioner of Immigration for the Port of San Francisco,

Appellee.

## ORDER ALLOWING APPEAL.

On motion of Stephen M. White, attorney for appellants in the above-entitled causes,—

IT IS HEREBY ORDERED, that an appeal to the United States Circuit Court of Appeals for the Ninth Circuit, from the order and judgment made and entered herein on the 17th day of December, 1923, be, and the same is hereby allowed, and that a certified transcript of the records, testimony, exhibits, stipulations and all proceedings be forthwith transmitted to the said United States Circuit Court of Appeals for the Ninth Circuit, in the manner and time prescribed by law.

Dated this 24th day of December, 1923.

HUNT,
United States District Judge.

[Endorsed]: Filed Jan. 11, 1924. Walter B. Maling, Clerk. By C. W. Calbreath, Deputy Clerk. [36]

---

In the Southern Division of the United States District Court for the Northern District of California, Second Division.

No. 18009.

DEA HONG, DEA CHUCK, DEA TON, DEA FONG,

Appellants,

vs.

JOHN D. NAGLE, as Commissioner of Immigration for the Port of San Francisco,

Appellee.

## CITATION ON APPEAL (COPY).

United States of America,—ss.

The President of the United States, to John D. Nagle, Commissioner of Immigration, Port of San Francisco, and John T. Williams, United States Attorney, GREETING:

You are hereby cited and admonished to be and appear at a United States Circuit Court of Appeals for the Ninth Circuit, to be holden at the city of San Francisco, in the State of California, within 30 days from the date hereof, pursuant to an order allowing appeal, of record in the Clerk's Office of the United States District Court for the Northern District of California, where Dea Hong, Dea Chuck, Dea Ton and Dea Fong are appellants and you are appellee, to show cause, if any *thereby,* why the decree rendered against the said appellants, as in the said order allowing appeal mentioned, should not be corrected, and why speedy justice should not be done to the parties in that behalf.

WITNESS, the Honorable JOHN S. PARTRIDGE, United States District Judge for the Southern Division of the Northern District of California, this 30th day of January, A. D., 1924.

JOHN S. PARTRIDGE,
United States District Judge.

[Endorsed]: Filed Jan. 30, 1924. Walter B. Maling, Clerk. By C. W. Calbreath, Deputy Clerk. [37]

In the Southern Division of the United States District Court for the Northern District of California, Second Division.

No. 18009.

DEA HONG, DEA CHUCK, DEA TON, DEA FONG,

Appellants,

vs.

JOHN D. NAGLE, as Commissioner of Immigration for the Port of San Francisco,

Appellee.

## STIPULATION AND ORDER RE WITHDRAWAL OF IMMIGRATION RECORD.

It is hereby stipulated and agreed by and between the attorney for the petitioner and appellants herein and the attorneys for the respondent and appellee herein, that the original Immigration record in evidence and considered as part and parcel of the petition for a writ of habeas corpus upon hearing of the demurrer in the above-entitled matter, may be withdrawn from the files of the Clerk of the above-entitled court and filed with the Clerk of the United States Circuit Court of Appeals in and for the Ninth Circuit, there to be considered as a part and parcel of the record on appeal in the above-entitled case with the same force and effect as if embodied in the transcript of the record, and so certified to by the Clerk of the court.

Dated San Francisco, California, January 30th, 1924.

JOHN T. WILLIAMS,
Attorney for Respondent and Appellee.
STEPHEN M. WHITE,
Attorney for Petitioner and Appellants. [38]

Upon reading and filing the foregoing stipulation, it is hereby ordered that the said Immigration record therein referred to may be withdrawn from the office of the Clerk of this Court and filed in the office of the United States Circuit Court of Appeals for the Ninth Judicial Circuit, said withdrawal to be made at the time the record on appeal herein is certified to by this Court.

Dated San Francisco, California, January 30th, 1924.

JOHN S. PARTRIDGE,
United States District Judge.

[Endorsed]: Filed Jan. 30, 1924. Walter B. Maling, Clerk. By C. W. Calbreath, Deputy Clerk. [39]

---

CERTIFICATE OF CLERK U. S. DISTRICT COURT TO TRANSCRIPT OF RECORD.

I, Walter B. Maling, Clerk of the United States District Court, for the Northern District of California do hereby certify the foregoing 39 pages numbered from 1 to 39, inclusive, contain a full, true and correct transcript of certain records and proceedings, in the matter of Dea Hong et al., on Habeas Corpus, No. 18009, as the same now remain on file and of record in this office; said transcript having been prepared pursuant to and in accordance with the praecipe for transcript on appeal (copy of which is embodied herein) and the instructions of the attorney for appellants herein.

I further certify that the cost for preparing and certifying the foregoing transcript on appeal is the sum of twelve dollars and ten cents ($12.10) and that the same has been paid to me by the attorney for appellant herein.

Annexed hereto is the original citation on appeal, issued herein (page 41).

IN WITNESS WHEREOF, I have hereunto set my hand and affixed the seal of said District Court, this 21st day of March, A. D. 1924.

[Seal]          WALTER B. MALING,

Clerk.

By C. M. Taylor,

Deputy Clerk.   [40]

---

In the Southern Division of the United States District Court for the Northern District of California, Second Division.

No. 18009.

DEA HONG, DEA CHUCK, DEA TON, DEA FONG,

Appellants,

vs.

JOHN D. NAGLE, as Commissioner of Immigration for the Port of San Francisco,

Appellee.

## CITATION ON APPEAL (ORIGINAL).

United States of America,—ss.

The President of the United States, to John D. Nagle, Commissioner of Immigration, Port of San Francisco, and John T. Williams, United States Attorney, GREETING:

You are hereby cited and admonished to be and appear at a United States Circuit Court of Appeals for the Ninth Circuit, to be holden at the city of San Francisco, in the State of California, within 30 days from the date hereof, pursuant to an order allowing an appeal, of record in the Clerk's office of the United States District Court for the Northern District of California, wherein Dea Hong, Dea Chuck, Dea Ton and Dea Fong are appellants and you are appellee, to show cause, if any *thereby,* why the decree rendered against the said appellants, as in the said order allowing appeal mentioned, should not be corrected, and why speedy justice should not be done to the parties in that behalf.

WITNESS, the Honorable JOHN S. PARTRIDGE, United States District Judge for the Southern Division of the Northern District of California, this 30th day of January, A. D., 1924.

JOHN S. PARTRIDGE,
United States District Judge. [41]

[Endorsed]: No. 18009. In the Southern Division of the United States District Court in and for the Northern District of California. Dea Hong

et al., Appellants, vs. John D. Nagle, etc., Appellee.
Citation on Appeal. Filed Jan. 30, 1924. Walter
B. Maling, Clerk. By C. W. Calbreath, Deputy
Clerk. [42]

---

In the Southern Division of the United States District Court for the Northern District of California, Second Division.

### No. 18009.

DEA HONG, DEA CHUCK, DEA TON, DEA FONG,

Appellants,

vs.

JOHN D. NAGLE, as Commissioner of Immigration for the Port of San Francisco,

Appellee.

## STIPULATION AND ORDER RE EXTENSION OF TIME FOR FILING COPY OF TRANSCRIPT OF RECORD.

It is hereby stipulated by and between Stephen
M. White, the attorney for the above-named appellants, and John T. Williams, the attorney for the
above-named appellee, that the appellants be
granted until the 1st day of April, 1924, within
which to file the certified copy of the Transcript
of Record in the above-entitled action with the
Clerk of the United States Circuit Court of Appeals for the Ninth Circuit.

Dated this 21st day of March, 1924.

STEPHEN M. WHITE,
Attorney for Appellants.
JOHN T. WILLIAMS,
Attorney for Appellee.

ORDER ALLOWING EXTENSION OF TIME.

Upon reading the foregoing stipulation and good cause appearing therefor, it is hereby ordered that the above-named appellants be allowed until the 1st day of April, 1924, with which to file the certified copy of the Transcript of Record in the above-entitled action, with the Clerk of the United States Circuit Court for the Ninth Circuit.

Dated this 21st day of March, 1924.

FRANK H. RUDKIN.
United States District Judge.

[Endorsed]: 4225. No. 18009. In the Southern Division of the United States District Court, in and for the Northern District of California. Dea Hong et al., Appellants, vs. John D. Nagle, etc., Appellee. Stipulation and Order Allowing Extension of Time. Filed Mar. 21, 1924. F. D. Monckton, Clerk.

———

[Endorsed]: No. 4225. United States Circuit Court of Appeals for the Ninth Circuit. Dea Hong, Dea Chuck, Dea Ton and Dea Fong, Appellants, vs. John D. Nagle, as Commissioner of Immigration, Port of San Francisco, Appellee. Transcript of Record. Upon Appeal from the

Southern Division of the United States District Court for the Northern District of California, Second Division.

Filed March 21, 1924.

F. D. MONCKTON,

Clerk of the United States Circuit Court of Appeals for the Ninth Circuit.

By Paul P. O'Brien,

Deputy Clerk.

No. 4225

IN THE

# United States Circuit Court of Appeals

FOR THE

NINTH CIRCUIT

---

DEA HONG, DEA CHUCK, DEA TON and DEA
FONG,

*Appellants,*

*vs.*

JOHN D. NAGLE, as Commissioner of Immigration, Port of San Francisco,

*Appellee.*

---

# BRIEF FOR APPELLANTS

STEPHEN M. WHITE,
*Attorney for Appellants.*

No. 4225

# United States Circuit Court of Appeals

FOR THE

NINTH CIRCUIT

---

DEA HONG, DEA CHUCK, DEA TON and DEA FONG,

*Appellants,*

vs.

JOHN D. NAGLE, as Commissioner of Immigration, Port of San Francisco,

*Appellee.*

---

**BRIEF FOR APPELLANTS.**

**Statement of the Case.**

This is an appeal from an order and judgment of the District Court, for the Northern District of California, sustaining the demurrer interposed and denying a petition for a writ of habeas corpus.

Dea Fong, Dea Hong, Dea Ton, and Dea Chuck, the appellants herein, applied to the United States Immigration authorities, for the Port of San Francisco, to enter the United States, as the sons of Dea Chung Wing, a native born citizen thereof. Their applications were denied by a Board of Special Inquiry, from whose decision an appeal was taken to the Secretary of Labor, Washington, D. C. The Secretary of Labor, thereafter affirmed the decision of the Board of Special Inquiry and ordered the deportation of the applicants.

A Petition for a Writ of Habeas Corpus was thereupon filed in the District Court for the release of the applicants from the custody of the Immigration authorities, with the result that the Court sustained the demurrer interposed and dismissed the petition.

## ARGUMENT.
### With Points and Authorities.

It is admitted that Dea Chung Wing, the alleged father of the applicants is a native born citizen of the United States. It is, however, maintained by the Board of Special Inquiry that the applicants are not entitled to admission to the United States, as the sons of Dea Chung Wing, for the reason that the evidence shows that he (Dea Chung Wing) was not married in 1900; that, the three oldest of the applicants having been born prior to 1900, his paternity to them is, therefore, precluded.

The finding of the Board of Special Inquiry (Exhibit "A", page 39), upon this point, is as follows:

> "The alleged father attempted to secure the admission of an alleged son, Dea Bow, at this port in 1911, record No. 10485/56. His application to land was denied by this office and his appeal was subsequently dismissed October 6, 1911, Bureau No. 53329/106, as it was brought to light in that record that certain testimony given by the alleged father and the alleged uncle before the United States District Court in 1900, shows very clearly that the alleged father was not then married and did not have the family which he now claims to have had at that time, and that statement certainly affects the admission of the three older applicants, which is thoroughly covered in the various reports on the subject in file 10485/56."

Referring to the decision of the Commissioner of Immigration in the case of Dea Bow, mentioned in the above finding and which has been made a part of the record (Exhibit "D", pages 53 and 54), we find that the following testimony of the alleged father, Dea Chung Wing, was brought to light:

> "Q. Who was living with you in your house besides your mother when your uncle was in China?
>
> A. No one else."

Now, upon that question and answer, the Board of Special Inquiry determined that Dea Chung Wing, the alleged father, was not married in 1900. We do not believe that the conclusion has been fairly drawn. It is to be noted that the question refers to a time when the uncle of Dea Chung Wing was in China. According to the undisputed testimony in the case of Dea Chung Wing, on the occasion of his hearing in the United States District Court, Habeas Corpus, No. 12029, his uncle was in China for approximately four months in 1895. The testimony (Transcript of record, pages 10 and 11) was as follows:

"The Referee—Q. What number is your uncle's house?

A. The 3rd house.

Q. Then, it is the next house to yours, is it?

A. Taking, this for my house, my uncle lives in the adjoining house, and then he lives also in the 6th house from me.

Q. Which house did he live in while he was in China, and when you saw him there?

A. He lived in the furthest house.

Q. All the time he was in China?

A. He first lived in the house nearest mine and then it leaked and then he moved into the other one.

Q. What part of the time did he live in the 3rd house?

A.   He moved into the house last year, before that time he lived in the 3rd house.

Q.   When did your uncle return to this country?

A.   I don't remember when he returned.

Q.   When did he leave China?

A.   I do not remember.

Q.   Tell me as near as you can.

A.   He left to come back here in 1895, in the 8th month (September).

Q.   And when did he arrive in China?

A.   In April.

Q.   Then he was there only four months?

A.   Yes, sir."

Therefore, the question as to who was living with Dea Chung Wing, the alleged father, when his uncle was in China, necessarily refers to the year 1895, as, according to the evidence, this was the only time the uncle was there.   Therefore, if, from Dea Chung Wing's statement to the effect that no one, save his mother, was living with him at that time, it is to be concluded that he was not married, the inference would be that he was not married in 1895.   What bearing, then, has this point upon the issue?

The undisputed evidence shows that the four applicants were born subsequent to the time that the uncle of Dea Chung Wing was in China; their birth dates being as follows:

> Dea Fong, November 27, 1895. (Exhibit "A", pg. 22).
>
> Dea Hong, December 3, 1897. (Exhibit "A", pg. 17).
>
> Dea Chuck, September 7, 1899. (Exhibit "A", pg. 13).
>
> Dea Ton, February 22, 1907. (Exhibit "A", pg. 9).

We, therefore, submit that it was not necessary for Dea Chung to have been married, when his uncle was in China, in order to claim paternity to these applicants. He, certainly, could have been married subsequent to that time and be the father of these persons.

Our conclusion, therefore, is that the most the Board of Special Inquiry could find on this issue is that the alleged father was not married in 1895, in which event his paternity to the applicants would not be precluded. Consequently, the Board of Special Inquiry, in finding that the alleged father was not married in 1900 has not based its conclusion upon the evidence and has therefore acted manifestly unfair and arbitrary. In the case of Kwock Jan Fat v. White, 253 U. S. 454, the Supreme Court has said:

> "While the decision by the Secretary of Labor on the exclusion of a Chinese person is final,

unless the proceedings were manifestly unfair or show manifest abuse of discretion, the decision must be made after a hearing in good faith and must find adequate support in the evidence.''

Furthermore, we contend that the testimony of Dea Chung Wing, the alleged father, as to who was living with him, does not fairly infer that he was not married, even when his uncle was in China. Was it necessary for his wife to have been living with him at that time? As we have heretofore pointed out, the uncle was in China for a period of about four months in 1895, and, certainly, during that time, Dea Chung Wing's wife could have been temporarily living in another part of China or could have been separated from her husband for other causes. The situation, at least, raised a question, as the very admission of the Board of Review, which acted for the Secretary of Labor in the matter, will show. We quote from the finding of the Board as follows (Exhibit ''A'' pages 89 and 90):

"The Board of Review is of the opinion that the discrepancies alone indicate that this case is not bona fide. There is another feature, however, which has been given considerable weight at the Port and which is discussed at length by counsel. This has to do with a statement made by the alleged father in 1900, when he was an applicant for admission to the United States, indicating that he did not have a wife and family living in China. It is claimed by the alleged father that he was married in 1891 and that sons were born in 1892, 1893, 1895, 1897, and 1899, as well as in subsequent years. In

1900 he was asked 'who was living with you in your house besides your mother when your uncle was in China' and answered 'no one else.' If the present testimony is true he must have had a wife, and three sons living with him at that time. This feature is believed by the Board of Review to indicate a reasonable possibility that the alleged father was not married in 1895 and as he does not claim to have been married subsequent to that date, there seems to be a grave question whether or not he ever was married at all. * * *."

In other words, the plain language of the Board of Review shows that the 1900 testimony of the alleged father created a doubt as to whether or not he was married in 1895 or at any time. Under these circumstances, we submit that the Board of Special Inquiry and the Board of Review should have inquired into the situation and sought an explanation from Dea Chung Wing, the alleged father, before drawing their conclusions. As the Court has said in Ex Parte Wong Foo, 230 Fed. 534, the inquiry of the Immigration authorities should be directed in good faith to the ascertainment of all the facts in the case.

It, clearly and evidently, appears to be a matter which was susceptible of explanation; at least, it was a matter, which was not impossible to reconcile. In other words, it was a presumption; rebuttable and not conclusive. Hence, we believe that Dea Chung Wing should have been given an opportunity to explain and the failure of the Immigration authorities to do so was manifestly unfair (Lum Hoy Kee v. Johnson, 281 Fed. 873).

Then, also, it is to be noted, from the entire record in the case, that, at no time, were Dea Chung Wing or the applicants confronted with the evidence or testimony, upon which the adverse finding, on this point was based, nor did any of them learn of the reason for same, until after the case was decided and closed. As a result, the applicants were deprived of the right to introduce evidence, which would tend to rebutt the conclusion of the Immigration authorities. The failure to confront Dea Chung Wing or the applicants with the evidence was a further manifestation of unfairness (Chew Hoy Quong v. White, 162 C. C. A. 103; 249 Fed. 869).

It is, also, to be noted, in the discussion of this point, that the Immigration authorities have clearly violated the Rules of the Department of Labor. Rule 3, Subdivision 4, governing the admission of Chinese, provides as follows:

> "Introduction of additional evidence — If upon examining the applicant and the witnesses appearing in his behalf, the board of special inquiry does not conclude that the applicant is admissible, notice shall be served upon the applicant or his attorney to that effect, such notice to state the respect or respects in which the evidence is deemed by the board of special inquiry to be insufficient. * * *"

Now, the hearing of these applicants was primarily conducted by a single inspector; the attorneys for the applicants having stipulated that this procedure could be followed, in place of having the primary hearing conducted by a Board of Special Inquiry, as required by law. At the conclusion of the examination, the following and only notice was addressed to the attorneys for the applicants:

> "You are hereby notified that these applicants have been held for a hearing before a Board of Special Inquiry, having failed to establish on primary inspection the relationship claimed. Applicant Dea Fong (5-5) signifies a desire to have his alleged father present during the board of special inquiry hearings. A period of ten days will be allowed for the introduction of all additional evidence to be presented to said Board of Special Inquiry, provided notice thereof is filed with this office within five days. Review of the record will not be permitted during the time allowed for the submission of further evidence." (Exhibit "A", page 33).

We submit that the plain language of the above recited notice utterly fails to state the respect or respects in which the applicants have not established their relationship and consequently their right to enter the United States. It merely states the conclusion of the inspector and we believe it to be an open violation of the above rule. The unfairness and injustice of this procedure is apparent. Naturally, the attorneys, upon receiving the notice, believed that the only issue involved was the relationship of the applicants to the alleged father. Hence any additional which was to be introduced would be on this issue. If, on the other hand, the attorneys for the applicants had been advised that the marital status of the alleged father was in question, then an effort would have been exerted to produce evidence in relation thereto. As a result, the alleged father was foreclosed of his right to produce evidence to rebutt the adverse finding of the immigration authorities as to his marital status. Necessarily this affected the applicants and was therefore unfair to them.

As a matter of fact, the Immigration authorities have conceded, on two distinct occasions, that Dea Chung Wing was married even prior to 1895. The first occasion was in 1909, in the case of Dea See, who, at that time, was admitted to the United States as the true and lawful son of the said Dea Chung Wing, and whose record of admission is made a part of this hearing (Exhibit "C"). As this person's birth occurred in 1892, it naturally follows that Dea Chung Wing, his father, was married prior thereto. The second confirmation occurred in 1922, when the same Dea See made application for a pre-investigation of his status to the Immigration authorities. The record of this investigation, which is made a part of this hearing (Exhibit "C"), shows that the Immigration authorities made the same concessions as on the occasion of his admission in 1909.

We do not contend that, inasmuch as the Immigration authorities have on two prior occasions confirmed the marital status, the alleged father is absolved from subsequent attack on this issue. We do, however, maintain that such confirmations, at least import prima facie verity and require the Immigration authorities to produce some evidence in order to defeat same. In Ex Parte Wong Yee Toon, 227 Fed. 247, the Court held that, although the act of the Immigration authorities in admitting an alien is not the equivalent of a certificate of status or residence and does not shift the burden of proof from the alien in subsequent deportation proceedings, nevertheless, the act imports prima facie verity and it cannot be treated as if it never existed. Some evidence must be produced to justify the Immigration officials denying to it its usual and appropriate effect. (Lee Hing v. Nagle, 295 Fed. 642.) Also, in the case of Liu Hop Fong v. United States, 209 U. S. 453, the Supreme Court held that where a Chinese was admitted on a certificate he cannot United States unless there is competent evidence to be deported for having fraudulently entered the overcome the legal effect of the certificate.

In the case at bar, the only evidence, which was offered to rebutt the prior adjudications of the Immigration authorities as to the marital status of the alleged father, was the testimony of Dea Chung Wing, heretofore discussed. As we have pointed out, this testimony, at the most, creates only a presumption and as such was and is rebuttable. In this connection, the record shows that an opportunity was never accorded the alleged father to rebutt same. Under the law therefore it was unfair to utilize it as evidence against these applicants and hence cannot be considered as evidence at all.

The situation may be clearly illustrated by a reference to the status of Dea See, who, as heretofore mentioned, was admitted to the United States in 1909, as the son of Dea Chung Wing. This person is, now, in China, as the records indicate (Exhibit "C"). When this persons returns to the United States, can it be maintained that the Immigration authorities will, then, be authorized to deport him, merely, upon the presumption that his father was not married? It appears to us that, in order for deportation to take place, it will be necessary for the Immigration authorities to confront Dea See with the evidence upon which the presumption is based, namely, the prior testimony in 1900 of his alleged father (Chew Hoy Quong v. White, 162 C. C. A. 103, 249 Fed. 869, supra). Furthermore, it will be necessary to accord him an opportunity to produce evidence to rebutt the presumption. Yet, Dea See is in a no more favorable position than these applicants, who have been denied these rights.

In connection with this point, it has been argued
by the Board of Review, which acted for the Secretary of Labor in deciding the cases of these applicants, that the Immigration authorities adjudicat-
ed the marital status of Dea Chung Wing, on the
two occasions mentioned, without giving any consideration to the 1900 testimony of this person. In
answer thereto, we submit that there is not the least
particle of evidence to show or indicate that that
testimony was overlooked and not considered. The
finding of the Board of Review is, therefore, purely
arbitrary. Indeed, we believe, in the absence of
evidence to the contrary, the only fair presumption
to draw is that the Immigration authorities did give
full consideration to the prior testimony of Dea
Chung Wing, when deciding the admissibility of his
son, Dea See. In this connection, it must be remembered that Dea See's right to enter the United
States was dependent upon the native status of his
father, Dea Chung Wing. The proof submitted, as
to the place of nativity of Dea Chung Wing, was a
decree of the United States District Court, Habeas
Corpus, No. 12029, in which proceeding it is, now,
claimed that such testimony was given as to destroy
the alleged marital status of this person. The record of Dea See (Exhibit "C") shows that the Immigration authorities were satisfied of the nativity
of Dea Chung Wing in the United States and, also,
that Dea See was his son; that his marriage at a
time to permit of his paternity to this person was

thereby admitted. Is it, now, fair to presume that the Immigration authorities were derelict in their duty at that time and did not refer to the above mentioned habeas corpus proceeding to investigate the claims of Dea Chung Wing? We hardly believe that the Courts are willing to sustain such a presumption. On the contrary, we consider that the Courts will always presume, in the absence of evidence to the contrary, that the Immigration authorities, in deciding on the admissibility of aliens, have carefully investigated all claims advanced by these persons. By way of dicta, we would say that it is a fundamental rule of the Immigration Department, in the case of every alien, to investigate the prior records and testimony of the principals, in order to ascertain whether or not a foundation has been laid for the admission of the applicant.

It may be argued, by counsel for appellee, that, even granting the existence of the marital status of Dea Chung Wing, nevertheless, the discrepancies developed in the case are sufficient to warrant an adverse decision. In answer thereto, we beg to refer to the finding of the Immigrant Inspector, who first examined these applicants upon their admissibility to the United States. It is, in part (Exhibit "A", page 28), as follows:

"In view of the 1900 testimony of alleged father, and the discrepancies above recited, it is recommended that these four cases be held for a Board of Special Inquiry, as it does not appear that the claimed relationship has been satisfactorily established."

To, again, refer to the finding of the Board of Special Inquiry (Exhibit "A", page 39), we quote as follows:

"The alleged father attempted to secure the admission of an alleged son, Dea Bow, at this port in 1911, record No. 10485/56. His application was denied by this office and his appeal was subsequently dismissed October 6, 1911, Bureau No. 53329/106, as it was brought to light in that record that certain testimony given by the alleged father before the United States District Court in 1900, shows very clearly that the alleged father was not then married and did not have the family which he now claims to have had at that time, and that statement certainly affects the admission of the three older applicants, which is thoroughly covered in the various reports on the subject in file 10485/56."

Lastly, referring to the finding of the Board of Review (Exhibit "A" page 89), which acted for the Secretary of Labor, we quote as follows:

"* * * These discrepancies, coupled with the quite natural doubt arising from the 1900 testimony of the latter (Dea Chung Wing), indicate conclusively to the Board of Review that these applicants should not be admitted."

Now, we contend that the plain language of the findings of the various Immigration authorities, who passed upon the right of these applicants to enter the United States, shows that the 1900 testimony of the alleged father, Dea Chung Wing, was a deciding factor in the case. Therefore, if it be admitted that this testimony is of no value in determining the existence of the marital status of the alleged father, then, this fact alone is sufficient to warrant a finding of unfairness. In the case of Quan Hing Sam v. White, 254 Fed. 402, (9th. Circuit Court), the denial of the applicant was based upon two grounds, namely:

1. That the applicant was not a dependent member of his father's household.

2. That the applicant failed to prove his relationship to the alleged father.

The Court held that the applicant could not be excluded on account of not being a dependent member of his father's household. The question then arose: "Was the decision of the Commissioner of Immigration and the Secretary of Labor unfair, notwithstanding the fact that the applicant had failed to prove the claimed relationship?" Upon this point, the Court said:

"Was this decision (decision of Commissioner of Immigration) based solely upon the objection that it had not been established that the appellant was the son of Quan Hay, a native born citizen of the United States, or was it influenced by the fact that Quan Hay was dead, and the appellant was not at the time of his arrival in the United States, a dependent member of his father's household, as required by rule 9 (f)? The exclusion under that rule appears to have been considered, and apparently was an element in the decision of the Inspector of Immigration and the Commissioner of Immigration at San Francisco and it is not clear that it did not influence the Department of Labor at Washington.

We are of the opinion that in such an inquiry it should distinctly appear that the Department was not influenced in it's decision by considerations not authorized by law. * * * (Ex parte Wong Foo, 230 Fed. 535.)

The situation in the above cited case appears to be the same as in the case at bar. The question in the latter being: "Were the Board of Special Inquiry and the Secretary of Labor influenced in their decisions by the fact that the alleged father of the applicants was not married, on account of his testimony in 1900, or were their decisions based solely upon the ground of discrepancies in the case?" It is sufficient to point to the heretofore mentioned findings of the various Immigration authorities, who passed upon this case, to ascertain the situation. It will be noted therefrom that special stress and emphasis are laid upon the 1900 testimony of the alleged father. Certainly, the decisions of these various officers do not distinctly show that this testimony had no influence upon their findings.

We, therefore, submit that, if it be admitted that the 1900 testimony of the alleged father does not fairly show that he was not married, then, the

Board of Special Inquiry and Board of Review, in utilizing this feature against the applicants have acted unfairly.

Now, as a matter of fact, are there such discrepancies in this case as would be sufficient to defeat the right of these applicants to enter the United States. The Board of Review, which acted for the Secretary of Labor in the matter, cites the following discrepancies (Exhibit "A", page 90):

"The alleged father claims that he has no brothers or sisters and apparently Dea Fong agrees with him in this respect. Dea Hong, however, claims that his father had one brother, who is dead. He names this alleged brother as Dea Leong Foon and states that he had three sons, all in the Strait Settlements. Dea Chuck agrees with the alleged father in this respect, while Dea Ton testified substantially the same as Dea Hong. This discrepancy is regarded by the Board of Review as particularly material.

According to the testimony of the alleged father a Chinese person named Dea Suey Bow is from his village in China. The alleged father states that this man was a resident of St. Louis, Mo.; that he returned to China last year to his village and married a second wife, his first wife having died. Dea Fong has knowledge of Dea Suey Bow but states that the latter has never been to the United States; in fact has never been away from the village. With this Dea Chuck agrees. Dea Hong and Dea Ton have no knowledge of this person. If these persons are what they claim to be and come from the same village in China as Dea Suey

Bow, it is not believed that this inconsistency would exist. There are other material discrepancies in the case particularly with reference to matters in the home village."

Referring to the first discrepancy cited by the Board of Review, we quote from the transcript of record as follows:

"Q. How many brothers and sisters have you?

A. None."—(Dea Chung Wing, alleged father (Exhibit "A", p. 25).

"Q. How many brothers and sisters has your father?

A. None."—(Dea Fong (Exhibit "A", p. 20).

"Q. How many brothers and sisters has your father?

A. He had one brother, but he died a long time ago."—(Dea Hong (Exhibit "A", p. 15).

"Q. How many brothers and sisters has your father?

A. None."—Dea Chuck (Exhibit "A", p. 11).

"Q. How many brothers and sisters has your father?

A. One brother. I don't know his name. He is dead. I don't know when he died."—(Dea Ton (Exhibit "A", p. 7).

We, now, submit that there is absolutely not the slightest ground for concluding that there is a discrepancy between the father and the applicants, or between the applicants, themselves, as to whether or not the alleged father has any brothers or sisters. The above recited testimony covers the entire evidence on the subject. It will be noted therefrom, that all the questions were placed in the present tense, the verb "has" being used throughout. The alleged father, Dea Fong, and Dea Chuck gave their answers accordingly. Dea Hong and Dea Ton answered with the explanation that the father had one brother, who died many years ago. In effect, therefore, each and every answer was the same, namely, that the father *has* no brothers or sisters. If the verb "has" is taken for what it only can imply, namely, the present, then manifestly, upon the very face of the questions and answers, there is positively no discrepancy.

As to the other alleged discrepancy, which has reference to a Chinese person, Dea Suey Bow, we quote from the transcript of record as follows:

"Q. You state your house is the 3d. in the 5th. row. Who lives in the 4th. house?

A. There are two vacant lots back of mine. Mine is the 3d. house—4th. and 5th. lots are vacant. On the 6th. lot is a house occupied by Dea Suey Bow.

Q. Was his house built before or after yours?

A. My house was built first.

Q. What is his age and occupation?

A. 30 odd, he returned to China from St. Louis, United States, last year."—(Dea Chung Wing, alleged father (Exhibit "A", p. 24).)

"Q. What is the age and occupation of Dea Suey Bow?

A. Little over 20; farming.

Q. Has he ever been away from the home village?

A. No.

Q. Was he ever in the United States?

A. No."—(Dea Fong (Exhibit "A", p. 19).)

Now, the Board of Review, in its above recited finding, states that Dea Chuck testified the same as Dea Fong, whose testimony we have just quoted, concerning Dea Suey Bow. This is clearly erroneous, as the following testimony will show:

"Q. What is the age and occupation of Dea Suey Bow?

A. About 35; farming.

Q. Has he ever been away from his own village?

A. No. Not that I know of.

Q. Did he ever come to the United States?

A. I don't know."—(Dea Chuck (Exhibit "A", p. 10).)

In other words, Dea Fong testified that Dea Suey Bow has never been to the United States, whereas, Dea Chuck states that he does not know whether or not this person has ever been to this country; evidently, therefore, their testimony is not the same. Then, also, the Board of Review finds that Dea Hong has no knowledge of Dea Suey Bow. This is, also, an erroneous finding. If we examine the entire testimony of Dea Hong (Exhibit "A", pp. 14-18) we will find that there is not a single particle of evidence concerning Dea Suey Bow, Dea Hong not having been asked a single question, concerning this person. Finally, the Board of Review has made a further erroneous finding, in that it states that Dea Ton has no knowledge of Dea Suey Bow. The testimony shows the following:

"Q. What is the age and occupation of Dea Suey Bow?

A. 30 odd; farming.

Q. Has he ever been away from that village?

A. I don't know.

Q. Was he ever in the United States?

A. I don't know."—(Dea Ton (Exhibit "A", p. 6).)

From the above recited testimony, it is evident that Dea Ton has knowledge of Dea Suey Bow.

Aside from the fact that the Board of Review has made numerous erroneous findings concerning Dea Suey Bow, has any material discrepancy developed from the testimony? In brief the testimony shows that Dea Chuck and Dea Ton know Dea Suey Bow, but do not know whether or not he has ever been to the United States. Dea Hong, not having been questioned about this person, volunteered no information on the subject. Apparently, therefore, the only discrepancy is between the alleged father and Dea Fong, the former having testified that Dea Suey Bow had been to the United States, whereas, the latter testified to the contrary. Now, the Board of Review has taken the view that, if the alleged father and Dea Fong come from the same village as Dea Suey Bow, they should know whether or not this person had ever been to the United States. In other words, the materiality and importance of the discrepancy rest upon the ground as to whether or not the principals come from the same village. Inasmuch as the Board of Review has cited the discrepancy as material, it has taken for granted that these persons are from the same village. In this particular, the Board is mistaken. The transcript of testimony (Exhibit "A", p. 24) shows the following:

"Q. How large is Fung Tung village?
A. 50 odd houses.

Q. How many houses do you own in that village?

A. Only one; located 3d. house, 5th. row, head or west.

Q. Is that an old house, or was it built for your family to move into?

A. It was built before we moved in.

Q. In what year did you say your family moved there?

A. (C-R-6)   1917.

Q. How many rooms in that house?

A. Ordinary 5 room house.

Q. What kind of floors?

A. Red tile.        ......

Q. How many rows in Fung Teung?

A. Eleven.

Q. How many houses in your row?

A. Four.

Q. Where do you get water?

A. From both the stream and the well. The well is on the west side. The stream is on the right or east side. Ai Gong village is in the rear or south of Fung Teung.

Q. Just prior to coming to this country, what room in your house did you occupy?

A. The parlor.

Q. What persons occupied the parlor besides you and your wife?

A. My mother.

Q. Are there two outside doors to that house?

A. Yes, large and small. The large door is on the east.

Q. Who occupied the bed-room on the large door side, just prior to your departure for this country.

A. My fifth son, Dea Chuck, and his family. The bedroom on the small door side was occupied by Dea Ton and his wife.

Q. Where did your 7th. son, Dea Heung, sleep?

A. With my wife and I in the parlor.

Q. Where is your father buried?

A. Yon San Doy, a hill about half a li south of Fung Teung.

Q. Is his grave marked in any manner?

A. Yes, with a little headstone with an inscription with his name.

Q. When did you last visit that grave?

A. 2nd. month of the present year.

Q. Who accompanied you on that visit?

A. All my sons, even the baby.

Q. You state your house is the third in the 5th. row. Who lives in the 4th. house?

A. There are two vacant lots back of mine. Mine is the 3d. house—4th. and 5th. lots are vacant. On the 6th. lot is a house occupied by Dea Suey Bow."—(Dea Chung Wing, alleged father.)

According to the above recited testimony, which has not been disputed by the immigration authorities, Dea Chung Wing, just prior to his departure from China for the United States, occupied a house in Fung Teung village, where, it is also shown, Dea Suey Bow occupied a house. Now, as to Dea Fong, who disagreed with his father as to whether or not Dea Suey Bow has ever been to the United States, the testimony is as follows:

"Q. How large is Ai Gong village?

A. 15 to 16 houses.

Q. Where is your house located in that village?

A. 3d. house, 3d. row, south side.

Q. Is that the house in which you now live with your three brothers?

A. Yes."—(Dea Fong (Exhibit "A", p. 20).)

Therefore, according to the testimony just recited, Dea Fong is from Ai Gong village.

The conclusion is, therefore, obvious. As we have heretofore pointed out, the only discrepancy concerning Dea Suey Bow is between the alleged father and Dea Fong. The materiality and importance of this discrepancy are, as the plain language of the Board of Review indicates, dependent upon the fact that the alleged father and Dea Fong come from the same village as Dea Suey Bow. But, as the transcript of testimony clearly shows, the alleged father and Dea Suey Bow come from the village of Fung Teung, whereas, Dea Fong comes from the village of Ai Gong. Therefore, according to the Board of Review's own argument, the discrepancy is immaterial and unimportant.

We believe that we have amply proven that the Board of Review, in urging the two discrepancies mentioned, has acted manifestly unfair. In the first place, we have pointed out that the alleged discrepancy, as to the brothers and sisters of the father of these applicants, does not exist. Secondly, we have shown that the Board of Review has not based its findings, as to the alleged discrepancy concerning the Chinese person, Dea Suey Bow, upon the evidence and consequently has made numerous erroneous findings in the matter; furthermore, the discrepancy, as it actually exists, is immaterial and unimportant. Under these facts, we submit that the law has been clearly defined. The courts have, on innumerable occasions, held that the immigration authorities have acted manifestly unfair and in an abuse of their discretion, where it has been shown that the excluding decision was not based upon the evidence. Be it sufficient to quote the language of the Supreme Court in the case of Kwock Jan Fat v. White, 253 U. S. 454:

"While the decision by the Secretary of Labor on the exclusion of a Chinese person is final, unless the proceedings were manifestly unfair or show manifest abuse of discretion, the decision must be made after a hearing in good faith and must find adequate support in the evidence."

It may be argued by counsel for appellee that, notwithstanding the fact that the discrepancies cited by the Board of Review are not supported by the evidence, nevertheless, there are other discrepancies, which are sufficient to defeat the right of these applicants to enter the United States. Whether or not this be the situation, we are not aware, nor do we believe that we should be concerned with same. The two discrepancies, which we have discussed, have been cited by the Board of Review as particularly material and, as a matter of fact, are the only two cited by this body. We believe that, at this juncture, it is only fair to presume that the Board of Review considers these the most important discrepancies in the case. Certainly, in any event, it cannot be denied that these were made a prominent factor in the Board of Review's decision. We, therefore, submit that it makes no difference whether or not other discrepancies exist, as long as it is shown that the discrepancies, which have been made a factor in the decision, are not supported by the evidence. In the case of Quan Hing Sam v. White, 254 Fed. 402, supra, where an applicant was excluded upon two grounds, one of which was erroneous, the Court adjudged the entire hearing before the immigration authorities as unfair. So, too, in the case of bar, we could admit that there are other discrepancies in the record, but the fact would remain that there were certain discrepancies, which were made part and parcel of the decision, and which were not supported by the evidence. In other words, the fact would remain that the Board of Review was influenced in its decision by considerations not authorized by law. In Ex Parte Wong Foo, 230 Fed. 534, the Court said:

> "The inquiry of the immigration authorities should be directed, of course, in good faith to the ascertainment of that fact (that the applicant is the son of an American citizen). The burden of proving such a relationship is entirely upon the applicant, but that burden should not be increased by throwing extraneous matter in the scale against him."

*Ex Parte Leong Wah Jan,* 230 Fed. 540;

*Ex Parte Ng Doo Wong,* 230 Fed. 751;

*Ex Parte Lee Dung Moo,* 230 Fed. 746.

It is true that the Board of Review, in its findings, states that there are other discrepancies in the case. Nevertheless, it does not specify these "other discrepancies", nor does its decision show that these would be sufficient of themselves to warrant exclusion of these applicants. Certainly, the Board of Review's decision does not distinctly show that it was not influenced by the two discrepancies.

which were specified and which we have, heretofore, shown as groundless and immaterial to the right of these applicants to enter the United States (Quan Hing Sam v. White, 254 Fed. 402, supra; Ex Parte Wong Foo, 230 Fed. 534, supra).

## CONCLUSION

We submit, in conclusion, that the facts of the case are sufficient to warrant a finding of unfairness on the part of the immigration authorities in deciding adversely to these applicants, the appellants, herein.

In the first place, it has been shown that the attack upon the marital status of the alleged father of these applicants was unwarranted. In this connection, it has been proven that the finding of the Board of Special Inquiry to the effect that the father was not married in 1900 was not supported by the evidence; that the evidence utilized by the Board of Special Inquiry, upon this point, could, at the most, only show that he was not married in 1895, in which event his paternity to these applicants would not be precluded. In our opinion, the erroneous finding of the Board of Special Inquiry on this feature is sufficient, in itself, to justify a decision, which would decree that the entire proceedings before the immigration authorities were unfair (Kwock Jan Fat v. White, 253 U. S. 454, supra; Quan Hing Sam v. White, 254 Fed. 402, supra; Ex parte Wong Foo, 230 Fed. 534, supra).

Furthermore, in utilizing the prior testimony of the alleged father against the applicants, the immigration authorities have acted manifestly unfair and abused their discretion in many respects. As proof of this, we believe that we have shown that the prior testimony of the alleged father created a presumption only that he was not married; indeed, the admission of the Board of Review, in its finding (Exhibit "A", pp. 89 and 90), is to this effect. Being a presumption, it was rebuttable. Notwithstanding, the applicants were not confronted with the evidence upon which the presumption was based, nor were they advised or did they learn of the evidence, until the case was decided and closed. In other words, they were absolutely foreclosed of their right to offer evidence to overcome the adverse finding on this issue. Under the decisions of Lum Hop Kee v. Johnson, 281 Fed. 873, supra, and Chew Hoy Quong v. White, 249 Fed. 869, supra, these facts clearly constitute unfairness. Then, also, the depriving of the applicants of their rights in this connection was an open violation of Rule 3, Subdivision 4 of the rules governing the admission of Chinese, in that neither the applicants or their attorneys were advised of the respect or respects in which the applicants were found inadmissible until after a final decision had been rendered. This being a rule of the Department it had the force of law and the immigration authorities, in failing to adhere to same, acted manifestly unfair. Inasmuch as the prior testimony of the alleged father has been unfairly utilized against these applicants, we submit that it should not be considered as evidence at all.

Having shown that the prior testimony was insufficient to defeat the right of these applicants to enter the United States and, also, having shown that it was unfairly utilized as evidence, we, now, submit that the entire hearing before the immigration authorities was unfair, notwithstanding, that other grounds for the exclusion of these persons may exist. The principle of law, in this connection, has been well defined; the decisions hold that where a finding of the immigration authorities has been based upon two grounds, one of which is invalid, then, the entire hearing as to the admissibility of the applicant is unfair (Quan Hing Sam v. White, 254 Fed. 402, supra; Ex Parte Wong Foo, 230 Fed. 534).

But, the only other ground urged by the immigration authorities against these applicants is certain discrepancies in the testimony of the principals in the case. The Board of Review, which acted for the Secretary of Labor, and, which consequently served as the highest tribunal in the proceeding, specified two discrepancies as being particularly material (Exhibit "A", p. 90). It is, therefore, reasonable to presume that these two discrepancies were considered by the Board to be the most important. We have discussed these at some length and as to one, namely, as to the brothers and sisters of the alleged father, we have shown that the testimony, on its very face, proves that there is no disagreement whatever. As to the other, namely, as to whether or not a Chinese person, Dea Suey Bow, has ever been to the United States, we have shown by the testimony and evidence of the principals that the Board of Review has made numerous erroneous findings. Aside from the erroneous findings and taking the discrepancy, as the evidence shows it to exist, we believe that we have proven, by merely following the Board of Review's own argument, that the disagreement is unimportant and immaterial.

Therefore, in urging these two discrepancies, the Board of Review has failed to adhere to the evidence. Its finding, therefore, is not supported by the evidence and the Board of Review's decision having been based upon such finding is, therefore, manifestly unfair to these applicants (Kwock Jan Fat, 253 U. S. 454).

Nor would the fact that there may be or actually are other discrepancies, have any effect upon this issue. As long as the two discrepancies specified by the Board of Review were made a factor in the adverse finding, it is sufficient. The only possible means by which it could be maintained that the "other discrepancies" were sufficient to justify the exclusion of these applicants, would be for the Board of Review to show by its finding that it was not influenced by the discrepancies specified (Quan Hing Sam v. White, 254 Fed. 402, supra; Ex Parte

Wong Foo, 230 Fed. 534). Of course, the very
fact that the Board did specify these two discrepancies, as being particularly material, would necessarily preclude it from making any such showing.

Finally, if the finding of the Board of Review,
as to the discrepancies mentioned, is erroneous and
not supported by the evidence, then, we submit
that the entire hearing of these applicants before
the immigration authorities should be adjudged unfair. As the record plainly indicates, these discrepancies were made part and parcel of the adverse finding. They were a prominent factor in the
decision. To again quote from the decision of the
Board of Review (Exhibit "A", p. 89):

> "These discrepancies, coupled up with the quite
> natural doubt arising from the 1900 testimony
> of the latter (the alleged father), indicate con-
> clusively to the Board of Review that these ap-
> plicants should not be admitted."

Therefore, even granting that the 1900 testimony
of the alleged father creates a doubt as to his
marital status, nevertheless, as the plain language
of the decision of the Board of Review indicates,
this feature was not deemed sufficient, of itself, to
deny the applicants admission to the United States.
Hence, the finding of the Board of Review, as to
the discrepancies, being invalid, the entire hearing
of these applicants before the immigration authorities should be adjudged unfair. In Quan Hing
Sam v. White, 254 Fed. 402, supra, the Court says:

"We are of the opinion that, in such an inquiry, it should distinctly appear that the Department was not influenced in its decision by considerations not authorized by law."
Ex Parte Wong Foo, 230 Fed. 534.

In the case at bar, it is evident that the decision of the Board of Review did not show that this body was not influenced by the two specified discrepancies, which we believe we have fully proven were not supported by the evidence and were therefore not authorized by law as a ground for the exclusion of these applicants.

Wherefore, appellants pray that the order and judgment of the District Court of Appeal be reversed with instructions to issue the Writ of Habeas Corpus as prayed for.

Respectfully submitted,

STEPHEN M. WHITE,

*Attorney for Appellants.*

IN THE

# United States Circuit Court of Appeals

### For the Ninth Circuit

DEA HONG, DEA CHUCK, DEA TON
and DEA FONG,

*Appellants,*

vs.

JOHN D. NAGLE, as Commissioner of
Immigration, Port of San Francisco,

*Appellee.*

# BRIEF OF APPELLEE

JOHN T. WILLIAMS,
*United States Attorney,*

T. J. SHERIDAN,
*Assistant United States Attorney,*
*Attorneys for Appellee.*

Neal, Stratford & Kerr, S. F.   41428

No. 4225

IN THE

United States Circuit Court of Appeals

For the Ninth Circuit

DEA HONG, DEA CHUCK, DEA TON
and DEA FONG,

*Appellants,*

VS.

JOHN D. NAGLE, as Commissioner of
Immigration, Port of San Francisco,

*Appellee.*

## BRIEF OF APPELLEE

### STATEMENT

This is an appeal in a Chinese immigration case, taken from the order and judgment of the United States District Court for the Northern District of California in a Habeas Corpus proceeding.

The petitioners are Chinese persons who applied to that court for a Writ of Habeas Corpus to relieve them from the custody of the Commissioner of Immigration at the Port of San Francisco, the Commissioner holding them for deportation as a result of a hearing before the Immigration Bureau.

The petition for Writ of Habeas Corpus showed that the petitioners arrived at the Port of San

Francisco on May 26, 1923, and thereupon made application to enter the United States as sons of one Dea Chung Wing, who was said to be a native-born citizen of the United States. The petition further showed that upon proceedings before the Immigration Bureau, the petitioners were denied entry and that the decision was upheld upon appeal to the Secretary of Labor. The claim is made that the action of the immigration authorities was in excess of authority committed to them, and that the denial of the application was an abuse of authority in two specified particulars: It is said that the excluding decision was based upon prior testimony of the alleged father given February 28, 1900, holding also that such prior testimony showed that the alleged father was not married in the year 1900 or prior thereto; and the petition alleges as a further particular that petitioners were denied admission without being accorded or granted an opportunity to prove their relationship to the aforesaid Dea Chung Wing, and that the Board acted arbitrarily and in abuse of discretion in that behalf. (Tr. of Rec., pp. 2-7.)

An order to show cause having been issued upon the petition, the appellee demurred thereto, whereupon by stipulation and order of the parties, it was agreed that the immigration records be filed as respondent's Exhibits "A", "B", "C", "D" and "E", and that the same be considered as a part of the original petition. Of these, Exhibit "A" is the record relating to the proceedings complained of and the others are related records.

There was a hearing of the case before a Board of Special Inquiry, with a result that the Chairman reviewed the case at length in making an adverse decision. He was joined by the two other members of the Board. The statement appears at pp. 37-41 of Exhibit "A"; it is too long to quote here, but the following is the concluding portion of the Chairman's statement and the statement of the two other members of the Board.

22186-5-5, 6, 7, 14

THE CHAIRMAN:

"* * * The Board invites a very careful review of the report of the primary inspector covering the discrepancies that developed at the primary hearing between the alleged father and the four applicants, and when the ages of the latter are taken into consideration, those discrepancies, each and every one of them, carry a great deal of weight, and are very material to the claim of relationship in these cases.

The alleged father attempted to secure the admission of an alleged son, Dea Bow, at this port in 1911, record No. 10485/86. His application to land was denied by this office, and his appeal was subsequently dismissed October 6, 1911, Bureau Number 53329/106, as it appears it was brought to light in that record that certain testimony given by the alleged father and the alleged uncle before the United States District Court in 1900, shows very clearly that the alleged father was not then married and did not have the family which he now claims to have at that time, and that statement certainly affects the admission of the three older applicants, which is thoroughly covered in the various reports on the subject in file 10485/56.

The four applicants are brought into the Board room for a physical comparison, and I am unable to find any resemblance between any two of them. There is nothing that would indicate that they are even slightly related. In fact, each one appears to be of an entirely different and distinct type.

After a careful consideration of all the evidence submitted and adduced in the applicants' behalf, it is my opinion that these four Chinamen are not even brothers as claimed, and that they are not the blood sons of Dea Chung Wing, and I therefore move that all four applicants be denied admission to the United States.''

INSPECTOR JACOBSEN:

''It appears that the showing made in behalf of the applicants is very unsatisfactory. The testimony of the alleged father in the Court proceedings (Habeas Corpus) which resulted in his discharge as a citizen in 1900, indicates reasonably that he has no such sons as the three oldest applicants. This testimony of the alleged father indicates that he might then not have been married, and if so the possibility of paternity is precluded, and furthermore there is such a radical difference between the estimated, apparent and claimed age of the youngest applicant as to lead to the conclusion that the relationship does not exist. The statements of the additional witness presented is not believed to be of sufficient weight to overcome the weight of the adverse features as pointed out by the Board.

The four applicants have been brought in before the Board, and it will be noted in comparing each and every one that there is no resemblance whatever between any two of them or between all of them, they appearing to be of entirely different types. I therefore second the motion to exclude all four applicants."

INSPECTOR SMITH:

"After comparing these four applicants I find no resemblance among any of them, and I do not believe that they are the sons of Dea Chung Wing, basing my opinion not alone on the dissimilarity of the applicants, but on account of the alleged father's statement in 1900 concerning his family, and the other discrepancies set forth. I therefore concur in the motion to exclude."

When the case was appealed to the Secretary of Labor, the Chairman of the Board of Review made the following decision and statement of the case which was approved and so ordered by the Second Assistant Secretary of Labor:

55245/589—San Francisco, September 12, 1923.

In re: DEA FONG, 27; DEA HONG, 25; DEA CHUCJ, 24 and DEA TON, 16.

This case comes before the Board of Review on appeal from an excluding decision rendered at San Francisco, California.

Attorneys Bouve & Parker have submitted

brief and the case has been argued orally before the Board by Attorney John T. Vance, Jr.

The citizenship of Dea Chung Wing, the alleged father, is conceded. The Board of Special Inquiry at Angel Island has excluded the applicants because it is not satisfied that the claimed relationship has been reasonably established. The reasons which have resulted in an excluding decision will be found set forth in the report of Inspector Garcia, page 30, and the memorandum of the Chairman of the Board, page 41, both indicated by markers.

The record contains the testimony of the four applicants, the alleged father, and of two other Chinese witnesses, one named Yee Jow and the other Fong Leong. Fong Leong testified before the primary inspector. This witness, who is very little older than three of the applicants, states that when he was in China recently, departing in 1921 and returning in 1923, he was invited by the alleged father to call at his house. He availed himself of this invitation and met the applicants as well as other members of the family. It is apparent that this witness is not qualified to testify as to the relationship in this case.

Yee Jow was introduced as an additional witness before the Board of Special Inquiry. His testimony is to the effect that he has known the alleged father since 1912. In 1913 he visited the alleged father's home to deliver some goods, and at that time met the applicants and other members of the family. He also claims that he visited the alleged father's home again in 1922 and 1923, in a social way, and met the applicants.

In connection with the testimony of the witness Yee Jow, it is noted that he came to the United States on the same boat as the applicants. He was asked, presumably while on the boat, "Did you visit any resident of this country who happened to be at his home during your recent stay in China, or did you visit the home of any such resident?" His answer to this inquiry was in the negative. In view of the fact that he was on the boat with these applicants, during the voyage from China, it seems reasonable to believe that he would have recalled and mentioned his visit to their home, if he had actually made it. The inconsistency was invited to his attention and his explanation was that he thought the inquiry pertained only to new acquaintances. It is believed that the circumstance discussed casts considerable doubt upon the *bona fides* of the testimony of this witness, which at best, is not of the strongest.

In the memoranda of the primary inspector and of the Chairman of the Board are set forth a number of discrepancies, which in the opinion of the Board of Review would not exist were the relationship as claimed. The discrepancies are set forth fully in the report of Inspector Garcia and are discussed in the summary of the Chairman and in the brief of counsel. The report of the Inspector is incorrect in one or two instances, which are pointed out by the Chairman and by the attorneys.

The alleged father claims that he has no brothers or sisters and apparently Dea Fong agrees with him in this respect. Dea Hong, however, claims that his father had one brother who is dead. He names this alleged brother as Dea Leong Foom and states that he had three sons, all in Straits Settlements. Dea Chuck agrees with the alleged father in this respect, while Dea Ton testified substantially the same as Dea Hong. This discrepancy is regarded by the Board of Review as particularly material.

According to the testimony of the alleged father a Chinese person named Dea Suey Bow is from his village in China. The alleged father states that this man was a resident of St. Louis, Mo.; that he returned to China last year to his village, and married a second wife, his first wife having died. Dea Fong has knowledge of Dea Suey Bow, but states that the latter has never been to the United States; in fact, has never been away from the home village. With this Dea Chuck agrees. Dea Hong and Dea Ton have no knowledge of this person. If these persons are what they claim to be and come from the same village in China as Dea Suey Bow, it is not believed that this inconsistency would exist. There are other material discrepancies in the case particularly with reference to matters in the home village.

The Board of Review is of the opinion that the discrepancies alone indicate that this case is not *bona fide*. There is another feature, however, which has been given considerable weight at the port and which is discussed at length by counsel. This has to do with a statement made by the alleged father in 1900, when he was an applicant for admission to the United States, indicating that he did not then have a wife and family living in China. It is claimed by the alleged father that he was married in 1891 and that sons were born in 1892, 1893, 1895, 1897 and 1899, as well as in subsequent years. In 1900 he was asked "who was living with you in your house besides your mother when your uncle was in China?" and answered, "no one else." If the present testimony is true he must have had a wife and three sons living with him at that time. This feature is believed by the Board of Review to indicate a reasonable possibility that the alleged father was not married in 1895, and as he does not claim to have been married subsequent to that date, there seems to be a grave question whether or not he ever was married at all. An examination of the 1900 testimony, before the immigration officials and before the court, on *habeas corpus,* shows that the then applicant was asked numerous questions regarding matters in his home village, and the Board of Review believes that if he had actually been married at that time some inkling of it would have been forthcoming in that examination.

An alleged son of Dea Chung Wing was admitted to the United States in 1909 and was granted the return privilege as a citizen in 1921. This person is claimed to have been born prior to 1895 and counsel naturally stresses his admission and the subsequent conceding of his status as an adjudication of the marital status of the alleged father for the purposes of the present proceeding. With this the Board of Review does not agree. Reference to the admission of the alleged son in 1909 and to the proceedings had when he was granted a return certificate in 1921 show quite plainly that the 1900 testimony of Dea Chung Wing was overlooked and was not given any consideration whatever. Irrespective of this, however, as previously stated, the Board of Review believes that the discrepancies in the present record indicate that the applicants are not the sons of Dea Chung Wing. These discrepancies, coupled up with the quite natural doubt arising from the 1900 testimony of the latter, indicate conclusively to the Board of Review that these applicants should not be admitted.

The Board of Review has gone over the record in this case together with the related files with care and has given most painstaking consideration to all of the evidence. It has reached the conclusion after such review and consideration that the right of the applicants to enter the United States has not been reasonably established.

It is recommended that the appeals be dismissed.

W. N.,<br>Chairman, Secy. & Comr.<br>Genl's Board of Review.

CEB/CS

So Ordered:

    ROBE CARL WHITE,
        2nd Asst. Secretary.

It thus appears that the precise question involved is: whether the Bureau of Immigration in deciding that petitioners were not the sons of Dea Chung

Wing and thus not entitled to entry, and basing its view upon an inspection of the applicants as well as upon discrepancies in their proof, is there sufficient in the record to authorize the Bureau to so find?

## ARGUMENT

THE RECORD OF THE PROCEEDINGS BEFORE THE IMMIGRATION AUTHORITIES SHOWS MANIFEST DISCREPANCIES AND CONTRADICTIONS IN THE STATEMENTS OF PETITIONERS AND ESPECIALLY IN THE STATEMENTS OF THEIR ALLEGED FATHER. ACCORDINGLY THE BUREAU OF IMMIGRATION WAS AUTHORIZED TO FIND AS IT DID.

It is submitted, *in limine* that in attacking the decision of the Bureau of Immigration, petitioners are confined in general to the allegations of their petition for a Writ of Habeas Corpus and should not now be heard to question the immigration proceedings except upon the grounds set forth in the petition.

*Ex parte Yoshimasi Nomura,* 197 Fed. 191.

The immigration authorities, in denying admission to the applicants, concede that their alleged father, Dea Chung Wing, is a citizen of the United States, but it was held, on the evidence submitted, that the applicants have not shown that they are the sons of Dea Chung Wing.

It is claimed by the alleged father that he was married in China in the year 1891 and that he is now the father of eight sons. These children were born, he states, in the years 1892, 1893, 1895, 1897, 1899 and in subsequent years.

In the year 1909 the alleged father secured the admission of Dea See, the son whom he claimed was born in 1892. In 1911 a second alleged son, Dea Bow, was an applicant for admission, this son claiming to have been born in the year 1893. The immigration authorities denied admission in the case of this last mentioned son. The present applicants are the sons who, it is claimed, were born in 1895, 1897, 1899 and 1907.

In the year 1900 the alleged father was himself an applicant for admission and his right to admission was then tested in *habeas corpus* proceedings. (United States District Court case No. 12029.) At the hearing of this matter before a Special Referee, three Chinese witnesses testified that the then applicant was born in San Francisco. One of these witnesses, Dea Leong Foon, stated that he was the paternal uncle of Dea Chung Wing. He testified that he was from the same village in China as Dea Chung Wing and his testimony covered much that transpired in China during the year 1895, it appearing from the testimony of the uncle that he was in China and at the home village during from the 4th, to the 11th, month of that year.

Dea Chung Wing, in his testimony before the

Referee, stated that his uncle was in China for a period of four months, from the 4th, to the 8th, month during the year 1895, but as the uncle had stated that he was in the home village from the 4th to the 11th month, it is more probable that the latter's statement is correct.

During the hearing before the Referee, Dea Chung Wing was asked: (Ex. "B", page 37.)

"Q. Who was living with you in your house besides your mother when your uncle was in China?

A. NO ONE ELSE."

It was brought out in the testimony that the uncle, his wife and two sons were visitors to the applicant's house and that on a number of occasions they took their meals there, the uncle and his sons eating with the applicant while the aunt took her meals with the applicant's mother. Although much of the testimony before the Referee had to do with the circumstances pertaining to the taking of meals at the applicant's house, it nowhere appears that the applicant's wife and the two sons—those born in 1892 and 1893—were mentioned.

Counsel suggests that during the time in question the wife might have been living in another part of China or might have been separated from her husband for other causes.

In the first place, it is highly improbable that such was the case. It would be an exceptional reason which would cause a wife and two children, aged three and two years, to be absent from the home of her husband. Further it appears that a third son, Dea Fong, was born in the 10th month of the year 1895—a month prior to the time when the uncle stated he left the village—and it also appears that all of these children were born in the home village. Viewed in the light of the probabilities it would seem that the absence of the wife and children from the home would have been a most extraordinary circumstance. *But in his surmise counsel overlooks the statement of the alleged father in the case of Dea Bow* (Ex. "D", page 42), as follows:

"Q. Dea Leong Foon was in your village and visited your home in K. S. 21 (1895)?

A. Yes.

Q. The court record shows you were asked at that time, 'Who was living with you in your house besides your mother when your uncle was in China' and your answer was, 'No one else'— is that correct?

A. No, I had a wife and three children at that time.

Q. But the record shows you stated 'No one else' but your mother was living with you?

A. That is not so.

Q. What did you state at that time?

A. I stated I had a wife and children at home.

Q. Your uncle, Dea Leong Foon, and his

wife would come and eat at your house sometimes while he was in China in K. S. 21?

A. Yes.

Q. You were asked when you arrived in K.
S. 26 (1900) if your uncle, Dea Leong Foon's
wife would come to your house and eat and you
said, 'Yes, occasionally,' is that right?

A. Yes.

Q. You were also asked, 'And would she eat
at the same table with you and your mother?'
You answered, 'My aunt ate with my mother,'
did you not?

A. Yes, sometimes I ate with my uncle and
my mother and my wife would eat with my
aunt.

Q. But you stated, 'My aunt ate with my
mother,' at that time?

A. She ate with my wife and my mother, the
children were very small at that time.

Q. You had three at the time when Dea
Leong Foon was there?

A. Yes.''

Thus the surmise of counsel is disposed of in view
of the positive assertion of the alleged husband and
father.

It has repeatedly been held by the courts that
even unimpeached evidence may be rejected under
certain circumstances. In the case of *Lee Sing Far
v. United States* (94 Fed. 634), for example, several
instances of the rejection of such evidence are given,

among them the decision in the case of *Ellwood v. Telegraph Co.* (45 N. Y. 549). In that decision the following language was used:

> "It is undoubtedly the general rule that where unimpeached witnesses testify distinctly and positively to a fact, and are uncontradicted, their testimony should be credited, and have the effect of overcoming a mere presumption. * * * But this rule is subject to many qualifications. There may be such a degree of improbability in the statements themselves as to deprive them of credit, however positively made. The witnesses, though unimpeached, may have such an interest in the question at issue as to affect their credibility, * * * and, furthermore, it is often a difficult question to decide when a witness is, in a legal sense, uncontradicted. He may be contradicted by circumstances as well as by statements of others contrary to his own. In such cases courts and juries are not bound to refrain from exercising their judgment, and blindly adopt the statements of a witness, for the simple reason that no other witness has denied them, and that the character of the witness is not impeached."

Again, in the case of *Quock Ting v. United States,* 140 U. S. 417; 11 Sup. Ct. 733, the Supreme Court said:

> "Undoubtedly, as a general rule, positive testimony to a particular fact, uncontradicted by any one, should control the decision of the court; but that rule admits of many exceptions. There may be such an inherent improbability in

the statements of a witness to induce the court
or jury to disregard his evidence, even in the
absence of any direct conflicting testimony. He
may be contradicted by the facts he states as
completely as by direct adverse testimony; and
there may be so many omissions in his account
of particular transactions, or his own conduct,
as to discredit his whole story. His manner,
too, of testifying may give rise to doubts of his
sincerity, and create the impression that he is
giving a wrong coloring to material facts. All
these things may properly be considered in determining the weight which should be given to
his statements, although there is no adverse verbal testimony adduced.''

It is contended by counsel that the immigration
authorities failed to confront the alleged father with
his prior testimony.

From the above it will be noted that the alleged
father was given an opportunity to explain his former testimony. Even if this had not been done it
is contended that such omission would not have
rendered the hearing unfair. This Court, speaking
through His Honor, Judge Gilbert, in the case of
*Jang Dao Theung v. Nagle,* 294 Fed. 872, said:

"The Low Joe Case (287 Fed. 545), it may be
observed, is quite dissimilar to the case at bar.
It does not hold, and it is not authority for the
proposition, that a hearing is unfair from the
mere fact that a witness is not questioned regarding his inconsistent prior testimony.''

The counsel for appellants contends that the hearing was unfair in that the notice of the failure of the applicants to satisfy the Board of Special Inquiry that the relationship claim had been established should have been more specific.

It cannot be said that the alleged father was unaware of the matter of his conflicting statement which arose at the time when his alleged son Dea Bow was denied admission. Further, he was present during part of the examination before the Board, it appearing that his alleged son Dea Fong had expressed the desire that his father be present.

Opportunity was given to submit any and all evidence which might have been submitted to prove the existence of the relationship and the record shows that an additional witness was presented and heard. The applicants were represented by attorney before the port officials and also before the Secretary when the case was heard on appeal. This was in accord with due process of law. (See *Gong Sic Or. v. White,* 278 Fed. 733.)

It is sufficient if the applicant before the immigration authorities is accorded a fair though summary hearing.

In the case of *Sibray v. United States,* 227 Fed. 1, the Court said:

"The act of 1907 contemplates a summary investigation, and not a judicial trial, and while the alien's right to be heard must be respected,

and the discretion of the officials must not be
abused, the formalities of procedure and the
rules governing the admissibility of evidence
have been much relaxed. *U. S. v. Uhl* (C. C. A.
2nd Cir.), 215 Fed. 573, 131 C. C. A. 641; *Choy
Gum v. Backus,* (C. C. A., 9th Cir.) 223 Fed.
492. We do not find anything fatally erroneous in the present record. The alien had counsel from the beginning, and had the opportunity
to call such witnesses as he wished or was able
to produce.''

To the same effect is the case of *Chin Shee v.
White,* 273 Fed. 801.

In the recent case of *Tulsidas v. Insular Collector
of Customs,* 262 U. S. 258, — L. Ed. —, the
Supreme Court said:

"It would seem, therefore, as if something
more is necessary to justify review than the
basis of a dispute. The law is in administration of a policy, which, while it confers a privilege, is concerned to prevent it from abuse, and
therefore has appointed officers to determine
the conditions of it and speedily determine
them, and on practical considerations; not to
subject them to litigious controversies, and dis-
putable, if not finical, distinctions.''

It is enough if essential justice be attained in
these cases. (*In re Madeiros,* 225 Fed. 764; *Shige-
zumi v. White,* 269 Fed. 258.)

The alleged father claims that he has no brothers
or sisters and Dea Fong agrees with him in this

respect. Dea Hong claims that his father had one brother who is dead. He names this alleged brother and states that he had three sons, all in Straits Settlements. Dea Chuck agrees with the alleged father in this respect, while Dea Ton testified substantially the same as Dea Hong.

Counsel contends that the questioning as to the brothers and sisters of the alleged father is in the present tense, the verb "has" being used throughout. The argument is directed toward showing that while the alleged father "has" no brother at the present time he "had" one formerly.

Attention is called to the testimony of the alleged father in the case of Dea Bow (Ex. "D", page 8), as follows:

"Q. How many blood brothers and sisters have you?

A. No brothers or sisters, I am the only child."

Thus, while it appears that the alleged father states that he is the only child, two of the applicants state he has a brother, adding that this brother has three sons.

It is shown by the testimony that the four applicants are from the same vicinity in China, it appearing that the alleged father has two houses, one in the Ai Gong village and the second in the Fung Teung village, otherwise known as the New Ai Gong village. The Ai Gong village, it further appears, is quite close to the new village, one of the applicants stating that the two villages are separated by "several pieces of rice land."

The testimony of the alleged father shows that one Dea Suey Bow lives in the house next to his in the Fung Teung village, there being two vacant lots between the two houses. It is claimed that Dea Ton and Dea Chuck have been living in the house in the Fung Teung village for about eight years, while the other two applicants still reside in the Ai Gong village.

The alleged father states that Dea Suey Bow was a resident of St. Louis, Mo., and returned to China last year, where he married a second wife, his first wife having died.

Dea Hong does not know who lives in the house described by the others as the house of Dea Suey Bow (Ex. "A", page 14); Dea Fong knows of Dea Suey Bow, but states that this man has never been to the United States and has married but once (Ex. "A", page 19); Dea Ton states that Dea Suey Bow has been married but once and that he does not know whether this man has ever been to the United States (Ex. "A", page 6); while Dea Chuck states that Dea Suey Chuck has been married twice, his last marriage taking place about a year ago, but he does not know whether this man has ever been to the United States. (Ex. "A", page 10.)

It is a remarkable circumstance that Dea Ton and

Dea Chuck, who claim to have lived in the next house to that of Dea Suey Bow, are in ignorance of the antecedents of this man to the extent shown, and it may be questioned that they are testifying from actual knowledge.

Counsel contends that as the immigration authorities admitted Dea See, the first claimed son of Dea Chung Wing, in 1909, that presumptively they considered the testimony before the Referee in the *habeas corpus* proceeding and that the marriage of Dea Chung Wing, and his paternity to Dea See, was thereby admitted.

It is quite clear from the records that the record in the court proceedings were not considered until the second alleged son, Dea Bow, applied for admission in 1911.

But assuming that the immigration authorities had considered the evidence before the Referee, they were not estopped from reaching a different conclusion on a later consideration of the same evidence.

In the case of *Lee Hing v. Nagle,* 295 Fed. 642, this Court, speaking through His Honor, Judge Hunt, said:

> "In *Pearson v. Williams,* 202 U. S. 281, 26 Sup. Ct. 608, 50 L. Ed. 1029, a board of special inquiry admitted immigrants and thereafter ordered them deported. The court held that the act of admission was not equivalent to a certificate of status or residence issued in accordance

with the provisions of some treaty or statute.
As was held by Judge Ross in *Ex parte Wong
Yee Toon* (D. C.), 227 Fed. 247, a certificate of
admission imports a *prima facie* verity, and is
not to be treated as though it never had existed,
and some evidence must be produced to justify
the immigration authorities denying to it its
usual and appropriate effect. But we are not
ready to hold that a mere admission of an alien
into the United States is in itself an evidentiary
fact, which will protect the alien against subsequent deportation upon the same evidence which
has once been held sufficient to call for his admission.''

Again, in the case of *White v. Chan Wy Sheung*,
270 Fed. 764, this Court said:

"It remains to be considered whether the
judgment of the court below is sustainable on
the ground on which it was based, that the department should have been bound by its own
prior adjudications in admitting the appellee's
father and his two brothers as citizens of the
United States. The board of immigration is
not a court. It is an instrument of the executive power, and its decisions do not in a technical sense constitute *res adjudicata* (*Pearson
v. Williams*, 202 U. S. 281, 26 Sup. Ct. 608, 50
L. Ed. 1029), and the department is not bound
by its prior decisions in admitting aliens to the
United States (*Haw Moy v. North*, 183 Fed. 89,
105 C. C. A. 381; *Lew Quen Wo v. United
States*, 184 Fed. 685, 106 C. C. A. 639; *Li Sing
v. United States*, 180 U. S. 486, 21 Sup. Ct. 449,
45 L. Ed. 634).

It will be noted from an examination of the record that the applicants before the immigration authorities were in no way prevented from testifying fully. Opportunity was afforded them to present witnesses and they were permitted to appeal to the Secretary of Labor from the decision of the Board which made the finding adverse to their admission. Thus no substantial right was denied them, and it is urged that they were accorded all the rights to which they were justly entitled.

It is clear that there was evidence, as the foregoing sets forth, to support the conclusion of the administrative officers.

It is well settled by the decisions that if there is any evidence, however slight, to support the findings of the administrative officers, such findings are not reviewable by the courts. (*Lee Hing v. Nagle,* 258 Fed. 23; *Antolish v. Paul,* 283 Fed. 957; *Soo Hoo Doo Hon v. Johnson,* 281 Fed. 870.)

In the case of *White v. Gregory,* 213 Fed. 768, this Court held:

"In reaching this conclusion the officers gave the aliens the hearing provided by the statute. This is as far as the Court can go in examining such proceedings. It will not inquire into the sufficiency of probative facts, or consider the reasons for the conclusions reached by the officers."

It was also said in the case of *Jeung Bock Hong et al. v. White,* 258 Fed. 23:

"The discrepancies in the testimony appear to be unimportant, but if taking them altogether the executive officers of the Department found that the evidence in support of the petitioners' right to land and enter the United States was so impaired as to render it unsatisfactory, the Court is not authorized to reverse that conclusion.

Accordingly it is submitted that the order and judgment of the District Court should be affirmed.

In sum there were contradictions and inconsistencies in the several statements of Dea Chung Wing. To enable him to bring in alleged sons in 1911 and in attempting to show relationship, he took the position that when his uncle visited his home in China in 1895 there were residing with his mother also his wife and young sons. He thus excluded the hypothesis that the wife and sons were then elsewhere or that he was then single and afterwards married. Having elected to take that position, he was apparently oblivious of the fact that in 1900 he had declared that at the visit of the uncle in 1895 there was no one else living with him and his mother. Clearly the immigration authorities had ample warrant to determine that the present claim of having a wife at that time and being the father of petitioners was fraudulent.

It is therefore clear that when the immigration authorities based their decision upon the appearance of the four applicants and upon the manifest contradictions in the testimony of the alleged father

in the proof adverted to, there was warrant for the
action of the Bureau. Its decision being thus within
its jurisdiction was final and should now be upheld.

Respectfully submitted,

JOHN T. WILLIAMS,
*United States Attorney,*

T. J. SHERIDAN,
*Asst. U. S. Attorney,*
*Attorneys for Appellee.*

# No. 4226

## United States
## Circuit Court of Appeals
### For the Ninth Circuit.

---

AMERICAN SURETY COMPANY OF NEW
YORK, a Corporation,

Plaintiff in Error,

vs.

THE STATE OF OREGON ON THE RELA-
TION OF HARRY HUMFELD,

Defendant in Error.

---

## Transcript of Record.

---

Upon Writ of Error to the United States District
Court of the District of Oregon.

---

Filmer Bros. Co. Print, 330 Jackson St., S. F., Cal.

# United States

# Circuit Court of Appeals

## For the Ninth Circuit.

AMERICAN SURETY COMPANY OF NEW
YORK, a Corporation,

Plaintiff in Error,

vs.

THE STATE OF OREGON ON THE RELA-
TION OF HARRY HUMFELD,

Defendant in Error.

# Transcript of Record.

Upon Writ of Error to the United States District
Court of the District of Oregon.

Filmer Bros. Co. Print, 330 Jackson St., S. F., Cal.

# INDEX TO THE PRINTED TRANSCRIPT OF RECORD.

[Clerk's Note: When deemed likely to be of an important nature, errors or doubtful matters appearing in the original certified record are printed literally in italic; and, likewise, cancelled matter appearing in the original certified record is printed and cancelled herein accordingly. When possible, an omission from the text is indicated by printing in italic the two words between which the omission seems to occur.]

Index.                    Page

Index. Page

Index.                    Page

Index. Page

Index.                           Page

Index.                    Page

## NAMES AND ADDRESSES OF ATTORNEYS OF RECORD.

WILLIAM S. NASH and S. J. GRAHAM, Yeon
Building, Portland, Oregon,
For the Plaintiff in Error.

BRONAUGH & BRONAUGH, Northwestern
Bank Building, Portland, Oregon, BEACH &
SIMON, Board of Trade Building, Portland,
Oregon, and ARTHUR A. GOLDSMITH,
Platt Building, Portland, Oregon,
For the Defendant in Error.

---

## CITATION ON WRIT OF ERROR.

United States of America,
District of Oregon,—ss.
To Harry Humfeld, Relator, GREETING :

You are hereby cited and admonished to be and
appear before the United States Circuit Court of
Appeals for the Ninth Circuit, at San Francisco,
California, within thirty days from the date hereof,
pursuant to a writ of error filed in the Clerk's office
of the District Court of the United States for the
District of Oregon, wherein American Surety Company of New York, a corporation, is plaintiff in
error and you are defendant in error, to show cause,
if any there be, why the judgment in the said writ
of error mentioned should not be corrected and
speedy justice should not be done to the parties in
that behalf.

Given under my hand, at Portland, in said District, this 3d day of December, in the year of our Lord, one thousand nine hundred and twenty-three.

R. S. BEAN,

Judge.  [1*]

United States of America,

State and District of Oregon,

County of Multnomah,—ss.

Service of the within citation on writ of error by certified copy thereof as required by law is hereby acknowledged at Portland, Oregon, this 3d day of December, 1923.

ARTHUR A. GOLDSMITH,

Of Attorneys for Defendant in Error.

[Endorsed]: No. L.-9004. 30,198. U n i t e d States District Court, District of Oregon. American Surety Company of New York, a Corporation, Plaintiff in Error, vs. State of Oregon on the Relation of Harry Humfeld, Defendant in Error. Citation on Writ of Error. U. S. District Court, District of Oregon. Filed Dec. 3, 1923. G. H. Marsh, Clerk.

---

*Page-number appearing at foot of page of original certified Transcript of Record.

In the United States Circuit Court of Appeals for the Ninth Circuit.

AMERICAN SURETY COMPANY OF NEW YORK, a Corporation,

Plaintiff in Error,

vs.

STATE OF OREGON on the Relation of HARRY HUMFELD,

Defendant in Error.

## WRIT OF ERROR.

The United States of America,—ss.

The President of the United States of America, to the Judge of the District Court of the United States for the District of Oregon, GREETING:

Because in the records and proceedings, as also in the rendition of the judgment of a plea which is in the District Court before the Honorable Robert S. Bean, one of you, between State of Oregon on the Relation of Harry Humfeld, plaintiff and defendant in error, and American Surety Company of New York, defendant and plaintiff in error, a manifest error hath happened to the great damage of the said plaintiff in error, as by complaint doth appear; and we, being willing that error, if any hath been, should be duly corrected, and full and speedy justice done to the parties aforesaid, and, in this behalf, do command you, if judgment be therein given, that then, under your seal, distinctly and openly, you send the record and proceedings afore-

said, with all things concerning the same, to the
United States Circuit Court of Appeals for the
Ninth Circuit, together with this writ, so that you
have the same at San Francisco, California, within
thirty days from the date hereof, in the said Circuit Court of Appeals to be then and there held;
that the record and proceedings aforesaid, being
then and there inspected, the said Circuit Court of
Appeals may cause further to be done therein to
correct that error, what of right and according to
the laws and customs of the United States of
America should be done.

WITNESS the Honorable WILLIAM HOW-
ARD TAFT, Chief Justice of the United States
this 3d day of December, 1923.

[Seal]                    G. H. MARSH,
Clerk of the District Court of the United States
    for the District of Oregon.

                    By F. L. Buck,
                    Chief Deputy.  [2]

[Endorsed]: No. ——. In the U. S. Circuit
Court of Appeals for the Ninth Circuit. American
Surety Company of New York, Plaintiff in Error,
vs. State of Oregon, etc., Defendant in Error.
Writ of Error. Filed December 3d, 1923. G. H.
Marsh, Clerk, United States District Court, Dis-
trict of Oregon. By F. L. Buck, Chief Deputy
Clerk.

In the District Court of the United States for the District of Oregon.

July Term, 1922.

BE IT REMEMBERED, that on the 31st day of August, 1922, there was duly filed in the District Court of the United States for the District of Oregon, a complaint, in words and figures as follows, to wit: [3]

In the District Court of the United States for the District of Oregon.

No. ——.

STATE OF OREGON on the Relation of HARRY HUMFELD,

Plaintiff,

vs.

AMERICAN SURETY COMPANY OF NEW YORK, a Corporation,

Defendant.

### COMPLAINT.

The relator, Harry Humfeld, brings this action in the name of the State of Oregon, for his benefit and for his cause of action against the defendant alleges as follows:

### I.

That at all times herein mentioned, relator was and now is a resident of the State of Oregon, residing therein, and a citizen of said state.

II.

That at all times herein mentioned, the defendant American Surety Company of New York was and now is a corporation organized and existing under the laws of the State of New York, and a citizen of said state.

III.

That this is a suit of a civil nature arising at law where the matter in controversy exceeds, exclusive of interest and costs, the sum of Three Thousand Dollars ($3000.00) and is between citizens of different states.

IV.

That heretofore and on the 21st day of June, 1918, a contract was entered in writing, between the Jordan Valley Land and Water Company, and the Desert Land Board of the State of Oregon, with reference to the construction of the Jordan Valley Irrigation Project in Malheur County, State of Oregon. That in order to insure the performance of said contract by the Jordan Valley Land and Water Company, and in pursuance of the statutes of the State of Oregon hereinafter set forth, and to secure the payment by said company to all persons supplying said company labor, materials or supplies for [4] use in the construction of said irrigation project and as a part of said contract, the Jordan Valley Land and Water Company as principal and the defendant as surety executed and delivered unto the said Desert Land Board of the State of Oregon, for the use and benefit of all persons supplying said Jordan Valley Land and Water

Company with labor, materials or supplies for the prosecution of said work, their certain bond wherein the defendant and the Jordan Valley Land and Water Company bound themselves jointly and severally in the penal sum of One Hundred Thousand Dollars ($100,000.00). Said bond, among other things, was conditioned upon the prompt payment by the principal of all persons supplying the said Jordan Valley Land and Water Company with labor or materials for any prosecution of the work provided by the aforementioned contract with the Desert Land Board for the State of Oregon. That said bond obligatory was duly executed by the Jordan Valley Land and Water Company, as principal, and the defendant as surety, and was accepted by the Desert Land Board of the State of Oregon, and the same formed a part of said contract above referred to, a copy of which said bond was and is in words and figures following, to wit:

KNOW ALL MEN BY THESE PRESENTS, That the Jordan Valley Land and Water Company, a corporation organized under the laws of Nevada and doing business in the State of Oregon, as principal, and American Surety Company of New York . . . a corporation formed and organized under the laws of the State of New York . . . and authorized to transact the surety business in the State of Oregon, as surety, are held and firmly bound to the State of Oregon in the full penal sum of One Hundred Thousand Dollars ($100,000.00), for the payment of which well and truly to be made, we hereby bind ourselves, our successors and assigns, jointly and severally, firmly by these presents.

Signed, sealed and dated this 17th day of August, 1918.

THE CONDITIONS OF THIS OBLIGATION ARE SUCH THAT: WHEREAS, the above-bounden principal has entered into an agreement with the Desert Land Board, acting for and on behalf of the State of Oregon, dated June 21, 1918, providing for the construction by said principal of an irrigation system, reservoirs, canals, flumes and other irrigation works and structures therein more particularly described, for what is known as the Jordan Valley Irrigation Project in Malheur [5] County, Oregon, which contract is hereby made a part hereof as fully as if set forth at length herein.

NOW, THEREFORE, if the said principal shall faithfully perform and discharge each and every of the conditions of said contract, by said principal to be kept and performed, as therein set forth and described, and shall comply with all of the terms and conditions thereof and shall not permit any lien or claim to be filed or prosecuted against said irrigation system, reservoirs, canals, flumes and other irrigation works and structures, and shall promptly make payments to all persons supplying it with labor or materials for any prosecution of the work provided for in said contract, this obligation shall be null and void, otherwise to remain in full force and effect.

IN WITNESS WHEREOF, the said principal and the said surety have caused this instrument to

be executed by its officers thereunto duly authorized on the day first above written.

[Seal]   JORDAN VALLEY LAND & WATER
CO.

By HERBERT G. WELLS,
Vice-President.

[Seal]   AMERICAN SURETY CO. OF NEW
YORK.

By HOMER H. SMITH,
Resident Vice-President.

Attest:   FRANK B. CROSS,
Secretary.

Attest:   CAREY F. MARTIN,
Resident Asst. Secretary.

HOMER H. SMITH,
Agent.

State of Oregon,
County of Marion,—ss.

I, Percy A. Cupper, state engineer and secretary
of the Desert Land Board of the State of Oregon,
and custodian of its records, do hereby certify that
the foregoing is a full, true and correct copy of that
certain bond given the State of Oregon by the Jordan
Valley Land and Water Company, as principal,
and the American Surety Company of New York,
as surety, in the penal sum of $100,000.00, condi-
tioned upon the faithful performance of the terms
of that certain agreement entered into by and between the State of Oregon and the Jordan Valley
Land and Water Company, dated June 21st, 1918,
providing for the construction of the Jordan Valley
Irrigation Project, and of the whole thereof, as

the same appears in the records of the Desert Land Board in my custody.

IN WITNESS WHEREOF, I have hereunto set my hand this 15th day of March, 1922.

PERCY A. CUPPER,

State Engineer, Secretary of the Desert Land Board.

By J. McALLISTER,

Assistant Secretary. [6]

### V.

That heretofore and pursuant to said contract of June 21, 1918, the Jordan Valley Land and Water Company entered into the performance of said contract, and commenced construction work on the Jordan Valley Irrigation Project, and did complete a considerable part of the work called for by said contract.

### VI.

That the legislature of the State of Oregon duly and regularly passed acts known as Chapter 342, General laws of 1921, wherein and whereby any person or the assignee of any person who has supplied labor or material to a contractor engaged on public work and who has posted a bond with the State of Oregon, municipal corporation or other subdivision, is authorized to institute an action against the surety on said bond on his own relation but in the name of the State of Oregon, and to prosecute the same to a final judgment and execution for his own use and benefit as the fact may appear.

## VII.

That heretofore and between the 1st day of April, 1920, and the 31st day of August, 1921, the relator, Harry Humfeld, at the special instance and request of the Jordan Valley Land and Water Company, performed work and labor for said Jordan Valley Land and Water Company, for a period of seventeen (17) months, in the construction and maintenance of said Jordan Valley Irrigation Project, as provided in the aforementioned contract between the Jordan Valley Land and Water Company, and the Desert Land Board of the State of Oregon, for which work and labor said Jordan Valley Land and Water Company promised and agreed to pay the relator Harry Humfeld, the sum of One Hundred Twenty Dollars ($120.00) per month for each month of said work and labor so performed. Said work and labor performed by the relator for the Jordan [7] Valley Land and Water Company was a necessary part of the construction of the said Jordan Valley Irrigation Project, and said work and labor performed by the relator as aforesaid was reasonably worth the said sum of One Hundred Twenty Dollars ($120.00) per month. Therefore, the said Jordan Valley Land and Water Company became indebted to the relator in the sum of Two Thousand Forty Dollars ($2040.00), no part of which sum has been paid; and there is now due, owing and unpaid the relator from the Jordan Valley Land and Water Company, the sum of Two Thousand Forty Dollars ($2,040.00), together with interest thereon from the

31st day of August, 1921, at the rate of six per
cent (6%) per annum, until paid.

## VIII.

That the defendant as surety upon the bond aforementioned is indebted to the relator in the sum of
Two Thousand Forty Dollars ($2,040.00), with in-
terest thereon at the rate of six per cent (6%) per
annum, from August 31, 1921, until paid.

## IX.

That the statute of the State of Oregon mentioned in paragraph V hereof, provides that in such
an action as is herein set out, the prevailing party
shall recover such attorney's fees therein as the
Court shall adjudge reasonable. That the sum of
Two Hundred Fifty Dollars ($250.00) is a reason-
able attorney's fee in said action.

For a second, separate and further action against
the defendant, relator complains and alleges as
follows:

## I.

Relator hereby repeats and incorporates by reference, as though fully set out herein, paragraphs
I, II, III, IV, V, and VI of his first cause of
action, as part of this cause of action.  [8]

## II.

That relator's assignor, E. I. du Pont de Nemours & Company, now is and at all times herein
mentioned was a corporation organized and existing
under and by virtue of the laws of the State of
Delaware.

## III.

That relator's assignor sold and delivered to

Jordan Valley Land and Water Company, at the special instance and request of said Jordan Valley Land and Water Company, blasting materials and supplies of the agreed value of Five Thousand Two Hundred Forty-five and 58/100 Dollars ($5,245.58), between the 3d day of October, 1919, and the 16th day of March, 1920. That said materials and supplies were used in the prosecution of the work as provided in the contract heretofore mentioned between the Desert Land Board of the State of Oregon and the said Jordan Valley Land and Water Company.

## IV.

That no part of said sum has been paid except the sum of Two Thousand Three Hundred Forty-four and 85/100 ($2,344.85) Dollars, and there is now due, owing and wholly unpaid the sum of Two Thousand Nine Hundred and 73/100 Dollars ($2,900.73), with interest thereon at the rate of six per cent (6%) per annum, from March 16, 1920, until paid.

## V.

That subsequent to the 16th day of March, 1920, and prior to the commencement of this action, E. I. du Pont de Nemours & Company, for a valuable consideration, sold, assigned, transferred and set over unto the relator herein, Harry Humfeld, all its right, title and interest in and to the claim above mentioned, and said relator is now the owner and holder thereof.

## VI.

That the defendant as surety upon the bond

aforementioned, [9] is indebted to the relator
in the sum of Two Thousand Nine Hundred and
73/100 Dollars ($2,900.73), with interest thereon
from the 16th day of March, 1920, at the rate of six
per cent (6%) per annum, until paid.

### VII.

That the statute of the State of Oregon, mentioned in paragraph V of the first cause of action,
provides that in such an action as herein set out,
the prevailing party shall recover such attorney's
fees therein as the Court shall adjudge reasonable.
That the sum of Three Hundred Dollars ($300.00)
is a reasonable attorney's fee in said action.

For a third, separate and further cause of action
against defendant, relator complains and alleges
as follows:

### I.

Relator hereby repeats and incorporates by reference, as though fully set out herein, paragraphs
I, II, III, IV, V, and VI of his first cause of action, as part of this cause of action.

### II.

That relator's assignor, The R. Hardesty Mfg.
Co., now is and at all times herein mentioned was
a corporation organized and existing under and by
virtue of the laws of the State of ———.

### III.

That relator's assignor, on or about the 10th day
of June, 1920, sold and delivered to Jordan Valley
Land and Water Company, at the special instance
and request of said Jordan Valley Land and Water
Company, three (3) Model 181 Hardesty Radial

Gates and three (3) Radial Gate Hoists, of the agreed value of One Thousand Five Hundred Nine and 31/100 Dollars ($1,509.31). That said gates and hoists were used in the prosecution of the   [10] construction work of the Jordan Valley Irrigation Project, as provided in the contract heretofore mentioned, between the Desert Land Board of the State of Oregon and the said Jordan Valley Land and Water Company.

### IV.

That no part of said sum of One Thousand Five Hundred Nine and 31/100 Dollars ($1,509.31) has been paid, and there is now due, owing and wholly unpaid The R. Hardesty Mfg. Co. from said Jordan Valley Land and Water Company, the sum of One Thousand Five Hundred Nine and 31/100 ($1,509.-31) with interest thereon at the rate of six per cent (6%) per annum, from July 10, 1920, until paid.

### V.

That subsequent to the 10th day of June, 1920, and prior to the commencement of this action, The R. Hardesty Mfg. Co. for a valuable consideration, sold, assigned, transferred and set over unto the relator herein, Harry Humfeld, all its right, title and interest in and to the claim above mentioned, and said relator is now the owner and holder thereof.

### VI.

That the defendant as surety upon the bond aforementioned, is indebted to the relator in the sum of One Thousand Five Hundred Nine and

31/100 Dollars ($1,509.31), with interest thereon
from the 10th day of July, 1920, at the rate of six
per cent (6%) per annum, until paid.

### VII.

That the statute of the State of Oregon, mentioned in paragraph V of the first cause of action,
provides that in such an action as is herein set out,
the prevailing party shall recover such attorney's
fees therein as the Court shall adjudge reasonable.
That the sum of Two Hundred Dollars ($200.00) is
a reasonable attorney's fee in said action.  [11]

For a fourth, separate and further cause of action, against the defendant, the relator complains
and alleges as follows:

### I.

Relator hereby repeats and incorporates by reference, as though fully set out herein, paragraphs
I, II, III, IV, V and VI of his first cause of action,
as a part of this cause of action.

### II.

That relator's assignor, Richard Murray, was and
now is a resident and citizen of the State of Oregon.

### III.

That heretofore and between the 1st day of May,
1920, and the 22d day of August, 1920, relator's
assignor performed work and labor for said Jordan
Valley Land and Water Company for a period of
three (3) months and twenty-two (22) days, in the
prosecution and maintenance of the construction
work of said Jordan Valley Irrigation Project, as
provided in the aforementioned contract between
the said Jordan Valley Land and Water Company

and the Desert Land Board of the State of Oregon, for which work and labor said Jordan Valley Land and Water Company promised and agreed to pay relator's assignor, Richard Murray, the sum of One Hundred Forty-five Dollars ($145.00) per month, for each month of such work and labor so performed. That said work and labor so performed by said Richard Murray was a necessary part of the construction work of the Jordan Valley Irrigation Project, and the said work and labor so performed was reasonably worth the sum of One Hundred Forty-five Dollars ($145.00) per month. Therefore, said Jordan Valley Land and Water Company became indebted to relator's assignor, Richard Murray, in the sum of Five Hundred Thirty-seven and 84/100 Dollars ($537.84), no part of which sum has been paid, and there is now due and owing, and wholly unpaid, the said Richard Murray from the said Jordan [12] Valley Land and Water Company, the sum of Five Hundred Thirty-seven and 84/100 Dollars ($537.84), together with interest thereon from the 22d day of August, 1920, at the rate of six per cent (6%) per annum, until paid.

IV.

That subsequent to the 22d day of August, 1920, and prior to the commencement of this action, the said Richard Murray, for a valuable consideration, sold, assigned, transferred and set over unto the relator herein, Harry Humfeld, all his right, title and interest in and to the claim above mentioned, and the said relator is now the owner and holder thereof.

## V.

That the defendant, as surety upon the bond aforementioned, is indebted to the relator in the sum of Five Hundred Thirty-seven and 84/100 Dollars ($537.84) with interest thereon from the 22d day of August, 1920, at the rate of six per cent (6%) per annum, until paid.

## VI.

That the statute of the State of Oregon, mentioned in paragraph V of the first cause of action, provides that in such an action as herein set out, the prevailing party shall recover such attorney's fees therein as the court shall adjudge a reasonable attorney's fee in said action.

For a fifth, separate and further cause of action against the defendant, relator complains and alleges as follows:

## I.

Relator hereby repeats and incorporates by reference, as though fully set out herein, paragraphs I, II, III, IV, V and VI of his first cause of action, as part of this cause of action.

## II.

That relator's assignor, C. C. Lehner, now is and at all times herein mentioned was a resident and citizen of the State of Idaho. [13]

## III.

That relator's assignor sold and delivered to Jordan Valley Land and Water Company, at the special instance and request of said Jordan Valley

Land and Water Company, meat for use in feeding the crews of men employed by said Jordan Valley Land and Water Company, in the construction of the Jordan Valley Irrigation Project, to the amount and value of One Hundred Seventy-three and 10/100 Dollars ($173.10). That said meat was sold and delivered as aforesaid, between the 1st day of April, 1920, and the 31st day of May, 1920. That said meat so sold and delivered was reasonably worth the sum of One Hundred Seventy-three and 10/100 Dollars ($173.10).

### IV.

That no part of said sum has been paid, and there is now due, owing and wholly unpaid said C. C. Lehner, from Jordan Valley Land and Water Company, the sum of One Hundred Seventy-three and 10/100 Dollars ($173.10), with interest thereon at the rate of six per cent (6%) per annum, from the 31st day of May, 1920, until paid.

### V.

That subsequent to the 31st day of May, 1920, and prior to the commencement of this action, C. C. Lehner, for a valuable consideration, sold, assigned, transferred and set over unto the relator herein, Harry Humfeld, all his right, title and interest in and to the claim above mentioned, and the relator is now the owner and holder thereof.

### VI.

That the defendant, as surety upon the bond aforementioned, is indebted to the relator in the sum of One Hundred Seventy-three and 10/100 Dollars ($173.10), together with interest thereon from the

31st day of May, 1920, at the rate of six per cent
(6%) per annum, until paid.

### VII.

That the statute of the State of Oregon, mentioned in  [14]  paragraph V of the first cause of
action, provides that in such an action as is herein
set out, the prevailing party shall recover such attorney's fees therein as the Court shall adjudge reasonable. That the sum of Twenty-five Dollars
($25.00) is a reasonable attorney's fee in said ac-
tion.

WHEREFORE, plaintiff, for the use and benefit
of the relator, Harry Humfeld, demands judgment
against the defendant for the sum of Seven Thousand One Hundred Sixty and 98/100 Dollars ($7,-
160.98), together with interest on Two Thousand
Forty Dollars ($2,040.00) thereof, from the 31st day
of August, 1921, at the rate of six per cent (6%)
per annum, until paid; together with interest on
Two Thousand Nine Hundred and 73/100 Dollars
($2,900.37) thereof, from the sixteenth day of
March, 1920, at the rate of six per cent (6%) per
annum, until paid; together with interest on One
Thousand Five Hundred Nine and 31/100 Dollars
($1,509.31) thereof, from the 10th day of July, 1920,
at the rate of six per cent (6%) per annum, until
paid; together with interest on Five Hundred
Thirty-seven and 84/100 Dollars ($537.84) thereof,
from the 22d day of August, 1920, at the rate of six
per cent (6%) per annum, until paid; together with
interest on One Hundred Seventy-three and 10/100
Dollars ($173.10) thereof from the 31st day of May,

1920, at the rate of six per cent (6%) per annum, until paid; and for the sum of Eight Hundred Seventy-five Dollars ($875.00) as attorney's fees herein, together with plaintiff's costs and disbursements of this action.

> BRONAUGH & BRONAUGH,
> BEACH & SIMON,
> ARTHUR A. GOLDSMITH,
> Attorneys for Plaintiff. [15]

State of Oregon,
County of Multnomah,—ss.

I, Harry Humfeld, being first duly sworn, on oath depose and say that I am the relator in the above-entitled action; and that the foregoing complaint is true as I verily believe.

> HARRY HUMFELD.

Subscribed and sworn to before me this 12th day of August, 1922.

> EARL C. BRONAUGH, Jr.,
> Notary Public for Oregon.

My commission expires Dec. 29, 1922.

Filed August 31, 1922. G. H. Marsh, Clerk. [16]

AND AFTERWARDS, to wit, on the 22d day of January, 1923, there was duly filed in said court a demurrer to the complaint in words and figures as follows, to wit:   [17]

In the District Court of the United States for the District of Oregon.

No. L.–9004.

STATE OF OREGON on the Relation of HARRY HUMFELD,

Plaintiff,

vs.

AMERICAN SURETY COMPANY OF NEW YORK, a Corporation,

Defendant.

DEMURRER TO COMPLAINT.

Comes now the defendant and demurs to the second, third, fourth and fifth causes of action set out in plaintiff's complaint on file herein on the following grounds:

1.   That plaintiff has not legal capacity to sue.

2.   That there is a defect of parties plaintiff.

3.   That sufficient facts are not stated to constitute a cause of action.

It appears upon the face of the complaint that the respective parties entitled to maintain the respective causes of action included in the complaint to which this demurrer is directed are E. I. du Pont de

Nemours & Company, The R. Hardesty Mfg. Co., Richard Murray and C. C. Lehner.

WM. S. NASH and
S. J. GRAHAM,
Attorneys for Defendant.

### STATEMENT OF POINTS.

The defendant will contend that the statutes of the State of Oregon at the time the bond was executed did not authorize an assignee to maintain an action upon a bond of the character of [18] the bond which is made the basis of the several causes of action and that the respective assignors named in plaintiff's second, third, fourth and fifth causes of action are the only parties who are authorized under the statute in force at the time the bond was executed to maintain said several causes of action.

WM. S. NASH and
S. J. GRAHAM,
Attorneys for Defendant.

District of Oregon,
County of Multnomah,—ss.

Due service of the within demurrer is hereby accepted in Multnomah County, Oregon, this 22d day of January, 1923, by receiving a copy thereof, duly certified to as such by S. J. Graham, of attorneys for defendant.

EARL C. BRONAUGH, Jr.,
Attorney for Plaintiff.

Filed January 22, 1923.   G. H. Marsh, Clerk.   [19]

AND AFTERWARDS, to wit, on Monday, the 5th day of February, 1923, the same being the 78th Judicial day of the regular November term of said Court,—Present, the Honorable ROBERT S. BEAN, United States District Judge, presiding,—the following proceedings were had in said cause, to wit:  [20]

In the District Court of the United States for the District of Oregon.

No. L.–9004.

February 5, 1923.

STATE OF OREGON ex rel. HARRY HUM-FELD

vs.

AMERICAN SURETY COMPANY OF NEW YORK.

MINUTES OF COURT—FEBRUARY 5, 1923—ORDER OVERRULING DEMURRER.

This cause was heard by the Court upon the demurrer of defendant to the second, third, fourth and fifth causes of action set out in plaintiff's complaint on file herein, plaintiff appearing by Mr. Arthur A. Goldsmith, of counsel, and defendant by Mr. Sidney Graham, of counsel, upon consideration whereof,—

IT IS ORDERED that said demurrer be and the same is hereby overruled.  [21]

AND AFTERWARDS, to wit, on the 5th day of February, 1923, there was duly filed in said court an opinion on demurrer, in words and figures as follows, to wit: [22]

In the District Court of the United States for the District of Oregon.

STATE OF OREGON on the Relation of HARRY HUMFELD,

Plaintiff,

vs.

AMERICAN SURETY COMPANY OF NEW YORK, a Corporation,

Defendant.

MEMORANDUM BY BEAN, DISTRICT JUDGE, ON DEMURRER TO COMPLAINT.

Portland, Oregon, February 5, 1923.

The demurrer will be overruled.

The claims of laborers and materialmen are assignable and the assignment carries the security and all the rights of the assignor. (Columbia Co. vs. Cons. Const., 83 Ore. 251.) The Oregon Act of 1921 (Chapter 342), is merely a legal declaration of the rule already existing and does not in any way impair the obligations of defendant's contract.

Filed February 5, 1923. G. H. Marsh, Clerk. [23]

AND AFTERWARDS, to wit, on the 6th day of March, 1923, there was duly filed in said court an answer, in words and figures as follows, to wit: [24]

In the District Court of the United States for the District of Oregon.

No. L.-9004.

STATE OF OREGON on the Relation of HARRY HUMFELD,

Plaintiff,

vs.

AMERICAN SURETY COMPANY OF NEW YORK, a Corporation,

Defendant.

ANSWER.

Comes now the defendant and for answer to plaintiff's first cause of action admits, denies and alleges:

I.

For answer to paragraph I denies any knowledge or information sufficient to form a belief as to the truth of the averments of paragraph I and therefore denies the same and the whole thereof.

II.

Admits paragraph II.

III.

Answering paragraph III admits that this is a suit of a civil nature arising at law where the matter in controversy exceeds exclusive of interest and costs the sum of $3000.00 and denies any knowledge or information sufficient to form a belief as to the truth of the remaining averments of said paragraph and therefore denies the remainder of said paragraph.

### IV.

Admits paragraph IV.

### V.

Admits paragraph V.

### VI.

Admits paragraph VI.

### VII.

Denies any knowledge or information sufficient to [25] form a belief as to the truth of the averments of paragraph VII and therefore denies the same and the whole thereof.

### VIII.

Denies paragraph VIII.

### IX.

Denies paragraph IX, and in this connection alleges that the statute referred to in said paragraph was enacted after the execution of the bond referred to in plaintiff's complaint; that at the time said bond was executed no such provision or statute was in force and effect; that the allowance of attorneys' fees under said statute enacted after the execution of said bond would impair the obligation of the contract of this defendant and would be violative of Section 21 of Article I of the Constitution of the State of Oregon and of Section 10 of Article I of the Constitution of the United States.

For answer to plaintiff's second cause of action this defendant admits and denies:

### I.

Answering paragraph I this defendant hereby repeats and incorporates by reference as though fully set out herein, its answers to paragraphs I, II, III, IV, V and VI of plaintiff's first cause of action.

### II.

Admits paragraph II.

### III.

Denies any knowledge or information sufficient to form a belief as to the truth of the averments of paragraph III and therefore denies the same and the whole thereof.

### IV.

Denies paragraph IV.  [26]

### V.

Denies any knowledge or information sufficient to form a belief as to the truth of the averments of paragraph V and therefore denies the same and the whole thereof.

### VI.

Denies paragraph VI.

### VII.

Denies paragraph VII, and in this connection alleges that the statute referred to in said paragraph was enacted after the execution of the bond referred to in plaintiff's complaint; that at the time said bond was executed no such provision or statute was in force and effect; that the allowance of attorneys' fees under said statute enacted after the execution of said bond would impair the obligation of the contract of this defendant and would be violative of Section 21 of Article I of the Constitution of the State of Oregon and of Section 10 of Article I of the Constitution of the United States.

For answer to plaintiff's third cause of action this defendant admits and denies:

### I.

Answering paragraph I this defendant hereby repeats and incorporates by reference as though fully set forth herein its answers to paragraphs I, II, III, IV, V and VI of the first cause of action.

### II.

Admits paragraph II.

### III.

Denies any knowledge or information sufficient to form a belief as to the truth of the averments of paragraph III and therefore denies the same and the whole thereof. [27]

### IV.

Denies any knowledge or information sufficient to form a belief as to the truth of the averments of paragraph IV and therefore denies the same and the whole thereof.

### V.

Denies any knowledge or information sufficient to form a belief as to the truth of the averments of paragraph V and therefore denies the same and the whole thereof.

### VI.

Denies paragraph VI.

### VII.

Denies paragraph VII, and in this connection alleges that the statute referred to in said paragraph was enacted after the execution of the bond referred to in plaintiff's complaint; that at the time said bond was executed no such provision or statute was in force and effect; that the allowance of attorneys' fees under said statute enacted after the execution of said bond would impair the obligation of the contract of this defendant and would be violative of Section 21 of Article I of the Constitution of the State of Oregon and of Section 10 of Article I of the Constitution of the United States.

For answer to the fourth cause of action this defendant admits and denies:

### I.

Answering paragraph I, this defendant hereby repeats and incorporates by reference as though fully set forth herein its answers to paragraphs I, II, III, IV, V and VI of the first cause of action.

### II.

Denies any knowledge or information sufficient to [28] form a belief as to the truth of the averments of paragraph II and therefore denies the same and the whole thereof.

### III.

Denies any knowledge or information sufficient to form a belief as to the truth of the averments of paragraph III and therefore denies the same and the whole thereof.

### IV.

Denies any knowledge or information sufficient to form a belief as to the truth of the averments of paragraph IV and therefor denies the same and the whole thereof.

### V.

Denies paragraph V.

### VI.

Denies paragraph VI, and in this connection alleges that the statute referred to in said paragraph was enacted after the execution of the bond referred to in plaintiff's complaint; that at the time said bond was executed no such provision or statute was in force and effect; that the allowance of attorneys' fees under said statute enacted after the execution of said bond would impair the obligation of the contract of this defendant and would be violative of Section 21 of Article I of the Constitution of the State of Oregon and of Section 10 of Article I of the Constitution of the United States.

For answer to plaintiff's fifth cause of action this defendant admits and denies:

### I.

Answering paragraph I, this defendant hereby repeats and incorporates by reference as though fully set forth herein its answers to paragraphs I, II, III, IV, V and VI of the first cause of action. [29]

### II.

Denies any knowledge or information sufficient to form a belief as to the truth of the averments

of paragraph II and therefore denies the same
and the whole thereof.

### III.

Denies any knowledge or information sufficient
to form a belief as to the truth of the averments
of paragraph III and therefore denies the same
and the whole thereof.

### IV.

Denies any knowledge or information sufficient
to form a belief as to the truth of the averments
of paragraph IV and therefore denies the same
and the whole thereof.

### V.

Denies any knowledge or information sufficient
to form a belief as to the truth of the averments
of paragraph V and therefore denies the same
and the whole thereof.

### VI.

Denies paragraph VI.

### VII.

Denies paragraph VII, and in this connection
alleges that the statute referred to in said paragraph was enacted after the execution of the bond
referred to in plaintiff's complaint; that at the
time said bond was executed no such provision
or statute was in force and effect; that the allowance of attorneys' fees under said statute enacted
after the execution of said bond would impair
the obligation of the contract of this defendant
and would be violative of Section 21 of Article
I of the Constitution of the State of Oregon and

of Section 10 of Article I of the Constitution of the United States.

For a further and separate defense to plaintiff's first cause of action this defendant alleges: [30]

I.

That on the 27th day of May, 1921, the contract of June 21, 1918, referred to in plaintiff's complaint by mutual consent of the parties thereto was rescinded and a new contract dated May 27, 1921, executed in lieu thereof.

II.

That pursuant to the contract entered into between the Jordan Valley Land and Water Company and the Desert Land Board of the State of Oregon on the 27th day of May, 1921, as aforesaid, the Desert Land Board on the 8th day of June, 1921, at a special meeting thereof held on said date, cancelled said bond set out in plaintiff's complaint and all liability thereunder, and accepted a new bond in lieu thereof.

WHEREFORE, this defendant having fully answered plaintiff's complaint prays that it may be dismissed with costs.

WM. S. NASH and
S. J. GRAHAM,
Attorneys for Defendant.

District of Oregon,
County of Multnomah,—ss.

I, W. J. Lyons, being first duly sworn, depose and say that I am the resident vice-president of American Surety Company of New York, defendant in the above-entitled action; and that the foregoing answer is true as I verily believe.

W. J. LYONS.

Subscribed and sworn to before me this 3d day of March, 1923.

[Seal]                           WM. S. NASH,
        Notary Public for the State of Oregon.

My commission expires April 4, 1924.   [31]

District of Oregon,
County of Multnomah,—ss.

Due service of the within answer is hereby accepted in Multnomah County, Oregon, this 3d day of March, 1923, by receiving a copy thereof, duly certified to as such by S. J. Graham, one of attorneys for defendant.

ARTHUR A. GOLDSMITH,<br>Of Attorneys for Plaintiff.

Filed March 6, 1923.  G. H. Marsh, Clerk.  [32]

---

AND AFTERWARDS, to wit, on the 11th day of June, 1923, there was duly filed in said court a stipulation waiving jury trial in words and figures as follows, to wit:  [33]

In the District Court of the United States for the District of Oregon.

No. L.-9004.

STATE OF OREGON on the Relation of HARRY HUMFELD,

Plaintiff,

vs.

AMERICAN SURETY COMPANY OF NEW YORK, a Corporation,

Defendant.

STIPULATION WAIVING JURY TRIAL.

It is hereby stipulated and agreed by and between the plaintiff and the defendant by the respective attorneys that the above-entitled action may be tried by the Court without a jury and the right of trial by jury is hereby expressly waived.

EARL C. BRONAUGH, Jr.,
Of Attorneys for Plaintiff,

S. J. GRAHAM,
Of Attorneys for Defendant.

It is stipulated and agreed that the foregoing stipulation may be filed *nunc pro tunc* as of the 1st day of the trial of the above-entitled cause.

EARL C. BRONAUGH, Jr.,
Of Attorneys for Plaintiff,

WM. S. NASH,
Of Attorneys for Defendant.

Filed January 12, 1924. G. H. Marsh, Clerk. *Nunc pro tunc* as of June 11, 1923. [34]

AND AFTERWARDS, to wit, on the 29th day of
October, 1923, there was duly filed in said
court an opinion of the Court, in words and
figures as follows, to wit:   [35]

In the District Court of the United States for the
District of Oregon.

STATE OF OREGON ex rel. HARRY HUM-
FELD,

Plaintiff,

vs.

AMERICAN SURETY COMPANY OF NEW
YORK, a Corporation,

Defendant.

## OPINION.

Portland, Oregon, October 29, 1923.

R. S. BEAN, District Judge:

This is an action on a bond executed by the defendant company in August, 1918, in pursuance of
a state statute (Sec. 6718 Ore. Laws), conditioned
that the Jordan Valley Land & Water Company
would faithfully perform and discharge each and
every condition of the contract entered into by
it with the state on January 22, 1918, for the
construction of what is known as the Jordan Valley
Irrigation project and would promptly make payments to all persons supplying labor or material
for the prosecution of the work.

The relator, Humfeld, worked for the Land &
Water Company from May 15, 1920, to September

26, 1921, at an agreed wage of $120.00 per month but it was not in prosecution of work covered by its contract with the state. His duty was to look after the system as far as completed, keep the ditches in order, make necessary repairs thereto, and apportion and divide the water to the users therefrom. It is true the system had not been completed and under the contract the Water Company was to retain possession and control of the work until accepted by state, but this did not render the defendant liable on its bond for the costs and expenses of operating the same. (Nat. Surety vs. U. S. 228 Fed. 577.)

The claim of $2900.75 is for powder furnished by the Du Pont Company for use in the construction of the work and is supported by the testimony. The plaintiff is therefore [36] entitled, as assignee thereof, to judgment for the amount with interest from March 16, 1920. (Pendleton vs. Jeffery & Bufton, 95 Or. 447–453.)

There is no evidence to support the other causes of action and as to them the plaintiff will be nonsuited.

The relator is entitled to his costs and disbursements but not attorney fees, a question heretofore reserved for further consideration. The state statute (Ch. 34, Laws 1921) providing for the recovery of attorney fees in actions of this kind was passed after the execution of the bond in suit, and therefore impairs the obligations thereof. The state may of course change the remedies. Whatever belongs merely to the remedy may be altered at any time by the state provided the alteration does not impair the obligation of a contract, but if that result is produced it is immaterial whether done by acting on the remedy or on the contract itself. It has been held that a state may legally impose a penalty on those who unsuccessfully and not in good faith defend their liability on a contract without thereby impairing the obligation of the contract (Fraternal Mystic Circle vs. Snyder, 227 U. S. 497), and that a state statute providing for the recovery of attorney fees in an action on a fire insurance policy issued prior to its enactment does not impair the obligation of the contract because insurance companies are engaged in business of such a general and public nature as to permit the police power of the state to be invoked in aid of the rights and duties growing out of the relation of the insurer and the insured. (Germania Fire Ins. vs. Bally, 173 Pac. 1052.)

But this case does not come within either of these rules. The defendant is not engaged in such a business nor is the provision for attorney fees imposed as a penalty for an [37] unsuccessful defense not made in good faith but as a mere consequence of the judgment. The law in force at the time the bond in suit was given became and was a part of the contract. The defendant's obligation was measured by the terms of the bond and the then existing law. The subsequent provision for the recovery of attorney's fees as a mere consequence of the suit was an addition to the contract and to defendant's liability thereunder. It is a requirement so onerous that the defendant company could justly decline to do business in the state on that condition, or refuse to write in the future bonds of the character of the one in question without adequate security to protect it on account of the added liability.

Judgment will be entered accordingly.

Filed October 29, 1923. G. H. Marsh, Clerk. [38]

———

AND AFTERWARDS, to wit, on the 3d day of November, 1923, there was duly filed in said court the findings of the Court, in words and figures as follows, to wit: [39]

In the District Court of the United States for the District of Oregon.

No. L.–9004.

STATE OF OREGON on the Relation of HARRY HUMFELD,

Plaintiff,

vs.

AMERICAN SURETY COMPANY OF NEW YORK, a Corporation,

Defendant.

### GENERAL FINDINGS.

This cause came on regularly for trial on the 11th and 12th days of June, 1923, Arthur A. Goldsmith and E. C. Bronaugh, Jr., appearing as counsel for the relator and Graham & Nash and Boardman appearing for the defendant. A trial by jury having been waived by stipulation of counsel for the respective parties, the cause was tried before the Court sitting without a jury, and evidence both oral and documentary was received on the part of the relator and on the part of the defendant, and the evidence being closed, and arguments, both oral and written having been made, the cause was submitted to the Court for consideration and decision, and being duly advised in the premises, I hereby make and file the following general finding:

The Court finds the issue for the relator on the second cause of action in the sum of $2,900.73, with interest thereon at the rate of six per cent per annum from March 16, 1920, together with relator's costs and disbursements incurred in said action, and in favor of defendant on the other causes of action set forth in complaint.

Let judgment be entered accordingly.

R. S. BEAN,

District Judge.

Dated this 3d day of November, 1923.

Due service of the within general finding is admitted this 3d day of November, 1923.

S. J. GRAHAM,

Of Attorneys for Defendant.

Filed November 3, 1923. G. H. Marsh, Clerk.

[40]

AND AFTERWARDS, to wit, on Saturday, the 3d day of November, 1923, the same being the 108th judicial day of the regular July term of said court,—Present, the Honorable ROBERT S. BEAN, United States District Judge, presiding,—the following proceedings were had in said cause, to wit: [41]

In the District Court of the United States for the District of Oregon.

No. L.–9004.

November 3, 1923.

STATE OF OREGON on the Relation of HARRY HUMFELD,

Plaintiff,

vs.

AMERICAN SURETY COMPANY OF NEW YORK, a Corporation,

Defendant.

MINUTES OF COURT—NOVEMBER 3, 1923—JUDGMENT.

This cause came on regularly for trial on the 11th and 12th days of June, 1923, Arthur A. Goldsmith and E. C. Bronaugh, Jr., appearing as counsel for the relator and Graham & Nash and Boardman for the defendant. A trial by jury having been waived by stipulation of counsel for the respective parties, the cause was tried before the Court sitting without a jury, and witnesses were examined on the part of the relator and on the part of the defendant, and the evidence being closed, and arguments both oral and written having been made, the cause was submitted to the Court for consideration and decision and after due deliberation thereon, the Court delivered its opinion and decision in writing dated October 29, 1923, and the same has been filed, and made its finding and it is

ORDERED, that judgment be entered in accordance therewith.

WHEREFORE, by reason of the law and in accordance with said finding, it is ORDERED AND ADJUDGED that the Relator, Harry Humfeld, do have and recover of and from American Surety Company of New York, the defendant, on the second cause of action set forth in the complaint the sum of $2,900.73, with interest thereon at the rate of six per cent per annum from March 16, 1920, together with relator's costs and disbursements [42] incurred in this action taxed at $98.81, and that plaintiff take nothing on the other causes of action set forth in said complaint.

R. S. BEAN,<br>Judge.

Due service of the within judgment is admitted this 2d day of November, 1923.

S. J. GRAHAM,<br>Attorney for Defendant.

Filed November 3, 1923. G. H. Marsh, Clerk.
[43]

AND AFTERWARDS, to wit, on Monday, the 12th day of November, 1923, the same being the 7th judicial day of the regular November term of said court,—Present, the Honorable ROBERT S. BEAN, United States District Judge, presiding,—the following proceedings were had in said cause, to wit: [44]

In the District Court of the United States for the District of Oregon.

No. L.–9004.

November 12, 1923.

STATE OF OREGON ex rel. HARRY HUMFELD

vs.

AMERICAN SURETY COMPANY OF NEW YORK, a Corporation,

MINUTES OF COURT—NOVEMBER 12, 1923— ORDER EXTENDING TIME TO AND INCLUDING NOVEMBER 28, 1923, TO FILE BILL OF EXCEPTIONS.

Now, at this day come the plaintiff by Mr. A. A. Goldsmith, of counsel, and the defendant by Mr. Sidney Graham, of counsel, whereupon on motion of defendant,

IT IS ORDERED that said defendant do have to and including November 28, 1923, to file a bill of exceptions herein, and that execution be and the same is hereby stayed till that date. [45]

AND AFTERWARDS, to wit, on the 28th day of November, 1923, there was duly filed in said court a stipulation for further time to submit bill of exceptions, in words and figures as follows, to wit:  [46]

In the District Court of the United States for the District of Oregon.

No. L.–9004.

STATE OF OREGON on the Relation of HARRY HUMFELD,

Plaintiff,

vs.

AMERICAN SURETY COMPANY OF NEW YORK, a Corporation,

Defendant.

STIPULATION EXTENDING TIME TO AND INCLUDING DECEMBER 4, 1923, TO FILE BILL OF EXCEPTIONS.

It is hereby stipulated and agreed by and between the parties hereto, through their respective attorneys of record, that the Court may make an order extending the time for filing the bill of exceptions herein to and including the 4th day of December, 1923, and staying execution on the judgment heretofore entered herein during said period of time.

Dated this 27th day of November, 1923.

ARTHUR A. GOLDSMITH,<br>Of Attorneys for Plaintiff.<br>WM. S. NASH,<br>Of Attorneys for Defendant.

Filed November 28, 1923. G. H. Marsh, Clerk.
[47]

———

AND AFTERWARDS, to wit, on the 3d day of
December, 1923, there was duly filed in said
court a petition for writ of error, in words and
figures as follows, to wit: [48]

In the District Court of the United States for the
District of Oregon.

No. L.–9004.

STATE OF OREGON on the Relation of HARRY
HUMFELD,

Plaintiff,

vs.

AMERICAN SURETY COMPANY OF NEW
YORK, a Corporation,

Defendant.

PETITION FOR WRIT OF ERROR.

To the Honorable Judges of the District Court of
the United States, for the District of Oregon:

The American Surety Company of New York, a
corporation, defendant in the above-entitled cause,
conceiving itself aggrieved by the final order and
judgment of this Court made and entered against
it and in favor of the plaintiff on the 3d day of
November, 1923, and rulings in said cause made as
set forth in its assignment of errors herein filed,
petitions said Court for an order allowing said defendant to prosecute a writ of error to the United

States Circuit Court of Appeals for the Ninth Circuit, for the reasons specified in the assignment of errors filed herewith under and in accordance with the rules of the United States Circuit Court of Appeals in that behalf made and provided, and also that an order be made fixing the amount of security which the plaintiff shall give and furnish upon said writ of error, and that upon giving such security all further proceedings in this court be suspended and stayed until the determination of said writ of error by the said United States Circuit Court of Appeals, and relative thereto defendant respectfully shows:

That by reason of the premises defendant alleges manifest error has happened to the great damage of the American Surety Company of New York, a corporation, defendant herein.

That defendant has filed herewith its assignment [49] of errors upon which it relies and will urge in the said Appellate Court:

WHEREFORE, defendant prays that a writ of error may issue out of the said United States Circuit Court of Appeals for the Ninth Circuit, to this court, for the correction of the errors so complained of, and that transcript of the records, proceedings, papers and all things concerning the same upon which said judgment was made, duly authenticated may be sent to the said United States Circuit Court of Appeals for the Ninth Circuit, to the end that said judgment be reversed and that defendant recover judgment as demanded in its complaint.

WM. S. NASH,
S. J. GRAHAM,
Attorneys for Defendant.

United States of America,
State and District of Oregon,
County of Multnomah,—ss.

Due service of the within petition for writ of error is hereby accepted in Multnomah County, Oregon, this 3d day of December, 1923, by receiving a copy thereof, duly certified to as such by S. J. Graham, of attorneys for defendant.

ARTHUR A. GOLDSMITH,

Of Attorneys for Plaintiff.

Filed December 3, 1923. G. H. Marsh, Clerk.
[50]

---

AND AFTERWARDS, to wit, on the 3d day of December, 1923, there was duly filed in said court an assignment of errors, in words and figures as follows, to wit: [51]

In the District Court of the United States for the District of Oregon.

STATE OF OREGON on the Relation of HARRY HUMFELD,

Plaintiff,

vs.

AMERICAN SURETY COMPANY OF NEW YORK, a Corporation,

Defendant.

ASSIGNMENT OF ERRORS.

Comes now the defendant above named, appearing

by. Wm. S. Nash and S. J. Graham, its attorneys, and says that the judgment and final order of this Court made and entered in the above-entitled cause on November 3, 1923, in favor of the plaintiff and against this defendant, is erroneous and against the just rights of said defendant, and files herein, together with its petition for a writ of error from said judgment and order, the following assignment of errors, which it avers occurred in the proceedings in said cause, upon which said final judment is based:

### I.

The Court erred in overruling the demurrer to the complaint for the reason that the complaint fails to state facts sufficient to constitute a cause of action. The action is on a bond given to insure the performance of a contract for the construction of a project under the Carey Act. The legislation accepting the Carey Act creates the liability and prescribes the remedy, which remedy is exclusive. The complaint fails to show that the remedy prescribed by the statute has been followed.

### II.

, The Court erred in finding the issue for the relator on the second cause of action in the sum of $2,900.73, with interest thereon at the rate of 6% per annum from March 16, 1920, and relator's costs and disbursements, and entering judgment [52] thereon for the reasons given under the preceding assignment and for the further reason that the evidence was insufficient to show that any of the material covered by said second cause of action was ordered or used by the Jordan Valley Land & Water Company in the prosecution of its work under its contract with the State of Oregon and/or was necessary for the prosecution of any of the work under the terms of the contract or the terms of the bond made the basis of the cause of action.

### III.

The Court erred in failing specially to find that there was no sufficient or competent evidence to show that the material was ordered or used by the Jordan Valley Land & Water Company for the prosecution of the work under the contract with the State of Oregon or was necessary for any of the prosecution of the work under the terms of the bond sued upon for the reason that the evidence is insufficient to show that the material was ordered by the Jordan Valley Land & Water Company and necessary in the prosecution of the work.

### IV.

The Court erred in not directing a judgment for the defendant for the reason that the complaint fails to state facts sufficient to constitue a cause of action and there was no sufficient evidence showing that the material had been ordered by the Jordan Land & Water Company for the necessary prosecution of the work embraced in its contract with the State of Oregon.

### V.

The Court erred in failing to make special findings as requested by the defendant for the reason given under Assignment of Error No. 1 and for the reason that the evidence was insufficient to justify any finding in favor of the relator. [53]

## VI.

The Court erred in entering judgment for the relator for the reason that the complaint did not state facts sufficient to constitute a cause of action and for the further reason that the evidence was insufficient to justify any judgment in favor of the relator and for the further reason that by entering judgment for the relator the liability on the bond was extended beyond the terms of the contract it was given to secure and beyond the provision of the Carey Act and the legislation of the State of Oregon accepting the Carey Act.

WHEREFORE, the plaintiff in error prays that the judgment of the Court be reversed and a judgment entered in its favor with costs dismissing the relator's complaint.

WM. S. NASH and
S. J. GRAHAM,
Attorneys for Plaintiff in Error.

United States of America,
State and District of Oregon,
County of Multnomah,—ss.

Due service of the within assignment of errors is hereby accepted in Multnomah County, Oregon, this 3d day of December, 1923, by receiving a copy thereof, duly certified to as such by S. J. Graham, of attorneys for defendant.

ARTHUR A. GOLDSMITH,
Of Attorneys for Plaintiff.

Filed December 3, 1923.  G. H. Marsh, Clerk.
[54]

AND AFTERWARDS, to wit, on Monday, the 3d
day of December, 1923, the same being the 24th
judicial day of the regular November term of
said court,—Present, the Honorable ROBERT
S. BEAN, United States District Judge, presiding,—the following proceedings were had in
said cause, to wit:  [55]

In the District Court of the United States for the
District of Oregon.

No. L.–9004.

STATE OF OREGON on the Relation of HARRY
HUMFELD,

Plaintiff,

vs.

AMERICAN SURETY COMPANY OF NEW
YORK, a Corporation,

Defendant.

MINUTES OF COURT—DECEMBER 3, 1923—
ORDER ALLOWING WRIT OF ERROR,
STAYING PROCEEDINGS AND FIXING
THE AMOUNT OF BOND.

This 3d day of December, 1923, came the defendant above named, American Surety Company of
New York, appearing by Wm. S. Nash and S. J.
Graham, its attorneys of record, and filed herein
and presented to the Court its petition praying for
the allowance of a writ of error from the decision
and judgment of this Court, made and entered
herein on the 3d day of November, 1923, in favor of

the relator above named and against said defendant, and the rulings made upon the trial of the above-entitled cause out of the United States Circuit Court of Appeals in and for the Ninth Circuit, to this court, together with its assignment of errors intended to be urged by it within due time, and also praying that a transcript of the record and proceedings and papers upon which the said judgment herein was rendered, duly authenticated, may be sent to the said Circuit Court of Appeals for the Ninth Circuit, and also praying that an order be made fixing the amount of security which defendant shall give and furnish upon said writ of error, and that upon the giving of such security all further proceedings in this court be suspended and stayed until the determination of said writ of error by the United States Circuit Court of Appeals for the Ninth Circuit, and that such other and further proceedings may be had as may be proper in the premises.

NOW, THEREFORE, on consideration thereof, this Court does allow said writ of error upon said defendant filing with the   [56]   clerk of this court a good and sufficient bond in the sum of Five Thousand ($5,000.00) Dollars, to the effect that if the said defendant, American Surety Company of New York, a corporation, shall prosecute the said writ of error to effect and answer all damages and costs if defendant fails to make its complaint good, then said bond to be void, otherwise to remain in full force and virtue, the said bond to be approved by the Court, and it is ordered that all further proceedings in this court be, and the same are, hereby suspended and stayed until the determination of said writ of error by the said United States Circuit Court of Appeals, and that said bond shall operate as a supersedeas bond.

Dated this 3d day of December, 1923.

R. S. BEAN,

Judge.

Filed December 3, 1923. G. H. Marsh, Clerk. [57]

----

AND AFTERWARDS, to wit, on the 3d day of December, 1923, there was duly filed in said court a supersedeas bond, in words and figures as follows, to wit: [58]

In the District Court of the United States for the District of Oregon.

No. L.-9004.

STATE OF OREGON on the Relation of HARRY HUMFELD,

Plaintiff,

vs.

AMERICAN SURETY COMPANY OF NEW YORK, a Corporation,

Defendant.

## BOND ON WRIT OF ERROR AND SUPERSE-DEAS BOND.

KNOW ALL MEN BY THESE PRESENTS, that we, the American Surety Company of New York, a corporation, principal, and Fidelity and Deposit Company of Maryland, a corporation, surety, are held and firmly bound unto Harry Humfeld, the above-named plaintiff, in the Sum of Five Thousand ($5,000.00) Dollars, to be paid to the said Harry Humfeld, his heirs, administrators and assigns, to which payment well and truly to be made we bind ourselves and each of us, jointly and severally, and our and each of our successors or assigns, firmly by these presents.

Sealed with our seals and dated this 3d day of December, 1923.

WHEREAS, the above-named American Surety Company of New York, a corporation, is prosecuting a writ of error to the United States Circuit Court of Appeals for the Ninth Circuit to reverse the judgment in the above-entitled cause by the District Court of the United States for the District of Oregon, entered on the 3d day of November, 1923.

NOW, the consideration of this obligation is such that if the above-named American Surety Company of New York, a corporation, shall prosecute said writ of error to effect, and answer all costs and damages if it shall fail to make good its complaint, then this obligation to be void; otherwise to remain in full force and effect.

AMERICAN SURETY COMPANY OF NEW YORK.

[Seal]                        By W. J. LYONS,
                        Resident Vice-President.

FIDELITY AND DEPOSIT COMPANY OF MARYLAND.

By R. E. PINNEY,   (Seal)
Attorney-in-Fact.

Examined and approved this 3d day of December, 1923.

R. S. BEAN,
Judge.   [59]

United States of America,
State and District of Oregon,
County of Multnomah,—ss.

Due service of the within bond on writ of error and supersedeas bond is hereby accepted in Multnomah County, Oregon, this 3d day of December, 1923, by receiving a copy thereof, duly certified to as such by S. J. Graham, of Attorneys for Defendant.

ARTHUR A. GOLDSMITH,
Of Attorneys for Plaintiff.

Filed December 3, 1923. G. H. Marsh, Clerk.
[60]

AND AFTERWARDS, to wit, on Wednesday, the
26th day of December, 1923, the same being the
42d judicial day of the regular November
term of said court,—Present, the Honorable
ROBERT S. BEAN, United States District
Judge, presiding,—the following proceedings
were had in said cause, to wit:  [61]

In the District Court of the United States for the
District of Oregon.

No. L.-9004.

STATE OF OREGON on Relation of HARRY
HUMFELD,

Plaintiff,

vs.

AMERICAN SURETY COMPANY OF NEW
YORK, a Corporation,

Defendant.

MINUTES OF COURT—DECEMBER 26, 1923—
ORDER SETTLING BILL OF EXCEP-
TIONS.

This cause comes on this day to be heard on the
bill of exceptions proposed by the defendant and
the amendment proposed by the relator, and it
appearing to the Court that the amendment should
not be allowed and that the bill of exceptions proposed by the defendant should be settled and allowed as and for a bill of exceptions in this cause,—

IT IS ORDERED that the bill of exceptions heretofore tendered by the defendant be and the same is hereby settled and allowed as and for a bill of exceptions and made a part of the records in this cause, and the amendment proposed by the relator be and the same is hereby denied.

IT IS FURTHER ORDERED that the entire deposition of A. J. Vance be sent up with the original papers on appeal.

Dated this 26th day of December, 1923.

R. S. BEAN,

Judge.

Filed December 26, 1923. G. H. Marsh, Clerk. [62]

---

AND AFTERWARDS, to wit, on the 26th day of December, 1923, there was duly filed in said court a bill of exceptions, in words and figures as follows, to wit: [63]

In the District Court of the United States for the District of Oregon.

STATE OF OREGON on the Relation of HARRY HUMFELD,

Plaintiff,

vs.

AMERICAN SURETY COMPANY OF NEW YORK, a Corporation,

Defendant.

## BILL OF EXCEPTIONS.

BE IT REMEMBERED, that heretofore, to wit, on June 11, 1923, the above-entitled action came regularly on for trial in the above court before the Honorable Robert S. Bean, one of the Judges thereof, sitting without a jury, a stipulation in writing waiving a jury having been heretofore filed with the clerk, the plaintiff appearing by Messrs. Arthur A. Goldsmith and E. C. Bronaugh, Jr., his attorneys, and the defendant appearing by Wm. S. Nash, S. J. Graham and H. H. Boardman, its attorneys, and thereupon the following proceedings were had and done, to wit:

## TESTIMONY OF HARRY HUMFELD, FOR PLAINTIFF.

HARRY HUMFELD, being first duly sworn, testified on behalf of the plaintiff as follows:

### Direct Examination.

I am the plaintiff or relator in this action and am a citizen of the United States and a resident of the State of Oregon. My occupation is assistant superintendent at the Umatilla Experiment Station. I was formerly employed by the Jordan Valley Land & Water Company upon what is known as the Jordan Valley Irrigation Project, located in the Southern part of Malheur County, Oregon.

The Jordan Valley Land & Water Company was engaged in the construction of the irrigation sys-

(Testimony of Harry Humfeld.)

tem on the project. I first became connected with the work April 1, 1920. The nature of my connection with the Jordan Valley Land & Water Company was [64] as water-master and looking after the operation of their system. I was employed by the chief engineer of the Jordan Valley Land & Water Company, Mr. Charles C. Smith, who was also general manager, I believe. At the time I was employed by the Jordan Valley Land & Water Company I was employed by the Jordan Valley Farms which was a sales company of the Jordan Valley Project.

On April 1, 1920, I was employed by Mr. Hooker, the president of the Jordan Valley Farms, to assist the settlers in getting their land settled and leveled for irrigation, and just to be on the project there, and help in cruising the land the Farms Company was selling. About the 15th of May the water-master then employed by the Jordan Valley Land & Water Company left and Mr. Smith asked me to take that besides working for the Jordan Valley Farms. I told him I would do so so long as it would be all right with Mr. Hooker. I was instructed to do anything to help the project being settled, and that was part of my work, and the operation of the system as far as it was completed was right near the work I was doing, and I would be able to take care of that at the same time, so I looked after that from then on.

I commenced work as water-master on the 15th day of May, 1920, and continued in such work

(Testimony of Harry Humfeld.)

until the company went into bankruptcy on September 26th, I believe, 1921. The nature of my work as water-master was to look after the system as far as completed. That consisted of feeder canals which delivered water into the reservoir, the Antelope Reservoir, and then was taken out from the reservoir and distributed on the Antelope Unit. At the time I commenced work as water-master the project was completed substantially so some water could be delivered on the Antelope Unit, about three thousand acres. The dam was completed about forty feet high in which to store water in the reservoir and a main canal running from that with a main lateral along the Antelope [65] Unit complete. I looked after the delivery of the water and looked after the storage of the water. My work upon the ditch or canal was mainly maintenance work. It consisted of the delivery of the water, seeing the ditches were kept in good shape, making repairs if necessary or hiring men to do the repairs if necessary. I made repairs which were mostly to the feeder canal and worked continuously at that work after May 15, 1920. At the same time, as stated, I was employed by the Jordan Valley Farms and laid out the ditches for that company for the settlers on their farm units there and helped them in getting their land leveled and laid out, advised them how to put in crops if necessary, and those that had no experience in irrigating helping them along in that line.

(Testimony of Harry Humfeld.)

I was to receive a salary from the Jordan Valley Farms of $175.00 and expenses, including my board and traveling expenses. As I understood it at the time I went to work for the Jordan Valley Land & Water Company, its arrangement was to pay half my wages. As I say, I put in half my time on their work. This arrangement, I believe, was made between Mr. Smith and Mr. Hooker. I had made arrangements with Mr. Smith that they would pay half the expenses. The Jordan Valley Land & Water Company was paying me $175.00 a month and they figured they were at that time paying $60.00 a month for my board. Later on I found a statement of the first half month of my wages, payroll turned in by Mr. Smith, which figured my wages $120.00 a month as their share. That was the understanding with Mr. Smith that the Jordan Valley Land & Water Company was to pay me $120.00 a month. There was nothing definite as to whether this included my expenses and everything, but these two companies were to adjust that between them. I put in my time wherever I deemed best and wherever it was necessary. This arrangement continued all the time as far as I knew. Mr. Smith was manager, general manager or chief engineer at the time he made this arrangement with me. I was never notified of any change in that arrangement by any of the officers or employees of the Jordan Valley Land & Water Company, nor was I ever notified   [66]   by any one on behalf of the Jordan Valley Land & Water Company subse-

(Testimony of Harry Humfeld.)

quent to May 15, 1920, that my services were no longer required by it, nor was I ever notified of any change in the arrangement as to compensation which continued from May 15, 1920, until September 26, 1921. I never received any pay from the Jordan Valley Land & Water Company. I received $100.00 from the Jordan Valley Farms on account of the first month. Then afterwards I collected some money on some grain sold and for some maintenance collected for them. I did this under the direction of Mr. Hooker, who was president of the Jordan Valley Farms, and used the money so collected for living expenses mostly. Mr. Hooker instructed me to apply the money on wages. In addition I received a $50.00 check from the Boise Title & Trust Company later on; some time during the latter part of August. I would not state definitely when; it seems to me August or September, 1921. I understood it came from the Jordan Valley Farms as proceeds from sales made through the Boise Title & Trust Company.

Plaintiff's Exhibits 1, 2, 3 and 4 were thereupon offer and received in evidence.

Mr. Bronaugh then said: There has been a stipulation entered into, if your Honor please, with the respective counsel that the assignments of the claims, that is, Mr. Humfeld's personal claim here may be deemed to have been identified by competent testimony, and the authority to execute such assignments by the respective parties or officials who executed the assignments on behalf of

(Testimony of Harry Humfeld.)

the assignors, that has been stipulated by counsel, and we will merely submit the assignments to Mr. Humfeld themselves, without any testimony as to their execution.

The stipulation referred to in the statement of Mr. Bronaugh was thereupon offered and received in evidence and marked Plaintiff's Exhibit 1.

Thereupon an assignment from the Du Pont de Namours Company was offered and received in evidence as Plaintiff's Exhibit 2 and an assignment from Richard Murray was offered and received in [67] evidence as Plaintiff's Exhibit 3, and an assignment from one Lehner was offered and received in evidence as Plaintiff's Exhibit 4.

The witness then testified further on direct examination:

While I was employed upon the Jordan Valley Irrigation Project I knew of certain powder and blasting supplies which were shipped to the Jordan Valley Land & Water Company for use on the project. These supplies were shipped from the DuPont Company and were on the project at the time I quit work. They were stored in a building and consisted of approximately around seven hundred kegs of black powder and thirty-two or thirty-six cases of dynamite. I understood they were purchased from the DuPont de Nemours Company. I know they were.

Cross-examination.

My home is at Hermiston, Oregon, where I have lived since April 1, 1922. Prior to that time I

(Testimony of Harry Humfeld.)

lived at Corvallis, Oregon. I first became acquainted with Mr. Hooker, of the Jordan Valley Farms, about December, 1917, in Portland, Oregon. My father resided at that time in Portland but I was going to school at Corvallis. I first heard of the Jordan Valley Farms, it seems to me, in the fall of '19 from my father. It is my understanding that it is a separate and distinct corporation from the Jordan Valley Land & Water Company. They are distinct corporations or companies. I knew the business the Jordan Valley Farms had on hand at that time which was selling the land of the Jordan Valley Project. I first heard of the Jordan Valley Land & Water Company from my father or from Mr. Hooker. My father was manager for a mortgage company which was considering making loans on the Jordan Valley Irrigation Project. He was making a loan to both the Jordan Valley Farms and the Jordan Valley Land & Water Company as I understood it. His company was the mortgage company for Oregon, which is a foreign corporation. I was not employed by the mortgage company [68] at any time. The study I was taking up at school along the line of farm projects, irrigation and drainage work, and I asked my father if there wasn't a chance to get with some project that he knew about. This was in the fall of 1919 and I was still in school. I had not worked as water-master before and had no experience as a water-master, though I knew what a water-master was as I had had experience in irrigation projects

(Testimony of Harry Humfeld.)

before I was in school. At that time I had been in school three years. I then talked with Mr. Hooker, president of the Jordan Valley Farms. I met him in the Imperial Hotel and he stated that he was looking for a man to take care of the settlers he was selling the land to; to lay out their ditches and give them general advice in farming. I made arrangements then with him to work with the Jordan Valley Farms at a compensation of $175.00 a month and expenses. The contract was not in writing and Mr. Hooker is dead. At that time he was representing the Jordan Valley Farms. After I had made the arrangement with him I commenced work April 1, 1920. I went first to the Jordan Valley Farms Company office at Boise and saw Mr. Maney, vice-president of the company, who said that Mr. Hooker left word for me to report to the chief engineer, Mr. Smith, on the Jordan Valley Project. I think I repeated the agreement I had with Mr. Hooker and that Mr. Maney understood the terms of the agreement. My compensation, as stated, was to come monthly. I went from Boise to the project. Considerable construction work was done and considerable construction was going on at the time. I reported to Mr. Smith, chief engineer on the project. He had nothing to do with the Jordan Valley Farms that I know of, nor any official position with that company that I know of. I told him that Mr. Hooker had told me to come down there and report to him. This was April 1, 1920. I got during May, $100.00

(Testimony of Harry Humfeld.)

on account from the Jordan Valley Farms. During the month of April [69] I worked on the project as a member of the surveying crew on the construction work. I had previously had some experience laying out ditches. I was chainman in the crew. I don't know whether I reported my arrangement with Mr. Hooker to Mr. Smith or not other than to tell him Mr. Hooker had sent me down. In the first part of May I worked the same as I did in April. Then the latter part of May I went up to the Antelope Unit and became watermaster on May 15th. I am familiar with the physical topography of the structure. I know where the Antelope Unit is and the map which you hand me is substantially a blue-print of the project. The surveying work I first did was located on the lower part of Jordan Creek, in section 3, township 30 south, in the southeast quarter, where the camp was. At that time the feeder canal was constructed and there was a dam at the Antelope Reservoir and the Antelope lateral, and the construction work was going on. The diversion dam was constructed and the construction work was going on on the lower canal—the lower unit canal. My father, as I understand it, had mortgages on privately owned land on the Antelope Unit and the irrigation system at that time. Thereupon the map was offered in evidence and marked Defendant's Exhibit "A." When I commenced as water-master I superintended part that was constructed far enough so as to be able to carry water, which was the feeder

(Testimony of Harry Humfeld.)

canal, which is everything but the lower unit.
The terminals of the ditch or lateral were in section 36, the northeast quarter. I did not know at
the time I first reported that Mr. Smith did not
represent the Jordan Valley Farms. I think I
ascertained this some time in May. The duty of a
water-master is to see that the water is delivered
to the settlers. If necessary ditch draggers are
employed, or if a small project, you drag the ditch
yourself, keep in repair and deliver the water to
the settlers. It was my duty to see that they received water they were entitled to. The water-
master's [70] job had nothing to do with the
construction work on the lower unit. It was only
and entirely maintenance work. It had nothing
to do with the construction work on the balance of
the system that had not been completed only in so
far as it is mentioned in the contract that the water
company shall operate the system until accepted
by the State of Oregon. However, the work I did
as water-master on this first part of the work had
been completed had nothing whatever to do with the
construction of the balance of the work. I made
repairs for the reason we had several breaks in
the feeder canal. There was one break that took
five and there was a break that took approximately
ten days to repair, and some minor breaks which
two or three men fixed. Thirty or forty days would
cover time spent in repairing breaks. I laid out
ditches for the settlers, which was work for the
Jordan Valley Farms Company. I put in approxi-

(Testimony of Harry Humfeld.)

mately half of my time in that manner. The settlers did not pay me for this survey work for the
reason the Jordan Valley Farms had an agreement to do such work for them. I made collections for the Jordan Valley Farms and accounted
to them for the collections. I reported this to
Mr. Hooker. I had several talks with Mr. Hooker
concerning payment for my services and the understanding was that the money would be available soon, and that I would be paid regularly.
This ran along until the company went into bankruptcy, a period of approximately 17 months. I
stayed in the project for the reason that I understood the company was arranging a loan either
with my father or other companies. My father
also advised me that he thought eventually they
would have plenty of money to finish the project
and no doubt I would get my wages. My father
never definitely asked me to look after his interests.
I kept an eye open of course. There was no one
else that I reported to other than Mr. Hooker and
Mr. Smith. I am acquainted with Mr. Vance and
Mr. Leland Vance. I told them I was on the project
as water-master. [71] I could not have made a
statement to either of them in May, 1920, and again
in August, 1920, that I was glad I was in the employ
of the Jordan Valley Farms and not in the employ
of the Jordan Valley Land & Water Company because I felt that my salary coming from that source
would be much more certain than if I had been employed by the Jordan Valley Land & Water Com-

(Testimony of Harry Humfeld.)

pany, for the reason that I was employed by both companies in August. I made such a statement about the first of May, I think, to Mr. Leland Vance, but never made such a statement to Mr. A. J. Vance. I had no agreement with Mr. A. J. Vance in regard to my services. Mr. Smith represented the Jordan Valley Land & Water Company at the time I made the agreement. He was not representing the Jordan Valley Farms.

### Redirect Examination.

Mr. Rice was water-master on the project from the time they started the water, which was I think about April 15th, until May 15th. He was employed by the Jordan Valley Land & Water Company. The Jordan Valley Farms never maintained a water-master there that I know of. Mr. Smith, chief engineer of the Jordan Valley Land & Water Company, asked me to act as water-master. He asked me to do this for the Jordan Valley Land & Water Company. He said that he would make arrangements with Mr. Hooker that the Jordan Valley Land & Water Company would pay half of my wages, which were $175.00 a month and expenses. I was charged $60.00 a month for my board. I had a car which the Jordan Valley Land & Water Company furnished.

From May 15th to June 5th when the construction work closed down I took orders from Mr. Smith. There was no one there after that until Mr. Vance came out and he was there for a few

(Testimony of Harry Humfeld.)

days in August, 1920. He understood I was water-master. We went over the project together, looked after some supplies there and it was [72] arranged that I should sell supplies if I could for the benefit of the Jordan Valley Land & Water Company and pay off some of the most urgent debts. I am familiar with the signature of Mr. A. J. Vance and the letter which you hand me is dated August 30, 1920, and was a letter I received through the mail from Mr. Vance. At that time I understood he was vice-president of the Jordan Valley Land & Water Company. The letter was thereupon offered in evidence and objected to on the ground that it was incompetent, irrelevant and immaterial and not properly identified. It was admitted subject to the objection and marked Plaintiff's Exhibit 5.

The witness further testified: I received another letter through the mails from Mr. A. J. Vance. It bears his signature and is dated October 18, 1920. The letter was thereupon offered and the same objection was interposed and the letter was marked Plaintiff's Exhibit 6.

The witness further testified: I never received any instructions from Mr. Vance during the summer of 1920 as to how to proceed with the work. I think we talked about the matter of my wages and expenses and he said that as soon as the company was able to obtain money and was able to go ahead with the construction work all the debts would be taken

(Testimony of Harry Humfeld.)

care of which would include my wages. He made that statement to me during August, 1920.

My father did not own any land on that project and does not own any now and has no connection with the Jordan Valley Land & Water Company only in so far as they were parties to an agreement to borrow money from his company for the construction project. The same state of facts exists with respect to the Jordan Valley Farms. My father owned no stock in either of these companies. As security for money borrowed by these companies he received some first mortgages on the land on the Antelope Unit; but I think that was all. [73] He has not taken any steps to foreclose these mortgages. He foreclosed on the Jordan Valley Land & Water Company and the Jordan Valley Farms, but he has not foreclosed on the individual purchase mortgages which he obtained. He has not taken over the management or operation of any of the land. He was appointed receiver for the company after the companies went into bankruptcy, and as such operated the system. At the time I was working on the project he had no interest in any land on that project.

As heretofore testified, I am familiar with the signature of A. J. Vance. His signature appears on Plaintiff's Exhibit 7 for identification.

### Recross-examination.

I did not see Mr. Vance sign Plaintiff's Exhibits 5 or 6. I received both through the mails. I have never been present when he signed any paper. I

(Testimony of Harry Humfeld.)

became familiar with his handwriting through seeing it on several contracts he signed as vice-president. I did not see him sign these, but there was
only one Mr. Vance, A. J. Vance, and of course for
a signature as plain as that it could hardly be mistaken for anyone else's signature. I never saw him
sign his signature, though, to anything as I recall,
and I couldn't say that I ever saw him write by
hand in my presence. What I know about his handwriting is only the letters I received through the mail
coming from the Boise office of the Jordan Valley
Land & Water Company. He was vice-president
and was personally at Boise at the time. I testify
that the signature is Mr. Vance's by reason of the
fact that I have received letters through the mail
that should have come from him and by reason of
the fact that I have seen contracts signed Jordan
Valley Land & Water Company. I did not witness
these contracts and I did not know who signed it.
I do not have any other documents in my possession
[74] or any other writing that I know positively
of my own knowledge that Mr. Vance ever signed.
I have never been with him when he wrote things
and I do not know his handwriting.

Redirect Examination.

At the time the letter of August 24th and the
other letters were written it was my understanding
that Mr. Vance was vice-president of the Jordan
Valley Land & Water Company. As far as I knew
he held that office, and I believe he was at Boise;
that is where his letters came from. Every one of

(Testimony of Harry Humfeld.)

these letters was signed Jordan Valley Land & Water Company by A. J. Vance. This company did not have another vice-president at that time. Previously Mr. Wells had been vice-president, but as I understand it, Mr. Wells no longer held that office and Mr. Vance was vice-president, but I don't know that because I wasn't there.

## TESTIMONY OF JOHN W. CUNNINGHAM, FOR PLAINTIFF.

JOHN W. CUNNINGHAM being first duly sworn, testified on behalf of the plaintiff as follows:

### Direct Examination.

I am a civil engineer and a member of the firm of Barr & Cunningham. I have been a civil engineer since 1908 and am practicing that profession in Portland at the present time.

I have heard of the Jordan Valley Land & Water Company and have been connected with it. I know some of its officers. I know Mr. Emil Tschiegs. He was secretary of the Jordan Valley Land & Water Company on or about the 4th day of February, 1920. Plaintiff's Exhibit 8 for identification, which bears date February 4, 1920, Order No. 190, bears the signature of Mr. Tschiegs. I believe that Mr. H. G. Wells was an officer of the Jordan Valley Land & Water Company during the month of February, 1920. I do not recall the [75] exact date that he ceased to be an officer, but believes it was some time after February, 1920. He was vice-president.

(Testimony of John W. Cunningham.)

Plaintiff's Exhibit 9 for identification, which purports to be a letter from the Jordan Valley Land & Water Company addressed to the DuPont de Nemours Company, has thereon the signature of Mr. H. G. Wells. Mr. Vance succeeded Mr. Wells as vice-president of the Jordan Valley Land & Water Company some time in the spring of 1920. I think he was an officer of the Jordan Valley Land & Water Company in August, 1920. I believe he held the office of vice-president. I know that the Jordan Valley Land & Water Company ordered powder and blasting supplies from the DuPont Company for use on the project of the Jordan Valley Land & Water Company in Malheur County. I cannot fix the exact dates of order or delivery, but know that two lots of powder were purchased; two carloads at different times. One of these carloads was purchased to be delivered during the late winter or early spring of 1920 and was delivered on the ground at the project. It was purchased from the DuPont Company. In addition to black blasting powder there was dynamite and black powder. I remember seeing the dynamite. I couldn't say positively whether there was any fuse. I do not know that there was black powder and dynamite which was delivered on the project in the late winter or spring of 1920 and which was ordered by the Jordan Valley Land & Water Company. There was one carload purchased in the late summer or fall of 1919 and one in the late winter or spring of 1920. At the time the second carload of blasting supplies was

(Testimony of John W. Cunningham.)

ordered delivered I had no connection with the company. I was representing the Desert Land Board of the State of Oregon as sort of inspector, you might call it, on the project, and was familiar with the different operations in that way. The powder and blasting supplies were actually used in connection with the project.

There was a party by the name of Charles B. Smith in [76] connection with the project as chief engineer and general manager of the Jordan Valley Land & Water Company. He acted in that capacity until the early spring of 1920.

I saw Mr. Harry Humfeld while I was on the project. He was sent out as a sort of agricultural expert to help the farmers on the project, and lay out their ditches for them, tell them how to irrigate, etc. Harry Humfeld also acted as water-master and had something to do with the maintenance of part of the property of the project. I think he had general charge of maintenance and repair work in connection with the project. I know that he had at least one man working under him as ditch-rider.

I was a representative of the Desert Land Board of the State of Oregon exclusively for a period from September, 1918, to about May, 1920, and from November, 1920, on until some time in 1921. There was a period from about May, 1919, until Mr. Smith took over affairs in November, 1919, that I was acting in a joint capacity for the State and the Jordan Valley Land & Water Company. I have no con-

(Testimony of John W. Cunningham.)
nection with the Jordan Valley Land & Water Company now.

### Cross-examination.

I first went out on the project to represent the Desert Land Board in September, 1918. There was an arrangement by which all money that was collected from the sale of the lands in the project was turned into a trust fund and disbursed to pay for construction. I had general supervision of the distribution of that money and approved the estimates. I also determined the sufficiency of the construction work which was done. The money came from the sale of lands in the project and was pursuant to a lien that the State Board had allowed on the land. The settlers really paid in a lot of money before they got anything. The state was a party to the contract which permitted that. I was appointed as a  [77] representative of the Desert Land Board. The state engineer is a member of the Desert Land Board and takes the most active interest in these lands. I had access to the original accounts of moneys paid in by the settlers and checked such accounts and kept a record and eventually audited them. I made complete reports as to how much money the settlers had paid in that had been expended on this work. It amounted to between two and three hundred thousand dollars as I recall it. During the period I was connected with the project I don't recall that the Jordan Valley Land & Water Company put any money into it. At the time I first went on the project certain construction work had

(Testimony of John W. Cunningham.)

been completed which I understand was paid for by the Jordan Valley Land & Water Company. I would say that this work probably cost them sixty or seventy thousand dollars. I know of offhand claims that the preliminary work of the Jordan Valley Land & Water Company cost $125,000.00 or some such figure, which represented the original investment and feeder canal and Antelope dam. I was not a member of the Desert Land Board. My duties were to represent it on the project, but there was also a period of time I also represented the Jordan Valley Land & Water Company. Its chief engineer proved to be unsatisfactory and by consent of both parties I was put in jointly with the understanding that it was simply a temporary appointment and I was to be superseded as soon as a satisfactory man could be found. My recollection is that in a letter Mr. H. G. Wells as vice-president of the Jordan Valley Land & Water Company authorized me to represent it. The state engineer knew that I had been requested to represent the Jordan Valley Land & Water Company. I think the board as a whole were informed and advised of the arrangement. The board were never advised of this in open meeting. Whatever I did in my official capacity jointly for the Jordan Valley Land & Water Company and the Desert Land Board was simply because of a discussion [78] with the state engineer. I acted on the project under that sort of authority for both parties from May, 1919, until November, 1919. In respect to the Jordan Valley Land & Water Com-

(Testimony of John W. Cunningham.)

pany my title was acting chief engineer and general manager. The actual construction was being done under a subcontract, and the arrangement was that the subcontractor said what he wanted in the way of materials and I simply approved them. In regard to the materials, I was, you might say, a rubber stamp on the orders of the subcontractor. I did not hire the labor and order the materials. This was done through another source. At that time I was representing both parties.

I became acquainted with Mr. A. J. Vance in September, 1919. I met him on the project. He was sent out from Oklahoma City as a personal representative of Mr. Maney, president of the company. I did not know Mr. Maney at that time and my information on that subject came from Mr. Vance.

Wells Brothers were a contracting firm who were subcontractors on the Jordan Valley Project. The contract was between the Jordan Valley Land & Water Company and the State of Oregon. There were other subcontracts. Wells Brothers commenced work on the project in the spring of 1919. The first work that they did was on the lower unit, main canal. At that time I was acting in a joint capacity. At the time the first work was done by them they were working under a contract which I disapproved. I later approved a contract, but cannot state the exact date. Mr. Wells being a vice-president of the Jordan Valley Land & Water Company of course had authority to represent it. The fact that he was acting both as contractor and as

(Testimony of John W. Cunningham.)

a member of the firm of Wells Bros. and as vice-president was the cause of quite a lot of wrangling. The first contract with him he signed as both party of the first part and party of the second part. I objected to that and [79] objected to the scope of the contract which I thought included entirely too much and was against the best interests of the company and the project. This first contract was not approved by me. Wells kept on working. I did not order the powder. All I know about it is what someone else told me, that is, about the ordering of it. I did not sign any order and I did not write any letters. I just heard there was powder ordered and some powder came; that is all I know. My recollection is that the first car-load of powder came during the time I was acting in the dual capacity. The second one was later; after Charles B. Smith had become Chief Engineer of the project. I did not keep track of how much of the powder was used and how much wasn't used. All the evidence I could give on that matter would be a guess. During the period that I was acting in the joint capacity there were certain things which I ordered direct which are not involved in this case. Mr. Wells was doing the work on the project at the time Harry Humfeld was employed there.

### Redirect Examination.

Wells Bros. had no credit and were not in a position to purchase supplies. For that reason the purchases were made in the name of the Jordan Valley Land & Water Company. To the best of

(Testimony of John W. Cunningham.)

my belief orders for blasting supplies and all such
materials were placed by Mr. Wells in the name
of the Jordan Valley Land & Water Company.
I could not say whether they were so placed by
him as an officer of that company. I believe, however, they were purchased by him in the name of
the Jordan Valley Land & Water Company. I have
a copy in my files of the second contract finally
approved between Wells Bros. and the Jordan Valley Land & Water Company which I will produce
later. The supplies used on the project were purchased by Wells in the name of the Jordan Land &
Water Company. To the best of my knowledge there
was no [80] money in connection with the project disbursed or checked out directly by Wells
Bros. Bills for labor and materials were paid by
the Jordan Valley Land & Water Company.
Charles B. Smith was employed by the Jordan
Valley Land & Water Company. Wells Bros. as I
stated, started to work in 1919 under a certain contract, which was later disapproved by me. I have
the first contract and the contract which was later
approved and will endeavor to produce both of the
contracts.

Thereupon Plaintiff's Exhibits 7 and 8 for
identification were offered and received in evidence,
as well as Plaintiff's Exhibits 11, 12, 13, 14 and 15.

## TESTIMONY OF J. L. McALLISTER, FOR PLAINTIFF.

J. L. McALLISTER, being first duly sworn, on behalf of the plaintiff testified as follows:

### Direct Examination.

I am assistant secretary for the Desert Land Board of Oregon and connected with the State Engineer's office. The Desert Land Board is an *ex-officio* board, made up of the Governor as chairman, the attorney general, the state treasurer, the secretary of state, the state engineer who is secretary *ex-officio* of the board, but I am assistant secretary, directly under the state engineer who is the official secretary.

I have handled the records of the Desert Land Board in connection with the Jordan Valley Irrigation Project. A majority of the area of the land under the project was government land, title to which was in the United States. The Jordan Valley Land & Water Company filed an application with the Desert Land Board, acting for and on behalf of the State, to secure the segregation or withdrawal of this Government land under the Carey Act, and the state filed these applications and secured the withdrawal of a certain area of desert [81] land that lays under this project. That was all done under the contract between the United States, the Department of the Interior of the State of Oregon. Then the applicant, the Land & Water Company, entered into a contract with

(Testimony of J. L. McAllister.)

the state through the Desert Land Board for the construction of the system necessary to reclaim this land. The Desert Land Board of the State of Oregon was a party to that contract which was in writing and executed in duplicate. The Desert Land Board has a copy of the contract. The contract I now produce is the contract entered into between the Desert Land Board of the State of Oregon and the Jordan Valley Land & Water Company and has been in the possession of the Desert Land Board since its execution. It was signed by the Governor as chairman and it is under the seal of the State Engineer as secretary. The state engineer at that time was Mr. John L. Lewis, Mr. Cupper's predecessor. It was executed on behalf of the Jordan Valley Land & Water Company, by J. W. Maney, president, Frank B. Cross, secretary, attested under the seal, and bears date June 21, 1918. There is one later contract entered into between these parties on approximately May 27, 1921, as I remember. This contract was cancelled in the early spring of 1921 as I remember it. The statute under which the contract was executed provided that six months' cessation of work without the sanction of the state would subject the contract to cancellation and forfeiture of the works that had been constructed thereunder; that six months expired after cessation of the work and under the statute the state declared cancellation in the spring of 1921, as I remember it. The notice of failure was given in November, 1921, and the

(Testimony of J. L. McAllister.)

forfeiture and cancellation was declared January 27, 1922. There was a prior cancellation of the contract and forfeiture, and the publication required under the statute was running, the four weeks of publication. During that time the company came before the board with a proposition to re-finance, and [82] these proceedings were stopped, and they were given a new contract. That is the contract that I mentioned of May 27, 1921. Then the contracts were not carried out and it was necessary for the state to start the forfeiture proceedings over again; that is what was done. The contract was thereupon received in evidence by the Court and marked Plaintiff's Exhibit 16, subject to the objection that it was incompetent, immaterial and irrelevant. In connection with the execution of this contract a bond was also executed. The bond was received in evidence and marked Plaintiff's Exhibit 17. The original bond was given to cover the contract dated in June.

The COURT.—The June contract was subsequently cancelled as I understand it; was cancelled and renewed and a new contract.

A. It was cancelled. Cancellation proceedings were started and while the period of publication was running they came in with this proposition to re-finance the contract and asked for a new contract.

The COURT.—What date was that?

A. That was May, 1921.

The COURT.—The new contract was May, 1921?

(Testimony of J. L. McAllister.)

Mr. GRAHAM.—A new bond was given at that time.  I think in May.

The COURT.—There was a new bond?

A. Yes.

The COURT.—That is after all these supplies were alleged to have been furnished.

Mr. GRAHAM.—I think it covers some services rendered after that.

Mr. BRONAUGH.—The plaintiff has a cause of action which runs to the 1st day of August, 1921. There is a certain period overlapping the cancellation of that contract.

The witness resumes his testimony:

The bond marked Plaintiff's Exhibit 17 was declared by the board cancelled as to future obligations, in May, 1921.  There was an official  [82½] order of the Desert Land Board to that effect at a meeting held June 8, 1921, at the time of the consideration of the new contract and acceptance of the new bond.  The minutes in part provide as follows: "And be it further ordered that the bond of the American Surety Company executed on behalf of the Jordan Valley Land & Water Company in favor of the Desert Land Board in the penal sum of $100,000, on or about August 7, 1918, covering the said state contract of June 21, 1918, be and the same is hereby declared cancelled, and the secretary is instructed to so advise the principal and surety."

The new contract with the state was executed but there was never any performance under it.

(Testimony of J. L. McAllister.)

The contract provided that the project should be financed within 60 days and they had a loan which was pending at the time under which the money was to have been received, and I believe the loan was not received and the finances were never available and no work was done under the contract. The cancellation proceeding that I have testified to referred to the old contract. The final cancellation and forfeiture covered both contracts. The old contract of 1918 was cancelled by the new contract. The bond was cancelled on June 8, 1921, by the action of the State Land Board, but I would limit that to this: The bond was never surrendered; the obligations under future contracts was limited; to that extent it was cancelled. The bond executed in 1918, marked Plaintiff's Exhibit 17, was never released or delivered to the Surety Company or principal. I am not familiar with the actual construction work on the Jordan Valley Project.

Cross-examination.

Defendant's Exhibit "B" for identification is a contract between the Department of the Interior and the State of Oregon under which the desert land under this project was segregated to the state for the purpose of reclamation. It expresses the obligation in writing [83] between the general government and the State of Oregon with the relation to the Jordan Valley Irrigation Project. It was received in evidence as Defendant's Exhibit "B" subject to the objection that it was irrelevant, in-

(Testimony of J. L. McAllister.)

competent and immaterial and no proper foundation.

Defendant's Exhibit "C" for identification is a printed copy of the rules and regulations of the Desert Land Board of Oregon pertaining to the reclamation, cultivation and settlement of lands withdrawn under the Carey Act.

The rules therein prescribed were in force and effect at and during the time of the Jordan Valley Irrigation Project. It was received in evidence and marked Defendant's Exhibit "C" subject to the objection that it was incompetent, irrelevant and immaterial and no proper foundation.

As assistant secretary of the Desert Land Board I am familiar with the rules and regulations of the Department of the Interior of the General government relating to Carey Act transactions. We published them in reports from time to time.

Defendant's Exhibit "D" for identification at pages 36, 37, 38, 39, 40 and 41 is a correct copy in pamphlet form of those rules, being the regulations of the Department concerning the reclamation of the Carey Act lands. These rules were in force and effect at the time of the Jordan Valley Irrigation Project.

Pages 36, 37, 38, 39, 40 and 41 of the pamphlet marked Defendant's Exhibit "D" for identification were thereupon received in evidence and marked Defendant's Exhibit "D."

The minutes of the Desert Land Board are kept in book form where they are signed by each member

(Testimony of J. L. McAllister.)

of the board. I do not have these books, but I have with me the original sheet copies of the minutes that are read and approved by each member of the board [84] from which they are copied into a book. These documents are original entries. I do not have the original minutes wherein the amount of the bond in this case was fixed. I believe that the contract itself provided for the amount of the bond to be filed and the nature.

Defendant's Exhibit "E" for identification are the original minutes of the various board meetings of the Desert Land Board affecting the Jordan Valley Land & Water Company Project from August 24, 1918, to January 30, 1923.

Defendant's Exhibit "E" for identification was then offered in evidence subject to the privilege to substitute copies. It was received in evidence and marked Defendant's Exhibit "E," subject to the objection that it was irrelevant, immaterial and incompetent.

Exhibit "E" includes a complete record of the minutes of the board relating to the transaction whereby the board ordered the forfeiture and cancellation of the contract with the Jordan Valley Land & Water Company, unless through error in taking them out of the files one has been overlooked. It should be in the minutes. The exhibit includes the proceedings of the Desert Land Board relating to the service of notice upon the Jordan Valley Land & Water Company concerning the forfeiture and contemplated sale of the unfinished works. It

(Testimony of J. L. McAllister.)

also shows the proceedings of the board pursuant to the notice wherein and whereby the unfinished work was sold to other parties.  In fact, the entire proceedings of the Desert Land Board under the act of the Legislature, where they forfeited the contract and sold the works, will be in these minutes.  With reference to the amounts of money expended in the creation and construction of this project, Mr. Cunningham who was the state's representative on the job, reported once each six months to the board in a bound report volume, and these reports [85] show the amount of money that was expended.  I have the reports and identify them as Defendant's Exhibits "F," "G," "H," "I" and "J" for identification.  They are part of the records of the Desert Land Board in my possession and in my care.  My office has the complete official records of the Desert Land Board in connection with the Jordan Valley Irrigation Project.  I do not have among my files, records and papers a contract concerning that project with the firm of Wells Bros.  I never saw such a contract, but I have heard that such a contract existed.  Such a contract was never presented to the office; was never before it.  There is no record of it ever having been approved or anything of that kind, or ever officially recognized at all.  I have a record of the money received under the provisions of the state contract.  Upon the sale of land they were to deposit a dollar an acre covering the area of the sale, and some money has been deposited and held pend-

(Testimony of J. L. McAllister.)

ing the approval of these contracts. The opening of the lands for entry before placing it in the reclamation fund is provided in the contract. Some money has gone into the reclamation fund. The total amount received is approximately $7200.00 and the amount turned into the reclamation fund is about $641.00. The moneys not transferred into the reclamation fund are held in a bank account and are transferred to the reclamation fund when the sale of the lands are approved and the contracts are approved. I do not have among my reports in connection with this project any order whereby any of these lands were ever opened to settlement in the lower unit. We did open an area in the upper Antelope Unit, but there was no order opening the lands to settlement in the lower unit. Settlers, however, did go in there and money was received from them in payment for contemplated water rights. There has not yet been any formal opening of the lower unit. The settlers have paid money but have not received title. The unfinished work was sold to the Jordan Valley [86] Irrigation District for One Dollar and a proposal to complete. I now have with me minutes of the meetings of the Desert Land Board held March 6th and May 24th, 1918. These are correct records and minutes of the Desert Land Board on the dates mentioned concerning the Jordan Valley Project. Thereupon offered in evidence and added to and made a part of Defendant's Exhibit "E," subject to the objection that any invalid contract between the Desert

(Testimony of J. L. McAllister.)

Land Board and the Jordan Valley Land & Water Company would not affect in any way the liability of the surety to the labor and materialmen on the bond.

The witness continues:

Defendant's Exhibit "K" for identification is part of the records of the Desert Land Board. It is the original bond given in 1921 and received in evidence marked Defendant's Exhibit "K."

Defendant's Exhibit "L" for identification is the new contract. It was received in evidence and marked Defendant's Exhibit "L."

Attached to Exhibit "E" are certain printed instruments. These are the authorization of the Board of Directors of the Jordan Valley Land & Water Company for the execution of the contract of May 27, 1921, which was the new contract. These were offered in evidence and marked Defendant's Exhibit "M."

No amendment or supplemental contract was ever made between the Jordan Valley Land & Water Company and the Desert Land Board concerning this project.

Defendant's Exhibit "N" for identification is a part of the records of the Desert Land Board and was a proposed contract for execution by and between the Desert Land Board and the Jordan Valley Land & Water Company under which the lien was to have been raised from seventy-one to one hundred per acre. That contract was made or drawn subject to the approval of the surety on the

(Testimony of J. L. McAllister.)

bond under the original contract, which approval
was to have been filed [87] in writing with the
Desert Land Board. It was not filed and the contract was never executed. The second contract that
was made between the Desert Land Board and the
Jordan Valley Land & Water Company was made
on the strength of a proposed loan that was to be
made. We have a copy in our records of the loan
agreement between the parties which was referred
to in the new state contract of May 27, 1921. A
copy of said agreement was thereupon received in
evidence and marked Defendant's Exhibit "O."
We also have a copy of the trust agreement under
which the moneys were to have been handled, which
is also referred to in the new state contract of 1921.
The trust agreement was received in evidence and
marked Defendant's Exhibit "P." Thereupon Defendant's Exhibit "N" for identification was offered and received in evidence and marked Defendant's Exhibit "N."

Redirect Examination.

No part of the irrigation system of the Jordan
Valley Project was ever completed under the terms
of the contract of 1918 and accepted by the Desert
Land Board. A part known as the Antelope Unit
was completed to a stage where water could be delivered to some of the settlers and water was delivered to some of the settlers. Water was delivered to the settlers during the spring and summer
of 1921 on what is known as the Antelope Unit.
The Jordan Valley Land & Water Company oper-

(Testimony of J. L. McAllister.)

ated the system and delivered the water as it was required to do under the contract. So far as any of the system was operated at all it was operated by the Jordan Valley Land & Water Company. It was necessary for the Land & Water Company to have somebody on the job to operate the system and deliver the water. They had contracted with these people to deliver the water. I have had considerable experience with irrigation projects and am familiar with them while in the process of construction and in operation after completion. It is a common and usual thing in the case of a newly constructed irrigation [88] system for there to be considerable repairs necessary during the first year or two after the completion by reason of breaks in the dams and ditches and canals. In order to avoid damage very close supervision must be given to the operation of the system in order not to overload the banks of the canals and in order to watch the structures that have not yet been puddled into place. The canals and structures are generally inspected daily by men who are employed as ditch-riders or inspectors whose duty it is to go over the system continually. The duties of a water-master are generally to see that the proper amount of water is turned into the system and to see that the system is not overloaded; that its capacity is not taxed to the breaking point in a new system especially, and to distribute that water throughout the system to the water users. In a newly constructed system placed in operation it is necessary and es-

(Testimony of J. L. McAllister.)

sential to have some person carry out the duties of a water-master as I have defined them.

## Recross-examination.

A water-master has something to do with water and there is no water until the work is completed substantially enough to put water in. A water-master is not generally used in the construction of an irrigation system. His duties arise afterwards. The irrigation project was completed substantially as to what is called the Antelope Unit, but not to the extent under the contract that it could be accepted as a completed unit. However, they are delivering some water through it now. Our department never reported to the Department of the Interior that the project was completed as to the Antelope Unit, nor did we ever get title to it, nor did the settlers ever get title to the Carey Act lands. Some government lands were included in the Antelope Unit. They were opened to settlement. No land in the lower unit was ever opened.

## TESTIMONY OF A. F. FLEGEL, FOR PLAINTIFF. [89]

A. F. FLEGEL, being first duly sworn, on behalf of the plaintiff testified as follows:

I have been engaged in the practice of law in the city of Portland for 30 years. My practice has been civil practice exclusively, with a great deal of court work.

In a case involving a suit upon a bond given in

(Testimony of A. F. Flegel.)

connection with a contract for public work, such as an irrigation project, where the contract calls for the execution and delivery of certain bonds to cover among other things any indebtedness the construction company may have for labor or materials furnished by third persons for use in the prosecution of the construction work, and in case of suit upon such bond to collect claims for labor and materials, the suit being brought in the United States District Court and being contested, providing attorneys' fees are allowed in that sort of action, it would be my opinion that an attorney's fee of $250.00 would be reasonable upon a claim involving the sum of $2040.00, and an attorney's fee of $350.00 to $400.00 upon a claim involving the sum of $2900.00, and an attorney's fee of $200.00 upon a claim involving the sum of $1509.00, and an attorney's fee of from $75.00 to $100.00 upon a claim involving the sum of $537.00, and an attorney's fee of $50.00 upon a claim involving the sum of $173.00.

## TESTIMONY OF JOHN W. CUNNINGHAM, FOR PLAINTIFF (RECALLED).

### Direct Examination.

During the period from October, 1919, through March of 1920, I acted as the representative of the Jordan Valley Land & Water Company and the Desert Land Board of the State of Oregon. J. W. Maney was president of the Jordan Valley Land & Water Company during February and March, 1920.

(Testimony of John W. Cunningham.)

He was not present on the project or at Boise, Idaho, during that period of time to my knowledge. [90]

Between October, 1919, and March 15, 1920, supplies were ordinarily ordered for the Jordan Valley Land & Water Company by either H. G. Wells or Emil Tschiegs. Mr. Tschiegs, as a matter of fact, was the bookkeeper of the company. He also had the title of secretary, and a common procedure in a contracting concern of that sort is for the bookkeeper to handle the ordering of the supplies.

Plaintiff's Exhibit 18 for identification is the second contract between the Jordan Valley Land & Water Company and Wells Bros. It was executed November 17, 1919, and approved by me. It was thereupon offered in evidence and marked Plaintiff's Exhibit 18.

### Cross-examination.

At the time this contract was made I was representing jointly the Desert Land Board and the Jordan Valley Land & Water Company. I signed it on behalf of the Jordan Valley Land & Water Company as Chief Engineer and General Manager, and at the same time I represented the state. I do not recall that I submitted the contract to the Board of Directors of the Jordan Valley Land & Water Company for their approval, or that I ever submitted it to them. The action was taken with full cognizance of the vice-president and secretary, officers of the company. I objected to Mr. Wells' first contract. While I was representing two par-

(Testimony of John W. Cunningham.)

ties, as far as that contract was concerned they had identical interests. I first went upon the project in September, 1918. Wells Bros. were not there at that time. They came in the spring of 1919. They did all the lower unit work, first under the contract which was objected to and later under the contract of November 17, 1919. The contract which I objected to was made in the spring of 1919 and never approved. While I protested against the contract Wells Bros. continued with the work and I was intermittently on the job. I knew the work was proceeding. I protested to the state engineer and [91] the Desert Land Board and numerous conferences were held in regard to the matter, but the work still went on and Wells Bros. did it. I presented the contract in evidence as Plaintiff's Exhibit 18 for the approval of the Desert Land Board. I believe it was approved. I did not hear Mr. McAllister's testimony, yet the contract was never approved or submitted to the Desert Land Board. Whether it was or whether it was not, as the representative of the Jordan Valley Land & Water Company and as the representative of the State of Oregon, I permitted the work to be done under the contract.

## DEPOSITION OF F. A. FLAGLER, FOR PLAINTIFF.

Pursuant to a written stipulation between the parties, the deposition of F. A. Flagler was taken before Daniel B. Trefethen, a notary public for

(Deposition of F. A. Flagler.)

the State of Washington, residing at Seattle, on direct and cross-interrogatories.

The witness was duly sworn and testified as follows:

## Direct Examination.

My name is F. A. Flagler. I am of legal age and reside at 809 East 62d Street, Seattle, Washington.

I am credit manager, Seattle District, for the E. I. DuPont de Nemours & Co. The Jordan Valley Land & Water Company ordered certain blasting supplies from the E. I. Du Pont de Nemours & Co., which were shipped in October, 1919, and consisted of the following materials:

560 kegs Dup. Black Blasting......2.22   $1243.20
2000# Red Cross Extra 40%.....18.71   374.20
4000# Stumping Powder.........15.71   628.40

The said prices on blasting powder and dynamite covered the delivery of material f. o. b. Homedale, Idaho.

6000 ft. Dreadnaught Fuse...12.15–15%....61.97
1–#4 Dupont Blasting Machine....40.00....40.00

[92]

The prices on the fuse and blasting machine were as the same was delivered f. o. b. Portland, Oregon.

All of the material delivered on the first order received from the Jordan Valley Land & Water Company was paid for with the exception of the freight on the fuse and blasting machine from Portland to Homedale, which amounted to $2.92.

We received a check on December 15, 1919, from the Jordan Valley Land & Water Company for

(Deposition of F. A. Flagler.)

$1899.30 and on February 16th gave them credit for freight of $445.55, representing the freight on the dynamite and black blasting powder which they paid at destination and which was for our account. We received another order from the Jordan Valley Land & Water Company on February 6, 1920, Order No. 190 dated February 4, 1920, for the following:

100 Ones—5000# Red Cross Extra 40% ⅞ x 8.
800 kegs Black Blasting Powder.

12000 ft. Dreadnaught Fust.

Plaintiff's Exhibit 8 is the order received from the Jordan Valley Land & Water Company.

Plaintiff's Exhibit 9 is a letter received February 19, 1920, from the Jordan Valley Land & Water Company in connection with the said order. The order was accepted. It did not give directions, but the letter received February 19, 1920, in evidence as Plaintiff's Exhibit 9, advised that shipment should be made to Homedale, Idaho. The price on the 5000 Red Cross Extra 40% was $18.28 per C# f. o. b. Homedale, Idaho. The price on the 800 kegs of Black Blasting Powder was $2.32 per keg f. o. b. Homedale, Idaho. However, if customer had not included in this carload shipment the 100 cases dynamite, the price per keg would have been $2.24, this because the railroad company charge the second class rate on full carloads of black blasting powder and first class rate on mixed carload of dynamite and black blasting powder. The price on 12000 Ft. of Dreadnaught Fuse was $12.15 per

(Deposition of F. A. Flagler.)

thousand feet, less 15% f. o. b. [93] Portland, Oregon. The above prices were the usual market price for such materials at Homedale, Idaho.

As far as I know no objections were ever made by the Jordan Valley Land & Water Company to these prices. The order referred to was shipped from our plant at DuPont, Washington, on March 2, 1920, via O. W. R. & N. R. R. Co. in car C. St. P. M. & O. #29498.

As heretofore stated, the Jordan Valley Land & Water Company was indebted to our company in the sum of $2.92, for a balance due for freight on blasting supplies shipped it in October, 1919, also $3.88 freight and blasting supplies shipped in March, 1920. The dynamite and black blasting powder shipped to them in October, 1919, was sold, delivered at Homedale, Idaho, and shipment went forward collect. In this carload shipment was also included 6000 ft. Dreadnaught Fuse and one Dupont #4 Blasting Machine, the freight on the entire shipment amounting to $448.47 which the Jordan Valley Land & Water Co. paid when shipment reached destination. In making settlement for this particular shipment made to them in October, 1919, they deducted the full amount of freight paid, namely, $448.47, while only $445.55 was for our account, a difference of $2.92, representing the freight on the fuse and blasting machine.

The material sold the Jordan Valley Land & Water Company was in accordance with our regular terms of 30 days net with no discount for cash.

(Deposition of F. A. Flagler.)

The freight item of $2.92 due us on the shipment in October, 1919, is still unpaid and also the dynamite on the black blasting powder and freight on the fuse shipped to them in March, 1920, are still unpaid. The balance due us at this time from the Jordan Valley Land & Water Company is $2900.73.

Exhibits 11, 12, 13 and 14, inclusive, are invoices covering these shipments, copies of which were mailed to the Jordan [94] Valley Land & Water Company, Boise, Idaho. Invoice #37166, which is in evidence as Plaintiff's Exhibit 14, covers our charges for 800 kegs Black Blasting Powder amounting to $1856.00; No. 37165 covers our charge for shipment of 5000# Red Cross Extra 40% amounting to $914.00; 12000 ft. Dreadnaught fuse $123.93; Invoice No. 37530 covers our charge for freight on 12000 ft. Dreadnaught Fuse from Portland, Oregon, to Homedale, Idaho; No. 33016 covers our charge for 6000# Dynamite, 6000 ft. fuse and 1–#4 Battery shipped from our plant at Dupont, Washington, October 1, 1919. No objections were ever made to these invoices, nor was the account ever disputed. Demands for payment of the account were made under dates of April 21st and May 7, 1920.

On August 26th we received a letter dated August 24, 1920, signed by the Jordan Valley Land & Water Company by A. J. Vance, Vice-president, which acknowledges the account, the letter being in evidence as Plaintiff's Exhibit 7. The letter of

(Deposition of F. A. Flagler.)

August 24, 1920, in evidence as Plaintiff's Exhibit 7, in part stated:

"As soon as we realize funds from this source your account will be promptly met, and paid in full."

This referred to the account which is owing the E. I. DuPont de Nemours & Co., which was assigned to the relator in this action. The supplies ordered were for the prosecution of work on what is known as the Jordan Valley Irrigation Project in Malheur County, Oregon.

### Cross-examination.

The order received from the Jordan Valley Land & Water Company was signed by Emil L. Tsehiegs. This order was later confirmed by H. G. Wells, Vice-president of the Jordan Valley Land & Water Company, which corresponds with his title on their letter-head.

## DEPOSITION OF H. M. LINSLEY, FOR PLAINTIFF.

Pursuant to a stipulation between the parties, the deposition of H. M. Linsley, a witness on behalf of the plaintiff, was [95] taken on direct and cross-interrogatories before Daniel B. Trefethen, a Notary Public for King County, Washington.

The witness was duly sworn and testified as follows:

### Direct Examination.

I am 53 years of age and reside at DuPont, Washington. I am a magazine-keeper for the E. I. Du-

(Deposition of H. M. Linsley.)

Pont de Nemours & Co. I was instructed during the months of February and March, 1920, by the Dupont Company to ship certain blasting supplies to the Jordan Valley Land & Water Company at Homedale, Idaho. The entire shipment was made on March 2, 1920, from DuPont, Washington, and consisted of

100 Ones, 5000 lbs.

Red Cross Extra 40% ⅞ x 8, 2–6Ms. 12000 ft.
   Dreadnaught Fuse,

800 kegs, du Pont standard #57, railroad black blasting powder.

It was shipped to the Jordan Valley Land & Water Company, Homedale, Owyhee County, Idaho, over the O. W. R. & N., care of Oregon Short Line, in car #C. St. P. M. & O. 29498, on the 2d day of March, 1920.

Plaintiff's Exhibit 15 is a correct bill of lading of the articles shipped.

Thereupon Mr. GOLDSMITH said: "At this time I have taken the matter up with the attorneys for the defendants and it will be stipulated that no jury is required in this case. This for the purpose of the record. A written stipulation is on file."

Thereupon Mr. BRONAUGH said: "As to plaintiff's fourth and fifth causes of action, I request that judgment of voluntary nonsuit be entered."

The plaintiff then rested.

Whereupon the defendant requested the Court specially to find as follows:

(Deposition of H. M. Linsley.)

1. That the services of Humfeld as water-master did not come within the scope of the bond sued upon. [96]

2. That there was no sufficient or competent evidence to show that the labor and material were ordered or used for the Jordan Valley Land & Water Company in the prosecution of the work or were necessary for any of the prosecution of the work under the terms of the bond sued upon.

In the event of refusal so to find, the defendant then and there requested an exception. The defendant further asked upon the whole record for a judgment in favor of the defendant. The request for special findings and for a judgment in favor of the defendant were taken under advisement and the defendant offered the following testimony:

## DEPOSITION OF A. J. VANCE, FOR DEFENDANT.

The deposition of A. J. Vance, a witness on behalf of the defendant, was taken before Pauline E. Thrower, a notary public residing at Oklahoma City, Oklahoma, upon written interrogatories and cross-interrogatories pursuant to a stipulation between the parties to this action.

The witness was first duly sworn and testified as follows:

Direct Examination.

The relator, Harry Humfeld, was employed by Mr. Hooker, President and Manager of the Jordan Valley Farms, and the Colonization Company with

(Deposition of A. J. Vance.)

a kind of loose arrangement and more or less vague understanding that while the Farms Company was responsible to him for his salary the funds to pay it with would be partly derived from collections of water charges against the settlers and a large part was to be paid by the settlers for special work in the way of helping them to locate their ditches and land lines, and doing other survey work for them, as well as special survey work in locating land lines and corners for the Colonization Company. He may have had a written contract with Mr. Hooker, but so far as I have any knowledge the contract was verbal. The contract with him was made [97] by the Colonization agent, Mr. Hooker, in behalf of the Jordan Valley Farms. I learned of the verbal understanding and arrangement from Mr. Cunningham, at Boise, Idaho, in March, 1920. I discussed the matter with Mr. Humfeld while on the project in May, 1920, and again in August, 1920, while driving with Mr. Harry Humfeld over the project. He again told me the details about his arrangement and stated that he was very glad that he was in the employ of the Jordan Valley Farms, because he felt that his salary coming from that source would be much more certain than it would be if he were employed by the Jordan Valley Land & Water Company. He at that time claimed that Jordan Valley Land & Water Company was expected to reimburse the Jordan Valley Farms for one-half of his salary, but never explained to me by what authority such arrangement was made or

(Deposition of A. J. Vance.)

by whom. In this conversation Mr. Harry Humfeld also stated that the Jordan Valley Land and Water Company would soon go broke and that his father, the elder Humfeld, and Mr. Hooker, the head of the Jordan Valley Farms organization, would take over the project, Mr. Humfeld, Senior, re-financing it and completing it, and on that account he was absolutely sure of getting all his salary.

I was never asked to approve the arrangement of his employment either by him or by Mr. Hooker. I never approved or agreed to any arrangement with Mr. Humfeld on behalf of the Jordan Valley Land & Water Company.

Probably one-half of Mr. Humfeld's time during the irrigation season, from April to September, was consumed in looking after the ditches and distribution of the water. The other one-half of such time and a large portion of the other months outside of the irrigation season were occupied in assisting the settlers with surveying and also in doing survey work for some of Mr. Hooker's cattle [98] companies, like the Owyhee Cattle Company. This work was not in any manner for the use or benefit of the Jordan Valley Land and Water Company. None of the work except the work in connection with the distribution of the water and the repair work on the ditches was for the benefit of the Jordan Valley Land & Water Company.

In a conversation I had with Mr. Harry Humfeld concerning his arrangement about acting as water-

(Testimony of A. J. Vance.)

master, he told me specifically that his duties as water-master did not require probably more than one-half his time and that he would put in the rest of his time doing special work for the settlers and for the Colonization Company, and that there would be enough money collected from the settlers to take care of the amount coming to him as water-master.

## DEPOSITION OF LELAND S. VANCE, FOR DEFENDANT.

The deposition of Leland S. Vance, a witness on behalf of the defendant, was taken before Pauline E. Thrower, a notary public residing at Oklahoma City, Oklahoma, upon written interrogatories and cross-interrogatories pursuant to a stipulation between the parties to this action.

The witness was first duly sworn and testified as follows:

### Direct Examination.

I know the relator, Harry Humfeld. I met him in March or April, 1920, on the Jordan Valley Irrigation Project. My acquaintance began in March or April, 1920, on the project and lasted until October, 1920. We worked together, ate and slept together a greater part of the time for six months.

He rendered work and labor on the project during the time he was there as water-master for the project and also did a lot of survey work for the settlers. He also did some work for some of the Hooker Cattle Companies. All I know about the arrangement or understanding or agreement under

(Testimony of Leland S. Vance.)

which he rendered the services is what he, himself, told me and what I heard others say. During the [99] time I was working on the project I had a conversation with him concerning the question of his salary and the manner in which it was to be paid. In fact, I had several conversations with him in April and May, 1920, on the project in which he stated he was to receive his salary from the Jordan Valley Farms Company; that he desired this arrangement himself, because he thought he was more sure of getting his money. He also said that I might not get my money as he thought the Jordan Valley Land & Water Company would go broke and that his father would re-finance the project, so he was sure of getting his money.

I do not know whether his agreement with the Jordan Valley Farms was oral or in writing. The Jordan Valley Farms is a separate and distinct company or corporation from the Jordan Valley Land & Water Company. It was a real estate organization for the purpose of selling the land on the project. A Mr. Hooker was in charge of the affairs of the Jordan Valley Farms. I do not know what interest the relator, Harry Humfeld, or his father had in the Jordan Valley Farms or what their business relationships, if any, were with said company.

Testimony closed.

In connection with the introduction of the testimony of A. J. Vance, which was taken by deposition pursuant to a stipulation between the parties,

Mr. Graham said: "We offer the deposition of A. J. Vance, the question: 'State if you know under what terms or conditions the plaintiff, Harry Humfeld, was acting or working as water-master on the project.'" The transcript of testimony of the court reporter then shows the answer of the witness to the foregoing question. Then Interrogatory 68 of the deposition is set out and the answer thereto: Interrogatory 69 and the answer thereto. Then the following statement by Mr. Graham: "We also wish to offer  [100]  Interrogatories 70 and 71 and answers: Interrogatory 72 and answer; 73, 74, 75, 76 and the answers to each of these interrogatories; Interrogatory 77 and answer; 78 and answer. The foregoing statement is made for the reason that it is contended by counsel for the relator that the statements made by counsel for the defendant constituted an offer of the entire deposition of the witness, Vance, and in any event, whether the statements amounted to an offer of the entire deposition the reception in evidence of the entire deposition followed as a matter of law on the ground that a party taking a deposition may not offer a part thereof. This Court does not determine this question but leaves it for the determination of the Appellate Court. The entire deposition of A. J. Vance is set up with the original papers.

True and correct copies of all of the exhibits received in evidence on behalf of the plaintiff in the order in which they were received are as follows:

PLAINTIFF'S EXHIBIT No. 1.

Stipulation Between Counsel Concerning Execution of Assignments to Humfeld. [101]

In the District Court of the United States for the District of Oregon.

No. L.–9004.

STATE OF OREGON on the Relation of HARRY HUMFELD,

Plaintiff,

vs.

AMERICAN SURETY COMPANY OF NEW YORK, a Corporation,

Defendant.

STIPULATION.

It is hereby stipulated and agreed by and between the parties hereto through their respective attorneys, that the assignments and the signatures to the assignments mentioned in relator's complaint on file herein may be deemed to have been identified by competent testimony and the authority to execute such assignments of the respective officials who executed the assignments on behalf of the respective assignors is hereby admitted.

BEACH & SIMON,
ARTHUR A. GOLDSMITH,
BRONAUGH & BRONAUGH,
Attorneys for Relator.

WM. S. NASH and
S. J. GRAHAM,
Attorneys for Defendant.

Dated this 4th day of April, 1923.

No. ——. Plffs. Ex. No. 1.

U. S. District Court, District of Oregon. Filed June 12, 1923. G. H. Marsh, Clerk. [102]


PLAINTIFF'S EXHIBIT No. 2.

Assignment from E. I. DuPont de Nemours & Co. to Humfeld.

KNOW ALL MEN BY THESE PRESENTS: That E. I. DuPont de Nemours & Company, a corporation, for valuable considerations to it paid by Harry Numfeld, of Portland, Oregon, the receipt whereof is hereby acknowledged, does hereby sell, assign, transfer and set over the said Harry Humfeld and unto his heirs and assigns forever, its certain claim against Jordan Valley Land & Water Company, which claim is in the sum of Twenty-nine Hundred and 73/100 ($2900.73) Dollars.

TO HAVE AND TO HOLD Unto the said Harry Humfeld, his heirs and assigns forever.

IN TESTIMONY WHEREOF, said E. I. DuPont de Nemours & Company has caused these presents to be signed by its Vice-president at Seattle, Washington.

O. K.—W. H. MASON.

E. I. DuPONT DE NEMOURS & COMPANY,
By W. H. WM. COYNE,
Vice-president.

No. ——. Plffs. Ex. 2.

U. S. District Court, District of Oregon. Filed June 12, 1923. G. H. Marsh, Clerk. [103]

PLAINTIFF'S EXHIBIT No. 3.

Assignment from Richard Murray to Humfeld.

KNOW ALL MEN BY THESE PRESENTS, That I, Richard Murray, of Oregon City, in the County of Clackamas, State of Oregon, in consideration of Ten Dollars ($10.00) and other valuable consideration, to me paid by Harry Humfeld, of Portland, Oregon, receipt whereof I do hereby acknowledge, do hereby assign and transfer to said Harry Humfeld all claims and demands which I now have against the Jordan Valley Land & Water Company, a Nevada corporation, for all sums of money due and owing to me from said corporation, for services performed and/or materials furnished said Jordan Valley Land & Water Company by me, in connection with and for use upon the Jordan Valley Irrigation Project, in accordance with the contract between said Jordan Valley Land & Water Company and the Desert Land Board of the State of Oregon.

TO HAVE AND TO HOLD the same to the said Harry Humfeld, with power to collect the same in his own name, and to his own use.

IT IS EXPRESSLY UNDERSTOOD, however, that I, the said Richard Murray, am forever to be kept and saved harmless by the said Harry Humfeld from all cost or charge hereafter in any way or manner for and from the expense of the collection of the sum and sums hereby sold and assigned.

IN WITNESS WHEREOF, these presents are executed by me the 15th day of February, A. D. 1922.

In the presence of:

RICHARD MURRAY.    (Seal)

W. L. MULVEY.

ANNIE L. HINDLE.

No. ——.   Plffs. Ex. 3.

U. S. District Court, District of Oregon.   Filed June 12, 1923.   G. H. Marsh, Clerk.   [104]

PLAINTIFF'S EXHIBIT No. 4.

Assignment from C. C. Lehner to Humfeld.

KNOW ALL MEN BY THESE PRESENTS, That I, C. C. Lehner, of Homedale, in the County of Owyhee, State of Idaho, in consideration of Ten Dollars ($10.00) and other valuable consideration, to me paid by Harry Humfeld, of Portland, Oregon, receipt whereof I do hereby acknowledge, do hereby assign and transfer to said Harry Humfeld all claims and demands which I now have against the Jordan Valley Land & Water Company, a Nevada corporation, for all sums of money due and owing to me from said corporation, for services performed and/or materials furnished said Jordan Valley Land & Water Company by me, in connection with and for use upon the Jordan Valley Irrigation Project, in accordance with the contract between said Jordan Valley Land & Water Company and the said Desert Land Board of the State of Oregon.

TO HAVE AND TO HOLD the same to the said Harry Humfeld, with power to collect the same in his own name, and to his own use.

IT IS EXPRESSLY UNDERSTOOD, however, that I, the said C. C. Lehner, am forever to be kept and saved harmless by the said Harry Humfeld from all cost or charge hereafter in any way or manner for and from the expense of the collection of the sum and sums hereby sold and assigned.

IN WITNESS WHEREOF, These presents are executed by me the 17th day of February, A. D. 1922.

In the presence of:

C. C. LEHNER. (Seal)

R. W. VANDERHOOF.

E. B. SNELL.

No. ——. Plffs. Ex. 4.

U. S. District Court, District of Oregon. Filed June 12, 1923. G. H. Marsh, Clerk. [105]

### PLAINTIFF'S EXHIBIT No. 5.

Letter Dated August 20, 1920, from Jordan Valley Land & Water Company to Humfeld.

PAID–UP CAPITAL STOCK $200,000.

J. W. Maney, President,

H. G. Wells, Vice-President.

E. J. Wells, Treasurer.

Frank B. Cross, Secretary.

IRRIGATED LANDS IN THE FAMOUS JORDAN VALLEY, MALHEUR COUNTY, ORE.

JORDAN VALLEY LAND & WATER CO. INCORPORATED.

Paul S. A. Bickel,
Chief Engineer and General Manager.

Box 1126.

Boise, Idaho, August 30, 1920.

Mr. Harry Humfeld,

Danner, Oregon.

Dear Mr. Humfeld:

I have decided that the best arrangements to make in regard to the board bills is for this company to settle with Mrs. Mathews as follows: First, pay all properly charged against this company on account of our regular employees, and then pay half of the amount due her on your account for board. As you get money in from the sale of the cement, you are authorized to apply it in that way.

I consider that this company is properly liable and owes half your board, and that the Farms Company owes the other half. For us to pay their half would be in the nature of an advance to them, or on their account. It would confuse the bookkeeping possibly, and as I have no accountant here, I do not care to pay anything now except regular company bills. Besides, there are a number of other small claims to be met, and it will crowd us to get in funds to meet those other small labor bills, after the board bill has been taken care of as mentioned above.

If you have sufficient money, I think it best to take care of those small labor bills which you have found it necessary to make in helping you out with your duties as water-master. Forward all receipts to this office, and for fear they might get lost in the mails keep a copy for your own records.

Incidentally, repay yourself the two dollars that

you spent for the drawing of receipt for Ivy, and send me receipted bill for the same.

There is nothing serious for a while at least in regard to the lien filed by Murray.

So far as you may be able to prevent, allow no one to sell or remove any materials belonging to the company, except the little building sold by Wells to the Basque, and get his receipt on account due him from J. V. L. & W. Co.

Yours truly,

J. V. L. & W. CO.,

By A. J. VANCE,

V–P.

No. ——. Plffs. Ex. 5.

U. S. District Court, District of Oregon. Filed June 12, 1923. G. H. Marsh, Clerk. [106]

PLAINTIFF'S EXHIBIT No. 6.

Letter from A. J. Vance to Humfeld, Dated October 18, 1920.

J. W. MANEY,          H. G. WELLS,

Oklahoma City, Okla.    Boise, Idaho.

JOHN MANEY,          E. J. WELLS,

Oklahoma City, Okla.    Boise, Idaho.

Boise, Idaho, Oct. 18, 1920.

MANEY BROTHERS & COMPANY,

Contractors,

Boise.

Mr. Harry Humfeld,

Danner, Oregon.

Dear Sir:

I have been informed that there is a good head

of water going down Jordan Creek, and none going through the feeder canal into the reservoir. If possible, we should make arrangements at once to catch all the water available for storage. In talking the matter over this morning with Mr. Smith, he says that about two days work with "four up" and a fresno at the head of the ditch, it can be put in perfectly good shape to run water thru.

Now, is such is the case, I will suggest that you get some settler who wants to do some work for a credit on his contract to do that work, and send in his bill for credit after you have OK'D the same. If such an arrangement cannot be made very soon, then get someone to do it for regular wages, and we will pay him the cash from this office upon presentation of his bill for as much as three days work for a man and a helper, but don't contract anything over about $40 for immediate payment, for we might have to divide the payment if you do, for we are skating on rather thin ice, when it comes to promising any money at all. However, we can take care of a small bill in as important a matter as this.

At any rate, manage in some way to get the water started thru the feeder canal, and then if possible keep it headed that way until the hard freezup comes on. Pay no attention to any objection that Murray might offer, as he has no legal means of preventing water from being carried thru "his ditch." I have had legal advice on that matter, and if he interferes, he will get in bad.

I started the new Ford car on the way to you

last Saturday, and presume you will have received it before this letter reaches you. It left here in perfect condition mechanically, and hope it will reach you in as good condition, and that you will have no trouble with it. It has never been damaged in any way whatever, except for the wear on the tires and top, and I have put on a full new set of tires lately, so you should have no trouble on that score. I thot it would be easier to keep in running condition over there than the Dodge, and for that reason should be more serviceable to you.

Will you kindly favor me with an early report on the material sold, the outlay of the cash received, and any other matters you may consider worth while? Hoping you will write me at once, I remain, with best regards to your family,

Yours truly,

A. J. VANCE.

No. ——. Plffs. Ex. 6.

U. S. District Court, District of Oregon. Filed June 12, 1923. G. H. Marsh, Clerk. [107]

PLAINTIFF'S EXHIBIT No. 7.

Letter from Jordan Valley Land & Water Company Dated August 24, 1920, to E. I. DuPont de Nemours & Co.

Paid-up Capital Stock $200,000.

J. W. Maney, President,

~~H. G. Wells,~~ Vice-President.

E. J. Wells, Treasurer.

Frank B. Cross, Secretary.

IRRIGATED LANDS IN THE FAMOUS JOR-
DAN VALLEY, MALHEUR COUNTY, ORE.
JORDAN VALLEY LAND & WATER CO.
Incorporated.

Box 1126

Paul S. A. Bickel,
    Chief Engineer and General Manager.

Boise, Idaho, August 24, 1920.

E. I. duPont de Nemours & Co.,
    Seattle, Washington.

Gentlemen:

Your Mr. H. G. Bostick just called on us to-day in regard to our account with your company. I regret that it is necessary to explain that this company's funds have been exhausted since about June 1st, and that we can't pay any bills, or resume work on the project until we complete a loan which we are now negotiating. This we hope to be able to do and resume operations by October 1st, possibly earlier.

As soon as we realize funds from this source your account will be promptly met, and paid in full.

Unfortunately, the former management of this company was too optimistic, and went a little too far on what looked to be good prospects for money coming in as fast as needed to carry on the work, but the failure of the colonization end of the project to sell lands as fast as was expected put this company behind.

We feel very confident that we will be in good going condition within a very short time.

Thanking you for your many favors, and hoping that we will be able to remit soon, we remain,

Yours truly,

JORDAN VALLEY LAND & WATER CO.,

By A. J. VANCE,

Vice-Pres't.

(Stamped: "RECEIVED August 26, 1920, Seattle, Office.")

No. ——. Plffs. Ex. 7.

U. S. District Court, District of Oregon. Filed June 12, 1923. G. H. Marsh, Clerk. [108]

Exhibit 1 for Identification. Arthur A. Goldsmith, of Attys. for Plaintiff.

PLAINTIFF'S EXHIBIT No. 8.

ORDER FOR POWDER.

H. G. Wells, Vice-President.

J. W. Maney, President.     E. J. Wells, Treasurer.

Paid-up Capital Stock $200,000.

JORDAN VALLEY LAND & WATER CO.

INCORPORATED.

Boise, Idaho.          2/4/20

Box 1126.                                    No. 190.

To Du Pont & Co.

Maynard Building, Seattle, Wash.

ship
Please ~~furnish~~ us with the following supplies or materials: By freight

ones
100 ~~cases~~ (5000 lbs) of Red Cross extra @ ~~18.28~~
~~per cwt.~~
40%—⅞x8.

800 kegs of R. R. Black Blasting Powder @ ~~2.24~~
~~ea.~~

12,000 feet dreadnaught fuse @ 12.15 per 1000 ft.
　　less 15% f. o. b. Portland.
Ship to: HOMEDALE, OWYHEE CO., ORE.
Quotations
F. O. B. HOMEDALE, Ida.
Stamped:　　　22267.
　　"M. O. No. 22268.
　　　　　　SED–244.
　　Agency No. SEB–245.
　　DEL'Y TICKET No. A6308.
　　SHIP (DATE)　　Will advise
　　EXPECT TO SHIP ——.
　　VIA O. W. R. & N. C/o O. S. L.　Prepay.

　　U. S. District Court, District of Oregon.　Filed
June 12, 1923.　G. H. Marsh, Clerk.
　　　　　　F. O. B.
　　　　　　POINT.
See attached letter.
　　Bostick.
Dynamite Homedale, Ore.
Blk. Pdr. Homedale, Ore.
Blstg.　Supls.　Portland,
　　Ore.
　　　　　　TERMS　　30 days NET.
Ship to— Advise later　Via　　　　freight.
　　No. ——.　Plffs. Ex. 8.
Send invoice with goods.　Mail monthly itemized
statement to our office, Box 1126, Boise, Idaho.
Indicate requisition number on all invoices and
statements.
　　JORDAN VALLEY LAND & WATER CO.
　　　　　　By EMIL L. TSCHIRGE.

All accounts paid by the 15th of month following delivery of goods. [109]

PLAINTIFF'S EXHIBIT No. 9.

Letter from Jordan Valley Land & Water Company to E. I. DuPont de Nemours & Co., Dated February 17, 1920.

J. W. Maney, President.

H. G. Wells, Vice-President.

E. J. Wells, Treasurer.

Frank B. Cross, Secretary.

Paid-up Capital Stock $200,000.

IRRIGATED LANDS IN THE FAMOUS JORDAN VALLEY, MALHEUR COUNTY, ORE.

JORDAN VALLEY LAND & WATER CO.
INCORPORATED.

Paul S. A. Bickel,      Box 1126.

Chief Engineer and General Manager.

Boise, Idaho, Feb. 17, 1920.

E. I. Du Pont de Nemours Co.,

Seattle, Washington.

Attention Mr. J. H. Willman, Mgr.

Dear Sir:

Our order for car of powder, being order #190, given to your Mr. Bostick in Boise under date of Feb. 4th, is to be shipped by you to Homedale, Idaho, at the earliest possible date, as road conditions have reached the points where we can now get this powder to the work and as we are badly in need of it, trust you will be able to get it out promptly.

Very truly yours,

JORDAN VALLEY LAND & WATER COMPANY.      By H. G. WELLS.

(Stamped): E. I. du Pont de Nemours & Company. Rec'd. Feb. 19, 1920. Seattle Office. Shipping Clerk.

No. ——. Plffs. Ex. 9.

(Pencil notation: "Advised Dupont as above 2–19–20.")

U. S. District Court, District of Oregon. Filed June 12, 1923. G. H. Marsh, Clerk.

Exhibit 2 for Identification, marked by Arthur A. Goldsmith, of Attorneys for Plaintiff. [110]

## PLAINTIFF'S EXHIBIT No. 10.

Stipulation Between Attorneys Concerning Depositions and Exhibits in Connection Therewith.

In the District Court of the United States for the District of Oregon.

L.–9004.

STATE OF OREGON on the Relation of HARRY HUMFELD,

Plaintiff,

vs.

AMERICAN SURETY COMPANY OF NEW YORK, a Corporation,

Defendant.

## STIPULATION.

It is hereby stipulated and agreed by and between the parties hereto, through their respective attorneys of record, that the signatures to the papers marked by Arthur A. Goldsmith, of attorneys for plaintiff, "Plaintiff's Exhibits 1 and 2" for identification, are the signatures of Emil L. Tschurge and H. G. Wells respectively.

It is further expressly stipulated that this stipulation shall not in any manner be deemed or taken as an admission by the defendant of the authority of said Tschurge and said Wells to sign said documents marked respectively "Plaintiff's Exhibits 1 and 2" for identification.

BRONAUGH & BRONAUGH,
BEACH & SIMON,
ARTHUR A. GOLDSMITH,
Attorneys for Relator.
WM. S. NASH, and
S. J. GRAHAM,
Attorneys for Defendant.

No. ——. Plffs. Ex. 10.

U. S. District Court, District of Oregon. Filed June 12, 1923. G. H. Marsh, Clerk. [111]

PLAINTIFF'S EXHIBIT No. 11.

Invoice Dated March 16, 1920, Covering Shipment of Supplies From E. I. DuPont de Nemours & Co.

Form 8469Y.

2/HC.

DU PONT.

EXPLOSIVES.

Please send all remittances, freight bills and other vouchers for credit to E. I. DU PONT DE NEMOURS & CO. INC., Hoge Bldg., Seattle, Wash. Interest charged on all bills not paid at maturity.

#37530.

## E. I. DU PONT DE NEMOURS & COMPANY, INCORPORATED.

Seattle, Wash., March 16, 1920.

Terms NET days net from date of invoice.

Sold to—JORDAN VALLEY LAND & WATER CO. Shipped to SAME.

Address—Boise, Idaho.

Destination — Homedale, Owyhee Co., Idaho

Customer's order No. 190. Dated

Loc Work—Jordan Valley, Oregon

Shipped from    Date shipped    B. O.    M. O.

F. O. B.    Salesman    Via    Car Int. & No.
MISCL.

Business    Block

Amount.

REFERRING TO DEBIT INVOICE #37165 —3/4/1920.

Freight Prepaid From Portland to Homedale, Idaho, on 12,000 Ft. Dreadnaught Fuse 223# at 1.69    3.77

War tax. 3%    .11

————

3.88

No. ——. Plffs. Ex. 11.

U. S. District Court, District of Oregon. Filed June 12, 1923. G. H. Marsh, Clerk. [112]

## PLAINTIFF'S EXHIBIT No. 12.

Invoice Dated October 3, 1919, Covering Shipment of Supplies from E. I. Du Pont de Nemours & Co.

Form 8469Y.

2/HC.

DU PONT.

EXPLOSIVES.

Please send all remittances, freight bills and other vouchers for credit to E. I. DuPont de Nemours & Co., Inc., Hoge Bldg., Seattle, Wash.

Interest charged on all bills not paid at maturity.

#33016.

## E. I. DU PONT DE NEMOURS & COMPANY, INCORPORATED.

Seattle, Wash. October 3, 1919.

Terms 30 days net 2%—10 days from date of invoice.

Sold to—JORDAN VALLEY LAND & WATER CO. Shipped to SAME.

Address—Box 1126, Boise, Idaho    Destination — Homedale, Owyhee Co., Idaho

Customer's order No. REQ. 119.    Loc. Work — Homedale, Owyhee Co., Idaho
Dated

Shipped from Dupont Mill & Man.    B. O. A47641    M. O. 6917
Date shipped 10-1-19

F. O. B. As Below.    Via    Car Int. & No. NP-26040

Salesman Bostick.

Business Con Block    SE-8

| | | Amount |
|---|---|---|
| 40 Ones—2000#Red Cross Extra 40% 7/8 x 8 | 18.71 | 374.20 |
| 80 Ones—4000# Repauno Stumping 1-3/8 x 8 | 15.71 | 628.40 |
| F. O. B. Homedale—Idaho. | | |
| 6000 Ft. Dreadnaught Fuse | 12.15–15% | 61.97 |
| 1—#4 Push Down DuPont Blasting Machine | 40.00 | 40.00 |
| F. O. B. Portland—Oregon. | | |
| | | 1104.57 |

Part of Carload.

See Invoice #33017—10/3/1919.

No. ——. Plffs. Ex. 12.

U. S. District Court, District of Oregon. Filed June 12, 1923. G. H. Marsh, Clerk. [113]

PLAINTIFF'S EXHIBIT No. 13.

Invoice Dated March 4, 1920, Covering Shipment of
Supplies From E. I. Du Pont de Nemours & Co.

(Stamped "MC.")

Agent's Copy.

Form 8469Y.                                No. 37165.

2–VII.

E. I. DU PONT DE NEMOURS & COMPANY,
INCORPORATED.

SE–8.          Seattle, Wash.     March 4, 1920.

Sold to—JORDAN VALLEY LAND & WATER
CO.

Terms 30 days net from date of invoice.

Address—Boise, Idaho                Shipped to Same
Customers' order #190
        (From DuPont Mill & Maga-    Destination — Homedale, Owyhee
        (     zine                            Co., Ida.
        (     B. O. A-6308 M. O.
        (     22267                   Loc. Work—Jordan Valley, Oregon
Shipt(  &   SED-244 Via              (Int.
        (Date  3/2/20  Prepay         Car( &
                                      (No.
                        CN.—SE.—8 Bostick

100 Ones 5,000# Red Cross Extra 40% 7/8
    x 8 @ 18.28                              914.00

        F. O. B. Homedale, Idaho.

12,000 Ft. Dreadnaught Fuse @ 12.15–15%    123.93

        F. O. B. Portland, Oregon.

                                        _____

                                          1037.93

Part Order.  See Invoice #37166—March 4, 1920.
             Order placed prior to March 1, 1920.

(Stamped: "Freight Prepaid $556.76 P. I. From
DuPont to Destination.")

(Stamped: "Charged  Customer  $3.88.  Seattle.
Invoice No. 37530.")

No. ——.  Plffs. Ex. 13.

U. S. District Court, District of Oregon. Filed June 12, 1923. G. H. Marsh, Clerk. [114]

PLAINTIFF'S EXHIBIT No. 14.

Invoice Dated March 4, 1920, Covering Shipment of Supplies From E. I. DuPont de Nemours & Co.

(Stamped "MC.")

Form 8469Y. No. 37166.

2–VII.

E. I. DU PONT DE NEMOURS & COMPANY, INCORPORATED.

AGENT'S COPY.

SE–8. Seattle, Wash. March 4, 1920.

Terms 30 days net
From date of Invoice.

Sold to—JORDAN VALLEY LAND & WATER CO.

SHIPPED TO SAME

| | |
|---|---|
| Address—Boise, Idaho. | Destination — Homedale, Owyhee, Ida. |
| Customers' order #190. | M. O. 22268 |
|           B. O. SEB—245 | Loc. Work—Jordan Valley, Ore. |
|   (From DuPont Mill | (Int. |
| Shipt(   & | Car( & |
|   (Date 3/2/20 | (No. |
|           Via | CN.—SE.—8     Bostick |
|     Prepay | |

800 Kegs DuPont Black Blast. "RR"

    @ 2.32                     $1856.00

F. O. B. HOMEDALE, Idaho.

Part order—See Invoice #37165—March 4, 1920.

Order placed prior to March 1, 1920.

Per Form 5405 Y Attached.

(Stamped: "Freight Prepaid $556.76 P. I. From DUPONT TO DESTINATION.")

No. ——. Plffs. Ex. 14.

U. S. District Court, District of Oregon. Filed June 12, 1923. G. H. Marsh, Clerk. [115]

PLAINTIFF'S EXHIBIT No. 15.

Bill of Lading Covering Shipment by Powder Company to Jordan Valley Land and Water Company.

Form 6135–2500–12–18.

## DU PONT WORKS.

Uniform Bill of Lading—Adopted by Carriers in Official Classification Territory Effective January 1, 1916.

OWRN&N.          Railroad Company.

Straight Bill of Lading—Original—Not Negotiable.

Shipper's No. 8023.

Agent's No. ——.

RECEIVED, subject to the classifications and tariffs in effect on the date of issue of this original Bill of Lading, at du Pont, Pierce Co., Washington, 3/2/20, 191—, from E. I. du Pont de Nemours & Co. Inc., the property described below, in apparent good order, except as noted (contents and condition of contents of packages unknown), marked, consigned and destined as indicated below, which said Company agrees to carry to its usual place of delivery at said destination, if on its road, otherwise to deliver to another carrier on the route to said destination. It is mutually agreed, as to each carrier of all or any of said property over all or any portion of said route to destination, and as to each party at any time interested in all or any of said property, that every service to be performed hereunder shall be subject to all the conditions, whether printed or written, herein contained (including conditions on back hereof) and which are agreed to by the shipper and accepted for himself and his assigns.

The Rate of Freight from ——————————

ο —————————— is in Cents per 100 Lbs. per —— per

s

(Mail Address—Not for Purposes of Delivery)

onsigned to Jordan Valley Land & Water Co.

estination—Homedale. State of Idaho. County
of Owyhee.

oute—OWR&N. c/o OSL. Car Initial CStPM
&O. Car No. 29498.

| No. Packages | Description of Articles and Special Marks | Class or Check Weight Rate—Column (Subject to Correction) |
|---|---|---|
| 100 | Cases High Explosives          TD | 6000# |

No. ——. Plffs. Ex. 15. [116]

| | | |
|---|---|---|
| 0 Kegs Black Powder, #57 RR | 21600# | If charges |
| Half Kegs Black Powder, | | prepaid, |
| Dunnage ............... | 40# | stamp her |
| Cases Black Powder........ | | Prepaid.'' |
| Cases Blasting Caps........ | | ..Prepaid.. |
| Cases Electric Blasting Caps | | Received $ |
| 2 Cases Safety Fuse. 12,000 | | ply in pr |
| ft. Dreadnaught 223#..... | | of the c |

(stamped "Freight   P a i d
3/2/20  $556.76
PRO ........ 30 ........
DATE ............ ......'')
27640

(Stamped: "This shipment accepted subject to Shipper's
Weight, Load and Count.'')

the   prop
scribed h

Agen
Per
(The signa
acknowle
the   amo
paid.)

————

Charges Ad

(Stamped: "This is to certify that this shipment, covered by the Trans-Continental Freight Bureau Weighing and Inspection Department Agreement No. 451 is properly described hereon, and the total gross weight upon which freight charges should be assessed is 27600 lbs.

Dunnage 40#
DUPONT & CO.
(Shipper's Signature.)
By F. E. SMITH.")

(Stamped: "The charges on this shipment will be collected from the shipper and should therefore be considered to be fully prepaid.

E. R. C.,
Agent.")

22267                SED–244.
M. O. ORDER No. 22268.   Agency Order No.
SEB–245.
(Stamped: "E. R. COLLINS,"
Agent.)
Per....A....1

This is to certify that the above articles are properly described by name and are packed and marked, and are in proper condition for transportation, according to the regulations prescribed by the Interstate Commerce Commission.

E. I. Du PONT de NEMOURS & CO., INC.,
Shippers.
Per  F. E. SMITH.
Per  T. M. H.

(This Bill of Lading is to be signed by the shipper and agent of the carrier issuing same.)

No. ——.   Plffs. Ex. 15.

U. S. District Court, District of Oregon. Filed June 12, 1923. G. H. Marsh, Clerk. [117]

PLAINTIFF'S EXHIBIT No. 16.

Contract of June 21, 1918, Between the Desert Land Board of the State of Oregon and the Jordan Valley Land & Water Company.

26 ~~FIFTH BIENNIAL REPORT~~.

#28

CONTRACT FOR CONSTRUCTION OF JORDAN VALLEY IRRIGATION SYSTEM.

This Agreement, Made and entered into, in duplicate, this 21st day of June, A. D. 1918, by and between the Desert Land Board of the State of Oregon, acting for and on behalf of the State of Oregon, the party of the first part, and Jordan Valley Land and Water Company, a corporation organized under the laws of the State of Nevada and doing business in the State of Oregon (hereinafter sometimes called the "Construction Company"), the party of the second part, Witnesseth: That

Whereas, the Construction Company has succeeded to all right, title and interest in what is known as the Jordan Valley Irrigation Project in Malheur County, Oregon, of the parties who submitted the application for the withdrawal under the Act of Congress commonly known as the Carey Act, and the Acts amendatory thereof and supplemental thereto, of certain public lands more particularly described in what is known as Oregon Segregation List No. 24 and in the Articles of Agreement between the United States and the State of Oregon, dated the 23d day of April, 1918, for reclamation under the said Acts of Congress and the laws of the State of Oregon enacted in furtherance thereof; and,

Whereas, the said Desert Land Board on the 24th day of May, 1918, did resolve to enter into a contract with the Construction Company for the construction of the works and structures, hereinafter described or referred to, on the terms herein set forth, which terms have been accepted by the Construction Company; and,

Whereas, the State Engineer of the State of Oregon, after due examination, has made and filed his report in writing, approving the feasibility of the proposed plan of reclamation, sufficiency and availability of the water supply, and reasonableness of the estimate of cost and the lien requested;

Now, therefore, in consideration of the premises and of the covenants and agreements, hereinafter contained and to be kept and performed by the parties hereto, respectively, the said parties have agreed and hereby do agree as follows:

## ARTICLE I.

### GENERAL COVENANTS AS TO CONSTRUCTION AND COMPENSATION.

The Construction Company agrees to furnish all the material and do all work required in the construction of said irrigation system, reservoirs, canals, flumes, and other irrigation works and structures, hereinafter more particularly described, in substantial compliance with the plans and specifica-

No. ——.   Plffs. Ex. 16.

U. S. District Court, District of Oregon.   Filed June 12, 1923.   G. H. Marsh, Clerk.   [118]

tions herein set forth, and such additional plans and specifications as may hereafter be approved by the State Engineer of the State of Oregon and filed with the Desert Land Board; and it will do all such work in a good, substantial and workmanlike manner, and accept as full compensation for such material and work and for the rights of way, water rights, works, structures, privileges and franchises, to be transferred to the Jordan Valley Water Company (hereinafter sometimes called the "Operating Company"), as hereinafter provided, the lien or liens hereby created and authorized to be created by the said Acts of Congress and the laws of the State of Oregon on the lands segregated from the public domain under the said Acts of Congress, hereinafter referred to as Carey Act lands and a list of which is hereto attached, marked Exhibit "A," and made a part hereof, and all proceeds from the sale of water rights, shares or interests in said irrigation system, such sales to be made under the terms and provisions hereof.

## ARTICLE II.

## GENERAL SPECIFICATIONS FOR CONSTRUCTION.

Section 1. Capacity of structures. The storage reservoir shall have a gross impounding capacity of three and five-tenths acre feet for each acre of land to be irrigated or reclaimed therefrom, which amount, in addition to the natural flow of the creeks which may be diverted into said irrigation system, or parts thereof, is deemed sufficient to reclaim the lands for which water rights, shares or interests in said irrigation system and stock in said Operating Company are hereby authorized to be sold; but every canal, flume, pipe-line, ditch, lateral and other structure of said irrigation system shall have a carrying capacity, when completed, sufficient to deliver simultaneously one-eightieth (1/80) of a cubic foot of water per second of time, measured at the head of the farmer's service lateral or ditch, for each acre of land to be irrigated therefrom.

Section 2. Lower Feeder Canal. The Lower Feeder Canal commences at a point on Jordan Creek in the Northeast Quarter (NE.¼) of Section Thirteen (13), Township Thirty (30) South, Range Forty-six (46) East, W. M., and extends in a general westerly direction for a distance of approximately nineteen miles to the Antelope Reservoir, and is designed to be used for carrying water from Jordan Creek to said Reservoir for storage purposes, and also for supplying water for reclaiming lands above said Antelope Reservoir but susceptible of irrigation from said canal. But it and all appurtenant structures, diversion dam and gates shall be constructed in accordance with such detailed plans and specifications as shall be approved by the State Engineer and filed with the Desert Land Board; and the canal shall have a carrying capacity sufficient to deliver into said Antelope Reservoir three and five-tenths acre feet of water during a period of one hundred (100) days for each acre of land depending on said reservoir for water for irrigation purposes, and for which water rights, shares or interests may be sold in said irrigation system by the Construction Company; and if water be supplied directly from said Lower Feeder Canal for the irrigation of lands above said Antelope Reservoir, it shall be constructed with an additional capacity sufficient to deliver to each acre of land for which water rights may be sold therein one-eightieth (1/80) of a cubic foot of water per second of time, measured at the head of the farmer's lateral or ditch.

Section 3. Antelope Reservoir. The Antelope Reservoir is situated in Townships Thirty (30) and Thirty-one (31) South, Range [119] Forty-five (45) East, W. M., and the impounding dam is situated in the Southwest Quarter (SW.¼) of the Northeast Quarter (NE.¼), and the Northwest Quarter (NW.¼) of the Southeast Quarter (SE.¼) of Section Thirty-two (32), Township Thirty (30) South, Range Forty-five (45) East. The dam shall be of earth fill construction, and it and all control works, spillways and appurtenant structures shall be of such design and according to such detailed plans and specifications as may be approved by the State Engineer and filed with the Desert Land Board, and when completed the Reservoir shall have a gross impounding or storage capacity of three and five-tenths acre-feet per acre for each acre of land depending thereon for water for irrigation purposes, and for which water rights may be sold by the Construction Company.

Sec. 4. Reservoir Outlet to Jordan Creek. The water from Antelope Reservoir may be discharged into the channel of Jack Creek and carried in the channel of said creek to a point near the northeast corner of Section Thirty-one (31), Township Thirty (30) South, Range Forty-five (45) East, W. M.; thence through a canal extending from Jack Creek to Jordan Creek. A suitable dam shall be constructed at the head of said canal, and the channel of Jack Creek between said diversion dam and reservoir shall be straightened and improved and the dam and canal above referred to constructed in accordance with such plans and specifications as may be approved by the State Engineer.

Sec. 5. Antelope West Canal. The Antelope West Canal has its initial point at the control works located at the outlet of the Antelope Reservoir, from which point it runs in a westerly and southerly direction to a point near the Southeast quarter (SE.¼) of Section Nine (9), Township Thirty-one (31) South, Range Forty-four (44) East, W. M. It shall have a capacity sufficient to deliver one-eightieth (1/80) of a cubic foot of water per second of time for each acre of land for which water is furnished through such canal for irrigation purposes, measured at the head of the farmer's service lateral or ditch, and shall be constructed according to such detailed plans and specifications as may be approved by the State Engineer and filed with the Desert Land Board.

Sec. 6. Main Canal for Lower Unit. The main canal for what is known as the Lower Unit has its intake on Jordan Creek at the diversion dam situated in the Northwest Quarter (NW.¼) of Section

Thirty-six (36), Township Thirty (30) South, Range Forty-four (44) East, W. M., and extends in a southerly and westerly direction approximately five miles to a point in the Southeast Quarter (SE.1/4) of Section Five (5), Township Thirty-one (31) South, Range Forty-three (43) East, W. M., where it divides into branches and laterals, which together with said main canal will be extended for carrying and conducting water to the lands in said Lower Unit in Townships 30 and 31 South, Ranges 42 and 43 East, W. M.

## DESERT LAND BOARD.

The said canals, diversion dam and all headgates and other appurtenant structures shall be of such design and accord to such plans and specifications as may be approved by the State Engineer and filed with the Desert Land Board, but shall have a capacity sufficient to deliver one-eightieth (1/80) of a cubic foot of water per second of time to each acre of land depending thereon for water for irrigation purposes, and for which water rights, shares or interests therein may be sold by the Construction Company, measured at the headgates of the farmer's service lateral or ditch.

Sec. 7. Other Structures, Distributing Canals and Laterals. There shall be constructed such distributing canals and subordinate [120] laterals as may be required to carry the water to within one-half mile, measured in direct line, of each quarter-section of land susceptible of irrigation by gravity flow from said irrigation system and included in the list of lands hereto attached as Exhibit "A," and such other lands as may be susceptible of irrigation from said irrigation system, and for which water rights, shares or interests therein may be sold by the Construction Company. Provided that coulees and draws and other natural waterways may be utilized as part of said irrigation system for carrying water, when the same can conveniently be done; but all such distributing canals and laterals, coulees and waterways and other structures shall substantially conform to the plans and specifications therefor approved, or that may hereafter be approved, by the State Engineer and filed with the Desert Land Board; provided that all structures shall be of standard design and construction and have the capacity required under this agreement, and all sub-laterals or distribution canals shall have such excess capacity as may be necessary to permit of rotating water, which plan of rotation shall be prepared by the second party, and receive the approval of the State Engineer before construction work is undertaken on any particular unit.

Changes in plans and specifications may be made, with the consent of the State Engineer, to meet field conditions or conditions or obstacles unforeseen when the original plans and specifications were approved.

Sec. 8. Measuring Devices. The Construction Company shall construct at the outlet of the reservoir and at or near the head of main canals and branch canals, and at such places as may be deemed necessary by its Chief Engineer for the proper management and operation of said irrigation system, all necessary headgates, weirs and measuring devices; but the location and design of all such structures and measuring devices shall be subject to the approval of the State Engineer of the State of Oregon. Suitable headgates and necessary measuring devices shall be installed by the Construction Company at or near the head of all necessary farmer's laterals or service ditches, provided that the Construction Company shall not be required to construct more than one headgate and install more than one measuring device for each entryman or purchaser of water rights, and all additional headgates and measuring devices desired by any entryman or purchaser of water rights shall be installed at his expense, but under the direction and supervision of the Chief Engineer of the Construction Company. And all such individual headgates and measuring devices shall be of a design approved by the State Engineer.

## DESERT LAND BOARD.

Sec. 9. More Detailed Plans to be Submitted. The Construction Company shall file with the State Engineer and Desert Land Board complete plans and specifications of all structures to be constructed hereunder; and the Construction Company shall, on demand of the State Engineer, furnish such other and further detailed specifications and plans as the State Engineer or the Desert Land Board may require.

## ARTICLE III.
### RIGHTS OF WAY.

Section 1. Over State and Carey Act Lands. The party of the first part hereby grants to the party of the second part rights of [121] way across all lands segregated, as aforesaid, from the public domain and described in said Exhibit "A" hereto attached, and across all lands owned by the State of Oregon or that may hereafter be ceded or granted to the State of Oregon by the United States, which said rights of way shall be equal to the actual width of the canal, flume, pipe-line, lateral, ditch, waste ditch, or other structure at its base from toe to toe of the embankment, together with a strip or strips of land adjacent thereto not exceeding fifty (50) feet in width along the main canal and thirty (30) feet in width for the main laterals, and a proportionate width along the smaller structures. Such rights of way shall be located by the Chief Engineer of the Construction Company, and approved by the State Engineer, and shall in all cases be sufficient for ingress and egress along said structures, and for all dams and flooded or submerged areas. And every owner of land irrigated from said irrigation system and the persons filing on said Carey Act land shall have the necessary rights of way for service laterals, ditches and waste ditches; but no more laterals, service or waste ditches shall be constructed across any premises than the Chief Engineer of the Construction Company may deem necessary; provided, however, that his determination shall be subject to review by the State Engineer, whose decision in the premises shall be final. Maps showing the location of all canals, laterals and other structures constructed by the Construction Company shall be filed with the Desert Land Board and in the office of the State Engineer, but the filing of such maps shall not be required prior to the lands being thrown open for entry or settlement, and all entries shall be made subject to such rights of way whether selected before or after the making of the entry.

Sec. 2. Over the Public Domain. The Construction Company shall file, if it or its predecessors in interest have not heretofore filed, in the proper United States Land Office application or applications in due form for rights of way under Sections 18 to 21 of the Act of Congress approved March 3, 1891 (28 Stat. 1085) over public lands of the United States not included in the lands segregated as aforesaid.

Sec. 3. Over Privately Owned Lands. The Construction Company shall obtain at its own cost and expense easements for rights of way over lands not included in Sections 1 and 2 of this Article, affected by any of the structures constructed by it hereunder.

## DESERT LAND BOARD.
### ARTICLE IV.

## APPROPRIATIONS OF WATER HELD BY CONSTRUCTION COMPANY.

The Construction Company covenants and agrees that all water rights and water appropriations held by it for use in connection with said Jordan Valley Irrigation Project were appropriated or acquired solely for the purpose of transferring the title thereto from the State to the individual entrymen, settlers and owners of land acquiring rights in said irrigation system for the reclamation of their respective tracts of land, and the water so appropriated or filed upon is hereby dedicated to the reclamation of the lands susceptible of irrigation from said irrigation system, as the same may finally be constructed; and each acre of land entitled to water from said irrigation system under any contract with the Construction Company for a share or interest in said irrigation system shall be entitled to receive its proportionate share of the water available for the irrigation thereof, based upon the number of acres entitled to share in such supply; provided that beneficial [122] use shall be the measure and the limit of the right; that the water appropriations now held by the Construction Company, as aforesaid, include the following applications and permits for water, to wit:

(a)  Application No. 2286, filed in the office of the State Engineer of the State of Oregon, for the right to store 127,000 acre feet of water of Jordan, Jack and Antelope Creeks in the said Antelope Reservoir.

(b)  Application No. 310, on file in the office of the State Engineer of Oregon, for the right to divert 750 cubic feet per second of the waters of Jordan, Jack and Antelope Creeks for the irrigation of lands under the canals hereinbefore described.

(c) Application No. 4723, on file in the office of the State Engineer of Oregon, for the right to divert and store 32,000 acre feet of the waters of Jordan and Boulder Creeks and other water courses for storage in the Canyon Reservoir.

(d) Permit No. 11584, issued by the State Engineer of the State of Idaho, for 20,000 acre feet of the waters of Jordan and Boulder Creeks for storage in Canyon Reservoir, and for the irrigation of lands below said reservoir.

(e) Permit No. R. 1, issued by the State Engineer of the State of Idaho, for 12,000 acre feet of water additional to Permit No. 11584, of the waters of Jordan and Boulder Creeks for storage in said Canyon Reservoir.

(f) Permit No. 8382, issued by the State Engineer of Idaho, for 300 cubic feet per second of the waters of Jordan Creek.

## ARTICLE V.
## ACCEPTANCE OF CONSTRUCTION WORK.

The party of the first part shall maintain during the period of construction one or more inspectors, whose duty it shall be to inspect and observe all work being done and material used in the construction of said irrigation system, and to enforce the provisions of this contract and the plans and specifications relative to such construction work, and to promptly reject all work and material that, in the opinion of the inspector, does not conform to the

requirements of this agreement and the plans and
specifications approved and filed hereunder. Upon
the completion of any of the structures or canals
which conveniently form a unit for construction
purposes, particularly,

(a)   The Lower Feeder Canal,

(b)   The Antelope Reservoir.

(c)   The Reservoir Outlet Canal,

(d)   The Antelope West Canal, with the
necessary branches and laterals,

(e)   The Main Canal on the Lower Unit,
with the necessary branches and laterals,  [123]

(f)   Any other canal or branch canal or
structure forming a substantial part of said
irrigation system and a reasonable unit for construction purposes, the Construction Company
shall be entitled to a final inspection and acceptance of such structure, canal or unit of
construction, if constructed in substantial accordance with the plans and specifications therefor, to the end that it may be officially and
authoritatively advised wherein, if at all, such
structure or unit does not, in the opinion of
the party of the first part, conform to such plans
and specifications and so that any variation or
departure therefrom may be promptly and
economically remedied while the equipment or
construction force is conveniently available
therefor. And in the event the one dollar per
acre is received by the State from the sale of
Carey Act land under said project is not sufficient to meet the expenses of such inspections

and examinations, the Construction Company shall advance monthly, upon demand of the State Engineer, the additional funds required to meet such expenses.

## ARTICLE VI.
## TRANSFER OF TITLE AND MANAGEMENT OF SYSTEM.

Section 1. Operating Company. It being necessary to provide a convenient method for vesting the management and control of said irrigation system, and parts thereof when completed sufficiently for operation or use, in the purchasers of water rights, it is hereby provided that before any of said Carey Act lands are thrown open for settlement or entry there shall be organized, at the expense of the Construction Company, under the laws of the State of Oregon, a corporation to be known as the Jordan Valley Water Company. The articles of incorporation, by-laws and organization meetings and contract or contracts, if any, between said Jordan Valley Water Company and the Construction Company shall be subject to the approval of the Attorney General and State Engineer of the State of Oregon. The authorized capital stock of said corporation shall be on the basis of one share of stock for each acre of land which it is estimated may ultimately be reclaimed from said irrigation system, and each share of stock when issued shall represent a water right for one acre of land, and for the purpose of incorporation such capital stock shall be fixed at forty thousand (40,000) shares of the nominal par value of One Dollar ($1.00) per share; but no stock shall be issued therein in excess of the amount authorized from time to time by the Desert Land Board, and the amount of stock authorized to be issued shall at all times be limited by the capacity of said irrigation system, as hereinbefore provided.

Section 2. Transfer of Title. Subject to the terms of this agreement and any amendments or supplemental agreements that may hereafter be entered into between the parties hereto, and without prejudice to the rights of the Construction Company or the liens, rights, franchises and privileges granted to the Construction Company by this agreement and by the said Acts of Congress and the laws of the State of Oregon, the Construction Company shall transfer and convey to said Jordan Valley Water Company the legal title to all rights of way, water rights and water appropriations now held by the Construction Company, in so far as the same may be required for the operation, management and maintenance of such portions of said irrigation system as shall from time to time be accepted by first party as completed, as provided in Article V hereof, or shall be sufficiently completed for operation and use. And upon the final completion of said irrigation system the legal [124] title to all said irrigation system, the legal title to all said irrigation works, rights of way and water rights forming an integral or necessary part of said irrigation system shall be transferred to and vested in said Jordan Valley Water Company, the Construction Company retaining only its right or interest to the unsold water rights therein, which shall be represented by stock in the Jordan Valley Water Company on the basis of one share of stock for each acre of land that may be reclaimed from the unsold water rights therein as fixed by the Desert Land Board on the basis hereinbefore provided.

Section 3. Transfer of Management. Whenever it is certified by the Chief Engineer of the Construction Company that certain portions of said irrigation system have been so far completed as to permit the operation thereof for delivery of water to those entitled to water therefrom, such portions shall, with the consent of the State Engineer, be transferred and turned over for operation to said Jordan Valley Water Company; but such transfer shall not release the Construction Company of its obligation as to the completion thereof until the same has been accepted as completed by the party of the first part. And the distribution and delivery of water, and the management, maintenance and upkeep of such portions of said system as shall be so transferred for operation, or as may be fully completed and accepted as completed by the party of the first part, shall be vested in said Jordan Valley Water Company, and the Construction Company shall not be responsible for the operation of or for the distribution or delivery of water from any portion of said irrigaion system so turned over to the Operating Company for operation, or as completed. Provided, however, that if the Construction Company operates any portion of said system before it is turned over as aforesaid, to the Operating

Company, it may charge and assess the purchasers of water rights, shares or interests in said irrigation system, whose lands are susceptible of irrigation from the portion so operated by the Construction Company, One Dollar ($1.00) per acre per annum for each acre of land entitled to water from the portion of the system so operated, and payment thereof may be required in advance of the delivery of water; and if the sum so raised shall be insufficient for the purpose of maintaining, operating and keeping in repair the portion of the system so operated, the Construction Company shall furnish all additional funds necessary to supply such deficiency.

Section 4. Stock of Operating Company Accepted as Payment for Transfer of Title. The property, right, and interests to be transferred by the Construction Company to the Operating Company, as hereinbefore provided, shall, as between said Companies, be considered as payment in full by the Construction Company for all the capital stock of the Operating Company, and said stock, subject to the limitations hereinbefore set forth on the issuance thereof, shall be subject to the order of the Construction Company, and within the said limitations shall be issued by the Operating Company, from time to time as ordered and directed by the Construction Company unto such person or persons as it may designate, all of whom shall be owners or entrymen of land susceptible of irrigation from said irrigation system, except in the case of qualifying shares for directors, and every certificate of stock, except as above stated, shall describe the land to which the water, which the holder thereof is entitled to receive, shall be dedicated and made appurtenant.' [125]

## ARTICLE VII.
## SALE OF WATER RIGHTS.

Section 1. Interest acquired by Purchaser. All applications for the purchase of water rights, shares, or interests in said irrigation system for the irrigation of lands susceptible of irrigation therefrom shall be made to the Construction Company, and it shall cause to be issued and delivered to each and every purchaser a share of stock in the Jordan Valley Water Company, for each and every acre of land for which a water right is purchased; and the interest of the purchaser in said irrigation system shall be evidenced by a certificate of stock in said Jordan Valley Water Company which shall entitle the holder thereof to receive his proportionate share of all water available for distribution by said Company, based upon the number of shares issued and outstanding, subject only to the provisions of the laws of the State of Oregon that water shall not be wasted and that no water user shall receive more water than is actually required for the proper irrigation of his land, and in no event more than two and one-half (2½) acre feet per acre during the irrigation season and one-half acre foot per acre for domestic and stock purposes during the non-irrigation season; and all water shall be delivered or distributed according to such rules and regulations as to the rotation or delivery of water in periods or intervals as may be prescribed by the Desert Land Board.

Section 2. Priority of Purchase Does not Give Priority of Right. The Construction Company agrees to sell, or contract to sell, such shares or water rights to the extent of the capacity of said irrigation system, as determined from time to time by the Desert Land Board, to qualified entrymen applying to enter said Carey Act Lands and to purchasers of State lands and owners of other lands susceptible of irrigation from said irrigation system, upon the terms herein provided, without preference or partiality; it being understood, however, that priority of application or purchase, or priority of entry or settlement, shall not give priority of right to water from said irrigation system as against subsequent applicants, purchasers, entrymen, or settlers, but that every purchaser of water rights or shares in said irrigation system shall be entitled only to his proportionate interest therein, as aforesaid, based upon the number of shares or water rights sold therein with the approval and consent of said Desert Land Board.

Section 3. Price of Shares or Water Rights. The Construction Company agrees that it will sell, or cause to be sold, such shares or water rights at the rate of Seventy-one Dollars ($71.00) per share, payable as follows:

In cash at the time of sale, $31.00 per share; On the first day of December, 1921, $5.00 per share; and a like sum on the first day of December of each year thereafter until the full amount of the purchase price has been paid.

All deferred payments shall bear interest, payable on December first of each year, at the rate of six per cent (6%) per annum from May 1, 1919; provided water be available by said date within one-half mile of the quarter section in which the lands of the purchaser are situated. And if water be not available as aforesaid on said date, there shall be a rebate of interest for a period equal to the delay in the delivery of such water at said point; and in no event shall any payment of either principal or interest other than the said cash payment, be required of any purchaser until after water has been made available, as herein provided, for the irrigation of the lands described in the contract or mortgage for such water rights or shares.

Sec. 4. Security for Deferred Payments. All deferred payments [126] for the purchase of shares or water rights shall be secured by a first mortgage or lien on the land to which such water rights are made appurtenant, including the water rights purchased, executed, acknowledged and recorded as required by the laws of the State of Oregon; and the certificate of stock in said Jordan Valley Water Company shall be endorsed over and delivered to the Construction Company as additional security for the payment of the balance of the purchase price, with interest as aforesaid. The form of the mortgage or contract with the accompanying notes shall be subject to the approval of the Desert Land Board.

Nothing herein contained shall be construed as preventing the sale by the Construction Company of shares or water rights upon terms more favorable than those above stated, and the purchaser shall have the privilege of making deferred payments before their due date, with a proportionate rebate of interest.

Sec. 5. Sale of Partial Water Rights. Pending the determination of the feasibility of constructing what is known as the Canyon Reservoir, which if constructed would supply storage water for lands situated under and susceptible of irrigation from the Lower Feeder Canal, the Construction Company may sell "partial water rights" for the irrigation of said lands, which water rights shall not entitle the holder thereof to any reservoir water but only to his proportionate part of the water available for distribution from said Lower Feeder Canal, not exceeding the amount actually required for the proper irrigation of such lands. The same shall be evidenced by stock in the Operating Company, but every certificate of stock issued for such water rights shall be plainly marked so as to indicate that the holder thereof is not entitled to stored water; and such partial water rights shall be sold at the rate of Forty-five Dollars ($45.00) per share, payable as follows:

In cash at the time of sale, $20.00 per share;

The balance shall be payable in installments at the times, and bearing the same rate of interest, and secured as in the case of deferred payments for the purchase of other water rights authorized to be sold hereunder.

Upon the construction of said Canyon Reservoir,

and stored water being made available for the use of the holders of such partial water rights, the right of such holders to receive water under previous contracts and their certificates of stock in the Operating Company for partial rights shall terminate, and they shall thereupon make application for full water rights, paying the difference between the cost of such partial water rights and the full water rights, to-wit: Twenty-six Dollars ($26.00) per acre, at such times and in such manner as may be fixed by the Desert Land Board. And thereupon there shall be issued to such holders new certificates of stock in the Operating Company, placing them on the same basis as other holders of water rights entitled to reservoir water.

Sec. 6. Increase in Price of Water Rights Not Promptly Purchased. Should any owner of land susceptible of irrigation from said irrigation system and not included in said Exhibit A, fail to purchase water rights on the terms, hereinbefore fixed, on or before the date water is available for the irrigation of such lands, such availability being determined as hereinbefore provided, the Construction Company shall be entitled to charge in addition to the price, hereinbefore [127] fixed, interest thereon at the rate of seven per cent (7%) per annum from the date water is available for the irrigation of such land.

Section 7. Escrow of Securities and Cash. It is expressly agreed that until otherwise ordered by the Desert Land Board, the cash received by the Construction Company from the sale of water rights and all mortgages or securities taken for the purchase price of water rights shall be deposited in escrow with the Boise Title and Trust Company of Boise, Idaho, as escrow holder or Trustee; and the cash so deposited with said Trustee shall be paid out by it in installments, from time to time, to the Construction Company, or its order, upon engineer's estimates or certificates as the work progresses for work done or materials used or purchased for use in the construction of said irrigation system and for necessary expenses of colonization and sale of water rights, provided that such engineer's estimates or certificates shall be countersigned or approved by the State Engineer or his duly authorized representative before payment by the Trustee. And the mortgages or other securities taken for the deferred payments of the purchase price shall not be delivered by said Trustee or escrow-holder except on the certificate of the State Engineer or of the Desert Land Board that water has been made available for the irrigation of the lands described in such mortgages or contracts; but such certificates shall be made and securities delivered from time to time as water is made available. Provided, that neither such securities nor the proceeds thereof, nor any cash remaining in the hands of the trustees shall be diverted or applied to other purposes until the water has been made available for all lands for which water rights have been sold, but the same shall be held by said trustee and paid out on estimates or certificates approved by the State Engineer, as aforesaid.

## ARTICLE VIII.

### SALE AND ENTRY OF CAREY ACT LANDS.

Section 1. Price. The party of the first part agrees to sell the lands described in said Exhibit A and herein generally referred to as Carey Act Lands, to such persons as are or may be entitled under the law to enter the same, for the sum of One Dollar ($1.00) per acre, which shall accompany the application for entry and shall be paid by the Construction Company out of the first cash payment made by the entryman or purchaser, and forwarded by the Construction Company to the Desert Land Board with the application for entry of the form described by such Board, and the contract with the Construction Company showing that the applicant has made the proper arrangements for the purchase of the necessary water rights, and the release of the construction lien.

Section 2. Opening Lands for Entry. The Construction Company being now actually engaged in the construction of said irrigation system and having already expended a large sum in construction work thereon, it is expressly agreed that upon the execution of this contract and the filing of the bond required to be filed hereunder, five thousand (5,000) acres of said Carey Act Lands shall immediately be thrown open for entry and settlement, as provided by law; provided that the Desert Land Board shall determine what lands shall be included in the list of lands so first opened for entry, but so far as practicable the lands for which water will first be made available shall be included in such list. And

said Board shall from time to time open other tracts
of said Carey Act lands for entry as the construction [128] work advances to insure a water supply therefor. But it is expressly agreed and understood that the party of the first part will not approve any application for entry or settlement on said Carey Act lands until the person or persons so applying shall furnish a certified copy of the contract entered into with the Construction Company for the purchase of shares or water rights in said irrigation system, on the basis of one share of stock in the Operating Company for each acre of irrigable land in the entry. And it is further agreed and understood that the Construction Company may accept applications for entry and for the purchase of water rights or shares in said irrigation system in excess of the acreage opened for entry for the time being, by the Desert Land Board, but not in excess of the estimated area susceptible of irrigation from said irrigation system; but such applications shall be accepted or acted on by the party of the first part only as and when such additional lands are opened for entry and authority given the Construction Company to sell water rights for the lands included in such applications.

## ARTICLE IX.
### DEFINITIONS.

For the purpose of this contract, "date of reclamation" shall be construed to be the date when water is first available for the use of the entryman or purchaser of water rights at the point where the farmer's lateral or service ditch commences; and water shall be deemed "available" for such entryman or purchaser when the irrigation system has been so far completed that it has a carrying capacity sufficient to deliver simultaneously one-eightieth (1/80) of a cubic foot of water per second for each acre of land entitled to water from said canal, lateral or structure under existing contract of purchase, and with a gross storage or impound capacity in said reservoir equal to three and five-tenths acre feet per acre for each acre of land entitled to water from such reservoir under existing contracts of purchase, and with a sufficient capacity in the Feeder Canal to fill such reservoir in a period of one hundred (100) days.

## ARTICLE X.
## APPLICATION FOR PATENT.

When water has been made available for any substantial part of the Carey Act lands described in Exhibit "A" hereto attached, or for lands under any unit of construction as herein defined, the party of the first part, upon request of the Construction Company, shall make application to the Department of the Interior, in due form, for the issuance of patent for said lands, the Construction Company supplying all necessary data and maps required by the party of the first part in connection with said application; the first party will do all such acts and things as may be required under the rules and regulations of the Department of the Interior for obtaining patent for said lands, after the Construction Company has caused the same to be reclaimed to the extent required by the said Acts of Congress before

patent can issue therefor.  And upon the issuance
of such patent, the party of the first part will
promptly convey by deed to the entrymen their respective tracts of land.

## ARTICLE XI.
## COMMENCING WORK AND COMPLETING SYSTEM.

The Construction Company shall begin the actual
construction [129] of said irrigation system
within six months from the date hereof, and prosecute such construction diligently and continuously
to completion as required by the laws of the State
of Oregon, and complete the structures to the extent
required by this agreement within five (5) years
from the date hereof; Provided that the rights of
the Construction Company under this contract shall
be subject to all the provisions of the existing laws
of the State of Oregon applicable thereto.

## ARTICLE XII.
## ESTIMATED COST AND LIEN FOR RECLA-MATION.

The party of the first part, to the full extent it
may be authorized to do so under the said Acts of
Congress, hereby declares, fixes and creates a lien
on and against the said lands so segregated from
the public domain under the said Act of Congress
known as the Carey Act and described in Exhibit "A"
hereto attached to the amount of Seventy-one Dollars
($71.00) per acre on each acre of land susceptible
of irrigation from said irrigation system as finally
completed, and  Three and one-half Dollars ($3.50)

per acre on each acre of said lands included in any entry not susceptible of irrigation from said irrigation system, which lien, with interest thereon at the rate of six per cent (6%) per annum, shall be valid on any against the separate legal subdivisions thereof for the amount aforesaid from the date of reclamation until disposed of or released to actual settlers. And for the purpose of showing the irrigable area in each legal subdivision the Construction Company shall make a topographical survey of said lands and furnish, prior to such lands being thrown open for entry, a map and a list, in duplicate, showing the irrigable and nonirrigable acreage in each legal subdivision; and the amount of the lien so authorized as aforesaid shall be determined from such surveys, maps and lists. The said sum of $3.50 per acre for nonirrigable land is made, and shall be deposited with said Trustee, as aforesaid; provided that $1.00 per acre, out of the first payment made by the purchaser or entryman for each acre of Carey Act land entered shall be transmitted by the Construction Company to the Desert Land Board with the application for entry.

## ARTICLE XIII.
### INCREASING CAPACITY OF SYSTEM.

The Construction Company shall be entitled at any time within five (5) years from the date hereof to increase the capacity of said system, or any part thereof, and to extend the same so as to irrigate and reclaim other lands not herein described or specially referred to; but every such enlargement, extension or additional construction shall be substantially in

accordance with the plans and specifications that
may be approved therefor by the State Engineer
of the State of Oregon. And it is specially agreed
'that this contract does not include the construction
of what is known as the Canyon Reservoir and what
is known as the Upper Feeder Canal, and that the
feasibility of constructing said reservoir and Upper
Feeder Canal shall hereafter be determined, and
the construction of said works and the price of
water rights therein shall be covered by a supplemental or independent contract between the parties
hereto, after the feasibility of constructing the same
has first been determined.

## ARTICLE XIV.
### MORTGAGE.

The right, title and interest of the Construction
Company [130] in said irrigation system, water
rights, reservoir, structures and stock of the Operating Company, and in the rights, franchises and lien
hereby created and granted, may be mortgaged or
otherwise pledged as security for the capital required in carrying out the terms of this agreement
to be kept and performed by the Construction Company, the form of the mortgage or deed of trust to
be approved by the Attorney-General of the State
of Oregon. But such mortgage shall contain suitable provisions for releasing the lien thereof and of
any contract or mortgage given for the purchase
price of water rights on any lands and the appurtenant water rights, upon payment of the full amount
of the purchase price of such water rights, and accrued interest thereon.

## ARTICLE XV.
## DELIVERY OF WATER TO PERSONS NOT ENTITLED THERETO.

It is expressly agreed that the Jordan Valley Water Company shall not deliver water from said irrigation system, or any part thereof, or permit the use of any water therefrom by any person who is not entitled thereto under the terms of this contract and under the terms of a contract of sale executed or authorized by the Construction Company.

## ARTICLE XVI.
## BOND.

The Construction Company having already expended a large sum of money in the construction of said irrigation system and in the acquisition of rights of ways and water rights, the amount of the bond required hereunder for the faithful performance of this agreement by the party of the second part shall be One Hundred Thousand Dollars ($100,000).

## ARTICLE XVII.
## HIGHWAYS.

It is expressly agreed that all sales of State lands and all entries of Carey Act lands under said irrigation system shall be made subject to a right of way, without compensation to the entryman or purchaser, for roads upon all exterior section lines and half-section lines, and such other roads as the Construction Company may deem necessary and as may be approved by the State Engineer, and that such rights of way along section lines shall be sixty feet in width, being thirty feet on either side of the section line, and for other roads forty feet in width. And to aid in the development of said irrigation project and the reclamation of said lands, the Construction Company agrees to contribute or donate Five Dollars ($5.00) per acre for each acre of irrigable land for which a full water right (including reservoir water) is sold in said irrigation system, except in what is known as the Lower Unit, where the amount shall be Fifteen Dollars ($15.00) per acre for five thousand (5,000) acres and Five Dollars ($5.00) per acre for all sales in such Lower Unit in excess of said acreage, to a Road Fund to be expended under the supervision of the party of the first part in the construction of roads and highways to, over, or from said irrigation project in such manner as may seem most advantageous for the development of said irrigation project and the several tracts or communities thereunder; that such contribution or donation shall be made from time to time as water becomes available [131] for the lands for which water rights have been sold, and shall consist of mortgages or water contracts received by the Construction Company for deferred payments on water rights; and the said Trustee shall be instructed, and it hereby is instructed, to deliver to first party or its nominees, for the benefit of such road fund, the proportionate amount of all mortgages or contracts for deferred payments for the sale of water rights.

## ARTICLE XVIII.
## GENERAL MANAGER AND CHIEF ENGINEER.

The Construction Company expressly agrees to appoint or elect a General Manager and Chief Engineer, satisfactory to the State Engineer, who shall have charge of the work to be done and performed by the Construction Company under this agreement, and to make such changes from time to time in such office as may be demanded by the State Engineer.

## ARTICLE XIX.
## AMENDMENTS.

This contract may be amended, altered, or added to by the mutual consent of the parties hereto at any time hereafter whenever, in the opinion of the said Desert Land Board, it appears expedient or proper, in view of the conditions then existing, that such amendments, alterations or changes should be made.

In witness whereof, the said Desert Land Board, acting for and on behalf of the State of Oregon, has caused this instrument to be executed by the Governor of said State as chairman of said Board, and attested under the seal of the secretary, and the said party of the second part has caused its name to be hereunto subscribed by its president, and its corporate seal affixed, attested by its secretary, the day and year first above written.

DESERT LAND BOARD OF OREGON.

(Signed)  JAMES WITHYCOMBE,

Governor and Chairman.

(Seal of State of Oregon)

Attest: JOHN H. LEWIS  (Signed),

Secretary.

JORDAN VALLEY LAND AND WATER
COMPANY,
(Signed)   By J. W. MANEY,
President.
(Corporate Seal)      FRANK B. CROSS,
Secretary.
Signed, sealed and delivered in the presence of:
(Signed)  OLIVER O. HAGA.   [132]

DESERT LAND BOARD.

State of Oklahoma,
County of Oklahoma,—ss.

On this 21st day of June, 1918, before me, appeared J. W. Maney, to me personally known, who, being duly sworn, did say that he is the President of Jordan Valley Land and Water Company, the corporation that executed the within instrument, and that the seal affixed to said instrument is the corporate seal of said corporation, and that said instrument was signed and sealed in behalf of said corporation by authority of its Board of Directors; and said W. J. Maney acknowledged said instrument to be the free act and deed of said corporation.

In Testimony Whereof, I have hereunto set my hand and affixed my official seal, this the day and year first in my certificate written.

[Notarial Seal]    WILLIS G. SHIELDS,
Notary Public for Oklahoma County, Residing at
301 Am. N. Bank, Oklahoma City, Okla.

My commission expires the 1st day of March, 1920.  [133]

State of Oregon,
County of Marion,—ss.

I, Percy A. Cupper, State Engineer and Secretary of the Desert Land Board of Oregon, do hereby certify that the above and foregoing copy of that certain agreement entered into on June 21, 1918, by and between the Jordan Valley Land and Water Company, and the Desert Land Board of Oregon, providing for the construction of the irrigation system for the reclamation of the lands included within the Jordan Valley Irrigation Project, is a full, true and correct copy of the original as the same appears in the records of my office and in my custody and of the whole thereof.

In Witness Whereof, I have hereunto set my hand this 14th day of June, 1923.

PERCY A. CUPPER,
State Engineer, Secretary.
By (Signed) J. L. McALLISTER.
J. L. McALLISTER,
Assistant Secretary. [134]

## PLAINTIFF'S EXHIBIT No 17.

Bond Dated August 17, 1918, Executed by the Jordan Valley Land & Water Company as Principal and the American Surety Company of New York as Surety.

KNOW ALL MEN BY THESE PRESENTS, That the Jordan Valley Land and Water Company, a corporation organized under the laws of Nevada and doing business in the State of Oregon, as principal, and American Surety Company of New York, a corporation formed and organized under the laws of the State of New York and authorized to transact the surety business in the State of Oregon, as surety, are held and firmly bound to the State of Oregon in the full penal sum of one hundred thousand ($100,000.00) dollars, for the payment of which well and truly to be made, we hereby bind ourselves, our successors and assigns, jointly and severally, firmly by these presents.

Signed, sealed and dated this 17th day of August, 1918.

THE CONDITIONS OF THIS OBLIGATION ARE SUCH THAT:

WHEREAS, the above bounden principal has entered into an agreement with the Desert Land Board, acting for and on behalf of the State of Oregon, dated June 21, 1918, providing for the construction by said principal of an irrigation system, reservoirs, canals, flumes and other irrigation works and structures therein more particularly described, for what is known as the Jordan Valley Irrigation Project in Malheur County, Oregon, which contract is hereby made a part hereof as fully as if set forth at length herein.

NOW, THEREFORE, if the said principal shall faithfully perform and discharge each and every of the conditions of said contract, by said principal to be kept and performed, as therein set forth and described, and shall comply with all of the terms and  conditions thereof and shall not permit any lien or claim to be filed or prosecuted against said irrigation system, reservoirs, canals, flumes and other irrigation works and structures, and shall promptly make payments to all persons supplying it

No. ———. Plffs. Ex. 17. [135]

U. S. District Court, District of Oregon. Filed June 12, 1923. G. H. Marsh, Clerk.

with labor or materials for any prosecution of the work provided for in said contract, this obligation shall be null and void, otherwise to remain in full force and effect.

IN WITNESS WHEREOF, the said principal and the said surety have caused this instrument to be executed by its officers thereunto duly authorized on the day first above written.

JORDAN VALLEY LAND & WATER CO.

(Seal)        By HERBERT G. WELLS,
                                    Vice-President.

(Seal)        Attest: FRANK B. CROSS,
                                    Secretary.

AMERICAN SURETY CO. OF NEW YORK.

By HOMER H. SMITH,
            Resident Vice-President.

Attest: CAREY F. MARTIN,
            Resident Asst. Secretary.

HOMER H. SMITH,
                                    Agent.

No. ———. Plffs. 17.

U. S. District Court, District of Oregon. Filed June 12, 1923. G. H. Marsh, Clerk. [136]

PLAINTIFF'S EXHIBIT No. 18.

Contract Dated November 17, 1919, Between Jordan Valley Land & Water Company and Wells Brothers.

U. S. District Court, District of Oregon.    Filed June 12, 1923.    G. H. Marsh, Clerk.

## JORDAN VALLEY LAND & WATER COMPANY.

### CONTRACT AND SPECIFICATIONS
for
### LOWER UNIT MAIN CANAL TO STATION
286+00.

THIS AGREEMENT, Made this 17th day of November, A. D. 1919, by and between the JORDAN VALLEY LAND & WATER COMPANY, a corporation, organized under the laws of the State of Nevada, and doing business in the State of Oregon, party of the first part, hereinafter called "the Company," and WELLS BROTHERS, a copartnership consisting of H. G. Wells and E. I. Wells, of Boise, Idaho, party of the second part, hereinafter called "The CONTRACTOR," WITNESSETH:

That the Contractor, in consideration of the payments to be made and the promises to be performed by the Company as hereinafter specified, hereby covenants and agrees to furnish all materials and labor except as hereafter particularly excepted, and to execute, construct, and finish in compliance with the contract between the Desert Land Board of the

State of Oregon dated June 21, 1918, and in compliance with the detailed plans mentioned hereafter and the specifications, and in a most substantial and workmanlike manner and to the satisfaction and acceptance of the Engineer, the following work and construction, to wit:

The construction of the Lower Unit Main Canal, Jordan Valley Project, from the diversion dam on Jordan Creek to the entrance transition of the flume across Jordan Creek, and from the outlet transition of said flume to Station 286+00 of the line now located and staked upon the ground, this work to include all grading, culverts, bridges and wasteways along the line of said canal, the flume crossing of Jordan Creek being specifically excluded.

The Plans for this Improvement consist of one sheet, entitled, "PROFILE OF LOWER UNIT MAIN CANAL," which, duly dated and identified by the signatures of both parties hereto, is hereby made a part of this contract and mutually cooperative therewith. It is understood that the profile shall later be supplemented by detailed plans of bridges, culverts, and other necessary structures which are to be built under this contract, the cost of which is covered by the unit prices for various classes of work herein stated.

IT IS MUTUALLY AGREED AS FOLLOWS BETWEEN THE PARTIES TO THIS CONTRACT:

GENERAL STIPULATIONS.

Company.

1. Whenever the word "Company" occurs in these specifications [137] the term shall specify

the Jordan Valley Land & Water Company, or its authorized officers.

Engineer.

2. Wherever the term "Engineer" occurs in these specifications, the term shall signify the Chief Engineer of the Jordan Valley Land &Water Company, said Engineer acting either directly or through an authorized assistant, whose instructions and decisions shall be limited by the particular duties entrusted to him.

Contractor.

3. Wherever the word "Contractor" occurs in these specifications, the term shall signify the party or parties contracting to perform the work contemplated under these plans and specifications as party of the second part.

Arbitrament.

4. The Engineer shall decide all questions which may arise between the parties hereto relative to the true intent and meaning of any of the provisions or stipulations contained in this agreement, or the amount or quantities, quality, character and classification of the work performed by the Contractor under this contract, and his decision in the nature of an award shall be final and binding upon both parties to this agreement.

Laying Out of Work.

5. The Contractor shall give forty-eight (48) hours' notice in writing, when he shall require the services of the Engineer for laying out any portion of the work under this Improvement. He shall furnish a man to assist in giving lines and

levels under the direction of the Engineer. He shall carefully preserve all stakes when set, together with all benchmarks or monuments existing along the lines of this Improvement. And in case any of them have to be replaced, unnecessarily, by the Engineer, the Contractor shall be charged the expense thereof and the same may be deducted from his estimate.

Inspection.

6. The Contractor shall not begin work on any portion of this Improvement without notifying the Engineer of his intention to do so. If an Inspector is placed in charge of the work, it is understood that he is the representative of the Engineer and it shall be his duties to direct the construcion of the work and the manner of carrying on the same, within the limitations of these specifications; also to inspect all materials used on the work and to accept or reject the same. No materials of any kind shall be used on any part of this Improvement until they have been inspected and approved by the Engineer or Inspector. All rejected material of whatever kind shall be removed from this Improvement by the Contractor within twenty-four (24) hours after its rejection, and shall not be used on this Improvement. Instructions given by the Inspector shall be respected and executed by the Contractor, but no Inspector shall have the power to waive the obligations resting upon the Contractor to furnish good material or do good work, as herein prescribed. Any omission to condemn any work at the time of its construction

shall not be construed as an acceptance of any defective work, but the Contractor shall at any time
prior to final acceptance, upon notice from the
Engineer to do so, tear out, remove, and properly
reconstruct, at his own cost, any portion of the
Improvement which the Engineer may decide defective; and the Contractor will be held wholly
responsible for the safety, proper construction and
sufficiency of the entire Improvement until the
same has been finally accepted by the Company.
Orders Given Contractor.

7. The Contractor shall have an authorized
representative on the ground and in charge of the
work, and when the Contractor himself is not present, orders will be given to such representative,
[138] or to superintendents, or overseers in immediate charge, and shall by them be received
and obeyed. If any person employed on the work
shall refuse or neglect to obey the instructions of
the Engineer in any way relating to the work, or
shall appear to the Engineer to be incompetent,
disorderly, or unfaithful, he shall, upon written
request of the Engineer, be at once discharged and
not again employed on any part of the work.
Sub-contracts.

8. Sub-contractors employed upon this work
shall in all cases be considered merely as foremen
employed by the Contractor, and liable to be ordered discharged by the Engineer for incompetency,
neglect of duty, or misconduct.
Change in Plans.

9. It is understood and agreed that the Com-

pany shall have the right to make such changes in the amount, dimensions or character of the work to be done as the emergency may demand, or as in the opinion of the Engineer the interest of the work may require. If any such changes or alterations shall diminish the quantity of the work to be done, they shall constitute a claim for damages for anticipated profits on the work that may be so dispensed with. If they increase the amount of the work to be done, such increase shall be paid for according to the quantity actually done and at the price established for similar work under this contract.

Prosecution of Work.

10. The work embraced in this Improvement is to be completed in all respects, ready for operation under fully capacity on or before May 1, 1920, unless the work be delayed by the party of the first part due to insufficiency of funds or other causes, in which case an extension of time shall be given as provided in Section 12.

Taking Over Work.

11. If, in the opinion of the Engineer, the Contractor is using defective material or improperly performing the work, and shall refuse to take up or reconstruct such work at his own cost, as shall have been rejected by the Engineer as defective or unsuitable, then the Engineer may order all work suspended and any work performed after such time of suspension shall not be accepted, and if the Contractor refuses to take up or reconstruct such defective work within twenty-four hours after no-

tice from the Engineer has been given to do so, then it shall be lawful for the Company to reconstruct at the expense of the Contractor such defective work and do all things necessary to that end, and to deduct the cost thereof from the unpaid part of the contract price to be paid to the contractor.

If it shall appear to the Engineer that the work to be done under this agreement has been abandoned or that the said work is unnecessarily delayed and will not be finished within the prescribed time, he shall so certify in writing to the Company, and the Company shall have the power to notify the Contractor to discontinue all work or any part thereof under this contract, and thereupon the Contractor shall discontinue said work and the Company shall thereupon have the power, by contract or otherwise, as it may determine, to employ such persons and to use such implements, tools, or materials of every description as may be found along the line of the work, and to purchase or obtain such additional implements, tools, and materials as they may deem necessary to complete the work, and charge the expense of all labor and material necessary for such completion to the Contractor. And the expense so charged will be deducted and paid by the Company out of such money as may then be due or may afterwards become due to the said Contractor under and by virtue of the contract for this improvement, and in case such expense is less than the sum [139] which would have been payable under said contract if the same had been fulfilled by the Contractor, then the Contractor shall be entitled to receive the difference, and in case such expense is greater, the Contractor shall pay the Company the amount of such excess so due, and his bond shall answer and be liable therefor.

Suspension of Work.

12. The Company reserves the right to suspend operations on the work or any part or parts thereof, temporarily. In the event of such temporary suspension, the Company shall give the Contractor five (5) days' written notice thereof, and the date for the completion of the contract shall
· be extended for a period of time equal to said temporary suspension period. The Contractor being familiar with the financial affairs of the Company and its method of financing this Improvement, it is understood and agreed that whenever the Company considers it advisable to diminish work or to cease work entirely, temporarily, by reason of lack of money immediately available for the payments of estimates for work and materials, it shall have the right to so instruct the Contractor, but in the event the Contractor sees fit to carry on the work at his own expense and risk, he shall be allowed so to do, and in case the Company does so instruct the Contractor to diminish or cease work temporarily, it shall serve automatically to extend the time of completion of the contract proportionately as such instructions shall provide.

Right of Way.

13. It is understood and agreed that the Company will provide the necessary right-of-way for

the work. The Contractor shall confine his operations to this right-of-way, and shall be liable for damages from trespassing outside of the right-of-way limits.

Contractor's Risk.

14. It is understood that the whole of the work to be performed under the contract for this improvement is to be done at the Contractor's risk, and that he is to assume the responsibility and risk of all loss or damage to materials or work which may arise from any cause whatsoever prior to final acceptance by the Company.

State Laws.

15. The Contractor agrees to follow and be governed by the laws of the State of Oregon covering the employment of labor, the payment of claims and cancellation of contract in so far as they apply to the work undertaken.

Damage Claims.

16. The Contractor agrees to indemnify and hold harmless the Company from any and all claims for damages of every nature and description arising from or through the operation of the Contractor or those in his employ, including all sub-contractors, including all claims for death or injury to persons and for injury or damage to the property or right of any person or persons or corporations, either municipal or private, and including any fines or penalties that may result or be imposed by any municipal authority as a result of the prosecution of the work under said contract, and the Contractor further agrees to indemnify and save the

Company harmless from any claim of the State or other authority for fees, compensation or industrial insurance for workmen injured or killed in connection with the prosecution of the work called for by this contract. And in the event of the failure of the Contractor to promptly secure a valid release of any and all such claims within such time as the Company may determine reasonable, then the Company may be and it is hereby empowered to settle or compromise such claims as best it can and charge the cost thereof to the Contractor as so much paid on this contract, provided, however, that if upon the completion of the work called for by the contract, any such claims are pending and unsettled, irrespective [140] of whether they are in litigation or not, the Contractor shall be privileged to furnish to the Company a surety bond covering the full amount of said claims, executed by a responsible surety company authorized to transact a general surety business in the State of Oregon for the purpose of indemnifying the Company from such claims, and thereupon the Company shall release and pay to the Contractor all moneys withheld as a protection against such claims, but such bond shall not operate to release the Contractor from the primary obligation in this paragraph of this contract.

Fees and Royalties.

17. All fees and royalties for any patented invention, device, article, or arrangement that may be used upon or be connected with the work, or any part of the work comprehended by these specifica-

tions, shall be paid by the Contractor. The Contractor shall and must protect and hold harmless the Company from any and all such claims, demands, damages, costs, disbursements, actions and proceedings arising or resulting from the use of any patented device, article or arrangement.

Contractor's Bills.

18. Before making said final or any other payment, the Company may pay for and charge to the Contractor all unpaid bills for labor, supplies, material, outfit, machinery, appliances and expenses incurred on account of said work, and sums so paid shall be deducted from amounts earned by the Contractor on the work, and if such payments exceed the earnings of the Contractor on the work, the Company shall recover such excess from the Contractor, and his bond shall be liable therefor.

Release.

19. As a condition to the final payment to the Contractor, he will execute and deliver to the Company in substance and form as submitted by it, full release from all liens, claims, and demands against the Company, growing out of or connected with the contract.

In case it is desirable to release the Contractor upon completion of the work under this contract, and there still be outstanding unsettled or disputed claims for labor or material, the Company may in its discretion allow the Contractor to furnish a guarantee and surety bond ample in amount to cover all outstanding claims or bills which may become a lien against the property. This provision shall, however, in no way waive the primary obligation of this contract.

Payments.

20. In consideration of the faithful performance of all the covenants, stipulations, and agreements in this contract to be kept and performed by said Contractor, the Company hereby covenants and agrees to pay the Contractor in accordance with the following schedule of prices :

1. For solid lava rock, designated as Class A, Two Dollars ($2.00) per cubic yard.

2. For all other excavated materials, designated as Class B, fifty cents ($.50) per cubic yard.

3. Clearing, grubbing, and burning right of way, Ten Dollars per acre. ($10.00.)

4. Re-inforced concrete masonry in place, 1: 2: 4: mixture, reinforcement to be furnished by Company, Twenty-eight Dollars ($28.00) per cubic yard. [141]

5. Concrete masonry in place, 1: 2½: 5 or leaner mixture, Twenty-five Dollars ($25.00) per cubic yard.

6. Rubble stone masonry in place, Fifteen Dollars ($15.00) per cubic yard.

7. Lumber in place for highway bridges, including fastenings, One Hundred and Ten Dollars ($110.00) per thousand feet board measure.

8. Dry paving or revetment along canal banks, One Dollar and Twenty-five ($1.25) per square yard.

9. For overhaul in excess a 200-foot free haul

limit, three cents ($.03) per cubic yard per station of 100 feet.

10. For backfilling around structures, Seventy-five cents ($.75) per cubic yard.

On or about the end of each calendar month the Engineer shall make an estimate of all material furnished or work done by the Contractor during the previous month, and the Company agrees to pay to the Contractor not later than the fifteenth (15th) day of the month succeeding the month in which the work was done, ninety (90%) per cent of the amount of said estimate, retaining the remaining ten (10%) per cent thereof until the works contemplated under the contract between the Desert Land Board of the State of Oregon and the Jordan Valley Land and Water Company, hereinbefore mentioned, be fully completed and finally accepted by the State Engineer of Oregon.

PROVIDED, however, that if approval in writing by the State Engineer, the provision for retaining ten (10%) per cent of said estimates until acceptance of the project may be waived, and this amount paid unto the Contractor upon completion and acceptance of the work called for under this contract.

Revision of Estimates.

21. No estimate under this contract (except final estimate mentioned above) shall be construed or considered as final or conclusive against the Company in respect to the amount of work done or material furnished, or compensation to be allowed therefor or payments made, but all such estimates

made before the final payment shall be construed and considered only as being altogether provisional, and same shall be subject to revision and adjustment, readjustment and correction by the Engineer for the Company, for errors or mistakes as to the determination of the amount of work done or material furnished under this contract, or amounts paid or the amount of work unfinished, or the amounts of material unfinished, or as to any other matter or thing connected therewith, and the values thereof, respectively, as well as the amount of compensation therefor, having reference to the uncompleted part of said work or the unfinished part of said material, as well as the work done or the material furnished.

Any omission to disapprove of work at the time of making any monthly or other estimate, shall not be construed as an acceptance of any defective work, and the Contractor at his own cost must remove and rebuild or make good any work which the Engineer may consider defectively executed.

Extra Work.

22. Any work necessary or incident to the carrying out of the work herein contracted, but which is clearly not indicated [142] in the plans and specifications nor covered by the intent and meaning of this agreement, and which cannot be classified and paid for under the unit prices agreed to, but which may be advantageously furnished or performed by the Contractor, shall be designated as "Extra Work" and shall be paid for by contract specially made or at actual cost of said work, as

determined by the Engineer's acount of material and labor, plus ten (10%) per cent for the Contractor's supervision, use of tools and equipment, and for profit. Extra work shall be performed or supplied by the Contractor only upon written order of the Engineer and all claims and demands for extra work must be presented to the Company by the Contractor for settlement before the fifth day of the month next succeeding the month in which the work is performed, and must be accompanied by the written order of the Engineer to do such extra work. Should the Contractor fail to do this, he will be considered as having abandoned his claim to extra compensation therefor.

## SPECIFICATIONS.

Canal Sections.

23. The canal sections are shown in the drawings, but the undetermined stability of the material that will form the canal banks may make it desirable during the progress of the work to vary the slopes and dimensions dependent thereon. Increase or decrease of quantities excavated as a result of such changes shall be covered in the estimates, and shall not otherwise affect the payments due to the Contractor.

The canal shall be excavated to the full depth and width required and must be finished to the prescribed lines and grades in a workmanlike manner. Runways shall not be cut into canal slopes below the proposed water level. Earth slopes shall be neatly finished with scrapers or similar appliances. Rock bottoms and banks must show no points of rock projecting more than 0.3 foot into the pre-scribed section. Above the water lines the rock will be allowed to stand at its deepest safe angle and no finishing will be required other than the removal of rock masses that are loose and liable to fall. Payment for excavation of canals will be made to the neat lines only as shown in the drawings or as established by the Engineer.

It is desired that the Contractor or his repre-sentative be present during the measurement of the material excavated. On written request of the Contractor, made by him within ten days after the receipt of any monthly estimate, a statement of the quantities and classifications between suc-cessive stations included in said estimate will be furnished him within ten days after the receipt of such request. This statement will be considered as satisfactory to the Contractor unless he files with the Engineer, in writing, specific objections thereto, with reasons therefor, within ten days after re-ceipt of said statement by the Contractor or his representative on the work. Failure to file such written objection with reason therefor within ten days shall be considered a waiver of all claims based on alleged erroneous estimate of quantities or in-correct classification of materials for the work covered by such statement.

Classification of Excavation.

24. All materials moved in the excavation of canals and for structures, and in the construction of embankments, will be measured in excavation only, to the neat lines shown in the drawings or

prescribed by the Engineer, and will be classified for payment as follows: [143]

Class A.   Solid ledge rock of a volcanic nature commonly called lava rock, or detached boulders of the same rock exceeding ten cubic feet in volume. This classification shall not include cemented gravel, hard pan, tufa, or other materials or loose rock existing in boulders of less than ten cubic feet, even though the methods of excavating and handling such material be the same as for lava rock.

Class B.   All material not included under Class A.

Preparation of Surfaces.

25.   The ground under all embankments that are to sustain water pressure, and the surface of all excavation that is to be used for embankments, shall be cleared of trees, brush, vegetable matter of every kind. The roots shall be grubbed and burned with other combustible materials that have been removed. The surface of the ground under the entire embankment shall be scored with a plow making open furrows not less than eight inches deep below the natural ground surface at intervals of not more than three feet. The cost of all work described in this paragraph shall be included in the unit prices bid for excavation.

Construction of Embankments.

26.   Embankments built with teams and scrapers or with dump wagons shall be made in layers not exceeding twelve inches in thickness and kept as level as practicable. The travel over the embankments during construction shall be so diverted as

to distribute the compacting effect to the best advantage. Any additional compacting required over that produced by ordinary travel in distributing the material will be ordered in writing and paid for as extra work under the provisions of paragraph 21. Embankments shall be built to the height designated by the Engineer to allow for settlement, and shall be leveled on top to a regular grade.

No embankments shall be made from frozen materials nor on frozen surfaces. Should the Engineer direct that unsuitable material be excavated and removed from the site of any embankment, the material thus excavated shall be paid for as excavation. When canal excavation precedes the building of structures, openings shall be left in the embankments at the site of these structures, and except when the construction of the structures is included in the contract, the Contractor will not be required to complete such omitted embankments. The cost of all work described in this paragraph, except as herein specified, shall be included in the prices bid for excavation.

Disposal of Materials.

27. All suitable materials excavated in the construction of canals and structures, or so much thereof as may be needed, shall be used in the construction of embankments and in backfilling around structures. When the canal is on sloping ground, all materials taken from the excavation shall be deposited on the lower side of the canal, unless otherwise shown in the drawings or directed

by the Engineer. When the canal is on level or nearly level ground, the material from the excavation shall be deposited in embankments on both sides to form the top portions of the waterway.

If there is an excess of material in excavation, it shall be used to strengthen the embankment on either side of the canal as may be directed by the Engineer. Material taken from cuts that is not suitable for embankments construction and surplus material may be wasted on the right of way owned by the Company, at such points as may be approved by the Engineer. Unless otherwise shown in the drawings or directed by the Engineer, no material shall be wasted in drainage channels, nor within six (6) feet of the edge   [144]   of the prescribed or actual canal cut. On side-hill locations all material wasted shall be placed on the lower side of the canal unless specific written authority is obtained from the Engineer to waste such material elsewhere. Waste banks shall be left with reasonably even and regular surfaces. Whenever directed by the Engineer, materials found in the excavation, such as sand, gravel, or stone that are suitable for use in structures or that are otherwise required for special purposes, shall be preserved and laid aside in some convenient place designated by him. Borrow Pits.

28. Where the canal excavation at any section does not furnish sufficient suitable material for embankments, the Engineer will designate where additional material shall be procured. Unless otherwise shown in the drawings or directed by

the Engineer, a berm of fifteen (15) feet shall be left between the outside toe of the embankment and the edge of the borrow pit, with provision for a side slope of 1½: 1 to the bottom of the borrow pit. Borrowed material will be measured in excavation only, and unless the Engineer gives the Contractor specific written orders to excavate other than Class B material from borrow pits, all material obtained from this source will be paid for at the unit price bid for Class B excavation, regardless of its actual character. Payment for excavation from borrow pits will be made for only such quantities as are required for embankments or backfilling, or such as by direction of the Engineer are excavated and wasted or laid aside.

Overhaul.

29. All material taken from the excavation and required for embankment or for other purposes shall be placed as directed by the Engineer. The limit of free haul will be 200 feet. Necessary haul over 200 feet will be paid for at the price bid per cubic yard per hundred feet additional haul, but no allowance will be made for overhaul is specifically ordered in writing by the Engineer. Where material is taken from borrow pits, the length of the haul will be measured along the shortest practicable route between the center of gravity of material as found in excavation and the center of gravity of material as deposited in each station. Where the material is taken from canal excavation, the length of the haul shall be understood to mean the distance measured along the center line of

the canal from the center of gravity of the material as found in excavation to the center of gravity of the material as required to be deposited.

Surface and Berm Ditches.

30. If, in the judgment of the Engineer, it should be necessary to construct the surface and berm drainage ditches along the lines of the canal, the Contractor shall perform such work and the excavation will be paid for at the unit prices bid in the schedules covering the excavation of the canal along which such surface and berm ditches are built.

Excavation for Structures.

31. Unless otherwise shown in the drawings, excavation for structures will be measured for payment to lines 1 foot outside of the foundation of the structures, and to slopes of 1: 1, provided that, where the character of the material cut into is such that it can be trimmed to the required lines of the concrete structure and the concrete placed against the sides of the excavation without    [145] the use of intervening forms, payment for excavation will not be made outside of the required limits of the concrete.

Backfilling.

32. The Contractor shall place and shall compact thoroughly all backfilling around structures. The compacting must be equivalent to that obtained by the tramping of well distributed scraper teams depositing the materials in layers not exceeding six inches thick when compacted. The material used for this purpose, the amount thereof and the

manner of depositing the same must be satisfactory to the Engineer. So far as practicable, the material moved in excavating for structures shall be used for backfilling, but when sufficient suitable material is not available from this source, additional material shall be obtained from borrow pits selected by the Engineer. Payment for backfilling will be made at the price per cubic yard bid therefor in the schedule.

Puddling.

33. Backfilling and embankment around structures within ten (10) feet of the structure shall be made with material approved by the Engineer, and where practicable, shall consist of sand and gravel with an admixture of clay equal to one-fourth to one-half the volume of the sand and gravel. The material shall be deposited in water of such depth as is approved by the Engineer unless the quantity of clay predominates, in which case the Engineer may in his discretion order the material deposited in layers of six inches or less, and compacted by tamping or rolling with the smallest quantity of water that will insure consolidation. Work of this character will be paid for as "Extra Work."

Blasting.

34. Any blasting that will probably injure the work will not be permitted, and any damage done to the work by blasting shall be repaired by the Contractor at his expense.

Concrete.

35. The order of erection of the concrete struc-

tures covered by this contract will be subject to
the approval of the Engineer. All concrete structures shall be carefully finished to the lines and
dimensions prescribed by the Engineer. The dimensions of each structure shown in the drawings
will be subject to such changes as may be found
necessary to adapt such structure to the conditions disclosed by the excavation for the same.

Concrete will in general be mixed in the proportions of 1 cubic foot (94 pounds) Portland Cement,
two cubic feet sand, and four cubic feet gravel
or crushed rock for reinforced work or thin wall
sections, and in the proportions of 1 cubic foot (94
pounds) Portland Cement, two and one-half cubic
feet sand and five cubic feet gravel or crushed
rock for heavier wall sections. The exact proportions shall be designated by the Engineer for each
particular case.

Reinforcing materials, guide angles and other
accessories will be furnished by the Company and
placed by the Contractor without extra charge.
Gates and hoists will be furnished by the Company
and placed by the Contractor under the provisions
for "Extra Work."

Concrete Materials.

36. All cement shall be of a brand approved
by the [146] Engineer, and must conform to the
latest standard specifications of the American Society for Testing Materials.

The fine aggregate shall consist of clean, hard,
sharp, silicious material and shall contain no organic
material and not more than five (5%) per cent by

weight of clay or loam or other foreign materials. The grains shall be well graded and of such size that all will pass a one-quarter mesh and not more than twenty (20%) per cent will pass a fifty mesh screen.

The coarse aggregate may consist of either broken stone or gravel. Individual stones must be clean, hard and tough, and free from dust and dirt or adhering scum or clay material. Coarse aggregate shall range in size from one-quarter inch up to one and one-half inches.

The Jordan Creek gravel, taken from the bed of the stream near the Ruby ranch or equal may be used as an aggregate, provided that if the proportions of fine and coarse are not satisfactory to give a mixture of maximum density, screening may be required.

For mixing concrete, the water shall be reasonably clean and free from organic matter, alkali or salts. Jordan Creek water may be used.

Concrete Forms.

37. Forms shall be constructed of sound lumber surfaced on one side and accurately built to lines and elevations shown upon the plans. Forms shall be rigidly nailed and braced and if after concrete has been placed, they show signs of bulging or sagging, that portion of the concrete shall be immediately removed on notice from the Engineer and rebuilt only after the forms have been properly supported. Forms shall be thoroughly tight to prevent leakage. All shavings and debris shall be removed and the forms thoroughly wetted before placing concrete against them.

Mixing and Placing Concrete.

38.   Concrete may be mixed either in a mechanical batch mixer or by hand on a level, water-tight platform.  If mixed by hand, the materials must be turned over at least twice dry and twice after wetting.  The method, consistency and sufficiency of mixing shall be subject to the approval of the Engineer.  If concrete is laid in freezing weather the material shall be heated and the work protected in such a manner that the temperature does not fall below 32 degrees for 72 hours after placing. All concrete shall be mixed in the dry, excavations being kept pumped out until the mixture has taken its final set.  Concrete shall be carefully deposited in such a manner that there is no separation of the stone and mortar.  As fast as deposited it shall be carefully spaded to remove air pockets and bring the mortar in thorough contact with the forms. Removal of Forms.

39.   Forms shall be removed as soon as the Engineer has decided that it is safe to do so, form wires slipped off beneath the surface, and all crevices and pockets neatly pointed off with a stiff mortar compound of one part cement to two parts sand.  Exposed surfaces shall be protected from the direct rays of the sun by a covering of canvas or earth, and kept continuously wet for a period of one week after placing the same.  [147] Rubble Masonry.

40.   Where masonry is called for it shall be rubble masonry, laid in cement mortar.  No stone shall be less than six (6) inches in thickness or

less than twelve (12) inches in its least horizontal dimension. In general one and two man stone (stones weighing from 60# to 200#) shall be used. Beds shall be prepared for all stones and mortar sufficient to fill all joints poured on the bed before the stone is placed. The stones shall be pushed into the mortar and worked into place with a firm bearing eliminating all pockets or openings. The spaces between stones shall be rammed full of concrete. Grouting of joints after stones are in place will not be allowed. Stones shall be so arranged in the wall as to give thorough bond in all directions, and no single stone shall extend for more than one-third of the thickness of the wall.

Faces of masonry walls shall not deviate more than three inches from the surface alignment. Joints shall be pointed to full and flush surfaces.

The mortar shall, in general, be mixed in the proportion of one (1) part by weight of Portland Cement to five (5) parts of aggregate. The aggregate shall be a well graded sand and gravel as it is found in Jordan Creek. The proportions of fine and coarse in the aggregate shall be such as will give a maximum density, and if bank run material does not give the desired grading, screening may be required. The exact proportions for mortar in different parts of the work shall be fixed by the Engineer. The price bid for masonry shall include the cost of all materials and labor.

Stone.

41. The stone used for masonry shall be hard, dark, fine grained lava rock, free from cracks, seams,

or porous spots. Sound float rock, free from earth, clay or vegetable matter, may be used. Otherwise all stone used shall be quarried by methods which will not cause shattering or injury. Stone shall be of roughly rectangular shape, without irregular projections or feather edges, and capable of being laid up with a minimum use of spalls or fillers. If necessary, facing stones shall be rough dressed to plane surfaces.

Wooden Structures.

42. The order of erection of the wooden structures covered by this contract will be subject to the approval of the Engineer. The lumber used shall be #1 Common fir under the grading rules of the West Coast Lumber Manufacturers' Association or yellow western pine of equal quality. The dimensions of each structure shown in the drawings may be changed to better adapt such structure to the conditions disclosed by the excavation for the same. Matching and resurfacing will be required only as indicated in the drawings. Where double floor or double wall planking is shown, the boards or planks shall be so placed that the second layer will cover the longitudinal joints of the first layer. No splicing of sills, or posts, or of other main timbers, except as shown in the drawings, will be allowed. The ends of all timbers butting against other timbers shall be cut true to the required shape. All exposed ends of timbers, planks, and boards shall be sawed off squarely wherever directed by the Engineer. Braces, planks, boards, battens, etc., shall be well nailed or spiked to each

sill, post or other. support with wire nails or spikes of the size best adapted to the dimensions of the members that are to be fastened together. Standard washers shall be used under the heads and nuts of all bolts. All bolts, spikes, [148] nails and the like required in the erection of the wooden structures shall be furnished by the Contractor. The Contractor shall properly place and attach to each structure all accessories that are necessary for its completion for service. In making payment for lumber furnished and placed by the Contractor the rates named in the contract for the various kinds of lumber will be applied to the net amount of lumber in the completed structures estimated by the thousand F. B. M. to the required dimensions of the completed work.

Dry Paving.

43. Where shown in the drawings and where directed by the Engineer, dry paving shall be placed on the embankment slopes and on the beds and banks of canals and other water courses. The rock used for paving shall be clean, hard, dense, and durable. The dimension of paving stones normal to the face of the pavement shall be not less than 8 inches. They shall have an average volume of not less than ⅔ of a cubic foot, not more than twenty-five (25%) per cent of the pieces being less than ½ of a cubic foot in volume.

Either boulders or quarried rock may be used in fulfilling the requirements as to quality and dimensions. If quarried rock is used, the stones shall have roughly squared, reasonably flat upper faces. The stones shall be bedded in a layer of sand and gravel or unscreened crushed rock, having an average thickness of not less than six (6) inches. They shall be hand placed with closed joints to the lines and grades established by the Engineer and the spaces between the stones shall be filled with spalls and gravel or crushed rock. The thickness of the paving, including the gravel layer, shall be not less than 10 inches. Payment for dry paving will be made at the unit prices per square yard bid therefor in the schedules.

Grouted Paving.

44. Where shown in the drawings and where directed by the Engineer, grouted paving shall be placed on the embankment slopes and on the beds and banks of canals and other water courses. The rock used for paving shall be clean, hard, dense, and durable. The dimension of paving stones normal to the face of the pavement shall not be less than $\frac{2}{3}$ of a cubic foot, not more than twenty-five (25%) per cent of the pieces being less than $\frac{1}{2}$ of a cubic foot in volume. Either boulders or quarried rock may be used if fulfilling the requirements as to quality and dimensions. If quarried rock is used, the stones shall have roughly squared reasonably flat, upper faces. The stones shall be imbedded in a layer of sand and gravel or unscreened crushed rock, having an average thickness of not less than four (4) inches.

They shall be hand placed with close joints to the lines and grades established by the Engineer and the spaces between the stones shall be filled

with spalls and gravel or crushed rock, from which
the sand or fine material has been removed by
screening, after which a mortar, composed of three
parts sand and one part cement, shall be poured
into the voids so as to form a water-tight surface.
After the cement mortar has been added, the paving
shall be kept moist for forty-eight hours after the
cement has reached its permanent set. The thickness of paving including a gravel layer shall be not
less than eight (8) inches. Payment for grouted
paving will be made at the unit prices per square
yard bid therefor in the schedules.

Concrete Pipe.

45. Where pipe was shown upon the plans for
drainage [149] structures or turnouts it shall
be pre-moulded, wet-mix concrete pipe. Concrete
pipe shall be made of Portland Cement and first
class, clean aggregates which shall conform to the
requirements for concrete materials stated elsewhere in these Specifications. Concrete pipe shall
be moulded preferably in metal forms, shall be
thoroughly tamped and of uniform shape, free
from cracks, porous spots, or other defects. They
shall be cured by frequent sprinkling with water
for 28 days before using.

Concrete pipe shall have well thicknesses and
supporting strength in accordance with the following table. Strength tests will be made by the
methods prescribed in the specifications of the
American Society for Testing Materials, Number
C–4–14.

| Diameter | Thickness of Wall. | Strength Pounds Per Lineal Foot. |
|----------|--------------------|----------------------------------|
| 10″ | 1 ″ | 1000 |
| 12″ | 1¼″ | 1000 |
| 14″ | 1½″ | 1200 |
| 16″ | 1¾″ | 1500 |
| 18″ | 2 ″ | 1800 |
| 20″ | 2¼″ | 2200 |
| 24″ | 2¾″ | 2700 |
| 30″ | 3½″ | 3300 |

IN WITNESS WHEREOF, the parties hereto have caused this agreement to be executed the day and year first above written.

JORDAN VALLEY LAND & WATER COMPANY,

Party of the First Part.

By JOHN W. CUNNINGHAM,

Chief Engineer & General Manager.

WELLS BROTHERS,

Party of the Second Part.

By H. G. WELLS.

Signed in the presence of:

————————————.

————————————.

(Corporate Seal) Attest: FRANK B. CROSS,

Secretary. [150]

True and correct copies of all of the exhibits received in evidence on behalf of the defendant in the order in which they were received are as follows:

## DEFENDANT'S EXHIBIT "A."

Blue-print of Jordan Valley Irrigation District. [151]

## DEFENDANT'S EXHIBIT "B."

Contract Between Department of the Interior and the State of Oregon Under Which the Desert Land Under the Project was Segregated to the State for the Purpose of Reclamation. [152]

U. S. Land Office, Vale, Oregon. Filed Apr. 29, 1914, at 2 o'clock P. M. Bruce R. Kester, Register.

FORM 5. 27

## ARTICLES OF AGREEMENT.

Between

## ALEXANDER T. VOGELSANG.

Acting Secretary of the Interior, for and on Behalf of the United States of America,

and

## DESERT LAND BOARD.

For and on Behalf of the State of Oregon.

These articles of agreement, made and entered into this 23d day of April, A. D. 1918, by and between ALEXANDER T. VOGELSANG, Acting Secretary of the Interior, for and on behalf of the United States of America, party of the first part, and Desert Land Board, for and on behalf of the State of Oregon, party of the second part,

WITNESSETH, that in consideration of the stipulations and agreements hereinafter made, and of the fact that said State has, under the provisions of Section 4 of the Act of Congress approved August 18, 1894, of the Act of Congress approved

June 11, 1896, of the Act of Congress approved March 3, 1901, through J. T. Johnson, its proper officer, thereunto duly authorized, presented its proper application for certain lands situated within said State and alleged to be desert in character, and particularly described as follows, to wit:

Segregation List No. 24.

(Here add list of lands and total area.)

No. ——.    Defts. Ex. "B."    Ident. B.

In District Court, State of Oregon.    Filed June 1, 1923.    G. H. Marsh, Clerk.    [153]

("29 Pages Listing Lands by Forty-acre Tracts, totaling 29,199.46 acres, omitted here.")

and has filed a map of said lands, and exhibited a plan showing the mode by which it is proposed that said lands shall be irrigated and reclaimed, and the source of the water to be used for that purpose, the said party of the first part contracts and agrees, and, by and with the consent and approval of Woodrow Wilson, President thereof, hereby binds the United States of America to donate, grant and patent to said State, or its assigns, free from cost for survey or prirce, any particular tract or tracts of said lands, whenever an ample supply of water is actually furnished in a substantial ditch or canal, or by artesian wells or reservoirs to reclaim the same, in accordance with the provisions of said acts of Congress, and with the regulations issued thereunder, and with the terms of this contract, at any time within ten years from the date of the approval of the said map of the lands.

It is further understood that said State shall not
lease any of said lands or use or dispose of the same
in any way whatever, except to secure their reclamation, cultivation, and settlement; and that in selling
and disposing of them for that purpose the said
State may sell or dispose of not more than 160 acres
to any one person, and then only to *bona fide* settlers
who are citizens of the United States, or who have
declared their intention to become such citizens;
and it is distinctly understood and fully agreed
that all persons acquiring rights to said lands from
said State prior to the issuance of patent, as hereinafter mentioned, will take the same subject to all requirements of said acts of Congress and to the
terms of this contract, and shall show full compliance therewith before they shall have any claim
[154] against the United States for a patent to
said lands.

It is further understood and agreed that said
State shall have full power, right, and authority
to enact such laws, and from time to time make and
enter into such contracts and agreements, and to
create and assume such obligations in relation to
and concerning said lands as may be necessary
to induce and cause such irrigation and reclamation thereof as is required by this contract and the
said Acts of Congress; but no such law, contract,
or obligation shall in any way bind or obligate the
United States to do or perform any act not clearly
directed and set forth in this contract and said
acts of Congress and then only after the require-

ments of said acts, the regulations thereunder, and this contract have been fully complied with.

Neither the approval of said application, map, and plan, nor the segregation of said land by the Secretary of the Interior, nor anything in this contract, or in the said acts of Congress, shall be so construed as to give said State any interest whatever in any lands upon which, at the date of filing of the map and plan hereinbefore referred to, there may be an actual settlement by a *bona fide* settler, qualified under the public land laws to acquire title thereto.

It is further understood and agreed that as soon as an ample supply of water is actually furnished in a substantial ditch or canal, or by artesian wells or reservoirs, to reclaim a particular tract or tracts of said lands, the said State, or its assigns, may make proof thereunder and according to such rules and regulations as may be prescribed therefor by the Secretary of the Interior, and as soon as such proof shall have been examined and found to be satisfactory, patents shall issue to said State, or to its assigns, for the tracts included in said proof.

The said State shall, out of the money arising from [155] its disposal of said lands, first reimburse itself for any and all costs and expenditures incurred by it in irrigating and reclaiming said lands, or in assisting its assigns in so doing, and any surplus then remaining after the payment of the cost of such reclamation shall be held as a trust fund to be applied to the reclamation of other desert lands within said State.

This contract is executed in duplicate, one copy of which shall be placed of record and remain on file with the Commissioner of the General Land Office, and the other shall be placed of record and remain on file with the proper officer of said State, and it shall be the duty of said State to cause a copy thereof, together with a copy of all rules and regulations issued thereunder or under said Acts of Congress, to be spread upon the deed records of each of the counties in said State in which any of said lands shall be situated.

In testimony whereof, the said parties have hereunto set their hands, the day and year first above written.

[Seal] ALEXANDER T. VOGELSANG,
Acting Secretary of the Interior.
STATE OF OREGON.
By DESERT LAND BOARD.
By OSWALD WEST,
Governor, Chairman.
Attest: JOHN H. LEWIS,
State Engineer, Secretary.

### APPROVAL.

TO ALL TO WHOM THESE PRESENTS SHALL COME, GREETING:

Know ye that I, Woodrow Wilson, President of the United States of America, do hereby approve and ratify the attached contract and agreement, made and entered into on the 23d day of April, 1918, by and between ALEXANDER T. VOGELSANG, Acting Secretary of the Interior, for and on behalf of the United States, and Oswald West, for and on behalf of the State of Oregon, under Section 4 of the Act of Congress approved August 18, 1894, the act approved June 11, 1896, and the act approved March 3, 1901.

X.    WOODROW WILSON. [156]

State of Oregon,
County of Marion,—ss.

I, Percy A. Cupper, State Engineer and Secretary of the Desert Land Board of Oregon do hereby certify that the above and foregoing copy of the Articles of Agreement, between the Secretary of the Interior for and on behalf of the United States of America, and the Desert Land Board for and on behalf of the State of Oregon, entered into April 23, 1918, wherein the lands embraced in Oregon Carey Act Segregation List Number 24 were withdrawn from public entry and held for reclamation under the Jordan Valley Irrigation Project, is a full, true and correct copy of the original as the same appears in the records of my office and in my custody and of the whole thereof, save and except the description of the lands involved by forty acre tracts.

In Witness Whereof, I have hereunto set my hand this 14th day of June, 1923.

PERCY A. CUPPER,
State Engineer, Secretary.
By J. L. McALLISTER,
Assistant Secretary. [157]

## DEFENDANT'S EXHIBIT "C."

Rules and Regulations of the Desert Land Board
Pertaining to the Reclamation, Cultivation
and Settlement of Lands Withdrawn Under the
Carey Act.

No. ——. Defts. Ex. "C."

U. S. District Court, District of Oregon. Filed
June 12, 1923. G. H. Marsh, Clerk.

## RULES AND REGULATIONS
### of the
## DESERT LAND BOARD

Pertaining to the Reclamation of Lands Accepted
by the State Under the Provisions of the
Carey Act.

In order that those desiring to settle upon and
cultivate lands reclaimed under the provisions of
the Carey Act, may be advised as to the method
of procedure required by the Board, these rules
and regulations have been adopted by the Desert
Land Board, based upon its interpretation of
the Federal and State Laws and regulations of the
U. S. Department of the Interior.

Section 16, Chapter 226, Laws of Oregon for
1909 provides: "The Board shall provide suitable
rules for the filing of applications for constructing
irrigation works, prescribing the nature of final
surveys and the gathering of engineering data upon
which the contract with the State is to be based,
the manner in which the plans and specifications
shall be submitted, and for the entry and payment

for the land and water rights by settlers and for the settlement or forfeiting of entry by settlers, and such other rules and regulations as are necessary to carry out the provisions of this Act.''

In all cases the word company shall be construed to mean Board, in connection with the Tumalo Project. [158]

Policy of the Board.

Rule 1. It will be the policy of the Board to guard equally the interest of the State, of the intending settler, and of the company which has the contract for the construction of the canal system and colonization of the lands thereunder, and in referring to the several parties in these rules, the company that is building the system shall be referred to as the "construction company" or the "company," the intending settler as "entryman" or "settler" and the Desert Land Board of Oregon, as the "Board."

Meetings of the Board.

Rule 2. The Board shall hold a regular meeting on each Tuesday, and special meetings will be held at such times as may be found necessary for the proper transaction of business. All communications relative to the affairs of the Board should be addressed to John H. Lewis, Secretary of the Desert Land Board, Salem, Oregon.

Who May Enter.

Rule 3. The right to enter land under the Carey Act does not depend directly upon the general land laws of the United States; no entryman will, therefore, be disqualified for entering land under the provisions of this act by reason of his having previously exhausted his rights under the general land laws of the United States.

Application.

Rule 4. Application to the State for entry of land, and for the purchase of water right and release of lien from the company must be made to the company. This application and contract shall be executed in triplicate and forwarded by the company to the Board within 30 days after execution, for approval and endorsement by the Board, and without such endorsement shall be void. [159] The company shall, at the time of transmitting such application and contracts, also transmit to the Board any payments or deposits required by law, contract, or these rules, and no application shall be approved until such payment or deposit has been received. One copy of each application and contract shall be retained by the Board and the remaining copies returned to the company who shall deliver one copy to the applicant. No land will be considered entered until the settler's application has been received and approved by the Board and the entry noted on the records of the Board, at Salem.

Filing Fee for Proofs of Land in Segregation Lists 6 and 19.

Rule 5. A fee of 50 cents per acre shall be required of all settlers making application for lands embraced in Segregation Lists Nos. 6 and 19, from and after January 1, 1911, said payment of 50 cents per acre to accompany the proof papers of each settler, and no proof shall be acted upon by the Board until such payment has been received. This payment to be deposited in the reclamation fund provided by law.

Location.

Rule 6. All filings or entries of land shall be made according to legal subdivisions; and the legal subdivisions constituting a filing under a Carey Act project shall be contiguous. But when a tract is isolated and not contiguous to other land open to entry, such isolated tract, together with other land within the segregation, in all not to exceed 160 acres, may, with the approval of the company and the Board, be filed upon. And an entryman may also file upon land under the provisions of these rules upon two or more Carey Act projects in the State, the total amount so filed not to exceed 160 acres.

Entries in List No. 11.

Rule 7. When the lands within the Deschutes Land Company's [160] Segregation shall have been opened to entry or sale, they may be entered in non-contiguous tracts without reference to the distance between said tracts, or, one entryman may make several entries for said lands not to exceed a total area of 160 acres; provided that residence, cultivation and settlement for the entire area entered may be performed on any one or more of the said tracts.

State Law on Qualifications of Entryman; Payment.

Rule 8. Section 13, Chapter 226, Laws of Oregon for 1909, reads as follows: "Any citizen of the United States, or any person having declared his intention to become such, over the age of 21 years, may make application, under oath, to the Board, upon forms prescribed by it, to enter any of the lands reclaimed under the provisions of this act, in an amount not to exceed 160 acres for any one person. Each application shall be accompanied by a contract, made and entered into by the applicant with the person, association, or corporation which has undertaken the reclamation of the tract in question, which contract shall show that the applicant has made proper arrangement for the purchase of the necessary water right, and the release of the construction lien. Each application to the Board, shall in addition be accompanied by a payment of not less than one dollar ($1.00) per acre for each acre included in the application, which payment shall be made by the contractor out of the first payment by the applicant, and shall be deposited by the Board with the State Treasurer, who shall credit the same to the 'reclamation fund' herein created. If the application is not approved, the one dollar payment shall be returned to the contractor." Settlement.

Rule 9. The Carey Act grants certain lands to the State upon condition that the State shall cause such lands "to be irrigated, reclaimed, occupied, and not less than 20 acres of each  [161]  160 acre tract, cultivated by actual settlers, * * * as thoroughly as is required of citizens who may enter under said desert land law." The contract between the State and the United States provides that the "State shall not lease any of said lands or use or dispose of the same in any way whatever, except to secure their reclamation, cultivation and settlement."

Residence.

Rule 10. Actual settler is defined to mean a person in the actual occupancy of the land, with his family, if married, with the intention of making the same his residence and using the land as his home.

Settlement, Cultivation—Proof.

Rule 11. Within three years from the date of the settler's application for entry of land, he shall become an actual resident upon the land applied for, with his family, if married, and maintain such residence in accordance with the rules of the Board until he has made proof of reclamation, cultivation and settlement. In making proof, under this rule, actual residence for at least three consecutive months prior to and including date of proof will be required.

Within three years from the date of the settler's application, at least one-eighth of the irrigable land applied for shall be actually cultivated and irrigated.

Within three years from the date of the settler's application, he shall appear before any officer in the State authorized to administer oaths, and make proof of reclamation, cultivation and settlement, upon forms approved by the Board, supported by affidavits of two credible witnesses, and shall file such proof with the Secretary of the Desert Land Board at Salem, Oregon. Such proof may be made at any time after the required residence and cultivation and prior to the expiration of the three-year period, provided the settler [162] is actually residing upon the land at the time of making proof.

Alternative Rule for Settlement, Cultivation and Proof.

Rule 12. Provided that in lieu of the above requirement as to settlement and cultivation, any settler may make proof of reclamation, cultivation and settlement on the lands embraced in his application within three years from the date of such application upon submitting proof, on forms approved by the Board, that the land has been enclosed with a substantial fence, and not less than one-fourth of the irrigable land embraced in the application, nor less than one-eighth of the total area of the land applied for has been actually cultivated by clearing, plowing and planting to crops and irrigated in a substantial, workmanlike manner to raise ordinary agricultural crops; that a substantial house, fit for human habitation, having a total floor space of not less than 200 square feet has been built thereon; and that the settler, with his family, if married, has resided upon the land embraced in his application for a period of one week immediately prior to and including date of proof; and the settler shall appear before any officer of the State authorized to administer oaths, and make proof of reclamation, cultivation and settlement upon forms approved by the Board, supported by affidavit of two credible witnesses and file the same with the Secretary of the Desert Land Board, at Salem, Oregon, on or before the expiration of such three-year period. Such proof may be made at any time after the required residence and cultivation, and prior to the expiration of the three-year period, provided the settler is actually residing upon his land at the time of making proof.

Extensions of Time to Make Proof.

Rule 13. The Board may, for good cause shown, extend the time to make proof. Requests for such extension should be in writing, accompanied by affidavit setting forth facts upon which the request for extension of time is based. It will be the policy of [163] the Board to reject applications under this rule, except in cases of special merit.

Assignments.

Rule 14. Assignment of the application and contract may be made but the assignee shall possess all qualifications of an original entryman. Such assignment should be executed in triplicate and should be a complete and proper assignment of all the applicant's right, title and interest in and to the application, contract and release of lien, if issued, and to the land. One copy should be filed with the company and one copy with the Board, accompanied by the assignee's affidavit Form D, and the written consent of the company to the assignment.

The assignee shall make and complete all proofs required by these rules.

Certificate of Proof.

Rule 15. Upon receipt and approval by the Board of satisfactory proof of reclamation, cultivation and settlement, the Board shall direct the Secretary to issue a certificate (Form C) showing that satisfactory proof has been received and approved, and such certificate shall be forwarded to the settler, except that when deed is issued at the same time as the certificate, the certificate shall be filed in the Board's records and the deed forwarded to the settler.

Lien for Reclamation—Release of Lien.

Rule 16. As the object in withdrawing the land from the operation of the United States General Land Laws is primarily for the purpose of affording proper security for the capital invested in the construction of the works for reclaiming the same from its desert condition, no one shall enter any of such land until he has first entered into a contract with the construction company for the purchase of the necessary water rights. The law provides that the water rights purchased by the entryman shall, as soon as [164] title passes from the United States to the State, become appurtenant to the land, and that the person, association or company furnishing waer for the same shall have a prior lien on said water right and land upon which said water is used, for all deferred payments for said water rights. As soon as the settler has completed the payment to the company of the amount of lien, the company shall execute and deliver to the settler, a full release of their lien and within 30 days from the execution of such release shall file a duplicate of such release with the Board.

Deeds.

Rule 17. After the issuance of Certificate of Proof, as provided in Rule 15, and the filing of duplicate Release of Lien, as provided in Rule 16, the Board will issue a deed, conforming to the State Law as cited in Rule 8, to the person named in the certificate, or his heirs; provided, however, that no deed will be issued until after the lands described in the certificates have been patented to the State by the United States; and provided further, that in case certificate has been issued and forwarded to the settler, such certificate shall be returned and filed with the Board prior to the issuance of deed.

Rule 17a. Any contract holder on the Tumalo Project who has paid not less than one-third the full purchase price specified in his contract and has received proper certificate of proof of reclamation, cultivation and settlement for the lands held under said contract may, at his option, request the Board to issue deed for said lands, and, if patent of the lands has been issued to the State, the Board may, at its discretion, issue quitclaim deed for such lands, receiving back a first mortgage for the full amount of the lien price then remaining unpaid.

Forfeiture of Rights of Entryman.

Rule 18. The rights of entryman before the

Board shall be [165] subject to forfeiture to the State for the following causes:

(1) Failure to reside upon, cultivate and improve the land embraced within said entry as provided by law and these rules;

(2) Failure to submit satisfactory proof of reclamation, cultivation and settlement within the time specified in these rules;

(3) Failure to purchase the necessary water right or release of lien from the construction company.

Forms Approved.

Rule 19. The following forms for proof of reclamation, cultivation and settlement; certificate of proof; deed, and affidavit of assignee are the forms approved by the Board for their respective purposes, as follows:

> A—New proof form.
>
> C—Certificate of Proof.
>
> Deed.
>
> D—Affidavit of Assignee.

Blank copies of such approved forms can be obtained without charge by writing the Secretary, Desert Land Board, Salem, Oregon. [166]

## RULES AND REGULATIONS
### for
## OPERATING AND MAINTAINING
### TUMALO PROJECT.

For convenience the term "Board" in these rules is meant to represent the Desert Land Board and the State of Oregon.

Rule 1. The Board agrees to furnish and deliver 1.8 acre feet of water at or within one-half mile of each 40-acre tract between the tenth day of June and the twenty-eighth day of August of each year, and during the balance of the irrigation season, between April 15 and October 15, not included in the above dates, the Board agrees to deliver an additional amount of .45 acre feet, making a total of 2¼ acre feet per acre during the entire irrigation season; provided, however, that there shall be sufficient water flowing in Tumalo Creek and available in Tumalo Reservoir to supply all the land entitled to receive water with 2¼ acre feet. In case of any shortage under this amount the Board agrees to furnish the water *pro rata* among the water users. In case, however, that the share allotted each water user is less than 1.8 acre feet, preference shall be given to those contract holders holding form No. 60, Preferred Vested Water Rights, to the amount of 1.8 acre feet as per the terms of the adjudication.

Rule 2. The Board agrees to furnish and deliver the amount of water stipulated at the most practicable point to be reached by gravity flow from its main canal, ditches or laterals. Said point of delivery shall be ascertained and determined by the Project Engineer or Project Manager, but may be changed by the Board after being so established, the necessary expenses, however, caused by such change shall be paid by the Board. In case of a dispute between the Project Engineer or Manager and the settler as to the [167] proper point of delivery, the question shall be submitted to the State Engineer, whose decision shall be final.

Rule 3. The Board reserves the right and option on its part to deliver said water to any settler or settlers under the rotation system by giving the settler ten days' notice in writing of its intention to do so.

Rule 4. All necessary ditches, gates or measuring devices to be installed by the settler after the water has passed the point of delivery will, upon request, be installed by the Board, but the cost will be charged to the settler and must be paid by him.

Rule 5. The settler will be required to put at least one-eighth of the irrigable area of the land embraced under his contract under cultivation within three years from the date of his contract and make the necessary proof of such cultivation to the Board, and make settlement in accordance with the rules of the Board. In all cases the Water Superintendent shall be a witness to the proof submitted.

Rule 6. Water delivered to each settler may be used for stock, domestic and irrigation purposes only, and only on the lands described in each contract, and for no other purpose whatsoever. The Board will furnish water periodically when necessary and possible during such times outside the irrigation season for stock and domestic purposes. The Board will not be held responsible for any shortage of water for stock and domestic purposes during the non-irrigation season when it is impossible or impracticable to run water through the ditches.

Rule 7. The settler will be expected to use all of the water and allow none to run to waste and must provide proper drainage for all waste waters entering his land. Water may be shut off from any settler who deliberately wastes his water or does not put same to beneficial use. [168]

Rule 8. The contract holder or settler will not be allowed to disturb, pollute or cause to become impure the water in any flume, canal or lateral, or allow any act to be done which may cause same to become so.

Rule 9. The Board may when necessary shut the water off from its canals, laterals or ditches for the purpose of repairing same and may have such reasonable time as may be necessary in which to make such repairs and for such interruption of water supply, the Board will not be liable to the settler.

Rule 10. Until further notice is given, the settler will be expected to pay an annual maintenance fee of $1.00 per acre, which money shall be placed in the Tumalo Maintenance Fund and shall be used only for the operation and maintenance of the Tumalo Project. This maintenance fee shall be due and paid as follows: 50 cents per acre on or before the fifteenth day of April of each year, and 50 cents per acre on or before the fifteenth day of October of each year.

Rule 11. The Board, or its authorized representative, shall have the right to enter upon the premises owned by the settler for the purpose of repairing, constructing or maintaining any of its canals, flumes, laterals or ditches, and also for the purpose of constructing, operating and maintaining any portion of its irrigation system such as telephone system, etc.

Rule 12. A notice of at least twenty-four (24) hours from the time the change is desired should be given by the water users in order to change the 'amount of water received.

Rule 13. When a water user is delinquent more ,than six (6) months on account of his maintenance dues, the water may be turned off and the terms of the contract enforced.

Rule 14. These rules and regulations may be altered or changed from time to time as occasion may demand, but always with the approval of the Board. [169]

## DEFENDANT'S EXHIBIT "D."
Rules and Regulations of Department of the Interior Concerning the Reclamation of the Carey Act Lands.

No. ——. Defts. Ex. "D."

U. S. District Court, District of Oregon. Filed June 12, 1923. G. H. Marsh, Clerk.

## REGULATIONS.

1. Under the provisions of the acts quoted the states and territories are allowed ten years from the date of the approval of the application for the segregation of the land by the Secretary of the Interior, in which to irrigate and reclaim them.

The Secretary of the Interior may, however, in his discretion, extend the time for irrigating and reclaiming the lands for a period of five years, or he may restore to the public domain the lands not reclaimed at the expiration of the ten years, or of the extended period.

2. The lands selected under these acts must all be desert lands as defined by the acts of 1877 and 1891, and the decisions and regulations of this department therein provided for.

Lands which produce native grasses sufficient in quantity, if unfed by grazing animals, to make an ordinary crop of hay in usual seasons, are not desert lands. Lands which will produce an agricultural crop of any kind in amount sufficient to make the cultivation reasonably remunerative are not desert. Lands containing sufficient moisture to produce a natural growth of trees are not to be classed as desert lands.

Lands occupied by *bona fide* settlers and lands containing valuable deposits of coal or other minerals are not subject to selection.

3. The second paragraph of Section 4, above quoted, provides that before the application of any state is allowed or any contract [170] or agreement is executed or any segregation of any of the land from the public domain is ordered by the Secretary of the Interior, the state shall file a map of the land selected and proposed to be irrigated, which shall exhibit 'a plan showing the mode of contemplated irrigation and the source of the water. In accordance with the requirements of the act, the

state must give full data to show that the proposed plan will be sufficient to thoroughly irrigate and reclaim the land and prepare it to raise ordinary agricultural crops; for which purpose a statement by the state engineer of the amount of water available for the plan of irrigation will be necessary. The other data required cannot be fully prescribed, as it will depend upon the nature of the plan submitted. All information necessary to enable this office to judge of its practicability for irrigating all the land selected must be submitted. Upon the filing of the map showing the plan of irrigation and the lands selected, such lands will be withheld from other disposition until final action is had thereon by the Secretary of the Interior. If such final action be a disapproval of the map and plan, the lands selected shall, without further order, be subject to disposition as if such reservation had never been made; and the local officers will make the appropriate notations on the tract books and plat books, opposite those previously made, in accordance with the requirements of paragraph 7.

4. The map must be on tracing linen, in duplicate, and must be drawn to a scale not greater than 1,000 feet to one inch. A smaller scale is desirable if the necessary information can be clearly shown. The map and field notes in duplicate must be filed in the local land office for the district in which the land is located. If the lands selected are located in more than one district, duplicate map and field notes need be filed in but one dis-

trict, and single sets in the others. Each legal subdivision of the land [171] selected should be clearly indicated on the map by a check mark, thus: √. The map and field notes must show the connections of *termini* of a canal or of the initial point of a reservoir with public survey corners, the connections with public survey corners, the connections with public survey corners wherever section or township lines are crossed by the proposed irrigation works, and must show full data to admit of retracing the lines of the survey of the irrigation works on the ground.

5. The map should bear an affidavit of the engineer who made or supervised the preparation of the map and plan, Form 1, page 39, and also of the officer authorized by the State to make its selections under the act, Form 2, page 39. The map should be accompanied by a list in triplicate of the lands selected, designated by legal subdivisions, properly summed up at the foot of each page, and at the end of the list. If the lands selected are located in more than one district, a list in triplicate must be filed in each office, describing the lands selected in that district. Clear carbon copies are preferred for the duplicate and triplicate lists. The lists should be dated and verified by a certificate of the selecting agent, Form 3, page 40. The party appearing as agent of the state must file with the register and receiver written and satisfactory evidence, under seal, of his authority to act in the premises; such evidence once filed need not be duplicated during the period for which the agent

was appointed. The state should number the lists in consecutive order, beginning with No. 1, regardless of the land office in which they are to be filed. Form of title page to be prefixed to the lists of selections will be found on page 39, marked "A." Lists received at this office containing erasures will not be filed, but will be returned in order that new ones may be prepared. When a township has not been subdivided, but has had its exteriors surveyed, the whole township may be designated, [172] omitting, however, the sections to which the state may be entitled under its grant of school lands. When the records are in such condition that the proper notations may be made, a section or a part of a section of unsurveyed land may be designated in the list; but no patent can issue thereon until the land has been surveyed.

6. A contract in the form herein prescribed (Form 5, page 40), in duplicate, signed by the state officer authorized to execute such contract must also be filed. A carbon copy of the contract will not be accepted. * The person who executes the contract on behalf of the state must furnish evidence of his authority to do so.

7. The lists must be carefully and critically examined by the register and receiver, and their accuracy tested by the plats and records of their office. When so examined and found correct in all respects, they will attach a certificate at the foot of each list (Form 4, page 40). The register must note on the map, lists, contracts, and all papers the name of the land office and the date of filing

over his written signature and will thereupon post the selections in ink in the tract book after the following manner: "Selected ——, 19—, by ——, the state ——, as desert land, Act of August 18, 1894, serial No. ——," and on the plats he will mark the tracts so selected, "State desert land selections." After the selections are properly posted and marked on the records, the lists, maps, and all papers will be transmitted to the General Land Office.

For rejected selections a new list will be required, upon which the register will note opposite each tract the objections appearing on the records and indorse thereon his reasons in full for refusing to certify the same. The state will be allowed to appeal in the manner provided for in the Rules of Practice. It is required that clear lists of approvals shall in each case be [173] made out by the selecting agents, if after the above examination one or more tracts have been rejected, showing clearly and without erasure the tracts to which the register is prepared to certify. On the map of lands selected the register will mark rejected such tracts as he has rejected on the lists.

8. When the canals or reservoirs required by the plan of irrigation cross public land not selected by the state, an application for right of way over such lands under Sections 18 to 21, act of March 3, 1891, (26 Stat. 1085), should be filed separately, in accordance with the regulations under said act.

9. In the preceding paragraphs instructions are given for the designation of the lands by the proper state authorities. Upon the approval of the map

of the lands and the plan of irrigation, the contract is executed by the Secretary of the Interior and approved by the President, as directed by the act. Upon the approval of the map and plan, the lands are reserved for the purposes of the act, said reservation dating from the date of the filing of the map and plan in the local land office. A duplicate of the approved map and plan, and of the list of lands, is transmitted for the files of the local land office, and a triplicate copy of the list is forwarded to the state authorities.

10. When patents are desired for any lands that have been segregated, the state should file in the local land office a list, to which is prefixed a certificate of the presiding officer of the State Land Board, or other officer of the state who may be charged with the duty of disposing of the lands which the state may obtain under the law (Form 6, page 42); and followed by an affidavit of the state engineer, or other state officer whose duty it may be to superintend the reclamation of the lands (Form 7, page 42).

11. The certificate of Form 6 is required in order to show that the state laws accepting the grant of the lands have been duly complied with.

12. The affidavit of Form 7 is required in order to show [174] compliance with the provisions of the law, that an ample supply of water has been actually furnished in a substantial ditch or canal, or by artesian wells or reservoirs, for each tract in the list, sufficient to thoroughly irrigate and reclaim it, and to prepare it to raise ordinary agri-

cultural crops. A separate statement by the state engineer must be furnished, giving all the facts as to the water supply and the nature, location, and completion of the irrigation works.

If there are some high points which it is not practicable to irrigate, the nature, extent, location, and area of such points should be fully stated. If no part of a legal subdivision is susceptible of irrigation, such legal subdivision must be relinquished. Lands upon which valuable deposits of coal or other minerals are discovered will not be patented to the state under these acts.

13. These lists will be called "lists for patent," and should be numbered by the state consecutively, beginning with No. 1. The list should also show, opposite each tract, the number of the approved segregation list in which it appears. The aggregate area should be stated at the foot of each page and at the end of the list.

14. Upon the filing of such list the local officers will place thereon the date of filing and note on the records opposite each tract listed: "list for patent serial No. ——, filed ——," giving the date.

15. When said list is filed in the local land office there shall also be filed by the state a notice, in duplicate, prepared for the signature of the register and receiver, describing the land by sections, and portions of sections, where less than a section is designated (Form 8, p. 42). This notice shall be published at the expense of the state once a week in each of nine consecutive [175] weeks, in a newspaper of established character and gen-

eral circulation, to be designated by the register as published nearest the land. One copy of said notice shall be posted in a conspicuous place in the local office for at least sixty days during the period of publication.

16. At the expiration of the period of publication the state shall file in the local office proof of said publication and of payment for the same. Thereupon the register and receiver shall forward the list for patent to the General Land Office, noting thereon any protests or contests which may have been filed, transmitting such papers, and submitting any recommendations they may deem proper. They will also forward proofs of publication, of payment therefor, and of the posting of the list in their office.

17. Before patents are issued for lands within the former Southern Ute and the Ute Indian Reservations in Colorado, the state will be required to pay the price $1.25 per acre, fixed by the acts of March 1, 1907; and February 24, 1909. The state will be advised of the number of acres which will be included in the patent and payment shall be made to the receiver of the proper land office, who will issue a receipt as in other cases. The money will be accounted for in the same manner as other moneys received from the disposal of such lands.

18. Upon the receipt of the papers in the General Land Office such action will be taken in each case as the showing may require, and all tracts that are free from valid protest or contest, and respecting which the law and regulations have been com-

plied with, will be certified to the Secretary of the Interior for approval and patenting.

FRED DENNETT,

Commissioner General Land Office.

Approved April 9, 1909.

R. A. BALLINGER,

Secretary of the Interior. [176]

## FORM 2.

State of ——,

County of ——,—ss.

——, being duly sworn, says he is the engineer under whose supervision the survey and plan hereon were made (or is the person employed to make, etc.); that the tracts shown hereon to be selected are each and every one desert land as contemplated by the act of Congress approved August 18, 1894 (28 Stat., 372–422), the act of June 11, 1896 (29 Stat., 434); and the act of March 3, 1901 (31 Stat., 1133–1188); *that he is well acquainted with the character of the land herein applied for, having personally examined same; that there is not to his knowledge within the limits thereof any vein or lode or quartz or other rock in place bearing gold, silver, cinnabar, lead, tin or copper, nor any deposit of coal, placer, cement, gravel, salt spring, or deposit of salt, or other valuable mineral deposit; that no portion of said land is claimed for mining purposes under the local customs or rules of miners, or otherwise; that no portion of said land is worked for mineral during any part of the year by any person or persons; that the said land is essentially non-mineral land and that the land is not occupied by any settler; that the plan of irrigation herewith submitted is accurately and fully represented in accordance with ascertained facts; that the system proposed is sufficient to thoroughly irrigate and reclaim said land and prepare it to raise ordinary crops; and that the survey of said system of irrigation is accurately represented upon this map and the accompanying field notes.

———————————————————.

Subscribed and sworn to before me this —— day of ——, 19—.

[Seal]                          ————————————————,

Notary Public.   [177]

## FORM 2.

State of ——,

County of ——,—ss.

——, being duly sworn, says that he is the —— (designation of office,) authorized by the state of —— to make desert land selections under the act of Congress approved August 18, 1894 (28 Stat., 372–422), the act of June 11, 1896 (29 Stat., 434), and the act of March 3, 1901 (31 Stat., 1133–1188); * that the plan of irrigation and survey, herewith is submitted under authority of the state of ——; and that the tracts shown hereon to be selected are each and every one desert land, as contemplated by the said acts of Congress, none being of the classes designated as timber or mineral lands.

Subscribed and sworn to before me this —— day of ——, 19—.

[Seal]                    ————————————————,

         Notary Public.

### A.

State of ——,

United States Land Office.

         ————, 19—.

·· ——, the duly authorized agent of the State of — -, under and by virtue of an act of Congress approved August 18, 1894 (28 Stat., 372–422), the act of June 11, 1896 (29 Stat., 434), and the act of March 3, 1901 (31 Stat., 1133–1188), * and in pursuance of the rules and regulations prescribed by the Secretary of the Interior, hereby makes and files the following list of desert public lands which the state is authorized [178] to select under the provisions of the said acts of Congress.

### FORM 3.

State of ——,

County of ——,—ss.

I, ——, being duly sworn, depose and say that I am —— (designation of office), authorized by the state of —— to make desert land selections under the act of Congress approved August 18, 1894 (28 Stat., 372–422), the act of June 11, 1896 (29 Stat., 434), and the act of March 3, 1901 (31 Stat., 1133–1188); *that the foregoing list of lands which I hereby select is a correct list of lands selected under said acts; that the lands are vacant, unappropriated, are not interdicted timber nor mineral lands, and are desert lands as contemplated by the said acts of Congress.

Subscribed and sworn to before me this —— day of ——, 19—.

[Seal]

——————————————,

Notary Public. [179]

## FORM 4.

United States Land Office,

——————————

——————, 19—.

We hereby certify that we have carefully and critically examined the foregoing list of lands selected ——, 19—, by ——, the duly authorized agent of the State of ——, under the provisions of the act of Congress approved August 18, 1894 (28 Stat., 372–422), the act of June 11, 1896 (29 Stat., 434), and the act of March 3, 1901 (31 Stat., 1133–1188); * that we have tested the accuracy of said list by the plats and records of this office, and that we find the same to be correct. And we further certify that the filing of said list is allowed and approved, and that the whole of said lands are surveyed public lands of the United States, and that the same are not nor is any part thereof returned and denominated as mineral or timber lands; nor is there any homestead or other valid claim to any portion of said lands on file or of record in this office; and that the said lands are, to the best of our knowledge and belief, desert lands, as contemplated by the said acts of Congress; and that the

fees, amounting to $——, have been paid upon the
said area of —— acres.

————————————————, Register.

————————————————, Receiver.

### FORM 5.

These articles of agreement, made and entered
into this —— *day of ——, *A. D. 19——, *by and
between ——, *Secretary of the Interior, for and
on behalf of the United States of America, party
of the first part, and —— for and on behalf of the
state of ——, party of the second part, witnesseth:

That in consideration of the stipulations and
agreements hereinafter made, and of the fact that
said state has, under the [180] provisions of
Section 4 of the act of Congress approved August
18, 1894, of the act of Congress approved June 11,
1896, and of the act of Congress approved March
3, 1901, **through ——, its proper officer, thereunto duly authorized, presented its proper application for certain lands situated within said state and
alleged to be desert in character and particularly
described as follows, to wit: List No. —— (here
insert list of lands and total area), and has filed
a map of said lands and exhibited a plan showing
the mode by which it is proposed the said lands
shall be irrigated and reclaimed and the source of
the water to be used for that purpose, the said
party of the first part contracts and agrees, and,
by and with the consent and approval of ——,
*president thereof, hereby binds the United States
of America to donate, grant, and patent to said
state, or to its assigns, free from cost for survey

or price,   * * *   any particular tract or tracts
of said lands, whenever an ample supply of water
is actually furnished in a substantial ditch or
canal, or by artesian wells or reservoirs, to reclaim
the same, in accordance with the provisions of
said act of Congress, and with the regulations issued thereunder, and with the terms of this contract, at any time within ten years from the date
of the approval of the said map of the lands.

It is further understood that said state shall not
lease any of said lands or use or dispose of the
same in any way whatever, except to secure their
reclamation, cultivation, and settlement; and that
in selling and disposing of them for that purpose
the said state may sell or dispose of not more than
160 acres to any one person, and then only to *bona
fide* settlers who are citizens of the United States
or who have decuared their intention to become
such citizens; and it is distinctly understood and
fully agreed that all persons acquiring title to said
lands from said state prior to the issuance of patent, as hereinafter mentioned, will take the same
subject to all the requirements of said acts of Congress and to the terms of  [181]  this contract,
and shall show full compliance therewith before
they shall have any claim against the United States
for a patent to said lands.

It is further understood and agreed that said
state shall have full power, right, and authority to
enact such laws, and from time to time to make
and enter into such contracts and agreements, and
to create and assume such obligations in relation to

and concerning said lands as may be necessary to induce and cause such irrigation and reclamation thereof as is required by this contract and the said acts of Congress; but no such law, contract, or obligation shall in any way bind or obligate the United States to do or perform any act not clearly directed and set forth in this contract and said acts of Congress, and then only after the requirements of said acts and contract have been fully complied with.

Neither the approval of said application, map, and plan, nor the segregation of said land by the Secretary of the Interior, nor anything in this contract, or in the said acts of Congress, shall be so construed as to give said state any interest whatever in any lands upon which, at the date of the filing of the map and plan hereinbefore referred to, there may be an actual settlement by a *bona fide* settler, qualified under the public land laws to acquire title thereto, or which are known to be valuable for their deposits of coal or other minerals.

It is further understood and agreed that as soon as an ample supply of water is actually furnished in a substantial ditch or canal, or by artesian wells or reservoirs, to reclaim a particular tract or tracts of said lands the said state or its assigns may make proof thereof under and according to such rules and regulations as may be prescribed therefor by the Secretary of the Interior, and as soon as such proof shall have been examined and found to be satisfactory, patents shall issue to said state, or to its assigns, for the tracts included in said proof.

The said state shall, out of the money arising from its disposal of said lands, first reimburse itself for any and all costs   [182]   and expenditures incurred by it in irrigating and reclaiming said lands, or in assisting its assigns in so doing; and any surplus then remaining after the payment of the cost of such reclamation shall be held as a trust fund, to be applied to the reclamation of other desert lands within said state.

This contract is executed in duplicate, one copy of which shall be placed of record and remain on file with the Commissioner of the General Land office, and the other shall be placed of record and remain on file with the proper officer of said state, and it shall be the duty of said state to cause a copy thereof, together with a copy of all rules and regulations issued thereunder or under said acts of Congress, to be spread upon the deed records of each of the counties in said state in which any of said lands shall be situated.

In testimony whereof the said parties have hereunto set their hands the day and year first herein written.

—————————————,
Secretary of the Interior.
State of ———.
By ———————————.

## APPROVAL.

To All to Whom These Presents shall Come, Greetings:

Know ye, that I, ——, *President of the United States of America, do hereby approve and ratify the attached contract and agreement, made and entered into on the —— *day of ——, *19—, *by and between ——, *Secretary of the Interior, for and on behalf of the United States, and ——, for and on behalf of the State of ——, under Section 4 of the act of Congress approved August 18, 1894, the act approved June 11, 1896, and the act approved March 3, 1901.  *  *

——————————————.  [183]

## FORMS FOR VERIFICATION AND PUBLICATION OF LISTS FOR PATENT.
### FORM 6.

I, ——, do hereby certify that I am the —— (designation of office), of the state of ——; that I am charged with the duty of disposing of the lands granted to the state in pursuance of Section 4, act of August 18, 1894 (28 Stat., 372–422), the act of June 11, 1896 (29 Stat., 434), and the act of March 3, 1901 (31 Stat., 1133–1188)*; and that the laws of the said state relating to the said grant from the United States have been complied with in all respects as to the following list of lands which is hereby submitted on behalf of the said state for the issuance of patent under said act of Congress.

_____.

(Here add list of lands.)

_____.

## FORM 7·
(To follow list of lands.)

State of ——,
County of ——,—ss.

——, being duly sworn, deposes and says that he is the —— (designation of office), of the state of ——, charged with the duty of supervising the reclamation of lands segregated under Section 4, act of August 18, 1894 (28 Stat., 372–422), the act of June 11, 1896 (29 Stat., 434), and the act of March 3, 1901 (31 Stat., 1133–1188), *that he has examined the lands designated on the foregoing list, and that an ample supply of water has been actually furnished (in a substantial ditch or canal, or by artesian wells or reservoirs) for each tract in said [184] list, sufficient to thoroughly irrigate and reclaim it and to prepare it to raise ordinary agricultural crops.

_____.

_____.


Subscribed and sworn to before me this —— day of ——, 19—.

[Seal]                    _____,

Notary Public.

## FORM FOR PUBLISHING NOTICE.
### FORM 8.
United States Land Office,

——————, 19——.

To Whom It may Concern:

Notice is hereby given that the state of ——— has filed in this office the following list of lands, to wit: ——— and has applied for a patent for said lands under the acts of August 18, 1894 (28 Stat., 372–422), June 11, 1896 (29 Stat., 434), and March 3, 1901, (31 Stat., 113–1188), *relating to the granting of not to exceed a million acres* * of arid land to each of certain states; and that the said list, with its accompanying proofs, is open for the inspection of all persons interested, and the public generally.

Within the next sixty days following the date of this notice, protests or contests against the claim of the state to any tract described in the list, on the ground of failure to comply with the law, on the ground of the non-desert character of the land on the ground of prior adverse right, or on the ground that the same is more valuable for mineral than for agricultural purposes, will be received and noted for report to the General Land Office at Washington, D. C.

——————————————————, Register.

——————————————————, Receiver.    [185]

DEFENDANT'S EXHIBIT "E."

No. ——. Defts. Ex. "E."

U. S. District Court, District of Oregon. Filed June 12, 1923. G. H. Marsh, Clerk.

Minutes of Various Board Meetings of the Desert Land Board Affecting the Jordan Valley Land & Water Company Project.

Salem, Oregon, March 6, 1918.

Special meeting of the Desert Land Board was held this day in the Board of Control room at 10 A. M.

Present: James Withycombe, Governor, Chairman;

Ben W. Olcott, Secretary of State;

Thos. B. Kay, State Treasurer;

Geo. M. Brown, Attorney General;

John H. Lewis, State Engineer, Secretary;

Percy A. Cupper, Asst. Secretary.

Thereupon the following proceedings were had, to wit:

Mr. Herbert G. Wells, representative of Maney Brothers Construction Company and of the Jordan Valley Land and Water Company, and Mr. Harley J. Hooker who has undertaken the sale of lands and water rights in the Jordan Valley Carey Act Project, appeared before the Board and requested that the Board execute a preliminary contract for the reclamation of the Carey Act lands in the Jordan Valley Irrigation Project and agree upon the terms of the final contract to be executed after the execution of a contract between the State and the United States for the reclamation of these lands.

Mr. Lewis explained the plan under which the company proposed to operate and after considerable discussion, it was ORDERED that the preliminary contract be executed by the Board and the Jordan Valley Land and Water Company and attach thereto a form of final contract to be executed upon the execution of a contract for the reclamation of the lands by the Secretary of the Interior. It was agreed that the lien should be fixed at $65.00 per acre, $15 per acre of which amount on the first 8000 acres of land sold and $10 per acre of the lien fixed on the remainder of the land, to be applied to the construction of a road from the railroad to the project; that a surety bond in the sum of $100,000 should be posted by the Jordan Valley [186] Land and Water Company to insure the completion of the project; that the Board should permit the sale of lands and water rights, provided, that all funds arising from such sales, together with notes and contracts secured in connection therewith should be placed in the hands of a trustee satisfactory to and to be approved by the Board and none of the moneys received from the sale of such lands shall be paid out until after the 8000 acres have been sold and then only for labor employed and material furnished in the construction of the project, upon the approval of the State Engineer. The Attorney General and the State Engineer were instructed to prepare the necessary contracts embodying the above provisions and such other provisions as they may deem necessary and submit the same for the approval of the Board.

Upon the request of Mr. Wells and his offer to pay one-half of the expenses, it was ORDERED that the State Engineer be instructed to go to Washington, D. C., to facilitate the execution of the contract between the Interior Department and the State and also to endeavor to interest the Interior Department in the Morson Land Company's project and the further investigation of the Deschutes Project. One-half of his expenses to be paid by Maney Brothers Company and the other half by the Desert Land Board.

\*    \*    \*    \*    \*    \*    \*    \*    \*

No further business appearing the Board adjourned.

JAMES WITHYCOMBE,
Governor, Chairman.
BEN W. OLCOTT,
Secretary of State.
THOS. B. KAY,
State Treasurer.
GEO. M. BROWN,
Attorney General.
JOHN H. LEWIS,
State Engineer, Secretary.
Attest: PERCY A. CUPPER,
Asst. Secretary. [187]

Salem, Oregon, May 3, 1918.

Special meeting of the Desert Land Board was held this day in the Capitol Building at 2:30 P. M. Present: James Withycombe, Governor, Chairman;

Ben W. Olcott, Secretary of State;

Thos. B. Kay, State Treasurer;

Geo. M. Brown, Attorney General;

John H. Lewis, State Engineer, Secretary;

Percy A. Cupper, Asst. Secretary.

Thereupon the following proceedings were had, to wit:

Under date of April 1, 1918, the Commissioner of the General Land Office transmitted through the Land Office at Vale, a list for rejection as to certain lands included in Oregon Segregation List No. 24, Jordan Valley Project. This list for rejection comprising approximately 2910 acres, includes tracts which lie above the proposed canal system of the project and are therefore rendered non-irrigable under the present proposed system.

It is hereby ORDERED that the Desert Land Board consent to the relinquishment of approximately 2910 acres from Oregon Segregation List No. 24 as filed with the Commissioner of the General Land Office for execution on or about April 29, 1914, and submitted for rejection by letter of the Commissioner to the Desert Land Board through the Land Office at Vale, under date of April 1, 1918.

No further business appearing, the Board adjourned.

> JAMES WITHYCOMBE,
> Governor, Chairman.
> BEN W. OLCOTT,
> Secretary of State.
> THOS. B. KAY,
> State Treasurer.
> GEO. M. BROWN,
> Attorney General.
> JOHN H. LEWIS,
> State Engineer, Secretary.

Attest: PERCY A. CUPPER,

> Assistant Secretary. [188]
> Salem, Oregon, May 24, 1918.

Special meeting of the Desert Land Board was held this day in the Board of Control room at 2 P. M.

Present: James Withycombe, Governor, Chairman;

Ben W. Olcott, Secretary of State;

Thos. B. Kay, State Treasurer;

Geo. M. Brown, Attorney General;

John H. Lewis, State Engineer, Secretary;

Percy A. Cupper, Asst. Secretary.

Thereupon the following proceedings were had, to wit:

Messrs. J. W. Maney, Oliver O. Haga, Paul S. A. Bickel, Harley J. Hooker and George Archibald appeared before the Board on behalf of the Jordan Valley Project.

Mr. Haga requested the Board for an increase of the lien as fixed by the order of the Board entered March 6, 1918, from $65 to $71 per acre. He said this increase was made necessary due to the fact that it was impossible to determine when the upper unit of the project would be constructed and it was therefore essential to the success of the lower unit that the works be independent of any canals which might be constructed for the upper unit for sufficient capacity for the complete reclamation of the lands in the lower unit and also on account of the rapidly increasing cost of labor and material necessary in the construction of the project. Mr. Haga also explained that it was not understood heretofore that the $1 per acre due the state under the statute should be deducted from the amount of the lien collected by the company. It was also explained that applications had been received for approximately 5,000 acres of land in the project and that this was sufficient as a basis for the proceeding of construction work.

In view of the uncertainty relative to the construction of the upper unit, it was requested that the $100,000 bond be posted as a Guaranty Fund for the reclamation of the lower unit only and that upon the acceptance of any portion thereof, that a corresponding [189] release of the bond shall be made. After careful consideration of the entire matter and upon the recommendation of the State Engineer, it was ORDERED that the lien should be fixed at $71 per irrigable acre, and 2.50 per waste acre, $15 per irrigable acre of which amount on the first 5000 acres of land sold and $5 per irrigable acre of the lien fixed on the remainder of the land to be applied to the construction of a road from the railroad to the project and on roads on and through the project, such roads to be designated by the Desert Land Board and the money expended in the construction thereof under the direction of said board; that out of the lien so fixed that $1 per acre for each and every acre of Carey Act land in the project shall be paid into the Oregon Irrigation Fund as provided by statute; that a surety bond in the sum of $100,000 should be posted by the Jordan Valley Land and Water Company to insure the reclamation of the lower unit of the project, it being understood that whenever any distinct unit, or portion of the project has been completed and accepted that the bond shall be reduced in proportion to the area thus accepted; that the Board should permit the sale of lands and water rights, provided, that all funds arising from such sales, together with notes and contracts secured in connection therewith should be placed in the hands of a trustee satisfactory to and to be approved by the Board and none of the moneys received from the sale of such lands shall be paid out until after 5000 acres have been sold and then only for labor employed, material furnished and incidental expenses in the construction of the project, upon the approval of the State Engineer.

It was further ORDERED that the Attorney General and the State Engineer prepare the necessary contracts in accordance herewith and the

Governor as Chairman and the State Engineer as Secretary be and the same are hereby directed and instructed to execute such contract on behalf of the Board. [190]

\*    \*    \*    \*    \*    \*    \*    \*    \*

No further business appearing, the Board adjourned.

JAMES WITHYCOMBE,
Governor, Chairman.

BEN W. OLCOTT,
Secretary of State.

THOS. B. KAY,
State Treasurer.

GEO. M. BROWN,
Attorney General.

JOHN H. LEWIS,
State Engineer.

Attest: PERCY A. CUPPER,
Asst. Secretary.    [191]

STATE OF OREGON.
LEGAL DEPARTMENT.
Salem.

August 17, 1918.

Honorable John H. Lewis,
State Engineer,
Capitol Building.

Dear Sir:

In compliance with your favor of the 9th instant, transmitting contract between the Desert Land Board and the Jordan Valley Land and Water Company, and requesting this office to prepare a bond to be executed guaranteeing the faithful per-

formance of said contract by said company, I have
prepared such bond and delivered one original and
two copies to Mr. Homer H. Smith, Resident Agent
of the American Surety Company of New York,
surety on said bond, for execution and herewith
hand you one original of said bond, together with
the contract above mentioned.

Very truly yours,

GEO. M. BROWN,

Attorney General.

By I. H. VAN WINKLE,

Assistant.

Enc.

IHV/T.   [192]

Salem, Oregon, August 24, 1918.

Special meeting of the Desert Land Board was
held this day in the Board of Control room at 10:30
A. M.

Present: James Withycombe, Governor, Chairman;
Ben W. Olcott, Secretary of State;
Thos. B. Kay, State Treasurer;
Geo. M. Brown, Attorney General;
John H. Lewis, State Engineer, Secretary;
Percy A. Cupper, Asst. Secretary.

Thereupon the following proceedings were had,
to wit:

The duly executed bond of the Jordan Valley Land
and Water Company for the faithful performance
of its contract was presented and accepted by the
Board. The request of the Company to have a representative of the Board and the State Engineer
appointed to inspect the works as the same are con-

structed and to approve for payment from the funds in escrow with the Boise Title & Trust Company was considered.

Mr. Baar of the firm of Baar & Cunningham was present and after considerable discussion it was ORDERED that the firm of Baar and Cunningham be designated as the representative of the Desert Land Board and the State Engineer with full authority under the direction of the State Engineer, to direct the detailed execution of the work and accept the same when constructed and to approve for payment the claims of the Jordan Valley Land and Water Company in accordance with the provisions of Section 7 of the contract, and also to prepare suitable lists of land for opening by the Board and to do any and all other things requiring attention on the project. For this service the firm of Baar & Cunningham shall receive compensation at the rate of $1,800 per annum, payable monthly, and which service and compensation shall begin September 1st and continue during the pleasure of the Board, it being understood that the compensation shall be paid ultimately from moneys arising from the $1.00 per acre [193] payable to the State at the time of the sale of Carey Act lands in case such funds are insufficient, the deficiency shall be supplied by the Jordan Valley Land & Water Company in accordance with the terms of Article 5 of the contract

No further business appearing, the Board adjourned.

JAMES WITHYCOMBE,
Governor, Chairman.

BEN W. OLCOTT,
Secretary of State.

THOS. B. KAY,
State Treasurer.

GEO. M. BROWN,
Attorney General.

JOHN H. LEWIS,
State Engineer.

Attest: PERCY A. CUPPER,
Asst. Secretary. [194]

Salem, Oregon, January 7, 1919.

Regular meeting of the Desert Land Board was held this day at 2 P. M. in the office of the Board of Control.

Present: James Withycombe, Governor, Chairman;
Ben W. Olcott, Secretary of State;
Percy A. Cupper, State Engineer, Secretary.

Thereupon the following proceedings were had, to wit:

\* \* \* \* \* \* \* \* \*

The claim of Baar & Cunningham for expenses from Portland in connection with the inspection of the Jordan Valley Project for the months of September, October and November, 1918, was approved.

No further business appearing, the Board adjourned.

JAMES WITHYCOMBE,
Governor, Chairman.

BEN W. OLCOTT,
Secretary of State.

PERCY A. CUPPER,
State Engineer. [195]

Salem, Oregon, January 15, 1919.

Special meeting of the Desert Land Board was held this day in the Capitol Building at 10:30 A. M. Present: James Withycombe, Governor, Chairman;

Ben W. Olcott, Secretary of State;

O. P. Hoff, State Treasurer;

Geo. M. Brown, Attorney General;

Percy A. Cupper, State Engineer, Secretary.

Thereupon the following proceedings were had, to wit:

\*　　\*　　\*　　\*　　\*　　\*　　\*　　\*　　\*

Mr. John W. Cunningham appeared before the Board and reported progress on the Jordan Valley Project and filed his report on the same.

Mr. Paul S. A. Bickel, Chief Engineer and General Manager for the Jordan Valley Project, was also present and gave the Board some information relative to the progress of the construction work.

No further business appearing, the Board adjourned.

JAMES WITHYCOMBE,
Governor, Chairman.

BEN W. OLCOTT,
Secretary of State.

O. P. HOFF,
State Treasurer.

GEO. M. BROWN,
Attorney General.

PERCY A. CUPPER,
State Engineer, Secretary.   [196]

Salem, Oregon, March 3, 1919.

A special meeting of the Desert Land Board was held this day in the Capitol Building at 10 o'clock A. M.

Present: Ben W. Olcott, Secretary of State;
O. P. Hoff, State Treasurer;
Percy A. Cupper, State Engineer;
I. H. Van Winkle, Representing George M. Brown, Attorney General.

Thereupon the following proceedings were had, to wit:

Copies of the forms of application, contract, note and mortgage of the Jordan Valley Land & Water Company were ordered approved.

No further business appearing, the meeting ad-journed.

BEN W. OLCOTT,
Secretary of State.

O. P. HOFF,
State Treasurer.

PERCY A. CUPPER,
State Engineer.

I. H. VAN WINKLE,
Representing George M. Brown, Attorney General.
[197]

Salem, Oregon, June 20, 1919.

A special meeting of the Desert Land Board was held this day in the Capitol Building at 2.00 P. M.

Present: Ben W. Olcott, Governor, Chairman;
Ben W. Olcott, Secretary of State;
O. P. Hoff, State Treasurer;
George M. Brown, Attorney General;
Percy A. Cupper, State Engineer, Secretary.
J. L. McAllister, Assistant Secretary.

Thereupon the following proceedings were had, to wit:

\*     \*     \*     \*     \*     \*     \*     \*     \*

By Board order entered August 24, 1918, the engineering firm of Baar & Cunningham was designated as the representative of the Board and State Engineer to direct the execution of the work and accept same when completed, to approve construction, claims, etc., said firm to receive compensation at the rate of $150.00 per month.

It now appearing that the above firm has assumed the duties of Project Engineer, which position was formerly held by Mr. P. S. A. Bickel of Boise, and that arrangements have been made whereby said firm will temporarily act in the dual capacity for the consideration of $350.00 per month, to be paid by the Jordan Valley Land & Water Company, the Desert Land Board contributing at the rate of $75.00 per month or so much thereof as may be available from moneys received from the Jordan Valley Project after paying the expenses of the Board in connection with the project work.

This arrangement being satisfactory to the State Engineer, whose approval must be had for the appointment of the Project Engineer under the terms of the contract between that State and Company, it was ordered that the above order of August 24th be amended accordingly to become effective on the date of the appointment of Baar & Cunningham as Project Engineer. [198]

J. L. McAllister having returned from service in the A. E. F. was reappointed to his former position as Assistant Secretary at a salary of $175.00 per month, $100 to be paid from the appropriation for the Desert Land Board and the balance from the moneys received from the Jordan Valley Project, said appointment to be effective from and after May 25th.

There appearing no further business, the meeting adjourned.

BEN W. OLCOTT,
                    Governor, Chairman.

BEN W. OLCOTT,
                    Secretary of State.

O. P. HOFF,
                    State Treasurer.

GEO. M. BROWN,
                    Attorney General.

PERCY A. CUPPER,
                    State Engineer, Secretary.

Attest: J. L. McALLISTER,
                    Assistant Secretary.    [199]

Salem, Oregon, July 16, 1919.

A special meeting of the Desert Land Board was held this day in the Capitol Building at 2:00 P. M. Present: Ben W. Olcott, Governor, Chairman;

        Ben W. Olcott, Secretary of State;

        O. P. Hoff, State Treasurer;

        George M. Brown, Attorney General;

        Percy A. Cupper, State Engineer, Secretary;

        J. L. McAllister, Assistant Secretary.

Thereupon the following proceedings were had, to wit:

Under date of July 1st, 1919, the Jordan Valley Land and Water Company filed a petition with the Board requesting the temporary withdrawal of certain public lands under the provisions of the Act of March 15, 1910 (36 Stat. 237).

It appearing that these public lands totaling 16,-862.19 acres, being intermingled with those segregated for reclamation in Oregon list No. 24, under the Carey Act, now being reclaimed under the Jordan Valley Project by the above petitioner, should be immediately withdrawn from entry pending the completion of surveys now under progress, to determine the advisability of reclaiming the same under the above project.

Therefore, be it ORDERED that the Secretary be instructed to prepare the necessary application for the temporary withdrawal of said lands to be designated as Oregon Segregation List No. 38, to be signed in triplicate by the Chairman and Secretary and filed with the local land office at Vale, Oregon.

\*   \*   \*   \*   \*   \*   \*   \*   \*

There appearing no further business, the meeting adjourned. [200]

> BEN W. OLCOTT,
> > Governor, Chairman.
> BEN W. OLCOTT,
> > Secretary of State.
> O. P. HOFF,
> > State Treasurer.
> GEO. M. BROWN,
> > Attorney General.
> PERCY A. CUPPER,
> > State Engineer, Secretary.
> Attest: J. L. McALLISTER,
> > Assistant Secretary. [201]

Salem, Oregon, October 8, 1919.

A special meeting of the Desert Land Board was held this day in the Capitol Building at 1:30 P. M. Present: Ben W. Olcott, Governor, Chairman;

Ben W. Olcott, Secretary of State;

O. P. Hoff, State Treasurer;

George M. Brown, Attorney General;

Percy A. Cupper, State Engineer, Secretary; .

J. L. McAllister, Assistant Secretary.

Thereupon the following proceedings were had, to wit:

Mr. A. J. Vance of Oklahoma City, representing Mr. J. W. Maney of the Jordan Valley Land and Water Company, Mr. Harley J. Hooker, who is handling the colonization of the Jordan Valley Project under a contract with the Jordan Valley Land and Water Company, and Mr. John W. Cunningham, who is representing the Board as inspector on the above project, also at present acting in the capacity of Project Engineer and General Manager, appeared before the Board and verbally requested an increase in the lien under the contract between the State and the Jordan Valley Land and Water Company, from $71.00 to $100.00 per acre on the unsold lands.

A short discussion was had relative to the question presented after which the representatives present were instructed to submit their proposition in writing in order that proper consideration could be given by the Board members prior to the meeting at which the question would come up for action by the Board.

.* &ast; &ast; &ast; &ast; &ast; &ast; ~ &ast;

There appearing no further business, the meeting adjourned. [202]

BEN W. OLCOTT,
Governor, Chairman.

BEN W. OLCOTT,
Secretary of State.

O. P. HOFF,
State Treasurer.

GEO. M. BROWN,
Attorney General.

PERCY A. CUPPER,
State Engineer, Secretary.

Attest: J. L. McALLISTER,
Assistant Secretary. [203]

Salem, Oregon, October 30, 1919.

A special meeting of the Desert Land Board was held this day in the Capitol Building at 10:30 A. M. Present: Ben W. Olcott, Governor, Chairman;

Ben W. Olcott, Secretary of State;

O. P. Hoff, State Treasurer;

George M. Brown, Attorney General;

Percy A. Cupper, State Engineer, Secretary;

J. L. McAllister, Assistant Secretary.

Thereupon the following proceedings were had, to wit:

An application was presented by the Jordan Valley Land and Water Company for an increase in lien on all unsold lands from $71.00 to $101.00 per acre. A statement and recommendation was submitted by the Secretary.

Mr. A. J. Vance, representing the Jordan Valley Land and Water Company, was present.

After due consideration, it was ORDERED that the lien be increased from $71.00 to $100.00 per acre on all unsold Carey Act Lands to be served from the Antelope Reservoir. The funds arising from the sale of land to be first applied as under the present arrangement to the cost of construction and colonization, after the completion of which the Jordan Valley Land and Water Company shall be entitled to $156,000.00. The balance, if any, shall be divided and applied as follows:

One-half thereof shall be paid to the Jordan Valley Land and Water Company and the remaining one-half thereof shall be turned over to the Desert Land Board to be expended for the general good of the project, it being understood that the cost of colonization under the Jordan Valley Farms contract is a legitimate charge against the project and shall include cost of financing up to an amount equal to $30.00 per acre, and that the cost of financing over and above the amount of $30.00 per acre shall be an additional charge against the project. [204]

It is also understood that the water rights to private lands in the project shall be sold under the same terms and conditions as the Carey Act land and that the terms of deferred payments shall be extended over a period of twenty (20) years.

And be it further ordered, that the Secretary be

and he hereby is instructed to prepare a supplemental agreement embodying the changes in the State Contract of June 21, 1918, necessitated hereby, and the Chairman and Secretary are hereby authorized to execute the same.

And be it further ordered that the increase of lien hereby granted shall be effective from the date of this order, provided, however, that the written consent of the American Surety Company of New York shall be subsequently filed with the Board otherwise this order shall be inoperative and the State Contract shall remain in its present form.

An invitation was presented to the Board by Mr. Harley J. Hooker, Sales Manager for the Jordan Valley Project to visit the Project, the construction of which is now in progress by the Jordan Valley Land and Water Company, also to visit some of the Idaho projects in the vicinity of Boise. Due to the fact that some of the Board members are extremely busy at this time in connection with other matters, also on account of the lateness of the season, the Secretary was instructed to advise Mr. Hooker that the Board members are all very anxious to visit the project and that if the invitation can be held over until spring, arrangements will be made to make the trip.

There appearing no further business the meeting [205] adjourned.

BEN W. OLCOTT,
Governor, Chairman.
BEN W. OLCOTT,
Secretary of State.
O. P. HOFF,
State Treasurer.
GEORGE M. BROWN,
Attorney General.
PERCY A. CUPPER,
State Engineer, Secretary.
Attest: J. L. McALLISTER,
Assistant Secretary.  [205½]

Salem, Oregon, February 4, 1920.

A special meeting of the Desert Land Board was held this day in the Capitol Building, at 4:00 o'clock P. M.

Present: Ben W. Olcott, Governor, Chairman;
Ben W. Olcott, Secretary of State;
O. P. Hoff, State Treasurer;
George M. Brown Attorney General;
Percy A. Cupper, State Engineer, Sec.;
J. L. McAllister, Assistant Sec.

Thereupon the following proceedings were had, to wit:

*      *      *      *      *      *      *      *

Application dated November 3, 1919, for the opening of lands for entry and sale was made by the Jordan Valley Land and Water Company. These lands are designated as List No. 1, and comprises 641.74 acres of Carey Act Land reclaimed under the Antelope Unit of the Jordan Valley Project.

The application appearing to be in proper form and in compliance with the requirements of the Board and the contract betwen the Company and the State,

It was, therefore, ordered that said List No. 1 be and the same is hereby opened for entry and sale and the secretary is hereby authorized to approve contracts covering the sale of the lands included therein.

\*　　\*　　\*　　～　　\*　　\*　　\*　　\*

No further business appearing, the meeting adjourned.

BEN W. OLCOTT,
Governor, Chairman.

BEN W. OLCOTT,
Secretary of State.

O. P. HOFF,
State Treasurer.

GEORGE M. BROWN,
Attorney General.

PERCY A. CUPPER,
State Engineer.

Attest: J. L. McALLISTER,
Assistant Secretary. [206]

Salem, Oregon, July 1, 1920.

A special meeting of the Desert Land Board was held this day in the Capitol Building, at 2:00 P. M.

Present: Ben W. Olcott, Governor, Chairman;

Sam A. Kozer, Secretary of State;

O. P. Hoff, State Treasurer;

George M. Brown, Attorney General;

Percy A. Cupper, State Engineer, Secretary;

J. L. McAllister, Assistant Secretary.

Thereupon the following proceedings were had, to wit:

\*    \*    \*    \*    \*    \*    \*    \*

The written approval of the American Surety Company, of New York, not having been filed under the provisions of Section 2, Article 3, of the Supplemental State Contract, dated February 2d, 1920, and authorized by Board order of October 30, 1919, the Secretary was instructed to advise the Jordan Valley Land and Water Company that the terms of said Supplemental Contract were never operative, and that the Board will require the Company to proceed with the construction of the project under the terms of the State Contract of June 21st, 1918.

There being no further business, the meeting ad-journed.

BEN W. OLCOTT,
Governor, Chairman.

SAM A. KOZER,
Secretary of State.

O. P. HOFF,
State Treasurer.

GEORGE M. BROWN,
Attorney General.

PERCY A. CUPPER,
State Engineer, Secretary.

Attest: J. L. McALLISTER,
Assistant Secretary. [207]

Salem, Oregon, October 19th, 1920.

A regular meeting of the Desert Land Board was held in the Capitol Building at 10:30 A. M., Tuesday, October 19th.

Present: Ben W. Olcott, Governor, Chairman;

Sam A. Kozer, Secretary of State;

Percy A. Cupper, State Engineer, Secretary;

J. L. McAllister, Assistant Secretary.

Thereupon the following proceedings were had, to wit:

\*      \*      \*      \*      \*      \*      \*      \*

It appearing that construction work on the Jordan Valley Project was suspended on or about June 1st, and while the Board and its Secretary, the State Engineer, have been diligent in their efforts to bring about a resumption of the work and a continuance in accordance with the terms of its contract with the Jordan Valley Land and Water Company, no assurance has been received to date that work will be resumed and prosecuted in accordance with the provisions of said contract.

It also appearing that the State Laws under which the above contract was written provided that a cessation of work without the Board's approval for a period of six months will forfeit to the State all rights under said contract,

It was therefore ORDERED that the Secretary be and he is hereby instructed to so notify the Jordan Valley Land and Water Company, contractor with the State, and principal in the One Hundred Thousand Dollar bond given for faithful performance of the terms thereof, also the American Surety Company of New York, as surety on said bond, and J. W. Maney, of Oklahoma City, President of the Jordan Valley Land and Water Company.

\*    \*    \*    \*    \*    \*    \*

[208]

No further business appearing, the meeting was adjourned.

BEN W. OLCOTT,
Governor, Chairman.

SAM A. KOZER,
Secretary of State.

PERCY A. CUPPER,
State Engineer, Secretary.

Attest: J. L. McALLISTER,
Assistant Secretary.    [209]

Salem, Oregon, January 24, 1921.

A special meeting of the Desert Land Board was held Friday, January 21st, at 11:00 o'clock A. M. Present: Ben W. Olcott, Governor, Chairman;

Sam A. Kozer, Secretary of State;

I. H. Van Winkle, Attorney General;

Percy A. Cupper, State Engineer, Secretary;

J. L. McAllister, Assistant Secretary.

Thereupon the following proceedings were had, to wit:

\*     \*     \*     \*     \*     \*     \*     \*

An application by the Jordan Valley Land and Water Company, bearing date of November 30, 1920, requesting an extension of time in which to resume construction work under its contract with the State providing for the construction of the Jordan Valley Irrigation Project, was presented for consideration. This application was laid on the table.

\*     \*     \*     ..     \*     \*     \*     ~

No further business appearing, the meeting was adjourned.

BEN W. OLCOTT,
Governor, Chairman.

SAM A. KOZER,
Secretary of State.

I. H. VAN WINKLE,
Attorney General.

PERCY A. CUPPER,
State Engineer, Secretary.

Attest: J. L. McALLISTER,
Assistant Secretary. [210]

Salem, Oregon, Capitol Building.

A special meeting of the Desert Land Board was held at 2:00 o'clock P. M., Friday, February 25th, 1921.

Present: Ben W. Olcott, Governor, Chairman;

Sam A. Kozer, Secretary of State;

O. P. Hoff, State Treasurer;

I. H. Van Winkle, Attorney General;

Percy A. Cupper, State Engineer, Secretary;

J. L. McAllister, Assistant Secretary.

Thereupon the following proceedings were had, to wit:

WHEREAS, a certain contract dated June 21, 1918, by and between the Desert Land Board, acting for and on behalf of the State of Oregon, and the Jordan Valley Land and Water Company, provides for the construction of the irrigation system for the Jordan Valley Irrigation Project in accordance with certain plans and specifications, and the State law authorizing the same, and

WHEREAS, on or about June 1, 1920, all construction work ceased and has not been resumed to date, which cessation is in direct violation of said contract of June 21, 1918, and the State Laws under which it is written, and

WHEREAS, written notice of cessation of work has been given as required by law, and more than sixty days has elapsed since the giving of such notice and said company has failed to proceed with the work or to conform to the specifications of its

contract with the State, and no extension of time
has been given,

WHEREAS, this and other breaches of the contract subjects the same to forfeiture, and under the
law it is the duty of the board so to declare,

NOW, THEREFORE, BE IT ORDERED:

That said contract of June 21, 1918, and all
works constructed for the reclamation of the Jordan Valley Irrigation Project, together with all
rights, incident thereto, are hereby declared forfeited to the State of Oregon as provided by law.
[211]

And it is further ORDERED that notice of this
declaration be given by publication once a week for
a period of four weeks in "The Jordan Valley Express," a newspaper of general circulation published
in the County of Malheur, State of Oregon, the
county of which the work is situated, and in the
"Statesman," a newspaper of general circulation
published in the City of Salem, Marion County,
Oregon, the seat of the State Capital.

And it is further ORDERED that upon the
tenth day of June, 1921, up to the hour of 10
o'clock in the forenoon of said day, proposals will
be received at the office of the Secretary of the
Desert Land Board in the Capitol Building in the
city of Salem, Marion County, Oregon, for the purchase of the incompleted works and for the completion of the irrigation works in accordance with
the plans and specifications therefor, which are
now on file and in the custody of the Secretary
of said Desert Land Board and open to the inspec-

tion of all persons interested, which plans and specifications and the condition therein contained are hereby by reference made a part of the notice. The Board reserves the right to reject any and all bids and the Secretary of the Board is hereby instructed to secure the publication of this declaration as hereinabove proivded.

\*        \*        \*        \*        \*        \*        \*        \*

No further business appearing, the meeting adjourned.

> BEN W. OLCOTT,
>> Governor, Chairman.
>
> SAM A. KOZER,
>> Secretary of State.
>
> O. P. HOFF,
>> State Treasurer.
>
> I. H. VAN WINKLE,
>> Attorney General.
>
> PERCY A. CUPPER,
>> State Engineer, Secretary.
>
> Attest: J. L. McALLISTER,
>> Assistant Secretary.    [212]

> Salem, Oregon, Capitol Building.

A special meeting of the Desert Land Board was held in the Capitol Building at 3:00 P. M., Wednesday, May 11th, 1921.

Present: Ben W. Olcott, Governor, Chairman;
> O. P. Hoff, State Treasurer;
> I. H. Van Winkle, Attorney General;
> Percy A. Cupper, State Engineer, Secretary;
> J. L. McAllister, Assistant Secretary.

Thereupon the following proceedings were had, to wit:

Mr. J. W. Maney, President of the Jordan Valley Land and Water Company, Mr. J. Humfeld, agent for the Mortgage Company for America, a Holland corporation, and Mr. John W. Cunningham, representative of the Board on the Jordan Valley Irrigation Project, appeared before the Board.

It appearing that on or about June 1st, 1920, construction work ceased under the Jordan Valley Land and Water Company's contract with the State, dated June 21st, 1918, also that by an order entered February 25th, 1921, said contract was declared forfeited by the State and that publication was being made in compliance with statutory provisions.

Mr. Maney submitted a plan by which he could raise approximately $100,000.00 for construction purposes, through a transfer of securities now held by the Mortgage Company for America, which amount would be expended in the reclamation of the lands under A, B, and C Laterals, under which all settlers now holding contracts could be taken care of. The plan would involve a new contract between the Jordan Valley Land and Water Company and the State, and the filing of a new bond thereunder. Mr. Maney also advised that a $25,-000.00 surety bond would be the maximum that he could get, also that if the Board would give him a new contract that would permit the carrying out of the proposed plan of financing, and accept a $25,-

000.00 [213] bond in lieu of the contract and bond heretofore given, he would stay on the project and personally supervise the construction work, at least to the extent necessary to take care of all the interests of all settlers who have heretofore purchased lands, and further, that no attempt would be made in the future to sell any land before the canals were constructed and a water supply available therefor.

In view of the representations made, the Board consented to accept the $25,000.00 surety bond, subject to the approval of the Attorney General, when filed, also to execute a new contract, the details of which the State Engineer and the Attorney General were requested to work out for later consideration.

No further business appearing, the meeting adjourned.

BEN W. OLCOTT,
Governor, Chairman.

O. P. HOFF,
State Treasurer.

I. H. VAN WINKLE,
Attorney General.

PERCY A. CUPPER,
State Engineer, Secretary.

Attest: J. L. McALLISTER,
Assistant Secretary.   [214]

Salem, Oregon, Capitol Building.

A special meeting of the Desert Land Board was held in the Capitol Building, Monday, June 8th, 1921, at 2:00 o'clock P. M.

Present: Ben W. Olcott, Governor, Chairman;

Sam A. Kozer, Secretary of State;

O. P. Hoff, State Treasurer;

I. H. Van Winkle, Attorney General;

J. L. McAllister, Assistant Secretary.

Thereupon the following proceedings were had, to wit:

The following resolution was adopted:

WHEREAS, at a meeting held February 25th, 1921, the Board declared the forfeiture of the contract between the State of Oregon, and the Jordan Valley Land and Water Company, dated June 21st, 1918, and providing for the construction of the Jordan Valley Irrigation Project, and

WHEREAS, Mr. J. W. Maney, President of the Jordan Valley Land and Water Company, recently submitted a proposal to the Board whereby construction work might be resumed on the project, which proposal contemplated a new State contract, under which certain securities might be hypothecated for the purpose of raising cash for construction work; a $25,000.00 surety bond filed, and the old $100,000.00 bond cancelled, and

WHEREAS, a new state contract has been prepared for execution by and between the Desert Land Board and the Jordan Valley Land and Water Company, also a trust agreement has been prepared for execution by and between the Desert

Land Board, the Jordan Valley Land and Water
Company, J. Humfeld, and the United States National Bank, of Portland, Oregon, wherein J. Humfeld is made Trustee under the State contract, and
the United States National Bank named as a de-
pository, **and**

WHEREAS, a certain loan agreement has been
executed by and between the Jordan Valley Land
and Water Company, the Jordan [215] Valley
Farms, and the Mortgage Company for America,
which contemplates the hypothecation of trust
fund securities as provided for in the State contract, subject to the approval of the Board.

NOW, THEREFORE, BE IT ORDERED:

That the new State contract be and the same is
hereby approved as prepared by the State Engineer and the Attorney General under date of May
27, 1921, and executed by the Jordan Valley Land
and Water Company, and the Chairman and Secretary are hereby authorized to execute the same in
duplicate, and be it Further ORDERED that the
trust agreement as prepared and executed by the
Jordan Valley Land and Water Company, J.
Humfeld and the United States National Bank,
of Portland, Oregon, under date of May 27, 1921,
be and the same is hereby approved, and the Chairman and Secretary are hereby authorized to execute the same in quadruplicate, and be it Further
ORDERED that that certain loan agrement executed by and between the Jordan Valley Land and
Water Company, the Jordan Valley Farms, and
the Mortgage Company for America, dated May

27, 1921, be and the same is hereby approved, and be it Further ORDERED that the new $25,000.00 bond given the State under the new State contract and approved by the Attorney General as to form, be and the same is hereby approved, and be it Further ORDERED that the bond of the AMERICAN SURETY COMPANY executed on behalf of the Jordan Valley Land and Water Company in favor of the Desert Land Board in the penal sum of $100,000.00, on or about August 7, 1918, covering the State contract of June 21, 1918, be and the same is hereby declared cancelled and the Secretary is instructed to so advise the principal and surety on said $100,000.00 bond.

\* \* \* \* \* \* \* \*

No further business appearing, the meeting adjourned. [216]

DESERT LAND BOARD OF OREGON,
By BEN W. OLCOTT,
Governor, Chairman,
SAM A. KOZER,
Secretary of State,
O. P. HOFF,
State Treasurer,
I. H. VAN WINKLE,
Attorney General.
Attest: J. L. McALLISTER,
Assistant Secretary. [217]

Salem, Oregon, Capitol Building.

A special meeting of the Desert Land Board was held in the Capitol Building, at two o'clock P. M., Friday, July 1st, 1921.

Present: Ben W. Olcott, Governor, Chairman;
Sam A. Kozer, Secretary of State;
O. P. Hoff, State Treasurer;
I. H. Van Winkle, Attorney General;
Percy A. Cupper, State Engineer, Secretary;
J. L. McAllister, Assistant Secretary.

Thereupon the following proceedings were had, to wit:

In the matter of the transfer of the cash and securities held by the trustees under the old State Contract of June 21st, 1918, covering the construction of the Jordan Valley Irrigation Project, to the trustee under the new State Contract of May 27, 1921, the following order was entered;

Be it ORDERED that the Boise Title and Trust Company, of Boise, Idaho, be and is hereby authorized to immediately transfer all cash, mortgages and securities now held by it under the provisions of the State Contract of June 21st, 1918, covering the construction of the Jordan Valley Irrigation Project, to Mr. J. Humfeld, United States National Bank Building, Portland, Oregon. This authorization is given in accordance with the provisions of the new State Contract of May 27th, 1921, also the new Trust agreement of the same date. The Secretary is hereby instructed to transmit a certified copy of this order, together with a copy of the new State Contract of May 27th, 1921, and of the new Trust Agreement of the same date, to the Boise Title and Trust Company, and to Mr. J. Humfeld.

\*      \*      \*          \*      \*      \*      \*

No further business appearing, the meeting adjourned. [218]

BEN W. OLCOTT,
Governor, Chairman.

SAM A. KOZER,
Secretary of State.

O. P. HOFF,
State Treasurer.

I. H. VAN WINKLE,
Attorney General.

PERCY A. CUPPER,
State Engineer-Secretary.

Attest: J. L. McAllister,
Assistant Secretary. [219]

Capitol Building, Salem, Oregon.

A special meeting of the Desert Land Board was held in the Capitol Building at 2:00 o'clock P. M., Thursday, November 17, 1921.

Present: Ben W. Olcott, Governor, Chairman;

Sam A. Kozer, Secretary of State;

O. P. Hoff, State Treasurer;

I. H. Van Winkle, Attorney General;

Percy A. Cupper, State Engineer, Secretary;

J. L. McAllister, Assistant Secretary.

Thereupon the following proceedings were had, to wit:

\*    \*    \*    \*    \*    \*    \*    \*    \*

It appearing that the Jordan Valley Land and Water Company is now in default under the terms of that certain contract executed by and between said company and the Board on June 21st, 1918, in that all construction work ceased on or about June 1st, 1920, and has not been resumed prior to the date hereof;

It also appearing that the Jordan Valley Land and Water Company is now in default under the terms of that certain contract executed by and between said Company and the Board on May 27th, 1921, in that the funds provided therein to be made immediately available for construction purposes have not as yet been made available, also in that the construction work has not been commenced within the time provided in said contract;

It further appearing that said agreement entered into by and between the Jordan Valley Land and Water Company, the Jordan Valley Farms, and the Mortgage Company of America, a copy of which was attached to and made a part of said State Contract of May 27th, 1921, therein referred to and designated the "Loan Contract," is not being carried out by the parties thereto;  [220]

It also appearing that there is some question as to the status of said contract of May 27th, 1921, for the reason, first, of the failure of said Loan Contract, and second, the fact that the said State Contract of May 27th, 1921, ws executed by the

President and Secretary of the Jordan Valley Land and Water Company without the authorization of its Board of Directors, and which authorization by said Board of Directors was not given, nor the contract ratified, until after notification by this Board of such failure to the said Jordan Valley Land and Water Company, and its surety under the $100,000 bond, the American Surety Company of New York;

It was therefore ORDERED that the Secretary be, and he hereby is, instructed to give notice, as required by statute, of the cessation of construction work under the contract of June 21st, 1918, by and between the State of Oregon, and the Jordan Valley Land and Water Company; also of the failure to begin construction work within the time provided, or to otherwise carry out the terms of that certain contract purporting to have been executed by and between the State of Oregon, and the Jordan Valley Land and Water Company, dated May 27th, 1921. Said notice to be given to the Jordan Valley Land and Water Company, the American Surety Company of New York, the Hartford Accident and Indemnity Company, and Mr. J. Humfeld.

No further business appearing, the meeting adjourned. [221]

BEN W. OLCOTT,
                Governor, Chairman.
SAM A. KOZER,
                Secretary of State.
O. P. HOFF,
                State Treasurer.
I. H. VAN WINKLE,
                Attorney General.
PERCY A. CUPPER,
        State Engineer-Secretary.
Attest:  J. L. McALLISTER,
        Assistant Secretary.   [222]

Capitol Building, Salem, Oregon.

A special meeting of the Desert Land Board was held in the Capitol Building at 2 o'clock P. M., Friday, January 27th, 1922.

Present:  Ben W. Olcott, Governor, Chairman.
          Sam A. Kozer, Secretary of State;
          O. P. Hoff, State Treasurer;
          I. H. Van Winkle, Attorney General;
          Percy A. Cupper, State Engineer, Secretary;
          J. L. McAllister, Assistant Secretary.

Thereupon the following proceedings were had, to wit:

WHEREAS, a certain contract dated June 21st, 1918, by and between the Desert Land Board, acting for and on behalf of the State of Oregon, and the Jordan Valley Land and Water Company, provides for the construction of the irrigation system for the Jordan Valley Irrigation Project in accordance with certain plans and specifications, and the State Law authorizing the same, and

WHEREAS, on or about June 1, 1920, all construction work ceased and has not been resumed to date, which cessation is in direct violation of said contract of June 21, 1918, and the State laws under which it was written, and

WHEREAS, a certain contract dated May 27, 1921, by and between the Desert Land Board, acting for and on behalf of the State of Oregon, and the Jordan Valley Land and Water Company, provides that certain funds should be immediately available for construction purposes, and that construction work should be resumed within sixty days from the date hereof, and

WHEREAS, no funds have been made available to date, and construction work has not been resumed as provided for in said contract of May 27, 1921, and

WHEREAS, written notice of the cessation of work under said contract of June 21, 1918, and of the failure to resume work and otherwise carry out the terms of said contract of May 27, 1921, has been given as required by law, and more than sixty days has [223] elapsed since the giving of such notice, and said company has failed to proceed with the work or to conform to the specifications of its contracts with the State, and no extension of time has been given, and

WHEREAS, This and other breaches of the contracts subject the same to forfeiture, and under the law it is the duty of the Board so to declare;

NOW, THEREFORE, BE IT ORDERED, That said contracts of June 21, 1918, and May 27, 1921, and all work constructed for the reclamation of the Jordan Valley Irrigation Project, together with all rights incident thereto, are hereby declared forfeited to the State of Oregon, as provided by law.

And it is further ORDERED, that notice of this declaration be given by publication once a week for a period of four weeks in the "Jordan Valley Express," a newspaper of general circulation published in the county of Malheur, State of Oregon, the county in which the work is situated, and in the "Oregon Statesman," a newspaper of general circulation, published in the city of Salem, Marion County, Oregon, the seat of the State Capital,

And it is further ORDERED, that upon the tenth day of May, 1922, up to the hour of 10:00 o'clock in the forenoon of said day, proposals will be received at the office of the Secretary of the Desert Land Board in the Capitol Building, in the city of Salem, Marion County, Oregon, for the purchase of the incompleted works and for the completion of the irrigation works in accordance with the plans and specifications therefor, which plans and specifications and the conditions therein contained are hereby by reference made a part of this notice. The board reserves the right to reject any and all bids, and the Secretary of the board is hereby instructed to  [224]  secure the publication of this declaration as herein provided.

\* \* \* \* \* \* \* \* \*

No further business appearing, the meeting adjourned.

> BEN W. OLCOTT,
>> Governor, Chairman.
>
> SAM A. KOZER,
>> Secretary of State.
>
> O. P. HOFF,
>> State Treasurer.
>
> I. H. VAN WINKLE,
>> Attorney General.
>
> PERCY A. CUPPER,
>> State Engineer-Secretary.
>
> Attest: J. L. McALLISTER,
>> Assistant Secretary.  [225]
>
> Salem, Oregon, Capitol Building.

A regular meeting of the Desert Land Board was held in the Capitol Building at two o'clock P. M., Tuesday, February 28, 1922.

Present: Ben W. Olcott, Governor, Chairman;
> Sam A. Kozer, Secretary of State;
> O. P. Hoff, State Treasurer;
> Percy A. Cupper, State Engineer-Secretary;
> J. L. McAllister, Assistant Secretary.

Thereupon the following proceedings were had, to wit:

\* \* \* \* \* \* \* \* \*

In view of the failure of the Jordan Valley Land and Water Company, the Jordan Valley Farms, and the Mortgage Company for America, to comply with the terms of certain contracts executed May 27, 1921, and providing for the completion of the Jordan Valley Irrigation Project, also in view of the cancellation of the State Contracts and the forfeiture of the works constructed thereunder to the State of Oregon, Be it ORDERED that the authorization given by the Board Order of July 1, 1921, for the transfer of cash and securities by the Boise Title and Trust Company, Trustee under the State Contract of June 21, 1918, to J. Humfeld, Trustee under the State Contract of May 27, 1921, be and the same is hereby withdrawn and declared annuled, and the secretary is hereby instructed to so notify the Boise Title and Trust Company.

\*    \*    \*    \*    \*    \*    \*    \*.    \*

No further business appearing, the meeting adjourned.

> BEN W. OLCOTT,
> > Governor, Chairman.
> SAM A. KOZER,
> > Secretary of State.
> O. P. HOFF,
> > State Treasurer.
> PERCY A. KUPPER,
> > State Engineer, Secretary.
> Attest: J. L. McALLISTER,
> > Assistant Secretary. [226]

Capitol Building, Salem, Oregon.

A special meeting of the Desert Land Board was held Thursday, May 4, 1922, at 2:00 o'clock P. M.

Present: Ben W. Olcott, Governor, Chairman;

Sam A. Kozer, Secretary of State;

O. P. Hoff, State Treasurer;

I. H. Van Winkle, Attorney General;

Percy A. Cupper, State Engineer Secretary;

J. L. McAllister, Assistant Secretary.

Thereupon the following proceedings were had, to wit:

\*    \*    \*    \*    \*    \*    \*    \*    \*

The present status of the Jordan Valley Irrigation Project was discussed and it appearing advisable in view of the complications that have arisen involving this project for a representative of the state to go over the project and consult with the settlers and their representatives who are organizing an irrigation district, with a view to the completion of the project,

It was therefore ORDERED that Mr. J. L. McAllister be and he hereby is authorized and directed to go to Boise, Idaho, and make such investigation, and to make due report of his findings and recommendations upon his return.

No further business appearing, the meeting adjourned.

BEN W. OLCOTT,
Governor, Chairman.
SAM A. KOZER,
Secretary of State.
O. P. HOFF,
State Treasurer.
I. H. VAN WINKLE,
Attorney General.
PERCY A. CUPPER,
State Engineer.
Attest: J. L. McALLISTER,
Assistant Secretary.   [227]

Salem, Oregon, Capitol Building.

A special meeting of the Desert Land Board was held at 10:00 o'clock A. M. Wednesday, May 10, 1922.

Present: Ben W. Olcott, Governor, Chairman;

Sam A. Kozer, Secretary of State;

O. P. Hoff, State Treasurer;

I. H. Van Winkle, Attorney General;

Percy A. Cupper, State Engineer, Secretary;

J. L. McAllister, Assistant Secretary.

Thereupon the following proceedings were had, to wit:

WHEREAS, on January 27, 1922, an order was entered by this Board cancelling the contracts of the Jordan Valley Land and Water Company, and declaring forfeiture of all works constructed thereunder, after having given due notice as required under Sec. 5585, Oregon Laws, which order fixed the time for receiving of bids as 10 o'clock A. M. May 10, 1922, and

WHEREAS, publication of said order has been duly made and the time has arrived for the receiving of bids for the purchase of the incompleted works and proposals for the completion of the same, and

WHEREAS, an Irrigation District has been organized embracing the lands of the Jordan Valley Project, by a unanimous vote of the land owners and qualified entrymen, which District is known as the Jordan Valley Irrigation District, and

WHEREAS, Mr. W. S. Bruce, representing the settlers on said project and the District then in process of organization, did make and file with this Board a bid for the purchase of the incompleted works and a proposal for the completion thereof, and

WHEREAS, said bid having been opened and it appearing to be the only bid or proposal filed,

Now, Therefore, BE IT ORDERED, that the bid of W. S. Bruce, representative of the Jordan Valley Irrigation District, then in process of organization and the settlers thereof, of One Dollar ($1.00), [228] and his proposal to finish the construction of said project in accordance with the plans and specifications heretofore adopted or to be adopted under a contract to be entered into by and between said District and the State of Oregon, be and the same is hereby accepted and the incompleted works and all forfeited rights and interests of the Jordan Valley Land and Water Company, are hereby ORDERED sold to the Jordan Valley Irrigation District, and

BE IT FURTHER ORDERED that the Secretary be and he hereby is instructed to prepare, in cooperation with officers of said District, all of the necessary details in connection with such transfer, and to work out the terms of an agreement covering the completion of the construction work to be executed by and between the Jordan Valley Irrigation District, and the State of Oregon, through the Desert Land Board.

No further business appearing, the meeting adjourned.

> BEN W. OLCOTT,
>> Governor, Chairman.
> SAM A. KOZER,
>> Secretary of State.
> O. P. HOFF,
>> State Treasurer.
> I. H. VAN WINKLE,
>> Attorney General.
> PERCY A. CUPPER,
> State Engineer, Secretary.

Attest: J. L. McALLISTER,
Assistant Secretary. [229]

Salem, Oregon, Capitol Building.

A special meeting of the Desert Land Board was held in the Capitol Building at two o'clock P. M., Monday, July 17, 1922.

Present: Sam A. Kozer, Secretary of State;

O. P. Hoff, State Treasurer;

Percy A. Cupper, State Engineer, Secretary;

J. L. McAllister, Assistant Secretary.

Thereupon the following proceedings were had, to wit:

The following representatives appeared before the Board:

J. H. Richards, representing the Trustee in Bankruptcy for the Jordan Valley Land and Water Company;

L. J. Aker, representing the Trustee in Bankruptcy for the Jordan Valley Farms;

F. H. Wegener, Trustee in Bankruptcy for the Jordan Valley Farms;

Wm. M. Morgan, Attorney for the Jordan Valley Irrigation District;

W. S. Bruce and Charles El Lanning, representing the Board of Directors of the Jordan Valley Irrigation District.

A general discussion was had relative to the present status of the affairs of the Jordan Valley Irrigation Project, and the interest of the Creditors of the Jordan Valley Land and Water Company, also as to what claims, if any, should be taken care of by the Irrigation District.

After all present had been heard, the matter was referred to the Attorney General and the State Engineer for further consideration.

No further business appearing, the meeting adjourned. [230]

(Minutes of July 17, 1922, continued.)

SAM A. KOZER,
Secretary of State.

O. P. HOFF,
State Treasurer.

PERCY A. CUPPER,
State Engineer, Secretary.

Attest: J. L. McALLISTER,
Assistant Secretary. [231]

Salem, Oregon, Capitol Building.

A special meeting of the Desert Land Board was held in the Capitol Building, Thursday, September 7, 1922, at 10:30 o'clock A. M.

Present: Ben W. Olcott, Governor, Chairman;

Sam A. Kozer, Secretary of State;

O. P. Hoff, State Treasurer;

I. H. Van Winkle, Attorney General;

Percy A. Cupper, State Engineer, Secretary;

J. L. McAllister, Assistant Secretary.

Thereupon the following proceedings were had, to wit:

WHEREAS, on July 14, 1922, the Mortgage Company for America, by its Agent, J. Humfeld, offered to deliver to the Jordan Valley Irrigation District the securities purchased at foreclosure sale in the case of Mortgage Company for America versus Jordan Valley Land and Water Company and Jordan Valley Farms, and to assign to the District, a certain deficiency judgment against these defendant companies for the payment of $117,000.00, and

WHEREAS, on July 21, 1922, the Jordan Valley Irrigation District, through its Board of Directors, by resolution accepted the offer of the Mortgage Company for America, and agreed to pay the amount of $117,000.00 subject to the approval of the Desert Land Board of Oregon, and

WHEREAS, by order of the District Court of the United States for the District of Oregon, entered July 14, 1922, in the above-mentioned case, on petition of J. Humfeld, Receiver, for the approval of his accounts, the following fees and disbursements were allowed, to wit: [232]

$3500.00, fee as Receiver for the Jordan Valley Land and Water Company;

3233.43, Receiver's disbursements for the Jordan Valley Land and Water Company;

750.00, fee as Receiver for The Jordan Valley Farms;

860.05, Receiver's disbursements for the Jordan Valley Farms;

750.00, fee for the services of the Attorney for the Receiver;

_____

$9093.48, Total.

And WHEREAS, to secure payment of said amount, the Receiver holds certain securities which under the terms of said Court Order are to be returned to said defendant Companies upon the payment of the amounts due the Receiver, and

WHEREAS, it appears to the Board that funds sufficient for the satisfaction of the Receiver's fees and disbursements should be realized from a sale of the property held as security therefor.

NOW, THEREFORE, BE IT ORDERED that the proposed purchase by the District be not approved under the Court Order of July 14, and

BE IT FURTHER ORDERED that the Secretary be, and he hereby is, instructed to notify the parties interested that it is the opinion of the Board that the fees and disbursements of the Receiver should be realized from a sale of the property held as security therefor.

WHEREAS, the contracts of the Jordan Valley Land and Water Company providing for the construction of the Jordan Valley Irrigation Project in Malheur County, have been cancelled, and all interests thereunder, including the incompleted works, have been forfeited to the State, as provided by law, and

WHEREAS, the forfeited works, and all rights-of-way, water rights and franchises have been duly sold to the Jordan Valley Irrigation District, as provided by law, and

WHEREAS, a conveyance of the forfeited property by the State to said District, also a construction contract providing for  [233]  the completion of the irrigation system, have been prepared and submitted by the Secretary.

NOW, THEREFORE, BE IT ORDERED that upon the approval by the Attorney General of the conveyance and construction contract as submitted, the Chairman and Secretary, be and they are hereby authorized and instructed to execute the same, provided the contract shall have first been executed in duplicate by said District, and the required bond filed and approved by the Attorney General.

And be it further ORDERED that the Assistant Secretary be, and he is hereby instructed to go to Boise, Idaho, and Jordan Valley for a conference with the Board of Directors of the Jordan Valley Irrigation District, and its Attorneys, relative to the construction contract, the conveyance herein authorized, also the proposed purchase by the District of the securities held by the Mortgage Company for America.

\* \* \* \* \* \* \* \* \*

No further business appearing, the meeting adjourned.

BEN W. OLCOTT,
Governor, Chairman.
SAM A. KOZER,
Secretary of State.
O. P. HOFF,
State Treasurer.
I. H. VAN WINKLE,
Attorney General.
PERCY A. CUPPER,
State Engineer, Secretary,
Attest: J. L. McALLISTER,
Assistant Secretary. [234]

Salem, Oregon, January 30, 1923.

A regular meeting of the Desert Land Board was held January 30th in the Capitol Building at 4:00 P. M.

Present:   Walter M. Pierce, Governor, Chairman;
Sam A. Kozer, Secretary of State;
O. P. Hoff, State Treasurer;
I. H. Van Winkle, Attorney General;
Percy A. Cupper, State Engineer, Sec'y;
J. L. McAllister, Assistant Secretary.

Thereupon the following proceedings were had, to wit:

WHEREAS, On July 16, 1919, this Board filed with the United States Land Office at Vale, Oregon, an application for the termporary withdrawal of certain lands located in Jordan Valley, Malheur County, and designated Oregon Carey Act Segregation list number 38, and,

WHEREAS, since the filing of said application the Jordan Valley Land and Water Company, the contractor with the State for the construction of the Jordan Valley Irrigation Project, which contemplated the reclamation of the lands above referred to has failed in the prosecution of the work in compliance with the terms of its contract and is now a bankrupt, and,

WHEREAS, a portion of the land included in the said list number 38 have subsequently been included within the boundaries of an irrigation district organized under the Oregon Irrigation Laws, known as the North Side Irrigation District, and,

WHEREAS, the canal system, for the reclamation of such lands together with other lands included in said district, having been constructed and entrymen having filed, or attempted to file, Desert Land entries covering a portion of said lands, and,

WHEREAS, it appears to be for the best interests of said district and the settlers involved that the State's application for segregation be amended so as to eliminate lands which are embraced within the boundaries of said district that the applications [235] for desert entries pending before the United States Land Office at Vale, be approved or that a preference right be given to such applicants to refile as soon as the lands are open for entry. Now, therefore, be it ordered that the State's application for segregation of the lands included in Oregon Carey Act segregation list number 38, filed July 16, 1919, be and the same is hereby amended so as to exclude the lands described as follows, to wit:

Township 30 South, Range 42 East, W. M.

Sec. 12 SW. ¼ ........................ 160 acres
Sec. 14 All ........................... 640 acres
Sec. 20 All ........................... 640 acres
Sec. 22 All ........................... 640 acres
Sec. 24 All ........................... 640 acres
Sec. 26 All ........................... 640 acres
Sec. 28 All ........................... 640 acres
Sec. 30 All ........................... 640 acres
Sec. 32 All ........................... 640 acres
Sec. 36 SW. ¼ of SW. ¼ ............... 40 acres

NE. ¼ ........................ 160 acres

N. ½ of SE. ¼ ................. 80 acres

SE. ¼ of E. ¼ ................. 40 acres

Township 30 South, Range 43 East, W. M.

Sec. 18 SW. ¼ ...................... 160 acres

S. ½ of SE. ¼ .................. 80 acres

Sec. 20 All ........................ 640 acres

Sec. 28 All ........................ 640 acres

Sec. 30 All ........................ 640 acres

Sec. 32 All ........    ............ 640 acres

Sec. 34 All ........................ 640 acres

Township 31 South Range 43 East, W. M.

Sec.   2 SE. ¼ ...................... 160 acres

NE. ¼ of SW. ¼ ............... 40 acres

NW. ¼ ....Estimated .......... 160 acres

NE. ¼ .....Estimated ......... 160 acres

_____

9,560 acres

And be it further ordered that the Honorable Commissioner of the General Land Office be, and he hereby is, requested to approve the applications now pending for desert land entry covering any of the above-described lands or that the applicants, all of whom are actual settlers under the Jordan Valley Carey Act Project, be given a preference right to refile on their respective selections as soon as said lands are open for entry.

*    *    *    *    *    *    *    *    *    *    *

[236]

There being no further business the meeting was adjourned.

WALTER M. PIERCE,
Governor, Chairman.

SAM A. KOZER,
Secretary of State.

O. P. HOFF,
.State Treasurer.

I. H. VAN WINKLE,
Attorney General.

PERCY A. CUPPER,
State Engineer, Sec'y.

Attest: J. L. McALLISTER,
Assistant Secretary.

State of Oregon,
County of Marion,—ss.

I, Percy A. Cupper, State Engineer and Secretary of the Desert Land Board of Oregon, do hereby certify that the above and foregoing copy of extracts from the minutes of the meetings of the Desert Land Board, showing all actions taken in connection with the Jordan Valley Irrigation Project during the period beginning March 6, 1918 and ending January 30, 1923, is a full, true and correct copy of the original as the same appears in the records of my office and in my custody and of the whole thereof.

In Witness Whereof, I have hereunto set my hand this 14th day of June, 1923.

PERCY A. CUPPER,
State Engineer, Secretary.

By J. L. McALLISTER,

J. L. McALLISTER,
Assistant Secretary.   [237]

## DEFENDANT'S EXHIBIT "K."

No. ——. Defts. Ex. "K."

U. S. District Court, District of Oregon. Filed June 12, 1923. G. H. Marsh, Clerk.

Bond Dated May 27, 1921, Executed by the Jordan Valley Land & Water Company as Principal and Hartford Accident & Indemnity Company as Surety.

47.

KNOW ALL MEN BY THESE PRESENTS, That the Jordan Valley Land and Water Company, a Corporation organized under the laws of Nevada and doing business in the State of Oregon, as principal, and Hartford Accident and Indemnity Co., of Hartford, Conn., a corporation, formed and organized under the laws of the State of Connecticut, and authorized to transact the surety business in the State of Oregon, as surety, are held and firmly bound to the State of Oregon in the full penal sum of twenty-five thousand ($25,000.00) dollars, for the payment of which well and truly to be made, we hereby bind ourselves, our successors and assigns, jointly and severally, firmly by these presents.

Signed, sealed, and dated this 27th day of May, 1921.

THE CONDITIONS OF THIS OBLIGATION ARE SUCH THAT:

WHEREAS, the above-bounden principal has entered into an agreement with the Desert Land Board, acting for and on behalf of the State of

Oregon, dated May 27, 1921, providing for the construction by said principal of an irrigation system, reservoirs, canals, flumes and other irrigation works and structures therein more particularly described, for what is known as the Jordan Valley Irrigation Project in Malheur County, Oregon, which contract is hereby made a part hereof as fully as if set forth at length herein.

NOW, THEREFORE, if the said principal shall faithfully perform and discharge each and every of the conditions of said contract, by said principal to be kept and performed, as therein set [238] forth and described, and shall comply with all the terms and conditions thereof and shall not permit any lien or claim to be filed or prosecuted against said irrigation system, reservoir, canals, flumes and other irrigation works and structures, and shall promptly make payments to all persons supplying it with labor or materials for any prosecution of the work provided for in said contract, this obligation shall be null and void, otherwise to remain in full force and effect.

IN WITNESS WHEREOF, the said principal and the said surety have caused this instrument to be executed by its officers thereunto duly authorized on the day first above written.

> JORDAN VALLEY LAND AND WATER COMPANY.
>
> By J. W. MANEY,
> President.
>
> [Seal]      Attest: EMIL L. TSCHIRGI,
> Secretary.

HARTFORD ACCIDENT AND INDEM-
NITY CO.,

By JOHN KER,

Attorney in Fact.

[Seal]           By HARRISON ALLEN,

Attorney in Fact.

Countersigned at Portland, Oregon, this 27th day
of May, 1921,

JOHN KER CO.,

Agents,

By JNO. KER,

Treas. Pres.   [239]

State of Oregon,
County of Marion,—ss.

I, Percy A. Cupper, State Engineer and Secretary of the Desert Land Board of Oregon, do hereby
certify that the above and foregoing copy of the
Bond  given May 27, 1921, wherein  the Jordan
Valley Land and Water Company, as principal,
and the Hartford Acident and Indemnity Company,
as surety, are bound to the State of Oregon in the
penal sum of Twenty-five Thousand Dollars, conditioned upon the faithful performance and discharge of the conditions of that certain contract
entered into on May 27, 1921, by and between said
principal and the Desert Land Board of Oregon,
providing for the re-financing and completion of
the Jordan Valley Irrigation Project, is a full, true
and correct copy of the original as the same appears
in the records of my office and in my custody and
of the whole thereof.

In Witness Whereof, I have hereunto set my hand this 14th day of June, 1923.

PERCY A. CUPPER,
State Engineer, Secretary.
By J. L. McALLISTER,
Assistant Secretary. [240]

DEFENDANT'S EXHIBIT "L."

No. ——. Defts. Ex. "L."

U. S. District Court, District of Oregon. Filed June 12, 1923. G. H. Marsh, Clerk.

Contract Dated May 27, 1921, Between Desert Land Board of the State of Oregon and the Jordan Valley Land & Water Company.

#44.

CONTRACT FOR CONSTRUCTION
of
JORDAN VALLEY PROJECT.

THIS AGREEMENT, made and entered into, in duplicate, this 27th day of May, A. D. 1921, by and between the DESERT LAND BOARD of the State of Oregon, acting for and on behalf of the State of Oregon (hereinafter sometimes called the "Board") the party of the first part, and JORDAN VALLEY LAND AND WATER COMPANY, a corporation organized under the laws of the State of Nevada and doing business in the State of Oregon (hereinafter sometimes called the "Construction Company") the party of the second part, witnesseth: That,

WHEREAS; the Jordan Valley Land and Water Company has heretofore under date of June 21,

1918, entered into a contract for the construction
of the Jordan Valley Irrigation Project, and has
collected and disbursed certain funds, and has constructed certain irrigation works and reclaimed
certain lands, which said contract and all works
constructed thereunder were, on or about February
25, 1921, declared forfeited by the party of the first
part; and

WHEREAS, a plan has been submitted by the
party of the second part whereby the lands for
which application has heretofore been made may be
supplied with water, or the settlers in interest transferred to reclaimed lands, which plan also contemplates the ultimate completion of the project;

NOW, THEREFORE, In consideration of the
premises and of the covenants and agreements,
hereinafter contained and to be kept and performed by the parties hereto, respectively, the said
parties have agreed and hereby do agree as follows:
[241]

## ARTICLE I.    #44.
### Transfer and Satisfaction of all Applicants for Land.

The Construction Company agrees to make immediately available approximately $93,000.00 to be
expended in the construction of the necessary
works for the complete reclamation of lands under
the "A" and "B" Laterals on the Lower Unit of
the Project, the remainder, if any, to be expended
in the construction of the "C" Lateral, and said
construction company will use his best endeavors
to have applicants for lands on the Lower Unit

select lands that may be served by the "A" and "B" Laterals, or that part of the "C" Lateral which may be constructed with the available funds, to the end that all persons who have heretofore made application for lands in the Lower Unit may secure water at the earliest possible date. Transfers of selection shall be made without additional cost to the applicant. The construction company further agrees that no further applications for water rights, shares of land, shall be received, or obligations to deliver additional water incurred, until all present applicants have been supplied or otherwise satisfied and the lands opened for entry and sale as hereinafter provided.

INSERT. Addition to Article I.

Said $93,000.00 to be deposited through the Trustee designated under the provisions hereof with the United States National Bank of Portland, Oregon, and designated "Jordan Valley Trust Fund," which shall be disbursed in the manner hereinafter set forth and more particularly specified in the Trust Agreement executed by and between the Board, the Construction Company, J. Humfeld, and the United States National Bank, of Portland, Oregon. It is mutually understood and agreed that the said $93,000.00 shall not be reduced to an amount less than $30,000.00, or the amount to which the present outstanding indebtedness of the Construction Company may be reduced.

No. ——. Defts. Ex. "L."

U. S. District Court, District of Oregon. Filed June 12, 1923. G. H. Marsh, Clerk. [242]

## ARTICLE II.

General Covenants as to Construction and Compensation.

The Construction Company agrees to furnish all material and do all work required in the construction of said irrigation system, reservoirs, canals, flumes, and other irrigation works and structures, hereinafter more particularly described, in substantial compliance with the plans and specifications herein set forth, and such additional plans and specifications as may hereafter be approved by the State Engineer of the State of Oregon and filed with the Desert Land Board; and it will do all such work in a good, substantial and workmanlike manner, and accept as full compensation for such material and work and for the rights of way, water rights, works, structures, privileges and franchises, to be transferred to the Jordan Valley Water Company (hereinafter sometimes called the "Operating Company") as hereinafter provided, the lien or liens hereby created and authorized to be created by the Act of Congress commonly known as the Carey Act, and the Acts amendatory thereof and supplemental thereto, and the laws of the State of Oregon on the lands segregated from the public domain under the said Acts of Congress, hereinafter referred to as Carey Act lands and a list of which is hereto attached, marked Exhibit "A," and made a part hereof, and all proceeds from the sale of water rights, shares or interests in said irrigation system, such sales to be made under the terms and provisions hereof.

## ARTICLE III.

### General Specifications for Construction.

Sec. 1. Lower Feeder Canal. The Lower Feeder Canal commences at a point on Jordan Creek in the Northeast Quarter (NE.1/4) of Section Thirteen (13), Township Thirty (30) South, Range Forty-six (46) East, W. M., and extends in a general westerly direction for a distance of approximately nineteen miles to the Antelope Reservoir, [243] and is designed to be used for carrying water from Jordan Creek to said Reservoir for storage purposes, and also for supplying water for reclaiming lands above said Antelope Reservoir but susceptible of irrigation from said canal. But it and all appurtenant structures, diversion dam and gates shall be constructed in accordance with such detailed plans and specifications as shall be approved by the State Engineer and filed with the Desert Land Board; and the canal shall have a carrying capacity sufficient to fill said Antelope Reservoir to the capacity hereinafter set forth and specified during a period of one hundred (100) days; and if water be supplied directly from said Lower Feeder Canal for the irrigation of lands above said Antelope Reservoir, it shall be constructed with an additional capacity sufficient to deliver to each acre of land for which water rights may be sold therein one-eightieth (1/80) of a cubic foot of water per second of time, measured at the head of the farmer's lateral or ditch.

Sec. 2. Antelope Reservoir. The Antelope Reservoir is situated in Township Thirty (30) and

Thirty-one (31) South, Range Forty-five (45) East, W. M., and the impounding dam is situated in the Southwest Quarter (SW¼) of the Northeast Quarter (NE.¼) and the Northwest Quarter NW.¼) of the Southeast Quarter (SE.¼) of Section Thirty-two (32) Township Thirty (30) South, Range Forty-five (45) East. The dam shall be of earth fill construction, and it and all control works, spillways and appurtenant structures shall be of such design and according to such detailed plans and specifications as may be approved by the State Engineer and filed with the Desert Land Board, and when completed the Reservoir shall have a gross impounding or storage capacity of three and five-tenths acre feet for each acre of land for which water rights are sold and which depends for its supply solely upon said reservoir, or for which water right contracts have been entered into by the Construction Company under date prior hereto. In view of the large proportion of the supply [244] which may be secured by direct diversion of the waters of Jordan Creek and Cow Creek, it is provided that for future sales of water rights for diversion at the Lower Unit diversion dam, there shall be a gross reservoir storage capacity of two acre feet for each acre of land for which water rights are hereafter sold.

Sec. 3. Reservoir Outlet to Jordan Creek. The water from Antelope Reservoir may be discharged into the channel of Jack Creek and carried in the improved channel of said creek or otherwise to a point of discharge into Jordan Creek. All these works shall be constructed in accordance with such plans and specifications as may be approved by the State Engineer.

Sec. 4. Antelope Canals. The Antelope West Canal has its initial point at the control works located at the outlet of the Antelope Reservoir, from which point it runs in a westerly direction to a point near the Southeast Quarter (SE.¼) of Section Nine (9), Township Thirty-one (31) South, Range Forty-four (44) East, W. M. It shall have a capacity sufficient to deliver one-eightieth (1/80) of a cubic foot of water per second of time for each acre of land for which water is furnished through such canal for irrigation purposes, measured at the head of the farmer's service lateral or ditch, and shall be constructed according to such detailed plans and specifications as may be approved by the State Engineer and filed with the Desert Land Board.

The Antelope North Canal diverts from the channel of Jack Creek below the outlet of the Antelope Reservoir and runs northwesterly to Jordan Creek where a portion of the water is carried across by a flume to irrigate lands north of Jordan Creek. The capacities of the Antelope North Canal shall be the same as above stated, and it shall similarly conform to approved plans and specifications. [245]

Sec. 5. Main Canal for Lower Unit. The main canal for what is known as the Lower Unit has its intake on Jordan Creek at the diversion dam situated in the Northwest Quarter (NW.¼) of Section Thirty-six (36) Township Thirty (30) South, Range Forty-three (43) East, W. M., and extends in a southerly direction to Jordan Creek, which is crossed by a flume near the center of Section One (1), Township Thirty-one (31) South, Range Forty-three (43) East, W. M., thence westerly along the south side of Jordan Creek for approximately five miles to a point in the Southwest Quarter (SW.¼) of Section Four (4), Township Thirty-one (31) South, Range Forty-three (43) East, W. M., where it divides into branches and laterals, which together with said main canal will be extended for carrying and conducting water to the lands in said Lower Unit in Townships 30 and 31 and 32, South, Ranges 42 and 43 East, W. M.

The said canals, diversion dam and all headgates and other appurtenant structures shall be of such design and according to such plans and specifications as may be approved by the State Engineer and filed with the Desert Land Board, but shall have a capacity sufficient to deliver one-eightieth (1/80) of a cubic foot of water per second of time to each acre of land depending thereon for water for irrigation purposes, and for which water rights, shares or interests therein may be sold by the Construction Company, measured at the headgates of the farmer's service lateral or ditch.

Sec. 6.  Other Structures.  Distributing Canals and Laterals.  There shall be constructed such distributing canals and subordinate laterals as may be required to carry the water to within one-half mile, measured in direct line, of each quarter section of land susceptible of irrigation by gravity flow from said irrigation system and included in Oregon Segregation List No. 24, and such other lands as may be susceptible of irrigation from said irrigation system, and for which water rights, shares or interests therein may be sold [246] by the Construction Company. Provided that coulees and draws and other natural water ways may be utilized as part of said irrigation system for carrying water, when the same can conveniently be done; but all such distributing canals and laterals, coulees and water ways and other structures shall substantially conform to the plans and specifications therefor approved, or that may hereafter be approved, by the State Engineer and filed with the Desert Land Board; provided that all structures shall be of standard design and construction and have the capacity required under this agreement, and all sub-laterals or distribution canals shall have such excess capacity as may be necessary to permit of rotating water, which plan of rotating shall be prepared by the second party, and receive the approval of the State Engineer before construction work is undertaken on any particular unit.

Changes in plans and specifications may be made, with the consent of the State Engineer, to meet field conditions or conditions or obstacles unforeseen when the original plans and specifications were approved.

Sec. 7. Measuring Devices. The Construction Company shall construct at the outlet of the reservoir and at or near the head of main canals and branch canals, and at such places as may be deemed necessary by the Chief Engineer for the proper management and operation of said irrigation system, all necessary headgates, weirs and measuring devices; but the locations and design of all such structures and measuring devices shall be subject to the approval of the State Engineer of the State of Oregon. Suitable headgates and necessary measuring devices shall be installed by the Construction Company at or near the head of all necessary farmer's laterals or service ditches, provided that the Construction Company shall not be required to construct more than one headgate and install more than one measuring device for each entryman or purchaser of water rights, and all additional headgates and measuring devices desired by any entryman or [247] purchaser of water rights shall be installed at his expense, but under the direction and supervision of the Chief Engineer of the Construction Company. And all such individual headgates and measuring devices shall be of a design approved by the State Engineer.

Sec. 8. More detailed Plans to be Submitted. The Construction Company shall file with the State Engineer and Desert Land Board complete detailed maps, profiles, plans and specifications, together with forms of contracts, sub-contracts or agreements for all canals, structures or units of work to be constructed hereunder, and shall not undertake any work or enter into any contract or sub-contract until the plans, specifications and agreements covering the same have been approved in writing by the State Engineer or his authorized representative.

## ARTICLE IV.
### Rights of Way.

Section 1. Over State and Carey Act Lands. The party of the first part hereby grants to the party of the second part, rights of way across all lands segregated, as aforesaid, from the public domain and described in said Exhibit "A" hereto attached, and across all lands owned by the State of Oregon, or that may hereafter be ceded or granted to the State of Oregon, or that may hereafter be ceded or granted to the State of Oregon by the United States, which said rights of way shall be equal to the actual width of the canal, flume, pipe-line, lateral, ditch, waste ditch or other structure at its base from toe to toe of the embankment, together with a strip or strips of land adjacent thereto not exceeding fifty (50) feet in width along the main canals and thirty (30) feet in width for the main laterals, and a proportionate width along the smaller structures. Such rights of way shall be located by the Chief Engineer, and shall in all cases be sufficient for ingress and egress along said structures, and for all dams and flooded or submerged areas. [248] And every owner of land irrigated from said irrigation system and the persons filing on said Carey Act Land shall have the necessary rights of way for service laterals, ditches and waste ditches; but no more laterals, service or waste ditches shall be constructed across any premises than the Chief Engineer of the Construction Company may deem necessary; provided, however, that his determination shall be subject to review by the State Engineer, whose decision in the premises shall be final. Maps showing the location of all canals, laterals, and other structures constructed by the Construction Company shall be filed with the Desert Land Board and in the office of the State Engineer, but the filing of such maps shall not be required prior to the lands being thrown open for entry or settlement, and all entries shall be made subject to such rights of way whether selected before or after the making of the entry.

Sec. 2. Over the Public Domain, The Construction Company shall file, if it or its predecessors in interest have not heretofore filed, in the proper United States Land Office application or applications in due form for rights of way under Sections 18 to 21 of the Act of Congress approved March 3, 1891 (26 Stat. 1085) over public lands of the United States not included in the lands segregated as aforesaid.

Sec. 3. Over Privately Owned Lands. The Construction Company shall obtain at its own cost and expense easements for rights of way over lands, not included in Sections 1 and 2 of this Article, affected by any of the structures constructed by it hereunder.

## ARTICLE V.

Appropriations of Water Held by Construction Company.

The Construction Company covenants and agrees that all water rights and water appropriations held by it for use in connection with said Jordan Valley Irrigation Project were appropriated or [249] acquired solely for the purposes of transferring the title thereto from the State to the individual entryman, settlers and owners of land acquiring rights in said irrigation system for the reclamation of their respective tracts of land, and the water so appropriated or filed upon is hereby dedicated to the reclamation of the lands susceptible of irrigation from said irrigation system, as the same may finally be constructed; and each acre of land entitled to water from said irrigation system under any contract with the Construction Company for a share or interest in said irrigation system shall be entitled to receive its proportionate share of the water available for the irrigation thereof, based upon the number of acres entitled to share in such supply; provided the beneficial use shall be the measure and the limit of the right; that the water appropriations now held by the Construction Company, as aforesaid, include the following applications and permits for water, to wit:

(a)  Application No. 2886, filed in the office of the State Engineer of the State of Oregon, for the right to store 127,000 acre feet of water of Jordan, Jack and Antelope Creeks in the said Antelope Reservoir.

(b)  Application No. 310 on file in the office of the State Engineer of Oregon, for the right to divert 750 cubic feet per second of the waters of Jordan, Jack and Antelope Creeks for the irrigation of lands under the canals hereinbefore described.

(c)   Application No. 4723, on file in the office of the State Engineer of Oregon for the right to divert and store 32,000 acre feet of the waters of Jordan and Boulder Creeks and other water courses for storage in the Canyon Reservoir.

(d)   Permit No. 11584, issued by the State Engineer of the State of Idaho, for 20,000 acre feet of the waters of Jordan and Boulder Creeks for storage in Canyon Reservoir, and for the irrigation of lands below said reservoir.

(e)   Permit No. R 1, issued by the State Engineer of the State of Idaho, for 12,000 acre feet of water additional to Permit No. 11584, of the waters of Jordan and Boulder Creeks for storage in said Canyon Reservoir.

(f)   Permit No. 8382, issued by the State Engineer of the State of Idaho, for 300 cubic feet per second of the waters of Jordan Creek.
[250]

## ARTICLE VI.

Obligations Involving Water Rights.

Heretofore, in connection with the acquisition of water rights and before the date of the contract, heretofore executed between the parties hereto, certain contracts were made disposing of water rights under the Jordan Valley Project. It is agreed that the following obligations shall be recognized and these rights to the extent set forth shall be exempt from the provisions for payment of money and securities into the Trust Fund, but as to the amount and character of the water right, the issuance of shares representing water rights and other administrative matters shall be upon the same basis as other actual purchasers of water rights.

1. An agreement with Jordan Valley Cattle Co., a corporation which shall be limited to the delivery of water, including stored water for seven hundred (700) acres of land at the Lower Unit Diversion Dam for use on North Side Lands.

2. An agreement with George R. Parks and Fred J. Palmer, which shall be limited to the delivery of water to two hundred and forty (240) acres for each, or a total of Four Hundred and Eighty (480) acres in the Lower Unit.

3. Contracts as follows, for delivery of water for an aggregate of One Thousand Seven Hundred Twelve and nine-hundreths (1712.09) acres in the Antelope Unit.

| | | |
|---|---|---|
| Eric Smith | 80 | acres |
| Albert N. Long et al. | 78.2 | |
| William Weber | 56 | |
| Good Beam | 93.3 | |
| Elijah C. Dillow | 40 | |
| E. Edith Wise | 39.1 | |
| Seburn P. Harris | 40 | |
| Alva S. Gulley | 40 | |
| Benjamin E. Johnson | 80 | |
| William S. Sinclair | 50.5 | |
| Oscar J. Martin | 36 | |

Ernest B. Alsop .............. 45
William S. Skinner ...........258.5
Jesse Anderson ............... 57.4
Antelope Cattle Co. ........... 80
Samuel B. Webb ............. 41.69
John Kovarnik ............... 60
Milas H. Smith ...............113.2
William M. Weber ............115.2
Joseph F. Lyonsmith .......... 40.
Theo. H. Wegener ............ 38
James T. Archibald ........... 80
Frank Rice .................150

——————

1,712.09  [251]

The foregoing contracts or agreements shall be subject to transfer or assignment only within the Unit within which they are now located.

### ARTICLE VII.

#### Acceptance of Construction Work.

The party of the first part shall maintain during the period of construction an authorized representative and such inspectors as are deemed necessary, whose duty it shall be to inspect and observe all work being done and material used in the construction of said irrigation system, and to enforce the provisions of this contract and the plans and specifications relative to such construction work, and to promptly reject all work and material, that in the opinion of the representative or inspector, does not conform to the requirements of this agreement and the plans and specifications approved and filed hereunder. Upon the completion of any of the structures or canals which conveniently form a unit for construction purposes, particularly,

(a)   The Lower Feeder Canal,

(b)   The Antelope Reservoir,

(c)   The Reservoir Outlet Canal,

(d)   The Antelope West Canal, with the necessary branches and laterals,

(e)   The Main Canal on the Lower Unit, with the necessary branches and laterals,

(f)   Any other canal or branch canal or structure forming a substantial part of said irrigation system,

and a reasonable unit for construction purposes, the Construction Company, shall be entitled to a final inspection and acceptance of such structure, canal or unit of construction, if constructed in substantial accordance with the plans and specifications therefor, to the end that it may be officially and authoritatively advised wherein, if at all, such structure or unit does not, in the opinion of the party of the first part, conform to such plans and specifications and so that any variation or departure therefrom may be promptly and economically [252] remedied while the equipment or construction force is conveniently available therefor. And in the event that the one dollar per acre received by the State from the sale of Carey Act Land under said project is not sufficient to meet the expenses of such inspections and examinations, the Construction Company shall advance monthly, upon the demand of the State Engineer, the additional funds required to meet such expenses.

## ARTICLE VIII.

### Transfer of Title and Management of System.

Section 1. Operating Company. It being necessary to provide a convenient method for vesting the management and control of said irrigation system, and parts thereof when completed sufficiently for operation or use, in the purchasers of water rights, there has heretofore been organized at the instance and expense of the Construction Company, and under the laws of the State of Oregon, a corporation known as the Jordan Valley Water Company. The articles of incorporation, by-laws and organization meetings and contract or contracts, if any, between said Jordan Valley Water Company and the Construction Company are subject to the approval of the Attorney General and State Engineer of the State of Oregon. The authorized capital stock of said corporation is and shall be on the basis of one share of stock for each acre of land which it is estimated may ultimately be reclaimed from said irrigation system, and each share of stock when issued represents a water right for one acre of land, and for the purpose of incorporation such capital stock is fixed at forty thousand (40,000) shares of the nominal par value of One Dollar ($1.00) per share; but no stock shall be issued therein in excess of the amount authorized from time to time by the Desert Land Board, and the amount of stock authorized to be issued shall at all times be limited by the capacity of said irrigation system, as hereinbefore provided. [253]

Section 2. Transfer of Title. Subject to the terms of this agreement and any amendments or supplemental agreements that may hereafter be entered into between the parties hereto, and without prejudice to the rights of the Construction Company or the liens, rights, franchises, and privileges granted to the Construction Company by this agreement and by the said Acts of Congress and the laws of the State of Oregon, the Construction Company shall transfer and convey to said Jordan Valley Water Company the legal title to all rights of way, water rights and water appropriations now held by the Construction Company, in so far as the same may be required for the operation, management and maintenance of such portions of said irrigation system as shall from time to time be accepted by first party as completed, as provided in Article VII hereof, or as shall be sufficiently completed for operation and use. And upon the final completion of said irrigation system the legal title to all said irrigation works, rights of way and water rights forming an integral or necessary part of said irrigation system shall be transferred to and vested in said Jordan Valley Water Company, the Construction Company retaining only its right or interest to the unsold water rights therein, which shall be represented by stock in the Jordan Valley Water Company on the basis of one share of stock for each acre of land that may be reclaimed from the unsold water rights therein as fixed by the Desert Land Board on the basis hereinbefore provided.

Section 3. Transfer of Management. Whenever it is certified by the Chief Engineer of the Construction Company that certain portions of said irrigation system have been so far completed as to permit the operation thereof for delivery of water to those entitled to water therefrom, such portions shall, with the consent of the State Engineer, be transferred and turned over for operation to said Jordan Valley Water Company; but such transfer shall not release the Construction [254] Company of its obligation as to the completion thereof until the same has been accepted as completed by the party of the first part. And the distribution and delivery of water, and the management, maintenance and upkeep of such portions of said system as shall be so transferred for operation, or as may be fully completed and accepted by the party of the first part, shall be vested in said Jordan Valley Water Company, and the Construction Company shall not be responsible for the operation of or for the distribution or delivery of water from any portion of said irrigation system so turned over to the Operating Company for operation, or as completed. Provided, however, that the Company shall upon order of the Desert Land Board turn over to said Jordan Valley Water Company or to an irrigation district organized in lieu thereof, as provided by law, the maintenance, operation and management of the irrigation system or any unit thereof, retaining only the right to dispose of water rights for additional lands up to the capacity of the irrigation

system as determined by the Desert Land Board.
Provided, however, that if the Construction Company operates any portion of said system before
it is turned over, as aforesaid, to the Operating
Company, it may charge and assess the purchasers
of water rights, shares or interest in said irrigation
system, whose lands are susceptible of irrigation
for the portion so operated by the Construction
Company, One Dollar ($1.00) per acre per annum
for each acre of land entitled to water from the
portion of the system so operated and payment
thereof may be required in advance of the delivery
of water; and if the sum so raised shall be insufficient for the purpose of maintaining, operating and
keeping in repair the portion of the system so
operated, the Construction Company shall furnish
all additional funds necessary to supply such deficiency.

Section 4. Stock of Operating Company Accepted
as Payment for Transfer of Title. The property,
rights, and interests to be transferred by the Construction Company to the Operating Company,
[255] as hereinbefore provided, shall, as between
said Companies, be considered as payment in full
by the Construction Company for all the capital
stock of the Operating Company, and said stock,
subject to the limitations hereinbefore set forth
on the issuance thereof, shall be subject to the
order of the Construction Company, and within the
said limitations shall be issued by the Operating
Company from time to time as ordered and directed
by the Construction Company unto such person

or persons as it may designate, all of whom shall be owners or entrymen of land susceptible of irrigation from said irrigation system, except in the case of qualifying shares for directors, and every certificate of stock, except as above stated, shall describe the land to which the water, which the holder hereof is entitled to receive, shall be dedicated and made appurtenant.

## ARTICLE IX.
### Sale of Water Rights.

Section 1. Interest Acquired by Purchaser. All applications for the purchase of water rights, shares, or interests in said irrigation system for the irrigation of lands susceptible of irrigation therefrom shall be made to the Construction Company, and it shall cause to be issued and delivered to each and every purchaser a share of stock in the Jordan Valley Water Company for each and every acre of land for which a water right is purchased; and the interest of the purchaser in said irrigation system shall be evidenced by a certificate of stock in said Jordan Valley Water Company which shall entitle the holder thereof to receive his proportionate share of all water available for distribution by said Company, based upon the number of shares issued and outstanding, subject only to the provisions of the laws of the State of Oregon that water shall not be wasted and that no water user shall receive more water than is actually required for the proper irrigation of his land, and in no event more than two and [256] one-half (2½) acre during the irrigation season and where no other supply is available, not more than one-half acre feet per acre for domestic and stock purposes during the nonirrigating season; and all water shall be delivered or distributed according to such rules and regulations as to the rotation or delivery of water in periods or intervals as may be prescribed by the Desert Land Board.

Section 2. Priority of Purchase does not give Priority of Right. The Construction Company agrees to sell, or contract to sell, such shares or water rights to the extent of the capacity of said irrigation system, as determined from time to time by the Desert Land Board, to qualified entrymen applying to enter said Carey Act lands and to purchasers of State lands and *owners of other lands,* susceptible of irrigation from said irrigation system, upon the terms herein provided, without preference or partiality; it being understood, however, that priority of application or purchase, or priority of entry or settlement, shall not give priority of right to water from said irrigation system as against subsequent applicants, purchasers, entrymen, or settlers, but that every purchaser of water rights or shares in said irrigation system shall be entitled only to his proportionate interest therein, as aforesaid, based upon the number of shares or water rights sold therein with the approval and consent of said Desert Land Board.

Section. 3. Price of Shares or Water Rights. The price of shares or water rights hereafter disposed of shall hereafter be fixed by the Desert Land Board for each tract of land to which the same is made appurtenant, not to exceed $85.00 per share for each share representing land for which stored water is furnished and not to exceed $45.00 per share for each share representing partial or flood water right for the irrigation of lands under the Lower Feeder Canal, payable as follows: [257]

Twenty-five per cent (25%) cash at the time of sale, and the remainder in ten equal annual payments, beginning on December 1st of the year following the year in which the sale is made, or in case water is not then available, on the first day of December of the year following the first irrigation season during which water is available.

Section 4. Deferred Payments. All deferred payments for water rights shall bear interest, payable on December first of each year, at the rate of six per cent (6%) per annum from date of sale, provided water be available by said date within one-half mile of the quarter section in which the lands of the purchaser are situated. And if the water be not available as aforesaid on said date, there shall be a rebate of interest for a period equal to the delay in the delivery of such water at said point; and in no event shall any payment of either principal or interest, other than the said cash payment, be required of any purchaser until after water has been made available, as herein provided, for the irrigation of the lands described in the contract or mortgage for such water rights or shares.

All deferred payments for the purchase of shares or water rights shall be secured by a first mortgage or lien on the land to which such water rights are made appurtenant, including the water rights purchased, executed, acknowledged and recorded as required by the laws of the State of Oregon; and the certificate of stock in said Jordan Valley Water Company shall be endorsed over and delivered to the Construction Company as additional security for the payment of the balance of the purchase price, with interest as aforesaid. The form of the mortgage or contract with the accompanying notes shall be subject to the approval of the Desert Land Board.

Nothing herein contained shall be construed as preventing [258] the sale by the Construction Company of shares or water rights upon the terms of payment more favorable than those above stated, and the purchasers shall have the privilege of making deferred payments before their due date, with a proportionate rebate of interest.

Section 5. Increase in Price if Water Rights not Promptly Purchased. Should any owner of land now deeded or privately owned and susceptible of irrigation from said irrigation system, fail to purchase water rights on the terms, hereinbefore fixed, on or before the date water is available for the irrigation of such lands, such availability being determined as hereinbefore provided, the Construction Company shall be entitled to charge in addition to the price, hereinbefore fixed, interest thereon at the rate of seven per cent (7%) per annum from the date water is available for the irrigation of such land.

Section 6. Escrow of Securities and Cash. It is expressly agreed that until otherwise ordered by the Desert Land Board, all cash hereafter received by the Construction Company from the sale of water rights under the system and all mortgages or securities taken for the purchase price of water rights shall be deposited in escrow with an escrow holder or Trustee to be selected and approved by the Desert Land Board, and upon the execution of this contract authority shall be given for the transfer of all cash, mortgages and securities now held by the Boise Title and Trust Company, of Boise, Idaho, to this Trustee.

The cash so deposited with said Trustee shall be paid out in installments, from time to time, to the Construction Company, or its order, upon Engineer's estimates or certificates as the work progresses for work done or materials used or purchased for use in the construction of said irrigation system and for necessary expenses of colonization and sale of water rights. Provided that such Engineer's estimate or certificates shall be countersigned or approved  [259]  by the State Engineer or his duly authorized representative before payment by the Trustee.

The mortgages or other securities taken for the deferred payments shall be held by the Trustee until such time as water has been made available for each and every tract of land under the system for which water has been sold, and as a guaranty of the completion of said system, and only after such completion shall the remaining securities upon the Certificate of the State Engineer or the Desert Land Board be delivered to the Construction Company.

Provided, that in order to provide funds for construction expenses, the Construction Company may hypothecate the securities covering deferred payments on water rights which are in the hands of the Trustee. Any contract under which hypothecation is contemplated shall be submitted to and approved by the Desert Land Board prior to the execution thereof, and all moneys received under such contract shall be paid into the Trust Fund held by said Trustee. No securities shall be released by the said Trustee except on specific instructions from the Desert Land Board designating the securities to be so released. Any contract or agreement involving hypothecation of securities shall include suitable provisions for discharging the lien upon individual holdings, and releasing any contract or mortgage given the purchase price of water rights upon the lands and the appurtenant water rights, upon payment of the full amount of the purchase price of such water rights and accrued interest thereon.

INSERT. Addition to Article IX.

It is mutually understood and agreed that the transaction whereby certain Trust Fund securities have heretofore been hypothecated and are being held by the Mortgage Company for America, shall be and the same is hereby recognized. [260]

The contract with the Jordan Valley Cattle Company, a corporation, for the delivery at the

Lower Unit Diversion Dam of water as herein provided to 1600 acres of land on the North side of Jordan Creek is hereby recognized with the understanding that sufficient storage capacity over and above that necessary to meet the requirements of this contract for other lands be provided for said 1600 acres.

### ARTICLE X.
### Sale and Entry of Carey Act Lands.

Section 1. Price. The party of the first part agrees to sell the lands of Oregon Segregation List No. 24 and other segregations which may be made in the future, herein generally referred to as Carey Act Lands, to such persons as are or may be entitled under the law to enter the same, for the sum of One Dollar ($1.00) per acre, which shall accompany the application for entry and shall be paid by the Construction Company out of the first cash payment made by the entryman or purchaser, and forwarded by the Construction Company to the Desert Land Board with the application for entry of the form prescribed by such Board, and the contract with the Construction Company showing that the applicant has made proper arrangement for the purchase of the necessary water rights, and the release of the construction lien.

Section 2. Opening Lands for Entry. The Desert Land Board shall open Carey Act lands for entry and sale as soon as the construction work advances to such an extent as to reasonably insure a delivery of water thereto, provided, however, that such opening to entry and sale shall apply only to substantial portions or units and the Desert Land Board shall be under no obligation to open individual or isolated tracts. But it is expressly agreed and understood that the party of the first part will not approve any application for entry or settlement on said Carey Act lands until the person or persons so applying [261] shall furnish a certified copy of the contract entered into with the Construction Company for the purchase of shares or water rights in said irrigation system, on the basis of one share of stock in the operating company for each acre of irrigable land in the entry.

## ARTICLE XI.
### Definitions.

For the purpose of this contract, "date of reclamation" shall be construed to be the date when water is first available for the use of the entryman or purchaser of water rights at the point where the farmer's lateral or service ditch commences; and water shall be deemed "available" for such entryman or purchaser when the irrigation system has been so far completed that the carrying capacities of canals and laterals, the Reservoir capacity, and the capacity of the Feeder canal are sufficient under the terms of this contract for the lands considered in addition to all lands for which water has previously been made available.

## ARTICLE XII.
### Application for Patent.

When water has been made available for any substantial part of the Carey Act lands described in Exhibit "A" hereto attached, or for lands under any unit of construction as herein defined, the party of the first part, upon request of the Construction Company, shall make application to the Department of the Interior, in due form, for the issuance of patent for said lands, the Construction Company supplying all necessary data and maps required by the party of the first part in connection with said application; and first party will do all such acts and things as may be required under the rules and regulations of the Department of the Interior for obtaining patent for said lands, after the Construction Company has caused the same to be reclaimed to the extent required by the said Acts of Congress before patent can issue therefor. And upon the issuance of such patent, the party of the [262] first part will promptly convey by deed to the entrymen their respective tracts of land, provided said entrymen have complied with the State requirements as to reclamation, cultivation and settlement.

## ARTICLE XIII.

### Commencing Work and Completing System.

The Construction Company shall resume the actual construction of said system within sixty days from date hereof, and prosecute such construction work diligently and continuously to completion as required by the laws of the State of Oregon and complete all structures to the extent required by this agreement on or before June 21, 1925.

It is mutually understood and agreed that a cessation of work under this contract for a period of six months, without the sanction of the Board, will forfeit to the State all rights hereunder. Provided that the rights of the Construction Company under this contract shall be subject to all the provisions of the existing laws of the State of Oregon applicable thereto. The Construction Company shall also conform to the laws of the State of Oregon in regard to the employment of labor and the payment of bills.

## ARTICLE XIV.
### Estimated Cost and Lien for Reclamation.

The party of the first part, to the full extent it may be authorized to do so under the said Acts of Congress, hereby declares, fixes and creates a lien on and against the said lands so segregated from the public domain under the said Act of Congress known as the Carey Act and included in Oregon Segregation List No 24, in the amounts hereafter to be fixed by the Board as herein provided, the maximum of which lien shall not exceed Eighty-five Dollars ($85.00) per acre on lands provided with full water rights, and Three Dollars and fifty cents ($3.50) per acre on non-irrigable lands included in any entered legal subdivision, which lien, with interest at [263] the rate of six per cent (6%) per annum, shall be valid on and against the separate legal subdivisions thereof for the amount aforesaid from the date of reclamation until disposed of or released to actual settlers. And for the purpose of showing the irrigable area in each subdivision the Construction Company shall make a topographical survey of said lands and furnish, prior to such lands being thrown open for entry, a map and a list, in duplicate, showing the irrigable and non-irrigable acreage in each legal subdivision; and the amount of the lien so authorized as aforesaid; Provided, that One Dollar ($1.00) per acre, out of the first payment made by the purchaser or entryman, for each acre of Carey Act Land entered shall be transmitted by the Construction Company to the Desert Land Board with the application for entry.

## ARTICLE XV.

### Increasing or Curtailing Capacity of System.

The Construction Company shall be entitled at any time before June 21, 1925, to increase the capacity of said system, or any part thereof, and to extend the same so as to irrigate and reclaim other lands not herein described or specially referred to; but every such enlargement, extension, or additional construction shall be substantially in accordance with the plans and specifications that may be approved therefor by the State Engineer of the State of Oregon. And it is specially agreed that this contract does not include the construction of what is known as the Canyon Reservoir and what is known as the Upper Feeder Canal, and the feasibility of constructing said reservoir and Upper Feeder Canal hereafter be determined, and the construction of said works and the price of water rights therein shall be covered by a supplemental or independent contract between the parties hereto, after the feasibility of constructing the same has first been determined. [264]

It is further specially agreed that the Construction Company shall be permitted to curtail the extent of the irrigation system to the extent of reclaiming only a portion of the Lower Unit lands, and if it shall appear upon the completion of any Unit or division of the system that all applicants for entry of lands and all purchasers of water rights are fully satisfied, and the system so far as completed has adequate capacity and conforms to the terms of this contract, then, after due application and proof of these facts, the Desert Land Board shall waive the requirement for the completion of the remainder of the system herein described.

## ARTICLE XVI.
### Mortgage.

The right, title and interest of the Construction Company in said irrigation system, water rights, reservoir, structures and unsold stock of the Operating Company, and in the rights, franchises, and lien hereby created and granted, may be mortgaged or otherwise pledged as security for the capital required in carrying out the terms of this agreement to be kept and performed by the Construction Company, the form of the mortgage or deed of trust to be approved by the Attorney General of the State of Oregon, and the substance of the same by the Desert Land Board. The proceeds from such mortgage shall be disbursed for construction purposes through the Trust Fund heretofore mentioned, and shall be subject to the control and supervision of the State Engineer or his representative. Such mortgage upon the system shall contain suitable provisions for protection of individual purchasers of water rights in case of foreclosure, and for releasing the lien thereof and of any contract or mortgage given for the purchase price of water rights on any lands and the appurtenant water rights, upon payment of the full amount of the purchase price of such water rights, and accrued interest thereon. [265]

## ARTICLE VII.

Delivery of Water to Persons Not Entitled Thereto.

It is expressly agreed that the Jordan Valley Water Company shall not deliver water from said irrigation system, or any part thereof, or permit the use of any water therefrom by any person who is not entitled thereto under the terms of this contract and under the terms of a contract of sale executed or authorized by the Construction Company.

## ARTICLE XVIII.

### Bond.

The party of the second part further agrees to file with the party of the first part on or before June 10th, 1921, a surety bond in the penal sum of Twenty-five Thousand Dollars ($25,000.00) as required by Section 5582, Oregon Laws, conditioned upon the faithful performance of the terms hereof, said bond to be subject to the approval of the party of the first part, whereupon the Board agrees to release the $100,000 bond heretofore given by the party of the second part.

## ARTICLE XIX.
### Highways.

It has been heretofore agreed that all sales of State Lands and all entries of Carey Act lands under said irrigation system shall be made subject to a right of way, without compensation to the entryman or purchaser, for roads upon all exterior section lines and half-section lines, and such other roads as the Construction Company may deem necessary and as may be approved by the State Engineer, and that such rights of way along section lines shall be sixty feet in width, being thirty feet on either side of the section line, and for other roads forty feet in width. And to aid in the development of said irrigation project and the reclamation of said lands, the Construction Company has agreed to contribute or donate Five Dollars ($5.00) [266] per acre for each acre of irrigable land for which a full water right (including reservoir water) is sold in said irrigation system, except in what is known as the Lower Unit, where the amount shall be Fifteen Dollars ($15.00) per acre for five thousand (5,000) acres and Five Dollars ($5.00) per acre for all sales in such Lower Unit in excess of said acreage, to a Road Fund to be expended under the supervision of the party of the first part in the construction of roads and highways to, over, or from said irrigation project in such manner as may seem most advantageous for the development of said irrigation project and the several tracts or communities thereunder; that such contribution or donation shall be made from time to time as water becomes available for the lands for which water rights have been sold, and shall consist of mortgages or water contracts received by the Construction Company for deferred payments on water rights; and the said Trustee shall be instructed, and it hereby is instructed, to deliver to first party or its nominees, for the benefit of such road fund, the proportionate amount of all mortgages or contracts for deferred payments for the sale of water rights.

In view of the increase in the cost of construction, and other unforeseen contingencies, the donation of these amounts for construction of roads appears to unduly handicap the financing of the project under present conditions, and it is hereby expressly agreed that the Desert Land Board in behalf of the State of Oregon will waive this provision, provided that suitable waivers, satisfactory to the Attorney General of Oregon be secured from all purchasers and all other interested parties. In any event, the provisions of this Article shall not apply to future sales and the Road Fund will not be collected under future water right contracts.

### ARTICLE XX.

#### General Manager and Chief Engineer.

The Construction Company expressly agrees to appoint or [267] elect a General Manager and a Chief Engineer who may or may not be the same party, satisfactory to the State Engineer, who shall have charge of the engineering and construction work to be done and performed by the Construction Company under this agreement, the disbursement of funds, subject to the terms of any escrow or trust agreement made in accordance with the terms hereof, and the actual management of the project, and the Construction Company agrees to make such changes from time to time in this office, or these offices, as may be demanded for cause by the State Engineer.

## ARTICLE XXI.

### Trust Agreement and Loan Contract Made Part Hereof.

Reference is here made to a certain contract of even date herewith made by and between The Mortgage Company for America, The Jordan Valley Land & Water Company, and the Jordan Valley Farms, for the hypothecation of securities for a loan of $117,000.00; also an agreement under even date herewith by and between the Board, Construction Company, J. Humfeld, and the U. S. National Bank of Portland, Oregon, providing for a Trust Fund and disbursements therefrom, both said agreements are hereby specifically referred to and made a part hereof.

## ARTICLE XXII.

### Amendments.

This contract may be amended, altered, or added to by the mutual consent of the parties hereto at any time hereafter, whenever, in the opinion of the said Desert Land Board, it appears expedient or proper, in view of the conditions then existing, that such amendments, alterations or changes should be made.

IN WITNESS WHEREOF, the said Desert
Land Board, acting for and on behalf of the State
of Oregon, has caused this instrument to be executed
by the Governor of said State as Chairman of said
Board, and attested under the seal of the Secretary,
and the said party of the second part has caused its
name to be hereunto subscribed by its [268]
President, and its corporate seal affixed, attested
by its Secretary, the day and year first above
written.

DESERT LAND BOARD OF OREGON.
By BEN W. OLCOTT,
Governor and Chairman.

[Seal]    Attest: PERCY A. CUPPER,
Secretary.

JORDAN VALLEY LAND AND WATER
COMPANY.
By W. J. MANEY,
President.

[Seal]    Attest: EMIL L. TSCHIRGI,
Secretary.

State of Oregon,
County of Marion,—ss.

I, Percy A. Cupper, State Engineer and Secretary of the Desert Land Board of Oregon, do hereby
certify that the above and foregoing copy of the
contract entered into May 27, 1921, by and between
the Jordan Valley Land and Water Company, and
the Desert Land Board of Oregon, providing for
the re-financing and completion of the Jordan Valley Irrigation Project, is a full, true and correct
copy of the original as the same appears in the

records of my office and in my custody and of the whole thereof.

IN WITNESS WHEREOF, I have hereunto set my hand this 14th day of June, 1923.

PERCY A. CUPPER,

State Engineer, Secretary.

By J. L. McALLISTER,

J. L. McALLISTER,

Assistant Secretary. [269]

DEFENDANT'S EXHIBIT "M."

No. ——. Defts. Ex. "M."

U. S. District Court, District of Oregon. Filed June 12, 1923. G. H. Marsh, Clerk.

Minutes of Special Meeting of the Directors of Jordan Valley Land & Water Company Authorizing Execution of Contract Dated May 27, 1921.

Minutes of Special Meeting of Directors of Jordan Valley Land and Water Company.

Held September 10th, 1921.

The Board of Directors of the Jordan Valley Land and Water Company met in special meeting in the office of Messrs. Richards and Haga, Idaho Building, Boise, Idaho, at 2:30 P. M., September 10, 1921.

All members of the Board were present, as follows:

J. W. Maney,

A. J. Vance,

Emil L. Tschirgi,

J. H. Richards,

O. O. Haga.

Mr. Maney called the meeting to order, and presided, and Emil L. Tschirgi recorded the proceedings.

Mr. Maney presented a contract dated May 27th, 1921, between the Desert Land Board of the State of Oregon and the Jordan Valley Land and Water Company, which had been executed by the proper officers of the State of Oregon, and the President and Secretary of the Company, and urged that the same be approved by the Board of Directors.

Whereupon, it was moved and seconded, and duly carried, that the contract between this Company and the Desert Land Board of the State of Oregon, dated May 27th, 1921, an executed copy of which is on file in the office of said Desert Land Board at [270] Salem, Oregon, and one executed copy of which is on file with the Secretary of the Company, be and the same is hereby ratified, approved and confirmed, and the action of the officers of this Company in executing said contract is likewise duly ratified, approved and confirmed.

There being no further business, the meeting adjourned.

EMIL L. TSCHIRGI,<br>Secretary.

State of Idaho,
County of Ada,—ss.

I, Emil L. Tschirgi, do hereby certify and declare that I am the Secretary of the Jordan Valley Land and Water Company; that the foregoing is a full, true and correct copy of the proceedings of the Board of Directors of the said Company, as shown by the minutes thereof, at a meeting of said Board held on the 10th day of September, 1921.

IN WITNESS WHEREOF, I have hereunto set my hand and the seal of this Company, this 10th day of September.

[Corporate Seal]  EMIL L. TSCHIRGI.  [271]

State of Oregon,
County of Marion,—ss.

I, Percy A. Cupper, State Engineer and Secretary of the Desert Land Board of Oregon, do hereby certify that the above and foregoing copy of the resolution of the Board of Directors of the Jordan Valley Land and Water Company authorizing the execution of the contract between said company and the Desert Land Board of Oregon, bearing date May 27, 1921, is a full, true and correct copy of a certified copy thereof as the same appears in the records of my office and in my custody and of the whole thereof.

In Witness Whereof, I have hereunto set my hand this 14th day of June, 1923.

PERCY A. CUPPER,
State Engineer, Secretary.
By J. L. McALLISTER,
J. L. McALLISTER,
Assistant Secretary.  [272]

DEFENDANT'S EXHIBIT "N."

No. ——.  Defts. Ex. "N."  Ident. "N."

U. S. District Court, District of Oregon.  Filed June 12, 1923.

Proposed Contract for Execution Between Desert
Land Board and Jordan Valley Land &
Water Company Increasing Water Shares
from $71.00 per Share to $100.00 per Share.

40

# AMENDMENT TO CONTRACT FOR CON-STRUCTION

of

# JORDAN VALLEY IRRIGATION SYSTEM.

THIS AGREEMENT, Made and entered into,
in duplicate, this 2d day of February, A. D. 1920,
by and between the DESERT LAND BOARD of
the State of Oregon, acting for and on behalf of the
State of Oregon, the party of the first part, and
JORDAN VALLEY LAND & WATER COM-PANY, a corporation organized under the laws of
the State of Nevada and doing business in the
State of Oregon (hereinafter sometimes called the
"Construction Company"), the party of the second
part, WITNESSETH, That,

WHEREAS, the parties hereto did heretofore
enter into a contract bearing date the 21st day of
June, A. D. 1918, for the construction of what is
known as the Jordan Valley Irrigation System,
and for the sale of shares of interests therein to
settlers and owners of land under said irrigation
system, to which contract reference is hereby made
for a full and complete statement of the terms and
provisions thereof; and,

WHEREAS, The Company did make and file
with the Desert Land Board an application for an

increase of lien supported by an estimate to complete construction, and

WHEREAS, The cost of labor and material re.quired in the construction of said irrigation system has greatly increased since said contract was entered into and conditions have arisen which, in the opinion of the Desert Land Board, renders it expedient [273] and proper that said contract should be amended in the particulars hereinafter stated.

NOW, THEREFORE, in consideration of the premises and the mutual covenants hereinafter contained, the parties hereto have agreed, and hereby do agree, as follows:

### ARTICLE I.

Section 1. Price of Shares of Water Rights. That the price or cost of shares, interests, or water rights covering lands to be served under the Antelope Reservoir, fixed by said contract dated June 21, 1918, at $71.00 per share is hereby increased from $71.00 per share to $100.00 per share, payable as follows: In cash at the time .of sale, $31.00 per share, on the first day of December, 1922, $1.80 per share, and a like sum on the first day of December, 1923, 1924, 1925, and 1926, and $4.00 per share on the first day of December of each year thereafter until the full amount of the purchase price has ben paid. But this increase in price shall not apply to what is designated in said contract as "Partial Water Rights," being water rights for lands situated under and irrigated from what is known as the Lower Feeder Canal.

All deferred payments shall bear interest, payable on December first of each year, at the rate of six per cent (6%) per annum from May 1st, 1920, provided water be available by said date within one-half mile of the quarter section in which the lands of the purchaser are situated. And if water be not available as aforesaid on said date, there shall be a rebate of interest for a period equal to the delay in the delivery of such water at said point; and in no event shall any payment of either principal or interest, other than the said cash payment, be required of any purchaser until after water has been made available, as herein provided, for the irrigation of the lands described in the [274] contract or mortgage for such water rights or shares.

Section 2. Estimated Cost and Lien For Reclamation. That the estimated cost and lien for reclamation, fixed by said contract at $71.00 per acre, is hereby increased to $100.00 per acre on all unsold lands to be served though the Antelope Reservoir.

## ARTICLE II.

Section 1. All proceeds from the sale of water rights shall be applied as provided in said contract of June 21st, 1918, and any surplus remaining in the trust fund shall be disposed of in the following manner; The Company shall be entitled to $156,000.00 after which any balance remaining shall be divided as follows: one-half thereof shall be paid to the Company, and the remaining one-half shall be turned over to the Desert Land Board to be expended for the general good of the project in a manner similar to the Road Fund.

Section 2. The increase in price of shares of water rights and in the Carey Act lien, hereinbefore authorized, shall apply to all lands, shares, interests, and water rights sold on and after the first day of November, 1919; but all sales made prior to said date shall be governed by said contract as it existed prior to this amendment.

## ARTICLE III.

Section 1. In order to provide funds available for construction expenses the Company may hypothecate the securities covering deferred payments on water right contracts which are now or hereafter may be in the hands of the Boise Title and Trust Company, as Trustee. Any contract under which hypothecation is contemplated shall be submitted to and approved by the Desert Land Board prior to the execution thereof, and all moneys received under such contract shall be paid into the Trust Fund held by said trustee. No securities shall be released by the said Trustee [275] except on specific instructions from the Desert Land Board, designating the securities to be so released.

Section 2. The said contract of June 21, 1918, and all the terms and provisions thereof, except as herein expressly modified, shall be and remain in full force and effect; Provided, however, that this agreement shall not be binding upon the party of the first part unless duly approved in writing by the American Surety Company of New York, on or before April 1st, 1920, said proof to be filed with the Desert Land Board.

IN WITNESS WHEREOF, The said Desert Land Board acting for and on behalf of the State of Oregon, has caused this instrument to be executed by the Governor of said State as Chairman of said Board, and attested under the seal of the Secretary, and the said party of the second part has caused its name to be hereunto subscribed by its President and its corporate seal affixed, attested by its Secretary, the day and year first above written.

DESERT LAND BOARD OF OREGON.

By ———————————,

Governor, and Chairman.

Attest: ———————————,

Secretary.

JORDAN VALLEY LAND & WATER COMPANY,

By ———————————,

President.

Attest: ———————————,

Secretary.    [276]

State of Oklahoma,

County of Oklahoma,—ss.

On this —— day of February, in the year 1920, before me appeared J. W. Maney, to me personally known, who, being duly sworn, did say that he is the President of Jordan Valley Land & Water Company, the corporation that executed the within instrument, and that the seal affixed to said instrument is the corporate seal of said corporation, and that said instrument was signed and sealed in behalf of said corporation by authority of its Board of Directors; and said J. W. Maney acknowledged said instrument to be the free act and deed of said corporation.

IN TESTIMONY WHEREOF, I have hereunto set my hand and affixed my official seal, this the day and year first in this my certificate written.

———————————,

Notary Public for Oklahoma County, Residing at ———.

My commission expires ———. [277]

Salem, Oregon, October 30, 1919.

A special meeting of the Desert Land Board was held this day in the Capitol Building at 10:30 A. M. Present: Ben W. Olcott, Governor, Chairman;

Ben W. Olcott, Secretary of State;

O. P. Hoff, State Treasurer;

George M. Brown, Attorney-General;

Percy A. Cupper, State Engineer, Sec'y;

J. L. McAllister, Assistant Sec'y.

Thereupon the following proceedings were had, to wit:

An application was presented by the Jordan Valley Land and Water Company for an increase in lien on all unsold lands from $71.00 to $101.00 per acre. A statement and recommendation was submitted by the Secretary.

Mr. A. J. Vance, representing the Jordan Valley Land and Water Company, was present.

After due consideration, it was ordered that the lien be increased from $71.00 to $100.00 per acre on all unsold Carey Act lands to be served from the Antelope Reservoir. The funds arising from the sale of lands to be first applied as under the present arrangement to the cost of construction and colonization, after the completion of which, the Jordan Valley Land and Water Company shall be entitled to $156,000.00. The balance, if any, shall be divided and applied as follows:

One-half thereof shall be paid to the Jordan Valley Land and Water Company and the remaining one-half thereof shall be turned over to the Desert Land Board to be expended for the general good of the Project, it being understood that the cost of colonization under the Jordan Valley Farms contract is a legitimate charge against the Project and shall include cost of financing up to an amount equal to $30.00 per acre, and that the cost of financing over and above the amount of $30.00 per acre shall be an additional charge against [278] the project.

It is understood tht the water rights to private lands in the project shall be sold under the same terms and conditions as the Carey Act Land and that the terms of deferred payments shall be extended over a period of twenty (20) years.

And be it further ORDERED, that the Secretary be and he hereby is instructed to prepare a supplemental agreement embodying the changes in the State Contract of June 21, 1918, necessitated hereby, and the Chairman and Secretary are hereby authorized to execute the same.

And be it further ordered that the increase of lien hereby granted shall be effective from the date of this order, provided, however, that the written consent of the American Surety Company of New York shall be subsequently filed with the Board, otherwise this order shall be inoperative and the State Contract shall remain in its present form.

(Consent never filed. Contract never executed—never operative.) [279]

State of Oregon,
County of Marion,—ss.

I, Percy A. Cupper, Secretary of the Desert Land Board, and custodian of its records, do hereby certify that the foregoing copy of the Board's Order, entered October 30th, 1919, granting an increase of lien on the Jordan Valley Project has been compared with the original as it appears of record on Page 166, Volume 3, Record of Minutes of the Desert Land Board, and that the same is a full, true and correct copy, and of the whole thereof.

PERCY A. CUPPER,
Secretary of the Desert Land Board.
By ————————,
Assistant Secretary.

State of Oregon,
County of Marion,—ss.

I, Percy A. Cupper, State Engineer and Secretary of the Desert Land Board of Oregon, do hereby certify that the above and foregoing copy of the proposed amendment to the contract of June 21, 1918, between the State, and the Jordan Valley Land and Water Company, providing for increasing the lien as fixed in said contract of June 21, 1918, under certain conditions which conditions were never met and the above and foregoing unexecuted copy is a full, true and correct copy of the proposed form as the same appears in the records of my office and in my custody and of the whole thereof.

In Witness Whereof, I have hereunto set my hand this 14th day of June, 1923.

PERCY A. CUPPER,

State Engineer, Secretary.

By J. L. McALLISTER.

J. L. McALLISTER,

Assistant Secretary.    [280]

DEFENDANT'S EXHIBIT "O."

No. ——. Defts. Ex. "O."

U. S. District Court, District of Oregon. Filed June 12, 1923. G. H. Marsh, Clerk.

Contract Dated May 27, 1921, Between Jordan Valley Land & Water Company and the Mortgage Company for America.

#45.

THIS MEMORANDUM OF AGREEMENT, Made and entered into the 27 day of May, 1921, by and between Jordan Valley Land and Water Company, a corporation organized and existing under the laws of the State of Nevada as party of the first part; Jordan Valley Farms, a corporation organized and existing under the laws of the State of Idaho, as party of the second part; and Mortgage Company for America, a corporation organized and existing under the laws of the Kingdom of the Netherlands, as party of the third part,

## WITNESSETH:

THAT for and in consideration of the agreement of the party of the third part to loan unto the party of the first part the sum of money hereinafter mentioned, and the payment of One Dollar made by the party of the third part to each of the parties of the first and second part, and other valuable consideration moving from the party of the third part to each of the other parties hereto, receipt of all which considerations is hereby acknowledged by each of the parties of the first and second part, it is hereby mutually agreed by and between the parties hereto as follows:

First. The parties of the first and second part, jointly and severally, covenant and agree that they will assign, transfer, set over and convey unto the party of the third part (or cause the same to be done) the entire irrigation system owned by the party of the first part in Jordan Valley, Malheur County, State of Oregon, including all dams, reservoirs, intakes, head-gates, canals, laterals, ditches, drains, weirs, gates, rights of way, sites for [281] any of the aforesaid purposes whether now actually used therefor or hold in contemplation of such uses in the future, and also all lands used or intended to be used in the operation of such irrigation system; it being the intention to include herein all of the properties, rights and franchises aforesaid now owned by the party of the first part or which may be acquired by it hereafter for use in connection with said irrigation system. Nothing in this paragraph contained, however, shall be con-

strued as limiting or putting any restraint upon
the sale, as elsewhere in this agreement provided,
of water rights to be appurtenant to, and used for
the irrigation of, lands under said irrigation system.

Second.   The parties of the first and second part,
jointly and severally, further covenant and agree
that they will assign, transfer, set over and convey
unto J. Humfeld of Portland, Oregon, as trustee
(the said Humfeld being the general agent in the
State of Oregon for the party of the third part)
all of the following described properties and assets,
to wit:

1. All water rights owned by or belonging to the
party of the first part or to any and all of its officers and directors personally, upon or appurtenant
to lands under said irrigation system, as well as all
their rights in and to the waters of Jordan Creek,
its tributaries and sources; and also any and all
title and interest that may hereafter be acquired
by the party of the first part, its officers and directors in and to such water rights.

2. A valid, unincumbered title to all lands owned
by the party of the first part and (or) the party of
the second part under Laterals A and B of the
lower unit of said irrigation system; and all mortgages held by or belonging to said parties or either
of them upon lands under said laterals, and lands
in this paragraph referred to consisting of not
less than three thousand acres.   It is intended to
include herein all mortgages upon any of said lands
now held by [282]  Boise Title & Trust Com-

pany in which the parties of the first and second part or either of them, have any interest.

3. All mortgages given by purchasers of water rights in connection with so-called Carey Act Lands located under any part of said irrigation system.

Third. All of the rights, franchises, and properties hereinabove mentioned, of every kind and nature, whether transferred to the party of the third part or to J. Humfeld as trustee, shall be held, subject to any disposal thereof provided for in this agreement, for the purpose of securing to the party of the third part the repayment to it by the parties of the first and second part of a loan in the sum of One Hundred and Seventeen Thousand Dollars ($117,000.00), Gold Coin of the United States of America, of the present standard value, as evidenced by the promissory note of the parties of the first and second part for said sum of One Hundred Seventeen Thousand Dollars ($117,-000.00), bearing date of April 1, 1921, and payable two (2) years after said date, with interest in like gold coin at the rate of eight per cent per annum, payable annually, as evidenced by two interest coupon notes payable, respectively, April 1, 1922, and April 1, 1923, and each being for the sum of Nine Thousand Three Hundred Sixty Dollars ($9,-360.00).

Fourth. The party of the third part agrees that upon the full and complete performance by the parties of the first and second part, of all and singular their covenants and agreements herein contained, and not otherwise, the party of the third part will pay unto the party of the first part said sum of One Hundred and Seventeen Thousand Dollars ($117,000.00), in the manner hereinafter provided subject to the penalties for default in payment of principal or interest or breach of covenant or condition of this agreement hereinafter set forth.

Fifth. All properties, lands and securities that shall be [283] transferred unto J. Humfeld as trustee under this agreement shall be held by him in trust to secure the repayment to the party of the third part of the loan contemplated by this agreement, and the faithful performance by the party of the first part and the party of the second part of all covenants and agreements entered into by them or either of them as respects the said loan.

Sixth. For the purposes of promoting the development of the irrigation system of the party of the first part, it is necessary that the irrigable lands conveyed to said J. Humfeld as trustee and also water rights be sold and for that purpose it is expressly agreed that said trustee shall be, and he hereby is invested with full and complete power to convey any and all such lands and water rights as may be sold by the party of the first part, it being understood that land and water rights are to be sold at such price as the party of the first part may designate, subject to the terms prescribed by the Desert Land Board of the State of Oregon, provided that no lands with appurtenant water rights are to be sold for less than Sixty Dollars ($60.00) per acre, without the written consent of said J. Humfeld, trustee, and it shall never be necessary, so long as title is vested in said trustee for any confirmatory conveyance to be executed by the party of the first part or the party of the second part, nor shall any grantee of any such land and water right be at all concerned about, or be under any obligation to see to, the application of any purchase price paid for any such lands or water rights, but all of such purchase price moneys shall be paid to the said trustee and the initial cash payment, which shall not be less than Twenty Dollars ($20.00) an acre, without the consent of said J. Humfeld, and so much of the subsequent installment payments on the purchase price mortgages as shall not reduce the principal of any mortgage below Forty Dollars ($40.00) per acre, shall be deposited by him in a sinking [284] fund to provide for the payment of the taxes and other public charges that may be levied upon the properties transferred to the party of the third part and or to the said trustee, and for the payment to the party of the third part of the interest accruing upon said loan of One Hundred Seventeen Thousand Dollars ($117,000.00). So long as the parties of the first and second part shall not be in default as respects any of their covenants herein contained, no part of said sinking fund shall be applied in payment of the principal of said loan, but any surplus in the sinking fund after providing for the payment of said taxes and interest shall be deposited in the general trust fund for application to the purposes provided for in this agreement. Neither the party of the third part nor the trustee shall be under any obligation to pay any taxes or other public charges upon any lands or other property transferred to the party of the third part or to the trustee, or to advance any money for such purposes, but either the party of the third part or the trustee may at its or his election pay any such taxes for the protection of the security of the party of the third part for the repayment of said loan, and any sums advanced by either the party of the third part or the trustee shall be immediately due and repayable, and shall bear interest at the rate of eight per cent per annum, and shall be repaid out of the first money coming into the hands of the trustee that may be applicable to the sinking fund or be otherwise available for such repayment.

Seventh. All of the mortgages given by the purchasers of said lands and water rights for deferred payments of purchase price thereof, shall be executed in favor of said J. Humfeld as Trustee, and shall be held by him as security for the payment of said loan of One Hundred Seventeen Thousand Dollars ($117,000.00). So much of the payments of principal and interest upon said mortgages as shall reduce the balance due on said mortgages to less than Forty [285] Dollars per acre, shall be deposited in a savings account in the United States National Bank of Portland, Oregon, and applied in payment of said One Hundred Seventeen Thousand Dollar loan at its maturity.

Eighth. The parties of the first and second part each covenant that they will sell the deeded land (that is, any lands other than Carey Act Lands) under said Laterals A and B to actual settlers only, and further covenant that not less than two-thirds of the irrigable portion of said lands shall be brought under cultivation within two years from the date of sale thereof.

Ninth. The party of the first part and the party of the second part shall each deliver unto the said J. Humfeld, trustee, a complete statement of the affairs and the condition of the business of said companies, respectively, at the date of this agreement, and shall also deliver to said trustee all money, notes, accounts and securities of said companies, respectively, and from and after the date of this agreement, and until the repayment of the loan herein provided for, and the repayment of all sums of money due from either of said parties to the party of the third part, at the date hereof, or arising out of this contract, the entire administration of the business of each of said parties of the first and second part shall be under the direction and supervision of said trustee, who shall manage, control, and administer the same until the income, proceeds of sale, and receipts of said business shall amount to a sum sufficient to repay all of said indebtedness to the party of the third part, provided, however, that the party of the first part and the party of the second part each agree to and shall give their full and best attention and service to the development and operation of the irrigation system, and to the selling of lands and water rights, and said trustee shall be under no obligation, except at his own election, to attend to the [286] actual operation of said irrigation system or to the selling of lands and water rights. It is understood and agreed that J. W. Maney shall be appointed and shall act as general manager of the irrigation project.

All costs of administration of said business while under the control of said trustee shall be charged to said companies, respectively, and may be paid by said trustee out of any moneys received by him for the account of either of said companies, without regard to the source from which the funds may be derived.

Tenth. The proceeds of said loan of One Hundred Seventeen Thousand Dollars ($117,000.00) to be made by the party of the third part to the party of the first part, shall be disbursed by the said trustee as follows, to wit:

1. To pay to the party of the third part all arrears of interest which became due January 1, 1921, on a note for Twenty-seven Thousand Dollars ($27,000.00) and on March 1, 1921, on a note for Fifty-five Thousand Dollars ($55,000.00) due from parties of the first and second part to the party of the third part, and all arrears of interest which became due January 1, 1921, on a note for Thirty-five Thousand Dollars ($35,000.00) due from Ascuenaga Livestock and Land Company to the party of the third part.

2. To pay to the party of the third part a consideration of four per cent of the face of the three notes last mentioned, as an advance payment of six months interest on said note as a consideration and

inducement to the party of the third part to accept prepayment before maturity of said notes and assign and transfer to Mortgage Bond Company of Portland, Oregon, all the notes, mortgages and other securities held by the party of the third part as security for the payment of said three notes, which assignments are to be made and which prepayment is accepted by the party of the third part [287] at the especial instance and for the accommodation of the party of the first part.

3. To pay to the party of the third part all the expenses incurred and to be incurred by it in making said loan of One Hundred Seventeen Thousand Dollars ($117,000.00), by way of inspection charges, attorneys' fees, recording fees, abstractors' charges and such like expenses incidental to the making of said loan.

4. To pay to the trustee such compensation for his services in administering said trust and for any services he may render to the party of the first part and or the party of the second part in connection with the said loan (with all of which the party of the third part is not concerned) as may be agreed upon between the parties of the first and second part and said trustee.

5. To deposit the remainder of the proceeds of said loan in the United States National Bank of Portland, Oregon, in a trust fund to be used for the extension and development of the Jordan Valley Irrigation System, as the same shall be done by the party of the first part. Said trust fund shall be disbursed by the said trustee as the work pro-

gresses, upon receipt by him of vouchers drawn by the general manager of said irrigation project, and approved by the authorized agent of the State of Oregon; provided that no checks drawn by said trustee upon said trust fund shall be valid unless accompanied by such vouchers. Said disbursements shall cover existing debts of the party of the first part incurred in the construction of the irrigation project as well as the cost of future extension and development work, including the reasonable expenses incident to the selling of lands, provided that the transfer of settlers from one tract of land to another shall not constitute a sale of the land and no commission shall be charged by the party of the second part for such transfers. [288]

Eleventh. There have been heretofore deposited with the State of Oregon by the party of the first part and or the party of the second part certain securities for a Road Fund in connection with said irrigation system. If the State shall cancel said road fund and redeliver said securities, then all of them shall be assigned to and deposited with said trustee for the further security of the party of the third part as respects the repayment to it of said loan.

Twelfth. Any share of the capital stock of the Jordan Valley Water Company that may be held by either the first or second party shall be assigned to said trustee with power to vote the same and during the existence of said loan said J. Humfeld shall be a director of said Jordan Valley Water Company.

Thirteenth. The party of the third part shall have a lien upon all of the lands and securities herein provided to be pledged as security for said loan, whether the same are assigned to the party of the third part or to said trustee, and in event of any default in the payment of principal and interest of said loan, may proceed, either in its own name or in the name of the trustee or jointly in its own name and that of the trustee, by any lawful means or process to foreclose its lien upon the whole or any part of its security, and sell the same and out of the proceeds of sale pay the expenses incident to the foreclosure and sale, including such attorneys' fees as the Court may adjudge reasonable to be allowed for such foreclosure, and apply the balance of such proceeds of sale towards the satisfaction of the indebtedness due to the party of the third part. Any such foreclosure shall be without prejudice to the rights of the owners of lands under said Irrigation Project with appurtenant water rights to receive water according to the provisions of the original water contracts under which the lands were sold by the party of the first part or the party of the second part. [289]

In case of any default of either the party of the first part or the party of the second part in the payment of any installment, either principal or interest, of the indebtedness due from them or either of them to the party of the third part, then, at its option, the party of the third part may declare the whole of the indebtedness owing to it by said parties and each of them to be immediately due and payable.

Fourteenth. In the event of any suit being instituted for the foreclosure of the lien of the party of the third part upon any of the property or securities herein referred to, the plaintiff may apply to the Court or Judge having jurisdiction of such matters for the appointment of a receiver to take charge of such property and securities and conserve and operate the same.

Fifteenth. If the parties of the first and second part shall well and truly pay or cause to be paid the whole amount of the principal and interest due or becoming due upon their promissory note for One Hundred Seventeen Thousand Dollars ($117,-000.00), and shall also pay or cause to be paid all the other sums payable by them and each of them under the terms of this agreement, and shall well and truly keep, perform and observe all their covenants and agreements herein contained, according to the true meaning and intent of this agreement, then and in that case the trustee and or the party of the third part at the cost and expense of the party of the first part shall enter satisfaction and discharge of any lien created by this contract, and thereafter so much of the properties and securities as may then remain undisposed of and in the custody or under the control of the said trustee or the party of the third part, shall be held by the trustee and disposed of by him in accordance with the provisions of a contract entered into between the Desert Land Board of the State of Oregon and the party of the first part for the construction of the Jordan Valley Project, a copy of which is attached to the Trust [290] agreement of even date herewith entered into between said Desert Land Board, the party of the first part, said trustee, and the United States National Bank, of Portland, Oregon.

Sixteenth. In case the trustees or any trustee hereafter appointed, shall at any time become incapable of action, a successor may be appointed by the party of the third part by an instrument duly executed and acknowledged by it, and a copy thereof delivered to each of the parties of the first and second part, and thereupon said new trustee shall, without further act, deed or conveyance, become vested with the trust property with like effect, as if originally named as trustee herein, provided that such new trustee shall be acceptable to the Desert Land Board of the State of Oregon. The trustee retiring shall, nevertheless, on written demand of the new trustee or of the party of the third part, execute and deliver an instrument or instruments conveying and transferring unto such new trustee, upon the trust herein expressed, all the trust property, powers, powers of trust of the trustee so retiring, and shall duly assign, transfer and deliver to the new trustee all properties and moneys held by such retiring trustee. Should any deed, conveyance or instrument in writing from either of the parties of the first or second part be required by any new trustee for more fully and certainly vesting in and confirming to such new trustee the trust property, then any and all such instruments shall, upon request of such new trustee, be made, executed, acknowledged and delivered by the party or parties of whom same is requested.

IN WITNESS WHEREOF, These presents, are executed the day and year first above written in four original parts.

> JORDAN VALLEY LAND & WATER COMPANY.
>
> > By J. W. MANEY,
> >
> > > President.

[Seal]          By EMIL TSCHIRGI,

> > > Secretary.
>
> JORDAN VALLEY FARMS.
>
> By HARLEY J. HOOKER,
>
> > President.

[Seal]      By THEODORE H. WEGENER,

> > Secretary.

Executed in the presence of

  EARL C. BRONAUGH,

  EARL C. BRONAUGH, Jr.,

> Witnesses to signatures of Harley J. Hooker and J. Humfeld. [291]

EDNA L. HICE,

FRED T. KOPKE,

> Witnesses to signature of Theodore H. Wegener and J. W. Maney and Emil Tschirgi.

> MORTGAGE COMPANY FOR AMERICA.
>
> > By J. HUMFELD, (Seal)
> >
> > > General Agent. [292]

State of Idaho,
County of Ada,—ss.

On this 2d day of June, 1921, before me appeared J. W. Maney, to me personally known, who being duly sworn did say that he is the secretary of Jordan Valley Land and Water Company, and Emil L. Tschirgi, to me personally known, who being duly sworn did say that he is the secretary of Jordan Valley Land and Water Company, and that the seal affixed to said instrument is the corporate seal of said corporation, and that said instrument was signed and sealed in behalf of said corporation by authority of its board of directors and said J. W. Maney and Emil L. Tschirgi acknowledged said instrument to be the free act and deed of said corporation.

IN TESTIMONY WHEREOF, I have hereunto set my hand and affixed my official seal this, the day and year first in this, my certificate, written.

[Seal]            EDNA L. HICE,

Notary Public for the State of Idaho, Residing at Boise, Ada Co.

State of Oregon,
County of Multnomah,—ss.

On this 4th day of June, 1921, before me appeared Harley J. Hooker, to me personally known, who being duly sworn did say that he is president of Jordan Valley Farms, a corporation organized and existing under the laws of the State of Idaho, and that the seal affixed to said instrument is the corporate seal of said corporation and that said instrument was signed and sealed in behalf of said corporation by authority of its Board of Directors, and said Harley J. Hooker acknowledged said instrument to be the free act and deed of said corporation.

IN TESTIMONY WHEREOF, I have hereunto set my hand and affixed my official seal this, the day and year first in this my certificate written.

[Seal]        EARL C. BRONAUGH, Jr.,

Notary Public for the State of Oregon.

My commission expires Dec. 29, 1922.   [293]

State of Idaho,

County of Ada,—ss.

On this 2d day of June, 1921, before me appeared Theodore H. Wegener, to me personally known, who being duly sworn did say, that he is the secretary of Jordan Valley Farms, a corporation duly organized and existing under the laws of the State of Idaho, and that the seal affixed to said instrument is the corporate seal of said corporation, and that said instrument was signed and sealed in behalf of said corporation by authority of its board of directors, and said Theodore H. Wegener acknowledged said instrument to be the free act and deed of said corporation.

IN TESTIMONY WHEREOF, I have hereunto set my hand and affixed my official seal this, the day and year first in this, my certificate, written.

[Seal]        EDNA L. HICE,

Notary Public for the State of Idaho.  Residing at Boise, Ada Co.

State of Oregon,
County of Multnomah,—ss.

On this 4th day of June, 1921, before me appeared J. Humfeld, to me personally known, who being duly sworn did say that he is general agent for the State of Oregon of Mortgage Company for America, a corporation duly organized and existing under the laws of the Kingdom of the Netherlands, and that said instrument was signed and sealed in behalf of said corporation by said J. Humfeld as its general agent for the State of Oregon, and said J. Humfeld acknowledged said instrument to be the free act and deed of said corporation.

IN TESTIMONY WHEREOF, I have hereunto set my hand and affixed my official seal, this, the day and year first in this, my certificate, written.

[Seal]        EARL C. BRONAUGH, Jr.,
        Notary Public for the State of Oregon.
My commission expires Dec. 29, 1922.

No. ——. Defts. "O."
U. S. District Court, District of Oregon. Filed June 12, 1923. [294]

State of Oregon,
County of Marion,—ss.

I, Percy A. Cupper, State Engineer, and Secretary of the Desert Land Board of Oregon, do hereby certify that the above and foregoing copy of that certain contract entered into May 27, 1921, by and between the Jordan Valley Land and Water Company, the Jordan Valley Farms, and the Mortgage Company for America wherein the loan of One Hundred and Seventeen Thousand Dollars was to have been made for the purpose of completing the construction of the Jordan Valley Land and Water Company, is a full, true and correct copy of a copy thereof as the same appears in the records of my office and in my custody and of the whole thereof.

In Witness Whereof, I have hereunto set my hand this 14th day of June, 1923.

PERCY A. CUPPER,

State Engineer.

By J. L. McALLISTER,

J. L. McALLISTER,

Assistant Secretary.   [295]

DEFENDANT'S EXHIBIT "P."

No. ——.   Defts. Ex. "P."

U. S. District Court, District of Oregon.   Filed June 12, 1923.   G. H. Marsh, Clerk.

Trust Agreement Dated May 27, 1921.

TRUST AGREEMENT.

#46

This Memoranda of Agreement made and entered into this 27th day of May, 1921, by and between the Desert Land Board, acting for and on behalf of the State of Oregon, hereinafter called the "Board," the Jordan Valley Land and Water Company, a corporation organized under the laws of the State of Nevada and doing business in the State of Oregon, hereinafter called the "Construction Company." J. Humfeld, Agent for the Mortgage Company for America in that certain agreement entered by and between the Construction Company, the Jordan Valley Farms, and the Mortgage Company for America whereby a mortgage was given covering the Jordan Valley Irrigation Project as security for a certain loan of $117,000.00, hereinafter called the "Trustee," and the United States National Bank of Portland, Oregon, hereinafter called the "Bank," WITNESSETH THAT:

WHEREAS, the Construction Company and the Board have entered into an agreement dated the 27 day of May, 1921, which provides for the continuation of the construction of the Jordan Valley Irrigation Project, located in Malheur County, State of Oregon, which contract is hereinafter designated the State Contract, a copy of which is hereto attached and made a part hereof, which contract provides that all cash and mortgages for securities taken for the purchase price of water rights shall be deposited in escrow with an escrow holder or trustee, to be selected and approved by the Board; which contract further provides that the irrigation system and all properties and rights of the construction company may be mortgaged and that all securities arising from the sale of project lands, may be hypothecated [296] for the purpose of securing money for carriyng on construction work, and

WHEREAS, an agreement has been made by and between the Construction Company and the Mortgage Company for America whereby a mortgage has been given covering said irrigation project as security for a certain loan in the amount of \$117,-000.00, a copy of which agreement is hereto attached and made a part hereof.

NOW, THEREFORE, in consideration of the premises and the mutual covenants and benefits herein provided, it is mutually understood and agreed by and between the parties hereto as follows:

First. The Board hereby agrees and by these presents selects and approves J. Humfeld, as trustee for the purpose of receiving and disbursing the cash and securities under the provisions of said State contract, and under the provisions of this agreement, who shall hold such office pending the payment of the loan heretofore mentioned, or until his successor has been duly appointed and qualified, to whom said J. Humfeld shall turn over all remaining cash and securities.

Second. J. Humfeld hereby agrees to assume and carry out the obligation as Trustee under said State contract, and under the further provisions herein contained, subject to the provisions of the said Loan Agreement for \$117,000.00. The Trustee further agrees that except as may be provided in said Loan Agreement no securities shall be assigned or delivered except upon the written approval of the Board, and that upon the payment of any loan under which any securities are hypothecated said securities remaining shall be returned to the Trust Fund herein specified; also that no payment shall be made from said Trust Fund except as herein provided. The Trustee further

agrees that he will render to the Board a monthly
statement of all receipts and disbursements of funds
coming into [297] his hands as Trustee hereunder.

Third. The Bank hereby agrees to receive and
disburse the money to be deposited in the Jordan
Valley Trust Fund as herein provided and further
that no payment shall be made from said Trust
Fund except as hereinafter provided.

Fourth. Any cash belonging to the Construction Company that may be received from Boise
Title and Trust Company, and so much of said loan
of $117,000.00 as may be contemplated by clause
5 of paragraph tenth of said loan contract shall
be deposited by the Trustee in the Bank in a Trust
Fund designated "Jordan Valley Trust Fund."
All other cash, mortgages, and securities coming
into the possession or control of the Trustee shall
be accounted for by him as provided in said loan
contract. All cash deposited in the "Jordan Valley
Trust Fund" shall be paid out by the Bank only
upon checks drawn by the Trustee and countersigned by the duly authorized representative of the
Board. The signature of the representative of
the Desert Land Board shall be full assurance to
the Bank that all necessary conditions precedent
to the issuing of said checks have been fully complied with. No checks shall be drawn by the Trustee except upon receipt by him of vouchers drawn
by the General Manager of the Irrigation Project,
and approved by the duly authorized representative
of the Board. Which vouchers shall be based upon

engineers' estimates or certificates as the work progresses, for work done or materials used or purchased for use in the construction of said irrigation system, and for necessary expenses of colonization and sale of water rights, which engineers' estimates or certificates shall be countersigned or approved by the State Engineer or his duly authorized representative. Any securities remaining in the possession of the Trustee after the repayment of said loan and the completion of the project shall be disposed of in accordance with the terms of the State Contract.  [298]

IN WITNESS WHEREOF, these presents are executed in quadruplicate the day and year first above written.

DESERT LAND BOARD OF OREGON.

By BEN W. OLCOTT,

Chairman.

[Seal]  Attest: PERCY A. CUPPER,

Secretary.

JORDAN VALLEY LAND AND WATER COMPANY.

By J. W. MANEY,

President.

J. HUMFELD,

Trustee.

[Seal]  Attest: EMIL L. TSCHIRGI,

Secretary.

## UNITED STATES NATIONAL BANK OF PORTLAND, OREGON.

By J. C. AINSWORTH,

President.

[Seal]   Attest: A. W. WRIGHT,

Secretary-Vice-President.

Approved as to form.

PLATT & PLATT,

MONTGOMERY & FALES,

Attorneys for the United States National Bank of Portland, Oregon.   [299]

State of Oregon,

County of Marion,—ss.

I, Percy A. Cupper, State Engineer, and Secretary of the Desert Land Board of Oregon, do hereby certify that the above and foregoing copy of the Trust Agreement entered into May 27, 1921, by and between the Desert Land Board of Oregon, the Jordan Valley Land and Water Company, J. Humfeld, and the United States National Bank of Portland, providing for the handling of funds derived through the One Hundred and Seventeen Thousand Dollar loan mentioned therein, is a full, true and correct copy of a copy thereof as the same appears in the records of my office and in my custody and of the whole thereof.

IN WITNESS WHEREOF, I have hereunto set my hand this 14th day of June, 1923.

PERCY A. CUPPER,

State Engineer, Secretary.

By J. L. McALLISTER,

J. L. McALLISTER,

Assistant Secretary.   [300]

Prior to the entry of judgment and on the 1st day of November, 1923, but subsequent to the opinion of the Court, the defendant in writing requested the Court specially to find and declare upon the whole record as a matter of law, as follows:

1. That there was no sufficient or competent evidence to show that any of the labor or material made the basis of plaintiff's cause of action was ordered or used by the Jordan Valley Land & Water Company in the prosecution of the work under its contract with the State of Oregon, or were necessary for the prosecution of any of the work under the terms of said contract or the terms of the bond sued upon.

2. That the complaint fails to state facts sufficient to constitute a cause of action and the evidence offered is insufficient to entitle the plaintiff to any judgment whatsoever.

3· That upon the whole record, judgment should be entered in favor of the defendant and against the plaintiff.

Thereafter and on the 3d day of November, 1923, judgment was entered in favor of the plaintiff in said action and against the defendant in said action in the sum of $2,900.73, with interest thereon at 6% per annum from March 21, 1920, and costs and disbursements.

The foregoing bill of exceptions contains all the evidence that was introduced and all the proceedings had on the trial of said cause.

And now within the time required by law and within the rules of this court, the defendant proposes the foregoing as and for its bill of exceptions and prays that the same may be settled and allowed as correct.

WM. S. NASH,
S. J. GRAHAM,
Attorneys for Defendant.

Settled and allowed December 26, 1923.

R. S. BEAN,
Judge.

Bill of exceptions lodged in clerk's office Dec. 20, 1923. G. H. Marsh, Clerk.

Filed December 26, 1923. G. H. Marsh, Clerk. [301]

---

In the District Court of the United States for the District of Oregon.

No. L.–9004.

STATE OF OREGON on the Relation of HARRY HUMFELD,

Plaintiff,

vs.

AMERICAN SURETY COMPANY OF NEW YORK, a Corporation,

Defendant.

STIPULATION RE TAKING OF DEPOSITIONS.

It is hereby stipulated and agreed by and between the parties hereto, through their respective attorneys of record, that the depositions of A. J. Vance and Leland S. Vance may be taken before Pauline E. Thrower, a notary public residing at Oklahoma City, Oklahoma, upon the written interrogatories and cross-interrogatories hereto attached; that the same may be returned to the clerk of the above-entitled court and may be introduced at the trial of this cause by either party hereto, the same as if said witnesses were personally present and testifying herein, subject, however, to objections on the grounds of immateriality, irrelevancy and incompetency, and that all objections to the manner and form of taking said depositions and the identification thereof are hereby waived.

It is further stipulated and agreed that the official signature and seal of said notary public shall be sufficient identification and certification of said depositions.

Dated this 17th day of May, 1923.

> BRONAUGH & BRONAUGH,
> BEACH & SIMON,
> ARTHUR A. GOLDSMITH,
> > Attorneys for Relator.
> WM. S. NASH and
> S. J. GRAHAM,
> > Attorneys for Defendant.    [302]

In the District Court of the United States for the District of Oregon.

No. L.–9004.

STATE OF OREGON on the Relation of HARRY HUMFELD,

Plaintiff,

vs.

AMERICAN SURETY COMPANY OF NEW YORK, a Corporation,

Defendant.

DEPOSITION OF A. J. VANCE, FOR DEFENDANT.

BE IT REMEMBERED, that pursuant to the stipulation hereto annexed, and on the 29th day of May, 1923, at my office in the county of Oklahoma, State of Oklahoma, before me, Pauline El Thrower, a notary public in and for the said county of Oklahoma, and State of Oklahoma, duly appointed and commissioned to administer oaths, etc., personally appeared A. J. Vance, a witness produced on behalf of the defendant, American Surety Company of New York, in the above-entitled suit, now pending in said court, who being by me first duly sworn to tell the truth, the whole truth and nothing but the truth, was then and there examined upon the following interrogatories and cross-interrogatories, and testified as follows:

Int. No. 1. State your name.

Answer. A. J. Vance.

Int. No. 2. Where do you reside?

Answer. In Oklahoma City, Oklahoma.

Int. No. 3. How long have you resided in Oklahoma City?

Answer. Twenty-three years.

Int. No. 4. State your age.

Answer. Fifty-three years.

Int. No. 5. State whether or not at any time you were ever in any manner associated with the Jordan Valley Land and Water Company.

Answer. For several months I was vice-president of the company.

Int. No. 6. State, if you know, the approximate date upon which you assumed the duties of vice-president of that company. [303]

Answer. About the first of May, 1920.

Int. No. 7. Where were you at that time?

Answer. In Boise, Idaho.

Int. No. 8. State whether or not you at that time were acquainted with the general nature and character of the work being conducted by the Jordan Valley Land and Water Company in Oregon.

Answer. Yes.

Int. No. 9. When did you first become acquainted with the nature and character of that particular project?

Answer. In September, 1919.

Int. No. 10. State how that came about.

Answer. In August, 1919, J. W. Maney employed me to go to Boise, Idaho, and look after his personal interests in connection with the Jordan Valley Land and Water Project, as well as the interests of his brother, John Maney, with instructions to visit the project, make investigations and report to him.

Int. No. 11. State, if you know, who you found in charge of the work on this project.

Answer. John W. Cunningham of Barr & Cunningham, of Portland, Oregon.

Int. No. 12. State, if you know, by what general or popular name this project was known.

Answer. Jordan Valley Irrigation Project.

Int. No. 13. You may state, if you know, the reason for Mr. Cunningham at that time representing or attempting to represent both the Desert Land Board of the State of Oregon and the Jordan Valley Land and Water Company.

Answer. Early in the spring of 1919, the Engineer representing the Desert Land Board of the State of Oregon resigned his position in connection with the Jordan Valley Irrigation Project and about the same time Mr. Bickle, the Engineer representing the Jordan Valley Land and Water Company on the Project also resigned. By agreement between Mr. Cupper, the State Engineer, and Mr. Wells, Vice-President of the Company, as a matter of economy, they decided to have Mr. Cunningham represent both the State and the Company.

Int. No. 14. State, if you know, how long Mr. Cunningham continued to also represent the interests of the Jordan Valley Land and Water Company on this project. [304]

Answer. This arrangement continued until about the first of November, 1919.

Int. No. 15. State, if you know, whether or not the Jordan Valley Land and Water Company secured an engineer to represent them alone.

Answer. Yes.

Int. No. 16. When?

Answer. About November 1, 1919.

Int. No. 17. State, if you know, by whom he was employed and the arrangement made for the services of this engineer.

Answer. I employed him myself.

Int. No. 18. Well, you mean you employed him as vice-president of the company?

Answer. No, I did not act as vice-president of the company, but as representative of Mr. Maney, president of the company, with the approval of the vice-president.

Int. No. 19. What was his engineer's name, if you know?

Answer. Charles P. Smith.

Int. No. 20. State, if you know, how long he continued to act as engineer and in what capacity to represent the Jordan Valley Land and Water Company on this project.

Answer. From about November 1, 1919, until the work on the project was discontinued, some time in July, 1920.

Int. No. 21. State, if you know, who the engineer was during that period of time representing the State of Oregon or the Desert Land Board.

Answer. John W. Cunningham.

Int. No. 22. State generally the nature of your work and duties in connection with this project prior to the time you were elected vice-president of the Jordan Valley Land and Water Company.

Answer. My duties in connection with this project were to look after any phase of the business affairs that would have a bearing on the interests of Maney Brothers and to secure a raise in the price of water rights or the provision in the price of water rights; this arrangement being made with the Desert Land Board. In other words to secure an alteration of the original contract with the State of Oregon, which I did; and to do anything I could to further the interests of the company in any way opportunity offered. [305]

Int. No. 23. Who was in charge of the affairs of the Jordan Valley Land and Water Company in connection with this particular project at the time you first went to Oregon or Idaho, as the case may be?

Answer. H. G. Wells, who was vice-president of the company and general manager in the absence of Mr. Maney.

Int. No. 24. State, if you know, how long he continued as the vice-president and general manager of the Jordan Valley Land and Water Company.

Answer. He continued to act as vice-president of the company until about May 1, 1920.

Int. No. 25. What occurred at that time?

Answer. About May 1, 1920, he resigned and I was elected vice-president of the company.

Int. No. 26. State, whether or not after that time Mr. Wells continued to have anything to do with the work on the project.

Answer. Mr. Wells continued the work on the

project until some time in July, 1920, when he left the project, the work being entirely shut down. The main force on the work, however, quit the latter part of June.

Int. No. 27. State, if you know, under what arrangement, if any, Mr. Wells continued to perform services in connection with this project.

Answer. Under the contract with the Company, approved by Mr. Cunningham in behalf of the Desert Land Board.

Int. No. 28. About when was that contract executed?

Answer. About the first of May, 1920.

Int. No. 29. Prior to that time, state, if you know, under what arrangement, if any, Mr. Wells was doing the construction work on this project.

Answer. Under a contract with Wells Brothers, as one party of the contract and Jordan Valley Land and Water Company as second party to the contract. Mr. Wells acted both as representative for Wells Brothers and representative of the Jordan Valley Land and Water Company, as vice-president. In other words, he made a contract in which he assumed to represent both parties to the contract.

Int. No. 30. State whether any objection was ever made to Mr. Wells doing the construction work on the project in question under this particular contract.

Answer. Yes. [306]

Int. No. 31. State, if you know, what objection was made.

Answer. Mr. Cunningham objected to this contract for the reason he thought it hardly fair or good business for Mr. Wells to assume to represent the company in making a contract with himself to do the work for the company.

Int. No. 32. State, if you know, when Mr. Cunningham first made any criticism or objection to this procedure.

Answer. His first objection was made to me early in September, 1919, the first time I met him and on every monthly visit afterwards until the arrangement was finally changed.

Int. No. 33. State, if you know, how long Mr. Wells did the construction work on this project under this objectionable contract before it was changed to satisfy Mr. Cunningham.

Answer. About one year, he having begun the work under this arrangement several months before my arrival in Boise.

Int. No. 34. State, if you know, about how long Mr. Wells continued to do the construction work on this project under this objectionable contract after Mr. Cunningham made his first objection.

Answer. About seven or eight months.

Int. No. 35. You may state, if you know, how long after Mr. Cunningham made his first objection to the contract it was before a new contract was formulated that was satisfactory to Mr. Cunningham.

Answer. About two months, but this contract was not signed by Mr. Wells; he refused to agree to some of the terms.

Int. No. 36. State, if you know, whether or not, Mr. Cunningham permitted Mr. Wells to carry on the construction work on this project under the objectionable contract and up to the time that the new contract was made.

Answer. He did.

Int. No. 37. State, if you know, what caused the delay in making the new contract with Wells Brothers after the first contract had been criticised by Mr. Cunningham.

Answer. It was the failure of Mr. Wells and Mr. Cunningham to agree on the price of some of the classifications of the work and also some other terms and conditions in the contract. [307]

Int. No. 38. State, if you know, whether or not Mr. Cunningham and Mr. Wells did finally agree upon these terms that were in question.

Answer. They did.

Int. No. 39. Who, if you know, was Mr. Cunningham representing in connection with the contract that Wells Brothers had made and was making?

Answer. He represented the State of Oregon or the Desert Land Board for the State of Oregon.

Int. No. 40. In what capacity, if you know?

Answer. He was the representative of the Engineering Department of the Desert Land Board of the State of Oregon.

Int. No. 41. State, if you know, the approximate date that the new contract was agreed upon between Mr. Cunningham and Wells Brothers.

Answer. In May, 1920.

Int. No. 42. State, if you know, whether or not this contract was reduced to writing.

Answer. It was.

Int. No. 43. State, if you know, whether or not it was signed and executed by Wells Brothers and also by Mr. Cunningham.

Answer. It was executed and signed by H. G. Wells and the Jordan Valley Land and Water Company and approved for the State of Oregon by Mr. Cunningham. However, I think this contract, as finally approved, was not between Wells Brothers, but between H. G. Wells and the company.

Int. No. 44. State, if you know, who prepared this written contract.

Answer. Mr. Cunningham had this contract prepared himself after considerable discussion with me and Mr. Wells.

Int. No. 45. In what manner did Mr. Cunningham approve this contract?

Answer. Mr. Cunningham approved it by signing it.

Int. No. 46. Did you see him sign it?

Answer. I did and handled the papers while the contract was being signed by all parties.

Int. No. 47. State, if you know, who signed the contract on behalf of Wells Brothers. [308]

Answer. Yes, I saw Mr. Wells sign the contract. behalf of himself—I think, rather than Wells Brothers.

Int. No. 48. Did you see him sign it?

Answer. Yes, I saw Mr. Wells sign the contract.

Int. No. 49. State, if you know, how many copies of this contract were made and signed.

Answer. There were four copies of this contract signed.

Int. No. 50. State, if you know, what became of these several copies.

Answer. The Jordan Valley Land and Water Company retained one copy, Mr. H. G. Wells one copy, one copy was forwarded to the Desert Land Board at Salem, Oregon, the receipt of which was later acknowledged by that office, and the fourth copy was kept by Mr. John W. Cunningham for his office files.

Int. No. 51. How long has it been since you have had the charge and custody or control of any of the books or records of the Jordan Valley Land and Water Company?

Answer. Nearly two years.

Int. No. 52. Do you know at this time where the copy of this contract, which was retained by the Jordan Valley Land and Water Company, is located?

Answer. The last time I saw it, it was in the file of the company's office at Boise. I do not know where it is now.

Int. No. 53. Have you recently made a search among the books, records and papers now in the hands of Mr. J. W. Maney, president of the Jordan Valley Land and Water Company, in Oklahoma City?

Answer. I have.

Int. No. 54. Were you successful?

Answer. No, I found a very large part of the records in the office at Boise when I left but not the contract.

Ind. No. 55. I will ask you to state, if you know,

how long the firm of Wells Brothers continued the construction work on this project under the contracts by you in your testimony.

Answer. Mr. Wells continued construction work on the project until some time in July, 1920. However, the larger part of the work had been shut down a few weeks earlier, some time in June. [309]

Int. No. 56. State, if you know, what occurred at that time relative to the continuance or noncontinuance of the work on this project.

Answer. The company failed to be able to get funds to carry on the work any further and were forced to discontinue the work.

Int. No. 57. State whether or not, if you know, the firm of Wells Brothers was operating during the construction work on this project under the contract to which you have referred in your testimony as having been criticised by Mr. Cunningham at the time you first went to Oregon.

Answer. Yes, they were operating under the objectionable contract at the time I arrived in Boise at the time of my first visit to the project and continued to do so, as formerly stated, up to about the first of May, 1920.

Int. No. 58. Are you acquainted with the plaintiff in this case, Harry Humfeld?

Answer. Yes.

Int. No. 59. Where and when did you first become acquainted with him?

Answer. On the project in the spring of 1920.

Int. No. 60. At that time were you acquainted with the elder Humfeld, father of Harry Humfeld?

Answer. Yes.

Int. No. 61. How long had you known him at that time?

Answer. Probably about six or seven months.

Int. No. 62. Where did you first become acquainted with him?

Answer. In Boise, Idaho.

Int. No. 63. State, if you know, what relationship the elder Humfeld had, if any, in connection with this project and the work being done on the project.

Answer. He had loaned a good many thousands of dollars on security on this project.

Int. No. 64. State, if you know, generally what the form or nature of these securities were.

Answer. They consisted of mortgages or deeded lands in the project, together with the water rights for such lands.

Int. No. 65. State, if you know, where the elder Mr. Humfeld lived at that time.

Answer. In Portland, Oregon. [310]

Int. No. 66. You may state the circumstances under which you first became acquainted with Harry Humfeld.

Answer. He was working in the capacity of water-master on the project and utility man in doing survey work for the settlers and locating lines and corners for the colonization company, of which Mr. Hooker was the head.

Int. No. 67. State, if you know, under what terms or

conditions the plaintiff, Harry Humfeld was acting or working as water-master on this project.

Answer. He was employed by Mr. Hooker, president and manager of the Jordan Valley Farms and the Colonization Company with a kind of a loose arrangement and more or less vague understanding that while the Farms Company was responsible to him for his salary, the funds to pay it with would be partly derived from collections of water charges against the settlers and a large part was to be paid by the settlers for special work in the way of helping them to locate their ditches and land lines and doing other survey work for them, as well as special survey work in locating land lines and corners for the Colonization Company.

Int. No. 68. State whether or not this arrangement or understanding was verbal or in writing.

Answer. Mr. Humfeld may have had a written contract with Mr. Hooker, but so far as I have any knowledge the contract was verbal.

Int. No. 69. State, if you know, by whom it was made.

Answer. It was made by the Colonization Agent, Mr. Hooker, in behalf of the Jordan Valley Farms.

Int. No. 70. State how you became cognizant of this verbal understanding or arrangement with the plaintiff, Harry Humfeld.

Answer. Mr. Cunningham first told me about it in the company's office at Boise, I think during his visit in March, 1920.

Int. No. 71. State whether or not you ever talked with the plaintiff, Harry Humfeld, about it.

Answer. I did, on the project in May, 1920, again in August, 1920, while driving with Mr. Harry Humfeld over the project. He again told me the details about his arrangement and stated that he was very glad that he was in the employ of the Jordan Valley Farms, because he felt that his salary coming from that source would be much more certain than it would be if he were employed by the Jordan Valley Land and Water Company. He at that time claimed that Jordan Valley Land and Water Company was expected to reimburse the Jordan Valley Farms for one-half of his [311] salary, but never explained to me by what authority such arrangement was made or by whom. In this conversation Mr. Harry Humfeld also stated that the Jordan Valley Land and Water Company would soon go broke and that his father, the elder Humfeld, and Mr. Hooker, the head of the Jordan Valley Farms organization, would take over the project, Mr. Humfeld, senior, refinancing it and completing it, and on that account he was absolutely sure of getting all his salary.

Int. No. 72. I will ask you to state whether or not you were requested to agree to and approve this arrangement.

Answer. No. I was never asked to approve the arrangement of his employment, either by him or by Mr. Hooker.

Int. No. 73. State whether or not after you were advised by Mr. Cunningham as to this arrangement or understanding with the plaintiff, and after you had talked with the plaintiff himself about it, you ever approved or agreed to the same on behalf of the Jordan Valley Land and Water Company?

Answer. I did not.

Int. No. 74. I direct your attention to the plaintiff's complaint in this case and to paragraph 7 of the first cause of action, wherein the plaintiff, Harry Humfeld claims to have rendered work and labor for the Jordan Valley Land and Water Company from the first day of April, 1920, to the 31st day of August, 1921, and will ask you to state, if you know, whether or not the said plaintiff performed any work or labor on this project besides the work which he may have done as water-master under the verbal arrangement.

Answer. Probably one-half of his time during the irrigation season from April to September was consumed in looking after the ditches and distribution of the water. The other one-half of such time and a large portion of the other months outside of the irrigation season were occupied in assisting the settlers with surveying and also in doing survey work for some of Mr. Hooker's cattle companies, like the Owyhee Cattle Company.

Int. No. 75. State whether or not that kind or class of work was in any manner for the use or benefit of the Jordan Valley Land and Water Company.

Answer. No. None of the work, except the work in connection with the distribution of the water and the repair work on the ditches was for the benefit of the Jordan Valley Land and Water Company.

Int. No. 76. What was your conversation with

the plaintiff, Harry Humfeld, in regard to his arrangement about acting as water-master?

Answer. Harry Humfeld told me specifically that his duties [312] as water-master did not require probably more than one-half his time and that he would put in the rest of his time doing special work for the settlers and for the Colonization Company, and that there would be enough money collected from the settlers to take care of the amount coming to him as water-master.

Int. No. 77. State, if you know, about when you had this conversation with the plaintiff.

Answer. This conversation occurred upon the occasion of my first visit with him on the project in May, 1920, and a similar conversation in July, 1920, on the project.

Int. No. 78. I will ask you to state whether or not it was under the terms and conditions stated by Mr. Humfeld in this conversation that you permitted him to act as water-master.

Answer. It was.

Int. No. 79. State, if you know, of what the transaction consists in collecting water charges to which Mr. Humfeld referred to in his conversation.

Answer. A charge of some agreed price per acre against the water users for each season.

Int. No. 80. State whether or not, if you know, the plaintiff, Harry Humfeld, did make collections of water charges during the time he was acting as water-master.

Answer. He did.

Int. No. 81. State whether or not the plaintiff, during any of this time that you were in charge of the affairs of the Jordan Valley Land and Water Company on this project ever paid to the company any sums so collected.

Answer. He did not.

Int. No. 82. State whether or not, during any of this time you ascertained or were able to ascertain the amount that the plaintiff had collected.

Answer. No.

Int. No. 83. State whether or not you ever made any request of the plaintiff to furnish you a statement of the amounts and items of water charges collected by him.

Answer. I did.

Int. No. 84. Did you ever receive from the plaintiff any detailed statement showing the amounts so collected?

Answer. I did not.

Int. No. 85. Did the plaintiff, during any of this time that you [313] were in charge of the affairs of the Jordan Valley Land and Water Company ever account to you for the amounts of the water charges collected by him?

Answer. He did not, more than to tell me he had made some collections.

Int. No. 86. State, if you know, what was the nature and character of the labor and work necessary in fulfilling the duties of the water-master.

Answer. In this case his duties were to look after the apportionment and distribution of the water among the different users, to keep the ditches up and look after any minor repairs that might be necessary in connection with the ditches.

Int. No. 87. I will ask you to state whether or not you had any conversation with the plaintiff, Harry Humfeld, and also with Mr. Cunningham, in the spring of 1920, concerning the plaintiff's personal presence in and about the project.

Answer. Yes.

Int. No. 88. State the substance of this conversation.

Answer. The plaintiff, Mr. Harry Humfeld, and Mr. Cunningham both told me that Mr. Humfeld's father was very anxious to have his son on the project to keep a check on the work and development on account of the heavy loans that he had made on securities on the project, in order to conserve his own interests and see that the money he was furnishing really went into the construction work, and Mr. Cunningham repeatedly told me that as a matter of policy, in order to secure Mr. Humfeld's further aid in financing the project, it would be good business to have his son on the project, although other help was already provided.

Int. No. 89. I will ask you to state whether or not, pursuant to this conversation with the plaintiff, and Mr. Cunningham, the plaintiff was by you permitted to act as water-master under the verbal understanding and arrangement already testified to.

Answer. He was.

Int. No. 90. I will ask you to state, if you know, how much work during this period of time, that is between the 1st day of April, 1920, and the 31st day of August, 1921, the plaintiff did direct for the settlers.

Answer. He told me in August, 1920, while with him on the project that he was getting enough work out of the settlers to take care of his living expenses, provided he could collect promptly for all of such work, but was behind in his collections at that time. I was never back on the project but once more after this occasion, some time during the winter and severed my connection with the company about the first of April, [314] 1921, at which time Mr. Maney came out to Boise and took personal charge of the affairs of the company. I had nothing to do with the company's business after that time.

Int. No. 91. I will ask you to state, if you know, whether or not the firm of Wells Brothers, or the individual members thereof, in carrying on the construction work on this project as testified to, were able to or did use their own credit in procuring labor and material.

Answer. They used their own credit, but their credit was based altogether on their promise that the Jordan Valley Land and Water Company would pay their estimates in cash, which would give the money to pay their bills, otherwise they had no credit.

Int. No. 92. State, if you know, whose credit the firm of Wells Brothers and the individual members thereof used in procuring labor and material and supplies for this project.

Answer. They used their own credit as far as

they could, and also the credit of the Jordan Valley Land and Water Company.

Int. No. 93. I direct your attention to the plaintiff's complaint in this case, especially paragraphs 3 and 4 of the second cause of action, wherein the plaintiff claims the sum of $2,973 on account of blasting materials and supplies procured from E. I. Du Pont de Nemours Co., and ask you whether or not you became acquainted with this transaction.

Answer. Yes, in a general way.

Int. No. 94. I will ask you to state whether or not, if you know, any part of this blasting material and supplies were used in the construction work on this project.

Answer. Yes, a part of it was.

Int. No. 95. I will ask you to state, if you know, approximately how much of it was not.

Answer. In a conversation with Mr. Smith, the Engineer, I asked him if he had a check on the amount of powder on hand, and he told me in the company's office in Boise during August or September, 1920, that there was about one-half carload of powder stored that had not been used.

Int. No. 96. State, if you know, where this unused powder was at the time construction work ceased.

Answer. It was stored in a magazine on the project.

Int. No. 97. Do you know what became of it after that?

Answer. I do not know.

Int. No. 98. In your testimony heretofore given you have referred [315] to the contract which was finally acceptable and approved by Mr. Cunningham, and under which the construction work was to be continued by the firm of Wells Brothers, and in relation to this testimony I will ask you to state your best recollection concerning the parties by whom the contract was finally made and executed.

Answer. The negotiations for several months were contained with the understanding or on the theory that the contract would be executed in the name of Wells Brothers, but my best recollection was that inasmuch as only one of the Wells Brothers was really interested in the work, and that there was in reality no such firm, that the contract was finally executed by and in the name of H. G. Wells.

Int. No. 99. State, if you know, what the nature and character of the general terms and provisions of the contract with Wells Brothers or H. G. Wells were that were in controversy between Mr. Cunningham and yourself.

Answer. The differences related principally to the prices on certain classifications of work and also as to the length of time of the contract.

A. J. VANCE.

Subscribed and sworn to before me by the said A. J. Vance, this 29th day of May, A. D. 1923.

[Seal]        PAULINE E. THROWER,

Notary Public.

My commission expires November 27, 1926.
[316]

Cross–Interrogatories Propounded to Witness
A. J. Vance.

C.–Int. No. 1. Is the contract which was passed
upon by Mr. Cunningham, between Jordan Valley
Land and Water Company and Wells Brothers,
dated November 17, 1919?

Answer. The only contract that was ever finally
executed by all parties and approved was the one
executed in May, 1920, and my recollection is that
it bore the date of execution at that time.

C.–Int. No. 2. Is it not a fact that even after the
execution of the contract of November 17, 1919,
that H. G. Wells continued as vice-president of the
Jordan Valley Land and Water Company with
power to order supplies and materials for the
project in the name of the Jordan Valley Land and
Water Company?

Answer. It is a fact that Mr. Wells continued
as vice-president of the company until about the
first of May, 1920, but it is not a fact that any
contract whatever was executed and approved in
November, 1919.

C.–Int. No. 3. When, if ever, was such power
taken away from H. G. Wells?

Answer. Mr. Wells' authority to act for the
company expired, of course, when he resigned as
vice-president about the first of May, 1920.

C.–Int. No. 4. Was there ever any authorization
of the contract of November 19, 1921, or of the
prior contract which you have referred to as having been objected to by Mr. Cunningham by resolution of the corporation or otherwise. If your an-

swer be yes, state when and where and under what circumstances the authorization was given.

Answer. No. There was never any authorization of any contract on November 19, 1919, by the Board of Directors of the Jordan Valley Land and Water Company?

C.–Int. No. 5. Was the contract ever ratified by the Board of Directors of Jordan Valley Land and Water Company?

Answer. The contract executed about May 1, 1920, was ratified by the Board of Directors of the Jordan Valley Land and Water Company.

C.–Int. No. 6. If so, when and where was it ratified and state under what circumstances.

Answer. This contract as finally agreed upon was submitted to Mr. Haga, counsel for the Jordan Valley Land and Water Company, also one of the directors of the company, was approved by him as company attorney and he prepared the papers formally approving and ratifying the contract for the Board of Directors. This contract was signed by Mr. Wells as contractor, by myself as vice-president, attested by the secretary of the company and approved by John W. Cunningham, on behalf of the State of Oregon. [317]

C.–Int. No. 7. Did you, as vice-president of the Jordan Valley Land and Water Company ever deny the liability of that company for the blasting supplies sold and delivered to it by E. I. Du Pont de Nemours & Co. during March of 1920?

Answer. No. I considered that a valid claim against the company.

C.–Int. No. 8. Did you not during the month of August, 1920, on behalf of Jordan Valley Land and Water Company as vice-president of that company, inform E. I. Du Pont de Nemours & Co. that its account would be paid promptly by the Jordan Valley Land and Water Company as soon as funds were obtained by that concern?

Answer. Yes, I did.

C.–Int. No. 9. Is it not a fact that the plaintiff, Harry Humfeld, was employed as water-master by Jordan Valley Land and Water Company continuously from May 1, 1920, to August 31, 1921?

Answer. If the plaintiff, Harry Humfeld, was ever employed as water-master for the Jordan Valley Land and Water Company, I have no knowledge or when, where, how or by whom it was done.

C.–Int. No. 10. Did you employ Harry Humfeld as water-master for Jordan Valley Land and Water Company?

Answer. I did not.

C.–Int. No. 11. If not, by whom was he so employed?

Answer. It was always my understanding that his employment was contracted for by Mr. Hooker.

C.–Int. No. 12. Did the person employing him have authority to do so in behalf of Jordan Valley Land and Water Company

Answer. No.

C.–Int. No. 13. Is it not a fact that the work and labor performed by Harry Humfeld as water-master was necessary to the ultimate completion of the construction work on the Jordan Valley Project?

Answer. No. I cannot see how his work of riding the ditches and distributing the water had anything at all to do with the construction work.

C.-Int. No. 14. Was it not necessary that such units of the Jordan Valley Project as had been completed should be maintained in operation and in good repair, in order that the construction work of the Jordan Valley Project might be completed in accordance with the terms of the contract between Jordan Valley Land and Water Company and the Desert Land Board of the State of Oregon, and in order that said construction work would be excepted by the Desert Land Board? [318]

Answer. The contract between the State and the Jordan Valley Land and Water Company for the building of this project is a very long document with many provisions and I do not remember all of the terms and conditions of that contract. I think this question can be better answered by referring to the contract.

C.-Int. No. 15. Did you not, during the period from April 1, 1920, to August 31, 1921, recognize the fact that Harry Humfeld was employed by Jordan Valley Land and Water Company?

Answer. No, but I did recognize the fact that the Jordan Valley Land and Water Company was to reimburse the Jordan Valley Farms, Mr. Hooker's organization, for one-half of Harry Humfeld's salary, and that the funds to take care of this obligation would be fully recovered from the collection of water rents from the water users.

C.-Int. No. 16. Did you not, during the summer

and fall of 1920, give Harry Humfeld instructions as to work which you desired him to do for the Jordan Valley Land and Water Company, and authorize him to employ men to do such work?

Answer. Yes, for some minor repairs.

C.–Int. No. 17. Was it not agreed by Jordan Valley Land and Water Company that Harry Humfeld was to receive a certain wage for his services as water-master, and that in addition thereto the Jordan Valley Land and Water Company was to pay a further sum for his board?

Answer. It was understood that about one-half of Harry Humfeld's time would be spent as water-master and paid for as described before. I *now* of no contract whereby the Jordan Valley Land and Water Company was to pay Harry Humfeld's board. But as a matter of fact, the Jordan Valley Farms had no funds with which to pay Humfeld's salary and he got behind with his board bill. Of course, it was necessary for him to have something to eat in order to stay on the job. I recognized that fact and got out with him and tried to help him sell some of the cement and other perishable articles belonging to the Jordan Valley Land and Water Company, in order to raise money to pay his board bill; both companies being entirely out of funds with which to meet any of their obligations and it was simply a question of getting by for a few weeks or a few months until Mr. Hooker and Mr. Humfeld Senior could raise the money as they had promised to do to resume construction work on the project and pay up all the outstanding bills.

For these reasons, regardless of whose obligation it might have been legally, I tried to help him on the job.

C.–Int. No. 18. State, if you know, what amount Harry Humfeld was to receive as wages from the Jordan Valley Land and  [319]  Water Company and what allowance he was to receive from Jordan Valley Land and Water Company for board?

Answer. I have forgotten what the exact amount was that Harry Humfeld said he was to receive for his work, but believe it was $125.00 per month, and as he stated, due him from the Jordan Valley Farms.

A. J. VANCE.

Subscribed and sworn to before me by the said A. J. Vance, this 29th day of May, A. D. 1923.

[Seal]          PAULINE E. THROWER,

Notary Public.

My commission expires November 27, 1926. [320]

State of Oklahoma,
County of Oklahoma,—ss.

I, Pauline E. Thrower, a Notary Public in and for said County and State, do hereby certify that the witness, A. J. Vance, in the foregoing deposition named, was by me duly sworn to testify the truth, the whole truth and nothing but the truth in said cause; that said deposition was taken in my office in said County of Oklahoma, State of Oklahoma, on the 29th day of May, 1923, between the hours of 4:30 P. M. and 6:00 P. M. of that day; that the answers of the said witness to the said interrogatories and cross-interrogatories were reduced to writing by me and when completed was by me carefully read to said witness and being by him corrected was by him subscribed in my presence.

IN WITNESS WHEREOF, I have hereunto set my hand and affixed my official seal this 30th day of May, 1923.

[Seal]    PAULINE E. THROWER,
Notary Public for Oklahoma.

My commission expires November 27, 1926.
[321]

---

In the District Court of the United States for the District of Oregon.

No. L.–9004.

STATE OF OREGON on the Relation of HARRY HUMFELD,

Plaintiff,

vs.

AMERICAN SURETY COMPANY OF NEW YORK, a Corporation,

Defendant.

DEPOSITION OF LELAND S. VANCE, FOR DEFENDANT.

BE IT REMEMBERED, that pursuant to the stipulation hereto annexed, and on the 29th day of May, 1923, at my office in the County of Oklahoma, State of Oklahoma, before me, Pauline E. Thrower, a notary public in and for the said county of Oklahoma and State of Oklahoma, duly appointed and commissioned to administer oaths, etc., personally appeared Leland S. Vance, a witness produced on behalf of the defendant, American Surety Company of New York, in the above-entitled suit now pending in said court, who being by me first duly sworn to tell the truth, the whole truth and nothing but the truth, was then and there examined upon the following written interrogatories and testified as follows:

Int. No. 1. State your name.

Answer. Leland S. Vance.

Int. No. 2. Where do you reside

Answer. Oklahoma City, Oklahoma.

Int. No. 3. How long have you resided in Oklahoma City, Oklahoma?

Answer. Twenty years.

Int. No. 4. State your age.

Answer. Twenty years.

Int. No. 5. State your occupation.

Answer. Real estate salesman.

Int. No. 6. State your relationship, if any, you bear to the witness, A. J. Vance.

Answer. A. J. Vance is my father.

Int. No. 7. State whether or not in the past you at any time [322] became acquainted with the construction work known as the Jordan Valley Irrigation Project in Oregon.

Answer. Yes.

Int. No. 8. State the date that you first became acquainted with this construction work?

Answer. September 1, 1919.

Int. No. 9. State what relationship, if any, your father, A. J. Vance, **had** with this project.

Answer. He looked after J. W. Maney's interests the first few months he was in Idaho and later became vice-president of the Jordan Valley Land and Water Company.

Int. No. 10. State whether or not you at any time ever did any work or performed any service in connection with this project.

Answer. I did.

Int. No. 11. State the nature of this labor and service performed by you, if any.

Answer. I was employed on the engineering crew on the project.

Int. No. 12. State during what period of time you rendered such service and labor, if any.

Answer. From September 1, 1919, to July 1, 1920.

Int. No. 13. State where such service and labor were rendered, if any.

Answer. On the Jordan Valley Irrigation Project.

Int. No. 14. State whether or not you know the plaintiff in this case, Harry Humfeld.

Answer. Yes, I do.

Int. No. 15. State where and when you first met him.

Answer. In March or April, 1920, on the project.

Int. No. 16. State whether during the period of time that you have testified you rendered labor and service on the Jordan Valley Irrigation Project in Oregon, you maintained your acquaintance with the plaintiff, Harry Humfeld.

Answer. My acquaintance with Harry Humfeld

began in March or April, 1920, on the project and lasted until October, 1920.

Int. No. 17. You may state the nature of your personal acquaintance and relationship to the plaintiff, Harry Humfeld, during the time you were working on the said project. [323]

Answer. We worked together, ate and slept together a greater part of the time for six months.

Int. No. 18. State, if you know, whether or not the plaintiff, Harry Humfeld, was engaged in any service or rendered any work and labor on this project during the time you were there.

Answer. He did.

Int. No. 19. If you answer the last above question in the affirmative, kindly state the nature and character of the labor and service performed by the plaintiff.

Answer. He worked as water-master for the project and also did a lot of survey work for the settlers. He also did some work for some of the Hooker Cattle Companies.

Int. No. 20. You may state, if you know, under what understanding, agreement or arrangement the plaintiff was rendering labor and service upon that project.

Answer. All I know about the arrangement was what Harry Humfeld himself told me and what I heard others say.

Int. No. 21. State whether or not during any of the time you were working on the project you had any conversation with the plaintiff Harry Humfeld, concerning the question of his salary and the manner in which it was to be paid.

Answer. Yes.

Int. No. 22. If you answer the last-above question in the affirmative, kindly state the conversation or conversations which you had with him, giving the time and place thereof.

Answer. I had several conversations with Harry Humfeld in April and May, 1920, on the project, in which he stated he was to receive his salary from the Jordan Valley Farms Company; that he desired this arrangement himself, because he thought he was more sure of getting his money. He also said that I might not get my money, as he thought the Jordan Valley Land and Water Company would go broke and that his father would re-finance the project, so he was sure of getting his money.

Int. No. 23. If in answering the last-above question you state that the defendant, Harry Humfeld, had a conversation with you in which he told you that he was employed by a corporation known as the Jordan Valley Farms, state, if you know, whether or not his understanding and agreement was in verbal or in writing.

Answer. I do not know. [324]

Int. No. 24. State, if you know, whether or not the Jordan Valley Farms is a separate and distinct company or corporation from the Jordan Valley Land and Water Company.

Answer. Yes.

Int. No. 25. If you answer the last-above question in the. affirmative, kindly state in detail what you know concerning the nature and character of the company known as the Jordan Valley Farms.

Answer. This company was a real estate organization for the purpose of selling the land on the project.

Int. No. 26. State, if you know, who was in charge of the affairs and interests of the Jordan Valley Farms.

Answer. Mr. Hooker.

Int. No. 27. State, if you know, what interest the plaintiff, Harry Humfeld, or his father, had in the company known as the Jordan Valley Farms, and what their business relationships to said company were, if you know.

Answer. I do not know.

LELAND S. VANCE.

Subscribed and sworn to before me by the said Leland S. Vance this 29th day of May, A. D. 1923.

[Seal]      PAULINE E. THROWER,

Notary Public.

My commission expires November 27, 1926.

[325]

State of Oklahoma,

County of Oklahoma,—ss.

I, Pauline E. Thrower, a notary public in and for said county and state, do hereby certify that the witness, Leland S. Vance, in the foregoing deposition named, was by me duly sworn to testify the truth, the whole truth and nothing but the truth in said cause; that said deposition was taken in my office in said county of Oklahoma, in the State of Oklahoma, on the 29th day of May, 1923, between the hours of 2:00 P. M., and 3:00 P. M.

of that day; that the answers of the said witness to the said interrogatories were reduced to writing by me and when completed was by me carefully read to said witness and being by him corrected was by him subscribed in my presence.

IN WITNESS WHEREOF, I have hereunto set my hand and affixed my official seal this 30th day of May, 1923.

[Seal]       PAULINE E. THROWER,
                    Notary Public for Oklahoma.

My commission expires November 27, 1926.

Filed June 2, 1923.  G. H. Marsh, Clerk.  [326]

———

AND AFTERWARDS, to wit, on the 7th day of January, 1924, there was duly filed in said court a praecipe for transcript, in words and figures as follows, to wit:  [327]

In the District Court of the United States for the District of Oregon.

No. L.–9004.

STATE OF OREGON on the Relation of HARRY HUMFELD,

                              Plaintiff,

              vs.

AMERICAN SURETY COMPANY OF NEW YORK, a Corporation,

                    Defendant.

## PRAECIPE FOR TRANSCRIPT ON WRIT OF ERROR.

To the Clerk of the Above-named Court:

Sir: Please prepare certified transcript on writ of error of the following pleadings, papers and orders:

1. Complaint.
2. Demurrer.
3. Order overruling demurrer.
4. Answer.
5. Reply.
6. Stipulation waiving trial by jury.
6–A. Opinion of Court.
7. Judgment.
8. Several orders extending time for serving bill of exceptions.
9. Bill of exceptions as settled by trial judge.
9–A. Order settling and allowing bill of exceptions.
10. Petition for writ of error.
11. Order allowing writ of error.
12. Assignment of errors.
13. Supersedeas bond and bond for costs.
14. Writ of error.
15. Citation on writ of error.
16. Deposition of A. J. Vance. [328]
17. Order extending time for filing record.
18. Praecipe for certified transcript.

Dated January 7, 1924.

WM. S. NASH and

S. J. GRAHAM,

Attorneys for Defendant.

Service of the within praecipe for transcript of record, by certified copy as prescribed by law, is hereby admitted at Portland, Oregon, this 7th day of January, 1924.

ARTHUR A. GOLDSMITH,
Of Attorneys for Plaintiff.

Filed January 7, 1924.  G. H. Marsh, Clerk.
[329]

---

## CERTIFICATE OF CLERK U. S. DISTRICT COURT TO TRANSCRIPT OF RECORD.

United States of America,
District of Oregon,—ss.

I, G. H. Marsh, Clerk of the District Court of the United States for the District of Oregon, pursuant to the foregoing writ of error and in obedience thereto, do hereby certify that the foregoing pages, numbered from 3 to 329, inclusive, constitute the transcript of record on the writ of error in the cause in said court in which the State of Oregon on the relation of Harry Humfeld is plaintiff and defendant in error and the American Surety Company of New York, a corporation, is defendant and plaintiff in error; that said transcript has been prepared by me in accordance with the praecipe for transcript filed in said cause, and that it is a full, true and correct transcript of the record and proceedings had in said court in said cause, designated by the said praecipe to be included therein, as the same appear of record and on file at my office and in my custody. I return to the United States Circuit Court of Appeals for the Ninth Circuit the original writ of error and citation filed in said cause with the said transcript of record annexed thereto.

I further certify that the cost of the foregoing transcript is Ninety-nine 15/100 Dollars and that the same has been paid by the said plaintiff in error.

In Testimony Whereof I have hereunto set my hand and affixed the seal of said court at Portland, in said district, this 19th day of March, 1924.

[Seal]            G. H. MARSH,
                         Clerk. [330]

---

[Endorsed]: No. 4226. United States Circuit Court of Appeals for the Ninth Circuit. American Surety Company of New York, a Corporation, Plaintiff in Error, vs. The State of Oregon on the Relation of Harry Humfeld, Defendant in Error. Transcript of Record. Upon Writ of Error to the United States District Court of the District of Oregon.

Filed March 22, 1924.

               F. D. MONCKTON,
Clerk of the United States Circuit Court of Appeals for the Ninth Circuit.
            By Paul P. O'Brien,
               Deputy Clerk.

In the District Court of the United States for the
District of Oregon.

No. L.–9004.

STATE OF OREGON on the Relation of HARRY
HUMFELD,

Plaintiff,

vs.

AMERICAN SURETY COMPANY OF NEW
YORK, a Corporation,

Defendant.

ORDER EXTENDING TIME TO AND IN-
CLUDING FEBRUARY 3, 1924, TO FILE
RECORD AND DOCKET CAUSE.

Now, at this day, for good cause shown, IT IS
ORDERED that the time for filing the transcript
of record in this cause and docketing the same in
the United States Circuit Court of Appeals for
the Ninth Circuit be, and the same is hereby, extended to and including the 3d day of February,
1924.

Dated December 31, 1923.

R. S. BEAN,
Judge.

[Endorsed]: No. L.–9004. In the District
Court of the United States for the District of
Oregon. State of Oregon on Relation of Harry
Humfeld, Plaintiff, vs. American Surety Company
of New York, a Corporation, Defendant. Filed
Jan. 3, 1924. F. D. Monckton, Clerk.

No. 4226. United States Circuit Court of Appeals for the Ninth Circuit. Order Under Subdivision 1 of Rule 16 Enlarging Time to and Including February 3, 1924, to File Record and Docket Cause. Refiled Mar. 22, 1924. F. D. Monckton, Clerk.

---

In the District Court of the United States for the District of Oregon.

No. L.–9004.

January 31, 1924.

THE STATE OF OREGON ex rel. HARRY HUMFELD

vs.

THE AMERICAN SURETY COMPANY OF NEW YORK.

ORDER EXTENDING TIME TO AND INCLUDING FEBRUARY 28, 1924, TO FILE RECORD AND DOCKET CAUSE.

Now, at this day, for good cause shown to the Court, IT IS ORDERED that the time for filing the transcript of record in this cause and docketing the same in the United States Circuit Court of Appeals for the Ninth Circuit be, and the same is hereby, extended to and including February 28, 1924.

R. S. BEAN,
Judge.

[Endorsed]: No. 4226. United States Circuit Court of Appeals for the Ninth Circuit. Order

Under Subdivision 1 of Rule 16 Enlarging Time to and Including February 28, 1924, to File Record and Docket Cause. Filed Mar. 22, 1924. F. D. Monckton, Clerk.

---

In the District Court of the United States for the District of Oregon.

No. L.–9004.

February 28, 1924.

STATE OF OREGON ex rel. HARRY HUM-
FELD,

vs.

THE AMERICAN SURETY COMPANY OF NEW YORK.

ORDER EXTENDING TIME TO AND IN-
CLUDING MARCH 31, 1924, TO FILE
RECORD AND DOCKET CAUSE.

Now at this day for good cause shown, IT IS ORDERED that the time for filing the transcript of record on writ of error in this cause and docketing the same in the United States Circuit Court of Appeals for the Ninth Circuit, be, and the same is hereby, extended to and including March 31, 1924.

R. S. BEAN,

Judge.

[Endorsed]: No. 4226. United States Circuit Court of Appeals for the Ninth Circuit. Order Under Subdivision 1 of Rule 16 Enlarging Time to and Including March 31, 1924, to File Record and Docket Cause. Filed Mar. 22, 1924. F. D. Monckton, Clerk.

No. 4226

# United States
# Circuit Court of Appeals
### For the Ninth Circuit.

AMERICAN SURETY COMPANY OF
NEW YORK, a corporation,

Plaintiff in Error,

vs.

THE STATE OF OREGON ON THE RE-
LATION OF HARRY HUMFELD,

Defendant in Error.

## BRIEF OF PLAINTIFF IN ERROR

Upon Writ of Error to the United States District
Court of the District of Oregon.

WM. S. NASH & S. J. GRAHAM,
Attorneys for Plaintiff in Error.

No. 4226

# United States
# Circuit Court of Appeals
### For the Ninth Circuit.

---

AMERICAN SURETY COMPANY OF
NEW YORK, a corporation,

Plaintiff in Error,

vs.

THE STATE OF OREGON ON THE RE-
LATION OF HARRY HUMFELD,

Defendant in Error.

---

## BRIEF OF PLAINTIFF IN ERROR

---

Upon Writ of Error to the United States District
Court of the District of Oregon.

---

## STATEMENT

On June 21, 1918, the Desert Land Board of the
State of Oregon entered into a contract with the Jordan Valley Land & Water Company, hereinafter referred to as the "company," for the construction of an
irrigation system to reclaim certain desert lands
which, under the provisions of the Carey Act, had
been withdrawn and segregated upon the application

of the company transmitted by the Desert Land Board to the Secretary of the Interior and by him approved.

Under date of August 17, 1918, in order to insure performance of the contract, the company as principal, and this plaintiff in error as surety, executed a bond to the State of Oregon in the penal sum of $100,-000.

Prior to the execution of the bond the company had spent a sum claimed by it to be in excess of $100,000 and conceded by the engineer representing the Desert Land Board to be $60,000 or $70,000 in preliminary construction work, and after the execution of the bond continued with the performance of the contract until some time in May, 1921, when a new contract was entered into between the company and the Desert Land Board and a new bond given with the company as principal and the Hartford Accident & Indemnity Company as surety. The new contract and new bond were dated May 27, 1921, and the minutes of a special meeting of the Desert Land Board show that on June 8, 1921, the Desert Land Board formally cancelled the bond of this plaintiff in error. The company did not complete the contract last entered into and it appears from the minutes of a special meeting of the Desert Land Board held at Salem on November 17, 1921, that the Secretary of the Board was ordered to give the notice required by the statutes of the State of Oregon of cessation of construction work under both contracts, that is, the contract of June 21, 1918, and the contract of May 27, 1921.

The minutes of the Desert Land Board then show

that at a meeting of the board held January 27, 1922, it was ordered that both of said construction contracts be cancelled; that notice thereof be published, and that upon the 10th day of May, 1922, the board would receive bids for the purchase of the incompleted works. It then appears from evidence in the record that the incompleted works were sold to the Jordan Valley Irrigation District for $1.00 and a proposal to complete the construction of the irrigation system.

On August 31, 1922, the defendant in error commenced this action against this plaintiff in error as surety upon the bond given to insure the performance of the contract of June 21, 1918, to recover the agreed value of certain alleged services rendered by him in connection with the construction of the irrigation system and as assignee of certain other labor and material claimants. He alleged in his complaint, in addition to the jurisdictional averments, the execution of the contract of June 21, 1918, and the bond dated August 17, 1918, the commencement of work under the terms of the construction contract and the rendition of services and the furnishing of material. A demurrer was interposed on the ground that the complaint failed to state facts sufficient to constitute a cause of action. The demurrer was overruled. The case came on for trial before the court without a jury. Plaintiff in error requested special findings of fact, which were denied. Plaintiff in error also asked for a directed judgment, which was also denied, and judgment was entered in favor of the defendant in error on the assigned claim of the Dupont Powder Company in the sum of $2900.75, from which judgment this writ of error is prosecuted.

The plaintiff in error will contend:

1. The statutes of the State of Oregon accepting the conditions of the Carey Act prescribe the character of contract to be entered into for reclamation of desert lands; the character of the bond to be given, and provide the remedy. The complaint fails to show that the remedy prescribed by the statute has been followed. In other words, it is the contention of the plaintiff in error that before any liability in favor of third parties can arise on a bond of the character of the one in controversy, it must appear that the incompleted works have been sold and that the state is not asserting any claim against the bond.

2. In the reclamation of desert lands withdrawn under the terms and provisions of the Carey Act, the state acts as the agent of the Federal Government. If the construction of an irrigation system on public lands be considered public works within the meaning of the Act of Congress approved February 24, 1905, 33 U. S. Statutes at large, chapter 278, page 811, the present action is either brought prematurely or is barred by limitation.

3. If this action may be maintained on the present pleading the fundamental, underlying purpose of Congress in enacting the Carey Act, that is, the reclamation of desert lands, would be defeated; and this for the reason that the primary and essential purpose of the bond, its purpose under the language of the statutes of the State of Oregon accepting the Carey Act, is to insure the performance of the construction contract.

## SPECIFICATION OF ERRORS

1.   The court erred in ovreruling the demurrer to the complaint, for the reason that it fails to state facts sufficient to constitute a cause of action.

>   Assignment of Error No. 1 (Transcript of Record, page 48).

2.   The court erred in entering judgment in any sum against the plaintiff in error.

>   Assignment of Errors No. 2 and No. 6 (Transcript of Record, page 48 and page 50).

3.   The court erred in failing to make special findings as requested by the defendant.

>   Assignment of Error No. 5 (Transcript of Record, page 49).

4.   The court erred in not directing a judgment for the defendant.

>   Assignment of Error No. 4 (Transcript of Record, page 49).

## ARGUMENT

1.   When work has been performed under a contract of the character of the one involved in this action, before any liability can arise to third parties on a bond given to insure performance of a contract, it must appear that the incompleted works have been sold and a deficiency exists and that the state is not asserting any claim against the bond.

Section 5576, Oregon Laws, provides as follows:

"ACCEPTING CONDITIONS OF 'CAREY
ACT.' The State of Oregon hereby accepts the
conditions of section 4 of an act of congress, entitled 'An act making appropriations for sundry
civil expenses of the government for the fiscal
year ending June 30, 1895, and for other purposes,' approved August 18, 1894, and amendments thereto, together with all grants of land to
the state under the provisions of the aforesaid
act."

Section 5582, Oregon Laws, provides as follows:

"CONTRACT AND LIEN FOR RECLA-
MATION. Upon the withdrawal of the land
by the department of the interior, it shall be the
duty of the board to enter a contract for the
reclamation of such land with the party submitting the application, which contract shall contain
plans and specifications of the proposed irrigation works; provided, that no contract shall be
executed by the board until after an examination
and report in writing by the state engineer concerning the feasibility of the proposed plan of
reclamation, sufficiency and availability of the
water supply, and reasonableness of the estimate of cost and the lien requested. Such contract shall provide for the sale of water right to
settlers on said land in satisfaction of the reclamation lien allowed. This contract shall not be
entered into on the part of the state until the
withdrawal of the lands by the department of
the interior and the filing of a satisfactory bond
on the part of the proposed contractor, which
bond shall be in a penal sum not less than two

per cent of the lien to be allowed, and shall be conditioned for the faithful performance of the provisions of the contract with the state. The board may, however, require the contractor to make a deposit at the time of application for entry of land by settlers to insure the transfer of the system in good condition and repair to the purchasers of water rights as herein provided, which deposit shall be returned by the board at the time of such transfer."

Section 5584, Oregon Laws, provides as follows:

"CONTRACT — TIME — FORFEITURE. No contract shall be made by the board which requires a greater time than five years for the construction of the works, and all contracts shall state that the work shall begin within six months from date of contract; that the contractor shall secure for the use and benefit of the reclamation system all necessary water rights, rights of way, reservoir sites, or other property necessary for its construction and operation; that construction shall be prosecuted diligently and continuously to completion; and that a cessation of work under the contract with the state for a period of six months, without the sanction of the board, will forfeit to the state all rights under said contract. The board shall have power to extend the time in which to begin the construction of works, or for the completion of work, on account of delay caused by physical or engineering difficulties beyond the power of the contractor to control."

Section 5585, Oregon Laws, provides as follows:

"CONTRACT FORFEITED TO STATE. Upon the failure of any parties, having contracts with the state for the construction of irrigation works, to begin the same within the time specified by the contract, or to complete the same within the time or in accordance with the specifications of the contract with the state, to the satisfaction of the board, it shall be the duty of the secretary to give such parties written notice of such failures; and if after a period of sixty days from the sending of such notice they shall have failed to proceed with the work or to conform to the specifications of their contract with the state, or secure an extension of time as herein provided, the contract of such parties and all works constructed thereunder shall be at once and thereby forfeited to the state. In case of any forfeiture, cancellation, or relinquishment of any contract to the state, it shall be the duty of the board so to declare and to give notice once each week, for a period of four weeks, in some newspaper of general circulation in the county in which the work is situated, and in one newspaper at the state capital in like manner and for a like period, of the forfeiture, cancellation, or relinquishment of said contract, and that upon a fixed day proposals will be received at the office of the board in the capitol building for the purchase of the incompleted works and for the completion of the irrigation works in accordance with such plans and specifications and such other conditions as may be prescribed by the board, the time for receiving said bids to be at least sixty days subsequent to the issuing of the last notice of forfeiture. The money received by the board from the sale of the partially completed works under the provisions of this act shall first be applied to the expenses incurred by the state in their forfeiture and disposal, and the surplus, if any exists, shall be paid to the original contractors with the state."

Under the terms of the above legislation the contract between the Desert Land Board and the company is a construction contract entered into for the purpose of reclaiming desert lands. The bond given is one to insure the performance of the contract. It is specifically required that it shall be in a penal sum of not less than 2% of the lien to be allowed. In the event that the contract is not carried out, it is the duty of the secretary of the Desert Land Board to give written notice of the failure to carry out the terms of the contract, and if after a period of sixty days from such notice the contractor fails to proceed with the work, the contract and all works constructed thereunder shall at once be forfeited to the state. In case of such forfeiture, notice shall be given once a week for a period of four weeks in some newspaper of general circulation in the county in which the work is situated and in one newspaper in the state capital of the forfeiture of said contract, and that upon a fixed day proposals will be received for the purchase of the incomplete works and for the completion of the irrigation works. The monies received from the sale shall be first applied to the expenses of the state incurred in the forfeiture and sale, and the surplus, if any, shall be paid to the original contractor.

We accordingly have a statutory enactment creating a liability upon the bond in the event of a default in the completion of the works by the construction company, declaring the purpose of the bond and providing the manner of its enforcement.

Under these circumstances, may one not a party to the contract bring an action upon such a bond, even though it contains conditions for his benefit? We submit that where the same statute creates a liability and provides a remedy that the remedy provided is exclusive and that the provisions in the bond respecting payment of labor and material claimants are to be disregarded as surplusage.

A similar question was before the Supreme Court of the State of Idaho in the case of Sauve vs. Title Guaranty and Surety Company, 29 Idaho 146, 158 Pac. Rep. 112. In that case Sauve commenced an action against the defendant on a bond given to insure the performance of a construction contract to reclaim desert lands withdrawn under the terms of the Carey Act. It appeared that originally a company known as the Big Lost River Land & Irrigation Company had entered into a contract to reclaim these lands. The company became insolvent and transferred its interests in the incompleted works to one George Speer. Speer entered into a new contract with the State of Idaho in which he agreed to complete the construction of the irrigation works and in which he assumed and agreed to carry out contracts previously made by the insolvent company with settlers on the project. To secure the fulfillment of the provisions of the contract, Speer, as principal, and the Title Guaranty & Surety Company, as surety, executed a bond to the State of Idaho. Sauve as one of the purchasers of water rights from the Big Lost

River Land & Irrigation Company brought the action against the surety to recover damages for failure to complete the project and furnish water. The Surety Company interposed a demurrer, which was sustained. It was contended that since Speer had failed to carry out the contracts of the settlers with his predecessors in interest which by the terms of his contract he assumed and agreed to carry out, the injured settler had a right of action on the bond. The Surety Company contended that the contract was simply a construction contract, and that the liability upon the bond extended merely to a failure on the part of Speer to complete the project according to the plans and specifications made a part of the contract. To use the language of the court in rendering the opinion:

> "In other words, it (the surety) contends that the liability upon the bond is limited under the statutes of this state to certain specific contingencies; that the statutes prescribe the method of enforcing such liability; that the statutory provisions are exclusive, and until the contingencies arise, and until the state has taken the action provided in the statutes, the bond is unenforceable."

The statutes of the State of Idaho referred to in the opinion are identical in substance with the statutes of the State of Oregon hereinbefore set out. The court held that the demurrer was properly sustained. Among other things, the court said at page 117 of the Pacific Reporter citation:

> "It (referring to the statute) also declares the purpose of the bond and provides the manner of its enforcement. The liability and the

remedy is created by the same statute. This being true, it would seem to us that the remedy provided in the statute is exclusive, and that the respondent company is in a position to insist upon the statutory remedy being followed. In Pollard v. Bailey, 87 U. S. (20 Wall.) 520-527, 22 L. Ed. 376, it was held that a general liability created by statute without a remedy may be enforced by an appropriate common-law action; but where the provision for the liability is coupled with a provision for a special remedy, that remedy, and that alone, must be employed."

The court also said at page 118:

"We are also satisfied that the contract entered into between Speer and the state was a construction contract for the construction of the irrigation project only, and that the bond given by the Title Guaranty & Surety Company was to secure the performance of this construction contract. To hold that covenants other than for the completion of the irrigation works are secured by the bond upon which this action is sought to be maintained, and to allow a recovery thereon, would result in reducing the bond below the 5 per cent of the estimated cost of the construction, and thereby defeat the purpose for which it was given."

In the instant case the contract which the bond is given to secure contains no provision for the payment of labor and material claimants. In the Sauve case the contractor specifically assumed and agreed to carry out the former contract of the Big Lost River Land & Irrigation Company with the settler, and the bond was conditioned upon the faithful performance of the terms and conditions of the contract.

We are not unmindful that sections 2991 and 6718, Oregon Laws, provide that in contracts made with the state a bond shall be furnished with a condition among other things that the contractor will promptly make payment to all persons supplying labor or materials. The State of Idaho has a similar provision. Section 7341, Idaho Compiled Statutes, 1919, is practically identical with the provisions existing in the State of Oregon, and bearing upon the proper construction to be given such a provision it is interesting to observe that the bond in controversy in the Sauve case did not contain a provision for the payment of labor and material claimants.

While that particular section of the Idaho statute was not directly involved or passed upon, yet the effect of the decision is that third parties, whether damaged settlers or unpaid labor and material claimants, have no remedy upon a Carey Act construction bond given to insure the faithful performance of a Carey Act construction contract.

Notwithstanding a contractor may have breached his contract, he should be dealt with fairly and should not lose the benefit of his labor and work without due and timely notice of the contemplated forfeiture of the contract and bond and after a bona fide sale of the incompleted works. Upon such a sale the state might receive a sufficient amount of money to complete the contract and pay all outstanding claims, in which event the contractor would not lose more than his time, money and labor expended up to the time that work on the project was by him discontinued.

It plainly appears from the decision that a contractor who has breached his contract still retains an equity in the project, and that upon a breach of the contract his equity can only be foreclosed in the manner exclusively provided by section 5585, Oregon Laws, and if the amount of money received by the state from the sale of the incompleted works is insufficient with which to complete the works, then and then only is a liability upon the bond established, and such liability is wholly in favor of the state. This being a specific and complete remedy and provided by the act which creates the right, such remedy is exclusive, and sections 2991 and 6718, Oregon Laws, are clearly inapplicable.

The opinion of the Idaho court makes it clear that an action may not be maintained on a Carey Act construction bond by third parties, no matter what their relationship may be to the construction company. In the Sauve case the settlers, who were damaged, were denied the right to maintain action upon the bond and there is even more reason for denying labor and material claimants such right. The labor and material claimants are not obliged to deal with the construction company, but on the other hand, a settler upon the land is obliged to give a lien upon his land in order to provide the funds with which to construct the irrigation project. Why, then, should a labor or material claimant occupy a better position or have a greater right than such a settler? It is evident that such is not the case, and that the reasoning in the Sauve case has closed the door to all third parties concerning suits upon Carey Act construction bonds and has given this right exclusively to the state, by virtue of the special and exclusive remedy provided by the act of the Legislature.

2. In the reclamation of desert lands withdrawn under the terms and provisions of the Carey Act, the state acts as the agent of the Federal Government, and if the condition of the bond providing for the payment of labor and material claimants is a proper condition in the bond, it is so under the provisions of the act of Congress approved February 24, 1905, 33 U. S. Statutes at Large, chapter 278. And under such act the present action is either brought prematurely or is barred by limitation.

This court in several cases has considered the Carey Act and its purpose.

In the case of Twin Falls Salmon River Land & Water Co. et al. vs. Caldwell et al., 242 Fed. 177, this court speaks of the general government in Carey Act projects acting through the state as its agency. This is, of course, inconsistent with the state acting in its sovereign capacity, and if the condition in the bond for the payment of labor and material claimants is a proper condition, we suggest it is so by virtue of the act of Congress providing for the protection of persons furnishing materials and labor for the construction of public works. The act of Congress in question expressly provides that if no suit is instituted by the United States within six months from the completion and final settlement of the contract, then labor and material claimants may institute action upon the bond to recover their claims, but that such suits must be brought in the courts of the United States, and not elsewhere, and be commenced within one year after the performance and final settlement of said contract and not later.

Under the facts in this case, the construction contract with the government, acting through the Desert Land Board, was not performed and completed, but on the other hand was breached, and literally, there has never been a final settlement between the contractor and either the government or its agency, the Desert Land Board, so the question of what constitutes a final settlement within the meaning of said act of Congress is material.

The Supreme Court of the United States in Illinois Surety Company vs. United States to the Use of Peeler et al., Trading as Faith Granite Company, 240 U. S. 214, and United States ex rel. Texas Portland Cement Company vs. McCord, 233 U. S. 157, has held in effect that a final settlement occurs when the amount to be paid the contractor or received by the government is fixed by the proper government official. It seems that the consent of the contractor is not essential for the purpose of a final settlement such as will start the statute of limitations.

In this case, if no final settlement has been made within the meaning of the act of Congress, the case is instituted prematurely, as the United States is given the exclusive right to bring the action for its own use and benefit during the first six months period after final settlement, and if no final settlement has been made, said six months period of time has not yet commenced to run.

On the other hand, if the declaration of forfeiture of the contract by the Desert Land Board and the subsequent sale of the incompleted works constitutes a final settlement within the meaning of the act of Congress, then the action is barred by the special statute of limitations provided by the act.

From the evidence it appears that the construction contract was forfeited by action of the Desert Land Board on February 25, 1921, and again on January 27, 1922, and that the sale of the incompleted works was confirmed on May 10, 1922. If the act of Congress referred to is applicable, it follows either that the action was prematurely instituted or that it is barred by the special statute of limitations contained in the act.

Interpreting this particular act of Congress, it is held that the limitation in the act is one that need not be pleaded to be taken advantage of.

The precise point was considered in the case of Baker Contract Co. et al. vs. United States for Use of Pennock et al., 204 Fed. 390. At page 397 the court said:

> "After a careful consideration of this statute, creating—as it does—a right of action, and at the same time fixing a limitation as to the time within which suit shall be instituted, we are of the opinion that such limitation is a condition precedent to the right to institute such action, which must be complied with in order to enable one to institute an action pursuant thereto. In other words, a right of action is granted provided suit is instituted within one year 'after the performance and final settlement of said contract

and not later.' It appearing that the Parkersburg & Marietta Sand Company has failed to comply with this requirement, we are of the opinion that the right of action and the remedy are both lost and that the defendant is not required to plead such limitation specially as a defense in order to defeat the complainant's right to recover."

And again in the case of United States vs. American Bonding Company, 42 App. D. C. 268, the court said:

"The present action was brought about three months after the final settlement between Smith and the United States. The statute creates the remedy; hence, strict compliance with its terms is a condition precedent to the right of action. Neither did defendant waive its right to object by pleading to the declaration, since the condition is jurisdictional."

3. If this action may be maintained, the terms and provisions of the Carey Act and the legislation of the State of Oregon accepting the Carey Act are in effect nullified.

The purpose of the Carey Act was to secure the reclamation of desert lands. In the act of the legislature accepting the provisions of the Carey Act it was specifically provided that a bond should be furnished by the contractor to insure the performance of his contract, which bond should be in a penal sum of not less than 2% of the lien to be allowed. If the present plaintiff may maintain his action, the security for the performance of the contract may be entirely frittered away. This was emphasized by the Supreme Court of Idaho in the Sauve case, where the court said at page 118 of the Pacific Reporter:

"We are also satisfied that the contract entered into between Speer and the state was a construction contract for the construction of the irrigation project only, and that the bond given by the Title Guaranty & Surety Company was to secure the performance of this construction contract. To hold that covenants other than for the completion of the irrigation works are secured by the bond upon which this action is sought to be maintained, and to allow a recovery thereon, would result in reducing the bond below the 5 per cent of the estimated cost of the construction, and thereby defeat the purpose for which it was given.

At the same page the Court said further:

"In our opinion, under the plain provisions of the statutes, all of the settlers on this project were entitled to the protection of this bond, and the entire amount of it was intended to guarantee the completion of the project. Therefore it cannot be resorted to for the purpose of reimbursing individual locators for damages sustained by the failure to complete the works, but should be resorted to by the state to the end that the irrigation project be completed for the benefit of all locators thereon."

The fundamental purpose of Congress in providing for the reclamation of arid lands should not be defeated.

Respectfully submitted,

WM. S. NASH and
S. J. GRAHAM,
Attorneys for Plaintiff in Error.

# United States
# Circuit Court of Appeals
### For the Ninth Circuit

---

AMERICAN SURETY COMPANY OF
NEW YORK, a corporation,
Plaintiff in Error,

vs.

THE STATE OF OREGON ON THE RE-
LATION OF HARRY HUMFELD,
Defendant in Error.

---

## BRIEF OF DEFENDANT IN ERROR

---

Upon Writ of Error to the United States District
Court of the District of Oregon.

ARTHUR A. GOLDSMITH,
BEACH & SIMON,
Attorneys for Defendant in Error.

WM. S. NASH & S. J. GRAHAM,
Attorneys for Plaintiff in Error.

BUSHONG & CO., PORTLAND

No. 4226

# United States
# Circuit Court of Appeals
## For the Ninth Circuit

AMERICAN SURETY COMPANY OF
NEW YORK, a corporation,

Plaintiff in Error,

vs.

THE STATE OF OREGON ON THE RE-
LATION OF HARRY HUMFELD,

Defendant in Error.

## BRIEF OF DEFENDANT IN ERROR

Upon Writ of Error to the United States District
Court of the District of Oregon.

Action was instituted by the defendant in error
on the relation of Harry Humfeld as the assignee of
a number of claims against the plaintiff in error as
surety on a bond in the penal sum of $100,000.00 given
by the Jordan Valley Land & Water Company to the
State of Oregon, which bond was executed by the
plaintiff in error as surety in August, 1918, to secure
the faithful performance of a contract entered into
by the Jordan Valley Land & Water Company with
the Desert Land Board of the State of Oregon, providing for the construction of an irrigation system,

known as the Jordan Valley Irrigation Project in
Malheur County, Oregon, a Carey Act project. The
bond was further conditioned that the principal would
promptly pay all persons supplying it with labor or
materials used in and for the prosecution of the work
provided for in such contract.

The Jordan Valley Land & Water Company de-
faulted on its contract with the Desert Land Board of
the State of Oregon and has failed to pay the claims
for labor and materials which form the basis of this
case. The claims set forth in the different causes of
action in the complaint arose out of labor performed
and materials furnished for the construction of the
Jordan Valley Irrigation project. These claims were
assigned to Harry Humfeld, the relator herein. It
was stipulated that the assignments of the claims
were properly executed by those having the requisite
authority. The testimony shows that the bond upon
which this action is based was never surrendered, nor
was it released as to past obligations, but that on
June 8, 1921, it was formally cancelled as to future
liabilities.

It was stipulated that the case should be tried by
the court below without a jury and it was so tried.
Judgment was rendered in favor of defendant in error
on the second cause of action which was based on the
assigned claim of the E. I. du Pont de Nemours &
Co. in the sum of $2900.75, with interest thereon at
the rate of six per cent per annum from March 16,
1920, and costs and disbursements. As judgment was
in favor of the plaintiff in error on the other causes
of action, they may be disregarded so far as this writ
of error is concerned.

The second cause of action, upon which judgment

was given .in favor of the defendant in error, was based on the assigned claim of the E. I. du Pont de Nemours & Co. against the plaintiff in error as surety on the bond of the Jordan Valley Land & Water Company, for a balance of $2900.75, with interest at six per cent per annum from March 16, 1920, for blasting supplies sold and delivered to the Jordan Valley Land & Water Company at its special instance and request for use in the construction of the irrigation project. All of the material was furnished between October 3, 1919, and March 16, 1920. The evidence fully substantiates this claim and is uncontradicted. The plaintiff in error is not contending that the second cause of action is not supported by the evidence or is not a valid claim against the principal on the bond, but contends that there should be no liability against it as surety, because the Statutes of the State of Oregon, accepting the provisions of the Carey Act, do not expressly provide for a bond conditioned among other things upon the payment of claims of material men and for labor.

## ARGUMENT

The entire argument of the plaintiff in error rests on the assumption that under a construction contract covering a Carey Act project, no form of bond could be legally given for the benefit of one who has furnished materials for the project. We submit that there is neither precedent nor principle to sustain such a proposition.

## ANSWER TO FIRST POINT OF PLAINTIFF IN ERROR

The first point raised by counsel for plaintiff in error is based on the case of Sauve vs. Title Guarantee & Surety Co., 29 Idaho 146, 158 Pac. 112. That was an action by a purchaser of water rights from a construction company, against the surety on the bond of the construction company to recover damages for failure to complete the irrigation project and furnish water. The surety company contended that the bond was given to secure merely a construction contract. A demurrer was interposed to this complaint and the demurrer sustained, and such action was affirmed by the Supreme Court. The plaintiff in the Sauve case contended that the contract, which the bond was given to secure, expressly provided that the principal on the bond would carry out the former contract between the construction company and the settlers, and that therefore it was different than the ordinary Carey Act construction contract. The Idaho Supreme Court held, however, that all settlers, whether they had purchased water rights under the former contract, or under the contract with Speer, would have equal protection under the bond and that in neither case would there be a right of action by an individual settler. It is rather difficult to see how such a decision has any bearing on the case at bar, which involves the right of a material man to recover on a bond expressly conditioned upon prompt payment of claims for material.

Plaintiff in error cites absolutely no authority where relief has been denied one furnishing materials to a construction company on a Carey Act project, where the bond expressly provides for the prompt payment of claims for labor and material. Plaintiff in error then proceeds to argue that there can be no recovery by the defendant in error in the instant case, on the theory that the Oregon Statutes with reference to Carey Act projects prohibit the execution of a bond conditioned upon the prompt payment for labor and material. In that connection it is interesting to note the language of Section 5582 Oregon Laws, concerning the bond to be posted by a construction company on a Carey Act project.

> " * * * This contract shall not be entered into on the part of the state until the withdrawal of the land by the department of the interior and the filing of a satisfactory bond on the part of the proposed contractor, which bond shall be in a penal sum of not less than two per cent of the lien to be allowed, and shall be conditioned for the faithful performance of the provisions of the contract with the state."

The statute does not say that the bond shall be limited to two per cent of the amount of the lien, but that it shall not be less than two per cent of the lien. It is argued by the plaintiff in error that Section 5584 and Section 5585 of Oregon Laws provide the liability of a construction company, as well as the remedies under the contract. Section 5585 expressly provides that if the contract is forfeited and the partly completed works are sold, the money arising from such sale shall be applied by the state to cover the expenses of the forfeiture and of selling the works, and the balance shall then be turned over to the contractor. No provision is made under the sections of the law cited by plaintiff in error which would afford any remedy for one who has furnished material for the project.

The sections of the law mentioned above should be read in connection with Sections 2991 and 6719, Oregon Laws.

Section 2991 Oregon Laws, provides as follows:

"CONTRACTORS ON PUBLIC WORK TO GIVE BOND FOR BENEFIT OF LABORERS AND MATERIALMEN — ENFORCEMENT. Hereafter any person or persons, firm or corporation, entering into a formal contract with the State of Oregon, or any municipality, county, or school district within said state, for the construction of any building, or the prosecution and completion of any work, or for repairs upon any building or work, shall be required before commencing such work to execute the usual penal bond with good and sufficient sureties, with the additional obligations that such contractor or contractors shall promptly make payments to all persons supplying him or them labor or materials for any prosecution of the work provided for in such contracts; and any person or persons making application therefor, and furnishing affidavit to the proper officer of such state, county, municipality, or school district, under the direction of whom said work is being or has been prosecuted, that labor or materials for the prosecution of such work has been supplied by him or them, and payment for the same has not been made, shall be furnished with a certified copy of said contract and bond, upon which said person or persons supplying such labor or materials shall have a right of action and shall be authorized to bring suit in the name of the State of Oregon, or any county, municipality, or school district within such state for his or their use and benefit, against said contractor and sureties, and to prosecute the same to final judgment and execution.

Section 6719, Oregon Laws, provides as follows:

"SUIT FOR LABOR AND MATERIAL ON PENAL UNDERTAKING. Any person who has supplied labor or material under the conditions herein provided, on making application to the proper officer in charge of such contract, together with a showing under oath what relation such person bears to such contract or its performance, shall receive a certified copy of such contract and bond, as herein provided, and is hereby authorized to institute an action against said contractor and sureties on his own relation, but in the name of the state of Oregon or the county, school district, municipality, municipal corporation, or other subdivision concerned, and to prosecute the same to final judgment and execution for his own use and benefit, as the fact may appear.

Amendment of 1921, Chapter 342, added the following:

"All claims and accounts for the furnishing or supplying of labor and material or either, to any contractor as herein provided, shall be assignable by instrument in writing and subscribed by the person furnishing or supplying such labor or material, and the assignee shall have the same right and remedy, against the contractor and the surety on the bond as is by this act given to or vested in such laborer or materialmen and upon application to the proper officer in charge of such contract, together with a proper showing under oath what relation the assignor bears or bore to such contract or its performance, and the facts of the assignment, such assignee shall receive a certified copy of such contract and bond and is hereby authorized to institute an action against said contractor and surety or sureties, on his or its relation, but in the name of the state of Oregon, or of the county, school district, municipality, municipal corporation or other subdivision concerned, and to prosecute the same to final judgment and execution for his or its own use and benefit, as the fact may appear.

"In any action as hereinbefore provided, the prevailing party shall recover such attorney fees therein as the court shall adjudge reasonable; provided, however, that all labor and material liens shall have preference and be superior to all other liens and claims of whatsoever kind' or nature created by this act."

It is admitted by plaintiff in error that the contract involved in the instant case was for the construction or prosecution and completion of work and was a formal contract entered into with the Desert Land Board acting for and on behalf of the State of Oregon. Section 2991 expressly provides that before commencing such work, the contractor shall execute the usual penal bond "with the additional obligations that such contractor or contractors shall promptly make payments to all persons supplying him or them with labor or materials for any prosecution of the work provided for in such contract." Both Section 2991, and Section 6719 before and after it was amended, authorize suit to be brought on such a bond, for his own benefit, by one furnishing materials. These sections of the statutes are construed and upheld by well considered Oregon cases.

Multnomah County vs. U. S. F. & C. Co., 87 Ore. 198; 170 Pac. 525;

School District No. 30 vs. Alameda Construction Co., 87 Ore. 132; 169 Pac. 507, 788.

Another reason why the position of the plaintiff in error cannot be sustained is that it is essential to make provisions for the prompt payment of claims of material men and labor in order that persons will deal with construction companies engaged in such work. It is clear that the ordinary lien for material could not be invoked against the land where a construction contract involves a Carey Act project or other public work. In lieu thereof, Sections 2991 and 6718 of the Oregon Laws provide that a bond shall be given which will protect material men and laborers. It is the policy of this state that material men and laborers be protected.

Clatsop County vs. Feldschau, et al., 101 Ore. 369, 199 Pac. 953.

Counsel for plaintiff in error call attention to the fact that the bond in the Sauve case contained no provision for the payment of labor and material claimants, although plaintiff in error states that the Idaho statute is similar to Sections 2991 and 6718 of the Oregon Laws. Because such a provision is absent from the bond in the Sauve case, it cannot be said that legally it is unenforcable. That question was not before the Idaho court.

As a concluding argument under the first point, counsel for plaintiff in error contend that a material man should not stand in a better position than a settler on the project. The answer to this argument is that in the case at bar the bond and Sections 2991 and 6719, Oregon Laws, expressly provide a remedy for the material man, while no such remedy is given to the settler. Another reason why a material man stands in a better position than a settler, is that the material man contributes something to the completion of the project, the end sought by all concerned. Furthermore, the public policy in this and other states seeks to insure the payment for labor and materials furnished. In a private undertaking the law provides for a specific lien for labor and material claimants. On public work, in lieu of such a lien, the law provides that a bond should be given for the prompt payment of the claims of laborers and material men.

Even though it were held that the provisions of Sections 2991, 6718 and 6719 were inapplicable where a construction contract covering a Carey Act project was involved, yet defendant in error should be entitled to a recovery on the bond executed by the plaintiff in error as surety. The surety company and the principal were competent to enter into the bond. The bond was not repugnant to the letter or policy of the law, but strictly in accordance with the general policy of the state providing for the prompt payment of labor and materials furnished for the prosecution of public works. The award of the contract was a sufficient consideration for the promise of the contractor and its surety to pay such claims. Such is the holding of the Oregon Supreme Court in the case of **Clat-**

sop County vs. Feldschau et al., 101 Ore. 369, 199 Pac.
953, 18 A. L. R. 1221.

The facts in that case are that the County of
Clatsop in entering into a contract for road construction required a bond which was broader in its terms
than was required by the Oregon Laws. The surety
company contended, that that part of the bond which
was in addition to what is required by statute was of
no force, and that the county was not authorized to
require such an additional stipulation. In the case at
bar, while the plaintiff in error admits that the provisions of Section 5582, Oregon Laws, requires the
execution of a bond conditioned upon the faithful performance of the contract, it contends that the provisions with reference to the prompt payment of
claims of laborers and materialmen are surplusage.
In answering this argument, the Supreme Court in
the Feldschau case, at pages 374 and 375 said:

"It is unquestioned that Feldschau voluntarily entered into a contract with Clatsop
County. The county was authorized to make
such contract. The surety company in the ordinary course of business and it may be fairly
assumed, for compensation, voluntarily obligated
itself as sponsor for Feldschau in the faithful performance of the contract, and the performance
of all of the conditions incorporated in the bond.
The parties were competent to enter into the undertaking. The bond was not repugnant to the
letter or policy of the law, but was strictly in accordance with the policy of the law in this state
to provide for the payment of labor and supplies
and expenses in the construction of public works.
Although the statute did not require all of the
conditions to be enumerated in the bond, the

county authorities were under a moral duty to protect persons with whom the contractor incurred such indebtedness in the performance of the work. The award of the contract for the improvement was a sufficient consideration for the promise of the contractor and his surety to pay such indebtedness. It is generally held that those furnishing supplies or extending credit for whose benefit such a bond is given may sue upon the bond on the principle that the third person for whose benefit a contract is made by another may maintain an action thereon, although the consideration does not directly move to such third person."

Clatsop County vs. Feldschau, et al., 101 Ore. 369 at 374 and 375.


## ANSWER TO SECOND POINT OF PLAINTIFF IN ERROR

The second contention of plaintiff in error is based on the proposition that the contract for which the bond is given is a contract with the Federal government for public work, rather than with the State of Oregon. The strategy of such an argument is clear. Plaintiff in error would like to invoke the limitations provided by the Federal statutes. The best that can be said about this point is that it is ingenious. While the court in the case of Twin Falls Salmon River Land & Water Co. vs. Caldwell, 242 Fed. 177, may speak of the general government acting through the agency of the state in furthering the reclamation of desert lands, it is no authority for the proposition that the contract entered into by the State with a construction company is a federal contract, as distinguished from a state contract, nor is it such a contract as would come within the provisions of the Act of Congress set out in 33 U. S. Statutes at Large, Chapter 278. In the first part of the brief of plaintiff in error, the statutes of the State of Oregon are set forth, under the provisions of which the contract was entered into between the Desert Land Board acting for the State of Oregon, and Jordan Valley Land & Water Company. Those are provisions of the Oregon law and not of the Federal government. The Federal government is in no sense a party to the contract between the construction company and the Desert Land Board. It is not liable under such a contract and is not entitled to any of the advantages. It is merely interested to the extent that when the construction work is complete, a patent will be issued to the state which in turn may issue patents to the settlers.

It is interesting to note that the court in the case of Twin Falls Salmon River Land & Water Co. vs. Caldwell, supra, expressly points out that **the state itself is authorized to make all necessary contracts for the reclamation of the land withdrawn under the provisions of the Carey Act.**

Since the Federal government is not a party to the contract with the construction company, and since the bond does not run to the United States, but to the State of Oregon, the provisions of the Act of Congress, found in 33 U. S. Statutes at Large, Chapter 278, certainly would not apply. Therefore it is unnecessary to discuss whether the action is premature or is barred by limitation under the provisions of the Federal statute.

## ANSWER TO THIRD POINT OF PLAINTIFF IN ERROR

As a final contention, plaintiff in error states that if the judgment of the Court below is sustained, the terms and provisions of the Carey Act and the legislation of the State of Oregon, accepting the Carey Act, are in effect nullified. We cannot see how the giving of a bond by a contractor, conditioned among other things, upon the prompt payment of the claims of laborers or material men can possibly interfere with the reclamation of desert land under Carey Act projects. In fact, it would appear that unless such a bond were given, very little progress could be made to reclaim desert land. Laborers and material men would hesitate to extend credit to a construction company involved in the hazardous undertaking of reclaiming desert land where there would be no lien on the land itself and no recourse to a bond. On the other hand, if, as in the case at bar, the state requires a bond, conditioned among other things upon the prompt payment of the claims of laborers and material men, the contractor will be able to obtain supplies, as the material man may feel reasonably sure that he will be paid for what he furnishes.

The main argument used by the plaintiff in error to sustain its third point is that if a material man can maintain an action on the bond, the security for the performance of the contract may be entirely frittered away. This conclusion is reached on the mistaken assumption that a bond in the penal sum of only two per cent of the lien is required, rather than a bond for **not less than two per cent** of the lien. There would be nothing to prevent the state, through the Desert

Land Board, from requiring a bond in a sum sufficient to be adequate security for the performance of the contract, as well as for the payment of the claims of laborers and material men. Such a bond is required on all public work, whether state or federal, and such requirement has not caused a cessation of such work.

The opinion in the Sauve case, quoted by plaintiff in error on page 19 of its brief, points out that if recovery for damages were allowed settlers, the bond would be reduced below the five per cent of the estimated cost of construction. Such argument would not apply to claims of laborers or material men which actually enter into the cost of construction. The payment of claims of laborers and material men tends towards the completion of the project under construction and certainly does not interfere with it. It is submitted that the requirements of the type of bond given in the case at bar will in no wise interfere with the fundamental purpose of Congress in providing for the reclamation of arid land.

## CONCLUSION

It is submitted that the judgment of the court below should be affirmed as the bond sued upon, by its express terms, provided for the payment of claims of material men. It was given in accordance with the express provisions of Sections 2991 and 6718 of Oregon Laws. Even though it were held that these sections of the law did not apply, yet in accordance with the decision of the cases of Clatsop County vs. Feldschau, supra, since the parties were competent to enter into the undertaking, which was based on a valid consideration, and was not contrary to the policy of the state, the surety should be bound by the express provisions of the undertaking.

Respectfully submitted,

ARTHUR A. GOLDSMITH,
BEACH & SIMON,
    Attorneys for Defendant in Error.

# United States
# Circuit Court of Appeals
## For the Ninth Circuit.

---

LOUIS H. REYFF, E. W. FREDERICK and
HARRY BIGBY,

> Plaintiffs in Error,

vs.

UNITED STATES OF AMERICA,

> Defendant in Error.

---

# Transcript of Record.

---

Upon Writ of Error to the United States District Court
of the Southern District of California,
Southern Division.

---

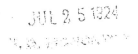
Filmer Bros. Co. Print, 330 Jackson St., S. F., Cal.

# No. 4227

## United States
## Circuit Court of Appeals
### For the Ninth Circuit.

LOUIS H. REYFF, E. W. FREDERICK and HARRY BIGBY,

> Plaintiffs in Error,

vs.

UNITED STATES OF AMERICA,

> Defendant in Error.

# Transcript of Record.

Upon Writ of Error to the United States District Court of the Southern District of California, Southern Division.

# INDEX TO THE PRINTED TRANSCRIPT OF RECORD.

[Clerk's Note: When deemed likely to be of an important nature, errors or doubtful matters appearing in the original certified record are printed literally in italic; and, likewise, cancelled matter appearing in the original certified record is printed and cancelled herein accordingly. When possible, an omission from the text is indicated by printing in italic the two words between which the omission seems to occur.]

## NAMES AND ADDRESSES OF ATTORNEYS OF RECORD.

For Plaintiffs in Error Louis H. Reyff, E. W. Fredrick and Harry Bigby:

R. G. RETALLICK, Esq., Fresno, California.

EDWARD A. O'DEA, Esq., 826–28–30 Phelan Building, San Francisco, California.

For Defendant in Error:

JOSEPH C. BURKE, Esq., United States Attorney, Federal Building, Los Angeles, California.

----

## WRIT OF ERROR (ORIGINAL).

### UNITED STATES OF AMERICA—ss.

The President of the United States of America, To the Honorable, the Judges of the District Court of the United States for the Southern District of California, GREETING:

Because, in the record and proceedings, as also in the rendition of the judgment of a plea which is in the said District Court, before you, or some of you, between Louis H. Reyff, E. W. Frederick and Harry Bigby, plaintiffs in error, and the United States of America, defendant in error, a manifest error hath happened, to the great damage of the said Louis M. Reyff, E. W. Frederick and Harry Bigby, plaintiffs in error, as by their complaint appears:

We, being willing that error, if any hath been, should be duly corrected, and full and speedy justice done to the parties aforesaid in this behalf, do command you, if judgment be therein given, that then, under your seal, distinctly and openly, you send the record and proceedings aforesaid, with all things concerning the same, to the United States Circuit Court of Appeals for the Ninth Circuit, together with this writ, so that you have the same at the City of San Francisco, in the State of California, within thirty days from the date hereof, in the said Circuit Court of Appeals, to be then and there held, that; the record and proceedings aforesaid being inspected, the said Circuit Court of Appeals may cause further to be done therein to correct that error, what of right, and according to the laws and customs of the United States, should be done.

WITNESS, the Honorable WILLIAM HOWARD TAFT, Chief Justice of the United States, the 28th day of November, in the year of our Lord one thousand nine hundred and twenty-three.

[Seal]　　　　CHAS. N. WILLIAMS,

Clerk of the United States District Court, Southern District of California.

R. S. Zimmerman,

Deputy.

Allowed by:

WM. P. JAMES,

District Judge, Southern District of California.

Nov. 28, 1923.

[Endorsed]: No. 821. United States District Court for the Southern District of California,

Northern Division. Louis H. Reyff, E. W. Frederick and Harry Bigby, Plaintiffs in Error, vs. United States of America, Defendant in Error. Original Writ of Error. Filed Nov. 28, 1923. Chas. N. Williams, Clerk. By R. S. Zimmerman, Deputy Clerk.

---

## CITATION ON WRIT OF ERROR (ORIGINAL).

### UNITED STATES OF AMERICA,—ss.

The President of the United States, To United States of America and to Joseph Burke, Esq., United States Attorney, and to Mark Herron, Esq., and E. I. McGann, Assistants to the United States Attorney, GREETING:

You are hereby cited and admonished to be and appear at a United States Circuit Court of Appeals for the Ninth Circuit, to be holden at the City of San Francisco, in the State of California, within thirty days from the date hereof, pursuant to a writ of error duly issued and now on file in the Clerk's office of the United States District Court for the Southern District of California, wherein Louis H. Reyff, E. W. Frederick and Harry Bigby are plaintiffs in error, and you are defendant in error, to show cause, if any there be, why the judgment rendered against the said plaintiffs in error, as in the said writ of error mentioned, should not be corrected, and why speedy justice should not be done to the parties in that behalf.

WITNESS, the Honorable WM. P. JAMES, United States District Judge for the Southern District of California, this 28th day of November, A. D. 1923.

WM. P. JAMES,<br>
United States District Judge.

Due service of a copy of the within citation is acknowledged this 28th day of November, A. D. 1923.

JOS. C. BURKE,<br>
U. S. Attorney.<br>
MARK L. HERRON,<br>
Asst. U. S. Atty.

[Endorsed]: No. 821. United States District Court for the Southern District of California. Louis H. Reyff, E. W. Frederick and Harry Bigby, Plaintiffs in Error, vs. United States of America, Defendant in Error. Original Citation on Writ of Error. Filed Nov. 28, 1923. Chas. N. Williams, Clerk. By R. S. Zimmerman, Deputy Clerk.

Rec'd copy of within this 28th day of November, 1923.

JOSEPH C. BURKE,<br>
U. S. Atty.<br>
MARK L. HERRON,<br>
Asst. U. S. Atty.

In the District Court of the United States in and for the Southern District of California, Northern Division.

THE UNITED STATES OF AMERICA,

Plaintiff,

vs.

LOUIS H. REYFF, E. W. FREDRICK and HARRY BIGBY,

Defendants.

## INFORMATION.

National Prohibition Act.

BE IT REMEMBERED, that Joseph C. Burke, United States Attorney for the Southern District of California, who prosecutes in behalf and with the authority of the United States, makes known to and informs the Court that heretofore, to wit, on or about the 16th day of May, A. D. 1923, one Louis H. Reyff, E. W. Fredrick and Harry Bigby, whose true names are, other than as herein stated, to the affiant unknown, at Fresno, Fresno County, California, in the division and district aforesaid, and within the jurisdiction of this court, did knowingly, willfully and unlawfully sell for beverage purposes to one C. W. Kittle, about one case of intoxicating liquor then and there containing alcohol in excess of one-half of one per cent by volume, at and for the agreed price of One Hundred ($100.00) Dollars, lawful money of the United

States; in violation of Section 3, Title II, of the National Prohibition Act of October 28, 1919;

Contrary to the form of the statute in such case made and provided, and against the peace and dignity of the United States of America.

## SECOND COUNT.

And now comes Joseph C. Burke, United States Attorney for the Southern District of California, who prosecutes in behalf and with the authority of the United States, and makes known to, and informs, [1*] the Court that heretofore, to wit, on or about the 16th day of May, A. D. 1923, one LOUIS H. REYFF, E. W. FREDRICK and HARRY BIGBY, whose true names are, other than as herein stated, to the affiant unknown, at Fresno, Fresno County, California, in the division and district aforesaid, and within the jurisdiction of this court, did knowingly, willfully and unlawfully have in their possession about one case and five bottles of intoxicating liquor, then and there containing alcohol in excess of one-half of one per cent by volume, for beverage purposes; in violation of Section 3, Title II, of the National Prohibition Act of October 28, 1919;

Contrary to the form of the statute in such case made and provided, and against the peace and dignity of the United States of America.

## THIRD COUNT.

And now comes Joseph C. Burke, United States Attorney for the Southern District of California,

---

*Page-number appearing at foot of page of original Certified Transcript of Record.

who prosecutes in behalf and with the authority of the United States, and makes known to, and informs, the Court that heretofore, to wit, on or about the 16th day of May, A. D. 1923, LOUIS H. REYFF, E. W. FREDRICK and HARRY BIGBY, whose true names are, other than as herein stated, to the affiant unknown, at Fresno, Fresno County, California, in the division and district aforesaid, and within the jurisdiction of this court, did knowingly, willfully and unlawfully transport in a certain Chalmers automobile bearing California State License No. 763229, Engine No. 37117, about one case and five quarts of intoxicating liquor for beverage purposes, then and there containing alcohol in excess of one-half of one per cent by volume; in violation of Section 3, Title II, of the National Prohibition Act of October 28, 1919;

Contrary to the form of the statute in such case made and provided, and against the peace and dignity of the United States of America. [2]

WHEREUPON, the said Attorney for the United States prays that due process of law may be awarded against the said defendants to make them answer the premises aforesaid.

JOSEPH C. BURKE,
United States Attorney.
MARK L. HERRON,
Assistant United States Attorney.

United States of America,
Southern District of California,—ss.

T. J. Niceley, Federal Prohibition Agent, being first duly sworn, on oath says: That he has read the foregoing information and that the matters contained therein are true in substance and in fact.

T. J. NICELEY.

Subscribed and sworn to before me this 22d day of May, A. D. 1923.

[Seal]                CHAS. N. WILLIAMS,
                      Clerk U. S. District Court.

[Endorsed]: No. 821—Crim. In the District Court of the United States for the Southern District of California, Northern Division. United States of America, Plaintiff, vs. Louis H. Reyff, E. W. Dredrick and Harry Bigby, Defendants. Information. Filed May 22, 1923. Chas. N. Williams, Clerk. By Louis J. Somers, Deputy. [3]

---

At a stated term, to wit, the November Term, A. D. 1923, of the District Court of the United States of America, within and for the Northern Division of the Southern District of California, held at the courtroom thereof, in the City of Fresno, on Monday, the 19th day of November, in the year of our Lord one thousand nine hundred and twenty-three. Present: The Honorable WM. P. JAMES, District Judge.

No. 821—CRIM. N. D.

UNITED STATES OF AMERICA,

Plaintiff,

vs.

LOUIS H. REYFF, F. W. FREDRICK and HARRY BIGBY,

Defendants.

## ARRAIGNMENT AND PLEA.

This cause coming on at this time for arraignment and plea of defendants herein; Mark L. Herron, Esq., Assistant United States Attorney, appearing as counsel for the Government; defendants Louis H. Reyff, F. W. Frederick and Harry Bigby being present in court with their attorney, R. G. Retallick, Esq., and Edw. A. O'Day, appearing as counsel for defendant Louis H. Reyff, and defendants having been called, waive the reading of the Information and state their names to be as given therein; and, upon being required to plead, each of said defendants interposes his plea of not guilty; now, good cause appearing therefor, it is by the Court ordered that this cause be continued to November 22d, 1923, for trial of defendants herein. [4]

In the District Court of the United States in and
for the Southern District of California, Northern Division.

## No. 821—CRIMINAL.

UNITED STATES OF AMERICA,

                                           Plaintiff,

    vs.

LOUIS H. REYFF, E. W. FREDERICK and
    HARRY BIGBY,

                                           Defendants.

## MOTION TO RETURN PROPERTY AND EX-
CLUDE EVIDENCE.

To the Honorable Above-entitled Court:
    The petition of E. W. Frederick respectfully
shows:

### I.

That at all the times herein mentioned he owned
and possessed a certain Chalmers Automobile, License No. 763–229, and that on the 16th day of May,
1923, he was in possession and control of said automobile in the City of Fresno, County of Fresno,
State of California.

### II.

That said automobile is of such construction that
in the rear of same there is a receptacle for the purpose of containing packages; that said receptacle
was closed and locked on said 16th day of May, 1923.

### III.

That on the 16th day of May, 1923, while your petitioner was in possession and control of said automobile, he and the defendant Reyff entered a garage located in the rear of No. 1041 T Street, in the City of Fresno, County of Fresno, State of California. That upon entering said garage, Federal Prohibition Enforcement Officers Nicely and Emrich jumped upon defendants, your petitioner's automobile, and illegally and unlawfully, without the authorization of a search-warrant, or order of any Court, and without any warrant for the arrest of your petitioner, and without witnessing any act or acts, committed in violation of the laws of the United States, [5] or of the State of California, and in violation of the defendant's rights guaranteed him by the Fourth and Fifth Amendments to the United States Constitution, and without seeing any liquor in plain sight, or otherwise, placed the defendant in custody, handcuffing him and proceeded to search his person, and by means of illegal and unlawful search violated his rights above referred to, said Federal Prohibition Enforcement officers proceeded to search his person and found thereon a key, and that they thereupon illegally and unlawfully, without the authority of a search-warrant, and in violation of the defendant's rights guaranteed him under the Fourth and Fifth Amendments to the United States Constitution, and against the will of your petitioner, took the said key and opened the rear receptacle to said automobile and found therein a case of Scotch whiskey, which they illegally and unlawfully seized and took the same away with them, and they profess to hold the same against the will of your petitioner as evidence of the violation of the law committed on the part of your petitioner, in the above-entitled case.

### IV.

That said whiskey is held without process of law, and is the property of the defendant, your petitioner, and he is entitled to its return. And that by reason thereof, and facts set forth, the defendant's rights under the Fourth and Fifth Amendments to the United States Constitution have been, and will be, violated unless the Court orders the return of said liquor, and its exclusion from evidence at the trial of said cause, and the suppression of all knowledge derived from said seizure of said liquor.

### V.

This petitioner further alleges that on said 16th day of May, 1923, his said automobile was seized by the said Federal Prohibition Enforcement Agents of the United States, in the manner hereinbefore particularly specified, and that the said Federal Prohibition Enforcement Officers still retain the control and custody of said automobile, and that said automobile is so held by them for the [6] reasons hereinbefore particularly specified, and without due process of law, and for no other reason, and your petitioner is entitled to the return of said automobile.

WHEREFORE, defendant, your petitioner, prays that the United States Attorney, Marshal,

Prohibition Enforcement Officers be notified, and the Court direct an order to said United States Attorney, Marshal, Clerk, and Prohibition Enforcement Officers, or any or either of them, to return the said property, to wit: One case of Scotch whiskey, and the said Chalmers automobile, to defendant, and to exclude the same and all knowledge derived, from the trial of said cause.

E. W. FREDRICK,

R. G. RETALLICK,

E. A. O'DEA,

Attorneys for Defendants.

[Indorsed]: No. 821—Criminal. In the District Court of the United States in and for the Southern District of California, Northern Division. United States of America, Plaintiff, vs. Louis H. Reyff, E. W. Frederick and Harry Bigby, Defendants. Motion to Return Property and Exclude Evidence. Filed Nov. 22, 1923. Chas. N. Williams, Clerk. By Murray E. Wire, Deputy Clerk. Edw. A. O'Day and R. G. Retallick, Attorneys for ———.
[7]

———

At a stated term, to wit, the November Term, A. D. 1923, of the District Court of the United States of America, within and for the Northern Division of the Southern District of California, held at the courtroom thereof, in the City of Fresno, on Thursday, the 22d day of November, in the year of our Lord one thousand nine hundred and twenty-three. Present: The Honorable WM. P. JAMES, District Judge.

## No. 821—CRIM. N. D.

UNITED STATES OF AMERICA,

Plaintiff,

vs.

LOUIS H. REYFF, F. W. FREDRICK and HARRY BIGBY,

Defendants.

### TRIAL.

This cause coming on at this time for trial of defendants Louis H. Reyff, F. W. Fredrick and Harry Bigby before this court and a jury to be impanelled herein; Mark L. Herron, Esq., Assistant United States Attorney, appearing as counsel for the Government; defendant Louis H. Reyff being present in court with his attorney Edw. A. O'Day, Esq., and defendant F. W. Fredrick and Harry Bigby being present in court with their attorney, R. G. Retallick, Esq., and counsel for defendant having made a motion to file petition for return of property, and counsel for the Government having objected to said motion, it is by the Court ordered that the ruling thereon be reserved until trial, and counsel for the respective parties having announced their readiness to proceed with the trial of this cause, it is by the Court ordered that the trial be proceeded with, and that a jury be impaneled herein, and thereupon the following twelve names were drawn from the jury-box, said names being as follows, to wit:

W. J. Archibald, C. F. Doyle, T. E. Mabee, Clark Hastie, Chas. Jasper, Ray Hutchison, Roderick W. Dallas, Edw. A. Leyden, F. C. Goodwin, T. O. Cavin and M. Saier and Benj. L. Sims, and said petit jurors having been called and sworn on *voir dire* and examined by the Court and by counsel for the Government for cause and passed [8] for cause; except M. Saier; and M. Saier having been excused for cause by the plaintiff, he knowing about the cause, it is by the Court ordered that one more name be drawn from the jury-box, said name being J. D. Heiskell, and said J. D. Heiskell having been called and sworn on *voir dire* and examined by the Court and by counsel for the Government and for the defendant, for cause, and passed for cause; and

Clark Hastie having been peremptorily challenged by counsel for the Government and by the Court excused, it is by the Court ordered that one more name be drawn from the jury-box, said name being P. H. McMurtry, and said P. H. McMurtry having been called and sworn on *voir dire* and examined by counsel for the Government and defendant for cause and passed for cause; and

Chas. Jasper having been peremptorily challenged by counsel for the defendant and by the Court excused;

It is by the Court ordered that one more name be drawn from the jury-box, said name being J. C. Young and said J. C. Young having been called and sworn on *voir dire* and examined by the Court and by counsel for the respective parties, and passed for cause, and said J. C. Young having been peremp-

torily challenged by counsel for the Government
and by the Court excused, it is by the Court ordered
that one more name be drawn from the jury-box,
said name being Fred Nelson, and said Fred Nelson
having been called and sworn on *voir dire* and examined by the Court and by counsel for the respective parties, and passed for cause, and said Fred
Nelson having been peremptorily challenged by
counsel for the Government and by the Court excused, it is by the Court ordered that one more name
be drawn, said name being C. B. Jackson, and said
C. B. Jackson having been called, and sworn on
*voir dire* and examined by counsel for the respective
parties for cause, and passed for cause, and counsel for the respective parties [9] not having desired
to peremptorily challenge the petit jurors now in the
box, it is by the Court ordered that said petit jurors
be sworn in a body as the jury to try this cause, said
petit jury, as sworn, consisting of the following-
named petit jurors, to wit:

## THE JURY.

| | | | |
|---|---|---|---|
| 1. | W. J. Archibald | 7. | F. C. Goodwin |
| 2. | C. F. Doyle | 8. | T. O. Cavin |
| 3. | T. E. Mahee | 9. | Benj. L. Sims |
| 4. | Ray Hutchison | 10. | J. D. Heiskell |
| 5. | Roderick W. Dallas | 11. | P. H. McMurtry |
| 6. | Edw. A. Leyden | 12. | C. B. Jackson |

and at the hour of 3:10 o'clock P. M. the Court
having excused the jury to the hour of 3:15 o'clock
P. M., and at the hour of 3:15 o'clock P. M. the
Court having reconvened and all being present as before; and

Mark L. Herron, Esq., having made a statement to the jury as to what the Government expects to be able to prove and defendant having waived a statement to the jury; and

C. W. Kettle having been called, sworn and having testified in behalf of the Government and subjected to direct examination by Mark L. Herron, Esq., on behalf of the Government; and

Defendant herein having renewed his motion to exclude evidence and for return of property seized herein, and said motion having been denied at this time, and an exception having been noted on behalf of defendant herein; and

Said C. W. Kettle having been cross-examined by Edw. A. O'Day, Esq., on behalf of the defendant; and

T. J. Niceley having been called, sworn and having testified in behalf of the Government and subjected to direct examination by Mark L. Herron, Esq., on behalf of the Government; and in connection with his testimony there having been offered and admitted for identification on behalf of the Government, the following exhibits, [10] to wit:

U. S. Ex. No. 1 for Ident.—Sack and contents,

U. S. Ex. No. 2 for Ident.—Bottle and contents,

and said T. J. Niceley having been cross-examined by Edw. A. O'Day on behalf of the defendant; and

Paul A. Emmrich having been called, sworn and having testified in behalf of the Government; subjected to direct examination and cross-examination by Mark L. Herron, Esq., and R. G. Retallick, Esq., on behalf of the Government and defendant, respectively; and

F. D. Stribling having been called, sworn and having testified in behalf of the Government and subjected to direct examination by Mark L. Herron, Esq., on behalf of the Government; and in connection with his testimony U. S. Exhibits Nos. 1 and 2 heretofore offered and admitted for identification having been admitted in evidence, and said F. D. Stribling having been cross-examined by R. G. Retallick, Esq., on behalf of the defendant; and

T. J. Niceley having been recalled and having testified in behalf of the Government and subjected to direct and cross-examination by Mark L. Herron, Esq., and R. G. Retallick, Esq., on behalf of the Government and defendants, respectively, and having also been cross-examined by Edw. A. O'Day, Esq., on behalf of his clients;

Now at the hour of 5:10 o'clock P. M., the Court declares a recess in this cause to the hour of 9:30 o'clock A. M. November 23d, 1923, and the Court thereupon excused the jurors herein until said time.
[11]

At a stated term, to wit, the November Term, A. D. 1923, of the District Court of the United States of America, within and for the Northern Division of the Southern District of California, held at the courtroom thereof, in the city of Fresno, on Friday, the 23 day of November, in the year of our Lord one thousand nine hundred and twenty-three. Present: The Honorable WM. P. JAMES, District Judge.

No. 821—CRIM. N. D.

UNITED STATES OF AMERICA,

Plaintiff,

vs.

LOUIS H. REYFF, F. W. FREDRICK and HARRY BIGBY,

Defendants.

TRIAL (CONTINUED).

This cause coming on at this time for further trial of defendants herein; Mark L. Herron, Esq., and Eugene McGann, Esq., Assistant United States Attorneys, appearing as counsel for the Government; defendant Louis H. Reyff being present in court with his attorney Edw. A. O'Day, Esq., and defendants F. W. Fredrick and Harry Bigby, being present in court with their attorney, R. G. Retallick, Esq., E. M. Walker being also present in court in his official capacity as stenographic reporter of the testimony and proceedings, and at the hour of 9:35 o'clock A. M. the Court having reconvened and all being present as before except the jury who is not present; and

Defendants having renewed their motion to exclude evidence, said motion having been made by Edw. A. O'Day, Esq., and said motion having been denied and an exception having been noted for the defendants; and

Edw. A. O'Day, Esq., having made a motion for a directed verdict as to defendant Harry Bigby and Mark. L. Herron, Esq., having argued in opposition to motion for said directed verdict, and the motion having been denied, and an exception having been noted on behalf of said defendant; and

Said Edw. A. O'Day, Esq., having made a motion for a directed verdict as to defendant Louis H. Reyff, and said motion having been denied and [12] an exception having been saved for said defendant; and

Said Edw. A. O'Day, Esq., having made a motion for a directed verdict as to defendant F. W. Fredrick, and said motion having been denied, and an exception having been saved for said defendant; and

At the hour of 10:05 o'clock A. M. the jury having taken the box and the Court having ordered that this trial be proceeded with; and

T. J. Nicely having resumed the stand and testified further on recross-examination by R. G. Retallick, Esq., and

The above motions having been renewed in the record; and

Defendant having rested; and

Government having rested; and

At the hour of 10:25 o'clock A. M., Mark L. Herron, Esq., having argued to the jury on behalf of the Government; and

At the hour of 10:37 o'clock A. M. Edw. A. O'Day, Esq., having argued to the jury on behalf of the defendants; and

At the hour of 10:58 o'clock A. M. Mark L. Herron, Esq., having argued to the jury on behalf of the Government in reply; and

At the hour of 11:10 o'clock A. M. the Court having instructed the jury with respect to the law involved in this cause and at the hour of 11:38 o'clock A. M. the jury having retired in charge of J. B. Henderson, bailiff, to deliberate upon their verdict;

Now, at the hour of 12:15 o'clock P. M. the jury returned into court and the roll of the jury having been called and all having answered present, and all being present as before, and the jury having been asked by the Court, through their foreman, if they have agreed upon a verdict, reply that they have so agreed, and, upon being required to present the same, present the following verdict which is as follows, to wit:

In the District Court of the United States in and
for the Southern District of California, Northern Division.

### No. 821—CRIM. N. D.

THE UNITED STATES OF AMERICA,

Plaintiff,

vs.

LOUIS H. REYFF, E. W. FREDRICK and
HARRY BIGBY,

Defendants.

### VERDICT.

We, the jury in [13] the above-entitled cause,
find the defendant Louis H. Reyff, guilty as charged
in the first count of the Information; guilty as
charged in the second count of the Information;
and guilty as charged in the third count of the Information; and we, the jury in the above-entitled
cause, find the defendant E. W. Fredrick, guilty
as charged in the first count of the Information;
guilty as charged in the second count of the Information and guilty as charged in the third count of
the Information; and we, the jury in the above-
entitled cause, find the defendant Harry Bigby,
guilty as charged in the first count of the Information; not guilty as charged in the second count of
the Information; and not guilty as charged in the
third count of the Information.

Fresno, California, November 23, 1923.

C. B. JACKSON,<br>Foreman.

and the verdict of guilty as to defendants Louis H. Reyff and F. W. Fredrick on all three counts having been presented and guilty as to defendant Harry Bigby on the first count and not guilty as to defendant Harry Bigby on the second and third counts having been presented and read by the clerk of the court as aforesaid, and ordered filed and entered therein, it is by the court ordered that this cause be continued to the hour of 10:00 o'clock A. M., November 26th, 1923, for sentence of defendants herein on the counts of which they have been found guilty, and it is further ordered by the Court that the petit jurors herein be excused from further attendance in this court until notified to be present. [14]

———

In the District Court of the United States in and for the Southern District of California, Northern Division.

No. 821—CRIM. N. D.

THE UNITED STATES OF AMERICA,

Plaintiff,

vs.

LOUIS H. REYFF, E. W. FREDRICK and HARRY BIGBY,

Defendants.

### VERDICT.

We, the jury in the above-entitled cause, find the defendant Louis H. Reyff, Guilty as charged in

the first count of the Information; Guilty as
charged in the second count of the Information;
and Guilty as charged in the third count of the Information; and we, the jury in the above-entitled
cause, find the defendant, E. W. Fredrick, Guilty
as charged in the first count of the Information;
Guilty as charged in the second count of the Information; and guilty as charged in the third count
of the Information; and we, the jury in the above-
entitled cause, find the defendant, Harry Bigby,
Guilty as charged in the first count of the Information; Not Guilty as charged in the second count of
the Information; and Not Guilty as charged in the
third count of the Information.

C. B. JACKSON,

Foreman.

Fresno, California, November 23, 1923.

Filed Nov. 23, 1923. Chas. N. Williams, Clerk.
Murray E. Wire, Deputy. [15]

———

In the District Court of the United States in and
for the Southern District of California, Northern Division.

No. 821—CRIMINAL.

UNITED STATES OF AMERICA,

Plaintiff,

vs.

LOUIS H. REYFF, E. W. FREDERICK and
HARRY BIGBY,

Defendants.

## MOTION FOR A NEW TRIAL.

Now come, Louis H. Reyff, E. W. Frederick and Harry Bigby, defendants in the above-entitled cause, and by Edward A. O'Dea and R. G. Retallick, their attorneys, move the Court to set aside the verdict rendered herein and to grant a new trial of said cause and for reasons therefor, show to the Court the following:

### I.

That the verdicts in said cause are contrary to law.

### II.

That the verdicts in said cause were not supported by the evidence in the case.

### III.

That the evidence in said cause is insufficient to justify any of said verdicts.

### IV.

That the Court erred upon the trial of said cause in deciding questions of law arising during the course of the trial, to which errors exceptions were duly taken.

### V.

That said Court upon the trial of said cause admitted incompetent evidence offered by the United States of America.

### VI.

That the Court improperly instructed the jury to the defendants' prejudice. [16]

Dated at Fresno, California, this 26th day of November, 1923.

L. F. REYFF,

E. W. FREDRICK,

HARRY BIGBY,

Defendants.

EDWARD A. O'DEA,

R. G. RETALLICK,

Attorneys for Defendants.

[Endorsed]: No. 821. In the United States District Court in and for the Northern Division of the Southern District of California. United States of America, Plaintiff, vs. Louis H. Reyff, E. W. Frederick and Harry Bigby, Defendants. Original Motion for a New Trial. Filed Nov. 26, 1923. Chas. N. Williams, Clerk. Murray E. Wire. Deputy. R. G. Retallick, Edward A. O'Dea, Attorneys for Defendants, 826–28–30 Phelan Building, Telephone Sutter 276, San Francisco.

Due service of the within motion for a new trial is hereby admitted this 26th day of Nov., 1923.

UNITED STATES ATTORNEYS.

By EUGENE T. McGANN,

Special Assistant United States Attorney.  [17]

In the District Court of the United States in and for the Southern District of California, Northern Division.

No. 821—CRIMINAL.

UNITED STATES OF AMERICA,

Plaintiff,

vs.

LOUIS H. REYFF, E. W. FREDERICK and HARRY BIGBY,

Defendants.

MOTION IN ARREST OF JUDGMENT.

Now come the defendants, Louis H. Reyff, E. W. Frederick and Harry Bigby, and respectfully move the Court to arrest and *without* judgment in the above-entitled cause and that the verdicts or verdict of conviction of said defendants heretofore given and made in the said cause be vacated and set aside and declared to be null and void for each of the following causes and reasons:

I.

That it appears on the face of the record that no judgment can legally be entered against these defendants or any or either of them for the following reasons.

1. *The* count one of the Information filed herein does not charge or state facts sufficient to constitute a public offense under the laws of the United States against the defendants or any or either of them.

2. That count two of the Information filed
herein does not charge or state facts sufficient to
constitute a public offense under the laws of the
United States against the defendants or any or
either of *the*. [18]

3. That count three of the Information filed
herein does not charge or state facts sufficient to
constitute a public offense under the laws of the
United States against the defendants or any or
either of them.

### II.

That this Court has no jurisdiction to pass judgment upon the defendants or either of them by
reason of the fact that Counts I–II and III of the
Information on file herein do not state public offenses under the laws of the United States.

WHEREFORE, by reason of the premises the
defendants pray this Honorable Court that the
judgment herein be arrested and withheld and that
the conviction of the defendants and each of them
be declared null and void.

Dated at Fresno, California, this 26th day of
November, 1923.

L. H. REYFF,

E. W. FREDRICK,

HARRY BIGBY,

Defendants.

EDWARD A. O'DEA,

R. G. RETALLICK,

Attorneys for Defendants.

[Endorsed]: No. 821—Criminal. In the District Court of the United States in and for the

Southern District of California, Northern Division. United States of America, Plaintiff, vs. Louis H. Reyff, E. W. Frederick, and Harry Bigby, Defendants. Original Motion in Arrest of Judgment. Filed Nov. 26, 1923. Chas. N. Williams, Clerk. Murray E. Wire, Deputy. R. G. Retallick, Edward A. O'Dea, Attorneys for Defendants, 826–28–30 Phelan Building. Telephone Sutter 276, San Francisco.

. Due service of the within motion in arrest of judgment is hereby admitted this 26th day of Nov. 1923.

UNITED STATES ATTORNEY.

By EUGENE T. McGANN,

Special Assistant United States Attorney. [19]

----

At a stated term, to wit, the November Term, A. D. 1923, of the District Court of the United States of America, within and for the Northern Division of the Southern District of California, held at the courtroom thereof, in the city of Fresno, on Monday the 26th day of November, in the year of our Lord one thousand nine hundred and twenty-three. Present: The Honorable WM. P. JAMES, District Judge.

No. 821—CRIM. N. D.

UNITED STATES OF AMERICA,

Plaintiff,

vs.

LOUIS H. REYFF, F. W. FREDRICK and HARRY BIGBY,

Defendants.

## SENTENCE.

This cause coming on at this time for sentence of defendants Louis H. Reyff and F. W. Fredrick on all counts of the Information and for sentence of defendant Harry Bigby on the first count thereof; Mark L. Herron, Esq., Assistant United States Attorney, appearing as counsel for the Government; defendants herein being present in court with their attorney R. G. Retallick, Esq., and said R. G. Retallick, Esq., having made a motion for a new trial and said motion having been overruled and an exception having been noted on behalf of defendants, and thereupon said R. G. Retallick, Esq., having made a motion in arrest of judgment, and said motion having been overruled, and an exception having been noted on behalf of the defendants, and said R. G. Retallick, Esq., having made a statement on behalf of defendants before sentence, it is by the Court ordered that defendants have thirty days within which to file bill of exceptions, and thereupon the Court pronounces sentence upon defendants herein for the offence of which they stand convicted, namely, violation of the National Prohibition Act of October 28th, 1919, and it is the judgment of the Court that each of said defendants Louis H. Reyff and F. W. Fredrick stand committed to the Fresno County Jail for the term and period of five (5) months on the first count [20] and pay unto the United States of America a fine in the sum of Ten Dollars on each of the second and third counts; and that defendant Harry Bigby stand committed to said Fresno County Jail for the term and period of three months on the first count. 6/234. [21]

---

In the District Court of the United States in and for the Southern District of California, Northern Division.

No. 821—CRIM. N. D.

UNITED STATES OF AMERICA,

Plaintiff,

vs.

LOUIS H. REYFF, F. W. FREDRICK and HARRY BIGBY,

Defendants.

## CERTIFICATE OF CLERK U. S. DISTRICT COURT TO JUDGMENT-ROLL.

I, Chas. N. Williams, Clerk of the United States District Court for the Southern District of California, do hereby certify the foregoing to be a full, true, and correct copy of an original Judgment entered in the above-entitled cause; and I do further certify that the papers hereto annexed constitute the judgment-roll in said cause.

ATTEST my hand and the seal of said District Court, this 1st day of December, A. D. 1923.

[Seal]      CHAS. N. WILLIAMS,

Clerk,

By B. B. Hansen,

Deputy Clerk.

[Endorsed]: No. 821–Crim. In the District Court of the United States for the Southern District of California, Northern Division. United States of America, Plaintiff, vs. Louis H. Reyff, F. W. Fredrick and Harry Bigby, Defendants. Judgment-roll. Filed Dec. 1, 1923. Chas. N. Williams, Clerk. By B. B. Hansen, Deputy Clerk. Recorded Min. Book No. 6, page 234. [22]

---

In the District Court of the United States for the Southern District of California, Northern Division.

### No. 821—CRIMINAL.

UNITED STATES OF AMERICA,

Plaintiff,

vs.

LOUIS H. REYFF, E. W. FREDERICK, and HARRY BIGBY,

Defendants.

### ASSIGNMENT OF ERRORS.

Louis H. Reyff, E. W. Frederick and Harry Bigby, defendants above named and plaintiffs in error herein, having petitioned for an order from said Court permitting them to procure a writ of error directed from the Circuit Court of Appeals for the Ninth Circuit, from the judgment and sentence entered in said cause against Louis H Reyff, E. W. Frederick and Harry Bigby, now makes and

files with the said petition the following assignment
of errors herein, upon which they and each of them
will apply for a reversal of said judgments and
sentences upon the said writ, and which said errors
and each of them are, to the great detriment, injury and prejudice of the said defendants, and each
of them, and in violation of the rights conferred
upon them by law; and they say that in the record
and proceedings in the above-entitled cause, upon
the hearing and determination thereof in the District Court of the United States for the Southern
District of California, there is manifest error in
this, to wit:

## I.

The Court erred in denying the motion made by
the defendant and plaintiff in error, E. W. Frederick, for the return of certain property, to wit, a case
of Scotch whiskey and four jars of intoxicating
liquor, upon the ground that said property was
seized from [23] the automobile of the defendant, E. W. Frederick without due process of law,
without the authorization of a search-warrant, or
warrant for the arrest of the said defendant, the
officers seizing same not having witnessed the commission of any crime in their presence and without
having seen any liquor in plain sight in said automobile and in violation of the defendant's right
guaranteed him under the 4th and 5th amendments
to the Constitution of the United States. Said motion was made before the trial, based upon an affidavit presented to the Court; said motion was made
during the trial and at the conclusion of the Gov-

ernment's case and the submission of all the evidence in the case. To the Court's order denying said motion the defendant Frederick then and there duly excepted.

## II.

The Court erred in denying the motion made by the defendant and plaintiff in error, E. W. Frederick, for the return of a Chalmers automobile seized by federal officers without due process of law, in that, said seizure of said automobile was based upon an unlawful search and seizure of certain property taken from said automobile without the authorization of a search-warrant or order of Court, or warrant for the arrest of the defendant, E. W. Frederick, or any person whomsoever, no crime having been committed in the presence of said federal officers and they not having seen any liquor in plain sight. To the Court's order denying said motion defendant and plaintiff in error Frederick duly excepted.

## III.

The Court erred in overruling the objection made by the defendants and each of them to the bringing in and exhibiting in a conspicuous place in front of the jury of certain bottles containing intoxicating liquors, which said objection was made upon the ground that the same was prejudicial to the rights of the defendants before the jury, and which bottles were so exhibited before any evidence whatsoever was introduced and while the said jury was [24] being empanelled, and said Court then and there erred in not requiring said bottles to be removed from the presence of the prospective jurors, to all of which the defendants then and there duly excepted.

### IV.

The Court erred in denying the motion of the defendants to exclude from evidence certain intoxicating liquors seized in violation of the constitutional rights of the defendants under the 4th and 5th amendments to the United States Constitution, as well as all knowledge derived from said search and seizure. Said motion was based upon the seizure of said intoxicating liquors from the automobile of the defendant Frederick, without the authorization of a search-warrant or order of Court, without a warrant for the arrest of any of the defendants, the arresting officers not having evidence sufficient to justify said seizure and search, they not having witnessed any violation of the law in their presence, and not having seen any liquor in plain sight or otherwise. Said motion was made before the trial and at each time said evidence was sought to be introduced during said trial. To the Court's order denying said motion, the defendants duly excepted.

### V.

The Court erred in admitting in evidence, over the objection of the defendants, one case of Scotch whiskey and four containers of liquor, said objection was based upon the ground that the evidence was obtained as a result of an illegal search and seizure of same out of an automobile in violation of the

defendants' constitutional rights. To the Court's
ruling the defendants then and there duly excepted.

### VI.

The Court erred in admitting the following testimony, over the objection of the defendants, upon the
ground that it was incompetent, irrelevant and immaterial and calling for a conclusion [25] of the
witness, and leading and suggestive and hearsay.

"Mr. HERRON.—Q. "Now, Mr. Nicely, at the
time you sent Mr. Kettle to see if he could make
those purchases of liquor, did you have reason to
believe that these defendants, or any one of them,
were engaged in the business of keeping or selling
intoxicating liquors?"

"Mr. RETALLICK.—"We object to that as incompetent, irrelevant and immaterial; calling for
a conclusion of the witness; leading and suggestive."

"The COURT.—"State, then, what information
you did have."

A. "I received a large number of complaints that
the defendant Bigby—

"Mr. RETALLICK.—"If your Honor please, we
object to this answer. Of course, I cannot object
to the question that the Court has asked. I object
to the answer on the ground that it is hearsay."

"The COURT.—"You may object to it if you
wish. I am allowing the evidence in view of your
motion to suppress evidence. If you will withdraw
the motion I will sustain the objection, but if the
motion stands, then they are entitled to show upon

what information he acted, to the extent that it was reasonable.''

Mr. O'DEA.—''The motion was made in behalf of the defendant Frederick. This is in relation to the conversation had with the defendant Bigby, and I submit it is immaterial and hearsay.''

''The COURT.—''You may act upon hearsay if it is generally reliable. If it ultimately proves to be reliable, then you may act upon it. It depends upon whether there was reasonable grounds existing to make the search. If I understand that you do not require that proof be made that they had reasonable ground to make the search then I will sustain the objection.''

Mr. O'DEA.—''We won't admit that.''

The COURT.—''The witness may answer.''

Mr. O'DEA.—''Note an exception.

A. ''I had received a large number of complaints that the defendant [26] Bigby had been dealing in intoxicating liquors.

Mr. HERRON.—Q. ''Don't state the language of it. You may say whether you had received complaints to the effect of it, but not the language.''

A. ''The people would go into this store where he was employed—''

Q. ''You had received complaints that he was selling liquor. That is as far as you may proceed.''

A. ''I had quite a number of them. I had also received complaints that the defendant Frederick was dealing in liquor, and I had arrested the defendant Frederick before, for the same thing.''

Mr. RETALLICK.—"I ask that that latter part be stricken out."

The COURT.—"It may be stricken.

Mr. O'DEA.—"And I would ask your Honor to instruct the jury not to consider that testimony."

The COURT.—"That may be stricken out as to the prior arrest of the defendant."

## VII.

The Court erred in denying the motions of the defendants and plaintiffs in error, made at the conclusion of the Government's case, which was at the conclusion of taking of all the testimony, to exclude all the evidence not legally obtained upon the ground that said evidence was taken without process of law. That the automobile which contained the liquor was searched and a seizure made therefrom without the authorization of a search-warrant, without any warrant for the arrest of the defendants or either of them, the officers not having witnessed the commission of any violation of the law, and not having seen any liquor in plain sight or otherwise. To the Court's order denying said motion the defendants then and there duly excepted.

## VIII.

The Court erred in denying the motion of the defendant and plaintiff in error Bigby for a directed verdict of not guilty of [27] all the counts set forth in the information, upon the grounds that the evidence was insufficient to sustain the charges contained therein. Said motion was made at the conclusion of the Government's case, which was at the conclusion of the taking of all the testimony in said case, to which ruling the defendant and plaintiff in error Bigby duly excepted.

The Court erred in denying the motion of the defendant and plaintiff in error Reyff for a directed verdict of not guilty of all the counts set forth in the information, upon the grounds that the evidence was insufficient to sustain the charges contained therein. Said motion was made at the conclusion of the Government's case, which was at the conclusion of the taking of all the testimony in said case, to which ruling the defendant and plaintiff in error, Reyff duly excepted.

## X.

The Court erred in denying the motion of the defendant Frederick for a directed verdict of not guilty of all of the counts set forth in the information, upon the grounds that the evidence was insufficient to sustain the charges that all of the evidence was taken in violation of the defendant's constitutional rights; that the liquor was taken from his automobile without a search-warrant, and without any crime having been committed in the presence of the officers making the arrest. Said motion was made at the conclusion of the Government's case, which was at the conclusion of the taking of all the testimony in said case, to which ruling the defendant and plaintiff in error duly excepted.

## XI.

The Court erred in denying the motion for a new trial on behalf of defendants and plaintiffs in error, in this:

(1)  That the verdicts in said cause are contrary to law.

(2)  That the verdicts in said cause were not supported by the evidence in the case. [28]

(3)  That the evidence in said cause is insufficient to justify any of said verdicts.

(4)  That the Court erred upon the trial of said cause in deciding questions of law arising during the course of the trial, to which errors exceptions were duly taken.

(5)  That said Court upon the trial of said cause admitted incompetent evidence offered by the United States of America.

(6)  That the Court improperly instructed the jury to the defendant's prejudice.

To which ruling on said motion for a new trial the defendants duly excepted.

### XII.

The Court erred in denying the motion in arrest of judgment on behalf of the defendants and plaintiffs in error, in this:  (1) . That it appears on the face of the record that no judgment can legally be entered against these defendants or any or either of them, for the following reasons:

That count one of the information filed herein does not charge or state facts sufficient to constitute a public offense under the laws of the United States against the defendants or any or either of them.

That count two of the information filed herein does not charge or state facts sufficient to constitute a public offense under the laws of the United States against the defendants or any or either of them.

That count three of the information filed herein does not charge or state facts sufficient to constitute a public offense under the laws of the United States against the defendants or any or either of them.

That this Court has no jurisdiction to pass judgment upon the defendants or either of them by reason of the fact that counts one, two and three of the information on file here do not state [29] public offenses under the laws of the United States.

To which ruling on defendants' said motion in arrest of judgment, defendants duly excepted.

R. G. RETTALICK,
EDWARD A. O'DEA,
Attorneys for Defendants.

[Indorsed]: No. 821—Criminal. In the District Court of the United States for the Southern District of California, Northern Division. United States of America, Plaintiff, v. Louis H. Reyff, E. W. Frederick and Harry Bigby, Defendants. Assignment of Errors. Rec'd copy of within this 28th day of November, 1923. Mark L. Herron, Asst. U. S. Atty. R. G. Retallick, of Fresno, California, and Edward A. O'Dea, Attorneys for Defendants. 826–28–30 Phelan Building. Telephone Sutter 276, San Francisco. [30]

In the District Court of the United States in and
for the Southern District of California, Northern Division.

No. 821—CRIMINAL.

UNITED STATES OF AMERICA,

Plaintiff,

vs.

LOUIS H. REYFF, E. W. FREDERICK and
HARRY BIGBY,

Defendants.

PETITION FOR WRIT OF ERROR AND SU-
PERSEDEAS.

Now come, Louis H. Reyff, E. W. Frederick and
Harry Bigby, the defendants herein, by their attorneys, Edward A. O'Dea and R. G. Retallick, and
say that on the 26th day of November, 1923, this
Court rendered judgment and sentence against the
defendants and each of them, in which judgment
and the proceedings had prior thereto certain errors
were permitted to the prejudice of the defendants
and each of them, all of which will more fully appear from the assignment of errors which is filed
with his petition.

WHEREFORE, the defendants pray that a writ
of error may issue in their behalf out of the United
States Circuit Court of Appeals for the Ninth Circuit, for the correction of the errors complained
of, and that a transcript of the record in this cause,

duly authenticated, may be sent to the Circuit Court of Appeals aforesaid, and that these defendants and each of them be awarded a supersedeas upon said judgment and all necessary and proper process including bail.

L. H. REYFF,

E. W. FREDERICK,

HARRY· BIGBY,

Defendants.

EDWARD A. O'DEA,

R. G. RETALLICK,

Attorneys for Defendants. [31]

[Indorsed]: No. 821—Criminal. In the District Court of the United States, in and for the Southern District of California, Northern Division. United States of America, Plaintiff, vs. Louis H. Reyff, E. W. Frederick and Harry Bigby, Defendants. Original Petition for Writ of Error and Supersedeas. Due service of the within petition for a writ of error and supersedeas is hereby admitted this 28th day of November, 1923. Joseph C. Burke, United States Attorney, Mark L. Herron, Assistant United States Attorney. Filed Nov. 28, 1923. Chas. N. Williams, Clerk. By R. S. Zimmerman, Deputy Clerk. R. G. Retallick and Edward A. O'Dea, Attorney for Defendants, 826–28–30 Phelan Building, Telephone Sutter 276, San Francisco. [32]

In the District Court of the United States in and
for the Southern District of California, Northern Division.

No. 821—CRIMINAL.

UNITED STATES OF AMERICA,

Plaintiff,

vs.

LOUIS H. REYFF, E. W. FREDERICK, and
HARRY BIGBY,

Defendants.

ORDER ALLOWING WRIT OF ERROR AND
SUPERSEDEAS.

The writ of error and supersedeas herein prayed
for by Louis H. Reyff, E. W. Frederick and Harry
Bigby, the plaintiffs in error, and defendants above
named, pending the decision upon said writ of
error, are hereby allowed and the defendants are
admitted to bail upon writ of error in the following sums to wit:

Louis H. Reyff, in the sum of Five Thousand Dollars;

E. W. Frederick, in the sum of Five Thousand Dollars;

Harry Bigby, in the sum of Five Thousand Dollars.

The bond for costs on the writ of error is hereby
fixed at the sum of Two Hundred Fifty Dollars
for each defendant.

Dated at Fresno, California, this 20th day of November, 1923.

WM. P. JAMES,
United States District Judge.

[Endorsed]: No. 821—Criminal. In the United States District Court for the Northern Division of the Southern District of California. United States of America, Plaintiff, vs. Louis H. Reyff, E. W. Frederick, and Harry Bigby, Defendants. Original Order Allowing Writ of Error and Supersedeas. Rec'd copy of within this 28th day of November, 1923. Mark L. Herron, Asst. U. S. Atty. Filed Nov. 28, 1923. Chas. N. Williams, Clerk. By R. S. Zimmerman, Deputy Clerk. R. G. Retallick, Fresno, California, and Edward A. O'Dea, Attorney for Defendants. 826–28–30 Phelan Building, Telephone Sutter 276, San Francisco. [33]

---

In the Northern Division of the United States District Court, the Southern District of California.

No. 821—CRIMINAL.

UNITED STATES OF AMERICA,

Plaintiff,

vs.

LOUIS H. REYFF, E. W. FREDERICK, and HARRY BIGBY,

Defendants.

## STIPULATION EXTENDING TIME IN WHICH TO LODGE AND SETTLE PROPOSED BILL OF EXCEPTIONS.

It is hereby stipulated by and between counsel for the above-mentioned parties that the defendants may have to and including the 26th day of January, 1924, in which to lodge and settle their proposed bill of exceptions upon order allowing a writ of error to the United States Circuit Court of Appeals in and for the Ninth Circuit.

Dated this 21st day of December, 1923.

JOSEPH C. BURKE,
United States Attorney.
MARK L. HERRON,
Asst. U. S. Atty.
EDWARD A. O'DEA,
R. G. RETALLICK,

Attorneys for Defendants, Louis H. Reyff, E. W. Frederick and Harry Bigby.

So ordered:

Dated this 21st day of December, 1923.

WM. P. JAMES,
United States District Judge.

[Endorsed]: No. 821—Criminal. In the Northern Division of the United States District Court for the Southern District of California. United States of America, Plaintiff, vs. Louis H. Reyff, E. W. Frederick and Harry Bigby, Defendants. Stipulation Extending Time in Which to Lodge and Settle Proposed Bill of Exceptions. Filed Dec. 21,

1923, at —— min. past —— o'clock —— M. Chas. N. Williams, Clerk. G. F. Gibson, Deputy. R. G. Retallick of Fresno, Cal., and Edward A. O'Dea, Attorneys for Defendants, 826–28–30 Phelan Building, Telephone Sutter 276, San Francisco. [34]

In the District Court of the United States in and for the Southern District of California, Northern Division.

No. 821.

UNITED STATES OF AMERICA,

Plaintiff,

vs.

LOUIS H. REYFF, E. W. FREDERICK and HARRY BIGBY,

Defendants.

## ORDER ALLOWING TEN DAYS TO SERVE AND FILE AMENDMENTS TO BILL OF EXCEPTIONS.

Upon motion of Joseph C. Burke, United States Attorney in and for the Southern District of California, and good cause appearing therefor, the plaintiff herein is hereby allowed ten days within which to serve and file its proposed amendments to the proposed bill of exceptions heretofore filed by the defendants in the above-entitled cause.

Dated this 10th day of January, 1924.

WM. P. JAMES,
United States District Judge.

[Endorsed]: No. 821. United States District Court, Southern District of California, Northern Division. United States of America, Plaintiff, vs. Louis H. Reyff, E. W. Frederick and Harry Bigby, Defendants. Order Filed Jan. 10, 1924, at 30 min. past 4 o'clock P. M. Chas. N. Williams, Clerk. G. F. Gibson, Deputy. [35]

---

In the District Court of the United States for the Southern District of California, Northern Division.

### No. 821—CRIMINAL.

UNITED STATES OF AMERICA,

Plaintiff,

vs.

LOUIS H. REYFF, E. W. FREDERICK, and HARRY BIGBY,

Defendants.

### ENGROSSED BILL OF EXCEPTIONS.

BE IT REMEMBERED, that heretofore the United States Attorney in and for the Southern District of California did file in the above-entitled court an information against the defendants, Louis H. Reyff, E. W. Frederick and Harry Bigby, and that thereafter the said Louis H. Reyff, E. W. Frederick and Harry Bigby appeared in court and upon being called to plead to said information, each of them pleaded Not Guilty as shown by the record herein.

AND BE IT FURTHER REMEMBERED, that the defendants, Louis H. Reyff, E. W. Frederick and Harry Bigby, having duly pleaded Not Guilty, and the cause being at issue, the same coming on for trial at Fresno, California, on Thursday, the 22d day of November, 1923, at two o'clock P. M., before the Honorable William P. James, District Judge of said court, and a jury duly impaneled, the United States being represented by Mark Herron, Esq., and E. T. McGann, Esq., Assistant United States Attorneys, and the defendants being represented by Edward A. O'Dea, Esq., and R. G. Retallick, Esq.

That before said cause came to issue and on the 22d day of November, 1923, and before the jury was impaneled in said cause, [36] the defendant, E. W. Frederick, filed and presented to the Court a motion for the return of property and exclusion of evidence: said motion is in the words and figures as follows, to wit:

"In the District Court of the United States in and for the Southern District of California, Northern Division.

No. 821—CRIMINAL.

UNITED STATES OF AMERICA,

Plaintiff,

vs.

LOUIS H. REYFF, E. W. FREDERICK, and HARRY BIGBY,

Defendants.

## MOTION TO RETURN PROPERTY AND EX-CLUDE EVIDENCE.

To the Honorable Above-entitled Court:

The petition of E. W. Frederick respectfully shows:

### I.

That at all the times herein mentioned he owned and possessed a certain Chalmers Automobile, License No. 763–229, and that on the 16th day of May, 1923, he was in possession and control of said automobile in the City of Fresno, County of Fresno, State of California.

### II.

That said automobile is of such construction that in the rear of same there is a receptacle for the purpose of containing packages; that said receptacle was closed and locked on said 16th day of May, 1923.

### III.

That on the 16th day of May, 1923, while your petitioner was in possession and control of said automobile, he and the defendant, [37] Reyff, entered a garage located in the rear of No. 1041 T Street, in the City of Fresno, County of Fresno, State of California. That upon entering said garage, Federal Prohibition Enforcement Officers Nicely and Emrich, jumped upon defendants, your petitioner's automobile, and illegally and unlawfully, without the authorization of a search-warrant, or order of any Court, and without any warrant for the arrest of your petitioner, and without witnessing any act or acts, committed in violation of the laws of the United States, or of the State of California, and in violation of the defendant's rights guaranteed him by the Fourth and Fifth Amendment to the United States Constitution, and without seeing any liquor in plain sight, or otherwise, placed the defendant in custody, handcuffing him and proceeded to search his person, and by means of illegal and unlawful search violated his rights above referred to, said Federal Prohibition Enforcement Officers proceeded to search his person and found thereon a key, and that they thereupon illegally and unlawfully, without the authority of a search-warrant, and in violation of the defendant's rights guaranteed him by the Fourth and Fifth Amendments to the United States Constitution, and against the will of your petitioner, took the said key and opened the rear receptacle to said automobile and found therein a case of Scotch whiskey, which they illegally and unlawfully seized and took the same away with them, and they profess to hold the same against the will of your petitioner as evidence of the violation of the law committed on the part of your petitioner, in the above-entitled case.

## IV.

That said whiskey is held without process of law, and is the property of the defendant, your petitioner, and he is entitled to its return. And that by reason thereof, and facts set forth, the defendant's rights under the Fourth and Fifth Amendments to the United States Constitution have been, and will be violated unless [38] the Court orders the return of said liquor, its exclusion from evidence at the trial of said cause, and the suppression of all knowledge derived from said seizure of said liquor.

This petitioner further alleges that on said 16th day of May, 1923, his said automobile was seized by the said Federal Prohibition Enforcement Agents of the United States, in the manner hereinbefore particularly specified, and that the said Federal Prohibition Enforcement Officers still retain the control and custody of said automobile, and that said automobile is so held by them for the reasons hereinbefore particularly specified, and without due process of law, and for no other reason, and your petitioner is entitled to the return of said automobile.

WHEREFORE, defendant, your petitioner prays that the United States Attorney, Marshal, Prohibition Enforcement Officers be notified, and the Court direct an order to said United States Attorney, Marshal, Clerk and Prohibition Enforcement Officers, or any or either of them, to return the said property, to wit: One case of Scotch whisky, and the said Chalmers automobile, to defendant, and to exclude the same and all knowledge derived from the trial of said cause.

E. W. FREDERICK.   [39]

State of California,
County of Fresno,—ss.

E. W. Frederick, being first duly sworn, deposes and says that he is one of the defendants in the above-entitled action; that he has read the foregoing motion for return of property and exclusion of evidence and knows the contents thereof; that the same is true of his own knowledge, except as those matters which are therein stated on information or belief; as to those matters that he believes it to be true.

E. W. FREDERICK.

R. G. RETALLICK,

E. A. O'DEA,

Attys. for Defts.

Subscribed and sworn to before me this 22d day of November, 1923.

[Seal] RUTH H. JACKSON, Notary Public in and for the County of Fresno, State of California.

[Endorsed]: Filed Nov. 22, 1923. Chas. N. Williams, Clerk. By Murray E. Wire, Deputy Clerk. [40]

At the time of the presentation of said motion, as above referred to, the following proceedings were had:

Mr. O'DEA.—If the Court please, the defendants desire to present a motion for the return of property and to exclude evidence.

Mr. HERRON.—To which the Government objects on the ground that the motion has not been made seasonably. I have been in communication with counsel all during the week, and this case has been on the calendar since Tuesday, and they have not indicated that such a motion would be filed. The Government must resist the filing of the motion at this time.

Mr. O'DEA.—This is a right that is accorded the defendants any time up to the time of trial.

Mr. HERRON.—Counsel is incorrectly quoting the law. The law distinctly states it must be seasonable.

The COURT.—What are the grounds?

Mr. O'DEA.—That the automobile of the defendant, Frederick, was searched without probable cause and without the authorization of a search-warrant, and without process of any kind.

Mr. HERRON.—If this contention should arise in the course of the trial, of course, then the Court could refuse to permit the evidence to be put in.

The COURT.—With that understanding, you may proceed, and you may have your objection.

Mr. O'DEA.—Your Honor is denying the objection.

The COURT.—No, I am not denying the objection. You may present your objection as the trial develops.

(Whereupon a jury was duly impaneled, during the course of which, after counsel for the Government had passed the jurors in the box for cause, the following proceedings were had.) [41]

### EXCEPTION No. 1.

Mr. RETALLICK.—It looks like at the present time the prohibition official is bringing into the courtroom certain bottles supposedly containing intoxicating liquors and placing them on the table in a conspicuous place right in front of the jury. We object to that as prejudicial to the rights of the defendants before this jury.

Mr. HERRON.—We are perfectly willing for the Court to instruct the jurors not to notice the bottles until the proper time for noticing them arrives.

The COURT.—Your objection has been noted. Proceed.

Mr. O'DEA.—Did your Honor overrule the objection?

The COURT.—Counsel has not offered any evidence as yet, and I am not assuming that the jury is taking note of anything that is not before them.

Mr. RETALLICK.—May we have an EXCEPTION to the Court's ruling?

That thereupon the following proceedings were had:

Mark Herron, Esq., Assistant United States Attorney, made an opening statement to the jury and counsel for the defendants waived an opening statement. The plaintiff, to maintain the issues on its part to be maintained, introduced and offered in evidence the following testimony, to wit:

## TESTIMONY OF C. W. KETTLE, FOR THE GOVERNMENT.

C. W. KETTLE, called for the United States, being sworn, testified as follows:

### Direct Examination.

My name is C. W. Kettle. On or about May 16, 1923, I was reporter for the "Fresno Herald" and I was living in Fresno. At that time, and prior to that particular date, I knew the colored man, Bigby.

(Testimony of C. W. Kettle.)

I [42] saw him on or about May 16, 1923. I saw him on the sidewalk opposite Shaddow's jewelry store. I went down to make some arrangements to get some liquor. When I first saw him, no other person was present. I had a conversation with him. The conversation I had with him (Bigby) ran something like this: I said, "Do you remember me?" and he said, "No, I don't." I said, "I bought some gin from you a little while back. I want to get another case." He said, "I haven't got any gin. You must be mistaken. I never sold you any gin." I (Kettle) said, "No, I am not mistaken." He (Bigby) said, "I haven't got any gin, but I think I can get you some whiskey." I (Kettle) said, "How much is it?" He said, "Just a minute, I will have to find out about that." He then went inside the jewelry store and came back out and said, "$100.00." I (Kettle) said, "Can you deliver it to my room?" He (Bigby) said, "When do you want it?" I (Kettle) said, "I want it to-night." He said, "I will have to find that out," and he went back in the store the second time and called Mr. Reyff out and introduced me to him and Reyff said, "Yes, we can deliver it to-night. Where do you want it?" I (Kettle) gave him the address of my house and Reyff said, "What time do you want it?" and I said, "Make it eight o'clock." He (Reyff) said, "Will you be there?" and I said, "Yes." He said, "All right, I will be there at eight." I then left the defendant. At eight o'clock,

(Testimony of C. W. Kettle.)

I was at my room at 1041 T Street. At that time, I saw the defendants, Frederick and Reyff. They were in their machine in front of the house. I had a conversation with them at that time. Frederick spoke to me and said, "I didn't know it was you I was bringing the liquor to." I don't remember the rest of the conversation right then but I told him to drive around to the garage in the rear. First, I asked him if he had the liquor there and he (Frederick) said, "Yes, it is in the rear of the car." Then I (Kettle) said, "Drive around to the garage and we will take it out there." We drove around to the garage and while doing so I (Kettle) counted out [43] $100 and gave it to Frederick. I first obtained the money from Mr. Nicely. Mr. Nicely took the serial numbers of the bills in my presence. We then drove around to the garage and Frederick still had the money in his hand. We pulled into the garage and got out on one side of the car and Frederick started to get out of the other. Reyff was in the center. The car was a roadster. I was on the right hand side and Frederick was driving on the left. The conversation took place while Frederick was seated in the automobile and Reyff was seated by his side. The conversation was not very loud. I think Mr. Reyff heard the conversation. He was seated between Frederick and myself in the automobile. After we got into the garage, Mr. Nicely and two deputies came from the rear of the garage. One man took hold of me and one took hold of each one of the other two. At that time, Mr. Frederick

(Testimony of C. W. Kettle.)
threw the money away and it went under the motor
car. I did not see him throw it away. I was on
the other side of the car. I heard something go
under the car and I heard one of the deputies say,
"Where is the money?" and he said, "What
money?"

### EXCEPTION No. 2.

At this point, Mr. O'Dea asked the Court to take
up for the Court's ruling, his Motion to Return
Property and Exclude Evidence, and obtained permission to cross-examine the witness on the question of the search and seizure of the automobile and
the seizure of certain property from the receptacle
of the automobile and in response to his questions
the witness testified as follows:

The prohibition officers in the garage did not exhibit any search-warrant to search the automobile
in question. I do not know whether they had a
warrant for the arrest of Frederick or anybody else.
I believe that the rear portion of the machine was
closed down. The money was not handed to Frederick in that garage. It was handed to him on the
outside. I do not know whether Prohibition Officer
Nicely or Prohibition Officer Emrich or anybody
[44] connected with them had any knowledge of
what had transpired from the time I left the house
and went into the garage. I do not know whether
they were conversant with what took place.

Mr. O'DEA.—I submit the motion.

COURT.—Had you told them about the bargain
you had made?

(Testimony of C. W. Kettle.)

WITNESS.—Yes, sir.

COURT.—You told them of the arrangements and the time and place where it was to be delivered?

WITNESS.—Yes, sir.

COURT.—And that was the reason that they were there?

WITNESS.—Yes, sir.

COURT.—Motion denied.

Mr. O'Dea.—May we have an EXCEPTION noted, if the Court please?

COURT.—Surely.

At this point, the direct examination was resumed and the witness testified further as follows:

One of the agents recovered the money from under the car. There was some scuffling at the time and Mr. Frederick and Mr. Reyff were handcuffed together.

On cross-examination, the witness testified as follows:

I have been residing in Los Angeles from the middle of last August up to the present time. I have known Mr. Nicely since some time early last spring. Before the raid in the garage I knew him, say, about two or three months. I don't know whether Mr. Nicely went into my home. On the morning of May 16th, 1923, certain people connected with the Police Department of this city and the Prohibition Department went into my room and got from there a case of gin. I was not charged with violating the "National Prohibition [45] Law" for the case of gin they took from my room. I

(Testimony of C. W. Kettle.)

don't know what time of the day it was. After they
went to my room, I had a conversation with Prohibition Officers Nicely and Emrich. I first had a
conversation with Nicely, afterwards with Emrich,
on the same day. They did not tell me that if I
helped them out there would be nothing done with
the case. I have never been in their employ. At
the instigation of the prohibition officers I went to
the store of the jeweler, Shaddow, Mr. Nicely said
that he knew that the colored boy was putting out
liquor, and he knew that I had bought from him,
and he asked me if I would go down there and make
another buy for him, and I said I would. I am
positive that he did not pay me or promise to pay me
for going down there. I knew I was not going to be
charged with violating the prohibition law. Mr.
Nicely said, "I got that liquor out of your room without a search-warrant, or anything else, and," he said,
"under the law I had no right to take it." Nicely
said, "Where did you get it?" I said, "I don't
know where I got it from." He said, "I know
where you got it and I will tell you where you got
it. I just want you to go down and buy another
one; will you do that?" I said, "Yes, I will go down
and buy another one." He previously told me that
when he found out the circumstances of the case
that he could not prosecute. Then I went to this
jewelry store. I saw the colored boy there. I told
him I wanted to get another case of gin. First, I
should say, I asked him if he remembered me, and
he said, "No, I don't believe I do." I said, "I

(Testimony of C. W. Kettle.)

bought some gin from you some time ago." First, he said, "No, you didn't, you are mistaken." Finally I told him some things which made him remember that I had, I guess. He said, "I haven't any gin, but I think we can get some liquor." I said, "What kind?" He said, "Scotch." I said, "How much?" He said, "I don't know exactly, just wait a minute, wait here a minute and I will see." He went into the store and came back out and said, "$100." I said, "Can you deliver it?" He said, [46] "When?" I said, "To-night." He said, "I will have to find that out, too." He went back in and that is when he brought Reyff out and introduced me to Reyff. Reyff says, "We can take care of you. When do you want it?" I said, "I want it to-night." He said, "What time?" I said, "That is immaterial." But I said, "Let us make it eight o'clock." He says, "All right, where do you want it?" and I told him and gave him this address at 1841 T Street. He said, "Will you be there?" I said, "I will be there," and he said, "All right, I will be up there." I had the case of gin in my house for beverage purposes. There were twelve bottles in the case of gin. I had that for about two weeks but not in that room. I had it on San Pablo Avenue. I did not get a permit to transport from San Pablo Avenue to my home. I knew it was in violation of the law to transport liquor from one place to another without securing a permit. I did not attempt to sell any of it. I was not drinking at the time. I was going to drink it. I brought

(Testimony of C. W. Kettle.)

it up to my room on the day of the arrest. I did
not tell the officers that I had moved liquor in violation of the law on that morning. I didn't tell him
at any time. I got it from Bigby. I didn't get
it from Bigby. I didn't get it from Reyff. I don't
know the fellow's name, I got it from. I made
arrangements to have it delivered on San Pablo
Avenue. I don't know the man's name that delivered it. I gave him the money for it. I made
the arrangements at the jewelry store with Bigby
about three or four weeks before I got the Scotch.
I saw Mr. Nicely between the time I made the
arrangements for the purchase and the time Mr.
Frederick was arrested. I saw him at Police Headquarters. He gave me the money and told me to
pay for the liquor and he asked me what arrangements had been made and I told him and he said,
"That is all: we will take care of the rest of it."
I told him what I was going to do. I did not tell
him that I was going to drive around the block. I
did not tell the officers to go into the garage. Mr.
Nicely told me that they would be there. [47] I
worked with police officers and prohibition officers
for the last fifteen years. I worked on prohibition
raids before. I secured evidence before. In
Fresno, Chicago, Kansas City and several places.
I did not particularly secure evidence for the Prohibition Department of the State of California
before. I have been with them when they have gone
on raids and things. I did not know whether they
were conducting a raid or obtaining evidence. I did

(Testimony of C. W. Kettle.)

not attempt to secure evidence until I was caught myself. I secured evidence in other places before, within the same month, before I went on this raid. When I bought the liquor I did not tell the prohibition officers where I purchased it. I have since learned that my landlady turned a report into the Police Department that I had liquor in my room. I had no inducement to purchase liquor from the Shaddow jewelry store. I was not paid any money at all. I had never received a dime. The serial numbers of the bills were taken down in my presence, by Mr. Nicely. They were put in a little book that he had in his pocket, at the Police Headquarters.

## TESTIMONY OF T. J. NICELEY, FOR THE GOVERNMENT.

T. J. NICELEY, called for the United States, being sworn testified as follows:

### Direct Examination.

I am a Federal Prohibition Agent. I was such on May 16, 1923. On that date, I saw all of the defendants. I saw the witness, Kettle. I first saw Mr. Frederick and Mr. Reyff at eight o'clock that evening in a garage on T Street. They drove into the garage in a Chalmers Roadster. After they got in the garage, we stepped over to the car. Mr. Kettle stepped out of the car; Mr. Reyff stayed in the car. Mr. Frederick was on the other side of the car and Agent Stribling stepped around on the

(Testimony of T. J. Niceley.)

other side of the car   [48]   near to Mr. Frederick,
and they started scuffling over there.   I went around
there then and we put the handcuffs on Mr. Frederick and Mr. Reyff and placed them under arrest
and then we started searching for some marked
money and Agent Stribling found it lying right
by the left front wheel under the car by the fender.
Agent Stribling picked it up.   I examined the bills,
when I gave them to Witness Kettle.   I made a
record of that examination.   I can tell what bills
they were.   They were as follows:   One was a $10
bill, serial No. V.-851246; another $10 bill, K-4767-
29-B; a $5 bill, L-41840135-A; a $5, Y-716344-D; a
$10 bill, N-39482-E; a $10 bill, K-394852-B; a $20
bill, K-884312; a $5 bill, L-36821332-A; a $5 bill,
H-227309849; a $10 bill, Y-839953-E; a $5 bill,
V-76446-E; a $5 bill, L-35589711-A.   This money
was picked up off the ground and the numbers
checked, that is, the number of the bills were read
off and checked with a notation that I had previously made.   I do not know where the money is
now.   It was my money and after it had been used,
I used it again.   Then I asked Mr. Frederick where
the case of liquor that he had was, and he said he
had no liquor; I asked him for the key for the rear
end of the automobile, the rear compartment.

### EXCEPTION No. 3.

Mr. O'DEA.—If the Court please, at this time I
want to renew my objection to this testimony as to
the seizure of the liquor, for the purpose of the
record, along with the motion heretofore made.

(Testimony of T. J. Niceley.)

The COURT.—The objection is overruled and you may take your exception.

Mr. O'DEA.—EXCEPTION.

The WITNESS.—(Continuing.) We unlocked the rear compartment to his automobile and took from this sack (indicating) with the letter "K" on it, and the liquor contained therein, and the one bottle of [49] liquor sitting on the table that has the white cap on it.

(Here the sack and the contents were marked "Government's Exhibit 1 for Identification," and the bottle as "Government's Exhibit 2 for Identification.")

WITNESS.—(Continuing.) We opened the compartment and found that sack containing that liquor in the car and then locked that compartment up and brought the car into the Federal Building here and took out the sack of liquor and brought it into the Federal Building. Later, I took this car in the back of the Federal Building here and called the garage man to come and get it. When he came after the car, I looked in the compartment behind the seat and found two of the jars there. I don't know which of these two jars it was. The jars were in the compartment behind the seat, with tools and other things. I have seen the other two jars. Those two jars were in the garage on M Street where Mr. Frederick took me later. Before I opened the rear compartment of the automobile, the defendants were placed under arrest. I had a conversation later with Mr. Frederick after he

(Testimony of T. J. Niceley.)

was arrested. Mr. Frederick and myself were present.

Mr. O'DEA.—Your Honor, we will object to that conversation as hearsay in so far as it affects the other defendants.

The COURT.—That will be understood. The jury will understand that—any statement made out of the presence of the other defendants cannot be received as against those defendants who were not present or who were not within hearing.

Mr. HERRON.—May I also ask that the jury be told if in the event the Government establishes agency between the defendants, in that event the acts shown to have been committed out of the presence of the principal would nevertheless be binding upon him. Each defendant is accessory to the other in this transaction, and I believe under the decisions where that situation develops a statement [50] of any one agent is binding upon his principal.

Mr. O'DEA.—That would be in a case of conspiracy, not in a case charging these defendants with sale.

The COURT.—We will endeavor to cover the matter by proper instructions.

The WITNESS.—(Continuing.) The defendant was under arrest at the time. His statement was in the nature of an admission. I told Mr. Frederick that he did not have to talk to me at all, that any conversation or anything that he told me was to be free and voluntary on his part and that there was no way that I could compel him to talk; that

(Testimony of T. J. Niceley.)

if he didn't want to he didn't have to say a word to me; that I wanted to ask him something about this; that I would like to get the rest of the liquor that he had. Nothing was said about felonies or misdemeanors. I told him that he could either be charged with conspiracy to violate the law, which was a more severe offense than transporting and selling. I told him in substance that if he would take me to where the liquor was that he wouldn't be charged with conspiracy. Prior to the conversation I have just recounted, I had another conversation with Mr. Frederick. Mr. Reyff was in there and I believe that Mr. Emrich was there. I made no threats or held out any promises of immunity to them as a result of anything that they might say. I did not advise them in so many words that what they might say would be used against them. I told Mr. Frederick that he didn't have to talk with me at any time; that he was not compelled to and that there was no way that I could compel him to talk to me. I don't remember of any conversation with Mr. Reyff at the time. He was sitting over on the other side of the office. I told Mr. Frederick that we had plenty of evidence there to convict him, that I would like to find out where the rest of the liquor was. He said, "Yes," that he knew we had plenty of evidence to convict him, but that he didn't want to be charged, [51] with the other liquor.

## EXCEPTION No. 4.

Mr. HERRON.—Now, Mr. Niceley, at the time you sent Mr. Kettle to see if he could make those

(Testimony of T. J. Niceley.)

purchases of liquor did you have reason to believe that these defendants, or any one of them, were engaged in the business of keeping or selling intoxicating liquor?

Mr. RETALLICK.—We object to that as incompetent, irrelevant and immaterial; calling for a conclusion of the witness; leading and suggestive.

The COURT.—State then what information you did have.

WITNESS.—I received a large number of complaints that the defendant Bigby—

Mr. RETALLICK.—If your Honor please, we object to this answer. Of course, I cannot object to the question that the Court has asked. I object to the answer on the ground that it is hearsay.

The COURT.—You may object to it if you wish. I am allowing the evidence in view of your motion to suppress evidence. If you will withdraw the motion I will sustain the objection, but if the motion stands then they are entitled to show upon what information he acted, to the extent that it was reasonable.

Mr. O'DEA.—The motion was made in behalf of the defendant, Frederick. This in relation to the conversation had with the defendant, Bigby, and I submit it is immaterial and hearsay.

The COURT.—You may act upon hearsay if it is generally reliable; if it ultimately proves to be reliable then you may act upon it. It depends upon whether there was reasonable ground existing to make the search. If I understand that you do not

(Testimony of T. J. Niceley.)

require that proof be made that they had reasonable ground to make the search, then I will sustain the objection. [52]

Mr. O'DEA.—We won't admit that.

The COURT.—The witness may answer.

Mr. O'DEA.—Note an EXCEPTION.

WITNESS.—I received a large number of complaints that the defendant, Bigby, had been dealing in intoxicating liquors.

WITNESS.—(Continuing.) I had quite a number of complaints that he was selling liquor. I also received complaints that the defendant, Frederick, was dealing in liquor. All of this transaction took place in the City of Fresno.

On cross-examination, the witness testified as follows: I did not pay a ten-cent piece, not any money of any kind to Kettle to procure the evidence against the defendant, Frederick, and the other two defendants. I did not tell you (Mr. O'Dea) in the presence of Mr. Retallick and in the presence of the Assistant United States Attorney that I paid to get that evidence. I never told you (Mr. Retallick) in the office of the United States Attorney in this building in Fresno on Monday or Tuesday last, in the presence of Mr. O'Dea, Mr. Herron and Mr. Retallick and possibly other persons that Kettle was paid $10.00. I told you that Mr. Kettle had not received a dime for obtaining this evidence. That is what I told you. I can tell you the exact language of the conversation if you want it. The

(Testimony of T. J. Niceley.)

$5.00 and $10.00 bills that I took the numbers of aggregating the amount I gave Kettle were found in my presence afterwards. They were found underneath right by the left front wheel of the Chalmers car in this garage on T Street. Kettle couldn't have the bills on him if they were under the car. I knew whether or not he had them on him immediately before he went into that garage. I did not see Kettle give that money to anybody. I did not see either the defendants, Frederick or Reyff, throw those bills on the floor. I do not know now of my own knowledge whether [53] Kettle ever gave those bills to either of the defendants. To go into that garage, I made arrangements with a lady who owns that property. The doctor's wife, to go out there and wait in that garage. To wait until this liquor was delivered. Her husband showed me how to get in the garage with the knowledge of Kettle. I went out to the place where Kettle was rooming at the request of the lady who owns the place. I did not open the door and go into his room. He opened the door for me and I went into his room. I found in there twelve bottles of gin in a pasteboard box. Then I came down to the postoffice and took the matter up with Mr. Mark Herron, Assistant United States Attorney and asked for a complaint for Kettle. He asked me the circumstances of the case and I told him the circumstances; that this lady had followed me out there and had opened the door and told me this liquor was there and I had got it. I didn't see Kettle between the time I seized the liquor

(Testimony of T. J. Niceley.)

in the room and the time I went to see the District Attorney. On that day I first saw Kettle at police headquarters some time after that. I had a conversation with him there. He asked me who got the liquor out of his room and I told him that I did. I did not tell Kettle to go up and see those people and try to procure some liquor from them to be used against them. I had knowledge that a violation of the law had occurred there. I had a Government agent go in there and get some liquor. I did not send the defendant, Kettle, to that place without any knowledge of my own that the law was being violated, to see whether or not I could procure a violation of the law. I sent a Government agent in there to get some liquor while I stood outside of the place. He got the liquor from A. D. Shaddow. He did not get the liquor from these defendants.

That was a week prior to the time of the raid. I have never arrested A. D. Shaddow for that offense. I asked this man to go and try to purchase liquor from a place where I knew the law was being violated. Kettle reported back the conversation he had with the colored boy who was only a porter. [54] And he reported back the conversation he had with the other party who was only a clerk in that place. I knew that A. D. Shaddow was the employer of these boys, and I made no attempt to prosecute him. I based my prosecution upon the ones that had violated the law. Although I had information a week before that a violation of the law had occurred there, I took no steps to prosecute because

(Testimony of T. J. Niceley.)

we use our own judgment as to whether there is
evidence sufficient to go to court. The evidence
has not been sufficient in that case. I went to the
garage to wait that evening with two other agents.
The other agent was Stribling. I waited until the
defendant went into the place. I do not know
whether Reyff participated in any sale that was to
be consummated. I do not know anything about the
arrangement between Kettle and the colored boy,
only what Kettle told me. I depended upon Kettle
for my information. At the police station, Kettle
was not a bit nervous. He did not look as if he
had been indulging in intoxicating liquor. He appeared very calm and cool. I told him first that
Mr. Mark Herron had advised me that I could not
prosecute him because I had no search-warrant to
go into that place. I told him I knew where he had
got that liquor at and asked him if he would go
down there and buy some liquor. There wasn't
two or three police officers there—I don't talk before two or three police officers. He had never
given me any information before. I have been at
the head of the Prohibition forces in Fresno for
three years and a half. During all that time he
has not given me any information at all.

## TESTIMONY OF PAUL A. EMRICH, FOR THE GOVERNMENT.

PAUL A. EMRICH, called for the United States, being first duly sworn, testified as follows:

### Direct Examination.

I am a Federal Prohibition Agent. That was my business on [55] May 16, 1923. I saw all of these defendants on the 16th of May, in a garage located on T Street, in the City of Fresno.

### EXCEPTION No. 5.

Mr. HERRON.—State to the Court and jury the circumstances under which you saw them.

WITNESS.—The circumstances of it were that I had knowledge of an anticipated sale at that place. I went to that garage in company with Mr. Stribling and Agent Niceley. About eight o'clock in drove a Chalmers roadster in which was Mr. Frederick and Mr. Reyff, I believe his name is, accompanied by Mr. Kettle. Mr. Kettle and he got out of the machine and Mr. Frederick had his right hand closed. They had been placed under arrest and I was about to search him for the marked money when he made a motion with his hand down towards the left front wheel of the Chalmers roadster. Mr. Stribling came around and was looking down where he had made this motion and picked up that marked money. We then opened up the back of the car and found that whiskey.

Mr. RETALLICK.—We object to this on the grounds heretofore stated, incompetent, irrelevant,

(Testimony of Paul A. Emrich.)

and immaterial. All of the evidence of the acts immediately preceding the seizure of this intoxicating liquor we believe to be incompetent, irrelevant and immaterial.

The COURT.—Objection overruled.

Mr. RETALLICK.—May we have our exception.

WITNESS.—They were placed under arrest, as stated before, and the car was taken over here to the Federal Building and they were brought into the office. Agent Niceley questioned them, and in particular I asked Mr. Frederick his occupation, as a matter of record, and he informed me distinctly that it was that of bootlegging.

WITNESS.—(Continuing.) Mr. Frederick informed me that he was a bootlegger, in the [56] evening here in Mr. Niceley's office in this building.

EXCEPTION No. 6.

Mr. HERRON.—Now, calling your attention to Government's Exhibit No. 1 for Identification, have you ever seen that before?

WITNESS.—I have.

Mr. HERRON.—Where did you first see that?

WITNESS.—In the back of that Chalmers roadster which drove into that garage on T Street in which Mr. Frederick and the other defendants were.

Mr. HERRON.—Did you examine the sack at that time?

Mr. O'DEA.—If the Court please, I renew my objection on the motion to suppress the evidence.

The COURT.—Overruled.

Mr. O'DEA.—EXCEPTION.

(Testimony of Paul A. Emrich.)

Mr. HERRON.—Will you step down, Mr. Emmrich, and look at the contents of that sack and see if it is the same as it was when you discovered it in the back of the automobile?

WITNESS.—(Witness examining.) Yes.

WITNESS.—(Continuing.) There were twelve bottles in it at that time as I remember. The money that was picked up was compared with the numbers that had been previously taken off the money in my presence in this building and they checked absolutely with the numbers of the money that Mr. Niceley had given Mr. Kettle to consummate the sale with.

On cross-examination, the witness testified as follows: As far as my knowledge goes, I don't know anything about Mr. Bigby in this transaction at all. H was not present at the time the machine stopped in the alley or the garage. My knowledge deals with [57] the other two defendants. Mr. Frederick told me he was a bootlegger in this building, in Mr. Niceley's office. I asked him his name and he said he didn't care to give it. He acted in a very sarcastic manner, and I said to him that if he didn't want to give it that we would get it anyway. I told him that didn't help him any, that he was caught, or words to that effect. Then I said, "What is your business"? and he said, "Bootlegging." And he said it in a very sarcastic manner. He did not seem to be joshing about it, he was very serious. In fact, he was very much impressed with the seriousness of the charge. He had not been handcuffed

(Testimony of Paul A. Emrich.)

with Mr. Reyff prior to the time that I had the
conversation with him. He was brought into Mr.
Niceley's office. I did not tell him that anything
he might say would be used against him. I was
merely interested in getting his name as a matter
of record. That was the extent of my conversation
with him. Later on, I heard a conversation between Mr. Frederick and Mr. Niceley. Something
was said about charging Mr. Frederick with conspiracy. It happened right outside of this door-
way here in the hall. Mr. Niceley and myself were
kind of talking about what would be the proper
thing to charge him with and Mr. Niceley said,
"This fellow has got more liquor," and so on like
that, "but he don't want to say where it is." Mr.
Niceley, himself, was talking about the difference
between selling, transportation, possession and conspiracy. He finally stated that he would tell Mr.
Niceley where this liquor was but he didn't want to
have it brought up as an additional charge against
him so he took him over to the garage, and we went
to get that liquor. I am positive that Mr. Niceley
did not get out the law and read it to him. I was
out to Mr. Kettle's house in the afternoon, when
the case of gin was secured. I did not know who
it belonged to and who lived there. After that, I
saw Mr. Kettle in the evening. I knew that Kettle
was not going to receive any consideration because
that is against the rules and regulations of our
[58] department to pay anybody for doing that
kind of work. At the time the automobile came

(Testimony of Paul A. Emrich.)

into the garage that night, Frederick was driving.
I know whose automobile it was. The car was
registered under the name of Frederick. I do not
claim that Mr. Reyff or Mr. Bigby had any interest
in the car whatsoever. Bigby was not in the vicinity that I know of. I know that Mr. Frederick
was handcuffed, but just what time it was, whether
the key had been gotten before he was handcuffed
or · after, I cannot state positively. We had advanced information that there was to be a delivery.
It was to such an extent that we, at least, figured
that probably we had information that the sale
had been consummated at that time. I knew of
my own knowledge that a sale had been consummated at that time because when Mr. Kettle got out
of the car he nodded his head and by that I knew
the sale had been made. I never saw any money
passed. I knew that a sale was completed then—
well, Mr. Frederick had the money there. The
money was found before the car was opened. After
finding the money, as near as I can remember,
Reyff and Frederick were handcuffed together.
While I was searching for the money, Mr. Kettle
was on the far side of the car close to the wall. I
was between Kettle and Frederick and had a flash-
light and held it there. I didn't watch Kettle—I
watched Frederick. I watched Kettle during this
time to see what he did. I could see him just standing there in a very calm manner, not making any
movement of any kind whatsoever. I have been
in this locality before in my official capacity. To

(Testimony of Paul A. Emrich.)
my knowledge, Mr. Kettle, other than this time, has not furnished any information. After the machine entered the place, it took a second or two to find that money. I know positively that Kettle did not throw the money because he was in sight of me and if he made any movement I would have seen it. Reyff did not throw the money there—I say Frederick threw it because I saw a very hasty motion of his hand. Like that (indicating) towards the floor. I said, "Where is that money?" and Stribling came [59] along and picked it up and says, "Here it is."

On redirect examination, the witness testified as follows: The liquor that I referred to on cross-examination—some of it is in the courtroom as I remember. It is those gallon jugs there. I think there are two.

## TESTIMONY OF F. D. STRIBLING, CALLED FOR THE GOVERNMENT.

F. D. STRIBLING, called on behalf of the United States, being sworn, testified as follows:

I am an Internal Revenue chemist, and I also hold a commission and badge as Federal agent. (Here counsel for the parties stipulated that Government's Exhibit No. 1 and No. 2 contain alcohol in excess of one-half of one per cent by volume.)

### EXCEPTION No. 7.

Mr. HERRON.—At this time we offer in evidence Government's Exhibit No. 1 and Government's Exhibit No. 2.

(Testimony of F. D. Stribling.)

Mr. O'DEA.—We object to their introduction on the same ground, if the Court please, that it was an illegal seizure in violation of the defendants' constitutional rights.

The COURT.—Do I understand you wish to offer any evidence in support of your motion outside of the presence of the jury?

Mr. RETALLICK.—We have some authorities we would like to call to your Honor's attention.

The COURT.—I mean on the question of evidence. That would not preclude you from introducing evidence, and I would excuse the jury for that purpose if you so desire. However, with that understanding, I will overrule the objection. [60]

(At the conclusion of the taking of testimony, in the absence of the jury, defendants renewed the objection, which the Court overruled and denied and to which the defendants noted an EXCEPTION.)

WITNESS.—(Continuing.) I saw these defendants in the garage. I don't know the address. There were present Agents Emrich and Niceley and defendants, Frederick and Reyff, and the witness, Kettle, and myself. I have forgotten the exact time. I was under the impression it was something after eight o'clock. Anyhow, it was dark when this car drove in. I went on the right-hand side of the car and Agent Niceley went on the right-hand side of the car and Agent Emrich went on the left-hand side of the car. I got hold of the witness, Kettle, and Agent Niceley caught hold of defendant, Reyff,

(Testimony of F. D. Stribling.)

and Agent Emrich caught hold of Frederick. It was agreed beforehand that I was to go after the money and the witness, Kettle, was to give me the information as to who had the money and as to where it was. Witness Kettle whispered, "Not Reyff," and indicating that defendant, Frederick, had the money. I was still holding to his arm and then went around on that side. That is, on the left-hand side of the car, and reached in the right-hand pocket, as it was my impression that the money was in the right-hand pocket of the defendant but the money was not there. As I was reaching in his right-hand pocket, he pulled the money out of his right hand and it brushed my hand; I then grabbed hold of his arm and I believe my exact words were, "Loose it, loose it," but he didn't want to turn it loose. We struggled there a few minutes and then something was said about the marshal. Then Agent Niceley showed his badge and then he quit struggling; but when he opened his right hand it was empty. Then I looked on the garage floor and the money was there and I had felt the bills in his hands just before that. I picked the bills up. I read off the numbers to Agent Niceley that he had put in his note-book, that were taken from the money before  [61]  it was given to the witness, Kettle, and the numbers corresponded. Then we came to the office occupied by Agent Niceley and I heard Agent Emrich ask the occupation of the defendant, Reyff. He also asked him his name, and the defendant, Reyff, refused to give his name.

(Testimony of F. D. Stribling.)

I believe he said that his occupation was a clerk or something of that kind. The same questions were asked of the defendant, Frederick, and Frederick gave his name and gave his occupation as a bootlegger. Government's Exhibit No. 1, judging from all appearances, is the liquor that was taken from the rear compartment of the Chalmers car. Government's Exhibit No. 2, from all appearances, it is the same.

On cross-examination, the witness testified as follows:

It took me a very short time to find the money after I grabbed hold of the defendant, Frederick. It was a very short time after the two defendants had arrived. Just as long as it would take those things to happen; a much shorter time than it takes to tell about it. I don't think it was more than a minute or possibly two minutes after the time they came in. The lights of the car were on. I couldn't see the money. It was comparatively dark inside of the garage, although the lights of the automobile were turned on. I didn't se the money until after I saw it on the floor. I couln't tell by the feel of the money how much it was. Apparently, it was several bills—I couldn't tell how many. I just judged it to be a roll of money. That's my opinion. I think I could tell at night-time when I put my hand in my pocket, whether or not I have a bill in my pocket or a piece of paper. I don't know as to the grade of the paper but if the paper was the same grade as the bills possibly I couldn't tell.

(Testimony of F. D. Stribling.)

Of course, it would be according to how much the bills had been used and how many hands they had passed through. Everybody knows that there is a difference between the feel of paper and bills. To a certain extent, I was a party to those arrangements whereby this man Kettle was to go and endeavor to purchase [62] this liquor. I heard the arrangements made all right. At the time he was given the money I heard what passed. I was not in Kettle's room when the gin was taken. I heard some general conversation that they had got the liquor in Kettle's room prior to that time, but I didn't know when. I did not hear any statement to the effect that Kettle would have to go and get some evidence to try and save himself. I did not understand that that was the situation from anything I observed that day. I knew that this liquor had been taken from him and I presumed that that had something to do with his going. It was not my impression that he was to receive any money although I don't know of any remarks that gave me that impression. I believe that I had heard that he was a reporter on the newspaper but I had forgotten. It was a presumption on my part I think that the finding of this liquor in his room had something to do with the arrangements that were being made. I didn't know exactly what the arrangements were that had been made.

On redirect examination, the witness testified as follows:

I didn't know anything at all about the arrange-

(Testimony of T. J. Niceley.)

ments, whether there had been any made or had not been. I didn't know that Kettle had been arrested. I knew that they found some stuff in his room. From general conversation I knew that intoxicating liquor had been found there before.

## TESTIMONY OF T. J. NICELEY, FOR THE GOVERNMENT (RECALLED).

T. J. NICELEY, recalled in behalf of the Government, being sworn, testified as follows:

### Direct Examination.

Government's Exhibit No. 1, to which my attention has been called—I examined that sack and its contents at the time of the seizure, in the garage. I opened the sack. I examined the sack [63] and its contents prior to coming into this courtroom. The contents of the sack are the same now as they were then. That sack and its contents has been since the time of its seizure in the garage, in the vault in the United States Marshal's office, under the control of Mr. Shannon. When I examined the bottles a few moments ago they were the same as when they were taken from the machine. Government's Exhibit No. 2 for Identification—I examined that bottle at the time it was seized—I examined it a few moments ago. It is the same now as at the time of the seizure. Subsequent to the evening of the occurrence that I have related, I had a conversation with defendant, Bigby. Mr. Walker, Collector of Internal Revenue, was present. I did not

(Testimony of T. J. Niceley.)

hold out to the defendant any promise of immunity
or hope of reward or make any arrests to induce
him to say anything which he might have said. The
conversation had between myself and him was entirely free and voluntary on that point. That was
after he was arrested; half an hour after he was
arrested. He was not handcuffed at any time. He
was being detained in the office while we completed
this case. In substance, I stated that anything he
said would be used against him in evidence. I told
him, "Harry"—I was joshing him and I said,
"Harry, I have been after you for a long time."
He said, "No, I don't think you have caught me,"
and he started to laughing. I said, "Harry, I
would like to talk to you, but," I says, "you don't
have to talk to me if you don't want to. I cannot
compel you to, but I would like to have a statement
from you in regard to your part in this transaction.
I know what it is, but I would like to have you tell
me," and he said, "I will tell you all about it."
I asked him if he knew this man Kettle and he said,
"No, I don't know him." I asked him if he ever
saw him before, and Mr. Kettle was standing in
the hallway and Mr. Bigby saw him. He said, "I
will tell you, Mr. Niceley, this man came down to
the jewelry store and said to me, "Do you remember
me?" and I told him, "No," I didn't remember
him. He said that he had bought a  [64]  case of
gin from me some time ago, and I said, "You never
bought any gin from me." He said he never
bought any gin from him and that he never sold

(Testimony of T. J. Niceley.)

him any gin and I said, "What did you tell him
at that time?" He said, "He wanted to buy some
gin and I told him I didn't have any gin, and I
told him that maybe I knew where I could get some
whiskey; that he asked him how much he could pay
for it, and this fellow said, "What's the price?"
and he said he would find out. He said he went
in the store and called out Mr. Reyff.

Mr. O'DEA.—We object to anything said about
Mr. Reyff or Mr. Frederick as hearsay.

Mr. HERRON.—I believe Mr. Niceley said he
called out Mr. Reyff.

The WITNESS.— I am relating the conversation
with Mr. Bigby as he told it to me.

Mr. RETALLICK.—Mr. Niceley is not testifying
now, but is narrating a statement that was made
to him, and I think that must be distinctly remembered.

Mr. HERRON.—The witness is relating what
Bigby said he did and only that, what he said he
did, and the ruling was agreeable to the objection,
sustaining it as to any other defendant, advising
the jury that they would consider it only as against
the person speaking and not against any other defendant not present.

The WITNESS.—He said that he then called
Mr. Reyff out of the store and introduced Mr. Reyff
to this man and told this man to make the arrangements with him for the delivery of this whiskey.
He says he didn't know anything about it any

(Testimony of T. J. Niceley.)

further than that; that he had nothing whatever to do with it.

WITNESS.—(Continuing.) I did not at any time place the witness, Kettle, under arrest, and my reason for failing to do so is that I was instructed by the United States District Attorney that I had no case on the ground that I had no proper search-warrant, and I [65] was pretty sore at the United States Attorney because I thought he was wrong.

On cross-examination, the witness testified, as follows:

I didn't know, as a matter of fact, that if Mr. Kettle hadn't had his room visited that day, and hadn't had some gin taken out by myself and the other Prohibition Officers that he wouldn't have been a party to the purchase of any liquor in the transaction. Mr. Kettle hadn't done anything of that kind before. I have already so stated. I think I know why he did it. He knew I was not going to get him into trouble for a violation of the prohibition law, because I told him I couldn't prosecute him. He told me about transporting intoxicating liquor from the San Pablo place to the place where I found it. I don't remember the testimony wherein he testified that he didn't tell me. I did not appeal to Mr. Herron to obtain his judgment as to whether or not there was any case against this man for transporting intoxicating liquor. It would not be a case of transporting against him unless he was caught at it. The only thing I consulted Mr.

(Testimony of T. J. Niceley.)

Herron about was the particular case of gin that was found in his room that day. I told Mr. Kettle at the time—he was leaving at the time—I told him that I could not prosecute him because Mark Herron would not let me. I told him I could not prosecute him because he would not let me prosecute, because I didn't have any search-warrant. I did not tell him I was sore. I first asked him where he got this liquor from—this gin—and he said, "Tom, I don't want to tell you." I said, I know where you got it, but I would like to have you go down and buy a case from this party so that I can prosecute the ones that are violating this law, the man that is selling it." He said he had made arrangements for the delivery of that gin through Mr. Bigby, but he didn't know who the man was that delivered it. At the time I arrested Mr. Bigby, I went out and got Mr. Kettle and took him in the room where Mr. Bigby was, and told Mr. Kettle to tell Mr. Bigby the transaction as [66] he told it and Mr. Kettle did so, standing right in the office here, in Room 8, the Internal Revenue office.

On redirect examination, the witness testified as follows:

I did not appeal the decision of the Assistant United States Attorney with reference to a search-warrant to a higher authority.

(That thereupon Mr. Herron announced, the Government rests, and the following proceedings were had.)

Mr. O'DEA.—May the jury be excluded while we make a motion?

The COURT.—The jury will be excused until ten o'clock to-morrow morning and we will convene at 9:30 and take up the motion.

### EXCEPTION No. 8

(Thereupon, the jury, having been admonished, a recess was had until Friday, November 23, 1923, at 9:30 A. M., and thereafter and on Friday, the 23d day of November, 1923, at 9:30 A. M. in the absence of the jury, the following proceedings were had.)

The COURT.—You may proceed with your motion.

Mr. O'DEA.—The defendants shall renew their motion to exclude all of the evidence which has not been legally obtained, not only the evidence set forth in this petition but as to the five or six additional bottles of liquor found in the automobile that we don't know anything about. Your Honor is doubtless familiar with the cases I have cited here, and these cases are authority for the decision that automobiles are in no different category than any other place that the law requires should be entered with due process of law, and the rules obtaining with respect to searches apply as well to an automobile as they do to private homes, places of business and so forth.

(Then ensued argument by Counsel, after which the following proceedings were had.)   [67]

The COURT.—Mr. O'Dea, however much my Judgment may differ from other decisions, I am prepared to hold that an automobile may be searched without a search-warrant where the officer has reasonable ground to believe it contains contraband, and where the surrounding circumstances are the same as in this case.

Mr. O'DEA.—Then I will submit the motion.

The COURT.—Very well.

Mr. O'DEA.—May I have an exception?

The COURT.—Certainly. In this case I think there are other angles and matters to be considered. Here is a case where the informant, to call him such, had actual knowledge of the sale that was about to be made, because he negotiated it; he made the arrangements, and in accordance with the arrangements he had made for the delivery of the liquor at a place, men appeared in an automobile and informed him that they had the liquor; the money was paid over, and the sale became complete. Now, that man, irrespective of any official character, had the right to make the arrest himself; he had the right to arrest the man. That would be sufficient, in my judgment, to constitute the commission of a misdemeanor, these thing having been done in his presence and with his actual knowledge. That being true, the officers acting upon the full information that all of these things that these men had done and the things that were being done, all the circumstances coinciding, that these men had produced the liquor at that time and they then had the money. I think they were justified in the action they took in arresting the men and seizing the liquor without a search-warrant. That is my position, and the order is made denying the motion, and an exception may be noted.

### EXCEPTION No. 9.

Mr. O'DEA.—The defendants wish to make a motion for a direct verdict on behalf of the defendant, Bigby, on all of the counts set forth in the information, upon the grounds that the  [68] evidence is insufficient to establish any of those offenses. I wish to call your Honor's attention particularly to the last two counts, transportation and possession. There is no evidence here that the defendant, Bigby, transported or possessed that liquor, or had anything to do with the facilitating of the transportation or possession of that liquor. Then I call your Honor's attention to the first count of the information charging him with the selling of that liquor. The only evidence is that he might have committed another misdemeanor set forth in the National Prohibition Law, the giving of information where it may be obtained.

The COURT.—There is in my opinion evidence sufficient to show that he aided in the sale, and under the statute he would be equally guilty. As to the second and third counts, I will hear from the District Attorney on them.

(Argument omitted.)

The COURT.—I will submit the matter to the jury under proper instructions to cover that.

Mr. O'DEA.—May we have an exception, if the Court please?

The COURT.—An exception may be noted.

### EXCEPTION No. 10.

Mr. O'DEA.—Now on behalf of the defendant, Reyff, we desire to ask for a directed verdict of Not Guilty, upon the ground that the evidence is insufficient to convict the defendant, Reyff, of selling the amount of liquor mentioned in the information to the informant, Kettle. From the evidence brought out on the witness-stand very little was said concerning Reyff. Through all of the testimony on the stand by the informant he didn't say that he paid the money to Reyff, and he gave no conversation that he had with Reyff.

The COURT.—Yes, he made the bargain to buy the liquor with Reyff. He made the bargain with him as to how much he had to [69] pay for it, and the time of delivery.

Mr. O'DEA.—We wish to submit the motion. I also desire to move for a directed verdict of not guilty, there being no evidence sufficient to convict the defendant, Reyff, of transportation and possession, because undoubtedly the evidence presented before this Court was that the defendant, Reyff, did not own the automobile, and there is no evidence here that he owned the liquor. He did not have the liquor under his control and did not have the automobile under his control. It is true the evidence showed that he rode with Frederick, but as far as owning the vehicle in which the liquor was transported, or owning the liquor itself, there is no evidence to justify a verdict of guilty. I submit that motion.

The COURT.—The motions will be denied, and you may have your exception.

Mr. O'DEA.—Note an exception.

### EXCEPTION No. 11.

Mr. O'DEA.—Then on behalf of the defendant, Frederick, I wish to ask for a directed verdict of not guilty, upon the ground that the evidence is insufficient to convict him of any charges set forth in the information, particularly upon the ground that all of the evidence received was taken in violation of his constitutional rights; that the liquor seized was taken from his automobile without a search-warrant, and without any crime having been committed in the presence of the officers making the arrest, and there was no warrant for the arrest of the defendant, Frederick. I submit that motion.

The COURT.—The motion will be denied.

Mr. O'DEA.—Exception.

(Thereafter, and 10:05 A. M. on said day, the jury came into  [70]  court and the following proceedings were had:)

Mr. RETALLICK.—May I ask the privilege of the Court to recall Mr. Niceley to examine him as to matters previously gone into already in this trial?

## TESTIMONY OF T. J. NICELEY, FOR THE GOVERNMENT (RECALLED FOR FURTHER CROSS-EXAMINATION).

T. J. NICELEY, recalled for further cross-examination by the defendants, testified as follows:

During my discussion with Mr. Kettle, I had a conversation with him relating to the payment of money for his services in this case. The conversation was had some short time before he left Fresno. I don't know just when it was. I told Mr. Kettle that if I could get money from a certain organization here in Fresno, that I would pay him $50.00. I recollect seeing an account in the newspaper. I remember at the time there were certain matters published in the "Fresno Bee" in connection with this case and in connection with Mr. Kettle's connection with it. Mr. Kettle did not advance any of the money that was used for the purpose of purchasing the liquor. On the morning of the 17th day of May, the day following the occurrence of this offense, I had a conversation with the reporter of the "Bee," whose name I do not know, with reference to this particular case particularly with reference to Mr. Kettle's participation in it. I do not know who was the reporter from the "Bee." It was somebody talking to me over the telephone. I don't know exactly what time of the day it was. To my best recollection it was the day following after this arrest. At the time I was in my office. I did not, at that time and place, tell the reporter that Kettle was a "stoolie" in the case, that was

(Testimony of T. J. Niceley.)

getting paid by the Government for his work. The "Fresno Bee" never quoted me correctly since it has been in Fresno. At that time and place, I stated that I would recommend that Mr. Kettle be paid $50.00 but that this would  [71]  only be re-imbursing him for the money that I said Kettle ac-tually paid out. I told them a lot of other things that I didn't think was any of their business and had nothing to do with the case. At that time and place I told this agent of the "Bee" that Kettle had worked with other Prohibition agents here, but it was not true—I did it for a purpose. I told them that for all I knew Kettle might have obtained the gin by arrangements with other agents for the purchase of the gin. I never told them that the gin was bootleg. The statement given to the re-porter of the "Fresno Bee" at the time was given by me in my own way, and was given for the pur-pose of stopping the reporters from monkeying with the affairs of my office. They insisted on com-ing into my office and wanting to know all about the case, and how it happened, and so forth, and I sim-ply told them that so they would let me alone. Mr. Kettle was never paid before he left here for his services in this case. I told him if I could get cer-tain people to raise the money that I would pay him $50, but he has never received a ten-cent piece.

On redirect examination, the witness testified as follows: The conversation was had with reference to the $50 after the transaction occurred. I never made any offer to Kettle at all. I simply asked him

(Testimony of T. J. Niceley.)

if he would go down and get the liquor so I could get the man who was selling the liquor. I never considered that the newspapers were entitled to know all of my business in connection with the enforcement of the law by my office. I have never considered it any of their business, especially the "Fresno Bee," which is a "wet" paper.

On recross-examination, the witness testified as follows: The talk about the $50 to Mr. Kettle was long prior to the time that this case came up for trial. It was just before he left Fresno, but I don't know just when. Kettle was never in custody to my knowledge. I do not know whether he will get the $50 or not. He won't get it unless the organizations I have in mind get the money. [72] If they do I will be very glad to give it to Mr. Kettle for what he has done in this case.

(That thereupon the following proceedings were had:)

### EXCEPTION No. 12.

Mr. RETALLICK.—We desire, if your Honor please, to renew certain motions heretofore made, out of the presence of the jury.

The COURT.—You simply wish to renew the motions that have heretofore been made?

Mr. O'DEA.—Yes, your Honor, just for the purpose of the record.

The COURT.—If you can, without disclosing them to the jury, you may state your motions into the record.

Mr. O'DEA.—We renew the motions that were made before the jury was present this morning.

Mr. RETALLICK.—Is it stipulated that that is sufficient?

Mr. HERRON.—Yes.

The COURT.—The motions may now appear in the same form as when made this morning, and the order denying the same, and the exception shown.

Mr. O'DEA.—Is that your case?

Mr. HERRON.—We concluded our case yesterday.

Mr. O'DEA.—That is our case, your Honor. The defendants rest.

(That thereupon counsel proceeded to argue the case, at the conclusion of which the Court instructed the jury and thereupon, at ————— the jury retired and ————— returned into the court with a verdict finding the defendant, Reyff, guilty of all the counts set forth in the information; the defendant, Frederick, guilty of all the counts set forth in the information, and the [73] defendant, Bigby, guilty of the charge set forth in Count I of the information and not guilty under Counts II and *II* of said information.)

(Thereupon the Court continued said case to the 26th day of November, 1923, for judgment. That, thereafter and on the 26th day of November, 1923, the day set by the Court for the pronouncement of sentence upon the defendants, the defendants were called to the bar of the Court to show and asked to show cause, if they had any, why sentence should not be pronounced upon them according to law. Thereupon, the attorneys for the defendants presented to the Court a motion for a new trial, which motion for a new trial is in words and figures following, to wit:

"Now come 'Louis H. Reyff, E. W. Frederick and Harry Bigby, defendants in the above-entitled cause, and by Edward A. O'Dea and R. G. Retallick, their attorneys, move the Court to set aside the verdict rendered herein and to grant a new trial of said cause and for reasons therefor show to the Court the following:

### I.

That the verdicts in said cause are contrary to law.

### II.

That the verdicts in said cause were not supported by the evidence in the case.

### III.

That the evidence in said cause is insufficient to justify any of said verdicts.

### IV.

That the Court erred upon the trial of said cause in deciding questions of law arising during the course of the trial, to which errors exceptions were duly taken.

### V.

That said Court upon the trial of said cause admitted incompetent [74] evidence offered by the United States of America.

### VI.

That the Court improperly instructed the jury to the defendants' prejudice.

Dated at Fresno, California, this 26th day of November, 1923.

> E. W. FREDERICK,
> LOUIS H. REYFF,
> HARRY BIGBY,
> > Defendants.
> EDWARD A. O'DEA,
> R. G. RETALLICK,
> Attorneys for Defendants.

[Endorsed]: Filed November 26, 1923. Chas. N. Williams, Clerk. Murray E. Wire, Deputy Clerk.

Due service of the within motion for a new trial is hereby admitted this 26th day of Nov. 1923.

> UNITED STATES ATTORNEY.
> By EUGENE T. McGANN,
> Special Assistant United States Attorney.

EXCEPTION No. 13.

Said motion for a new trial was argued by R. G. Retallick, Esq., one of the attorneys for the defendants and was submitted to the Court for its decision and after due consideration the Court denied the motion for a new trial and the defendants then and there duly and regularly EXCEPTED. [75]

Thereafter, on the same day, R. G. Retallick, Esq., one of the attorneys for the defendants, presented to the Court a motion in arrest of judgment which motion was in the words and figures following, to wit:

"Now come the defendants, Louis H. Reyff, E. W. Frederick and Harry Bigby, and respectfully

move the Court to arrest and withhold judgment
in the above-entitled cause and that the verdicts or
verdict of conviction of said defendants heretofore
given and made in the said cause be vacated and set
aside and declared to be null and void for each of
the following causes and reasons:

### I.

That it appears on the face of the record that no
judgment can legally be entered against these defendants, or any or either of them for the following reasons:

1. That Count One of the Information filed
herein does not charge or state facts sufficient to
constitute a public offense under the laws of the
United States against the defendants or any or
either of them.

2. That Count Two of the Information filed
herein does not charge or state facts sufficient to
constitute a public offense under the laws of the
United States against the defendants or any or
either of them.

3. That Count Three of the Information filed
herein does not charge or state facts sufficient to
constitute a public offense under the laws of the
United States against the defendants or any or
either of them.

### II.

That this Court has no jurisdiction to pass judgment upon the defendants or either of them by
reason of the fact that Counts I, II and *II* of the
Information on file herein do not state public offenses under the laws of the United States.

WHEREFORE, by reason of the premises the defendants pray [76] this Honorable Court that the judgment herein be arrested and withheld and that the conviction of the defendants and each of them be declared null and void.

Dated at Fresno, California, this 26th day of November, 1923.

E. W. FREDERICK,

LOUIS H. REYFF,

HARRY BIGBY,

Defendants.

EDWARD A. O'DEA and

R. G. RETALLICK,

Attorneys for Defendants."

[Endorsed]: Filed November 26, 1923. Chas. N. Williams, Clerk. Murray E. Wire, Deputy Clerk.

Due service of the within motion in arrest of judgment is hereby admitted this 26th day of Nov. 1923.

UNITED STATES ATTORNEY.

By EUGENE T. McGANN,

Special Assistant United States Attorney.

EXCEPTION No. 14.

Said motion in arrest of judgment was argued by R. G. Retallick, Esq., one of the attorneys for the defendants, and was submitted to the Court for its decision and after due consideration, the Court denied the motion in arrest of judgment and the defendants then and there duly and regularly EXCEPTED.

And thereupon the Court rendered its judgments and sentences upon the defendants and granted to said defendants time in which to [77] lodge and settle their bill of exceptions. Said time was granted and was extended by the stipulation of the parties and orders of the Court to and including the 26th day of January, 1924.

Said defendants hereby present the foregoing as their bill of exceptions herein and respectfully ask that the same be allowed, signed and sealed and made a part of the record in this case.

Dated this 28th day of December, 1923.

> EDWARD A. O'DEA,
> RICHARD G. RETALLICK,
> Attorneys for Defendants. [78]

---

In the District Court of the United States for the Southern District of California, Northern Division.

## No. 821—CRIMINAL.

UNITED STATES OF AMERICA,

Plaintiff,

vs.

LOUIS H. REYFF, E. W. FREDERICK and HARRY BIGBY,

Defendants.

## NOTICE OF PRESENTATION OF BILL OF EXCEPTIONS.

To Joseph Burke, Esq., United States Attorney, and to Mark Herron, Esq., and E. T. McGann, Esq., Assistant United States Attorneys:

You will please take notice that the foregoing

constitutes and is the proposed bill of exceptions of the defendants in the above-entitled cause, and the said defendants will apply to the said Court to allow said bill of exceptions and to sign and seal the same as the bill of exceptions herein.

> EDWARD A. O'DEA,
> RICHARD G. RETALLICK,
> Attorneys for Defendants.    [79]

---

In the District Court of the United States for the Southern District of California, Northern Division.

### No. 821—CRIMINAL.

UNITED STATES OF AMERICA,

> Plaintiff,

vs.

LOUIS H. REYFF, E. W. FREDERICK and HARRY BIGBY,

> Defendants.

### STIPULATION RE BILL OF EXCEPTIONS.

It is hereby stipulated and agreed that the foregoing bill of exceptions is correct and that the same may be signed, settled, allowed and sealed by the Court.

Dated this 19th day of January, 1924.

> EUGENE T. McGANN,
> Spec. Asst. United States Attorney.
> EDWARD A. O'DEA,
> RICHARD G. RETALLICK,
> Attorneys for Defendants.    [80]

In the District Court of the United States for the Southern District of California, Northern Division.

No. 821—CRIMINAL.

UNITED STATES OF AMERICA,

Plaintiff,

vs.

LOUIS H. REYFF, E. W. FREDERICK and HARRY BIGBY,

Defendants.

ORDER SETTLING BILL OF EXCEPTIONS.

This bill of exceptions having been duly presented to the Court within the time allowed by law and the rules of the Court and within the time extended by the Court by orders duly and regularly made is now signed, sealed and made a part of the records in this case and is allowed as correct.

Dated this 19th day of January, 1924.

WM. P. JAMES,

United States District Judge.

[Endorsed]: No. 821—Criminal. In the District Court of the United States for the Southern District of California, Northern Division. United States of America, Plaintiff, vs. Louis H. Reyff, E. W. Frederick and Harry Bigby, Defendants. Engrossed Bill of Exceptions. Filed Jan. 19, 1924, at —— min. past —— o'clock — M. Chas. N. Williams, Clerk. G. F. Gibson, Deputy. R. G. Retallick, Fresno and Edward A. O'Dea, Attorneys for

Defendants, 826–28–30 Phelan Building, Telephone
Sutter 276, San Francisco.   [81]

---

In the District Court of the United States, in and
for the Southern District of California, Northern Division.

No. 821—CRIMINAL.

UNITED STATES OF AMERICA,

Plaintiff,

vs.

E. W. FREDERICK,

Defendant.

BOND ON WRIT OF ERROR (E. W. FRED-
ERICK).

KNOW ALL MEN BY THESE PRESENTS:
That I, E. W. Frederick, of the County of Fresno,
State of California, as principal, and Aram Joseph
and A. S. Shaddow, of the County of Fresno, State
of California, as sureties, are held and firmly bound
unto the United States of America in the full and
just sum of Five Thousand ($5,000.00) Dollars, to
be paid to the United States of America, to which
payment well and truly to be made we bind ourselves, our heirs, executors, and administrators,
jointly and severally by these presents.

Sealed with our seals and dated this 29th day of
November, in the year of our Lord one thousand
nine hundred and twenty-three.

WHEREAS, lately on the 26th day of November, 1923, at the November term of District Court of the United States for the Southern District of California, Northern Division, in a cause pending in said court, between the United States of America, plaintiff, and E. W. Frederick, Louis H. Reyff, and Harry Bigby, defendants, a judgment and sentence was rendered and entered against said E. W. Frederick, Louis H. Reyff, and Harry Bigby, and whereas said defendants thereafter obtained a writ of eror directed to the United States of America and the United States Attorney for the Southern District of California before the United States Circuit Court of Appeals for the Ninth Circuit, to reverse the judgment and sentence in the aforesaid suit, and a citation directed to the said United States of America, and to the United States attorney for the Southern District of California, citing and [82] admonishing the United States of America and said United States attorney to be and appear in the United States Circuit Court of Appeals for the Ninth Circuit, at San Francisco, California, pursuant to the terms and at the time fixed in said citation, which citation has been fully served.

WHEREAS the said E. W. Frederick has been admitted to bail pending decision upon said writ of error in the sum of Five Thousand ($5,000.00) Dollars.

NOW, THEREFORE, the condition of said obligation is such that if the said E. W. Frederick shall appear either in person or by his attorney in the United States Circuit Court of Appeals for the Ninth Circuit when said cause is reached for argument or when required by law or by the rule of said court and from day to day thereafter in said court until said cause shall be finally disposed of and shall abide by and obey the judgment and orders made by the said Court of Appeals in said cause and shall surrender himself in execution of the judgment and sentence appealed from as said Court may direct, if the judgment and sentence against him shall be affirmed by said United States Circuit Court of Appeals and if the said E. W. Frederick shall appear for trial in the District Court of the United States for the Southern District of California, Northern Division, on such day or days as may be appointed for a retrial of said cause by said District Court and abide by and obey all orders made by said District Court, provided the judgment and sentence against him shall be reversed by the said Court of Appeals, then the obligation to be void; otherwise to remain in full force, virtue and effect.

E. W. FREDERICK,
Principal.

ARAM JOSEPH,
Surety.

A. S. SHADDOW,
Sureties.

————————————,
Sureties.

Signed, sealed and acknowledged before me this the 29th day of November, 1923.

[Seal] SAMUEL F. HOLLINS,

U. S. Commissioner. [83]

United States of America,

Southern District of California,—ss.

Aram Joseph, whose name is subscribed to the foregoing undertaking as one of the sureties thereof, being first duly sworn, deposes and says:

That I am a householder in said district and reside at 427 Fulton Street in the City of Fresno, County of Fresno, State of California, and my occupation, a fruit broker.

That I am worth the sum of $5,000.00, the sum in said undertaking specified as the penalty thereof, over and above all my debts and liabilities and exclusive of property exempt from execution and that my property now standing of record in my name is as follows:

Real Property:

Lots 10, 11 and 11½ in Block 5, of the City of Fresno, County of Fresno, State of California. Value $12,000.00 Mtges., $2,900.00.

27½ acres vineyard in Woodlake District, Tulare County, California. Value $12,000.00, free and clear.

Personal Property:

$3,200 Liberty bonds.

$8,000.00 secured and unsecured notes.

That my total net assets, above all liabilities and obligations on other bonds, is the sum of $32,000.00.

That I am surety upon no outstanding penal bonds (made within one year from date); now in force, aggregating Total Penalty: $ none.

ARAM JOSEPH.

Subscribed and sworn to before me this 29th day of November, 1923.

[Seal]     SAMUEL F. HOLLINS,
United States Commissioner for the Southern District of California.   [84]

United States of America,
Southern District of California,—ss.

A. S. Shaddow, whose name is subscribed to the foregoing undertaking as one of the sureties thereof, being first duly sworn, deposes and says:

That I am a householder in said district and reside at 801 Vassar Street in the City of Fresno, County of Fresno, State of California, and am by occupation a merchant.

That I am worth the sum of $5,000.00 *Dollars,* the sum in said undertaking specified as the penalty thereof, over and above all my debts and liabilities and exclusive of property exempt from execution and that my property, now standing of record in my name, consists as follows:

Real Estate, described as follows, to wit:

A contract interest or equity 40-acre vineyard being E. ½ of the W. ½ of the SW. ¼ of Section 21, Township Fourteen South, Range 20 East, M. D. B. & M. Valued at $31,000.00. Encumbrances, $14,800.00.

A contract interest in 40-acre vineyard in Madera

County, being the NE. 1/4 of the SE. 1/4 of Section 36, T. 12 South, Range 17 East, M. D. B. & M. Valued at $40,000.00. Encumbrances, $11,250.00.

Lot 75x100 feet on the NE. corner of Belmont and Yosemite Avenues in the City of Fresno. Valued at $5,500.00. Mtge. $1,500.00.

Lot on the SW. corner of Dean and Butler Avenues in the City of Fresno, valued at $1,000.00. No mortgages.

5-acre ranch at Kerman, California. Valued at $1500.00. Free and clear.

2-acre fig orchard in the Forkner Fig Gardens. Valued at $2500.00. Encumbrances, $1,000.00.

Personal Property:

Net value of jewelry store at Mariposa and Fulton Streets in Fresno, California, together with fixtures and lease, $50,000.00, all standing in my name.

That my total net assets, above all liabilities and obligations [85] on other bonds, is the sum of $86,200.00; that I am surety upon six outstanding penal bonds (made within one year from date, these bonds) now in force, aggregating total penalty of $15,750.00.

A. S. SHADDOW.

Subscribed and sworn to before me this 29th day of November, 1923.

[Seal]          SAMUEL F. HOLLINS,
United States Commissioner. [86]

Examined and recommended for approval as provided in Rule No. 29.

R. G. RETALLICK,<br>Attorney for Defendants.

I hereby approve the foregoing bond this the 30th day of November, 1923.

WM. P. JAMES,

Judge.

I hereby approve the foregoing bond as to form.

JOSEPH C. BURKE,

United States Attorney.

MARK L. HERRON,

Asst. U. S. Attorney.

[Endorsed]: No. 821—Criminal. In the District Court of the United States, in and for the Southern District of California, Northern Division. United States of America, Plaintiff, vs. E. W. Frederick, Defendants. Bond to Appear on Writ of Error. Filed Nov. 30, 1923, at —— min. past —— o'clock — M. Chas. N. Williams, Clerk. Louis J. Somers, Deputy. R. G. Retallick, 531 Brix Bldg., Fresno, Cal. [87]

———

In the District Court of the United States in and for the Southern District of California, Northern Division.

No. 821.

UNITED STATES OF AMERICA,

Plaintiff,

vs.

LOUIS H. REYFF,

Defendant.

## BOND ON WRIT OF ERROR (HARRY BIGBY).

KNOW ALL MEN BY THESE PRESENTS: That I, Louis H. Reyff, of the County of Fresno, State of California, as principal, and A. S. Shaddow and J. D. Wirt, of the County of Fresno, State of California, as sureties, are held and firmly bound unto the United States of America in the full and just sum of Five Thousand ($5000.00) Dollars, to be paid to the United States of America, to which payment well and truly to be made we bind ourselves, our heirs, executors, and administrators, jointly and severally by these presents.

Sealed with our seals and dated this 29th day of November, in the year of our Lord one thousand nine hundred and twenty-three.

WHEREAS, lately on the 26th day of November, 1923, at the November term of District Court of the United States for the Southern District of California, Northern Division, in a cause pending in said court, between the United States of America, Plaintiff, and Louis H. Reyff, E. W. Frederick and Harry Bigby defendants, a judgment and sentence was rendered and entered against said Louis H. Reyff, E. W. Frederick and Harry Bigby, and whereas said defendants thereafter obtained a writ of error directed to the United States of America and the United States Attorney for the Southern District of California before the United States Circuit Court of Appeals for the Ninth Circuit, to reverse the judgment and sentence in the afore-

said suit, and a citation directed to the said *America*
and to the United States Attorney for the Southern
District of California citing and  [88]   admonishing the United States of America and said United
States Attorney to be and appear in the United
States Circuit Court of Appeals for the Ninth
Circuit, at San Francisco, California, pursuant to
the terms and at the time fixed in said citation
which citation has been fully served.

WHEREAS, the said Harry Bigby has been
admitted to bail pending decision upon said writ of
error in the sum of Five Thousand ($5000.00)
Dollars.

NOW, THEREFORE, the condition of said obligation is such that if the said Harry Bigby shall appear either in person or by his attorneys in the
United States Circuit Court of Appeals for the Ninth
Circuit when said case is reached for argument or
when required by law or by rule of said court
and from day to day thereafter in said court until
said cause shall be finally disposed of and shall abide
by and obey the judgment and orders made by the
said Court of Appeals in said cause and shall surrender himself in execution of the judgment and
sentence appealed from as said Court may direct,
if the judgment and sentence against him shall be
affirmed by said United States Circuit Court of
Appeals and if the said Harry Bigby shall appear
for trial in the District Court of the United States
for the Southern District of California, Northern
Division, on such day or days as may be appointed
for a retrial of said cause by said District Court,
provided the judgment and sentence against him

shall be reversed by the said Court of Appeals, then the obligation to be void; otherwise to remain in full force, virtue and effect.

LOUIS H. REYFF,
Principal.

A. S. SHADDOW,
Sureties.

J. D. WIRT,
Sureties.

Signed, sealed and acknowledged before me this the 29th day of November, 1923.

[Seal] SAMUEL F. HOLLINS,
U. S. Commissioner. [89]

United States of America,
Southern District of California,—ss.

A. S. Shaddow, whose name is subscribed to the foregoing undertaking as one of the sureties thereof, being first duly sworn, deposes and says:

That I am a householder in said district and reside at 801 Vassar Street in the City of Fresno, County of Fresno, State of California, and am by occupation a merchant.

That I am worth the sum of $5,000.00 *Dollars,* the sum in said undertaking specified as the penalty thereof, over and above all my debts and liabilities and exclusive of property exempt from execution and that my property, now standing of record in my name consists as follows:

Real Estate, described as follows, to wit:

A contract interest or equity 40 acre vineyard being E. ½ of the W. ½ of the SW. ¼ of Section 21, Township Fourteen South, Range 20 East M. D. B.

& M. Valued at $31,000.00. Encumbrances, $14,-800.00.

A contract interest in 40 acre vineyard in Madera County, being the NE. ¼ of the SE. ¼ of Section 36, T. 12 South, Range 17 East, M. D. B. & M. Valued at $40,000.00. Encumbrances, $11,250.00.

Lot 75x100 feet on the NE. corner of Belmont and Yosemite Avenues in the City of Fresno. Valued at $5500.00. Mtge. $1500.00.

Lot on the SW. corner of Dean and Butler Avenues in the City of Fresno. Valued at $1,000.00. No mortgages.

5 acre ranch at Kerman, California. Valued at $1500.00. Free and clear.

2 acre fig orchard in the Forkner Fig Gardens. Valued at $2,500.00. Encumbrances, $1000.00.

Personal Property:

Net value of jewelry store at Mariposa and Fulton Street in Fresno, California, together with fixtures and lease $50,000.00, all standing in my name.

That my total net assets, above all liabilities and obligations [90] on other bonds, is the sum of $86,200, that I am surety upon six outstanding penal bonds (made within one year from date these bonds) now in force, aggregating total penalty of $15,750.

A. S. SHADDOW.

Subscribed and sworn to before me this 29th day of November, 1923.

[Seal]  SAMUEL F. HOLLINS,
United States Commissioner. [91]

United States of America,
Southern District of California,—ss.

J. D. Wirt, whose name is subscribed to the fore-going undertaking as one of the sureties thereof, being first duly sworn, deposes and says:

That I am a householder in said district and reside at 3435 Palm Avenue, City of Fresno, County of Fresno, State of California, and by occupation a merchant.

That I am worth the sum of $5,000.00 *Dollars,* the sum in said undertaking specified as the penalty thereof, over and above all my debts and liabilities and exclusive of property exempt from execution and that my property, now standing of record in my name, consists in part as follows:

Real Estate, described as follows, to wit:

Lot No. Six (6) of Montpellier Tract, in the City of Fresno, County of Fresno, State of California. Valued at $20,000.00. Encumbrances of $5,000.00.

½ interest in lot eighty-six of West Fresno Tract of the City of Fresno, County of Fresno, State of California. Valued at $6,000.00 and encumbered to the amount of $1500.00. Value of equity $2250.00.

$1500 contract equity in house at 1235 Harrison Street in the City of Fresno, County of Fresno, State of California.

Personal Property:

¼ interest in the Samuel's Cigar Store of Fresno California, a copartnership. Interest valued at $20,000.00.

That my total net assets, above all liabilities and obligations on other bonds, is the sum of $22,600.00. That I am surety upon 6 outstanding penal bonds (made within one year from date) now in force, aggregating Total Penalty, $20,750.00.

J. D. WIRT.

Subscribed and sworn to before me this 29th day of November.

[Seal] SAMUEL F. HOLLINS,
United States Commissioner for the Southern District of California.    [92]

Examined and recommended for approval as provided in Rule No. 29.

R. G. RETALLICK,
Attorney for Defendants.

I hereby approve the foregoing bond this the 30th day of November, 1923.

WM. P. JAMES,
Judge.

I hereby approve the foregoing bond as to form.

JOSEPH C. BURKE,
United States Attorney
MARK L. HERRON,
Asst. U. S. Attorney.

[Endorsed]: 821—Criminal. In the District Court of the United States, in and for the Southern District of California, Northern Division. United States of America, Plaintiff, vs. Harry Bigby, Defendants. Bond to Appear on Writ of Error. Filed Nov. 30, 1923, at —— min. past —— o'clock

— M. Chas. N. Williams, Clerk. Louis J. Somers, Deputy. R. G. Retallick, 531 Brix Bldg., Fresno, Cal. [93]

———

In the District Court of the United States in and for the Southern District of California, Northern Division.

No. 821.

UNITED STATES OF AMERICA,

Plaintiff,

vs.

HARRY BIGBY,

Defendant.

BOND ON WRIT OF ERROR (LOUIS H. REYFF).

KNOW ALL MEN BY THESE PRESENTS: That I, Harry Bigby, of the County of Fresno, State of California, as principal, and A. S. Shaddow and J. D. Wirt, of the County of Fresno, State of California, as sureties, are held and firmly bound unto the United States of America in the full and just sum of Five Thousand ($5000.00) Dollars, to be paid to the United States of America, to which payment well and truly to be made we bind ourselves, our heirs, executors, and administrators, jointly and severally by these presents.

Sealed with our seals and dated this 29th day of November, in the year of our Lord one thousand nine hundred and twenty-three.

WHEREAS, lately on the 26th day of November, 1923, at the November term of District Court of the United States for the Southern District of California, Northern Division, in a cause pending in said Court, between the United States of America, Plaintiff, and Harry Bigby, E. W. Frederick, and Louis H. Reyff, Defendants, a judgment and sentence was rendered and entered against said Harry Bigby, E. W. Frederick, Louis H. Reyff, and whereas said defendants thereafter obtained a writ of error directed to the United States of America and the United States Attorney for the Southern District of California before the United States Circuit Court of Appeals for the Ninth Circuit to reverse the judgment and sentence in the aforesaid suit, and a citation directed to the said United States *of United States* of America and to the United States Attorney for the Southern District of California citing and [94] admonishing the United States of America and the said United States Attorney to be and appear in the United States Circuit Court of Appeals for the Ninth Circuit, at San Francisco, California, pursuant to the terms and at the time fixed in said citation, which citation has been fully served.

WHEREAS the said Louis H. Reyff has been admitted to bail pending decision upon said writ of error in the sum of Five Thousand ($5000.00) Dollars.

NOW, THEREFORE, the condition of said obligation is such that if the said Louis H. Reyff shall appear either in person or by his attorneys in the

United States Circuit Court of Appeals for the
Ninth Circuit when said cause is reached for argument or when required by law or by rule of said
court and from day to day thereafter in said court
until said cause shall be finally disposed of, and
shall abide by and obey the judgment and orders
made by said Court of Appeals in said cause and
shall surrender himself in execution of the judgment and sentence appealed from as said Court may
direct, if the judgment and sentence against him
shall be affirmed by said United States Circuit
Court of Appeals and if said Louis H. Reyff shall
appear for trial in the District Court of the United
States for the Southern District of California,
Northern Division, on such day or days as may be
appointed for a retrial of said cause by said District Court and abide by and obey all orders made by
said District Court, provided the judgment and sentence against him shall be reversed by the said
Court of Appeals, then the obligation to be void;
otherwise to remain in full force, virtue and effect.

HARRY BIGBY,

Principal.

A. S. SHADDOW,

Sureties.

J. D. WIRT,

Sureties.

Signed, sealed and acknowledged before me this
the 29th day of November, 1923.

[Seal]     SAMUEL F. HOLLINS,

U. S. Commissioner.   [95]

United States of America,

Southern District of California,—ss.

A. S. Shaddow, whose name is subscribed to the foregoing undertaking as one of the sureties thereof, being first duly sworn, deposes and says:

That I am a householder in said district and reside at 801 Vassar Street in the City of Fresno, County of Fresno, State of California, and am by occupation a merchant.

That I am worth the sum of $5000.00 *Dollars,* the sum in said undertaking specified as the penalty thereof, over and above all my debts and liabilities and exclusive of property exempt from execution and that my property, now standing of record in my name, consists as follows:

Real Estate, described as follows, to wit:

A contract interest or equity 40 acre vineyard being E. ½ of the W. ½ of the SW. ¼ of Section 21, Township Fourteen South, Range 20 East, M. D. B. & M. Valued at $31,000.00. Encumbrances, $14,-800.00.

A contract interest in 40 acre vineyard in Madera County, being the NE. ¼ of the SE. ¼ of Section 36, T. 12 South, Range 17 East, M. D. B. & M.. Valued at $40,000.00. Encumbrances, $11,250.00.

Lot 75x100 feet on the NE. corner of Belmont and Yosemite Avenues in the City of Fresno. Valued at $5500.00. Mtge. $1500.00.

Lot on the SW. corner of Dean and Butler Avenues in the City of Fresno. Valued at $1,000.00, No mortgages.

5 acre ranch at Kerman, California. Valued at $1,500.00. Free and clear.

2 acre fig orchard in the Forkner Fig Gardens. Valued at $2,500.00. Encumbrances, $1,000.00.

Personal Property:

Net value of jewelry store at Mariposa and Fulton Street in Fresno, California, together with fixtures and lease, $50,000.00, all standing in my name.

That my total net assets, above all liabilities and obligations [96] on other bonds, is the sum of $86,200.00, that I am surety upon six outstanding penal bonds (made within one year from *date these* bonds) now in force, aggregating total penalty of $15,750.00.

A. S. SHADDOW.

Subscribed and sworn before me this 29th day of November, 1923.

[Seal] SAMUEL F. HOLLINS,
United States Commissioner. [97]

United States of America,
Southern District of California,—ss.

J. D. Wirt, whose name is subscribed to the foregoing undertaking as one of the sureties thereof, being first duly sworn, deposes and says:

That I am a householder in said district and reside at 3435 Palm Avenue, City of Fresno, County of Fresno, State of California, and by occupation a merchant.

That I am worth the sum of $5,000.00 *Dollars,* the sum in said undertaking specified as the penalty thereof, over and above all my debts and liabilities and exclusive of property exempt from execution and that my property, now standing of record in my name, consists in part as follows:

Real estate, described as follows, to wit:

Lot No. Six (6) of Montpellier Tract, in the City of Fresno, County of Fresno, State of California, Valued at $20,000.00. Encumbrances of $5,000.00.

½-interest in lot eighty-six of West Fresno Tract of the City of Fresno, County of Fresno, State of California. Valued at $6,000.00 and encumbered to the amount of $1,500.00. Value of equity, $2,250.00.

$1,500 contract equity in house at 1235 Harrison Street, in the City of Fresno, County of Fresno, State of California.

Personal Property:

¼-interest in the Samuel's Cigar Store of Fresno, California, a copartnership, interest valued at $20,-000.00.

That my total net assets, above all liabilities and obligations on other bonds, is the sum of $22,600.00. That I am surety upon 6 outstanding penal bonds (made within one year from date) now in force, aggregating Total Penalty, $20,750.00.

J. D. WIRT.

Subscribed and sworn to before me this 29th day of November.

[Seal]     SAMUEL F. HOLLINS,

United States Commissioner for the Southern District of California. [98]

Examined and recommended for approval as provided in Rule No. 29.

R. G. RETALLICK,<br>Attorney for Defendants.

I hereby approve the foregoing bond this the 30th day of November, 1923.

> WM. P. JAMES,
>> Judge.

I hereby approve the foregoing bond as to form.

> JOSEPH C. BURKE,
>> United States Attorney.
> MARK L. HERRON,
>> Asst. U. S. Attorney.

[Endorsed]: No. 821—Criminal. In the District Court of the United States, in and for the Southern District of California, Northern Division. United States of America, Plaintiff, vs. Louis H. Reyff, Defendants. Bond to Appear on Writ of Error. Filed Nov. 30, 1923, at —— min. past —— o'clock. — M. Chas. N. Williams, Clerk, Louis J. Somers, Deputy. R. G. Retallick, 531 Brix Bldg., Fresno, Cal. [99]

---

In the District Court of the United States, in and for the Southern District of California, Northern Division.

## No. 821—CRIMINAL.

UNITED STATES OF AMERICA,

> Plaintiff,

vs.

LOUIS H. REYFF, E. W. FRERERICK and HARRY BIGBY,

> Defendants.

COST BOND ON APPEAL (HARRY BIGBY).

KNOW ALL MEN BY THESE PRESENTS:
That we, E. W. Frederick, as principal, and J. D.
Wirt, of Fresno, Fresno County, California, and
A. S. Shaddow, of Fresno, Fresno County, California, as sureties, are firmly bound unto the United
States of America in the full and just sum of Two
Hundred and Fifty ($250.00) Dollars to be paid
to the said United States of America, to which payment well and truly to be made, we bind ourselves,
our heirs, executors and administrators, jointly
and severally, by these presents.

Sealed with our seals and dated this 29th day of
November, in the year of our Lord one thousand
nine hundred and twenty-three.

WHEREAS, lately, on the 26th day of Novem-
ber, 1923, at the November term of the District
Court of the United States, for the Southern
District of California, Northern Division, in a
cause pending in said court between the United
States of America, plaintiff, and Louis H. Reyff,
E. W. Frederick and Harry Bigby, defendants, a
judgment and sentence were rendered against the
said Louis H. Reyff, E. W. Frederick and Harry
Bigby, and whereas, said Louis H. Reyff, E. W.
Frederick and Harry Bigby, thereafter obtained
a writ of error directed to the said United States
of America and the United States Attorney for the
Southern District of California before the United
States Circuit Court of Appeals, [100] for the
Ninth Circuit, to reverse the judgments and sen-

tences in the aforesaid suit, and a citation directed to the said United States of America and to the United States Attorney, for the Southern District of California, citing and admonishing the United States of America and the said United States Attorney to be and appear in the United States Circuit Court of Appeals for the Ninth Circuit, at San Francisco, California, pursuant to the terms and at the time fixed in said citation;

Now, the condition of the above obligation is such that if the said Harry Bigby shall prosecute said proceedings under said writ of error to effect and answer all damages and costs, if he fail to make his plea good, then the above obligation to be void; otherwise to remain in full force and effect.

HARRY BIGBY,

Principal.

A. S. SHADDOW,

J. D. WIRT,

Sureties.

Signed, sealed and acknowledged before me this 29th day of November, 1923.

[Seal]     SAMUEL F. HOLLINS,

U. S. Commissioner.   [101]

United States of America,
Southern District of California,—ss.

J. D. Wirt, whose name is subscribed to the foregoing undertaking as one of the sureties thereof, being first duly sworn, deposes and says:

That I am a householder in said district and reside at 3435 Palm Avenue, City of Fresno, County of Fresno, State of California, and by occupation a merchant.

That I am worth the sum of $250.00 *Dollars,* the sum in said undertaking specified as the penalty thereof, over and above all my debts and liabilities and exclusive of property exempt from execution and that my property, now standing of record in my name, consists in part as follows:

Real Estate, described as follows, to wit:

Lot No. Six (6) of Montpellier Tract, in the City of Fresno, County of Fresno, State of California. Valued at $20,000.00. Encumbrances of $5,000.00.

½-interest in lot eighty-six of West Fresno Tract of the City of Fresno, County of Fresno, State of California. Valued at $6,000.00 and encumbered to the amount of $1500.00. Value of equity, $2250.00.

$1,500 contract equity in house at 1235 Harrison Street, in the City of Fresno, County of Fresno, State of California.

Personal Property:

¼-interest in the Samuel's Cigar Store of Fresno, California, a copartnership, interest valued at $20,-000.00

That my total net assets, above all liabilities and obligations on other bonds, is the sum of $22,600.00. That I am surety upon 6 outstanding penal bonds (made within one year from date now in force), aggregating total penalty of $20,750.00

J. D. WIRT.

Subscribed and sworn to before me this 29th day of November, 1923.

[Seal]   SAMUEL F. HOLLINS,

United States Commissioner for the Southern District of California.   [102]

United States of America,

Southern District of California,—ss.

A. S. Shaddow, whose name is subscribed to the foregoing undertaking as one of the sureties thereof, being first duly sworn, deposes and says:

That I am a householder in said district and reside at 801 Vassar Street in the City of Fresno, County of Fresno, State of California, and am by occupation a merchant.

That I am worth the sum of $250.00 *Dollars,* the sum in said undertaking specified as the penalty thereof, over and above all my debts and liabilities and exclusive of property exempt from execution and that my property, now standing of record in my name, consists as follows:

Real Estate, described as follows, to wit:

A contract interest or equity 40-acre vineyard being E. ½ of W. ½ of SW. ¼ of Section 21, Township Fourteen South, Range 20 East, M. D. B. & M. Valued at $31,000.00. Encumbrances, $14,800.00.

A contract interest in 40-acre vineyard in Madera County, being the NE. ¼ of the SE. ¼ of Section 36, T. 12 South, Range 17 East, M. D. B. & M. Valued at $40,000.00. Encumbrances $11,250.00.

Lot 75x100 feet on the NE. corner of Belmont

and Yosemite Avenues in the City of Fresno. Valued at $5,500.00. Mtge., $1,500.00.

Lot on the SW. corner of Dean and Butler Avenues in the City of Fresno. Valued at $1,000.00. No mortgages.

5-acre ranch at Kerman, California. Valued at $1,500.00. Free and clear.

2-acre fig orchard in the Forkner Fig Gardens. Valued at $2,500.00. Encumbrances $1,000.00.

Personal property:

Net value of jewelry store at Mariposa and Fulton Street in Fresno, California, together with fixtures and lease $50,000.00, all standing in my name.

That my total net assets, above all liabilities and obligations [103] on other bonds, is the sum of $86,200, that I am surety upon six outstanding penal bonds (made within one year from date these bonds) now in force, aggregating total penalty of $15,750.00.

A. S. SHADDOW.

Subscribed and sworn to before me this 29th day of November, 1923.

[Seal]          SAMUEL F. HOLLINS,
United States Commissioner.

Examined and recommended for approval as provided in Rule No. 29.

R. G. RETALLICK,<br>Attorney for Defendants.

I hereby approve the foregoing bond this the 30th day of November, 1923.

WM. P. JAMES,<br>Judge.

I hereby approve the foregoing bond as to form.

JOSEPH C. BURKE,

United States Attorney,

MARK L. HERRON,

Asst. U. S. Attorney.

[Endorsed]: No. 821—Criminal. In the District Court of the United States, in and for the Southern District of California, Northern Division. United States of America, Plaintiff, vs. Louis H. Reyff, E. W. Frederick, and Harry Bigby, Defendants. Cost Bond on Appeal. *Bond of Louis H. Reyff.* Filed Nov. 30, 1923, at —— min. past —— o'clock — M. Chas. N. Williams, Clerk. Louis J. Somers, Deputy. R. G. Retallick, Attorney at Law, 531 Brix Bldg., Fresno, Cal. [104]

---

In the District Court of the United States, in and for the Southern District of California, Northern Division.

No. 821—CRIMINAL.

UNITED STATES OF AMERICA,

Plaintiff,

vs.

LOUIS H. REYFF, E. W. FREDERICK, and HARRY BIGBY,

Defendants.

## COST BOND ON APPEAL (E. W. FREDER-
## ICK).

KNOW ALL MEN BY THESE PRESENTS: That we, Louis H. Reyff, as principal, and J. D. Wirt, of Fresno, Fresno County, California, and A. S. Shaddow, of Fresno, Fresno County, California, as sureties, are firmly bound unto the United States of America in the full and just sum of Two Hundred and Fifty ($250.00) Dollars to be paid to the said United States of America, to which payment well and truly to be made, we bind ourselves, our heirs, executors and administrators, jointly and severally, by these presents.

Sealed with our seals and dated this 29th day of November, in the year of our Lord one thousand nine hundred and twenty-three.

WHEREAS, lately, on the 26th day of November, 1923, at the November term of the District Court of the United States, for the Southern District of California, Northern Division, in a cause pending in said court between the United States of America, plaintiff, and Louis H. Reyff, E. W. Frederick and Harry Bigby, defendants, a judgment and sentence were rendered against the said Louis H. Reyff, E. W. Frederick and Harry Bigby, and whereas, said Louis H. Reyff, E. W. Frederick and Harry Bigby, thereafter obtained a writ of error directed to the said United States of America and the United States Attorney for the Southern District of California before the United States Circuit Court of

Appeals, [105] for the Ninth Circuit, to reverse the judgments and sentences in the aforesaid suit, and a citation directed to the said United States of America and to the United States Attorney, for the Southern District of California, citing and admonishing the United States of America and the said United States Attorney to be and appear in the United States Circuit Court of Appeals, for the Ninth Circuit, at San Francisco, California, pursuant to the terms and at the time fixed in said citation;

Now, the condition of the above obligation is such that if the said E. W. Frederick shall prosecute said proceedings under said writ of error, to effect and answer all damages and costs, if he fail to make his plea good, then the above obligation to be void; otherwise to remain in full force and effect.

E. W. FREDERICK,

Principal.

A. S. SHADDOW,

J. D. WIRT,

Sureties.

Signed, sealed and acknowledged before me this 29th day of November, 1923.

[Seal] SAMUEL F. HOLLINS,

U. S. Commissioner. [106]

United States of America,

Southern District of California,—ss.

J. D. Wirt, whose name is subscribed to the foregoing undertaking as one of the sureties thereof, being first duly sworn, deposes and says:

That I am a householder in·said district and reside at 3435 Palm Avenue, City of Fresno, County of Fresno, State of California, and by occupation a merchant.

That I am worth the sum of $250.00 *Dollars,* the sum in said undertaking specified as the penalty thereof, over and above all my debts and liabilities and exclusive of property exempt from execution and that my property, now standing of record in my name, consists in part as follows:

Real Estate, described as follows, to wit:

Lot No. six (6) of Montpellier Tract, in the City of Fresno, County of Fresno, State of California. Valued at $20.000.00. Encumbrances of $5.000.00

½ interest in lot eighty-six of West Fresno Tract of the City of Fresno, County of Fresno, State of California. Valued at $6.000.00 and encumbered to the amount of $1500.00. Value of Equity, $2250.00.

$1500 Contract equity in house at 1235 Harrison Street in the City of Fresno, County of Fresno, State of California.

Personal Property:

¼ interest in the Samuel's Cigar Store of Fresno, California, a copartnership, interest valued at $20.000.00.

That my total net assets, above all liabilities and obligations on other bonds, is the sum of $22,600.00. That I am surety upon 6 outstanding penal bonds made within one year from date now in force, aggregating total penalty of $20.750.00.

J. D. WIRT.

Subscribed and sworn to before me this 29th day of November, 1923.

[Seal]               SAMUEL F. HOLLINS,
United States Commissioner for the Southern District of California. [107]

United States of America,
Southern District of California,—ss.

A. S. Shaddow, whose name is subscribed to the foregoing undertaking as one of the sureties thereof, being first duly sworn, deposes and says:

That I am a householder in said district and reside at 801 Vassar Street in the City of Fresno, County of Fresno, State of California, and am by occupation a merchant.

That I am worth the sum of $250.00 Dollars, the sum in said undertaking specified as the penalty thereof, over and above all my debts and liabilities and exclusive of property exempt from execution and that my property, now standing of record in my name, consists as follows:

Real Estate, described as follows, to wit:

A contract interest or equity 40 acre vineyard being E.½ of the W.½ of the SW.¼ of Section 21, Township Fourteen South, Range 20 East, M. D. B. & M. Valued at $31,000.00. Encumbrances, $14,-800.00.

A contract interest in 40 acre vineyard in Madera County, being the NE.¼ of the SE¼ of Section 36, T. 12 South, Range 17 East, M. D. B. & M. Valed at $40.000.00. Encumberances $11,250.00.

Lot 75x100 feet on the NE. corner of Belmont

and Yosemite Avenues in the City of Fresno. Valued at $5500.00 Mtge. $1500.00.

Lot on the SW. corner of Dean and Butler Avenues in the City of Fresno, Valued at $1.000.00 No mortgages.

5 acre ranch at Kerman, California, Valued at $1500.00. Free and clear.

2 acre fig orchard in the Forkner Fig Gardens. Valued at $2500.00   Encumbrances $1,000.00.

Personal Property:

Net value of jewelry store at Mariposa and Fulton Streets in Fresno, California, together with fixtures and lease $50.000.00, all standing in my name.

That my total net assets, above all liabilities and obligations [108]  on other bonds, is the sum of $86.200, that I am surety upon six outstanding penal bonds (made within one year from date these bonds) now in force, aggregating total penalty of $15.750.00.

A. S. SHADDOW.

Subscribed and sworn to before me this 29th day of November, 1923.

[Seal]        SAMUEL F. HOLLINS,
United States Commissioner.

Examined and recommended for approval as provided in Rule No. 29.

R. G. RETALLICK,
Attorney for Defendants.

I hereby approve the foregoing bond this the 30th day of November, 1923.

WM. P. JAMES,
Judge.

I hereby approve the foregoing bond as to form.

JOSEPH C. BURKE,
United States Attorney.

MARK L. HERRON,
Asst. U. S. Attorney.

[Endorsed]: No. 821—Criminal. In the District Court of the United States, in and for the Southern District of California, Northern Division. United States of America, Plaintiff, vs. Louis H. Reyff, E. W. Frederick and Harry Bigby, Defendants. Cost Bond on Appeal. Bond of E. W. Frederick. Filed Nov. 30, 1923, at —— min. past —— o'clock — M. Chas. N. Williams, Clerk. Louis J. Somers, Deputy. R. G. Retallick, Attorney at Law, 531 Brix Bldg., Fresno, Cal. [109]

In the District Court of the United States, in and for the Southern District of California, Northern Division.

No. 821—CRIMINAL.

UNITED STATES OF AMERICA,

Plaintiff,

vs.

LOUIS H. REYFF, E. W. FREDERICK, and HARRY BIGBY,

Defendants.

COST BOND ON APPEAL (LOUIS H. REYFF).

KNOW ALL MEN BY THESE PRESENTS: That we, Harry Bigby, as principal, and J. D.

Wirt, of Fresno, Fresno County, California, and
A. S. Shaddow, of Fresno, Fresno County, California, as sureties, are firmly bound unto the United
States of America in the full and just sum of Two
Hundred and Fifty ($250.00) Dollars to be paid to
the said United States of America to which payment
well and truly to be made, we bind ourselves, our
heirs, executors and administrators, jointly and
severally, by these presents.

Sealed with our seals and dated this 29th day of
November, in the year of our Lord one thousand
nine hundred and twenty-three.

WHEREAS, lately, on the 26th day of November,
1923, at the November term of the District Court
of the United States, for the Southern District of
California, Northern Division, in a cause pending
in said court between the United States of America,
plaintiff, and Louis H. Reyff, E. W. Frederick and
Harry Bigby, defendants, judgment and sentence
were rendered against the said Louis H. Reyff, E.
W. Frederick and Harry Bigby, and whereas, said
Louis H. Reyff, E. W. Frederick and Harry Bigby,
thereafter obtained a writ of error directed to the
said United States of America and the United
States Attorney for the Southern District of California before the United States Circuit Court of
Appeals, [110]  for the Ninth Circuit, to reverse
the judgments and sentences in the aforesaid suit,
and a citation directed to the said United States of
America and to the United States Attorney, for
the Southern District of California, citing and admonishing the United States of America and the

said United States Attorney to be and appear in
the United States Circuit Court of Appeals, for the
Ninth Circuit, at San Francisco, California, pursuant to the terms and at the time fixed in said
citation:

Now the condition of the above obligation is such
that if the said Louis H. Reyff shall prosecute said
proceedings under said writ of error, to effect and
answer all damages and costs, if he fail to make
his plea good, then the above obligation to be void;
otherwise to remain in full force and effect.

LOUIS H. REYFF,

Principal.

A. S. SHADDOW,

J. D. WIRT,

Sureties.

Signed, sealed and acknowledged before me this
29th day of November, 1923.

[Seal] SAMUEL F. HOLLINS,

U. S. Commissioner. [111]

United States of America,
Southern District of California,—ss.

J. D. Wirt, whose name is subscribed to the foregoing undertaking as one of the sureties thereof,
being first duly sworn, deposes and says:

That I am a householder in said district and
reside at 3435 Palm Avenue, City of Fresno, County
of Fresno, State of California, and by occupation
a merchant.

That I am worth the sum of $250.00 *Dollars,* the
sum in said undertaking specified as the penalty

thereof, over and above all my debts and liabilities and exclusive of property exempt from execution and that my property, now standing of record in my name, consists in part as follows:

Real Estate, described as follows, to wit:

Lot No. Six (6) of Montpellier Tract, in the City of Fresno, County of Fresno, State of California. Valued at $20.000.00. Encumbrances of $5.000.00.

½ interest in lot eighty-six of west Fresno Tract of the City of Fresno, County of Fresno, State of California. Valued at $6.000.00 and encumbered to the amount of $1500.00. Value of Equity, $2250.00.

$1500 contract equity in house at 1235 Harrison Street in the City of Fresno, County of Fresno, State of California.

Personal Property:

¼ interest in the Samuel's Cigar Store of Fresno, California, a copartnership, interest valued at $20.000.00.

That my total net assets, above all liabilities and obligations on other bonds, is the sum of $22.600.00. That I am surety upon 6 outstanding penal bonds (made within one year from date now in force), aggregating total penalty of $20.750.00.

J. D. WIRT.

Subscribed and sworn to before me this 29th day of November, 1923.

[Seal]    SAMUEL F. HOLLINS,
United States Commissioner for the Southern District of California.    [112]

United States of America,
Southern District of California,—ss.

A. S. Shaddow, whose name is subscribed to the foregoing undertaking as one of the sureties thereof, being first duly sworn, deposes and says:

That I am a householder in said district and reside at 801 Vassar Street in the City of Fresno, County of Fresno, State of California, and am by occupation a merchant.

That I am worth the sum of $250.00 *Dollars,* the sum of said undertaking specified as the penalty thereof, over and above all my debts and liabilities and exclusive of property exempt from execution and that my property, now standing of record in my name, consists as follows:

Real Estate, described as follows, to wit:

A contract interest or equity 40 acre vineyard being E.½ of the W.½ of the SW.¼ of Section 21, Township Fourteen South, Range 20 East, M. D. B. & M. Valued at $31.000.00. Encumbrances $14.800.00.

A contract interest in 40 acre vineyard in Madera County, being the NE.¼ of the SE.¼ of Section 36, T. 12 South, Range 17 East, M. D. B. & M. Valued at $40,000.00. Encumbrances $11,250.00.

Lot 75x100 feet on the NE. corner of Belmont and Yosemite Avenues in the City of Fresno, Valued at $5500.00. Mtge. $1500.00.

Lot on the SW. corner of Dean and Butler Avenues in the City of Fresno. Valued at $1.000.00. No mortgages.

5 acre ranch at Kerman, California. Valued at $1500.00. Free and clear.

2 acre fig orchard in the Forkner Fig Gardens. Valued at $2500.00. Encumbrances $1.000.00.

Personal Property:

Net value of jewelry store at Mariposa and Fulton Streets in Fresno, California, together with fixtures and lease $50.000.00 all standing in my name.

That my total net assets, above all liabilities and obligations [113] on other bonds, is the sum of $86.200, that I am surety upon six outstanding penal bonds (made within one year from date *these bonds*) now in force, aggregating total penalty of $15.750.00.

A. S. SHADDOW.

Subscribed and sworn to before me this 29th day of November, 1923.

[Seal]      SAMUEL F. HOLLINS,
United States Commissioner.

Examined and recommended for approval as provided in Rule No. 29.

R. G. RETALLICK,
Attorney for Defendants.

I hereby approve the foregoing bond this the 30th day of November, 1923.

WM. P. JAMES,
Judge.

I hereby approve the foregoing bond as to form.

JOSEPH C. BURKE,
United States Attorney.
MARK L. HERRON,
Asst. U. S. Attorney.

[Endorsed]: No. 821—Criminal. In the District Court of the United States, in and for the Southern District of California, Northern District. United States of America, Plaintiff, vs. Louis H. Reyff, E. W. Frederick, and Harry Bigby. Cost Bond on Appeal. *Bond of Harry Bigby.* Filed Nov. 30, 1923, at —— min. past —— o'clock — M. Chas. N. Williams, Clerk. Louis J. Somers, Deputy. R. G. Retallick, Attorney at Law, 531 Brix Bldg., Fresno, Cal. [114]

---

In the District Court of the United States for the Southern District of California, Northern Division.

### No. 821—CRIMINAL.

UNITED STATES OF AMERICA,

Plaintiff,

vs.

LOUIS H. REYFF, E. W. FREDERICK and HARRY BIGBY,

Defendants.

## PRAECIPE (FOR TRANSCRIPT ON WRIT OF ERROR).

To the Clerk of said Court:

Sir: Please prepare the transcript of record upon writ of error in the above-entitled cause.

1. Information.
2. Arraignment of defendants.
3. Pleas of defendants.

4. Petition for return of property and exclusion of evidence.
5. Order denying motion to return property and exclude evidence.
6. Record of the trial (minutes of November 22d and 23d, 1923).
7. Verdict of the jury.
8. Judgment of the Court.
9. Motions for new trial and in arrest of judgment.
10. Orders denying motions for new trial and arrest of judgment.
11. Clerk's certificate to judgment-roll.
12. Petition for writ of error.
13. Assignment of errors.
14. Citation on writ of error.
15. Return thereto.
16. Order allowing writ of error and supersedeas.
17. Supersedeas bonds.
18. Cost bonds on appeal.
19. Bill of exceptions. [115]
20. Writ of error (original).
21. Clerk's certificate to transcript of record.
22. Stipulations and orders extending time in which to lodge and settle bill of exceptions.
23. Order extending time in which to file transcript of record.

EDWARD A. O'DEA,
RICHARD G. RETALLICK,
Attorneys for Defendants.

[Endorsed]: No. 821—Criminal. In the District Court of the United States for the Southern

District of California, Northern Division. United States of America, Plaintiff, vs. Louis H. Reyff, E. W. Frederick and Harry Bigby, Defendants. Praecipe (for Transcript on Writ of Error). Filed Dec. 31, 1923, at —— min. past 2 o'clock P. M. Chas N. Williams, Clerk. G. F. Gibson, Deputy. R. G. Retallick, Fresno, and Edward A. O'Dea, Attorneys for Defendants. 826–28–30 Phelan Building, Telephone Sutter 276, San Francisco. [116]

———

In the District Court of the United States in and for the Southern District of California, Northern Division.

No. 821—CRIM.—N. D.

UNITED STATES OF AMERICA,

Plaintiff,

vs.

LOUIS H. REYFF, E. W. FREDRICK and HARRY BIGBY,

Defendants.

CERTIFICATE OF CLERK U. S. DISTRICT COURT TO TRANSCRIPT OF RECORD.

I, Chas. N. Williams, Clerk of the United States District Court for the Southern District of California, do hereby certify the foregoing volume containing 116 pages, numbered from 1 to 116, inclusive, to be the Transcript of Record on Writ of Error in the above-entitled cause, and contains a full, true and correct copy of the information, arraignment and plea of defendants, motion to return property and exclude evidence, minutes of the trial, including order denying motion to return property and exclude evidence, verdict of the jury, motion for a new trial, motion in arrest of judgment, judgment of the court, clerk's certificate to judgment-roll, assignment of errors, petition for writ of error and supersedeas, order allowing writ of error and supersedeas, stipulation extending time in which to lodge and settle proposed bill of exceptions, order, engrossed bill of exceptions, supersedeas bonds, cost bonds an appeal, and praecipe for transcript on writ of error. Said record also contains the original citation and original writ of error.

I DO FURTHER CERTIFY that the fees of the Clerk for comparing and correcting the foregoing record on writ of error amount to $35.45, and that said amount has been paid me by the plaintiff in error herein.

IN TESTIMONY WHEREOF, I have hereunto set my hand and affixed the Seal of the District Court of the United States of America, in and for the Southern District of California, [117] this 4th day of March, in the year of our Lord one thousand nine hundred and twenty-four, and of our Independence the one hundred and forty-eighth.

[Seal]　　　　CHAS. N. WILLIAMS,

Clerk of the District Court of the United States of America, in and for the Southern District of California, Southern Division.

By R. S. Zimmerman,

Deputy Clerk. [118]

[Endorsed]: No. 4227. United States Circuit Court of Appeals for the Ninth Circuit. Louis H. Reyff, E. W. Frederick and Harry Bigby, Plaintiffs in Error, vs. United States of America, Defendant in Error. Transcript of Record. Upon Writ of Error to the United States District Court of the Southern District of California, Southern Division.

Received March 15, 1924.

F. D. MONCKTON,

Clerk.

Filed March 25, 1924.

F. D. MONCKTON,

Clerk of the United States Circuit Court of Appeals for the Ninth Circuit.

By Paul P. O'Brien,

Deputy Clerk.

# No. 4227

IN THE

# United States Circuit Court of Appeals

### For the Ninth Circuit

---

LOUIS H. REYFF, E. W. FREDERICK and HARRY
BIGBY,

*Plaintiffs in Error,*

VS.

UNITED STATES OF AMERICA,

*Defendant in Error.*

---

## BRIEF FOR PLAINTIFFS IN ERROR.

---

EDWARD A. O'DEA,
RICHARD G. RETALLICK,
*Attorneys for Plaintiffs in Error.*

# United States Circuit Court of Appeals

### For the Ninth Circuit

---

Louis H. Reyff, E. W. Frederick and Harry
Bigby,

*Plaintiffs in Error,*

vs.

United States of America,

*Defendant in Error.*

---

## BRIEF FOR PLAINTIFFS IN ERROR.

---

## I.

### Statement of the Case.

The plaintiffs in error were charged by information with violations of the "National Prohibition Act". The information contained three counts. The first count charged the plaintiffs in error with having sold to one, C. W. Kittle, on the 16th day of May, 1923, in the City of Fresno, County of Fresno, in the Northern Division of the Southern District of California, a case of intoxicating liquor containing alcohol in excess of a half of one per cent. by volume for the agreed price of one hundred and No/100 ($100.00) dollars, lawful money of the

United States. That said liquor was sold for beverage purposes in violation of Section 3, Title II of the "National Prohibition Act" of October 28, 1919. The second count charged the plaintiffs in error on the last mentioned date, at the above mentioned place, with knowingly, wilfully and unlawfully having in their possession about one case and five bottles of intoxicating liquor, then and there containing alcohol in excess of one-half of one per cent. by volume for beverage purposes; in violation of Section 3, Title II, of the "National Prohibition Act" of October 28, 1919. The third count charged the plaintiffs in error, on the above mentioned date and at the above mentioned place, with knowingly, wilfully and unlawfully transporting in a certain Chalmers automobile, bearing California State License No. 763229, Engine No. 37117, about one case and five quarts of intoxicating liquor for beverage purposes, containing alcohol in excess of one-half of one per cent. by volume; in violation of Section 3, Title II of the "National Prohibition Act" of October 28, 1919. (Trans. Rec. pages 5 to 8.)

The information was filed by the United States Attorney on the 22nd day of May, 1923. That to the said information each of the plaintiffs in error pleaded Not Guilty to each of the counts set forth therein. (Trans. Rec. pages 5 to 9.) That before the trial of said cause E. W. Frederick, one of the plaintiffs in error, on the 22nd day of November, 1923, filed a petition for the return of certain property and the exclusion of evidence alleging therein an unlawful search without the authorization of any search warrant of the automobile of plaintiff in error and an unlawful seizure therefrom of certain property and the securing, at the same time, certain information in violation of plaintiff in error, E. W. Frederick's, rights under the Fourth and Fifth Amendments to the Constitution of the United States, which said property, so taken, and the information and knowledge, so obtained, were made the basis of the prosecution of the plaintiff in error, E. W. Frederick, and his conviction on the charges set forth in the information on file in said cause. (Trans. Rec. pages 10 to 13.)

That the Government resisted said petition and the Court, after hearing said petition, ordered the ruling on same reserved until trial. (Trans. Rec. pages 14 and 54.)

On the 22nd and 23rd days of May, 1923, the plaintiffs in error were tried before a jury and on the 23rd day of May, 1923, the jury, returned verdicts against the plaintiffs in error, as follows:

"We, the jury in the above entitled cause, find the defendant, Louis H. Reyff, Guilty as charged in the first count of the information; Guilty as charged in the second count of the information; and Guilty as charged in the third count of the information; and we, the jury in the above entitled cause, find the defendant, E. W. Frederick, Guilty as charged in the first count of the information; Guilty as charged in the second count of the information and Guilty as charged in the third count of the information; and we, the jury in the above entitled cause, find the defendant, Harry Bigby, Guilty as charged in the first count of the information; Not Guilty as charged in the second count of the information; and Not Guilty as charged in the third count of the information.

C. B. Jackson,
Foreman."

(Trans. Rec. pages 23 and 24.)

That upon the trial of said cause, plaintiff in error, E. W. Frederick, renewed his motion for the return of property and the exclusion of evidence and plaintiffs in error moved that the evidence obtained from the illegal search and seizure be excluded and timely objections were interposed upon each occasion that the evidence seized was offered or that information derived from said search and seizure was testified to. The grounds of said motions were set forth in plaintiff in error, E. W. Frederick's, petition to return property and exclude evidence and the objections were made upon the ground that the evidence seized and the information obtained were in violation of plaintiffs' in error constitutional rights. On each occasion the Court denied said motions and overruled said objections, to which rulings plaintiffs in error duly excepted. (Trans. Rec. pages 58, 59, 64, 65, 74, 78 and 79.) And, at the conclusion of the evidence, which was at the end of the Government's case, the plaintiffs in error renewed their motion to exclude all the evidence which had not been legally obtained, not only the evidence set forth in the petition but also five or six additional bottles of liquor found in the automobile of plaintiff in error, E. W. Frederick, upon the grounds heretofore set forth. The Court, after hearing argument, denied said motion and plaintiffs in error duly excepted. (Trans. Rec. pages 88, 89, 95 and 96.) And, plaintiff in error, E. W. Frederick, asked for a directed verdict of Not Guilty of the charges contained in the information upon the ground of the insufficiency of the evidence in that all of the evidence received was taken in violation of his constitutional rights. The Court denied this motion and plaintiff in error duly excepted. (Trans. Rec. pages 92, 95 and 96.)

At the conclusion of the Government's case, plaintiff in error, Harry Bigby, made a motion for a directed verdict of Not Guilty on each of the counts set forth in the information on the ground that the evidence was insufficient to establish any of those offenses and directed the Court's attention to the count charging him with the unlawful sale of intoxicating liquor and pointed out that all the evidence showed was that he might have committed another misdemeanor set forth in the National Prohibition Law, to-wit, the giving of information where liquor may be obtained. The Court denied said motions, to which plaintiff in error took an exception. (Trans. Rec. pages 90, 91, 95 and 96.) That a statement and a discussion of the evidence upon this subject is set forth in another portion of this brief.

At the conclusion of the Government's case, plaintiff in error, Louis H. Reyff, made a motion for a directed verdict of Not Guilty on each of the counts set forth in the information upon the ground that the evidence was insufficient to convict the defendant of the charges contained therein and setting forth at said time his reasons for said motions. The Court denied said motions to which plaintiff in error duly excepted. (Trans. Rec. pages 91, 92, 95 and 96.) A statement and a discussion of the evidence upon this subject is also set forth in another portion of this brief.

In like manner, at the conclusion of the Government's case, plaintiff in error, E. W. Frederick, made a motion for a directed verdict of Not Guilty on each of the counts set forth in the information upon the ground of the insufficiency of the evidence. The Court denied said motions to which plaintiff in error duly excepted. (Trans. Rec. 92, 96 and 96.)

Thereafter and on the 26th day of November, 1923, the plaintiffs in error each interposed a motion for a new trial; also a motion in arrest of judgment; each of which motions as to each defendant and plaintiff in error were by the Court denied. (Trans. Rec. pages 25 to 30 and 97 to 100.) Whereupon the Court sentenced plaintiffs in error, Louis H. Reyff and E. W. Frederick, to a term of five months in the Fresno County Jail on the first count of the information and sentenced each to pay unto the United States of America a fine in the sum of ten and No/100 dollars on each of the second and third counts contained in said information. (Trans. Rec. page 30.) And the Court sentenced plaintiff in error, Harry Bigby, to a term of three months in the Fresno County Jail on the first count of the information. (Trans. Rec. pages 30 and 31.) A writ of error was thereupon sued out by each of the plaintiffs in error to review the judgment and proceedings of the trial Court.

----

## II.

### Specifications of the Errors Relied Upon.

### I.

The Court erred in denying the motion made by the defendant and plaintiff in error, E. W. Frederick, for the return of certain property, to wit, a case of Scotch whiskey and four jars of intoxicating liquor, upon the ground that said property was seized from the automobile of the defendant, E. W. Frederick, without due process of law, without the authorization of a search warrant, or warrant for the arrest of the defendant, the officers seizing same not having witnessed the commission of any crime in their presence and without having seen any liquor in plain sight in said automobile and in violation of the defendant's right guaranteed him under the Fourth and Fifth Amendments to the Constitution of the United States. Said motion was made before the trial, based upon an affidavit presented to the Court; said motion was made during the trial and at the conclusion of the Government's case and the submission of all the evidence in the case.

To the Court's order denying said motion the defendant, Frederick, then and there duly excepted.

---

## II.

The Court erred in denying the motion made by the defendant and plaintiff in error, E. W. Frederick, for the return of a Chalmers automobile seized by Federal officers without due process of law, in that, said seizure of said automobile was based upon an unlawful search and seizure of certain property taken from said automobile without the authorization of a search warrant or order of Court, or warrant for the arrest of the defendant, E. W. Frederick, or any person whomsoever, no crime having been committed in the presence of said Federal officers and they not having seen any liquor in plain sight.

To the Court's order denying said motion, defendant and plaintiff in error, Frederick, duly excepted.

---

## III.

The Court erred in overruling the objection made by the defendants and each of them to the bringing in and exhibiting in a conspicuous place in front of the jury of certain bottles containing intoxicating liquors, which said objection was made upon the ground that the same was prejudicial to the rights of the defendants before the jury, and which bottles were so exhibited before any evidence whatsoever was introduced and while the said jury was being empanelled, and said Court then and there erred in not requiring said bottles to be removed from the presence of the prospective jurrors, to all of which the defendants then and there duly excepted.

## IV.

The Court erred in denying the motion of the defendants to exclude from evidence certain intoxicating liquors seized in violation of the constitutional rights of the defendants under the Fourth and Fifth Amendments to the United States Constitution, as well as all knowledge derived from said search and seizure. Said motion was based upon the seizure of said intoxicating liquors from the automobile of the defendant, Frederick, without the authorization of a search warrant or order of Court, without a warrant for the arrest of any of the defendants, the arresting officers not having evidence sufficient to justify said seizure and search, they not having witnessed any violation of the law in their presence, and not having seen any liquor in plain sight or otherwise. Said motion was made before the trial and at each time said evidence was sought to be introduced during said trial.

To the Court's order denying said motion, the defendant duly excepted.

----

## V.

The Court erred in admitting in evidence, over the objection of the defendants, one case of Scotch whiskey and four containers of liquor, said objection was based upon the ground that the evidence was obtained as a result of an illegal search and seizure of same out of an automobile in violation of the defendants' constitutional rights.

To the Court's ruling, the defendants then and there duly excepted.

----

## VI.

The Court erred in admitting the following testimony, over the objection of the defendants, upon the ground that it was incompetent, irrelevant and immaterial and calling for a conclusion of the witness, and leading and suggestive and hearsay:

"Mr. HERRON. Q. Now, Mr. Nicely, at the time you sent Mr. Kettle to see if he could make those purchases of liquor, did you have reason to believe that these defendants, or any one of them, were engaged in the businesse of keeping or selling intoxicating liquors?

Mr. RETALLICK. We object to that as incompetent, irrelevant and immaterial; calling for a conclusion of the witness; leading and suggestive.

The COURT. State, then, what information you did have.

A. I received a large number of complaints that the defendant, Bigby—

Mr. RETALLICK. If your Honor please, we object to this answer. Of course, I can not object to the question that the Court has asked. I object to the answer on the ground that it is hearsay.

The COURT. You may object to it if you wish. I am allowing the evidence in view of your motion to suppress evidence. If you will withdraw the motion I will sustain the objection, but if the motion stands then they are entitled to show upon what information he acted, to the extent that it was reasonable.

Mr. O'DEA. The motion was made in behalf of the defendant, Frederick. This is in relation to the conversation had with the defendant, Bigby, and I submit it is immaterial and hearsay.

The COURT. You may act upon hearsay if it is generally reliable. If it ultimately proves to be reliable, then you may act upon it. It depends upon whether there was reasonable grounds existing to make the search. If I understand that you do not require that proof be made that they had reasonable ground to make the search then I will sustain the objection.

Mr. O'DEA. We won't admit that.

The COURT. The witness may answer.

Mr. O'DEA. Note an exception.

A. I had received a large number of complaints that the defendant, Bigby, had been dealing in intoxicating liquors.

Mr. HERRON. Q. Don't state the language of it. You may say whether you had received complaints to the effect of it, but not the language.

A. The people would go into this store where he was employed—

Q. You had received complaints that he was selling liquor. That is as far as you may proceed.

A. I had quite a number of them. I had also received complaints that the defendant, Frederick, was dealing in liquor, and I had arrested the defendant, Frederick, before, for the same thing.

Mr. RETALLICK. I ask that that latter part be stricken out.

The COURT. It may be stricken.

Mr. O'DEA. And I would ask your Honor to instruct the jury not to consider that testimony.

The COURT. That may be stricken out as to the prior arrest of the defendant.

---

## VII.

The Court erred in denying the motions of the defendants and plaintiffs in error, made at the conclusion of the Government's case, which was at the conclusion of taking of all the testimony, to exclude all the evidence not legally obtained upon the ground that said evidence was taken without process of law. That the automobile which contained the liquor was searched and a seizure made therefrom without the authorization of a search warrant, without any warrant for the arrest of the defendants or either of them, the officers not having witnessed the commission of any violation of the law, and not having seen any liquor in plain sight or otherwise.

To the Court's order denying said motion, the defendants then and there duly excepted.

---

## VIII.

The Court erred in denying the motion of the defendant and plaintiff in error, Bigby, for a directed verdict of Not Guilty of all the counts set forth in the information, upon the grounds that the evidence was insufficient to sustain the charges contained therein. Said motion was made at the conclusion of the Government's case, which was at the conclusion of the taking of all the testimony in said case, to which ruling the defendant and plaintiff in error, Bigby, duly excepted.

---

## IX.

The Court erred in denying the motion of the defendant and plaintiff in error, Reyff, for a directed verdict of Not Guilty of all the counts set forth in the information, upon the grounds that the evidence was insufficient to sustain the charges contained therein. Said motion was made at the conclusion of the taking of all the testimony in said case, to which ruling the defendant and plaintiff in error, Reyff, duly excepted.

## X.

The Court erred in denying the motion of the defendant, Frederick, for a directed verdict of Not Guilty of all of the counts set forth in the information, upon the grounds that the evidence was insufficient to sustain the charges; that all of the evidence was taken in violation of the defendant's constitutional rights; that the liquor was taken from his automobile without a search warrant, and without any crime having been committed in the presence of the officers making the arrest. Said motion was made at the conclusion of the Government's case, which was at the conclusion of the taking of all the testimony in said case, to which ruling the defendant and plaintiff in error duly excepted.

---

## XI.

The Court erred in denying the motion for a new trial on behalf of defendants and plaintiffs in error, in this:

1. That the verdicts in said cause are contrary to law.

2. That the verdicts in said cause were not supported by the evidence in the case.

3. That the evidence in said cause is insufficient to justify any of said verdicts.

4. That the Court erred upon the trial of said cause in deciding questions of law arising during

the course of the trial, to which errors exceptions were duly taken.

5.  That said Court upon the trial of said cause admitted incompetent evidence offered by the United States of America.

6.  That the Court improperly instructed the jury to the defendants' prejudice.

To which ruling on said motion for a new trial, the defendants duly excepted.

----

## XII.

The Court erred in denying the motion in arrest of judgment on behalf of the defendants and plaintiffs in error, in this:

1.  That it appears on the face of the record that no judgment can legally be entered against these defendants or any or either of them, for the following reasons:

That Count One of the Information filed herein does not charge or state facts sufficient to constitute a public offense under the laws of the United States against the defendants or any or either of them.

That Count Two of the Information filed herein does not charge or state facts sufficient to constitute a public offense under the laws of the United States against the defendants or any or either of them.

That Count Three of the Information filed herein does not charge or state facts sufficient to constitute a public offense under the laws of the United States against the defendants or any or either of them.

That this Court has no jurisdiction to pass judgment upon the defendants or either of them by reason of the fact that Counts One, Two and Three of the Information on file herein do not state public offenses under the laws of the United States.

To which ruling on defendants' said motion in arrest of judgment, defendants duly excepted.

---

## III.
### Argument.
### I.

**THE COURT ERRED IN ADMITTING IN EVIDENCE PROPERTY TAKEN FROM THE PERSON OF THE DEFENDANT, E. W. FREDERICK, AND FROM HIS AUTOMOBILE AND THE INFORMATION WAS OBTAINED THEREBY IN VIOLATION OF THE FOURTH AND FIFTH AMENDMENTS TO THE CONSTITUTION OF THE UNITED STATES, BECAUSE THE SEARCH AND SEIZURE WAS UNREASONABLE FOR THE FEDERAL PROHIBITION ENFORCEMENT OFFICERS HAD NO SEARCH WARRANT TO SEARCH THE PERSON OR THE AUTOMOBILE OF THE SAID DEFENDANT.**

(Assignment of Errors I, II, IV, V, VI, VII, and X, Trans. Rec. pages 32 to 39.)

This point is raised by plaintiff in error, E. W. Frederick's, motion to return property and to exclude evidence made before the trial (Trans. Rec. pages 10, 11, 12, 13, 14, 50, 51, 52 and 53) and his execptions to the denial of said motion by the trial Court on two occasions. (Trans. Rec. pages 59, 89,

95 and 96.) The question was also raised by plaintiffs' in error timely objections to the introduction of evidence obtained from the search and seizure described in plaintiff in error, E. W. Frederick's, motion as illegal (Trans. Rec. pages 64, 65, 66, 67, 68, 69, 74, 78 and 79) on each occasion when each witness testified to same. To the Court's orders overruling said objections plaintiffs in error duly excepted. (See portions Trans. Rec. last referred to.) The question is further raised by plaintiff in error, E. W. Frederick, when at the conclusion of the taking of testimony, which was at the end of the Government's case, he asked for a directed verdict of Not Guilty of all the charges contained in the information on account of the insufficiency of the evidence because said evidence was taken in violation of his constitutional rights. The Court denied said motion and plaintiff in error, E. W. Frederick, excepted to said denial. (Trans. Rec. pages 92, 95 and 96.) *The trial Court was thoroughly advised of the said motion and its purport.*

*The procedure adopted by plaintiffs in error in raising the constitutional questions herein involved is in conformity with the rules laid down by the United States Supreme Court in the following cases:*

Amos v. U. S., 255 U. S. 315;

Gouled v. U. S. 255 U. S, 298;

Weeks v. U. S., 232 U. S. 383;

*and was duly and regularly presented to the trial Court.*

Plaintiff in error, in his petition for the return of property and exclusion of evidence, alleged

> *That on the 16th day of May, 1923, he owned,* *possessed and was in control of a certain Chalmers automobile, License No. 763229 in the City of Fresno, County of Fresno, State of California: That said automobile is of such construction that in the rear of same there is a receptacle for the purpose of containing packages; that said receptacle was closed and locked on the 16th day of May, 1923.* (Trans. Rec. page 10.)

That on the last mentioned date while plaintiff in error was in possession and control of said automobile, his petition alleges:

> "That he and Reyff entered a garage located in the rear of No. 1041 'T' Street, in the City of Fresno, County of Fresno, State of California. That upon entering said garage, Federal Prohibition Enforcement Officers jumped upon defendant's, your petitioner's automobile and illegally and unlawfully, without the authorization of a search warrant, or order of any Court, and without any warrant for the arrest of your petitioner, and without witnessing any act or acts in violation of the laws of the United States, or of the State of California, and in violation of the defendant's rights guaranteed him by the Fourth and Fifth Amendments to the United States Constitution, and without seeing any liquor in plain sight or otherwise, placed the defendant in custody and proceeded to search his person and by means of the illegal and unlawful search violated his rights above referred to, said Federal Prohibition Enforcement Officers proceeded to search his person and found thereon a key, and that

> they thereupon, illegally and unlawfully, without the authority of a search warrant, and in violation of the defendant's rights under the Fourth and Fifth Amendments to the United States Constitution, and against the will of your petitioner took the said key and opened the rear receptacle to said automobile and found therein a case of Scotch Whiskey which they, illegally and unlawfully seized and took the same away with them." (Trans. Rec. pages 5, 11 and 12.)

Then follows therein an allegation that the whiskey is held without process of law; is the property of the defendant and that he is entitled to its return; that if it is not returned and excluded from evidence at the trial and that the knowledge derived from the search and seizure is not suppressed his rights under the Fourth and Fifth Amendments to the United States Constitution will be violated. Then the petitioner alleges further that his automobile was seized at the same time in the manner set forth in the petition. And then follows the ordinary prayer for the return of the property and the exclusion and suppression of the evidence. (Trans. Rec. pages 10, 11, 12, 50 to 53.)

The information charges in the first count that plaintiffs in error sold about one case of intoxicating liquor; in the second count they are charged with possessing one case and five bottles of intoxicating liquor; and the third count charges them with transporting a case and five quarts of intoxicating liquor. (Trans. Rec. pages 10 to 13 inc.) (It will be noted that the information in this regard is very vague and indefinite and runs counter to the decision of Guilbeau v. United States, 288 Fed. 231.) The testimony adduced at the trial is conflicting and unsatisfactory concerning any intoxicating liquor in excess of a sack containing certain bottles. Two of the Government's witnesses do not mention any other liquor than that contained in the sack at all, while witness Emrich says: "there were twelve bottles in it (referring to the sack) as I remember". (Trans. Rec. page 75.) And, Nicely, the Government agent in charge of matters, testified:

"We unlocked the rear compartment to his automobile, and took from this sack (indicating) the liquor contained therein, and the bottle of liquor setting on the table which has the white cap on it * * * and then locked the compartment up and brought the car to the Federal Building and took out the sack of liquor and brought it into the Federal Building * * * When he came after the car, I looked into the compartment behind the seat and found two of the jars there. * * * I have seen the other two jars. Those two jars were in the garage on 'M' Street where Mr. Frederick took me later." (Trans. Rec. page 65.)

Plaintiff in error therefore can be excused for not mentioning additional liquor in excess of the case of Scotch in his motion but this situation was adjusted by his other objections and motions. (See Trans. Rec. pages 64 to 69, 74, 78 and 79.)

Plaintiffs in error contented themselves with the motion to return property and exclude evidence and the objections and motions above referred to, and rested their respective causes upon the Government's case. *It is not disputed by the Government that there was no search warrant to search the automobile of plaintiff in error, E. W. Frederick; the Federal prohibition enforcement officers did not have a warrant for the arrest of any of the plaintiffs in error; that the automobile of plaintiff in error, E. W. Frederick, was closed and locked; and there was no intoxicating liquor in plain sight nor were the Federal prohibition enforcement officers advised by any of their senses that a crime was being committed in their presence, such as smelling liquor,* etc. In fact none of the witnesses for the Government saw any intoxicating liquor until after the arrest of plaintiffs in error, E. W. Frederick and Louis H. Reyff, and after the Federal prohibition enforcement officers had searched the person of E. W. Frederick without the authorization of a search warrant or warrant for his arrest and found in one of his pockets a key with which they unlocked the receptacle in the rear portion of his automobile.

The government filed no answer or counter affidavit controverting the allegations set forth in the petition of plaintiff in error, E. W. Frederick, to return property and exclude evidence, but upon the trial sought to justify the conduct of its agents to establish the legality of the search by the following testimony. Their star witness, Kettle, was first called and testified that he was a reporter for the Fresno Herald and that:

"On the morning of May 16, 1923, certain people connected with the Prohibition and Police Department went into my room and got from there a case of gin." (Trans. Rec. page 59.)

"* * * I have since learned that my landlady turned a report into the police department that I had liquor in my room." (Trans. Rec. page 63.)

"* * * I had the case of gin in my house for beverage purposes. There were twelve bottles in the case of gin. I had that for about two weeks but not in that room. I had it on San Pablo Avenue. I did not get a permit to transport from San Pablo Avenue to my home. I knew it was in violation of the law to transport liquor from one place to another without securing a permit. I did not attempt to sell any of it. I was not drinking at the time. I was going to drink it. *I brought it to my home on the day of the arrest.*" (Trans. Rec. pages 61 and 62.)

Then the witness, Kettle, made two different statements concerning the person from whom he obtained the liquor. First stating:

*"I got it from Bigby."* (Then saying.) *"I didn't get it from Bigby. I didn't get it from Reyff.* I don't know the fellow's name I got it from. I made arrangements to have it delivered on San Pablo Avenue. I don't know the man's name that delivered it. I gave him the money for it. I made the arrangements at the jewelry store with Bigby about three or four weeks before I got the Scotch." (Trans. Rec. page 62.)

The witness, Kettle, also testified:

"I knew I was not going to be charged with violating the prohibition law. Mr. Nicely said 'I got that liquor out of your room without a search warrant, or anything else'. And he said 'Under the law I had no right to take it'. Nicely said, 'Where did you get it?' I said, 'I don't know where I got it from'. He said, 'I know where you got it and I will tell you where you got it. I just want you to go down and buy another one. Will you do that?' I said, 'Yes, I will go down and buy another one'." (Trans. Rec. page 60.)

The career of witness Kettle on May 16, 1923, went through a peculiar, if not a phenomenal, transition. From one pursued by the minions of the law he became the pursuer *on the same day*. Escaping arrest as a bootlegger, he assumed the role of a law enforcer with full powers to secure evidence, and may it please you, in order to legalize a winking at the Fourth and Fifth Amendments to the United States Constitution, it is contended that he was empowered to make a lawful arrest in enforcing the Statutes of Congress under the powers delegated to them by the Constitution of the United States.

Of his previous experience witness Kettle presents two versions. He said:

"I did not attempt to secure evidence until I was caught myself." (Trans. Rec. page 63.)

And in the same breath he stated:

"I secured evidence in other places before, within the same month before I went on this raid." (Trans. Rec. page 63.)

He also stated:

"I worked for Police Officers and Prohibition Officers for the last fifteen years. I worked on Prohibition raids before. I secured evidence before. In Fresno, Chicago, Kansas City and several places. I did not particularly secure evidence for the Prohibition Department of the State of California before." (Trans. Rec. page 62.)

The first statement must be taken as true for agent Nicely testified in referring to Kettle:

"He had never given me any information before. I have been at the head of the Prohibition forces in Fresno for three years and a half. During all that time he has not given me any information at all." (Trans. Rec. page 72.)

The following statement of F. D. Stribling, Internal Revenue Chemist and Federal Agent, a Government witness, would also seem to verify witness Kettle's first statement:

"I did not hear any statement to the effect that Kettle would have to go and get some evidence to try and save himself. I did not understand that that was the situation from anything I observed that day. I know that this liquor had been taken from him and I presumed that that had something to do with his going. It was not my impression that he was to receive any money although I don't know of any remarks that gave me that impression * * *. It was a presumption on my part, I think, that the finding of this liquor in his room had something to do with the arrangements that were being made." (Trans. Rec. page 82.)

At any rate, whether he was converted and volunteered his services in a neophyte's fervor, whether he was intimidated and driven on with a whip will always remain a mystery. However, he said:

> "At the instigation of the prohibition officers, I went to the store of the jeweler, Shaddow." (Trans. Rec. page 60.)

It might be well to observe again at this time that the witness Kettle displayed an unusual degree of moderation and complacency in hearing from the lips of a prohibition agent that he had taken twelve bottles of gin from his room without any warrant or right in law and in total disregard of the rights guaranteed him by the Fourth and Fifth Amendments to the United States Constitution and to thus embark on a series of acts and a course of conduct that showed such unusual zeal, that it well nigh bordered on entrapment, condemned by this Court in no uncertain language in the cases of

> Peterson v. U. S., 255 Fed. 433;
> Sam Yick v. U. S., 240 Fed. 60;
> Wo Wai v. U. S., 223 Fed. 412.

Thereupon, the witness, Kettle, went to the citadel of the notorious bootlegger Shaddow and instead of apprehending the captain himself made his advances to two boy employees; one a colored porter and the other a clerk. The record again is the best medium of narrating what occurred. (It should be borne in mind that everything in this case transpired on the day of the seizure of the gin from Kettle's room.)  Kettle said:

"I saw Bigby on the sidewalk opposite Shaddow's jewelry store.  I went down to make some arrangements to get some liquor.  When I first saw him no other person was present.  I had a conversation with him.  The conversation ran something like this: Kettle said: 'Do you remember me?'  Bibgy said: 'No, I don't.'  Kettle said: 'I bought some gin from you a while back.  I want to get another case.'  Bigby said: 'I haven't got any gin.  You must be mistaken.  I never sold you any gin.'  Kettle said: 'No, I am not mistaken.'  Bigby said: 'I haven't got any gin, *I think I can get you some whiskey.*'  Kettle said: 'How much is it?'  Bigby said: 'Just a minute, *I will have to find out about that.*'  Bigby then went inside the jewelry store and came back and said: '$100.00.'  Then Kettle said: *'Can you deliver it to my room?'*  Bigby said: 'When do you want it?'  Kettle said: 'I want it tonight.'  Bigby said: *'I will have to find that out.'*  And he went back into the store a second time and called Mr. Reyff out and introduced me to him.  And Reyff said: *'Yes, we can deliver it tonight.'*  I gave them the address to my house and Reyff said: 'What time do you want it?'  And I said: 'Make it eight o'clock.'  Reyff said: 'Will you be there?'  And I said: 'Yes'.  I then left the defendant."  (Trans. Rec. page 56.)

Then Kettle got in touch with his principal, Nicely.  This is how he puts it:

"I saw Mr. Nicely between the time I made the arrangements for the purchase and the time Mr. Frederick was arrested.  I saw him at police headquarters.  He gave me the money and told me to pay for the liquor and he asked me what arrangements had been made and I told him and he said: 'That is all. We will take care of the rest of it.' I told him what I was going to do. I did not tell him that I was going to drive around the block. I did not tell the officers to go into the garage. Mr. Nicely told me that they would be there.'' (Trans. Rec. page 62.)

And, again, Kettle swore:

"I first obtained the money from Mr. Nicely. Mr. Nicely took the serial numbers of the bills in my presence. (Trans. Rec. page 57.)

Following Mr. Kettle's story, he says:

"At eight o'clock I was at my room at 1041 'T' Street. At that time, I saw the defendants, Frederick and Reyff. They were in their machine in front of the house. I had a conversation with them at that time. Frederick spoke to me and said: 'I didn't know it was you I was bringing the liquor to.' I don't remember the rest of the conversation right then, but I told him to drive around to the garage in the rear. First, I asked him if he had the liquor there and he (Frederick) said, 'Yes, it is in the rear of the car.' Then, I said, 'Drive around to the garage and we will take it out there.' We drove around to the garage and while doing so I counted out $100.00 and gave it to Frederick. * * * We then drove around to the garage and Frederick still had the money in his hand. We pulled into the garage and got out on one side of the car and Frederick started to get out of the other. Reyff was in the center. The car was a roadster. I was on the right hand side and Frederick was driving on the left. The conversation took place while Reyff was seated by his side. The conversation was not very

loud. I think Mr. Reyff heard the conversation. He was seated between Mr. Frederick
and myself in the automobile. After we got
into the garage, Mr. Nicely and two deputies
came from the rear of the garage. One man
took hold of me and one took hold of each of
the other two. At that time, Mr. Frederick
threw the money away and it went under the
motor car. I did not see him throw it away.
I was on the other side of the car. I heard
something go under the car and I heard one
of the deputies say: 'Where is the money?'
And he said: 'What money?' * * * The prohibition officers in the garage did not exhibit
any search warrant to search the automobile in
question. I did not know whether they had a
warrant for the arrest of Frederick or anybody else. I believe that the rear portion of
the machine was closed down. The money was
not handed to Frederick in that garage. It was
handed to him on the outside. *I do not know
whether Prohibition Officer Nicely or Prohibition Officer Emrich or anybody connected
with them had any knowledge of what transpired from the time I left the house and went
into the garage. I do not know whether they
were conversant with what took place.*" (Trans.
Rec. pages 56 to 58, inc.)

Here the Court questioned the witness:

"The COURT. Had you told them the bargain
you had made?

WITNESS. Yes, sir.

The COURT. You told them of the arrangements and the time and place they were to be
delivered?

WITNESS. Yes, sir.

The COURT. And that was the reason they
were there?

WITNESS. Yes, sir.'' (Trans. Rec. pages 58 and 59.)

Kettle's testimony is the gist of the evidence in the case. Witness Kettle was the only person who could have any direct knowledge as to what transpired before the defendants, Reyff and Frederick, were placed under arrest. No other witnesses claimed to be present when Kettle had his alleged conversations with plaintiffs in error, Bigby and Reyff, at Shaddow's jewelry store. The Government officers did not see Kettle enter Shaddow's jewelry store and except for his word they did not even know that he was there. It is true agent Nicely marked a certain number of bills, aggregating a hundred dollars, but neither agent Nicely nor the other Government witnesses knew what Kettle did with those bills. They did not hear the alleged conversations which Kettle said were had with plaintiffs in error, Frederick and Reyff, before the search and seizure. They did not know, neither did Kettle know, that there was intoxicating liquor in the automobile of plaintiff in error, E. W. Frederick; at no time was there any liquor in sight and we believe that the prohibition officers were not legally justified in arresting any of the plaintiffs in error upon the word of a man who had just been apprehended in a violation of the same law for which plaintiffs in error were arrested, and who was so much interested that he was seeking to extricate himself from the situation he was then in at the expense of plaintiffs in error.

It should also be borne in mind that plaintiffs in error, Reyff and Frederick, were assaulted and placed under arrest before even the prohibition enforcement officers had time to procure their information from their decoy.

This statement of fact is predicated upon the following testimony:

Prohibition Agent Nicely testified:

"I first saw Mr. Frederick and Mr. Reyff at 8 o'clock that evening in a garage on 'T' Street. They drove into the garage in a Chalmers roadster. After they got into the garage we stepped over to the car. Mr. Kettle stepped out of the car; Mr. Reyff stayed in the car. Mr. Frederick was on the other side of the car and Agent Stribling stepped around on the other side of the car near to Mr. Frederick *and they started scuffling over there. I went around there then and we put the handcuffs on Mr. Frederick and Mr. Reyff and placed them under arrest and then we started searching for some marked money and Agent Stribling found it lying right by the left front wheel under the car by the fender. Agent Stribling picked it up.* I examined the bills when I gave them to witness Kettle. * * * This money was picked up off the ground and the numbers checked, that is, the number of the bills were read off and checked with the notation that I had previously made. I do not know where the money is now. It was my money and after it had been used I used it again, then I asked Mr. Frederick where the case of liquor that he had was. *And he said he had no liquor.* I asked him for the key for the rear end of the automobile, the rear compartment."

"We unlocked the rear compartment to his automobile and took from this sack with letter 'K' on it the liquor contained therein and the one bottle of liquor sitting on the table." (Trans. Rec. pages 63, 64 and 65.)

Again the same witness testified:

"Before I opened the rear compartment of the automobile, the defendants were placed under arrest." (Trans. Rec. page 65.)

The same witness said:

"I did not see Kettle give that money to anybody. I did not see either the defendants, Frederick or Reyff, throw that money on the floor. I do not know now of my own knowledge whether Kettle ever gave those bills to either of the defendants." (Trans. Rec. page 70.)

Finally on the same subject, the same witness said:

"I do not know whether Reyff participated in any sale which was to be consummated. *I do not know anything about the arrangements between Kettle and the colored boy, only what Kettle told me. I depended upon Kettle for my information.*" (Trans. Rec. page 72.)

In a similar vein Prohibition Enforcement Officer Emrich testified:

"I had knowledge of an anticipated sale at that place. I went to the garage in company with Mr. Stribling and Agent Nicely. About 8 o'clock in drove a Chalmers roadster, in which was Mr. Frederick and Mr. Reyff, accompanied by Mr. Kettle. Mr. Kettle and he got out of the machine and Mr. Frederick had his right hand closed. *'They had been placed under arrest'*, and I was about to search them for the marked money when he made a motion with his hand down towards the left front wheel of the Chalmers roadster. Mr. Stribling came around and was looking down where he made this motion and picked up that marked money. We then opened up the back of the car and found that whiskey.'' (Trans. Rec. page 73.)

And again the same witness at another time said:

"As far as my knowledge goes I don't know anything about Mr. Bigby in this transaction at all. He was not present at the time the machine stopped in the alley or the garage.'' (Trans. Rec. page 75.)

And finally this witness testified:

"I do not claim that Mr. Reyff or Mr. Bigby had any interest in the car whatsoever. Bigby was not in the vicinity that I know of. I know that Mr. Frederick was handcuffed, but just what time it was, whether the key had been gotten before he was handcuffed or after I can not state positively. *We had advanced information that there was to be a delivery. It was to such an extent that we, at least figured that probably we had information that the sale had been consummated at that time.* I knew of my own knowledge that a sale had been consummated at that time because when Mr. Kettle got out of the car he nodded his head and by that I knew the sale had been consummated. I never saw any money passed. I knew a sale was completed then, * * * well, Mr. Frederick had the money there.'' (Trans. Rec. page 77.)

And lastly F. D. Stribling, the third Government officer testifying upon the subject under discussion, said:

"I saw these defendants in the garage. I don't know the address. There were present Agents Emrich and Nicely and defendants, Frederick and Reyff and the witness Kettle and myself. * * * I was under the impression that it was something about 8 o'clock anyhow, it was dark when this car drove in. I went on the right hand side of the car and Agent Nicely went on the right hand side of the car. I got hold of the witness Kettle and Agent Nicely caught hold of defendant, Reyff, and Agent Emrich caught hold of Frederick. It was agreed before hand that I was to go after the money and the witness Kettle was to give me the information as to who had the money and as to where it was. Witness Kettle whispered, not Reyff, and indicating that defendant, Frederick had the money. I was still holding to his arm and then went around on that side, that is, on the left hand side of the car and reached in the right hand pocket as it was my impression that the money was in the right hand pocket of the defendant but the money was not there. As I was reaching in his right hand pocket he pulled the money out of his right hand and it brushed my hand; I then grabbed hold of his right arm, and I believe my exact words were 'Loose it! Loose it!' but he didn't want to turn it loose." (Trans. Rec. page 80.)

At this time a very significant remark was made and an action unnecessarily long delayed took place.

"We struggled there a few minutes and then something was said about the marshal. Then

Agent Nicely showed his badge and then he quit struggling; but when he opened his right hand it was empty. Then I looked on the garage floor and the money was there and I had felt the bills in his hand just before that." (Trans. Rec. page 80.)

The Court, in finally determining the motion for the return of property and exclusion of evidence, said:

"I think that there are other angles and matters to be considered. Here is a case where the informant, to call him such, had actual knowledge of the sale that was about to be made, because he negotiated it; he made the arrangements and in accordance with the arrangements he had made for the delivery of the liquor at a place men appeared in an automobile and informed him that they had the liquor. The money was paid over and the sale became complete. Now, that man, irrespective of any official character had the right to make the arrest himself; he had the right to arrest the man. That would be sufficient, in my judgment, to constitute the commission of a misdemeanor, these things having been done in his presence and with his actual knowledge. That being true, the officers acting upon the full information that all of these things that these men had done and the things that were being done, all the circumstances coinciding that these men had produced the liquor at that time and they then had the money. I think they were justified in the action they took in arresting the men and seizing the liquor without a search warrant." (Trans. Rec. pages 89 and 90.)

We must disregard what the search brought forth as having no bearing at all upon the legality of the search and seizure, and we deem it not necessary to fortify this statement by authorities, which are manifold, and in passing it might be well to observe that the Courts of this country have always abhorred the doctrine: "That the end justifies the means", cognizant as they·must be, of the evils that in other times lurked therein. We respectfully submit that the hearsay of Kettle, characterized as information, relied upon by the Government was of the most vicious and questionable character, for, except by subsequent results, the arresting officers had no means of judging of its truth or falsity or of his reliability. They had never received information from him before, in fact, they hardly knew him. He was interested, which alone would create presumptions against the truth of what he might say, having been apprehended for a similar offense the same day himself. He was not a sworn officer of the United States and was accountable only to his own liberty for his actions.

———

**The Search and Seizure in the Instant Case Was Illegal—Was Unreasonable—Because the Person of E. W. Frederick and His Automobile Were Searched and a Seizure Made Therefrom Without the Authorization of Any Search Warrant.**

The search was in violation of the Fourth and Fifth Amendments to the United States Constitution, which are as follows:

*"The right of the people to be secure in their persons, houses, papers and effects, against unreasonable searches and seizures, shall not be violated, and no warrants shall issue, but upon probable cause, supported by Oath or Affirmation, and particularly describing the place to be searched and the persons or things to be seized."* (Fourth Amendment to the United States Constitution.)

*"Nor shall any person be subject for the same offense to be twice put in jeopardy of life or limb; nor shall be compelled in any Criminal Case to be a witness against himself nor be deprived of life, liberty or property without due process of law."* (Part of the Fifth Amendment to the United States Constitution.)

We believe that the following authorities justify us in declaring the search and seizure in the instant case unconstitutional and illegal:

Amos v. U. S., 255 U. S. 315;

Gouled v. U. S., 255 U. S. 298;

Silverthorne Lumber Co. v. U. S., 251 U. S. 155;

Weeks v. U. S., 232 U. S. 383;

Boyd v. U. S., 116 U. S. 616;

Temperani v. U. S., 299 Fed. 365 (C. C. A. 9th Circuit);

Legman v. U. S., 295 Fed. 474 (C. C. A. 3rd Circuit);

Miucki v. U. S., 289 Fed. 47 (C. C. A. 7th Circuit);

Pressley v. U. S., 289 Fed. 477 (C. C. A. 5th Circuit);

Jozwich v. U. S., 288 Fed. 831 (C. C. A. 7th Circuit);

Ganci v. U. S., 287 Fed. 60 (C. C. A. 2nd Circuit);

Salada v. U. S., 286 Fed. 125 (C. C. A. 6th Circuit);

Murphy v. U. S., 285 Fed. 801 (C. C. A. 7th Circuit);

Snyder v. U. S., 285 Fed. 1 (C. C. A. 4th Circuit);

Woods v. U. S., 279 Fed. 706 (C. C. A. 4th Circuit);

Giles v. U. S., 284 Fed. 208 (C. C. A. 1st Circuit);

Berry v. U. S., 275 Fed. 680 (C. C. A. 7th Circuit);

Veeder v. U. S., 252 Fed. 415 (C. C. A. 7th Circuit);

Ripper v. U. S., 178 Fed. 24 (C. C. A. 8th Circuit);

U. S. v. Sievers, 292 Fed. 394;

U. S. v. Myers, 287 Fed. 260;

U. S. v. Jozwich, 285 Fed. 789;

U. S. v. Falloco, 277 Fed. 75;

U. S. v. Mitchell, 274 Fed. 128;

U. S. v. Kelih, 272 Fed. 484;

U. S. v. Slusser, 270 Fed. 818;

U. S. v. Abrams, 230 Fed. 313;

U. S. v. McHie, 194 Fed. 894;

State v. Owens, 259 S. W. 100 (Mo.);

Hughes v. The State, 238 S. W. 588 (Tenn.);

State v. Dist. Court, etc., 225 Pac. 1000
(Mont.);

State v. Gibbons, 203 Pac. 390 (Wash.);

Hoyer v. The State, 193 N. W. 89 (Wis.);

State v. One Hudson Cabriolet, 190 N. Y. S.
481 (N. Y.);

People v. De Vasto, 190 N. Y. S. 816 (N. Y.);

Douglas v. The State, 110 S. E. 168 (Ga.);

Tucker v. The State, 90 So. 845 (Miss.);

People v. Marxhausen, 171 N. W. 557
(Mich.).

In the leading case of Gouled v. United States,
255 U. S. 298, the learned Justice says, on page
308 of his opinion:

> "The working of the Fourth Amendment implies that search warrants were in familiar use, when the Constitution was adopted, and plainly, that when issued 'Upon probable cause', supported by oath or affirmation and particularly describing the place to be searched and the persons and things to be seized, searches and seizures made under them are to be regarded as not unreasonable, and therefore not prohibited by the Amendment. Searches and seizures are as Constitutional under the Amendment when made under valid search warrants as they are Unconstitutional because unreasonable when made without them—the permission of the Amendment has the same Constitutional warrant as the prohibition has, and the definition of the former restrains the scope of the latter."

And on page 304 thereof, the same Judge said:

> "It would not be possible to add to the emphasis with which the framers of our Con-

stitution and this Court (in Boyd v. United States, 116 U. S. 616; 25 L. Ed. 746; 6 Sup. Ct. Rep. 524, in Weeks v. United States, Ann. Cas. 1915C, 1177, and in Silverthorne Lumber Co. v. United States, 251 U. S. 385; 64 L. Ed. 319; 40 Sup. Ct. Rep. 182), have declared the importance to political liberty and to the welfare of our Country of the due observance of the rights guaranteed under the Constitution by these two Amendments. The effect of the decisions cited is: That such rights are declared to be indispensable to the 'full enjoyment of personal security, personal liberty, and private property'; that they are to be regarded of the very essence of constitutional liberty; and that the guaranty of them is as imporant and as imperative as are the guarantees of other fundamental rights of the individual citizen,— the right to trial by jury, to the writ of habeas corpus, and to due process of law. It has been repeatedly decided that these Amendments should receive a liberal construction, so as to prevent stealthy encroachment upon or 'gradual depreciation' of the rights secured by them, by imperceptible practice of Courts, or by well-intentioned but mistakenly over-zealous executive officers.''

And again on page 306, the Court says:

"Is the admission of such paper in evidence against the same person when indicted for crime, a violation of the Fifth Amendment?

Upon authority of the Boyd case, supra, this second question must also be answered in the affirmative. In practice the result is the same, to one accused of crime, whether he is obliged to supply evidence against himself or whether such evidence be obtained by an illegal search of his premises and seizure of his private papers. In either case he is the unwilling source of the evidence and the Fifth Amendment forbids that he shall be compelled to be a witness against himself.''

The authorities cited above approach the principles here involved from various angles. The Gouled and Silverthorne Lumber Company and Woods cases treated of an illegal seizure from a man's private office. The Boyd case treats of an illegal production of papers belonging to the defendant. The Weeks, Temperani, Jozwich, Ganci, Pressley and Mitchell cases treat of illegal searches and seizures from the homes of defendants. The Amos, Salata, Murphy and Muicki cases condemn searches and seizures without search warrants from the places of business of the accused. The Berry case is authority for the proposition that Federal agents, without the authority of a search warrant have no right to search the ice-box of a soft drink parlor. The Snyder case forbids the search of an individual's person, even though a bottle was seen protruding from the defendant's pocket, without the authorization of a search warrant. The cases of United States v. Myers; Hughes v. The State; Douglas v. The State; Hoyer v. The State, and The State v. One Hudson Cabriolet proclaim the search of automobiles, without the authorization of a search warrant, illegal.

The principles enunciated in the case of Boyd v. The United States, 116 U. S. 616, and reaffirmed in the celebrated case of Gouled v. The United States, quoted supra, and followed in opinions by every Circuit Court of the United States, as well as by numerous State jurisdictions apply with equal force to protect the people against illegal and unlawful searches, seizures and arrests in automobiles and other vehicles.

## A

### Section 26 of the National Prohibition Act Does Not Authorize a Violation of the Fourth and Fifth Amendments to the United States Constitution.

Section 26 of the National Prohibition Act provides:

> "When the commissioner, his assistants, inspectors or any officer of the law shall discover any person in the act of transporting in violation of the law, intoxicating liquors in any wagon, buggy, automobile, water or aircraft, or other vehicle, it shall be his duty to seize any and all intoxicating liquors found therein being transported contrary to law. Whenever intoxicating liquors transported or possessed illegally shall be seized by any officer he shall take possession of the vehicle and team or automobile, boat, air or watercraft, or any other conveyance and shall arrest any person in charge thereof."

Sec. 26, Title II, Act October 28, 1919 (Barnes' Federal Code Cum. Supp. 1923, page 740).

*Does this Section authorize a Federal prohibition enforcement officer to stop an automobile or search one already stopped for the purpose of ascertaining whether it is being used as a means of transporting liquor?*

If it does, it subjects the people to as much tyranny from over-zealous officers and members of fanatical self-constituted law enforcement organizations as the people endured in pre-revolutionary days. It would also render the driver or occupant of an automobile or other vehicle a prey, to the criminals who infest the public streets and highways and who utilize modern means of transportation to commit murders and robberies. For if one may be stopped on the highway and arrested without a warrant by Government officers or persons pretending to be such, who do not announce their authority or purpose, then one cannot defend himself or flee from peril until he becomes convinced that the person stopping him had not the right to do so. For if one, even though innocent of any wrong doing, does not stop or submit to a search he risks violence at the hands of the officer who thinks he has the right to stop him or, if one stops when hailed, expecting a search, and the person stopping him is not an officer the occupant of the automobile is already at the mercy of the robber intent upon his plunder.

We do not think that this was the intention of the lawmakers and if it was, we respectfully submit that such a law would soon be declared unconstitutional and would go the way of some of the revenue statutes which sought to nullify the effect of the Fourth and Fifth Amendments to the United States Constitution. For such a construction is violative, not only of the United States Constitution but of the Common Law and is condemned in the decisions of this country and England from Semaynes case decided in England in 1604 (5 Co. Rep. 91: English Ruling Cases, Vol. II, page 631), to the Act of Congress of June 15, 1917. In all the decisions on the question of the service of warrants or other process there is one uniform note—that the authority and purpose of the arresting officer *must* first be given before any breaking can be made or arrest effectuated.

"In all cases when the King is a party, the Sheriff (if the doors be not opened) may break the party's house, either to arrest him or to do other execution of the King's process. If otherwise, he cannot enter. But before he breaks it he ought to signify the cause of his coming and making request to open doors." "And that appears well by the Statute of Westm. I Chap. 17, which is but an affirmance of the Common Law as hereafter appears, for the law without a default in the owner abhors the destruction of the breaking of any house by which great damage and inconvenience might ensue to the party when no default is in him; for perhaps he did not know of the process of which, if he had notice, it is to be presumed that he would obey, and that appears by the Book in 18 Ed. II on Execut. 252, where it is said, that the King's Officer who comes to do execution may open the doors, which are shut, and break them if he cannot have the keys; which proves that he ought first to demand them, 7 Ed. III, 16;" * * * "By force of a capias on an indictment to trespass, the Sheriff may break his house to arrest him; but in such case if he breaks the house, when he may enter without breaking it, (that is on request made, or if he may open the door without breaking it), he is a trespasser.''

Semaynes Case, 5 Co. Rep. 91;

English Ruling Cases, Col. II, page 631.

This case is here cited to demonstrate the English insistence upon due process of law in serving process and the necessity of notice to the persons to be arrested of the authority and the purpose of the person making the arrest. By analogy we must assume that the same rules should be applied in cases such as the instant one. And if a sheriff with the King's writ in his hand issued by a judicial officer was obliged to take these precautions in consideration of the rights of his fellow subjects, how much more rigid should be the rules regulating the conduct of petty officers in making arrests for petty offenses.

An officer can never determine for himself what constitutes probable cause and in cases of misdemeanor he should always have a warrant, unless he sees a crime committed in his presence. Hearsay, no matter how reliable, does not constitute probable cause, and if an officer is informed by some person else that a crime has been committed, he should take that person to a magistrate or appropriate judicial authority and have a warrant issued upon that person's sworn testimony.

It has been held, in re Kellam's case, 55 Kan. Rep. 700:

"That a statute conferring authority upon the police officers of a City to make an arrest so far as it attempts to authorize an arrest without a warrant for misdemeanors not committed in the view of the officer, and merely upon suspicion, is unconstitutional and void.''

On page 702, the Court said:

"This provision guarantees protection against unreasonable arrests and when it was placed in the Constitution, and in fact ever since that time, an arrest for a minor offense without a warrant and not in view of the officer was deemed to be unreasonable and unlawful. Under the Common Law arrests without warrant were not permitted, except for offenses committed in the view of the officer; and in cases of felony actually committed the officer might also arrest upon a reasonable suspicion." "The liberty of a citizen was so highly regarded, however, that the officer arresting the supposed felon without warrant, must have acted in good faith, and upon grounds of probable suspicion that the person arrested was the actual felon.''

And on pages 703-4, the same Court said:

"If an arrest cannot be made or justified on a warrant resting only on hearsay or belief, how can an arrest for a petty offense without a warrant upon the mere suspicion of an officer, not resting even on hearsay or belief be justified. He may be irresponsible, have heard only an idle rumor, and may be actuated by malice or some unworthy motive, *and to give an officer unlimited authority to arrest without a warrant in all cases upon mere suspicion is unreasonable and a clear infringement of the constitutional rights of the people. It is in effect, a revival of the odious general warrants which placed the liberty of every man in the hands of every petty officer, and which long ago received judicial condemnation.*"

**We Submit That the Proper Construction to Place Upon Section 26 is That an Officer Cannot Be Said to Have Discovered a Person in the Illegal Act of Transporting Intoxicating Liquor Unless He Has Personal Knowledge of It.**

Such a construction is not repugnant to the language of the Fourth and Fifth Amendments to the United States Constitution.

It was so held in the case of United States v. Slusser, 270 Fed. 818.

In this case the facts were somewhat similar to the case at bar, an automobile was standing in the defendant's garage with liquor in it. The Federal officers entered the garage without a search warrant. The defendant was arrested and his automibile seized. The Court holding on page 821 of said reports:

> "A seizure without warrant in a private garage pursuant to an unauthorized search upon the charge of a mere statutory misdemeanor, is an unlawful seizure and cannot be made the basis of a valid forfeiture under the 26th section of the Volstead Law. The right of an officer of the law to enter to arrest for, prevent, felony or breach of the peace, in which actual or threatened violence is an essential element, is not here in issue."

So also in the case of State v. One Hudson Cabriolet Automobile, 190 N. Y. Supp. 841, in a case similar to the instant case, the Court held:

> "If an officer actually sees, or has before him direct tangible proof that liquors are being transported unlawfully in a given vehicle, he may seize that vehicle and the contents thereof and arrest the person in charge. In such a case he finds *or discovers* within the meaning of the

statute. But if he merely suspects or believes, or without suspicion or belief seizes or searches for the purpose of obtaining knowledge, his act is unjustified, and unwarranted by the statute; for if the statute should be otherwise construed it would be in my opinion null and void.''

The Court had under consideration a New York Statute similar to the quoted portions of Section 26 of the National prohibition law and included in his opinion the following excerpt, taken from an opinion handed down by the Attorney General for the State of New York on May 4, 1921:

"At Common Law, a person can be arrested for a misdemeanor only when it was committed in the presence of the person making it. Under the language quoted, it seems to me that the common law powers of the officer are not extended by the provision that he shall make an arrest and a seizure when he shall discover a person in an illegal act. The statute does not authorize a seizure or the arrest where he has suspicion that the law is being violated, or where *he has information only,* although if put in proper form, it would form the basis for the issue of a warrant.''

"I think the officer cannot be said to have discovered a person in the illegal act unless he has personal knowledge of it. I believe therefore that a peace officer had no right to stop an automobile or other conveyance for the purpose of ascertaining whether it is being used as a means of transporting liquor illegally.''

Neither can the arrest and search be justified upon the theory that a crime was committed in the presence of the officers.

## B.

**An Officer Cannot Make an Arrest for a Misdemeanor Not Committed in His Presence, Without a Warrant.**

The record shows that the prohibition enforcement officers and Kettle, did not see, hear, taste, smell or touch any intoxicating liquor until after plaintiffs in error Reyff and Frederick had been arrested and none of said witnesses had any personal knowledge that plaintiffs in error Reyff and Frederick had said liquor in their possession or were transporting same on the date set forth in the information. Neither had either of the prohibition enforcement officers any personal knowledge or information derived from the operation of their five senses that arrangements were being made for the sale of intoxicating liquor. Kettle claims that he made certain arrangements for the sale of certain intoxicating liquor, with all three plaintiffs in error. If that be so, that fact would not give the Federal prohibition enforcement officers the right to determine whether or not Kettle was telling the truth and make an arrest of the plaintiffs in error upon his say so, but they should have taken Kettle to the United States Commissioner and have him make a sworn complaint against plaintiffs in error, then they should have secured the approval of the United States District Attorney in writing, and then, if the Judge or United States Commissioner saw fit, a warrant for the arrest of plaintiffs in error could be issued. Only such a procedure constitutes due process of law. For Section 29, Chapter 252 of the

Act of May 28, 1896, 29 Stat. 184 (Barnes' Federal Code, Section 1415, page 322), provides:

"Warrants for arrests for violation of Internal Revenue laws may be issued by United States Commissioners upon the sworn complaint of a United States district attorney, assistant United States district attorney, collector, or deputy collector of internal revenue, or private citizen, but no such warrant of arrest shall be issued upon the sworn statement of a private citizen unless first approved in writing by a United States district attorney."

We respectfully submit that Sections 2 and 28 of the National Prohibition Act, and Section 1014 of the Revised Statutes contemplate the procedure set forth in the Act of May 28, 1896, cited supra, in cases such as the one at bar.

For the law contemplates that for every injury there is a redress and that the accuser must face consequences as well as the accused, if said accuser makes false accusations. The arrest of a citizen is such an infraction of his legal rights that it cannot be effectuated except by the sworn complaint before a judicial tribunal of some one who can be prosecuted for perjury if his charges are false. Then that judicial tribunal must determine whether there is probable cause before it issues any warrant depriving a citizen of his liberty. And to delegate to petty officers the right to determine whether they shall arrest and cast a man into prison upon the mere statements of an informer, caught red-handed in a violation of the law on the same day, is not authorized by the Common Law and was not the intention of the framers of the Constitution of the United States, who placed the Fourth and Fifth Amendments there to guard against just such methods.

In passing upon a set of circumstances very similar to the case under discussion, the Circuit Court of Appeals, of the Seventh Circuit, in the case of Veeder v. United States, 252 Fed. page 418, the Court says:

> "No search warrant shall be issued unless the judge has first been furnished with facts under oath—not suspicions, beliefs, or surmises—but facts which, when the law if properly applied to them, tend to establish probable cause for believing that the legal conclusion is right. The inviolability of the accused's home is to be determined by the facts, not by rumor, suspicion, or guess work. If the facts afford the legal basis for the search warrant the accused must take the consequences. But equally there must be consequences for the accuser to face. If the sworn accusation is based on fiction, the accuser must take the chance of being punished for perjury. Hence the necessity of a sworn statement of facts, because one can not be convicted of perjury for having a belief, though the belief be utterly unfounded in fact and law."

The authorities are manifold that arrests made, such as the case at bar, are unconstitutional and void. See:

Elk v. United States, 177 U. S. 529;

Snyder v. United States, 285 Fed. 1;

Berry v. United States, 275 Fed. 680;

United States v. Myers, 287 Fed. 260;

United States v. Slusser, 270 Fed. 818;

Hughes v. The State, 238 S. W. 588 (Tenn.);

Douglass v. The State, 110 S. E. 168 (Ga.);

Hoyer v. The State, 193 N. W. 89 (Wis.);

State v. Gibbons, 203 Pac. 390 (Wash.);

State v. One Hudson Cabriolet, 190 N. Y. Sup. 481 (N. Y.);

United States v. McHie, 194 Fed. 894;

State v. The District Court, 225 Pac. 1000 (Mont.);

In re Kellam, 55 Kan. 700 (Kan.);

Commonwealth v. Wright, 158 Mass. 149 (Mass.);

McLennon, v. Richardson, 81 Mass. 74 (Mass.);

People v. Glennon, 74 N. Y. Sup. 794 (N. Y.).

In the case of John Bald Elk v. United States, 177 U. S. 529, the facts were that three policemen under verbal orders to arrest another policeman for, an alleged violation of the law, to-wit, a misdemeanor, firing arms in Pine Ridge Reservation, when no charge had been formally made against him, and no warrant had issued for his arrest, attempted to make the arrest, carrying arms with them, and when he refused to go they tried to oblige him to do so by force. He fired and killed one of them and was arrested, was tried for murder and convicted. The Court below had instructed the jury that the defendant had no right to resist arrest and that the policemen had the right to arrest him without warrant.

The Supreme Court held:

"We think the Court clearly erred in charging the jury that the policemen had the right to arrest the plaintiff in error and to use such force as was necessary to accomplish the arrest and that the plaintiff in error had no right to resist it."

"So an officer at common law was not authorized to make an arrest without a warrant for a mere misdemeanor not committed in his presence. (Citing authorities.) If the officer had no right to arrest, the other party might resist the illegal attempt to arrest him, using no more force than was absolutely necessary to repel the assault constituting the attempt to arrest."

And on page 535 of the reports, the Court states:

"Referring to the laws of South Dakota, we find no authority for making such an arrest without a warrant. The law upon the subject of arrests in that State is contained in the Compiled Laws of South Dakota, 1887, Section 7134 and the following sections, and it will be seen that the common law is therein substantially enacted." * * * "No rule or regulation for government of Indians upon a reservation has been cited, nor have we found any, which prohibits the firing of a gun there, 'for fun', nor do we find any law, rule, or regulation which authorizes an arrest without warrant, of an Indian not charged even with the commission of a misdemeanor, nor does it anywhere appear that Gleason had authority to issue a warrant for an alleged violation of the rules or regulations."

So it was also held in the case of Snyder v. United States, 285 Fed. 1:

"In this case, Snyder was standing in one of the public streets of Wheeling, West Virginia, when he was approached by a Federal prohibition officer, who observed the inside pocket of his overcoat bulging out and the neck of a bottle protruding therefrom. The prohibition officer walked up to him, placed his hand on Snyder's shoulder, remarked that 'he had beat him to it', and forcibly lifted the bottle halfway out of his pocket with the other hand, and finding it to contain a liquid of the appearance of whiskey, placed him under arrest and took him in spite of his protest into a nearby store, searched him and found three other similar bottles. The defendant petitioned the Court for a suppression of the evidence, the District Attorney filed an answer admitting the arrest without a warrant, but denied its unlawful nature upon the ground that the offense charged, to-wit, transportation of liquor, was committed in the presence of the officer.''

The Circuit Court had this to say:

"That an officer may not make an arrest for a misdemeanor not committed in his presence without a warrant, has been so frequently decided as not to require citation of authority. It is equally fundamental that a citizen may not be arrested on suspicion of having committed a misdemeanor and have his person searched by force, without a warrant of arrest. If therefore, the arresting officer in this case had no other justification of the arrest than the mere suspicion that a bottle, only the neck of which he could see protruding from the pocket of defendant's coat contained intoxicating liquor, then it would seem to follow without much question that the arrest and search, without having secured a warrant were illegal. And that his only justification was his suspicion is admitted by the evidence of the arresting officer himself. If the bottle had been empty, or it had contained any one of a dozen innoxious liquids, the act of the officer would, admittedly have been an unlawful invasion of the personal liberty of the defendant. That it happened in this instance to contain whiskey we think *neither justifies the assault nor condemns the principle which makes such an act unlawful.*"

And likewise in the case of Berry v. United States, 275 Fed. 680; here the plaintiffs in error were convicted of *selling beer* in violation of the Volstead act. Government agents purchased two bottles containing some sort of liquid and drank the contents. They were permitted, over the objection, to say that what they drank was beer. At the trial the Government agents testified that they were not chemists, attempted no analysis, and established no expert qualifications to measure the alcoholic contents of the liquid by drinking it. The same agents took two other and similar bottles from the ice chest in the defendant's place. They had no search warrant. One of the bottles was analyzed afterwards by the chemist for the Government and upon analysis was found to contain alcohol in excess of the amount permitted by the National Prohibition Act. The bottle and contents were admitted over the objection of the defendants as exhibits in evidence.

The Court said:

"So the conviction is plainly bottomed on the exhibit and the chemist's testimony, that is, on the evidence which would never have had any existence but for the Government's violation of the restraint put on it by the Fourth

Amendment. Cases of this kind must be judged as if the illegal seizure had never been made."

In the case of Commonwealth v. Wright, 158 Mass. 149, it was held:

"It is suggested that the statutory misdemeanor . of having in one's possession short lobsters with intent to sell them is a continuing offense, which is being committed while such possession continues and that therefore an officer who sees any person in possession of such lobsters with intent to sell them can arrest such person without a warrant, as for a misdemeanor committed in his presence. We are of the opinion that such statutory misdemeanors of this kind, not amounting to a breach of the peace there is no authority in an officer to arrest without a warrant unless it is given by statute."

And in. the case of People v. Glennon, 75 N. Y. Sup. 794, the Court decided as follows:

"That a policeman was not direlict in his duties by reason of failure to search a house of ill fame and arrest the keeper thereof on mere suspicion and without either a warrant to arrest or a search warrant. The Court saying: The law does not tolerate the idea that anyone may be arrested by a police officer for an alleged criminal offense of the grade of misdemeanor, except on a warrant duly obtained from a magistrate, unless the offense was committed in the view of the officer. If a police officer knows facts which show that a criminal offense of the grade of misdemeanor has been committed, *but which he did not see committed then there is only one course for him to pursue:* that is his duty to go before a magistrate and make a written complaint under oath of such facts and obtain a warrant and then make the arrest with such warrant. *If the officer does not know such facts, but some person who professes to know them tells him of them, the officer can not obtain a warrant, much less make an arrest without a warrant on such hearsay."*

In the case of Hughes v. State, Supreme Court of Tennessee, 238 S. W. 588. This case is particularly interesting and instructive because it applies the law in the seizure of liquor in automobiles and the arrest of persons therefrom.

What the Court said is found on page 595 of the Report:

"It follows, therefore, that it can not be said that the plaintiff in error was in the commission of an offense in the presence of the officers, so as to justify the arrest merely from the fact that when the arrest was effected it was found that he was actually committing the offense. Neither is it sufficient to justify the arrest that the officer had information justifying him in the belief that an offense was being committed, for the facts constituting the offense must have been within the knowledge of the officer, and that knowledge must have been revealed in the officer's presence. To illustrate: If a person has in his possession a concealed weapon upon his person, but if there is no evidence of that fact apparent to an officer, his arrest would be unwarranted. The plaintiff in error may have been, as it was subsequently developed, engaged in the transportation of liquor in violation of the law, but the fact of his having liquor was not evident to the officer making the arrest. It must be held, therefore, that the arrest can not be justified upon the ground of the commission of an offense in the presence of the officer.''

To similar purport are the cases of Hoyer v. State, Supreme Court of Wisconsin, 193 N. W. 89 and State v. Gibbons, Supreme Court of Washington, 203 Pac. 390. These cases are extremely important because they discuss seizures of liquor from automobiles and arrests of persons therein. They were decided since the passage of the National Prohibition Act, and apply the principles set forth in the cases cited in this subdivision of this brief in the same manner.

But the case of the most importance, because it decides the question of unlawful arrest without warrant, under a statement of facts identical with the case at bar, is the case of Douglass v. State, decided by the Supreme Court of Georgia and is found in 110 S. E. 168.

The facts briefly stated were as follows:

*The plaintiff in error was tried and convicted of murder. On the day of the homicide the sheriff and others met an informant by name of Ivans, the sheriff offering the informant a reward of $25.00 for each automobile containing whiskey caught by means of aid from the informant. All parties separated and that night the informant phoned to the sheriff that he had information that there would be a car of whiskey at three o'clock at Nickajack Gap. Informant said that he met one Headrick who came to him and asked him if he wanted some whiskey,* *to which he replied in the affirmative. That Headrick introduced h\m to Douglas and Willie Burt; that he had made a contract with Douglass and Willie Burt for 26 gallons of whiskey* TO BE DELIVERED TO HIM *at or near Headrick's house in Chattanooga Valley the following morning. The informant, Ivans, did not know Douglass or Burt prior to this time. Ivans held no official position at this time but testified that the sheriff was to give him a commission as deputy sheriff the next day. Ivans testified further* THAT HE HAD BEEN IN TROUBLE IN CHATTANOOGA FOR SELLING LIQUOR. HE HAD BEEN IN THE LIQUOR BUSINESS TWO OR THREE MONTHS BEFORE THIS HOMICIDE AND KNEW HE WAS VIOLATING THE LAW. HE SAID HE ARRANGED FOR THESE COUNTRY BOYS TO BRING THE WHISKEY AND HIS AIM WAS TO TRAP THEM. *Informant said that he and plaintiff in error and others would be at the designated point in a Ford car. The sheriff organized a party to go in search of plaintiff in error at Nickajack Gap. On approaching said place some of the party saw an automobile with the top down standing at the side of the road, but saw at first no person in or about the car. As the posse approached the car, the sheriff said "boys what are you loaded with? What have you got in this car?" And two men sprang from the shadow of the running board. One escaped. The sheriff at this time threw his flash light on the other man, the plaintiff in error. They went together and the shooting commenced. The sheriff was killed. After the shooting it was discovered* *that the Ford automobile contained 26 gallons of whiskey. The sheriff had no search warrant and no warrant for the arrest of the plaintiff in error. The plaintiff in error was not informed that the sheriff and his posse were officers or were undertaking to arrest them or to search their car for whiskey. The plaintiff in error testified that he shot in self defense, believing that the sheriff and posse were hold up men and were going to take what Douglass and his friend had. The lower Court instructed the jury that the sheriff had the right to arrest and that plaintiff in error was in duty bound to submit to arrest.*

The Court's opinion upon the charge of the lower Court is to be found on page 173 of the Report and is as follows:

"The charge was an instruction on the law of arrest without a warrant, when the accused was attempting to escape, or the crime was committed in the presence of the officer, etc. Was this error requiring the grant of a new trial? Under all the facts of this case we think it was. The evidence adduced on the trial as to how the killing occurred and the facts and circumstances which preceeded it are, for all practical purpose, without conflict. The facts in this case demonstrate that the sheriff entertained an erroneous idea as to his right to make an arrest for a misdemeanor without a warrant and without disclosing his official character. It should be obvious to all fair minded and law abiding citizens that it is as equally important for arresting officers to confine themselves within their legal rights in making arrests as it is the duty of the citizen to peacefully submit when a legal arrest is made or sought to be made. The binding force of the law must rest upon all alike, the good and the bad, the public official and the private citizen. For the arrest of one charged with a misdemeanor, our penal code, Section 917 declares when, and when only an officer may make an arrest without a warrant, to-wit:

" 'An arrest may be made for a crime by an officer, either under a warrant, or without a warrant if the offense is committed in his presence, or the offender is endeavoring to escape or for other cause there is likely to be a failure of justice for want of an officer to issue a warrant.'

"If the offense is a felony, greater latitude is allowed; but this question need not be considered in the present case. We will undertake to examine carefully the statute just quoted, as applied to the facts of the case. The arrest was sought to be made by an officer, and on the trial of the cause the legality of the arrest was properly made an issue under the statute in question. Admittedly the officer was without a warrant. First: Was the offense committed in his presence? Under the authority of Pickett v. State, 99 Pa. 12; 25 S. E. 608; 59 Am. St. Rep. 226, this question must be answered in the negative. There it was held that,

" 'An arresting officer has no authority, without a warrant, upon mere information that another is carrying a concealed pistol, to arrest the latter and search his person for the purpose of ascertaining whether or not he is in fact violating the law prohibiting carrying concealed weapons. Even if he was so doing, the offense was not, in legal contemplation, committed in the presence of the officer and such an arrest and search are unauthorized by law, and are within the meaning of the Constitution unreasonable.'

"There the offense for which the arrest was undertaken, as in this case, was a misdemeanor. In the opinion, Mr. Justice Lumpkin said:

" 'The right of the people to be secure in their persons, houses, papers and effects, against unreasonable searches and seizures, shall not be violated. Code, Sec. 5008. (Code 1910, Sec. 6372.) If any search is unreasonable and obnoxious to our fundamental law, it is one of the kind with which we are now dealing. Even if the person did in fact have a pistol concealed about his person, the fact not being discoverable without a search, the offense of thus carrying it was not, in legal contemplation committed in the presence of the officer, and the latter violated a sacred constitutional right of the citizen in assuming to exercise a pretended authority to search his person in order to expose his suspected criminality.' "

We respectfully submit that if there is a distinction at all, in the case under discussion and the case last quoted it is in the conduct of the plaintiffs in error, who when pounced upon in the darkness of the garage did not resort to violence in resisting an unquestionable illegal arrest. In each case the parties were trapped; a former violator of the law did the trapping. Ivans was promised $25.00 and a position; Kettle was not to be prosecuted and Government Agent Nicely intended to procure funds for him for his work from some private organization. (Trans. Rec. page 95.) In each case the officers depended entirely upon the arrangements which the informants in each case said they had made; they each depended upon the information of the informant. In each case a short time elapsed between the making of arrangements and the attempted delivery of liquor. And in each case the officers delayed in announcing their authority. And finally in each case as the result of an unlawful and illegal arrest and a subsequent illegal search, intoxicating liquor was found.

Applying the law expostulated in all of the decisions cited in this subdivision of the brief, we can come to no other conclusion than that no crime was committed in the presence of the arresting officers to authorize them to arrest plaintiffs in error, Reyff and Frederick, and to search the person and property of plaintiff in error, Frederick, without the authorization of a warrant.

Nor is the case of Lambert v. United States, 282 Fed. Rep. page 413, decided by this Circuit on August 7, 1922, an authority against our contention. We respectfully submit however that under this decision the Federal officers are granted greater powers than under any of the decisions cited, but this decision is not authority for the principle that an officer may act upon information wherein he has had no opportunity of judging of its truth or falsity and it does not say that a Federal officer or a peace officer can arrest a citizen without a warrant, for a misdemeanor not committed in his presence. In the Lambert case the Federal officers received information from an informant that Lambert had whiskey in his automobile, the informant saw a liquid which looked like whiskey, saw the defendant go in and out of saloons, notified the Federal prohibition enforcement officers, who went to the automobile of Lambert, which was parked in a public street in Reno, Nevada, and saw the container, in which the informant had told them the whiskey was placed and saw also a quart bottle full of redish liquid. They ascertained therefore that the information given by the informant was correct and came to the conclusion that a crime was being committed in their presence from seeing a liquid which they had every reason for believing was an intoxicating liquor and only when they had verified the information given by the informant by the evidence of their own senses did they make an arrest. In the case at bar neither Kettle nor the Federal officers ever saw any intoxicating liquor, nor anything which looked like it; neither Kettle nor the prohibition enforcement officers actually knew whether the plaintiff in error, Frederick, had liquor in his automobile and he was assaulted and arrested by the Federal prohibition enforcement officers before they had any tangible evidence of a violation of the law. In the Lambert case there was a discovery of the liquor before the search, while in the instant case it took the illegal and unlawful search to make the discovery. Furthermore, in the Lambert case the informant was a law abiding citizen, who had no other object than to see the law enforced, while in the instant case the informant was one who was himself detected in a violation of the same law on the same day and who could have anyone of several ulterior motives in bringing about the arrests of plaintiffs in error. In the Lambert case there was no element of an entrapment, while in this case the informant, Kettle, was sent out to trap the plaintiffs in error. In the Lambert case the Federal prohibition officers had no opportunity to procure either search warrants or a warrant for the arrest of Lambert, while in the instant case, if the prohibition enforcement officers believed they had probable cause to arrest the plaintiffs in error or to search any automobile which plaintiff in error, Reyff, might be in at the place designated for the meeting by the informant, the Federal prohibition enforcement officers, if they really believed the statements of the informant, Kettle, we repeat had ample opportunity, to-wit, most of a whole day, to take the witness, Kettle, before a United States Commissioner, who would pass upon Kettle's evidence and determine whether or not there was probable cause to issue a warrant. If there was not probable cause the Government should proceed no further. If the Commissioner found that there was probable cause the Government and plaintiffs in error would each be protected. The Government by having a legal search made, and plaintiffs in error, if Kettle's testimony were false, would be in position to prosecute him for perjury. By the conduct of the prohibition enforcement officers in not taking the informant, Kettle, to a United States Commissioner proves that they were not sure of him or of the truthfulness of his statements and they awaited the illegal search to ascertain whether or not his statements were true and

"It was against such prying on the chance of discovery, that the Constitutional Amendment was intended to protect the people."

U. S. v. Slusser, 270 Fed. 819.

## C.

### There Was Not Such a Crime Committed in the Presence of the Informant Kettle That Would Give Him a Right to Arrest Plaintiffs in Error Without a Warrant.

This question has been interjected into the case by the remarks of the Court, partly based on the suggestion of counsel for the Government at the trial of the case.

In the first place, there is nothing in the United States Constitution or any of the statutes of Congress which gives a private citizen the right to make an arrest for a misdemeanor committed against the laws of the United States.

There are many statutes which authorize both Federal and State officers to perform acts outside the duties pertaining to their offices. (See Revised Statutes, Sections 1014, 1750, 1758, 1778, 2165, 2181, 3066, 3833, 4522, 4546, 4556, 4559, 4606 5270 and 5280.)

But there is no statute or other authority authorizing a private person, under any circumstances, to arrest another for a violation of a Federal Statute. We believe such authorization absolutely indispensible.

The Act of May 28, 1896, C. 252, Sec. 19, 29 Stat. 184 (Barnes Federal Code, Sec. 1415, page 322), quoted in full supra, provides the only manner in which a private citizen may effectuate an arrest for a violation of the Internal Revenue laws, which must be by warrant based upon a sworn complaint, and approved in writing by the United States District Attorney.

It was held in the case of Kurtz v. Moffitt, 115 U. S. 487, at page 505:

"Upon full consideration of the question, and examination of the statutes, army regulations, and other authorities cited in the elaborate argument for the Respondents, or otherwise known to us, we are of opinion that by the existing law a peace officer or private citizen has no authority as such, and without the order or direction of a military officer to arrest or detain a deserter from the Army of the United States. Whether it is expedient for the public welfare and the good of the Army that such authority should be conferred is a matter for the determination of Congress."

The foregoing decision is authority for the principle that if Congress does not empower peace officers of States or private citizens to enforce any Act of Congress or rule of the military authorities, that said persons have then no authority to make arrests either with or without warrants.

Sections 2 and 28 of the National Prohibition Act prescribe the manner in which legal arrests for violations of the National Prohibition Law under Governmental authority may be brought about. And they can be legalized in no other manner.

### Under the State Law Kettle as a Private Citizen Would Not Have Any Right to Arrest Plaintiffs in Error Without a Warrant.

The first subdivision of Section 837 of the Penal Code of the State of California provides:

> "That a private person may arrest another for an offense committed or attempted in his presence."

The arguments contained in subdivisions "A" and "B" of this brief apply with equal vigor to the instant subject under discussion. In fact the people would face greater dangers if by Governmental authority an unsworn person, in this case an informant, without badge of authority, were given the right to search automobiles and stop vehicles on the public highway and make arrests without warrants.

It should be borne in mind also that no crime was committed in the presence of Kettle, because he was not aware of the presence of intoxicating liquor by the operation of any of his five senses, at any time before the arrest heretofore described was effected.

In the case of People v. Denby, 108 Cal. page 54, the Court held:

> "That one who was not a peace officer has no right to arrest, or attempt to arrest a person for begging, and the person so arrested is justified in resisting such arrest, or in an assault made in attempting to free himself from unlawful detention upon ascertaining that the person arresting him is not an officer authorized to make the arrest."

In that case the prosecuting witness who was a railroad special police officer, but not a peace officer, testified that he saw the defendant soliciting alms from the passengers on the cars. Witness saw him through the windows but did not hear what he said. He, however, asked witness for some money, when witness arrested him and took him to the depot, as he says, "quite a length back south from where I arrested him."

Section 647 of the Penal Code defined who are vagrants and designated every beggar who solicits alms as a business as coming within the purview of the statute.

With the facts cited above in mind the Court on page 57 of the reports said:

> "There is nothing in the testimony showing or tending to show that the defendant committed or attempted to commit the public offense of vagrancy in the presence of the prosecuting witness. The statute makes it an offense for a healthy beggar to solicit alms as a business. For one to ask assistance on one occasion does not make him a vagrant."

And, lastly, we believe we should call this Court's attention to the late case of State ex. el. rel. Sadler v. The District Court of the Eighth Judicial Dist. in and for Cascade County, Montana, 225 Pac. Rep. page 1000, Advance Sheets Vol. 225, No. 5.

> The facts in this case were that two persons who were employed by the County Attorney to obtain evidence in the prosecution of cases involving a violation of the law relating to intoxicating liquors, were at Sunburst, Montana, and

there saw the Relator on the train going to
Sweet Grass. They got on the train and at
Sweet Grass the Relator got off on the left hand
side of the train looking towards the engine.
The relator had a black grip or hand bag.
They followed him to a place on the Canadian
line where there was a sign "Taxi Office" over
the door. Soon thereafter, they saw Sadler
near the train talking with a young man who
had an automobile. The young man picked up
the grip and carried it to the train, then he set
it down and relator picked it up and, using
both hands threw the same upon the platform
of the Pullman car and got aboard. The two
persons above mentioned boarded the train and
on the way to Great Falls, Mont. had a conversation with Sadler in which he informed them
that he had made five extra trips to Sweet
Grass, besides his regular runs up to Canada,
for liquor since Thanksgiving, and that on those
trips he got some good stuff, and also that if
his friend, a banker at Calgary, was appointed
Governor General of liquor at Alberta, he
would make more money than any man in the
State of Montana. The relator was a railway
conductor and his regular run was between
Great Falls and Sweet Grass, although he was
not then in charge of the train but a mere passenger. When the train arrived at Great Falls,
one of the men employed by the County Attorney got off first and Sadler carrying his grip,
next, followed by the other employee of the
County Attorney. Then one of the persons last
described stepped in front of relator and told
him he was under arrest and that he wanted to
search his grip. The relator told him that he
could not search his grip without a search warrant and tried to push one of said persons
aside. Whittaker, one of the persons attempting the arrest testified that the reason he arrested Sadler at the depot, was that he was

pretty certain that there was liquor in the grip from the things that he had seen, by Sadler's own actions and people that he had heard talk about it. After Relator was placed under arrest he was searched and a revolver and liquor was found in the grip.

**The Statutes of Montana Contain a Provision Exactly the Same as Section 837 of the Penal Code of This State Relating to Arrests by Private Citizens Without Warrants.**

The Court on page 1002 of the Report, says:

"The authority of a private person to arrest without a warrant is more limited than that of an officer. (Graham v. State, 143 Ga. 440; 85 S. E. 328.) It is not even contended by any party hereto that Whittaker or Larson was an officer. From all the facts and circumstances heretofore set forth, occurring up to the time relator was arrested by Whittaker, we can not say that they were sufficient to constitute probable cause to justify the belief in a reasonable man that a misdemeanor was being committed in his presence, which is essential for even an officer to arrest without a warrant; and this being so the arrest of relator was unlawful and consequently the search and seizure of the grip and revolver were unlawful." * * * "In the instant case there is no evidence that liquor of any kind had been used by Sadler at or immediately prior to his arrest, and the grip was never opened in the presence of Whittaker, and he did not know what it contained; he did not even know it was heavy, except from the manner in which the relator placed the same upon the train, and Whittaker had no information whatever as to Relator's mission to Sweet Grass. His only information was based upon the suspicion of others."

The last cited cases, similar in many aspects to the case at bar, would seem to give Kettle, in the instant case, no right to make an arrest, under the circumstances set forth in the record. If he had such a nebulous right to make an arrest, he had no right to provoke a violation of the law so as to enable him to arrest some one, and he was under a much higher obligation to prevent the commission of a misdemeanor than he was to bring about an arrest even of the plaintiffs in error.

It seems to us that the section of the California law last referred to has for its object the prevention of affrays and breaches of the peace committed in the presence of a private person upon the supposition, that they require immediate attention which would not await the arrival of duly constituted authorities.

Further discussion on this subject serves no useful purpose for a casual glance at the record shows that Kettle was not acting in his own behalf or at his own desire but at the instigation of the Federal prohibition enforcement officers who were co-operating with him in an endeavor to evade the operation of the Fourth and Fifth Amendments to the United States Constitution, in engaging in a course of conduct condemned alike in the cases of Gouled v. United States, quoted supra, Temperani v. United States, 299 Fed. page 365, and United States v. Falloco, 277 Fed. 75.

In the case of Temperani v. United States this Court put its finger on a similar attempt to evade the Fourth and Fifth Amendments when it said:

"Laying all pretense aside the officers entered the garage, not to apprehend an offender for committing an offense within their presence but to make a search of the premises to obtain tangible evidence to go before a jury. And whatever necessity may exist for enforcing the National Prohibition Act or other laws, the violation of rights guaranteed by the Constitution can not be tolerated or condoned."

The question raised in this subdivision of this brief affect each count and each defendant named in the information. The counts charging transportation and possession were actually based upon the evidence obtained from the illegal search and seizure. The count of sale depended as well on said search and seizure. By the illegal search and seizure there was a corroboration of the testimony of the witness, Kettle, which testimony standing alone would not be sufficient to convict any of the defendants, because there would not be even a semblance of proof of delivery in the count of sale. Plaintiffs in error Reyff and Bigby stood on plaintiff in error Frederick's petition to return property and exclude evidence. They had no other course. According to this Court's decision in the case of Libera v. United States, 299 Fed. page 300, plaintiffs in error could do naught else but to stand mute and content themselves with their motions and objections. By their taking the stand to deny the allegation of sale would necessarily lead at least one defendant to admit, upon cross-examination, the possession of intoxicating liquor. And evidence therefore would be furnished by them. The plaintiffs in error upon the trial faced a dilemma; if they took the stand to deny the sale they would necessarily have to admit the possession, perhaps the transportation of intoxicating liquor upon cross-examination; if they did not take the stand Kettle's word had to go uncontradicted, hence the result obtained.

In the cases of Gouled v. United States, 255 U. S. 298; Weeks v. United States, 232 U. S. 383; Woods v. United States, 279 Fed. 706, and Berry v. United States, 275 Fed. 680, the Court held:

> That to admit evidence procured from defendant from an illegal seizure would in effect compel him to become a witness against himself in violation of the Fifth Amendment to the United States Constitution.

In the case of Woods v. United States, the defendant was convicted of several counts of sale of narcotics in violation of the Harrison Narcotic Act. The Government agents, by means of a void search warrant obtained certain pill boxes of a character, which an informant testified on the witness stand, were used by Woods in selling him narcotics. The lower Court denied the defendant's motion to exclude evidence. The higher Court, although the informant testified on the witness stand, that he was sold narcotics by the defendant, said:

> "The warrant being thus void, nothing that was procured under it could be used as evidence against the defendant. To allow this to be

done would be in effect to compel the defendant to become a witness against himself in violation of the Fifth Amendment to the United States Constitution.''

In each of the cases cited above the Court's action in deciding the constitutional question went to the whole judgment. The Courts evidently believing that if the evidence obtained by the illegal search and seizure was not the real basis of the charges against the defendants, said evidence thus obtained was of such corroborative character that it went a long way to substantiate the charges and precluded the defendants from being fairly tried.

Consequently we believe that if the search and seizure was illegal, it affects all counts charged in the information as well as all of the defendants.

It is respectfully submitted that for the reasons stated in this brief, that the search and seizure was in violation of the constitutional rights of plaintiffs in error. That the automobile of plaintiff in error, Frederick, should have been ordered to him because it was taken from him in violation of his rights and without due process of law and that the judgment of the lower Court should be reversed.

## II.

**THE EVIDENCE WAS INSUFFICIENT TO CONVICT ANY OF THE DEFENDANTS OF THE SALE OF A CASE OF IN-TOXICATING LIQUOR TO ONE C. W. KETTLE.**

(Assignment of errors Nos. VIII, IX and X.)

This point is raised by plaintiffs in error's motions made at the conclusion of the Government's case, which was at the conclusion of the taking of all the testimony; for directed verdicts of Not Guilty upon the ground that the evidence was insufficient to establish said offense. (Trans. Rec. pages 90 to 92.) And in behalf of plaintiffs in error Bigby and Reyff particular reasons were pointed out.

The conviction of each of the defendants upon this charge was based almost entirely upon the testimony of C. W. Kettle. This testimony is set out at length in the first subdivision of this brief. According to the evidence of the witness Kettle: At the instigation of prohibition enforcement officer Nicely, he went to the jewelry store of one Shaddow, where plaintiffs in error Bigby and Reyff were employed. He met Bigby first and sought to convince him that on a previous occasion he had sold him gin. Plaintiff in error Bigby disclaimed this. Finally, Kettle induced Bigby to make inquiries in the jewelry store if it would be possible to get him a case of Scotch that day. Bigby also made inquiry for Kettle as to the price of a case of Scotch and finally brought Kettle to Reyff, whereupon Reyff informed Kettle that he could get him a case of

Scotch and the price would be $100. Arrangements were made, according to Kettle, to deliver the Scotch to him at his house at eight o'clock that night. At eight o'clock Kettle met Reyff and plaintiff in error Frederick. They were in an automobile in front of Kettle's house. Kettle asked Frederick if he had the liquor and Frederick said, "Yes, it is in the car." Then Kettle said, "Drive around to the garage and we will take it out there." While Frederick was doing so Kettle counted out $100 and gave it to Frederick. Frederick, Reyff and Kettle drove into the garage, where they were pounced upon by Federal prohibition agents before there was any attempt to deliver the liquor. At no time did Kettle see any intoxicating liquor and but for the statement made by plaintiff in error, Frederick, he did not know whether plaintiff in error Frederick had any liquor with him and was in a position to make a delivery.

**To Constitute a Sale Under Section 3 of the National Prohibition Act There Must Be Delivery.**

Section 3 of the Notional Prohibition Act provides:

> "That no person shall on or after the date when the 18th Amendment to the Constitution of the United States goes into effect, manufacture, sell, barter, transport, import, export, deliver, furnish, or possess any intoxicating liquor, except as authorized in this Act, and all the provisions of this Act shall be liberally construed to the end that the use of intoxicating liquor, as a beverage, may be prevented."
> Sec. 3, Title II, Act of October 28, 1919.

(Barnes Federal Code, Cum. Supp. 1923, Sec. 8351-b, page 732.)

Under this section the United States Attorney picked out three offenses and charged the plaintiffs in error with selling, transporting and possessing intoxicating liquor. He did not charge them with any of the other acts set forth in said section and therefore any consideration of them should be excluded in deciding what the words sale, possession and transportation mean. But here we are alone concerned with the word "sale" and what constitutes a sale.

Sales of intoxicating liquor are forbidden by the act. Such contracts of sale obviously can not be enforced in a Court of law.

*It has been held that no contract can be enforced in the Courts of the United States, no matter where made or where to be executed, if it is in violation of the laws of the United States, or is in contravention of the public policy of the Government, or in conflict with subsisting treaties.*

> Kenneth et al. v. Chambers, 55 U. S. 38;
> Hannay v. Eve, 3 Cranch. 7 U. S. 242;
> The President, etc., of the Bank of the United States v. Owens, 27 U. S. (2 Peters) 537;
> Miller v. Ammon, 145 U. S. 421.

As the decisions say, the law will not do anything to enforce an illegal contract, so also it is not unreasonable to conclude that the law will not create a crime in making an agreement of sale the completed act, unless so provided by statute.

To constitute the crime of sale there should be a delivery of the prohibited thing, in the present case a delivery of the intoxicating liquor. So it was held in the case of Riley v. State, 43 Miss. 414:

> "A sale is not constituted by a mere agreement to sell. There must be a delivery of the liquor. But the payment need not actually be made, for a sale on credit is within the prohibition of selling though the law would not enforce its payment."

So also in the case of Pulse v. State, 24 Tenn. Rep. 108.

The facts in that case were that Pulse was indicted for selling a quart of whiskey to Wesley, a slave, without the permission of the master of said slave. It appeared that Pulse had sold a barrel of whiskey to a slave, without the consent of his master and had employed an agent to deliver it to him. The whiskey was intercepted before it was delivered. The judge charged the jury that a sale without a delivery would complete the offense created by the Act of 1842. The defendant was found guilty and appealed. The learned judge said in reversing the lower Court:

> "It is contended that a delivery is not necessary to constitute a valid sale, but that upon a contract to sell upon a price agreed upon the sale is good, and may be enforced upon the payment or tender of the consideration, though

no delivery has been made. This reasoning is true in the abstract; but to apply it to the one under consideration would be *reductio ad absurdum;* the principle is only applicable to cases of legal contract which can be enforced in courts of justice. Here there is no such contract because, first it is made with a slave who has no power to contract and, second, it is made in direct violation of the provisions of the statute. It is therefore void and no contract at all. Again the evil intended to be suppressed by the statute was the consumption of spirits by slaves, to the detriment of their moral character and the danger of the peace of the community. A contract of sale without a delivery could by no possibility be attended by any such evils nor any other within the meaning and purview of the law."

So Black on intoxicating liquors says on page 472:

"On the trial of an indictment for unlawfully selling liquor, an actual delivery of the liquor must be proved, and evidence of the mere agreement to sell is not sufficient, but it is not necessary to aver or prove that the liquor was paid for because a sale on credit is as much a violation of the law as a sale for cash."

So also it was held in the case of Emerson v. Noble, 32 Me. 381.

A review of the record will disclose that the witnesses referred to "the sale that was to be consummated, a contemplated sale, etc." A sale that was to be consummated, a contemplated sale and an agreement of sale is not prohibited by Section 3 of Title II of the National Prohibition Act, the violation of which plaintiffs in error were all charged and convicted. In narcotic cases the crux of the offense of selling narcotics is not in the receipt of marked money or of something else of value, but it is the delivery of the narcotics and the physical transfer of possession which constitutes the offense, and so also the distribution, dissemination, and delivery of the forbidden article is the offense at which the National prohibition law is directed. There are numerous acts, other than those mentioned in Section 3 of the National Prohibition Act which the said act forbids. When the act therefore refers to a sale it means a sale according to the technical definition of the term.

We submit therefore that since there was no proof of delivery, the liquor having been intercepted before it could have been delivered, that the motions of plaintiffs in error for directed verdicts should have prevailed.

---

### III.

**THE COURT ERRED IN DENYING PLAINTIFF IN ERROR BIGBY'S MOTION FOR A DIRECTED VERDICT OF NOT GUILTY ON THE GROUND THAT THE EVIDENCE WAS INSUFFICIENT TO CONVICT HIM OF ANY OFFENSE GREATER THAN A VIOLATION OF SECTION 19 OF TITLE II OF THE NATIONAL PROHIBITION ACT.**

(Assignment of error number VIII.)

This point is raised by plaintiff in error Bigby's motion at the conclusion of the Government's case, which was at the conclusion of taking of all the testimony, for a directed verdict of Not Guilty, upon the ground that there was no evidence sufficient to convict him of the count charging sale. The only evidence is that he might have committed another misdemeanor set forth in the National prohibition laws, to-wit, the giving of information where liquor might be obtained. (Trans. Rec. page 90.)

As far as the plaintiff in error Bigby is concerned the testimony is very meagre. Kettle said that he went to the store of jeweler Shaddow and there saw Bigby. That he went there at the instigation of prohibition enforcement officer Nicely. That he told Bigby that he had sold him some gin on a previous occasion, which Bigby disclaimed. He then asked for some gin and Bigby said: "I haven't got any gin but I think I can get you some whiskey." Kettle asked the price. Bigby said: "Wait a moment, I will have to find out about that." He went inside the jewelry store and came back and said $100. Kettle said: "Can you deliver it to my room?" Bigby said: "When do you want it?" Kettle said: "I want it tonight." Bigby said: "I will have to find that out." He then went back into the store a second time and called Mr. Reyff out and introduced me to him. And Reyff said: "Yes we can deliver it tonight."

That ends all mention of the plaintiff in error, Bigby, in anything which Kettle said transpired. He was not present at the time of the arrest of plaintiffs in error Reyff and Frederick. He did not meet Kettle at 8 o'clock. No agency was proven between him and Frederick. He did not receive any money, nor was he present when the money was paid. Whatever he did was at the request of Kettle. He was therefore, if in the contemplation of the law the agent of Kettle, the alleged purchaser. He did not make any terms with Kettle, but according to Kettle's testimony he found out for Kettle that whiskey could be procured, the price of same and if and when it could be delivered. Without Kettle's solicitation and importunity neither he nor plaintiff in error Reyff would have been involved in the offenses for which they were convicted. We believe that under the law and under the facts as shown by the record that Bigby was not guilty of selling intoxicating liquor. For it has been repeatedly held that one who purchases liquor for another with money furnished by the latter and who has no interest in the liquor, is not guilty of selling intoxicating liquor:

Partin v. Com., 140 Ky. 146;

People v. Winkler, 174 Cal. 133;

Page v. State, 102 Miss. 743; 59 So. 884;

People v. Driver, 174 Mich. 214; 140 N. W. 515;

Chance v. State, 210 S. W. 208 (Tex.);

Harris v. State, 113 Miss. 457;

Clay v. State, 144 S. W. 280 (Tex.);

State v. Provencher, 160 N. W. 673 (Minn.);

State v. Lynch, 81 Ohio St. 336; 90 N. E. 935;

Chinn v. Com., 17 Ky. L. Rep. 1205; 33 S. W. 1117;

Ball v. Com., 28 Ky. L. Rep. 1344; 91 S. W. 1123;

Rigsby v. State, 64 Tex. Cim. 504; 142 S. W. 901.

At best, according to Kettle's testimony the defendant Bigby could not be convicted of any offense greater than that provided in Section 19, Title II of the National Prohibition Act, which is as follows:

"No person shall solicit or receive, nor knowingly permit his employee to solicit or receive, from any person, any order for liquor or give any information of how liquor may be obtained in violation of this Act." Act October 28, 1919, c. 85, Title II, Sec. 19. (Barnes Federal Code. 1923 Cum. Supp. pages 737 and 738.)

We submit that if plaintiff in error was guilty of any offense at all, it was a violation of the section of the prohibition law last cited and we submit that the Court erred in refusing to direct the jury to acquit on the ground of the insufficiency of the evidence, the evidence only showing this offense.

---

### Conclusion.

It is respectfully submitted that for the reasons stated in this brief, to-wit: The illegality of the search of plaintiff in error Frederick's person and automobile, and the seizures therefrom, which was made the basis of all the counts set forth in the information against each of the defendants in violation of the Fourth and Fifth Amendments to the United States Constitution; and on account of the insufficiency of the evidence to convict the plaintiffs in error of the charges set forth in the information, that the judgment of the lower Court should be reversed.

Dated, San Francisco,
  September 23, 1924.

> EDWARD A. O'DEA,
> RICHARD G. RETALLICK,
>   *Attorneys for Plaintiffs in Error.*

IN THE

## United States

# Circuit Court of Appeals,

## FOR THE NINTH CIRCUIT.

---

Louis H. Reyff, E. W. Frederick and
  Harry Bigby,
            *Plaintiffs in Error,*
            *vs.*
United States of America,
            *Defendant in Error.*

---

### BRIEF FOR DEFENDANT IN ERROR.

---

JOSEPH C. BURKE,
            *United States Attorney.*
MARK L. HERRON,
      *Assistant United States Attorney.*
JOHN R. LAYNG,
      *Special Assistant U. S. Attorney.*
*Attorneys for Defendant in Error.*

Parker, Stone & Baird Co., Law Printers, 232 New High St., Los Angeles.

# Circuit C

---

Louis H. Reyff, E.
Harry Bigby,

United States of Ar

    *I*

---

## BRIEF FOR

## STATEM

The plaintiffs in e
with violations of th
out in the brief of ｐ
certain articles were
plaintiffs in error co
mobile of the defen
vention of the pro
Amendments to the

Louis H. Reyff, E. W. Frederick and
Harry Bigby,
                    *Plaintiffs in Error,*
            *vs.*
United States of America,
                    *Defendant in Error.*

## BRIEF FOR DEFENDANT IN ERROR.

## STATEMENT OF THE CASE.

### I.

The plaintiffs in error were charged by information with violations of the "National Prohibition Act" as set out in the brief of plaintiffs in error. Upon the trial certain articles were introduced in evidence which the plaintiffs in error contend were seized from the automobile of the defendant E. W. Fredericks in contravention of the provisions of the Fourth and Fifth Amendments to the Constitution of the United States.

The defendant in error concedes that the plaintiff in error adopted such procedure as to properly raise the constitutional question involved.

## II.

On the morning of May 16, 1923, certain officers of the Prohibition Department entered the room of one C. W. Kettle without a search warrant and took therefrom a case of gin. [Tr. p. 59.] The fact of this seizure was communicated to the United States attorney and a complaint asked for the arrest of Kettle. [Tr. p. 70.] The United States attorney advised that Kettle could not be prosecuted because his room had been entered by federal officers without a search warrant, which fact was communicated to Kettle. [Tr. p. 60.]

At the time of the seizure Agent Niceley interrogated Kettle as to where the liquor seized had been obtained, telling Kettle that he (Niceley) knew where it had been obtained and that he wished Kettle to buy another case from the same place. This Kettle agreed to do. [Tr. p. 60.]

The case of gin seized had been purchased some two weeks prior to the seizure by Kettle, he having made arrangements with defendant Bigby at the jewelry store of A. D. Shadow to have the liquor delivered on San Pablo avenue, Fresno. It was there delivered by a man whom Kettle did not know and was by Kettle removed from San Pablo avenue to the room where it was seized by the prohibition agents. [Tr. pp. 61 and 62.] In addition to the sale of gin to Kettle from the store of Shadow, Shadow had from the premises sold liquor to a government agent. [Tr. p. 71.]

Acceding to the request of Agent Niceley, Kettle went to the store of Shadow and there encountered defendant Harry Bigby. Kettle engaged Bigby in conversation, telling him that he wanted to get another case of gin, and asked Bigby if he remembered him, Kettle. Bigby responded that he did not; Kettle assured him that he bought a case of gin from him (Bigby) some time before; thereupon Bigby said, "I haven't any gin but I think we can get some liquor—Scotch liquor." Being asked what the price would be, he replied, "I don't know exactly. Just wait a minute and I will see." He then went into the store, came out and said the price would be $100. Kettle asked if he could deliver that evening. Bigby informed Kettle that he would "Have to see about that," went into the store, returned with the defendant Reyff, whom he introduced to Kettle. Reyff asked Kettle when he wanted the delivery made and Kettle asked that it be made at eight o'clock at 1041 T street on May 16, 1923, and agreed to be there at that hour. [Tr. pp. 60, 61.]

These negotiations were reported by Kettle to Agent Niceley, [Tr. pp. 62 and 71], who furnished Kettle with $100 in bills, the serial numbers of which had been taken [Tr. pp. 62 and 64].

At eight o'clock, in conformity with his agreement, Kettle was at 1041 T street and there saw defendants Frederick and Reyff seated in Frederick's automobile in front of the house. When Frederick saw him he said, "I didn't know it was you I was bringing the liquor to." Kettle asked if Frederick had the liquor there and he replied, "Yes, it is in the rear of the car." Kettle directed Frederick to "Drive around to the garage and we will take it (the liquor) out there." *As they so did Kettle counted out $100 and gave it to Frederick, it being the money he had obtained from Agent Niceley* [Tr. p. 57]. As they drove into the garage, Frederick retained the money in his hand. Kettle got out upon one side of the machine, Frederick started to get out on the other and Reyff remained seated in the roadster where he had been sitting between the other two men [Tr. p. 57].

Agents Niceley and Emerick and F. D. Stribling were in the garage when the car entered it. Agents Niceley and Stribling approached the car on the right hand side, and Agent Emerick on the left. As Kettle got out of the car he nodded his head indicating to Agent Emerick that the sale had been made [Tr. p. 77].

Agent Stribling seized Kettle, Agent Niceley the defendant Reyff, and Agent Emerick the defendant Frederick. Kettle whispered to Agent Stribling, "Not Reyff," and indicated that defendant Frederick had the money. Agent Stribling reached into Frederick's right hand pocket thinking the money might be there, but as he did so Frederick who retained the money in his right hand, brushed the agent's hand. A struggle ensued. Frederick later opened his hand; it was empty. Agent Stribling thereupon looked on the garage floor and found money there, which he picked up and discovered to be the money which had previously been given by Niceley to Kettle [Tr. p. 80]. Frederick and Reyff were placed under arrest [Tr. pp. 64, 77 and 81].

Agent Niceley then asked Frederick where the case of liquor was. He said he had no liquor. Niceley asked him for the key for the rear compartment of the automobile [Tr. p. 64]. The rear compartment was opened and from it was taken a sack containing certain intoxicating liquor introduced in evidence upon the trial of the cause [Tr. p. 65].

## ARGUMENT.

### I.

**It Is the First Position of Defendant in Error That at the Time of the Search of Frederick's Automobile, and the Seizure of the Liquor Therein Contained, the Liquor Was the Property of Kettle.**

Defendant in error bases this contention upon the following statement of facts, hereinbefore referred to in detail:

Defendants Bibgy and Reyff took the order for and agreed to deliver to witness Kettle at 1041 T street, on May 16, 1923, at the hour of eight o'clock, a case of Scotch whiskey for the sum of $100.00. At eight o'clock defendants Frederick and Reyff appeared at the appointed place in Frederick's automobile and Frederick addressed Kettle saying: "I didn't know it was you I was bringing the liquor to." Kettle asked if Frederick had the liquor there and he replied, "Yes, it is in the rear of the car." Kettle then said, "Drive around to the garage and we will take it out there." *As they were driving from the front of the house to the garage Kettle counted out and gave to Frederick the $100 agreed purchase price.*

It is the contention of the defendant in error that arrangements for the sale of the liquor having been made, the liquor having been brought in the automobile of Frederick's to the point agreed on, at the agreed time, the fact that the liquor was there having been made known to Kettle, the purchase price having been paid and Kettle having thereafter exercised dominion over the liquor,—in that he directed Frederick to drive to the garage, saying, "We will take it out there,"— the liquor had become the property of Kettle. To this effect is South Carolina v. Small, 82 S. C. 93, 44 L. R. A., N. S. 451, the court saying:

> "A sale of intoxicating liquor is effected by a soliciting agent, who takes the order and receives the price, although the order is sent to his principal at another place to be filled, where nothing remains to be done but the shipping of the liquor, which the principal holds as bailie for the purchaser."

Which case cites with approval Commonwealth v. Hess, 148 Pa. 98, 17 L. R. A. 181, 31 Am. St. Rep. 810, 23 Alt. 977, where the court said:

> "The acceptance of the order * * * (for intoxicating liquor) is effective to pass the title as between the vendor and vendee. In such case the

vendee has the right of property. * * * Under all the authorities the vendor acts as bailie, and not as owner, in carrying or delivering the goods.' The sale was complete and it was only as bailie that Shuman & Company was to ship the liquor."

It is thus the contention of defendant in error that under the circumstances an actual delivery was not necessary to the consummation of the sale but that such a delivery was nevertheless made.

## II.

It Is the Second Position of Defendant in Error That Since at the Time of the Search of Frederick's Automobile and the Seizure of the Liquor Therein Contained, the Liquor Was the Property of Kettle, That the Rights of the Defendants Were Not Invaded by Taking From Frederick's Car the Said Liquor.

In the case of Hurwitz v. the United States, 299 Fed. 449, at page 452, a case arising in the Eighth Circuit, the testimony adduced upon trial showed:

A narcotic agent furnished one "Lulu Armstead with $50 with which to buy a bottle of cocaine and a bottle of morphine from the defendant, and induced her to request him over the telephone to bring it to her home at nine o'clock in the forenoon the following day. About that hour the agent and police officers secreted themselves in a nearby house. The doctor arrived in his automobile at the appointed hour. He went into the house. Lulu Armstead, her husband and another woman who was present testified that she gave the doctor the $50. The bills were marked. He put the money in his pocket, and they testified he said the drugs were in his car and he would go out and get them. As he left the house he was immediately arrested by those who were in hiding. The $50 was found on his person. They discovered that Lulu Armstead did not have the drugs. They then went to the doctor's automobile and found in it a bottle of morphine and a bottle of cocaine. The doctor testified that the money was paid to him on an account owed by Lulu Armstead for the drug treatment which he had administered to her several months before that. She denied that he had treated her but admitted that she was an addict. * * *"

It was assigned as error:

"That the two bottles were found in the car without a search warrant having been sued out, and that their seizure was unlawful, and that the bottles with their contents, which were offered in evidence, and all testimony pertaining thereto, should have been excluded."

The court said:

"We consider the objection without merit. There was sufficient evidence to sustain the conclusion that the bottles of morphine and cocaine had been purchased by Lulu Armstead and were her property, that is, there was a completed sale and not an executory contract for a sale; and the jury so found in rendering a verdict of guilty. Hatch v. Oil Co., 100 U. S. 124, 25 L. Ed. 554; Leonard v. David, 1 Black 476, 483, 17 L. Ed. 222; Hammer v. United States, 249 Fed. 336, 161 C. C. A. 344; Railway Co. v. Railway Co., 209 Fed. 758, 760, 126 C. C. A. 482. We cannot see how the rights of the defendant were invaded by taking from his car these two bottles of drugs that had been sold to Lulu Armstead."

## III.

**It Is the Third Position of Defendant in Error That Even Though the Search of Frederick's Automobile and the Seizure of the Liquor Therein Contained Were Not Justified Upon the Ground That the Liquor Seized Was the Property of Kettle, Search Was Nevertheless Lawful in That Under All of the Circumstances It Was Reasonable.**

Defendant in error rests squarely upon the proposition that the Prohibition of the Fourth and Fifth Amendments to the Constitution of the United States runs against only unreasonable searches and seizures (United States v. Lambert, 284 Fed. 417), and that the search of defendant's automobile under the facts and circumstances of this case was reasonable. Clearly Kettle, who had theretofore bought liquor through the Agency of Bigby from the store of Shadow, was justified after arrangements had been made with Reyff and Bigby at the same store to deliver a case of liquor to him at eight o'clock on a day certain, in believing that the defendants at the time they arrived at 1041 T street were engaged in the crime of unlawfully trans-

porting intoxicating liquor which belief was made
certain by Frederick's statement that the "Liquor was
in the rear of the car." The arrangements for the
delivery having been made known by Kettle to Agent
Niceley before the arrival of defendant's automobile
at Kettle's home, and the fact that the purchase price
of the liquor had passed having been disclosed to
Agent Emerick as prearranged by the nod of Kettle's
head, we submit that the officers were in the language
of U. S. v. Lambert "Amply justified in believing"
that defendants Reyff and Frederick "were actively engaged in the commission of the crime defined and de-
nounced by the National Prohibition Act and that they
were therefore justified in arresting them and in seizing the automobile by means of which they were committing the offense."

## IV.

### There Remains to Be Considered the Contention of Defendant That Defendants Were Entrapped Into the Commission of the Offense of Which They Were Found Guilty.

The court instructed the jury:

"It is not unlawful or illegal for the government
to arrange to have a person procure evidence for them
under such circumstances as is stated to have been
done by the evidence here. I mean that with a qualification. It is not legal or proper for a government
officer or a police officer to persuade another to commit a crime where the other has not a willingness, intent, or desire, or disposition to do it, but it is lawful
and legal for the law enforcement officers, if they have
information as to a crime being committed, to get the

evidence by procuring someone to act for them, as it is said that the witness Kettle acted here,—to procure evidence and the offense is none the less genuine where it is committed under those circumstances than had the conditions here alleged been brought about through the act of an entire stranger to the government, so I say that while the government has not the right to persuade a person to do a crime—to put the idea in their head in the first place,—if the idea never was there,—and then to furnish means to carry it into effect, then there would be no crime; but if a person has the disposition and is only waiting for the opportunity to carry it into effect, it is not unlawful for the government to furnish the opportunity of the committing of the act charged."

To this instruction the defendants offered no objection and the jury having by its verdict found 'the defendants guilty, it is the contention of defendant in error that the matter is concluded thereby.

## Conclusion.

It is respectfully urged that since the search of plaintiffs in error's automobile and the seizures therefrom were not unlawful, it follows that the evidence was amply sufficient to convict the plaintiffs in error of the charges set forth in the information, and that the judgment of the Lower Court should therefore be sustained.

Dated at Los Angeles, California, this 6th day of October, A. D. 1924.

JOSEPH C. BURKE,
*United States Attorney.*

MARK L. HERRON,
*Assistant United States Attorney.*

JOHN R. LAYNG,
*Special Assistant U. S. Attorney.*

# No. 4227

IN THE

# United States Circuit Court of Appeals

### For the Ninth Circuit

---

LOUIS H. REYFF, E. W. FREDERICK and HARRY
BIGBY,

*Plaintiffs in Error,*

VS.

UNITED STATES OF AMERICA,

*Defendant in Error.*

---

## PETITION FOR A REHEARING
## ON BEHALF OF PLAINTIFFS IN ERROR.

---

EDWARD A. O'DEA,
RICHARD G. RETALLICK,
Phelan Building, San Francisco,
*Attorneys for Plaintiffs in Error*
*and Petitioners.*

No. 4227

# United States Circuit Court of Appeals

### For the Ninth Circuit

---

LOUIS H. REYFF, E. W. FREDERICK and HARRY
BIGBY,

*Plaintiffs in Error,*

vs.

UNITED STATES OF AMERICA,

*Defendant in Error.*

---

## PETITION FOR A REHEARING
## ON BEHALF OF PLAINTIFFS IN ERROR.

---

*To the Honorable William B. Gilbert, Presiding
Judge, and the Associate Judges of the United
States Circuit Court of Appeals for the Ninth
Circuit:*

The plaintiffs in error, Louis H. Reyff, E. W.
Frederick and Harry Bigby, respectfully petition
the United States Circuit Court of Appeals for the
Ninth Circuit for a rehearing of the above entitled
cause, following the judgment and opinion filed therein on November 3, 1924, whereby the judgment of the
United States District Court for the Southern District of California was affirmed; and in that behalf
we respectfully ask and urge that further considera-

tion should be given to certain propositions of law declared in the opinion of the Court and that a rehearing should be granted for the following reasons:

## I.

THERE WAS NO VIOLATION OF THE "NATIONAL PROHIBITION ACT" COMMITTED IN THE PRESENCE OF THE ARRESTING FEDERAL OFFICERS BY PLAINTIFFS IN ERROR, REYFF AND FREDERICK, WHICH COULD LEGALLY JUSTIFY SAID OFFICERS IN ARRESTING PLAINTIFFS IN ERROR, REYFF AND FREDERICK, WITHOUT THE AUTHORIZATION OF A WARRANT AND BEFORE A SEARCH WAS HAD OF PLAINTIFF IN ERROR, FREDERICK'S, AUTOMOBILE AND A SEIZURE MADE THEREFROM.

It is respectfully submitted that this Court in its opinion did not pass upon the question above stated but held instead, first incorporating in said opinion part of Section 26 of Title II of the Act of October 28, 1919, the following,

"here although the officers had not seen the liquor they had knowledge that the defendants were in the act of transporting the same contrary to law. They were aware of the contract which Kettle had made for the purchase of the liquor. Before they seized it, they had obtained possession of the money that Frederick had received from Kettle and upon his arrest had dropped upon the garage floor, and they had been informed by Kettle that the liquor was in the rear of the car. All the circumstances indicated to the officers that the car had been brought into the garage for the purpose of delivering the liquor as prearranged. A case in point is Ash v. United States, 299 Fed. 277, where it was held that an officer may, if facts and circumstances patent to him are such as would reasonably lead him to believe that the law was being violated by unlawful transportation of intoxicating liquor, search an automobile and seize the liquor and arrest the person transporting the same without a search warrant. Of like import is Milam v. United States, 296 Fed. 629.''

It seems proper at this time to call this Court's attention to the conditions existent in the cases of Ash v. United States, 299 Fed. 277; Milam v. United States, 296 Fed. 629 and Hurwitz v. United States, 299 Fed. 499, which are not present in the case under discussion.

(The case of Hurwitz v. United States, it is true, was not cited in this particular portion of the Court's opinion, but its language seems to bear upon this question and was cited by this Court in another portion of its opinion.)

The Circuit Court of Appeals for the Fourth Circuit in Milam v. United States, 296 Fed. 629, decided,

"That Federal Prohibition Officers, having definite information that professional criminals were conveying in a motor car a quantity of whiskey along a certain road about a certain time, were on the watch to intercept it. They stopped the defendant's truck, opened it, and found, instead of whiskey, Chinamen in the course of unlawful transportation. Assuming that this was a search of the truck, under these circumstances we hold that the search was not unreasonable and that the evidence obtained was competent.''

It should be noted that the case last cited arose in the Commonwealth of Virginia, wherein Federal Prohibition Officers by the Statutes of that State are permitted to search under the circumstances as above set forth, if the powers of peace officers of the State wherein the offense is committed is to be conceded to them in enforcing the "National Prohibition Act."

Cited below is the Statute as set forth in Section 4629 Hurst's Annotated Pocket Code of Virginia, 4th Edition (1920):

"The deputies and inspectors appointed by the commissioner of prohibition provided for in this Act shall have power to administer oaths, take affidavits and examine records, and with a warrant, enter buildings, and *without a warrant may enter freight yards, passenger depots, baggage and storage rooms of any common carrier, and may enter any train, baggage, express, Pullman or freight car and any boat, automobile, or other conveyance, whether of like kind or not, where there is reason to believe* that the law relating to ardent spirits is being violated. Such deputies and inspectors may call to their aid in securing such information and in making such search, any officer of the law whose duty it is to enforce the law prohibiting the sale of ardent spirits."

The Prohibition Enforcement Officers by virtue of the Statutes of Virginia, granting them the powers that peace officers have in enforcing the laws in the respective states, would be authorized to make the arrest in Virginia and the same would constitute due process of law; but the officers in the instant case derive no such powers by virtue of the laws of the State of California, which under Section 837 of its Penal Code, only authorizes a peace officer to make an arrest without a warrant for a public offense not amounting to a felony committed or attempted in his presence.

The case of Ash v. United States, 299 Fed. 277, likewise decided by the Circuit Court of Appeals of the Fourth Circuit, although arising in the State of West Virginia, loses its force as an independent authority by the language of the decision itself found on page 279. It seems merely a reiteration of the language of that Court in the case of Milam v. United States cited supra, which is as follows:

> "In cases of this character, if the facts and circumstances then patent to him would reasonably lead an officer to believe that the law was being violated by the unlawful transportation of intoxicating liquors, he is authorized to seize and hold the same, and cause the arrest of the person so transporting. *This is the spirit and decision of this court rendered at the February term 1924 in Milam et al. v. United States, 296 Fed. 629, to which, and the authorities therein cited, reference is made and under that decision the testimony of the officers in this case was properly received.*"

At this time, it should be noted also, that in the case last cited the defendant made no objection to a search of his car, and that the door to same was unlocked. In the instant case the plaintiffs in error, Reyff and Frederick, were manhandled, detained and arrested before any search was made of the car.

The rear portion of the car was locked and it required a search of the person of plaintiff in error, Frederick to obtain the key with which the Federal Prohibition Enforcement Officers unlocked the car.

Again, in Hurwitz v. United States, 299 Fed. 453, there was a prosecution arising in the State of Missouri for violations of the "Harrison Anti Narcotic Act." Aside from the fact that violations of this Statute constitute a felony and in that respect differ from the instant case, there is a statute in Missouri granting to peace officers of that State the right to arrest persons accused of violations of the opium laws of that State without the authorization of a warrant. It is section 3623 of the Revised Statutes of Missouri (1919) and it is as follows:

"It shall and may be lawful for any sheriff, constable or other officer of justice, to seize upon, secure and remove any device, apparatus or instrument of any kind, character or description whatsoever, used and employed for the purposes of the unlawful smoking of opium or any other deadly drug, or of the unlawful use of opium as aforesaid, and *to arrest with or without a warrant* any person using or employing the same and the said court upon hearing the parties, if they should appear, if satisfied that such opium, device, apparatus or instrument was employed and used for the purposes of unlawful smoking of opium or any other deadly drug, or of unlawful use of opium as aforesaid, shall adjudge the same forfeited and order it to be publicly destroyed, and at the same time order reasonable costs and charges to the seizing officer, to be paid by the owner or possessor of such device, apparatus or instrument, or in case of his default, or in case he can not be found to be paid as costs as are now paid on indictment, and such adjudication shall be exclusive evidence to establish the legality of such seizure in any court of this Commonwealth.''

(Laws 1911, page 200.)

We respectfully submit that as the cases last cited are based upon statutes which have no existence in the State of California, that the Federal Prohibition Officers deriving their powers directly from the Constitution of the United States and the Act of October 28, 1919, and indirectly perhaps as National peace officers, from the Statutes of California, had no right to arrest the plaintiffs in error, Reyff and Frederick, without a warrant. It must be emphasized that the plaintiffs in error were arrested first. Were detained first. The person of plaintiff in error, Frederick, was searched first before any search was made of the automobile in question, or any seizure had been made therefrom, and that said Prohibition Enforcement Officers had not only not seen any liquor, but they were not advised by the operation of any of their senses that there was liquor in the automobile or that any crime was committed in their presence.

In this regard note the nebulous character of the testimony of Prohibition Enforcement Officer Emrich.

''We had advance information that there was to be a delivery. It was to such an extent that we, at least figured that *probably we had infor-*

*mation* that the sale had been consummated at that time.''

(Trans. Rec. page 77.)

In similar vein is the testimony of Prohibition Enforcement Officer Nicely,

"I did not see Kettle give that money to anybody. I did not see either the defendants, Frederick or Reyff throw that money on the floor. I do not know of my own knowledge whether Kettle ever gave those bills to either of the defendants.''

(Trans. Rec. page 70.)

And the third witness, Stribling, testified as follows:

"I saw those defendants in the garage. I don't know the address. There were present agents, Emrich, Nicely and the defendants, Frederick and Reyff, and the witness Kettle and myself. * * * I was under the impression that it was something about 8 o'clock anyhow, it was dark when this car drove in. I went on the right hand side of the car. I got hold of the witness Kettle and Agent Nicely caught hold of defendant Reyff and agent Emrich caught hold of Frederick. It was agreed beforehand that I was to go after the money and the witness Kettle was to give me the information as to who had the money and as to where it was.''

(Trans. Rec. page 80.)

From these excerpts of the testimony it is unquestionably a fact that the arrest, detention, and manhandling of the plaintiffs in error, Reyff and Frederick, were illegal, were done without due process of law and in contravention of their rights under the Fourth and Fifth Amendments to the Constitution of the United States.

The illegal conduct of the officers, in arresting plaintiffs in error without a warrant was not legalized by the result obtained by the subsequent search and seizure and so it was held by the Supreme Court of the United States in the case of Silverthorne Lumber Company v. United States, 251 U. S. 155.

We respectfully submit that the arrest of the plaintiffs in error, Reyff and Frederick, in the instant case was in contravention of the common law rule that in cases of misdemeanor an officer can make an arrest without a warrant only when the misdemeanor is committed or attempted in his presence which rule is also the law of the State of California and has been reiterated in the following cases:

Elk v. United States, 177 U. S. 529;

White v. United States, lately decided by this Circuit;

Temperani v. United States, 299 Fed. 365 (9th Circuit);

Miucki v. United States, 289 Fed. 447 (7th Circuit);

Ganci v. United States, 287 Fed. 60 (2nd Circuit);

Snyder v. United States, 285 Fed. 1 (4th Circuit);

Berry v. United States, 275 Fed. 680 (7th
   Circuit);

United States v. Myers, 287 Fed. 260;

United States v. McHie, 194 Fed. 894;

People v. Denby, 108 Cal. 54;

State v. Owens, 259 S. W. 100 (Mo.);

Hughes v. The State, 238 S. W. 588 (Tenn.);

Douglas v. The State, 110 S. E. 168 (Ga.);

Hoyer v. The State, 193 N. W. 89 (Wis.);

State v. Gibbons, 203 Pac. 390 (Wash.);

State v. One Hudson Cabriolet, 190 N. Y. S.
   481 (N. Y.);

State v. District Court, 225 Pac. 1000 (Mont.);

Commonwealth v. Wright, 158 Mass. 149;

McLennon v. Richardson, 81 Mass. 74;

In re Kellam, 55 Kas. 700.

---

## II.

DID CONGRESS INTEND TO ABROGATE THE FOURTH AND
FIFTH AMENDMENTS TO THE UNITED STATES CONSTI-
TUTION AND DUE PROCESS OF LAW IN THE ENACT-
MENT OF SECTION 26 OF THE "NATIONAL PROHIBI-
TION ACT", WHEN USING THE FOLLOWING PHRASES:
"WHEN THE COMMISSIONER, HIS ASSISTANTS, IN-
SPECTORS OR ANY OFFICER OF THE LAW SHALL DIS-
COVER ANY PERSON IN THE ACT OF TRANSPORTING,
IN VIOLATION OF THE LAW, INTOXICATING LIQUORS,
ETC."

In the original brief of plaintiffs in error the
question was raised as to when, under Section 26
of the "National Prohibition Act", part of which

was cited by this Court in its opinion, the commissioner, his assistants or inspectors may be said to have discovered a person in the act of transporting liquors in violation of the law, etc.

Does this section authorize the officers named to act upon their own initiative and ascertain for themselves upon mere whim or caprice whether or not a given automobile is transporting intoxicating liquors? Does it authorize the officers mentioned to act upon suspicion? Can such officers act upon the information of another or hearsay? And lastly, must the officers actually witness the commission of this misdemeanor in their presence before they are authorized to search an automobile for intoxicating liquors without a warrant?

No decision was made upon these points. It is the contention of plaintiffs in error that the Constitution of the United States protects the occupants of an automobile against trespasses and submission to arbitrary conduct on the part of petty officers to the same extent at least that it protects the occupant of an office as in the case of Gouled v. United States, 255 U. S. 298, or a store as in the case of Amos v. United States, 255 U. S. 315, or of the person. And it is the further contention of plaintiffs in error that Section 26 of the "National Prohibition Act" was not intended to dispense with the Fourth and Fifth Amendments to the United States Constitution or to take this misdemeanor for purposes of search and seizure out of its proper sphere and place it in the category of felonies for the purpose of enforcing the Eighteenth Amendment to the United States Constitution in contravention of the common law rule and the decisions cited supra. We contend that Section 26 means that when an officer has legally discovered a person in the illegal act of transporting intoxicating liquor, that then he has a right to arrest that person, seize the vehicle and the intoxicating liquor being transported. In other words, it means that when an officer has personal knowledge, obtained by the operation of his five senses or any reliable one of them, that the misdemeanor of transporting intoxicating liquor is being committed in his presence that then, and then only, can he make an arrest. And the Attorney General for the State of New York in interpreting a similar law of that State so held in an opinion handed down by him on May 4, 1921:

> "At common law a person can be arrested for a misdemeanor only when it was committed in the presence of the person making it. Under the language quoted, it seems to me that the common law powers of the officer are not extended by the provision that he shall make an arrest and a seizure when he shall discover a person in an illegal act. The statute does not authorize a seizure where he has a suspicion that the law is being violated *or where he has information only, although if in proper form it would form the basis for the issuance of a warrant.*"

> "I think the officer can not be said to have discovered a person in the illegal act unless he has personal knowledge of it. I believe there-

fore that a peace officer had no right to stop an automobile or other conveyance for the purpose of ascertaining whether it is being used as a means of transporting liquor illegally.''

And it was so held in the case of State v. One Hudson Cabriolet Automobile, 100 N. Y. Supp. 841. In the opinion in this case may be found excerpts quoted from the opinion of the Attorney General last cited.

---

## III.

**THE EVIDENCE WAS INSUFFICIENT TO CONVICT ANY OF THE PLAINTIFFS IN ERROR OF THE SALE OF A CASE OF INTOXICATING LIQUOR TO THE PERSON NAMED IN THE INFORMATION.**

The proof of the consummation of a sale in this case was necessarily involved in the discussion set out in the last two subdivisions of this petition, for by expunging the evidence obtained by the seizure from plaintiff in error Frederick's automobile, there would be not the slightest corroboration of the testimony of the witness Kettle, a doubtful character. Neither could Kettle claim that a sale had been made, in violation of the National Prohibition Act, if he had not received the intoxicating liquor.

A sale presupposes a contract, the first requisite of which is: there must be a meeting of minds. That Kettle had no intention of purchasing intoxicating liquor, in reality, from plaintiffs in error the record demonstrates beyond doubt. And he, by posting the prohibition agents in and about his garage, rendered impossible any hope of delivery, without which there could be no common law sale. And sales of this character *must come within the common law rule,* for the law creates no substitutes or estoppels in favor of either party, but leaves them to the rigorous ancient requisites of a common law rule. It has been held

> *"that no contract can be enforced in the courts of the United States, no matter where made or where to be executed, if it is in violation of the laws of the United States, or in contravention of the public policy of the Government or in conflict with subsisting treaties."*

Kenneth et al. v. Chambers, 55 U. S. 38;

Hanney v. Eve, 3 Cranch. 7 U. S. 242;

The President etc., of the Bank of the United States v. Owens, 27 U. S. (2 Peters) 537;

Miller v. Ammon, 145 U. S. 421;

Riley v. The State, 43 Miss. 414;

Pulse v. State, 24 Tenn. Rep. 108;

Black on Intoxicating Liquors, page 472.

It is respectfully submitted that this Court did not decide the question last urged, but said in its opinion:

> "On behalf of defendant Frederick it is contended that the liquor was his, that title had not passed to Kettle, and that the seizure thereof, without a search warrant, was made without authority of law. At the time when the automobile entered the garage the negotiations between Kettle and the defendants were no longer in the class of executory agreements, they had

resulted in a sale whereby the right and title to the liquor had passed to the purchaser. The terms had been agreed upon and complied with. The purchase money had been paid, and nothing remained to be done but to deliver the property at the place agreed upon, and the property had been brought to that place, to be taken out of the automobile and placed upon the floor of the garage. Hammer v. United States, 249 Fed. 336; Hatch v. Oil Co., 100 U. S. 124, 131; Hurwitz v. United States, 299 Fed. 449.''

In the case of Hammer v. United States, cited in this Court's opinion, it should be noted that there the defendant delivered the drugs to an agency over which he had no control; that agency was to perform the ministerial act of handing the package which had been segregated by the sender to the purchaser upon his payment of the stipulated price, while in the instant case there was no delivery at the place agreed upon. Plaintiffs in error never for a moment lost control of the contents of the automobile, before same was seized by the prohibition agents. If there was a prior agreement, plaintiffs in error repented of it, and refused to abide by it and if the Federal Agents had not opened the rear compartment of the automobile of plaintiff in error Frederick, but had let the plaintiffs in error go on their way, no Court in the land would compel them to live up to the alleged agreement, claimed by Kettle.

The delivery of the prohibited thing to the purchaser constitutes the crime. If the prohibited thing had been delivered, but there had been no immediate payment of the purchase price there would yet be a sale.

See Black on Intoxicating Liquors, page 472;

Riley v. The State, 43 Miss. 414;

Pulse v. The State, 24 Tenn. Rep. 108;

Emerson v. Noble, 32 Me. 381.

There is another angle to this question, which plaintiffs in error did not develop in the opening brief, it is suggested by the testimony of Prohibition Agent Nicely, which is:

"We unlocked the rear compartment to his automobile and took from this sack (indicating) with the letter 'K' on it, and the liquor contained therein, and the one bottle of liquor sitting on the table that has the white cap on it.  *  *  *  (Here the sack and the contents were marked 'Government's Exhibit I for identification,' and the bottle as Government's Exhibit 2 for Identification')  *  *  *  We opened the compartment and found that sack containing that liquor in the car and then locked that compartment up and brought the car into the Federal Building here and took out the sack of liquor and brought it into the Federal Building. Later, I took this car in the back of the Federal Building here and called the garage man to come and get it. When he came after the car, I looked in the compartment behind the seat and found two of the jars there. I don't know which of these two jars it was. The jars were in the compartment behind the seat, with tools and other things."

(Trans. Rec. page 65.)

This case in this last respect differs from the cases of Hammer v. United States, 249 Fed. 336;

and Hurwitz v. United States, 299 Fed. 449, for
in each of the latter cases, there was ready for delivery in wrapped up packages the exact amount
of the goods agreed upon; and in each instance
there was no more than that amount.

From the testimony last quoted it would appear
that from all the liquor found in the automobile,
plaintiffs in error were to make up a case.

A case has been defined by the Standard Dictionary

"as anything intended to inclose or contain
something. A box and the quantity or number
contained in it; a set; as a case of wine, of glass
or knives or the like."

It will be noted that from the testimony of the
witness Kettle no information can be obtained as to
how many bottles he intended to purchase in the
case. Plaintiffs in error therefore from all the
Scotch whiskey in the automobile had to select some
to fill the required order. Something therefore remained to be done upon the part of the vendor before title could pass, for it must be admitted that if
the vendee was to make the selection, there could
be no sale until that selection was made and so it
has been held.

"The vendor does not comply with his contract by the tender or delivery of either more or
less than the exact quantity contracted for, or by
sending the goods sold mixed with other goods.
As a general rule, the buyer is entitled to refuse the whole of the goods if they exceed the
quantity agreed, and the vendor has no right
to insist upon the buyer's acceptance of all, or

upon the buyer's selecting out of a larger quantity delivered. In Dixon v. Fletcher, 3 M. and W. 146, the declaration alleged an order by defendant for the purchase on his account of 200 bales of cotton, and a shipment to him of 206 bales, and the defendant's refusal to receive said cotton, or 'any part thereof', the court allowed the party to amend his declaration, holding it to be insufficient for want of an averment that the plaintiffs were ready and willing to deliver the 200 bales only. So, in Hart v. Mills, 15 M. and W. 85, where an order was given for two dozen of wine, and four dozen were sent, it was held that the whole might be returned. *In Cunliffe v. Harrison, 6 Ex. 903, a purchase made of 10 hdds. of claret, and the vendor sent 15. Held, that the contract of the vendor was not performed, 'For the person to whom they are sent can not tell which are the 10 that are to be his; and it is no answer to the objection to say that he may choose which 10 he likes, for that would be to force a new contract upon him'."*

Benjamin on Sales, 4th American Edition, · page 800, Section 689.

In conclusion it is earnestly contended that the considerations hereinabove adverted to should induce this Court to grant a rehearing of the instant case.

Dated, San Francisco,
December 3, 1924.

Respectfully submitted,
EDWARD A. O'DEA,
RICHARD G. RETALLICK,
*Attorneys for Plaintiffs in Error and Petitioners.*

### Certificate of Counsel.

I hereby certify that I am of counsel for plaintiffs in error and petitioners in the above entitled cause and that in my judgment the foregoing petition for a rehearing is well founded in point of law as well as in fact and that said petition for a rehearing is not interposed for delay.

Dated, San Francisco,
    December 3, 1924.

Edward A. O'Dea,
    *Of Counsel for Plaintiffs in Error and Petitioners.*

# No. 4220

## United States
# Circuit Court of Appeals
### For the Ninth Circuit.

AKHAY KUMAR MOZUMDAR,

Appellant,

vs.

UNITED STATES OF AMERICA,

Appellee.

# Transcript of Record.

Upon Appeal from the United States District Court for
the Southern District of California,
Southern Division.

Parker, Stone & Baird Co., Law Printers, Los Angeles.

**No.**

# United States
# Circuit Court of Appeals
### For the Ninth Circuit.

AKHAY KUMAR MOZUMDAR,

Appellant,

vs.

UNITED STATES OF AMERICA,

Appellee.

# Transcript of Record.

**Upon Appeal from the United States District Court for the Southern District of California, Southern Division.**

Parker, Stone & Baird Co., Law Printers, Los Angeles.

# INDEX.

[Clerk's Note: When deemed likely to be of an important nature, errors or doubtful matters appearing in the original record are printed literally in italic; and, likewise, cancelled matter appearing in the original record is printed and cancelled herein accordingly. When possible, an omission from the text is indicated by printing in italics the two words between which the omission seems to occur.]

## Names and Addresses of Attorneys.

For Defendant and Appellant:

S. G. PANDIT, 5135 Range View avenue, Los Angeles, California.

For Plaintiff and Appellee:

JOSEPH C. BURKE, United States Attorney, Los Angeles, California.

ROBERT B. CAMARILLO, Assistant United States Attorney, Los Angeles, California.

J. E. SIMPSON, Assistant United States Attorney, Los Angeles, California.

IN THE DISTRICT COURT OF THE UNITED
STATES SOUTHERN DISTRICT OF
CALIFORNIA, SOUTHERN
DIVISION

NO. H-5-J EQUITY

| | | |
|---|---|---|
| UNITED STATES OF AMERICA ) | | |
| ) | | |
| Plaintiff ) | | |
| ) | | |
| v. ) | CITATION | |
| ) | | |
| AKHAY KUMAR MOZUMDAR ) | | |
| ) | | |
| Defendant ) | | |

UNITED STATES OF AMERICA, ss:

The President of the United States to The United
States of America, GREETING:

To The United States of America:

You are hereby cited and admonished to be and appear at the United States Circuit Court of Appeals for the Ninth Circuit, at the city of San Francisco, in the State of California, within thirty days from the service of this citation, pursuant to an appeal duly allowed by the District Court of the United States in and for the Southern District of California, and filed in the Clerk's office of said court on the 4th day of March, 1924, in a cause, numbered H 5 J Equity, wherein Akhay Kumar Mozumdar is appellant and you appellee, to show cause if any why the decree rendered against the said appellant as in said appeal mentioned should not be corrected, and why speedy justice should not be done to the party in that behalf.

Witness t he Honorable William P. James, Judge of the District Court of the United States, in and for the Southern District of California, this 4th day of March. 1924, and of the Independence of the United States, the one hundred and forty-eighth.

Wm. P. James,

Judge.

Service of the within citation and receipt of a copy is hereby admitted this 4th day of March, 1924.

Joseph C. Burke

United States Attorney.

J. E. Simpson

Asst. United States Attorney.

Solicitor for Appellee.

[Endorsed]: NO. H 5 J EQUITY IN THE DISTRICT COURT OF THE UNITED STATES SOUTHERN DISTRICT OF CALIFORNIA SOUTHERN DIVISION UNITED STATES OF AMERICA Plaintiff v. AKHAY KUMAR MOZUMDAR Defendant CITATION FILED MAR 4 1924 CHAS. N. WILLIAMS Clerk By R S Zimmerman Deputy Clerk S. G. PANDIT Solicitor for Defendant 5135 Rangeview Ave. Los Angeles, Calif. Phone: Garfield 2557 Eq R B

## IN THE DISTRICT COURT OF THE UNITED STATES SOUTHERN DISTRICT OF CALIFORNIA SOUTHERN DIVISION

UNITED STATES OF AMERICA )
                              ) No. H 5 ⌐ Equity
              Plaintiff  )   AGREED
                              ) STATEMENT
          vs.               ) ON APPEAL
                              ) Under Equity
AKHAY KUMAR MOZUMDAR )   Rule No. 77
                              )
            Defendant  )

Come now the parties to the above entitled cause and by an agreed statement hereinafter set forth, pursuant to the provisions of Rule 77, present for determination upon appeal from the above entitled Court to the United States Court of Appeals for the Ninth Circuit, the issues hereinafter stated:

This is a suit in equity by the United States of America, plaintiff, against Akhay Kumar Mozumdar, defendant, to cancel, under section 15 of the Naturalization Act of June 29, 1906 (34 Stat. L., Part 1, p. 601), the certificate of naturalization of this defendant, and to cancel the order of the United States District Court for the Eastern District of Washington admitting said defendant to citizenship, dated the 30th day of June, 1913.

The cause was submitted upon plaintiff's Petition for Cancellation and defendant's Motion to Dismiss. The questions in the case arose out of the following facts:

On the 12th day of April, 1906, defendant filed a Declaration of Intention, in due form, to become a naturalized citizen of the United States. On the 11th day of July, 1912, said defendant filed a petition to be naturalized as a citizen of the United States in the United States District Court for the Eastern District of Washington. On the 28th day of December, 1912, said petition of defendant came on regularly for hearing before said District court of the United States; at said hearing said defendant testified under oath that he was a native of India and that his ancestors for generations before him were natives of that country; objection to defendant's naturalization was filed by George W. Tyler Esq., duly appointed, qualified and acting Naturalization Examiner, United States Department of Commerce and Labor, for the State of Washington, on the ground that being a Hindu, defendant was not a white person within the meaning of section 2169, Revised Statutes of the United States, and not entitled under the Naturalization laws to citizenship; said objection was by the court sustained, and said petition of said defendant to be naturalized as a citizen of the United States was by the Court denied, with leave to file a petition for a rehearing if defendant were so advised. Defendant filed such petition for rehearing on December 30, 1912; and the said District Court for the Eastern District of Washington, on the 6th day of January, 1913, made an order "That the said petition be and the same is hereby granted, to the end that a full presentation of the legal question involved may be made to the court before final action is taken.

The sole question involved on the rehearing is, is a Hindu a free white person within the meaning of the naturalization laws of the United States." The matter came on regularly for a rehearing on February 24, 1913, when said Naturalization Examiner of the United States was again present in open court representing the Bureau of Naturalization; that at that time this defendant testified under oath that he came from the Northern part of India, that he was a high caste Hindu of pure blood, and that he considered himself a member of the Aryan race; said representative of the Government again objected orally and by brief filed with the Court to defendant's admission to citizenship on the ground that he was not a free white person within the meaning of section 2169, Revised Statutes of the United States. The Court overruled the Government's reiterated objection, based on its brief and argument, and entered the following order:

"This matter coming on this day to be heard on petition for a rehearing,

IT IS CONSIDERED, ORDERED AND ADJUDGED by the court that the order heretofore made and entered on the 26th day of December, 1912, denying "the application of said petitioner to become a citizen of the United States be, and the same is hereby set aside.

"IT IS FURTHER ORDERED, that said application be and the same is hereby granted and that said petitioner be admitted to citizenship upon taking the oath prescribed by law."

On the 28th day of March, 1923, George W. Tyler, Esq., Naturalization Examiner aforesaid, made affidavit that "Affiant verily believes and therefore states the fact to be that citizenship in the United States was illegally procured by Akhay Kumar Mozumdar, as held by the Supreme Court of the United States during the October 1922, Term, February 19, 1923, No. 202, in the case entitled: The United States, appellant, vs. Bhagat Singh Thind."

Thereafter the United States Attorney for the Southern District of California filed, on the 8th day of August, 1923, in the United States District Court for the Southern District of California, on behalf of the United States, a petition for cancellation of defendant's naturalization, wherein said United States Attorney alleged:

"That your petitioner is informed and believes and upon such information and belief alleges that the said order and decree of court and certificate of naturalization were illegally procured from said Court in this, that said defendant was at all times herein mentioned a high caste Hindu of full Indian blood and not a white person entitled to be naturalized under the provisions of section 2169 of the Revised Statutes of the United States.

"That prior to the institution of this suit, a certain affidavit showing cause therefor was received by the United States Attorney for the Southern District of California, made by George W. Tyler, a duly appointed, qualified and acting examiner of the Bureau of Naturalization, United States Department of Labor."

And the petition prayed:

"That a decree may be entered cancelling said order of said District Court and said certificate of naturalization, and any and all copies thereof that may have been issued and for such other and further relief as to the Court may seem just and meet in the premises."

On the 8th day of October, 1923, this defendant moved said District Court for the Southern District of California "to dismiss the petition filed in the above cause, because said petition does not state any matter of equity entitling plaintiff to the relief prayed for, nor are the facts as stated sufficient to entitle plaintiff to any relief against this defendant."

The motion was called up on the 15th day of October, 1923, before the Honorable William P. James, District Judge, and was submitted on briefs filed by the parties. Thereafter, to-wit, on November 30, 1923, the Court filed its conclusions in words and figures following:

H 5 J EQUITY

OPINION

A petition was filed in this court by the United States Attorney asking that cancellation be decreed of a certificate of naturalization issued to defendant on the 30th day of June, 1913, by the United States District Court of the Eastern District of Washington. The right to maintain the proceeding is asserted under the provisions of the act of June 29, 1906, (Stat. at L. Vol.

34, page 601) Section 15 of which declares that it shall be the duty of the United States District Attorneys in their respective districts, and in the judicial district in which the naturalized citizen may reside at the time of bringing of the suit, to institute proceedings "for the purpose of setting aside and canceling the certificate of citizenship on the ground of fraud or on the ground that such certificate of citizenship was illegally procured." The petition in its further allegations sets forth that the certificate of naturalization of the defendant was illegally procured in that defendant was "a high caste Hindu of full Indian blood and not a white person." The petition has attached to it a photographic copy of the petition for naturalization as the same was presented to the District Court for the Eastern District of Washington. In the petition for naturalization defendant set forth that he was born in Calcutta, India, and that he was a subject of George V, King of Great Britain and Ireland. The petition here further shows that, upon the application of the defendant being presented to the District Court in the Eastern District of Washington, objection was made by the United States Naturalization Examiner to the granting of the application, on the ground that defendant was not eligible to citizenship in this country; that an order was made denying the application and that later the court granted a rehearing, stating in the order that the sole question involved on rehearing was: "Is a Hindu 'a free white person' within the meaning of the naturalization laws of the United States?" Upon the matter being presented a second time it is made to appear that the applicant then testified that he came from the northern part of India, that he was a high caste Hindu of pure blood and that "he considered himself a member of the Aryan race." Certificate of naturalization was then issued to him over the objection of the Naturalization Examiner.

The defendant appears and moves to dismiss the bill on the ground that facts are not stated sufficient to warrant the making of the decree prayed for. In his brief counsel for the defendant questions the right of the District Attorney to file the petition, insisting that, conceding that the District Court erred in granting the cerificate of naturalization, no such "irregularity" is shown as authorizes this action to be instituted under the provisions of the statute hereinbefore referred to. He insists that the District Court having had jurisdiction to determine the facts on the application of an alien for citizenship, its judgment may not be attacked in a separate proceeding such as has been here instituted. He carries the proposition even further by the argument that the decision of a court in a naturalization matter is conclusive as to the facts touching the qualifications of the applicant. The validity of these contentions may be conceded to a limited extent: That is, where a petition for naturalization, by a person who claims to fall within the class of eligibles, is presented to the court having jurisdiction to hear it, the decision of the judge made upon a conflict of the evidence would not be open to review and would present no case of irregularity such as would authorize the prosecution of a proceeding like this. Where, however, the case is that the person presenting himself as an applicant for citizenship admits that he belongs to a particular race, members of which are not eligible for naturalization, then no question of conflict of evidence arises and, upon the applicant's own petition or testimony, or both, naturalization must be denied. In Luria v. United States, 231 U. S. 24, which is among the cases cited by the defendant, the Supreme Court, considering the provisions of the section referred to, said that those provisions did not affect or disturb rights acquired through "lawful naturalization." In United States v. Nopoulos, 225 Federal 656, the District judge held that the section provides for the annulment, by appropriate judicial proceedings, of merely colorable rights of citizenship to which their possessors never were lawfully entitled." In United States v. Mulvey, 232 Federal 513 (C. C. A. 2nd), it was held that the word "illegal" meant "contrary to law." See also, as defining the word, United States v. Plaistow, 189 Federal 1010. In Grahl v. United States, 261 Federal 487 (C. C. A. 7th) the court said:

"'Illegally' means 'contrary to law.' If Section 2171 in truth forbids the admission of alien enemies to citizenship, the action of the court in admitting them is contrary to law; and the decree of the court, based on a misconstruction of the statute, involves an error of law, for which the decree should be vacated."

In United States v. Ginsberg, 243 U. S. 472, the United States brought suit in the District Court of the

Western District of Missouri to cancel a certificate of citizenship of one Ginsberg, a native of Russia. One of the grounds alleged was a lack of residence for the required time. To quote the opinion of the Supreme Court in that case:

> "No alien has the slightest right to naturalization unless all statutory requirements are complied with; and every certificate of citizenship must be treated as granted upon condition that the Government may challenge it as provided in Section 15 and demand its cancellation unless issued in accordance with such requirements. If procured when prescribed qualifications have no existence in fact, it is illegally procured; a manifest mistake by the judge cannot supply these nor render their existence non-essential."

The latter decision, made by the court of last resort, is ample authority to authorize relief to be granted in this case, assuming that lack of qualification in the applicant for naturalization appears. The cases of the United States vs. Lenore (D. C.) 207 Fed. 865, and United States v. Rockteschell, 208 Fed. 530 (C. C. A. 9th), which furnish some support to the defendant's position, must be considered, in the light of the Ginsberg decision, as being without weight.

Coming then to the question as to whether it appears that the defendant, at the time he made his application for citizenship, was an ineligible person. The Supreme Court has settled that question also, in a decision which is at all points applicable here. In the case of United States vs. Bhagat Singh Thind, 261 U. S.

204, the question was certified by the Circuit Court of Appeals of the 9th Circuit to the Supreme Court for advice, in the following terms:

"(1) Is a high caste Hindu, of full Indian blood, born at Amrit Sar, Punjab, India, a 'white person,' within the meaning of Section 2169 Revised Statutes "?

The Supreme Court had, just previously, in Ozawa v. U. S. 260 U. S. 178, determined that a person of the Japanese race, born in Japan, was not eligible to citizenship. Referring in the Ozawa case to the terms of the statute (2169 R. S.), which authorizes the admission to citizenship of aliens who are "free white persons," the court said that the color test alone was not conclusive, but that the words should be held to import a "racial and not an individual test," declaring, however, that while the words "white person" might be synonymous with the words "a person of the Caucasian race," such a conclusion did not entirely dispose of the problem, the court saying:

"Controversies have arisen and will no doubt arise again in respect of the proper classification of individuals in border line cases. The effect of the conclusion that the words 'white person' mean a Caucasian is not to establish a sharp line of demarcation between those who are entitled and those who are not entitled to naturalization, but rather a zone of more or less debatable ground outside of which, upon the one hand, are those clearly eligible, and outside of which, upon the other hand, are those clearly ineligible to citizenship."

When the Thind case was presented later, the court reaffirmed its interpretation of the words "white person" as made in the Ozawa case, and said that the mere ability of an applicant to establish a line of descent from a Caucasian ancestor could not conclude the inquiry, because the word "Caucasian" was a conventional word of much flexibility. Justice Sutherland's able opinion in the Thind case is well worth perusal, but for the reason that brevity is a consideration here, only salient fragments will be reproduced. The opinion calls attention to the fact that when the words "white person" were placed in the statute they were being used by legislators as "words of common speech and not of scientific origin"; that they should still be so understood and applied; that it was impracticable and illogical to depend upon proof of a line of ancestry, having root in alleged Caucasian forefathers, as determinative of the question. And in that connection the learned justice declared:

"It may be true that the blond Scandinavian and the brown Hindu have a common ancestor in the dim reaches of antiquity, but the average man knows perfectly well that there are unmistakable and profound differences between them today; and it is not impossible, if that common ancestor could be materialized in the flesh, we should discover that he was himself sufficiently differentiated from both of his descendants to preclude his racial classification with either. The question for determination is not therefore, whether by the speculative processes of ethnological reasoning we may present a probability to the scientific mind that they have the same origin, but whether we can satisfy the common understanding that they are now the same or sufficiently the same to justify the interpreters of a statute—written in the words of common speech, for common understanding, by unscientific men—in classifying them together in the statutory category as white persons."

The court stated further that the applicant there considered claimed eligibility because of the "sole fact that he is of high caste Hindu stock, born in Punjab, one of the extreme northwest districts of India, and classified by certain scientific authorities as of the Caucasian or Aryan race." It was pointed out that writers on the subject of ethnology discredited the Aryan theory as a racial basis, the court saying: "The term 'Aryan' has to do with linguistic and not at all with physical characteristics" and that the word "Caucasian" was of scarce better repute. And the court concludes that "the words of familiar speech, which were used by the original framers of the law, were intended to include only the type of man whom they knew as white"; that "the immigration of that day was almost exclusively from the British Isles and northwestern Europe.......... When they extended the privilege of American citizenship to 'any alien, being a free white person,' it was these immigrants—bone of their bone and flesh of their flesh—and their kind whom they must have had affirmatively in mind"; hence that the words "free white persons" were to be interpreted "in acord with the understanding of the common man, synonymous with the word 'Caucasion' only as that word is popularly understood." And said the court: "Whatever may be the speculations of ethnologists, it does not include the body of people to whom the appellee belongs. It is a matter of familiar observation and knowledge that the physical group characteristics of the Hindus render them readily distinguishable from the various groups of persons in this country recognized as white."

Counsel for the defendant is inclined to be critical of the decision of the Supreme Court, unmindful evidently that an alien, when he lands on the shores of this country, comes with no right at all of any natural kind to have extended to him the privilege of citizenship. That privilege is in the nature of a bounty, which this Government may confer or withhold at its option, and without the support of any reason whatsoever.

By the highest authority in the land it has been determined that a person of the Hindu race is not eligible for citizenship. In view of that decision, upon the facts alleged in the petition here, the District Court granting the certificate of naturalization was not presented with a subject as to whose application any determination could be made except to deny it; and the certificate of naturalization should therefore be held to have been "illegally procured."

The motion to dismiss should be overruled and an order will be entered accordingly. Defendant may answer within five days after receiving notice of the ruling, if he so desires.

Dated November 30, 1923.        Wm. P. James,
                                                District Judge.

That notice of said ruling was duly sent to defendant's counsel, but no answer was filed by the defendant.

On December 10, 1923, plaintiff filed its praecipe for entry of defendant's default in the office of the Clerk of said United States District Court for the Southern District of California. No default was entered, however, at any time.

Thereafter, to-wit, on December 16, 1923, and in pursuance of said conclusions, the Court entered its Decree in favor of the plaintiff and against the defendant, canceling his certificate of naturalization and canceling the order of the United States District Court for the Eastern District of Washington admitting defendant to citizenship, which decree was filed with the Clerk of said Court and entered on December 16, 1923, and is in words and figures as follows:

"(Title of Court and Cause)

"A final decree having been presented to the court at this time in this case for signature, said decree is signed by the court and ordered filed and entered herein, the entry thereof being as follows to wit:

"(Title of Court and Cause)

"No. H 5 J Equity

"FINAL DECREE

"This cause came on regularly to be heard at this term of the court in Los Angeles, California, and was submitted to the court; and the court, after due consideration thereof, having made and entered its order that judgment be entered for the plaintiff as prayed for in plaintiff's complaint.

"NOW, THEREFORE, IT IS ORDERED, ADJUDGED AND DECREED that the order of the United States District Court for the Eastern District of Washington, heretofore entered granting the petition of the defendant Akhay Kumar Mozumdar, for naturalization as a citizen of the United States and admitting the said Akhay Kumar Mozumdar to become a citizen of the United States, is hereby set aside and cancelled;

"And it is further ORDERED, ADJUDGED AND DECREED that the said certificate of naturalization and citizenship and any and all copies thereof procured and issued by virtue of the order of the said United States District Court for the Eastern District of Washington be and the same hereby are cancelled and set aside;

"And it is further ORDERED, ADJUDGED AND DECREED that the clerk of the court transmit a certified copy of this decree to the court from which the said certificate of citizenship and naturalization was procured.

Dated December 18, 1923.

Wm. P. James<br>United States District Judge."

DECREE ENTERED AND RECORDED DECEMBER 18, 1923. CHAS. N. WILLIAMS, Clerk; by Murray E. Wire, Deputy Clerk.

Thereafter the Clerk of said court forwarded two certified copies of said decree to the Bureau of Naturalization and one certified copy to the Clerk of the United States District Court for the Eastern District of Washington.

Thereafter, to-wit, on the 4th day of March, 1924, defendant filed his petition for appeal and assignment of errors, which are in words and figures as follows:

No. H 5 J Equity

Petition for Appeal

To the Honorable William P. James, District Judge:

The above-named Akhay Kumar Mozumdar feeling himself aggrieved by the final decree entered in the above entitled cause on the 18th day of December, 1923, does hereby appeal from said decree to the Circuit Court of Appeals for the Ninth Circuit for the reasons set forth in the assignment of errors filed herewith, and he prays that his appeal be allowed and that a citation be issued as provided by law, and that a transcript of the record, proceedings and papers upon which said decree was based, duly authenticated, may be sent to the United States Circuit Court of Appeals for the Ninth Circuit, sitting at San Francisco.

And your petitioner further prays that the proper order touching the security, if any, to be required of him to perfect his appeal and to operate as a supersedeas, be made.

Dated March 4, 1924.

S. G. PANDIT,

Solicitor for Defendant.

No. H 5 J Equity
Assignment of Errors

Now comes the defendant in the above-entitled cause and files the following assignment of errors upon which he will rely in his prosecution of the appeal in the above entitled cause, from the decree made by this honorable court on the 18th day of December, 1923.

That the United States District Court for the Southern District of California, Southern Division, erred in the following particulars, to-wit:

1. The Court erred in not holding that the bill of complaint does not state facts sufficient to constitute a cause of action and in denying defendant's motion to dismiss.

2. The Court erred in not holding that there has been a binding adjudication of the matters and things set forth in the bill of complaint herein; said negative holding of the Court being contrary to the law.

3. The Court erred in holding that the order and decree of court and certificate of naturalization were illegally procured by this defendant from the United States District Court for the Eastern District of Washington.

4. The Court erred in decreeing the setting aside and cancellation of the order of the United States District Court for the Eastern District of Washington admitting this defendant to citizenship.

5. The Court erred in decreeing defendant's certificate of naturalization cancelled and set aside.

6. The decree is contrary to law.

WHEREFORE, defendant prays that the decree of the District Court for the Southern District of California may be reversed, and said Court directed to dismiss the bill and vacate its order canceling defendant's certificate of citizenship and that certified copies of such vacating order be directed to be sent by the clerk of said District Court to the Bureau of Naturalization and to the United States District Court for the Eastern District of Washington.

S. G. PANDIT,

Solicitor for Defendant.

No. H 5 J Equity

Order Allowing Appeal

On motion of S. G. Pandit, solicitor and counsel for defendant, it is hereby ordered that an appeal to the United States Circuit Court of Appeals for the Ninth Circuit from the order and decree made and entered herein on the 18th day of December, 1923, be and the same is hereby allowed, and that a certified transcript of the record be forthwith transmitted to said United States Circuit Court of Appeals for the Ninth Circuit.

It is further ordered that the appeal shall operate as a supersedeas and that a bond for costs be given in the amount of $250.

Dated this 4th day of March, 1924.

Wm. P. James

District Judge.

Approved as to form as provided in Rule 45. Joseph C. Burke, United States Attorney J. E. Simpson, Asst. U. S. Atty. Solicitors for Plaintiff.

Service of the within order and receipt of a copy is hereby admitted this 4th day of March, 1924.

> Joseph C. Burke
> United States Attorney.
> J. E. Simpson
> Asst. United States Attorney
> Solicitors for Appellee.

IN THE DISTRICT COURT OF THE UNITED STATES SOUTHERN DISTRICT OF CALIFORNIA SOUTHERN DIVISION

NO. H-5-J EQUITY

| | | |
|---|---|---|
| UNITED STATES OF AMERICA ) | | |
| ) | | |
| Plaintiff ) | | |
| v. ) | BOND ON | |
| ) | APPEAL | |
| AKHAY KUMAR MOZUMDAR ) | | |
| ) | | |
| Defendant ) | | |

KNOW ALL MEN BY THESE PRESENTS, that we Akhay Kumar Mozumdar, as principal, and Henry A. Shurra by occupation Moving Picture Co., Mgr., residing at 1002 McKenzie Ave., Los Angeles, in the Southern District of California, and Mrs. Annie J. Lipp by occupation Housewife, residing at 1001 Armour Ave., Los Angeles, in the Southern District of California, as sureties, are held and firmly bound unto the United States of America in the sum of Two Hundred Fifty ($250.00) Dollars, lawful money of the United States, to be paid to them and their respective executors, administrators and successors; to which payment, well and truly to be made, we bind ourselves and each of us, jointly and severally, and each of our heirs, executors and administrators by these presents.

Sealed with our seals and dated this 6th day of March. 1924.

Whereas the above named Akhay Kumar Mozumdar has petitioned for an appeal to the United States Circuit Court of Appeals for the Ninth Circuit to reverse the judgment of the District Court of the United States for the Southern District of California, Southern Division, in the above entitled cause:

Now, therefore, the condition of this obligation is such that if the above named Akhay Kumar Mozumdar shall prosecute his said appeal to effect and answer all costs if he fail to make good his plea, then this obligation shall be void; otherwise to remain in full force and effect.

Akhay Kumar Mozumdar (SEAL)
Henry A. Shurra (SEAL)
Mrs. A. J. Lipp (SEAL)

STATE OF CALIFORNIA )
) ss.
COUNTY OF LOS ANGELES )

On this 6th day of March. 1924, personally appeared before me Henry A. Shurra, and Mrs. Annie J. Lipp, respectively known to me to be persons described in and who duly executed the foregoing instrument as parties thereto, and respectively acknowledged, each for himself, that they executed the same as their free act and deed for the purposes therein set forth.

And the said Henry A. Shurra, and Mrs. Annie J. Lipp, being by me duly sworn, says, each for himself and not for the other, that he is a resident and householder of the said county of Los Angeles, in the Southern District of California, and that he is worth the sum of $500.00 over and above his just debts and legal liability and property exempt from execution.

Examined and recommended for approval as provided in Rule 29.

(SEAL)                    S. G. Pandit, Solicitor.

Subscribed and Sworn to before be this 6th day of March, 1924.

S. G. Pandit,

Notary Public in and for the County of Los Angeles,
    State of California.

The within bond is approved both as to sufficiency and form this 6th day of March, 1924.

Bledsoe

Judge

IN THE DISTRICT COURT OF THE UNITED
STATES SOUTHERN DISTRICT OF
CALIFORNIA SOUTHERN
DIVISION

NO. H-5-J EQUITY

UNITED STATES OF AMERICA )
         )
      Plaintiff )
         )
    v.     )STIPULATION
         )
AKHAY KUMAR MOZUMDAR )
         )
     Defendant )

It is stipulated between attorneys for plaintiff and
defendant that the foregoing is a true and correct
statement on appeal, and contains all the records necessary for complete determination of the issues involved
in this cause; and that the same may be used as a true
and correct statement of the case on appeal in pursuance of Equity Rule number Seventy-seven.

      Joseph C. Burke
       United States Attorney.
      J. E. Simpson
     Asst. United States Attorney.
      S. G. PANDIT,
       Attorney for Defendant.

Approved and allowed as an agreed statement of
the case on appeal, this 4th day of March, 1924.

       Wm. P. James
        District Judge.

[Endorsed:] NO H 5 J EQUITY IN THE DIS-
TRICT COURT OF THE UNITED STATES
SOUTHERN DISTRICT OF CALIFORNIA
SOUTHERN DIVISION UNITED STATES OF
AMERICA Plaintiff v. AKHAY KUMAR MOZUM-
DAR Defendant AGREED STATEMENT ON AP-
PEAL FILED Mar 6, 1924 CHAS. N. WIL-
LIAMS, Clerk By L J Cordes Deputy Clerk S. G.
PANDIT Solicitor for Defendant 5135 Rangeview
Ave. Los Angeles, Calif. Phone: Garfield 2557.


IN THE DISTRICT COURT OF THE UNITED
STATES SOUTHERN DISTRICT OF
CALIFORNIA SOUTHERN
DIVISION

| | | |
|---|---|---|
| UNITED STATES OF AMERICA ) | | |
| ) | | |
| Plaintiff ) | NO. H-5-J | |
| ) | EQUITY | |
| v. ) | CERTIFICATE | |
| ) | OF CLERK | |
| AKHAY KUMAR MOZUMDAR ) | OF COURT | |
| ) | | |
| Defendant ) | | |

I, Charles N. Williams, Clerk of the United States
District Court for the Southern District of California,
do hereby certify the foregoing volume containing 26
pages, numbered from 1 to 26 inclusive, to be the
Transcript of Record on Appeal in the above-entitled
cause, as printed by the Appellant and presented to me
for comparison and certification, and that the same
has been compared and corrected by me and contains

a full, true and correct copy of the Agreed Statement on Appeal under Equity Rule No. 77.

I DO FURTHER CERTIFY that the fees of the clerk for comparing, correcting and certifying the foregoing Record on Appeal, amount to $        , and that said amount has been paid me by the appellant herein.

IN TESTIMONY WHEREOF, I have hereunto set my hand and affixed the Seal of the District Court of the United States of America, in and for the Southern District of California, Southern Division, this        day of                in the year of our Lord One Thousand Nine Hundred and Twenty-four, and of our Independence the One Hundred and Forty-eighth.

(SEAL)                    Charles N. Williams.

Clerk of the District Court of the United States of America, in and for the Southern District of California.

By..........................

Deputy.

# No. 4229.

IN THE

## United States

# Circuit Court of Appeals,

## FOR THE NINTH CIRCUIT.

---

Akhay Kumar Mozumdar,
                                        *Appellant,*

*vs.*

United States of America,
                                        *Appellee.*

---

## BRIEF FOR THE APPELLANT.

---

S. G. PANDIT,
*Solicitor and Counsel for Appellant.*

---

Parker, Stone & Baird Co., Law Printers, 232 New High St., Los Angeles.

No. 4229.

IN THE

United States

# Circuit Court of Appeals,

## FOR THE NINTH CIRCUIT.

Akhay Kumar Mozumdar,
*Appellant,*

*vs.*

United States of America,
*Appellee.*

## BRIEF FOR THE APPELLANT.

## STATEMENT OF THE CASE.

This is an appeal from the final decree [Printed Transcript, pp. 17-18], in an equity suit wherein the United States of America, under section 15 of the Naturalization Act of June 29, 1906, sought (1) to cancel the certificate of naturalization of Akhay Kumar Mozumdar, appellant herein, and (2) to cancel the order [P. T., p. 6] of the District Court of the United States for the Eastern District of Washington, dated June 13, 1913, admitting said appellant to citizenship.

The petition for cancellation [P. T., p. 7], filed on August 8, 1923, in the District Court of the United

States for the Southern District of California, Southern Division, alleged that appellant's certificate of citizenship and the order and decree of court granting same were illegally procured by appellant, in that he "was at all times herein mentioned a high caste Hindu of full Indian blood and not a white person entitled to be naturalized under the provisions of section 2169 of the Revised Statutes of the United States."

On October 8, 1923, appellant moved the court below to dismiss the government's petition on the following grounds [P. T., p. 8]: (1) that said petition did not state any matter of equity entitling the government to the relief prayed for, and (2) that the facts as stated were not sufficient to entitle the government to any relief against this appellant. Said motion was overruled by the court on November 30, 1923 [P. T., pp. 16-17].

On December 10, 1923, the government filed its praecipe for the entry of appellant's default, which the clerk of the District Court declined to enter [P. T., p. 17].

On December 16, 1923, the court entered its final decree in favor of the government and against this appellant, canceling his certificate of naturalization and the order of the United States District Court for the Eastern District of Washington made ten years previously. From said final decree this appeal was taken on March 4, 1924.

## INTRODUCTION.

This case is noteworthy in that it involves much more than the rights of an individual. The answer to the question whether or not appellant shall continue to be a citizen will settle the status of all those who, belonging to the Caucasian peoples of Asia, have been duly and regularly admitted to citizenship in this country by courts of competent jurisdiction after a contest by the government in every case to evoke the most thorough consideration.

The case of the United States against Bhagat Singh Thind, 261 U. S. 204, did not determine the question. For the impropriety of a cancellation suit under section 15 of the Act of June 29, 1906, was not suggested and did not occur to the trial or appellate courts. Hence it is not a precedent which the court is bound to follow when the impropriety of the remedy is urged, as in this case. Cosgrove v. Wayne Circuit Judge, 144 Mich. 682, 108 N. W. 361. For a decision affirming or reversing a judgment is of no controlling force in a subsequent case as to any question involved but not argued nor presented, and left unnoticed or not passed on by the court. Salt Lake Inv. Co. v. Oregon Short Line R. Co., 46 Utah 203, 148 Pac. 439. Nor can a mere concession of counsel in a former case be regarded as a judicial establishment of the point conceded. State v. Keokuk etc. R. Co., 99 Mo. 30, 12 S. W. 290, 6 L. R. A. 222 (aff. 152 U. S. 301, 14 Sup. Ct, 592, 38 L. Ed. 450). And it has been repeatedly held that even though a point was involved in an earlier case and should have been decided, the case is not a precedent as to such point if it was not actually considered and decided. Moinet v. Burnham, 143 Mich. 489, 106 N. W. 1126; Atwood v. Sault Ste. Marie, 141 Mich. 295, 104 N. W. 649; Pav. Co. v. Realty Co. (Cal.), 195 Pac. 1058; Matter of Dunning, 213 Ill. App. 602. Nor are any of the precedents to be found precisely similar to the case at bar.

Here the government, with full knowledge of the facts, acquiesced in the decision of the Naturalization Court, adverse to its contention, for a period of ten years. No fraud or misconduct on the part of the appellant has been recently, or at any time, discovered by the government as the means whereby he procured his citizenship. No appeal was taken nor a cancellation suit instituted during all this time. The judgment of the District Court for the Eastern District of Washington has become final for a number of years. The appellant was required in 1913 to renounce absolutely and forever all allegiance to every foreign government and particularly to George V. King of Great Britain and Ireland at the suggestion of the government of the United States; for no divided allegiance would be tolerated by its laws. *In re* Haas, 242 Fed. 739.

If the court below were correct, the man without a country would be transferred from the realm of poetry into the domain of law, since an affirmance of the

decision here appealed from would declare the law
of the United States as expounded by its Court of
Appeals, to be that there exists under the jurisdiction
of the United States an innocent and law-abiding class
of persons who are strangers and aliens here and in
every other nation of the globe. There can be nothing
in law or in fact to justify or necessitate so extraordinary a result.

## SPECIFICATION OF ERROR.

The court erred in overruling appellant's motion to
dismiss the petition for cancellation of his citizenship.

## POINTS.

I. The purpose of the Act of June 29, 1906, was
to combat fraud and perjury in naturalization proceedings by the applicant for naturalization or his
witnesses, and illegality by court officials dominated
by party politics.

II. Appellant's certificate was not "illegally procured."

III. The judgment admitting this appellant to citizenship in 1913 is *res adjudicata* to and against the
appellee.

IV. The appellee is barred by its laches from seeking its remedy in a court of equity.

V. The appellee is estopped by its long-continued
acquiescence in the judgment admitting this appellant
to citizenship from now challenging his certificate of
naturalization.

VI. The contentions of the appellee are untenable.

## ARGUMENT.

### I.

### Purpose of Act of June 29, 1906.

"The purpose of the Act of 1906 was to stop the flagrant abuses and frauds ·which had become scandalous, by providing safeguards and a strict and uniform procedure. The act was the result of the labors of a commission appointed by an executive order of President Roosevelt, issued March 1, 1905. The commission consisted of one officer each from the Departments of State, Justice, Commerce and Labor. · Their report was transmitted to Congress by the President on December 5, 1905 (H. Doc. No. 44, 59th Cong., 1st sess.), and its recommendations formed the basis of·· the bill which became the act under consideration.

"In its report the commission quoted from the report of the Attorney General for 1903 the following language contained in a report of Mr. Van Deuzen, Special Examiner of the Department of Justice:

" 'The evidence is overwhelming that the general administration of the naturalization laws has been contemptuous, perfunctory, indifferent, lax, and unintelligent, and in many cases, especially in inferior state courts, corrupt.'

"The chief motive which led to fraudulent naturalization was the desire to vote, which caused corrupt politicians to encourage perjury and commit bribery under the guise of paying the naturalization fees, especially just before election. Another motive was found in the labor laws and the rules of some labor unions which prevented the employment of aliens in certains classes of work. Another motive was the desire of aliens to go abroad under the protection of the United States. There was no uniformity in the actual admission of aliens to citizenship by reason of the fact that they were admitted by many different courts, State and Federal, with no uniform procedure, many of them of inferior jurisdiction and presided over by inferior judges, and in practice the entire proceedings were often turned over to the clerk of the court. *It was to correct these abuses that the Act of 1906 was framed.* Mr. Bonynge, in presenting the bill to the house, referred to the great amount of fraud which had grown up under the old law and to the appointment of a special prosecuting attorney who in two years had secured 685 convictions and the cancellation of 1,916 fraudulent certificates." Ozawa v. United States, 43 Sup. Ct. 338. Brief of the Solicitor General 13-15.

In 1902 fraudulent and illegal practices in the naturalization of aliens were discovered in the city of St. Louis, Missouri. Some of these misdoings are recounted in Dolan v. United States, 133 Fed. 440, 69 C. C. A. 274. Investigation showed such practices to be common in other cities. Certificates were issued on sham and spurious proceedings. Clerks of courts issued certificates of citizenship without any proceeding in court whatever and frabricated a judicial record to support the certificates. It was even discovered that some clerks were engaged in a regular brokerage business in certificates of naturalization. Certificates were also sold to aliens residing abroad who had never been in the United States. The results of these investigations were gathered in an elaborate report which was presented to Congress and resulted in the passage of the Act of 1906. Congressional Record, Vol. 40, part of page 7036; House Documents Vol. 44 (Miscellaneous), 59th Congress, 1st Session.

The mischievous practices which the statute was intended to correct fell into two general classes: First, the obtaining of certificates of naturalization through the deception of the court by means of perjury and subornation of perjury—such certificates being *procured by fraud*. Second, *false and spurios certificates were obtained without any judicial proceeding whatever, or by a proceeding in court which was itself sham and spurious*. Certificates thus obtained are accurately described as having been *"illegally procured."* United States v. Lenore, 207 Fed. 865, 866-870.

> "Probably the most serious development of this investigation is the disclosure of the fact that many thousands of certificates have been issued to aliens by courts having no jurisdiction in naturalization matters." C. V. C. Van Deusen, Special Examiner in Relation to Naturalization, in his report of November 4, 1903. House Document No. 9, 58th Congress, 2d Session.

> "Experience and investigation had taught that the *wide-spread frauds in naturalization, which*

*led to the passage of the Act of June 29, 1906,*
were in large measure due to the diversities in
local practice, *the carelessness of those charged
with duties in this connection,* and *the prevalence
of perjured testimony* in cases of this character."
United States v. Ness, 245 U. S. 319, 324.

## II.

### Appellant's Certificate Was Not "Illegally Procured."

Section 21 of the Naturalization Regulations promulgated by the Secretary of Labor under the authority of section 28, Act of June 29, 1906, provides:

"Clerks of courts shall not receive declarations
of intention or file petitions for naturalization
from other aliens than white persons. * * *
Any alien other than a Chinese person, who
claims that he is a *white person* in the sense in
which that term is used in section 2169 Revised
Statutes, should be allowed if he insists upon it
after an explanation is made showing him the risk
of denial to file his declaration or petition, as the
case may be, leaving *the issue to be determined
by the court.*"

The Supreme Court in United States v. Ginsberg,
243 U S. 472, says of section 2169 R. S.:

"Prior to 1906 'the uniform rule of naturalization' authorized by the Constitution was found in
the Act of 1802 and a few amendments thereto.
This enumerated *only general controlling principles.*"

Appellant respectfully submits that in the application of such general principles to concrete cases and in making their findings from proofs adduced at such hearings, the courts are compelled to bring their discretion to bear thereon. And discretionary rulings of courts, even if erroneous, cannot be "illegal" nor unlawful, and can only be corrected by appeal or writ of error; and to them section 15 has no application.

It would seem, moreover, that "illegality" has reference to the omission or disregard of the plain and detailed statutory requirements of the *prescribed proceedings* of a "simple and comprehensive code" as is the Act of June 29, 1906, which "prescribes the exact character of proof to be adduced." United States v. Ness, 245 U. S. 319.

It has been held by the courts that if citizenship is granted, and the judgment is not tainted with any fraud or misconduct of the party in whose favor it is entered, such judgment is final and conclusive against attacks in courts of co-ordinate jurisdiction. Last Chance Mining Co. v. Tyler Mining Co., 157 U. S. 683, 691, 15 Sup. Ct. 733, 39 L. Ed. 859; approved in Johannessen v. United States, 225 U. S. 227, 238, 32 Sup. Ct. 613, 56 L. Ed. 1066. For the word *procure,* according to Webster's International Dictionary, means to contrive, to bring about, to effect (as a favor to be granted). And in Nash v. Douglass, 12 Abb. Prac. (N. S.) 187, 190, the court says:

"The word *procure*, as used in the pleadings in an action, and acted on by the courts, *imports an initial, active and wrongful effort.*"

"Illegally procured" means procured by subornation or some other illegal means used to impose upon the court; it does not mean that the certificate was issued through "error of law," says Judge Hand in United States v. Luria, 184 Fed. 643, 647.

The writer of the article dealing with this subject in *Corpus Juris,* after carefully weighing the diversity of decisions in the interpretation of the phrase "illegally procured" of the naturalization statute, says, at 2 C. J. 1126:

"ILLEGALLY PROCURED. While there is some difference of opinion as to the meaning of the term 'illegally procured,' the better rule seems to be that it imports a certificate issued without authority of law, and, in effect, false and spurious; not an error of law, but subornation or some other illegal means to impose on the court. When a certificate is issued as the result of a judicial hearing in a good faith attempt to exercise the jurisdiction conferred by the act of Congress, it is not open to attack in another court of coordinate jurisdiction simply by reason of alleged errors which may have occurred in the court pursuant to whose judgment the certificate was issued. Errors of that kind can properly be reached only by appeal or writ of error."

The Supreme Court in Johannessen v. United States, 225 U. S. 227, 242, said of section 15 of the Act of 1906:

> "It (the act) merely provides that on good cause shown, the question whether one who claims the privileges of citizenship under the certificate of a court has procured that certificate through *fraud or other illegal contrivance,* shall be examined and determined in orderly judicial proceedings."

Says Chief Justice Marshall:

> "A judgment cannot be unlawful unless that judgment is an absolute nullity; and it is not a nullity if the court has general jurisdiction of the subject although it should be erroneous." *Ex parte* Watkins, 3 Pet. 203, 7 L. Ed. 650.

In sustaining the lower court in its dismissal of the government's petition for cancellation of a seaman's citizenship on the charge of "illegality," this honorable court said, in United States v. Rockteschell, 125 C. C. A. 532, 208 Fed. 530, at page 536:

> "The correctness of a finding of fact, so long as the same is within the bounds of reason, involves no question of law, and cannot be reviewed or disturbed."

A perusal of the opinion of the learned naturalization court at 207 Fed. 115, in the matter of Akhay Kumar Mozumdar, will suffice to show that the finding of that court was within the bounds of reason.

The District Courts for the Northern and for the Southern Districts of California, and State and Federal Courts in various parts of the country have approved of and followed the reasoning of Judge Rudkin in the case of this appellant. That conclusion had, moreover, become well established by judicial and executive concurrence and legislative acquiescence.

It is a significant fact that even with regard to some of the semi-prescribed proceedings of the Naturalization Act of 1906, except when there was evident misconduct in procuring the certificate on the part of the naturalized citizen, the appellate courts even when decreeing cancellation have hesitated and abstained from laying down any general rule regarding cancellation of certificates on the ground of illegal procurement thereof. For example, in the case of United States v. Cantini, 212 Fed. 925, the Circuit Court of Appeals prefaced its order of cancellation with these words:

"Recognizing the difficulties of the present controversy, and disclaiming the intention to lay down a general rule * * *."

The Circuit Court of Appeals, for the Second Circuit, in United States v. Mulvey, 232 Fed. 513, said at page 516:

"We think that each case of this kind must be decided according to its own circumstances."

It may be further noted that several courts and judges have been quite emphatic in holding that where the facts are before the court, its findings thereon cannot be disturbed by resort to section 15, even in the matter of prescribed proceedings, if there was any room for the exercise of the court's discretion in relation to the question raised at the hearing of the petition for naturalization.

The District Court for the Eastern District of Michigan, in the case of United States v. Nechman, 183 Fed. 788, 790, said:

"There is an entire absence of testimony that any fraud was perpetrated upon the court, or that there was any illegality by which Nechman's certificate was procured. There is, therefore, nothing in section 15 of the statute of 1906 which would warrant this court in cancelling the certificate. The facts were all directly before the court and it passed its judgment upon them. 'The judgments of courts may not be impeached for any facts, whether involving fraud or collusion, or not, or even perjury, which were necessarily before the court and passed upon.' The Acorn, 2 Abb. 435, 445, Fed. Cas. No. 29; U. S. v. Gleason, 90 Fed. 778, 83 C. C. A. 272; Spratt v. Spratt, 4 Pet. 393, 7 L. Ed. 272; Hilton v. Guyot, 159 U. S. 207, 16 Sup. Ct. 139, 40 L. Ed. 95; U. S. v. Throckmorton, 98 U. S. 66, 25 L. Ed. 93."

The Circuit Court of Appeals, for the Ninth Circuit, in United States v. Rocktechell, 125 C. C. A. 532, 208 Fed. 530, 534, 535 (where the government sought cancellation of a seaman's certificate on the ground of "illegality", because of alleged non-continuous residence for five years before petitioning for naturalization), said, in affirming the decision of the lower court in dismissing the cancellation petition:

> "It is not for a court in a proceeding of this character to review or set aside *findings of the court of original jurisdiction*, based upon conflicting evidence, or *upon evidence reasonably susceptible to different inferences.*
>
> "The controlling question is whether the respondent misrepresented or wilfully withheld from the court any of the concrete probative facts."

In United States v. Shanahan, 232 Fed. 169, Judge Dickinson, in dismissing the cancellation petition, said:

> "Congress in pursuance of its constitutional power 'to establish a uniform rule of naturalization' has provided us with our present system. These laws confine the power to certain courts, and impose the duty upon the District Courts of admitting to citizenship. Certain things are preliminarily essential to the exercise of this power. These are the jurisdictional facts. One of them is a previous declaration of the intention of the applicant to become a citizen. Another is that he shall within the prescribed time thereafter file his petition in the required form, and his petition must be verified by the affidavits of at least two credible witnesses, who are themselves citizens, to the fact of residence, etc. What follows is a matter of 'proofs'. In other words it is a finding of facts from evidence. This is a judicial act, or a judgment, the memory of which is preserved in the records of the court * * * When an applicant

has met all the requirements of the law, the privilege accorded him ripens into a right. It is his legal right to submit his petition and proofs to the court as the constituted tribunal to pass upon them. If certain facts appear to the satisfaction of the court, he is entitled to citizenship.

"In similar proceedings like findings made by an official or tribunal other than a judge or a court are not disturbed because a different conclusion might have been reached on the facts. The courts will not assume to sit in judgment to review findings of fact which it is the duty of another tribunal to make. This is the established rule. United States v. Rodgers, 191 Fed. 970, 112 C. C. A. 382. Why should not the same rule apply to a finding by a judge or a court? The principle remains the same when the court in one form of proceeding is asked to review its findings made in the course of another proceeding.

"The rule, of course, has its limitations. These are well recognized. They have their practical application in the provision of the law for cancellations. If the certificate was procured by fraud, it may be cancelled. So likewise if it was 'illegally procured.' The absence from the record of any of the jurisdictional facts would make the certificate 'unlawful,' because issued without warrant of law. *The moment, however, we get beyond the record and the jurisdictional facts we get into the domain of the 'proofs.'* In the first place, we have no record of what these were, and in any event, in the absence of fraud, or an abuse of power by the tribunal which has passed upon them, we are doing nothing else than hearing the evidence over again and retrying the case on its facts. * * *

"However this may be, the conclusion reached is that the court, when it admitted this applicant, was 'satisfied' of the fact of residence, and, being so satisfied, it was proper to admit him to citizenship, and we see no justification for cancelling the certificate because of the fact (even if it were the fact) that from a view of part of the proofs which were then before the court we differed in our judgment of the weight of the evidence."

In the case of United States v. Albertini, 206 Fed. 133, 135, the District Court of Montana said that the term ('illegally procured') imports a certificate issued by a court without jurisdiction or in violation of the law's procedure—without a petition, or witnesses, or notice (to the Government), or hearing for example. And the court further held that section 15 of the Act of 1906 does not add to or detract from the rights and remedies of the Government as they existed prior to the statute.

In presenting the bill (which became the Act of June 29, 1906), to the House, Mr. Bonynge, who had it in charge, spoke of the provisions of section 15 as providing for the *cancellation of certificates fraudulently obtained,* and said that that which the section provides for *"can be done now* (*i. e.* without any special aid from section 15) *as decided by the Federal Courts."* 40 Congressional Record, 7873-7874.

The Circuit Court of Appeals for the Fifth Circuit, in the case of United States v. Dolla, 177 Fed. 101, says of the Act of June 29, 1906:

> "The power vested in the court to grant or order the same (citizenship) is on proof to the *satisfaction* of the court, with the petitioner and witness as necessary exhibits—that is to say the question of admission is committed to the *discretion* of the courts—*and discretionary rulings of courts are not reviewable.*"

### III.

### Res Adjudicata.

The United States District Court for the Eastern District of Washington is a court of general jurisdiction having jurisdiction of naturalization causes, and it possessed in 1913 full jurisdiction over Mozumdar who had applied therein for citizenship. The government of the United States had notice of Mozumdar's application, appeared by its naturalization examiner, contested the application, made argument, filed brief, cross-examined witnesses, appeared and contested at the re-hearing of the case and acquiesced in the judgment of the court. (P. T. pp. 5-6.) The court filed a written opinion which was reported at 207 Fed. 115. The judgment was not reversed upon appeal nor was it vacated. No proceeding prescribed by statute was neglected in the naturalization of Mozumdar. Therefore there was nothing illegal or contrary to law in the proceedings, nor was there any manifest error committed by the court. Hence, the judgment of the court, even if it were erroneous in matters addressed to its discretion on proofs submitted at the hearing, is conclusive. 7 Co. 76; 1 Pet. 340; 9 Cow. 227; 3 Binn. 410; 6 Pick. 435; 4 Johns. Ch. 460; 106 N. Y. 604; 81 Va. 677; 82 Ga. 168; 7 L. R. A. 577; 11 L. R. A. 155, 308.

In support of our contention may be quoted the well-known maxims:

*"Nemo debet bis vexari pro eadem causa."*
*"Interest reipublicae ut sit finis litium."*
*"Res judicata facit ex albo nigrum, ex nigro album, ex curvo rectum, ex recto curvum."*

It is a general principle that a decision by a court of competent jurisdiction, of matters put in issue before it, is binding and conclusive upon all other courts of concurrent power, and between parties and their privies. This principle pervades not only our own, but all other systems of jurisprudence, and has become a rule of universal law, founded on the soundest policy, and is necessary for the repose and peace of society and the maintenance of civil order. 168 U. S. 48; 125 U. S. 702; 7 Wall. 107.

In Spratt v. Spratt, 4 Pet. 393, 7 L. Ed. 897, Chief Justice Marshall pointed out that the statutes "Submit the decision on the right of aliens to admission as citizens to courts of record. They are to receive testimony, to compare it with the law, and to judge on both law and fact. This judgment is entered on record as the judgment of the court. It seems to us, if it be legal in form, to close all inquiry, and, like every other judgment to be complete evidence of its own validity."

In Mutual Benefit etc. Co. v. Tisdale, 91 U. S. 245, 23 L. Ed. 314, Hunt, J., said that the certificate of citizenship "is against all the world a judgment of citizenship."

Says the District Court of Montana, in United States v. Albertini, 206 Fed. 133, referring to section 15:

"The design is to enable the government to exercise some supervision over the proceedings, some watchfulness, and in its discretion to oppose, contest and convert the proceedings into those actually adversary. It may be that if this discretion be so exercised the judgment and certificate would be *res judicata* in the matter of fraud intrinsic the record."

In the case of Johannessen v. United States, 225 U. S. 227, (a cancellation suit under section 15), Mr. Justice Pitney, speaking for the court, said at pages 237-238:

"What may be the effect of a judgment allowing naturalization in a case where the Government has appeared and litigated the matter does not now concern us. (See 2 Black, Judgments, section 534a). What we have to say relates to such a case as is presented by the present record, which is the ordinary case of an alien appearing before one of the courts designated by law for the purpose, and, without notice to the Government and without opportunity, to say nothing of duty, on the part of the Government to appear, submitting his application for naturalization with '*ex parte*' proofs in support thereof, and thus procuring a certificate of citizenship. In view of the great number of aliens thus applying at irregular times in the various courts of record of the several states and in the Federal Circuit and District Courts throughout the Union, and bringing their applications on to summary hearing without previous notice to the Government of the United States or to the public, it is of course impossible that the public interests should be adequately represented, and in our opinion the sections quoted from the Revised Statutes are not open to any construction that would give a conclusive effect to such an investigation *when conducted at the instance of and controlled by the interested individual alone.*

"The foundation of the doctrine of '*res judicata,*' or estopped by judgment, is that both parties have had their day in court. 2 Black, Judgments, sections 500, 504. The general principle was clearly expressed by Mr. Justice Harlan, speaking for this court in Southern Pacific Railway Co. v. United States, 168 U. S. 1, 48:

'That a right, question or fact *distinctly put in issue and directly determined by a court of competent jurisdiction,* as a ground of recovery, *cannot be disputed in a subsequent suit* between the same parties or their privies.' "

Page 241:

"The act (of June 29, 1906), does not purport
to deprive a litigant of the fruits of a successful
controversy in the courts."

## IV.

### The Appellee Is Barred by Its Laches in Seeking Its Remedy in a Court of Equity.

When the state invokes the power of equity to establish its rights, it may be denied relief on the ground of its laches.

State v. Livingstone, 164 Iowa 31, 145 N. W. 91.

Laches may be imputed to the commonwealth as well
as to an individual. *In re* Bailey's Estate, 241 Pa. 230,
88 Atl. 428; Atty. Gen. v. Central R. Co. 68 N. J. Eq.
198, 59 Atl. 348; Atty. Gen. v. Delaware etc. R. Co.,
27 N. J. Eq. 1 (aff. 27 N. J. Eq. 631); Pittsburgh R.
Co. v. Carrick, 259 Pa. 333; Commonwealth v. Bala
etc. Turnp. Co., 153 Pa. 47; 25 Atl. 1105.

In equity it is the rule that when the court is asked
to lend its aid in the enforcement of a demand that
has become stale, there must be some cogent and
weighty reasons presented why it has been permitted
to become so. Good faith, conscience, and reasonable
diligence of the party seeking relief are the elements
that call a court of equity into action. In the absence of those elements the court becomes passive and
refuses to extend its relief or aid. McDearmon v.
Burnham, 158 Ill. 62, 41 N. E. 1094.

The existence or non-existence as the case may be, of many facts or conditions will give to a state the right to declare forfeited or to cancel and annul the charter of a corporation under its laws. Any breach of a condition upon which the charter was granted, however, may be waived by the state and the corporation continue under the charter the same as if no breach occurred, and *thereafter the cause for forfeiture cannot be insisted upon by the state.* People v. Ulster Co. 128 N. Y. 240, 28 N. E. 635; People v. Manhattan Co. 9 Wend. 361 (N. Y.); Foster v. Joilet, 27 Fed. 899. And long delay in taking advantage of a ground of forfeiture has been held sufficient to constitute a waiver. People v. Oakland Bank, 1 Dougl. 282 (Mich.).

In this case there has been a delay of ten years in bringing the cancellation suit without any reason whatever being assigned to explain or justify the laches. Such delay is unreasonable and bars the remedy. Moreover, there was no difficulty in reviewing the naturalization order of the court of original jurisdiction by an appeal as from a chancery decree. This has been done in many cases. Furthermore, an action under section 15 "is in no sense an appeal from or review of the proceedings upon the petition. It is an independent action based upon fraud or illegality in the procurement of the certificate. Therefore it cannot be permitted to perform the office of an appeal." U. S. v. Milder, (C. C. A. 8), 284 Fed. 571.

## V.

### Estoppel.

The doctrine of equitable estoppel is frequently applied to transactions in which it is found that it would be unconscionable to permit a person to maintain a position inconsistent with one in which he has acquiesced. *The rule is well recognized that when a party with full knowledge, or with sufficient notice or means of knowledge, of his rights, and of all the material facts, remains inactive for a considerable time or abstains from impeaching the transaction so that the other party is induced to suppose that it is recognized, this is acquiescence, and the transaction though originally impeachable, becomes unimpeachable.* Rothschild v. Title Guarantee & Trust Co., 204 N. Y. 458, 97 N. E. 879, 41 L. R. A. (N. S.) 740. .Note: 9 L. R. A. 609.

Ignorance of his legal rights will not prevent one's conduct from working an estoppel if he has full knowledge of the facts. Rogers v. Portland etc. St. Ry., 100 Me. 86, 60 Atl. 713, 70 L. R. A. 574; Storrs v. Barker, 6 Johns. Ch. (N. Y.) 166, 10 Am. Dec. 316 and note. Note: 48 L. R. A. (N. S.) 773.

> "The whole office of an equitable estoppel is to protect one from a loss which, but for the estoppel, he could not escape." 10 R. C. L. 698 (quoted with approval by this court in the Tampico, 270 Fed. 537 at p. 542).

A state department in a matter of procedure and within the scope of departmental powers, may be estopped. Chicago etc. R. Co. v. Dey, 35 Fed. 866, 1 L. R. A. 744.

In this case the executive department of the Government had full knowledge of the facts, had due notice, appeared and contested, and after a judgment adverse to its claims neither appealed nor sued for cancellation of appellant's certificate for ten years. Such inaction could not but induce the belief that there was no further objection forthcoming from the appellee and that it had acquiesced in the judgment of the naturalization court. Hence, the appellee is now estopped from impeaching the judgment of the District Court of the Eastern District of Washington or the certificate based thereon, or from subjecting the appellant to the loss of a possession of acknowledged worth—citizenship of the greatest country in the world and the right to vote therein.

## VI.

### The Contentions of the Appellee Are Untenable.

It may be that counsel for the appellee will present to this Honorable Court some of their contentions made elsewhere. We shall, therefore, revert to them briefly in this place:

(a) Chinese or Japanese cases since 1882—of those admittedly belonging to the Mongolian or Yellow race —are no precedents for this case.

The Act of May 6, 1882, c. 126, Sec. 14, 22 Stat. 61 (U. S. Comp. St. 1901 p. 1333), expressly forbade the naturalization of Chinamen; and the courts even before 1882 had construed Sec. 2169, Revised Statutes, as excluding Mongolians from naturalization. See *In re* Ah Yup (1875), 5 Sawy. 155, Fed. Cas. No. 104. A certificate of naturalization issued, *after 1882,* to a Mongolian—and Chinese and Japanese are admittedly and obviously Mongolians—is issued in violation of the *obvious and express mandate* of the law, and therefore unlawful and void on its face. Chinese and Japanese belong to the Mongolian or Yellow race and are, therefore, inadmissible to citizenship in the United States, where citizenship is an exclusive privilege of white men and Africans. Section 2169 Revised Statutes; Ozawa v. United States, 260 U. S. 178.

There is no parallel between these cases and the case at bar. There has been no express and obvious law forbidding the admission of Hindus to citizenship. The words "white persons" do not clearly or manifestly exclude Hindus. Indeed, with the exception of one or two cases, federal and state courts have consistently held for at least twenty years, that Hindus are Caucasians and therefore of the white race. And such is also the consensus of learned opinion in the world.

(b) The reasoning of the Hon. William P. James in the opinion filed in this case (P. T. pp. 8-17), may be exhibited in the form of the following syllogism:

Mozumdar is an ineligible alien;

Certificate granted an ineligible alien is illegally procured;

Therefore, certificate granted Mozumdar is illegally procured.

Referring to the text of the opinion (at page 10, P. T., last lines), it is evident that the court overlooked the fact that the precise and only issue between Mozumdar and the naturalization examiner was as to whether a Hindu is or is not a free white person— Mozumdar asserting the affirmative and *claiming to be a white person.* (P. T. p. 6, lines 1-3). The naturalization court heard the evidence, weighed it, and decided that it preponderated in favor of Mozumdar's claim and so made the order (P. T. p. 6 last 4 lines) admitting him to citizenship. 207 Fed. 115.

(P. T. p. 11, lines 1 to 5): The learned judge overlooks the obvious fact that until the decision in the case of United States v. Bhagat Singh Thind the preponderance of judicial opinion was that Hindus were eligible to citizenship. The executive department of the Government as well as Congress had acquiesced in such interpretation of section 2169 by the courts; and it was just *the* question fought out in every Hindu naturalization case. This is an equity case, and therein obvious and outstanding *facts* cannot be waved out of existence by any presumptions. For here conscience must rule; as the purpose of equity is to mitigate the hardships which assail and at times mar the working of the law. Hence, the petition could not have been denied by the eminent jurist who presided over the naturalization court "upon the applicant's own petition or testimony, or both," without violating the dictates of his own reason or conscience, in view of the testimony presented at the hearing, where both sides were represented and issue was joined on this very question of eligibility. 207 Fed. 115.

It has been held that where the law is changed by judicial decision, such change will not affect transactions made with reference to the law as it stood previous to such change. Metzger v. Greiner, 29 Ohio Cir. Ct. R. 447. And that as judicial construction of a statute has the same effect on existing rights as would be given a legislative amendment, adjudications which seem to render Revised Statutes Sec. 2502 unconstitutional, will not be given a retroactive effect on a franchise founded on a good consideration and granted when this statute is not questioned. State v. Oakwood St. Ry., 30 Ohio Cir. Ct. R. 632.

Moreover, the authority of precedents must yield to the force of reason and the paramount demands of justice and the decencies of civilized society. Norton v. Randolph, 40 L. R. A. (N. S.) 129, Am. Cas. 1915 A. 714, 58 So. 283, 176 Ala. 381.

(P. T. p. 11 middle of page): In the Nopoulos case, 225 Fed. 656, the opinion, towards the end, goes on to say:

"In United States v. Plaistow, 189 Fed. 1010, the court says: 'The term illegally procured is not limited to irregularity of procedure, but also denotes the determination by the court contrary to law of the matter submitted to it. Tiedt v. Carstensen, 61 Iowa 334, 16 N. W. 214.' "

Evidently, the Plaistow opinion erred in its definition of "illegality," as did the Nopoulos opinion which followed it. For the Supreme Court of Iowa has consistently held to exactly the opposite view regarding the meaning of "illegality" from what it is made out to have held in the aforementioned cases which profess to follow it. Here are the words of the Iowa court:

"When the law prescribes proceedings to be had by an officer or tribunal in cases pending before them, the omission of such proceedings is in violation of law, and the court or officer omitting them would, therefore, act illegally. * * * But *if a discretion is conferred upon the inferior tribunal, its exercise cannot be illegal.* If it be clothed with authority to decide upon facts submitted to it, the decision is not illegal, whatever it may be, if the subject-matter and parties are within its jurisdiction; for the law entrusts the decision to the discretion of the tribunal. * * * *The distinction between erroneous proceedings which are termed 'illegalities,' and erroneous decisions of fact, is obvious.* See Smith v. Board of Supervisors, 30 Iowa 531; McCollister v. Shuey *et al.,* 24 Iowa 362; Jordan v. Hayne *et al.,* 36 Iowa 9." Tiedt v. Carstensen, 61 Iowa 334, 116 N. Y. 214.

This disposes of the Nopoulos and Plaistow cases as authorities on the point to support which they are cited in the opinion of the lower court. We may, however, quote from the opinion of the Supreme Court of Iowa in another case:

> *"The statute contains no other provision as to how these matters shall be inquired into and determined;* but as said in Wood v. Farmer, 69 Iowa 537, 'It is a familiar rule of law that authority to do an act implies authority to do all other acts necessary to be done in executing the power conferred. The law will always presume the existence of authority to do acts incidental and necessary to the discharge of lawful power.' We think it clear that the defendant board *did have power, by proper investigation, to determine,* etc." Iowa Eclectic Medical College Association v. Schrader, 20 L. R. A. 355, 358.

> *"The board* (of examiners) *having jurisdiction to determine this question of fact, and having determined it, upon full investigation and evidence* by unanimous vote, *we must hold their action legal, even though we might reach a different conclusion on the facts,* if it were our province to consider them." Iowa Eclectic Medical College Association v. Schrader, 20 L. R. A. 355, 359.

Thus it is obvious that "illegality" may arise in a court *acting* contrary to law in *proceedings prescribed* by the law. But there can be no illegality in an erroneous decision of a matter of fact where the law confers discretion on the court in deciding. And whether or not there is any discretion conferred in deciding the presence or absence of certain statutory conditions laid down by the Act of 1906, the question under section 2169 Revised Statutes, as to whether an applicant is white is preeminently a matter addressed to the discretion of the naturalization court.

The opinion in the Mulvey case declines to lay down any general rule, and emphasizes the fact that each case of this kind must be determined on its own circumstances. The case was decided by a divided court and Judge Hough wrote a vigorous dissenting opinion.

The Circuit Court of Appeals for the Second Circuit in United States v. Meyer, 241 Fed. 305, 154 C. C. A. 185, Ann. Cas. 1918 C. 704; and District Courts in *In re* Nananga, 242 Fed. 737; *In re* Weisz, 250 Fed. 1008; *In re* Pollock, 257 350; and *In re* Kreutzer *et al.,* 241 Fed. 985, took the opposite view in construing the statute to that adopted by the court in Grahl v. United States, 261 Fed. 487. Further, "The Department of Justice was requested by the Department of Labor to take the matter (of the construction of section 2171) to the Supreme Court of the United States, and the Department of Justice replied that after consideration of the subject it declined to take the case to the Suprefe Court." *In re* Kreutzer, 241 Fed. 985.

In every one of the cases cited in the learned opinion (P. T. pp. 11-13), the cancellation suit was filed almost on the heels of the naturalization order, and no acquiescence in the order of the naturalization court, nor laches, were exhibited by the Government.

(P. T. p. 12 lines 3-4): The question of "lack of residence for the required time" is a question of *quantity* requiring the exercise of much less of the faculty of discretion in determining, than the question of whether the applicant is a white person, which refers to *quality* and is not susceptible to mechanical measurement.

The quotation from the Ginsberg opinion on p. 11 (P. T.) lines 6-15, is made up of *obiter dicta*. Moreover, a careful perusal of the reported opinion at 243 U. S. 472 reveals the fact that the learned justice in writing the opinion, had throughout, reference to the prescribed proceedings of the Act of 1906—"a code of procedure" which "specifies with circumstantiality the *manner* ('and not otherwise') in which an alien may be admitted to become a citizen of the United States; what his preliminary declaration shall be; form and contents of his sworn petition to the court and witnesses by whom it must be verified," etc. —all "with the studied purpose *to avoid well-known abuses*." The words quoted by the Honorable William P. James on page 11 do not refer to "the general controlling principles found in the Act of 1802 and a few amendments thereto," wherein Sec. 2169 belongs.

Referring to the words quoted on page 11 (P. T.) we submit that the learned justice in writing his opinion did not contemplate that the Government should challenge a certificate for "illegality" years after the judgment had become final. And we venture to think that there was no *manifest mistake* made by Judge Rudkin in admitting Mozumdar to citizenship, especially in view of the fact that the Supreme Court is supposed (at p. 13, last 10 lines, printed transcript) to place Mozumdar among individuals in border line cases with respect to whom "controversies have arisen and will no doubt arise again." He evidently falls, in the view of the court, in the zone of more or less debatable ground, and is, in the opinion of the learned Justice Sutherland, neither clearly eligible not clearly ineligible. Under these circumstances how could the naturalization court avoid perplexity or doubt? And how could it off-hand deny the petition on the "applicant's own petition or testimony, or both;" or obviate "conflict of evidence"?

In view of what is said in the preceding lines, the statement of Judge James at page 16, lines 5 to 9 from bottom of page (P. T.) seems to us to be too sweeping. Jurisdiction is the power to determine a cause or controversy and necessarily includes the power to decide it correctly as well as incorrectly. It does not relate to the rights of the parties as between each other but to the power of the court.

> "Jurisdiction of a question is the lawful power to enter upon the consideration of, and to decide it. It is not limited to making correct decisions.

It necessarily, includes the power to decide an issue wrong as well as right." Foltz v. St. Louis and S. F. Ry. Co., 8 C. C. A. 635, 60 Fed. 316, 318.

"When the District Court of Comanche county had acquired jurisdiction of the prisoner and of the charge against him and the question arose in what manner the grand jury should be selected, that issue could not have been beyond the limits of its jurisdiction. The law had conferred upon it the power, and had imposed upon it the duty to try the petitioner for his alleged offense and the decision of that question was indispensable to such a trial. That court could not have lawfully stopped and refused to determine the issue. If it decided that question wrong, its action may have been error, but it was nevertheless the exercise of its lawful jurisdiction." *Ex parte* Moran, 75 C. C. A. 396, 144 Fed. 594, 604.

Mr. Justice Bradley, in speaking for the Supreme Court in Hans Nielsen, petitioner, 131 U. S. 176, 183, 184, distinguished between erroneous and void judgments, saying:

"The distinction between the case of a mere error in law, and of one in which the judgment is void, is pointed out in *Ex parte* Siebold, 100 U. S. 371, 375, and is illustrated by the case of *Ex parte* Parks, as compared with the cases of Lange and Snow. *In the case of Parks there was an alleged misconstruction of a statute. We held that to be a mere error in law, the court having juris-*

*diction of the case.* In the cases of Lange and Snow there was a denial or invasion of a constitutional right."

In State v. State, 12 Pet. (U. S.) 718, it is said:

"Jurisdiction is the power to hear and determine the subject-matter in controversy between the parties to the suit; to adjudicate or exercise any judicial power over them; the question is whether, in the case before a court their action is judicial or extra-judicial; with or without authority of law to render a judgment or decree upon the rights of the litigant parties. If the law confers the power to render a judgment or decree, then the court has jurisdiction."

In *Ex parte* Watkins, 32 U. S. 568, the rule is laid down that:

"The jurisdiction of the court can never depend upon its decision upon the merits of the case brought before it, but upon its right to hear and decide it at all."

This language was quoted with approval in United States v. Maney, 61 Fed. 140.

The Supreme Court of California in Chase v. Christianson, 41 Cal. 253, says:

"It is not the particular decision which makes up jurisdiction, but it is the authority to decide the question at all. Otherwise the distinction between erroneous exercise of jurisdiction on the one hand, and the total want of it on the other must be obliterated."

In Buckley v. Superior Ct. 96 Cal. 119, 31 Pac. 8, the lower court had granted a motion to dismiss an appeal taken to it from the judgment of a justice's court. The appeal was in all respects regularly taken, and the Superior Court, under the law, should not have dismissed the appeal. Speaking of the action of the court in dismissing the appeal it was said:

> "If it had jurisdiction to hear the motion, and as to that matter there can be no question, then the ruling upon the motion was simply an exercise of that jurisdiction; and however erroneous such ruling might be, it would be only an error of law, in no manner subject to review by an original proceeding in this court. *In this case the court had jurisdiction to hear the motion, and it would be an absurdity to say that upon submission of the matter the court had jurisdiction to deny the motion to dismiss the appeal, but no jurisdiction to grant it."*

In Sherer v. Superior Court, 96 Cal. 653, 31 Pac. 565, the Superior Court had erroneously stricken out an answer filed by a defendant, and entered judgment against him without any further trial, in a case appealed from a justice's court. The court, upon the application for a writ of *certiorari,* said:

> "Jurisdiction is the power to hear and determine, and does not depend upon the rightfulness of the decision made. The court in this case had the power, and in the regular course of proceeding in the disposition of the case before it, was actually called upon to determine, as a matter of law,

whether or not the answer of petitioner was properly filed, and whether he was legally in default in the action; and the fact that the court erred in such decision does not render its judgment void."

Each of the two last cited cases was a case where no right of appeal existed, and the petitioner was without redress as to the action of the lower court founded upon a pure error of law.

In White v. Superior Court, 110 Cal. 60, 42 Pac. 480, the court quoted with approval from Von Roun v. Superior Court, 58 Cal. 358, this language:

"If the order is one which the court had power to make, it is not for use to inquire whether this power was properly exercised or not. The writ of review is not a writ of error."

To the same effect is History Company v. Light, 97 Cal. 56, 31 Pac. 627.

### Conclusion.

It would seem that there was no illegal procuring of the certificate of naturalization by the appellant in 1913; that the District Court for the Eastern District of Washington did not act illegally nor in excess of its jurisdiction, nor committed manifest mistake, nor was bound to decide one way only, nor was its decision beyond the bounds of reason, when it admitted appellant to citizenship; nor was there any abuse of its power by that court. The government's petition is without merit, and the lower court erred in overruling the motion to dismiss said petition.

It is, therefore, most earnestly urged by counsel for appellant that in the light of the decisions above cited, and the manifest error of the lower court in the premises, this Honorable Court will reverse the decree, with such directions as justice and equity may require.

Respectfully submitted,

S. G. PANDIT,
*Solicitor and Counsel for Appellant.*

Dated, Los Angeles, April 15, 1924.

Italics throughout the foregoing brief are ours.

S. G. PANDIT.

# No. 4229.

IN THE

# United States
# Circuit Court of Appeals,

## FOR THE NINTH CIRCUIT.

---

Akhay Kumar Mozumdar,

*Appellant,*

*vs.*

United States of America,

*Appellee.*

---

## BRIEF OF APPELLEE.

---

Joseph C. Burke,
United States Attorney.
J. Edwin Simpson,
Assistant U. S. Attorney.
*Attorneys and Solicitors for Appellee.*

---

Parker, Stone & Baird Co., Law Printers, 232 New High St., Los Angeles.

Akhay Kumar Mozumdar,
>*Appellant,*

*vs.*

United States of America,
>*Appellee.*

## BRIEF OF APPELLEE.

Appellant raises five contentions as a basis for reversing the decree of the District Court and propounds the same contentions as error on the part of the District Court in denying the appellant's motion to dismiss the bill of complaint.

These contentions are:

1.   That the purpose of the Act of June 29, 1906, under which this complaint was filed was to combat fraud, perjury, and illegality by court officials dominated by party politics.

2.   That appellant's certificate was not "illegally procured."

3. That the judgment admitting appellant to citizenship in 1913 is *res adjudicata* to and against the appellee.

4. That appellee is barred by its laches from seeking the remedy of cancellation in a court of equity.

5. That appellee is estopped by its long continued acquiescence in the judgment admitting this appellant to citizenship from now challenging his certificate of naturalization.

Considering these contentions in the order in which they appear in appellant's opening brief, we find that appellant procured a certificate of naturalization in 1913; that thereafter this proceeding was instituted to cancel and annul the order made for the issuance of the certificate and to cancel the certificate on the grounds that they were "illegally procured." Appellant moved to dismiss the bill on the ground that the bill of complaint did not state facts sufficient to constitute a cause for cancellation. The motion to dismiss was denied, and upon the failure of the appellant to file an answer within the time allowed by law, a decree was made and entered directing that the said certificate and order granting the certificate be set aside, annulled and cancelled. [P. T., pp. 17 and 18.]

I.

The section of the Act of June 29, 1906, which appellant contends does not authorize this proceeding provides in part as follows:

"Section 15. That it shall be the duty of the
United States district attorneys for the respective
districts, upon affidavit showing good cause therefor, to institute proceedings in any court having
jurisdiction to naturalize aliens in the judicial district in which the naturalized citizen may reside
at the time of bringing the suit, for the purpose
of setting aside and canceling the certificate of
citizenship *on the ground of fraud* or *on the
ground that such certificate of citizenship was illegally procured.*"

It will be observed that this section provides two
grounds for cancelling certificates of citizenship, viz:
fraud and illegality. Admittedly orders and certificates procured through sharp practices, deceit, misrepresentation, perjury, or bribery fall within the first
class. Certificates procured without authority of law
or "illegally procured" and not tainted with fraud fall
within the second class. This proceeding attacks appellant's certificate and the order granting the certificate on the ground that it was procured illegally.
No fraud is charged, and we are here not interested
in the purpose of the act as it applies to fraudulent
certificates and orders, but only as it applies to certificates procured illegally. It is the contention of
appellee that judicial interpretations of this section of
the act do not sustain appellant's contention of the
purpose of the act as applied to illegal certificates. In
the discussion contained herein of appellant's arguments, appellee feels that the cases cited under the
second contention refute appellant's first contention,

and no further consideration will at this point of the controversy be given to appellant's first contention.

Before passing to a consideration of appellant's second contention, appellee desires to call to the attention of this Honorable Court the rule that citizenship is not a natural right to which aliens are entitled, but rather it is a privilege in the nature of a gift or bounty which may be granted, withheld, or taken away, with reason, without reason, or for such cause as Congress may prescribe.

United States v. Ginsberg, 243 U. S. 472, 475.

All of the statutory qualifications and requirements prescribed by Congress must be strictly complied with. If there be any doubt whether such statutory qualifications exist, that doubt is resolved in favor of the Government.

United States v. Ginsberg, *supra;*
United States v. Griminger, 236 Fed. 285.

With these propositions in mind, consideration may next be given to the second contention of appellant.

## II.

### Appellant's Certificate Was "Illegally Procured".

Considering the second contention of appellant, appellee contends that an order of naturalization and a certificate procured thereunder, if "illegally procured," is subject to cancellation under Section 15; that a certificate is "illegally procured" when procured by an alien who is not qualified or admissible to citizenship by reason of race, residence or lack of other statutory requirements, and that the appellant was not qualified to become a citizen and his certificate should, therefore, be cancelled.

Appellant contends that the certificate procured by him was legally procured and argues that before a certificate is subject to cancellation on the ground of illegality, there must be subornation or an error in procedure. Admittedly, if there be subornation, bribery or misrepresentation, there would not only be illegality but also fraud. If the proceedings be irregular, there might also be illegality, but likewise if the alien is not qualified by reason of race, residence, morals or attachment to the principles of the Constitution, there is illegality. The burden of initiating the proceedings to procure citizenship is upon the alien. He is the one who seeks to become a citizen and represents to the court that he is an eligible person. If a certificate is issued to him by the court upon his showing and representations, it is "procured by him."

The question then arises, "when is a certificate 'illegally procured'?" The term "illegal" has been held to mean "contrary to law."

> United States v. Mulvey—232 Fed. 513 (C. C. A 2nd);
> United States v. Plaistow, 189 Fed. 1010.

In the case of Grahl v. United States, 261 Fed. 487 (C. C. A. 7th), the court said,

" 'Illegally' means 'contrary to law.' If Section 2171 in truth forbids the admission of alien enemies to citizenship, the action of the court in admitting them is contrary to law; *and the decree of the court, based on a misconstruction of the statute,* involves an error of law, for which the decree should be vacated."

In the case of the United States v. Ginsberg, *supra,* suit was filed to cancel a certificate of citizenship issued to an alien who had not fulfilled the statutory requirement of residence. The question at issue was whether a certificate was "illegally procured" and should be cancelled under section 15 of the Act of June 29, 1906, when the uncontradicted evidence at the hearing on the petition showed undisputably that the petitioner was not qualified by residence for citizenship. The Supreme Court in holding that a certificate procured under such circumstances was "illegally procured," when the court or judge who heard the petition and ordered the certificate misapplied the law and facts, used the following language:

"No alien has the slightest right to naturalization unless all statutory requirements are complied with; and every certificate of citizenship must be treated as granted upon condition that the Government may challenge it as provided in Section 15 and demand its cancellation unless issued in accordance with such requirements. If procured when *prescribed qualifications have no existence in fact, it is illegally procured;* a manifest mistake by the judge cannot supply these nor render their existence non-essential."

This latter decision by the court of last resort and the decisions of the above cited Circuit Courts did not consider that fraud, deceit, perjury, bribery, subornation or error in procedure were the only cases in which illegality exists. These elements were not even within the issues of the cases, and appellee, therefore, contends that those cases furnish ample authority not only in refutation of appellant's first point as to the purpose of the act, but also for the proposition that a certificate procured by a person not qualified for citizenship is "illegally procured."

The precise question involved here has been passed upon in three other cases decided in the District Court for the Southern District of California: United States v. Mandel, decided by the Honorable Wm. P. James; United States v. Mohan Singh, and United States v. Pandit, decided by the Honorable Benjamin F. Bledsoe. In the two latter cases, counsel for the appellant herein appeared as counsel for Mohan Singh, and *in propria persona* in the Pandit case. Motions to dismiss were filed by the defendants, and in denying these motions, the learned judge had the following to say:

> "The only question remaining is whether or not an order made admitting such a person to citizenship after full and fair consideration by the court, is an order susceptible of being cancelled under and pursuant to the provisions of section 15 of the Naturalization Law of 1906 as being an instance of a certificate of citizenship "illegally procured." Much learned and technical argument has been indulged in to support the contention that

upon a full and fair hearing, where all the facts were presented to the court, where the Government was represented and made opposition to the order of admission, and where no fraud was involved, the Government may not, under and pursuant to the terms of said Section 15, successfully seek the annulment of the citizenship granted.

"The precise matter has been directly passed upon by Judge James of this court, in two cases, United States v. Mozumdar, No. E-5-J Equity, opinion filed November 30th, 1923, and United States v. Mandel, No. B-90-T, Northern Division, opinion filed December 6th, 1923. Reference to those opinions, the conclusions of which, supported by my own independent investigations, meet with my approval, should suffice as authority for the rulings had herein. Citing United States v. Plaistow, 189 Fed. 1010, Grahl v. United States, 261 Fed. 487, and other cases hereinafter referred to, he held that where a petition for naturalization is presented to a court having jurisdiction to hear it, by a person claiming to fall within the class of eligibles under the law, a decision based upon a mere conflict of evidence would present no case of irregularity or illegal procurement susceptible of cancellation under the terms of section 15. 'Where, however, the case is that the person presenting himself as an applicant for citizenship admits that he belongs to a particular race, members of which are not eligible for naturalization, then no question of conflict of evidence arises and upon the applicant's own petition or testimony, or both, naturalization must be denied.' The granting of it under the circumstances last detailed would not effect a 'lawful naturalization,' (Luria v. United States, 231 U. S., 9, 24.), and only a 'lawful naturalization' is immune from attack under the terms of section 15.

"On the main point, argued to the effect that the granting of citizenship to defendants hereinabove named, under the conditions obtaining, was not an illegal procurement of citizenship, it would seem that the rulings of the United States Supreme Court in United States v. Ness, 245 U. S. 325, and United States v. Ginsberg, 243 U. S. 472, and of the Second Circuit in United States v. Mulvey, C. C. A., 232 Fed. 513, are conclusive and require this court to deny the respective motions to dismiss."

As pointed out by these learned judges of the District Court, the case of Luria v. United States, 231 U. S. 9, 24, cited by appellant, held that the provisions of the Act of June 29, 1906, did not affect or disturb rights acquired through "lawful" naturalization.

The learned district judge in the case of the United States v. Nopoulos, 225 Fed. 656, held that Section 15, "provides for the annulment by appropriate judicial proceedings of *merely colorable rights of citizenships to which their possessors never were lawfully entitled.*" As above pointed out, if the alien was not entitled to citizenship by reason of lack of qualification, a certificate procured by him is "illegally procured." The next consideration is, therefore, whether the appellant was qualified for citizenship.

Section 4 of the Act provides, "that an alien may be admitted to become a citizen in the following manner and not otherwise." This was formerly section 2165 of the Revised Statutes and may, therefore, be considered as applicable to and governing section 2169, which provides as follows:

"Provisions of this title shall apply to aliens being free white persons and to aliens of African nativity and to persons of African descent."

No contention is raised herein that appellant is an alien of African nativity or a person of African descent. It is admitted that he claims to be a free white person and that his certificate of citizenship was procured upon his representation that he was such. The complaint herein alleges:

"That the said order and decree of court and certificate of naturalization were illegally procured from said court in question in this that said defendant was at all times herein mentioned a high caste Hindu of full Indian blood, and not a white person entitled to be naturalized under the provisions of section 2169 of the Revised Statutes of the United States."

The motion to dismiss admitted these allegations of the complaint and no further argument should be necessary to establish the proposition that a high caste Hindu of full Indian blood is not a free white person. The Supreme Court of the United States in the case of the United States v. Thind, 261 U. S. 204, decided once and for all that Hindus are not free white persons and are, therefore, not eligible to citizenship as such. The Supreme Court in that case did not make the law, but it simply applied the law as it has been for a long period of years to a particular race and determined that members of that race were not free white persons eligible to citizenship.

Clearly, therefore, appellant was not eligible to citizenship when he procured his certificate and the order and certificate could give him no more than merley "colorable rights of citizenship," to which he was never lawfully entitled. United States v. Nopoulos, 225 Fed. 656. The undisputed evidence at the hearing for citizenship showed that he was not eligible to citizenship and that naturalization should, therefore, have been denied. Having, however, been procured, it was "illegally procured" and must in this proceeding be cancelled. .

The learned judge of the District Court, therefore, properly denied appellant's motion to dismiss and ordered cancellation of the certificate and annulment of the order upon the grounds that they were "illegally procured," unless the remaining contentions of appellant are sufficient to defeat this proceeding.

### III.

The contentions of appellant in his third and fifth points, viz.: *res adjudicata* and estoppel, are predicated upon two hypotheses.:

(1) That the certificate was *legally procured*.

(2) That the Government could have appealed from the order granting citizenship.

Appellee has herein above answered the first hypothesis of appellant and established the proposition that a certificate procured by an ineligible alien is "illegally procured." The second hypothesis of appellant is likewise unsupported by judicial authority or reason.

Appellant has not directed the attention of the court to any provision of law authorizing an appeal from the order granting naturalization. Congress has not provided for appeals by the Government in such cases, but has, by section 15, of the Act of June 29, 1906, provided for annulment and cancellation by a *direct attack* upon the order, granting citizenship, and the certificate issued pursuant thereto, in an independent suit.

Before pointing out the unsoundness of appellant's contentions as disproved by judicial decisions, appellee desires to point out that the foundation of the doctrine of estoppel is that one party has negligently, wilfully, or fraudulently misled another to his injury by certain acts or words. That the person asserting the estoppel must have been misled to his damage is fundamental. Leather Manufacturers National Bank v. Morgan, 117 U. S. 96. An estoppel *in pais* operates only in favor of a person who has been misled to his injury. Katchun v. Duncan, 96 U. S. 659. There is nothing in this record disclosing any injury or damage to appellant by reason of any act of appellee.

In the case of the United States v. Johannessen, 225 U. S. 227, the Supreme Court considered the question of *res adjudicata* and estoppel by judgment as applied to an action brought under section 15 of the Act of June 29, 1906, when the naturalization hearing was not adversary. In deciding that these defenses did not prevent a proceeding under section 15, the Supreme Court, page 236, had the following to say:

"It was long ago held in this court, in a case arising upon the early acts of Congress which submitted to courts of record the right of aliens to admission as citizens, that the judgment of such a court upon the question was, like every other judgment, complete evidence of its own validity. Spratt v. Spratt, 4 Pet. 393, 409. This decision, however, goes no further than to establish the immunity of such a judgment from collateral attack. See also Campbell v. Gordon, 6 Cranch, 176.

"It does not follow that Congress may not authorize a direct attack upon certificates of citizenship in an independent proceeding such as is authorized by section 15 of the Act of 1906. Appellant's contention involves the notion that because the naturalization proceedings result in a judgment, the United States is for all purposes concluded thereby, even in the case of fraud or illegality for which the applicant for naturalization is responsible."

Admittedly, appellant was responsible for the procurement of the certificate procured by him, for it was upon his representation that he was properly qualified that the certificate was issued.

We quote, for the information of the court, the following passages from the opinion of the Supreme Court in the Johannessen case:

"In United States v. Beebe, 127 U. S. 338, 342; Mr. Justice Lamar, speaking for this court, said: 'It may now be accepted as settled that the United

States can properly proceed by bill in equity to have a judicial decree of nullity and an order of cancellation of a patent issued in mistake or obtained by fraud, where the Government has a direct interest, or is under an obligation respecting the relief invoked.' See also Noble v. Union River Logging R. R. Co., 147 U. S. 165, 175, and cases cited." (Page 239),

and at page 241:

"The act does not purport to deprive a litigant of the fruits of a successful controversy in the courts; for, as already shown, the proceedings for naturalization are not in any proper sense adversary proceedings, but are *ex parte* and conducted by the applicant for his own benefit. The act in effect provides for a new form of judicial review of a question that is in form, but not in substance, concluded by the previous record, and under conditions affording to the party whose rights are brought into question full opportunity to be heard."

and again at page 242:

"The act makes nothing fraudulent or unlawful that was honest and lawful when it was done."

The Supreme Court in the Johannessen case did not determine whether its rulings were applicable to a case in which the naturalization hearing was adversary. This question was, however, directly presented to the court in the case of the United States v. Ness, 245 U. S. 319. In that case the question presented to the court was:

"Whether an order entered in a proceeding to which the United States became a party under section 11 is *res adjudicata* as to matters actually litigated therein, so that the certificate of naturalization cannot be set aside under section 15 as having been 'illegally procured'?"

that is to say, whether sections 11 and 15 afford the United States alternative or cumulative means of protection against illegal or fraudulent naturalization under the Act of June 29, 1906. In determining that these sections afforded cumulative protection or relief, the Supreme Court used the following language:

"The remedy afforded by Sec. 15 for setting aside certificates of naturalization is broader than that afforded in equity, independently of statute, to set aside judgments, United States v. Throckmorton, 98 U. S. 61; Kibbe v. Benson, 17 Wall. 624; but it is narrower in scope than the protection offered under section 11." (Page 325),

and at page 327:

"Section 11, unlike Sec. 15, does not specifically provide that action thereunder shall be taken by the United States district attorneys; and if appearance under Section 11 on behalf of the Government should be held to create an estoppel, no good reason appears why it should not arise equally whether the appearance is by the duly authorized examiner or by the United States attorney. But in our opinion Secs. 11 and 15 were designed to afford cumulative protection against fraudulent or illegal naturalization."

Appellee believes that these cases decided by the Supreme Court of the United States show clearly that the arguments of appellant, that the order or judgment is *res adjudicata* and that the Government is estopped from bringing this proceeding, are untenable. As above pointed out, appellant's hypothesis for these arguments is that the Government has a right of appeal from the order. The following language used by the Supreme Court in the *Ness* case shows that no such right of appeal exists:

> "For Congress did not see fit to provide a direct review by writ of error or appeal."

As pointed out in the footnote to the Ness case, at page 326, the provision inserted in the Act for appeals was stricken therefrom.

> "The bill submitted by the commission on naturalization provided for such appellate proceedings and its proposal was recommended to the House by the committee on immigration and naturalization as Sec. 13 (Report of February 6, 1906, p. 5); but after debate in the committee of the whole (40 Cong. Rec., pp. 7784-7787) was stricken from the bill. The bill proposed by the commission and recommended by the house committee contained in addition (as Sec. 17) the provision for cancellation proceedings enacted as Sec. 15."

See also to the same effect as applied to proceedings brought under Section 15, United States v. Milder, 284 Fed. 571, C. C. A. 8th; United States v. Koopmans, 290 Fed. 545.

It has been held in numerous cases involving grants, surveys, or patents to land, that the United States is not estopped by reason of its acts nor the acts of its officials or agents. United States v. Jeems Bayou Hunting & Fishing Club, 260 U. S. 561, Cramer v. United States, 261 U. S. 219.

The cases cited by appellant in support of his points of *res adjudicata* and estoppel do not support his contentions, but in view of the above cited cases, it must follow that his contentions are insupportable by judicial authority.

## IV.

## The Appellee Is Not Barred by Laches From Prosecuting This Proceeding.

In support of his fourth point that the appellee is barred by laches from prosecuting this proceeding, appellant has not cited one case or statute of limitations to establish the laches. The doctrine of laches is, of course, an equitable doctrine of the legal defense of statute of limitations. Appellant has cited no statute of limitations applicable to this proceeding. He has cited state cases in support of his point that laches may be imputed to the commonwealth as well as to an individual. Whatever might be the statutory rule in some states, making the state subject to statutes of limitations, there is no such rule as to the United States. Statutes of limitations do not run against the United States. Gibson v. Chouteau, 13 Wall. 92.

Neither the statute of limitations nor the equitable doctrine of lapse of time can have any effect against the United States. Simmons v. Ogle, 105 U. S. 271.

Statutes of limitations have no force in actions brought by the Federal Government to enforce a public right or to assert a public interest. U. S. v. Beebe, 127 U. S. 338.

Since, therefore, this point is here advanced on a motion to dismiss, which challenges only defects appearing on the fact of the pleading, and nothing appears from the face of the pleadings herein which discloses that this action would be barred by a statute of limitations or laches; since there is no statute of limitations or laches applicable to this proceeding or to actions brought by the United States, and since no right of appeal by the Government was provided and therefore no statute of limitations or doctrine of laches applicable to the limitation of appeals or writs of error exists, it must follow that the United States is not barred by laches from prosecuting this proceeding, and that appellant's fourth contention is insupportable.

## V.

### The Contentions of Appellee Are Sustained by Statute, Judicial Authority and Reason.

Appellant in his sixth point endeavors to point out wherein certain arguments of appellee are untenable. We shall therefore refer briefly to these points.

(a) The argument of appellee is not based upon any statutory provision or judicial authority referring to Chinese or Japanese. Appellee's case is based upon the allegations of the complaint, admitted by the motion to dismiss, that the appellant is a high caste Hindu and not a free white person. That such a person is not admissible to citizenship cannot now be questioned.

United States v. Thind, 261 U. S. 204.

(b) The reasoning of the Honorable Wm. P. James in the opinion filed in this case is sound and logical and replete with judicial learning. The position of the Honorable Judge is unanswerable. It is, briefly, that an order for naturalization and a certificate of citizenship issued pursuant thereto are subject to cancellation under the provisions of Section 15 of the Act of June 29, 1906, if "illegally procured"; that an order and certificate procured by an alien ineligible to citizenship by reason of race is "illegally procured"; that appellant is admittedly ineligible to citizenship by reason of race, and that, therefore, his certificate must be cancelled, and the order granting citizenship annulled. It is submitted that the learned judge did not err in denying the motion to dismiss, and that the decisions of the Honorable Benjamin F. Bledsoe in the Mohan Singh and Pandit cases approving the conclusions of Judge James were correct and sustained by judicial authority.

The state cases cited by appellant are not applicable to this proceeding, which is especially prescribed by statute providing for the cancellation of merely colorable rights to which the alien was never lawfully entitled.

### Conclusion.

It would seem that the certificate of naturalization procured by appellant and the order admitting appellant to citizenship were subject to cancellation if "illegally procured"; that they were "illegally procured" because the defendant was a person not entitled to citizenship, and that this procedure to cancel the order and certificate is proper under the provisions of section 15 of the Act of June 29, 1906; that the order is not *res adjudicata* nor is the Government estopped by reason of any matters appearing on the face of the pleadings, nor is the Government barred by laches. The Government's complaint was, therefore, properly upheld by the lower court and no error committed in denying the motion to dismiss.

It is therefore respectfully submitted that in view of the failure of appellant to support his contentions and in light of the decisions cited herein by appellee and the sound judicial findings of the lower court, that this Honorable Court should sustain the decree and deny this appeal.

Respectfully submitted,

JOSEPH C. BURKE,
United States Attorney.

J. EDWIN SIMPSON,
Assistant U. S. Attorney.
*Attorneys and Solicitors for Appellee.*

Italics throughout the foregoing brief are ours.

J. EDWIN SIMPSON.

Lightning Source UK Ltd.
Milton Keynes UK
UKHW030231030219
336548UK00006B/797/P